THE CAMBRIDGE HISTORY OF THE
ENGLISH SHORT STORY

The Cambridge History of the English Short Story is the first comprehensive volume to capture the literary history of the English short story. Charting the origins and generic evolution of the English short story to the present day, this is the first history of its kind to present the development of the genre. There is no other single book that provides such an overview.

Written by international experts in the field, this book covers numerous transnational and historical connections between writers, modes and forms of transmission.

Suitable for English Literature students and scholars of the English short story generally, it will become a standard work of reference in its field.

DOMINIC HEAD is Professor of Modern English Literature at the University of Nottingham, where he served as Head of School from 2007 to 2010. He has written extensively on twentieth-century and contemporary literature and is the author of *The Modernist Short Story* (Cambridge University Press, 1992), *The Cambridge Introduction to Modern British Fiction, 1950–2000* (Cambridge University Press, 2002) and editor of *The Cambridge Guide to Literature in English*, third edition (Cambridge University Press, 2006).

THE CAMBRIDGE HISTORY
OF THE
ENGLISH SHORT STORY

Edited by

DOMINIC HEAD

CAMBRIDGE
UNIVERSITY PRESS

University Printing House, Cambridge CB2 8BS, United Kingdom

One Liberty Plaza, 20th Floor, New York, NY 10006, USA

477 Williamstown Road, Port Melbourne, VIC 3207, Australia

314-321, 3rd Floor, Plot 3, Splendor Forum, Jasola District Centre, New Delhi - 110025, India

103 Penang Road, #05-06/07, Visioncrest Commercial, Singapore 238467

Cambridge University Press is part of the University of Cambridge.

It furthers the University's mission by disseminating knowledge in the pursuit of education, learning and research at the highest international levels of excellence.

www.cambridge.org
Information on this title: www.cambridge.org/9781316618042
10.1017/9781316711712

© Cambridge University Press 2016

This publication is in copyright. Subject to statutory exception and to the provisions of relevant collective licensing agreements, no reproduction of any part may take place without the written permission of Cambridge University Press.

First published 2016
First paperback edition 2021

A catalogue record for this publication is available from the British Library

Library of Congress Cataloging in Publication data
NAMES: Head, Dominic, editor.
TITLE: The Cambridge History of the English Short Story / edited by Dominic Head.
DESCRIPTION: Cambridge, England ; New York : Cambridge University Press, 2016.
IDENTIFIERS: LCCN 2016017979 | ISBN 9781107167421 (hardback)
SUBJECTS: LCSH: Short stories, English – History and criticism. | English fiction × History and criticism. | Short story. | BISAC: LITERARY CRITICISM / European / English, Irish, Scottish, Welsh.
CLASSIFICATION: LCC PR829 .C19 2016 | DDC 823/.0109–dc23
LC record available at https://lccn.loc.gov/2016017979

ISBN 978-1-107-16742-1 Hardback
ISBN 978-1-316-61804-2 Paperback

Cambridge University Press has no responsibility for the persistence or accuracy of URLs for external or third-party internet websites referred to in this publication, and does not guarantee that any content on such websites is, or will remain, accurate or appropriate.

Contents

List of Contributors   page ix
Acknowledgements   x
A Note on the Texts   xi

Introduction   1
DOMINIC HEAD

1 · Early-Modern Diversity: The Origins of English Short Fiction   16
BARBARA KORTE

2 · Short Prose Narratives of the Eighteenth and Nineteenth Centuries   32
DONALD J. NEWMAN

3 · Gothic and Victorian Supernatural Tales   49
JESSICA COX

4 · The Victorian Potboiler: Novelists Writing Short Stories   67
SOPHIE GILMARTIN

5 · Fable, Myth and Folk Tale: The Writing of Oral and Traditional Story Forms   84
ANDREW HARRISON

6 · The Colonial Short Story, Adventure and the Exotic   100
ROBERT HAMPSON

7 · The *Yellow Book* Circle and the Culture of the Literary Magazine   118
WINNIE CHAN

Contents

8 · The Modernist Short Story: Fractured Perspectives   *135*
CLAIRE DREWERY

9 · War Stories: The Short Story in the First and Second World Wars   *152*
ANN-MARIE EINHAUS

10 · The Short Story in Ireland to 1945: A National Literature   *168*
HEATHER INGMAN

11 · The Short Story in Ireland since 1945: A Modernizing Tradition   *185*
HEATHER INGMAN

12 · The Short Story in Scotland: From Oral Tale to Dialectal Style   *202*
TIMOTHY C. BAKER

13 · The Short Story in Wales: Cultivated Regionalism   *219*
JANE AARON

14 · The Understated Art, English Style   *235*
DEAN BALDWIN

15 · The Rural Tradition in the English Short Story   *252*
DOMINIC HEAD

16 · Metropolitan Modernity: Stories of London   *269*
NEAL ALEXANDER

17 · Gender and Genre: Short Fiction, Feminism and Female Experience   *286*
SABINE COELSCH-FOISNER

18 · Queer Short Stories: An Inverted History   *304*
BRETT JOSEF GRUBISIC AND CARELLIN BROOKS

19 · Stories of Jewish Identity: Survivors, Exiles and Cosmopolitans   *323*
AXEL STÄHLER

20 · New Voices: Multicultural Short Stories   *341*
ABIGAIL WARD

Contents

21 · Settler Stories: Postcolonial Short Fiction 358
VICTORIA KUTTAINEN

22 · After Empire: Postcolonial Short Fiction and the Oral Tradition 377
JOHN THIEME

23 · Ghost Stories and Supernatural Tales 395
RUTH ROBBINS

24 · The Detective Story: Order from Chaos 411
ANDREW MAUNDER

25 · Frontiers: Science Fiction and the British Marketplace 429
PAUL MARCH-RUSSELL

26 · Weird Stories: The Potency of Horror and Fantasy 447
ROGER LUCKHURST

27 · Experimentalism: Self-Reflexive and Postmodernist Stories 464
DAVID JAMES

28 · Satirical Stories: Estrangement and Social Critique 481
SANDIE BYRNE

29 · Comedic Short Fiction 498
RICHARD BRADFORD

30 · Short Story Cycles: Between the Novel and the Story Collection 513
GERALD LYNCH

31 · The Novella: Between the Novel and the Story 530
GERRI KIMBER

32 · The Short Story Visualized: Adaptations and Screenplays 547
LINDA COSTANZO CAHIR

33 · The Short Story Anthology: Shaping the Canon 564
LYNDA PRESCOTT

Contents

34 · The Institution of Creative Writing   581
AILSA COX

35 · Short Story Futures   598
JULIAN MURPHET

Select Bibliography   615
Index   625

Contributors

JANE AARON, University of South Wales
NEAL ALEXANDER, Aberystwyth University
TIMOTHY C. BAKER, University of Aberdeen
DEAN BALDWIN, Pennsylvania State University
RICHARD BRADFORD, University of Ulster
CARELLIN BROOKS, University of British Columbia
SANDIE BYRNE, Kellogg College, Oxford
LINDA COSTANZO CAHIR, Kean University
WINNIE CHAN, Virginia Commonwealth University
SABINE COELSCH-FOISNER, University of Salzburg
AILSA COX, Edge Hill University
JESSICA COX, Brunel University London
CLAIRE DREWERY, Sheffield Hallam University
ANN-MARIE EINHAUS, Northumbria University
SOPHIE GILMARTIN, Royal Holloway, University of London
BRETT JOSEF GRUBISIC, University of British Columbia
ROBERT HAMPSON, Royal Holloway, University of London
ANDREW HARRISON, University of Nottingham
DOMINIC HEAD, University of Nottingham
HEATHER INGMAN, Trinity College, the University of Dublin
DAVID JAMES, Queen Mary, University of London
GERRI KIMBER, University of Northampton
BARBARA KORTE, University of Freiburg
VICTORIA KUTTAINEN, James Cook University
ROGER LUCKHURST, Birkbeck College
GERALD LYNCH, University of Ottawa
PAUL MARCH-RUSSELL, University of Kent
ANDREW MAUNDER, University of Hertfordshire
JULIAN MURPHET, University of New South Wales
DONALD J. NEWMAN, retired professor of English
LYNDA PRESCOTT, The Open University
RUTH ROBBINS, Leeds Metropolitan University
AXEL STÄHLER, University of Kent
JOHN THIEME, University of East Anglia
ABIGAIL WARD, University of Nottingham

Acknowledgements

The sure editorial hand of Ray Ryan has been invaluable throughout this project. I am also grateful to Victoria Parrin for her diligence in overseeing production as the Content Manager of the volume, and especially to Caroline Drake for her rigorous copy-editing.

Many thanks are due to the anonymous readers of the prospectus for this volume, and to the contributors, who have participated in a collaborative spirit over an extended period, with great patience, helping to realize the initial vision.

The greatest debt is to my family, Tricia, Felicity and Oliver.

A Note on the Texts

The date given for individual short stories is usually that of first book publication, unless it is clear from the discussion that the earlier publishing history is under consideration. There are some exceptions: for example, in the case of much later posthumous publication, the date of a story's composition is given to retain the historical logic of a discussion. Italics are used for any individual story or novella first published in book form as a separate title.

Introduction

DOMINIC HEAD

In establishing the credentials of the short story, especially as a modern written form significantly boosted by magazine culture in the eighteenth and nineteenth centuries, it is often felt necessary to make comparisons between the novel and the short story, comparisons that have tended to put the short story in the shade of the novel, a form assumed to be more technically sophisticated. The comparison can work in the other direction, however, to highlight the distinctive nature of shorter forms of fiction.

One of the evident problems with academic criticism of the novel in recent decades has been the overemphasis on topical or thematic interest at the expense of style or technique. The overemphasis is understandable, given the particular phase of intellectual history: critics have sought to eradicate the shortcomings inherent in successive critical movements – such as the New Criticism and structuralism – movements with a formalist focus that encouraged the neglect of contextual and historical questions. Successive critical approaches gaining purchase from the 1980s – Marxism, feminism, postcolonialism, ecocriticism – have served to swing the pendulum back towards questions of content, so that the contexts that generated topical points of foci for the novel necessarily became central to the key debates. This does not necessarily signify a neglect of formal and stylistic matters; but there has been a felt need for critics of the novel to still the swing of the pendulum, and to address questions of form and style within a properly mapped historical and contextual setting.

Where the short story is concerned, this apparent tension between attention to form and attention to content/context presents a rather different problem. This volume tries to excavate the 'pre-history' of the modern short story in its early chapters; even so, it must be acknowledged that, as a modern printed form, the short story is a relatively new phenomenon (compared with the longer history of the novel), which makes the specific nature of its different (and compressed) historical phases harder to trace. This problem is compounded by the relative dearth of critical interest in the short story, and by the clear emphasis in the extant criticism on formal attributes. This has helped create the impression that there is something 'timeless' about short fiction, but also something formulaic in its recurring stylistic features. The task for the short story critic, then, to pursue the metaphor of the pendulum, is to cause it to swing in the opposite direction from the swing now discernible in novel criticism. The prior critical emphasis on form signals the fact that a genuine History of short fiction remains to be written. This identifies the gap that this volume helps to fill.

This volume takes its place alongside companion Cambridge Histories of the English novel and English poetry. Like those volumes, it serves to interrogate the 'English' literary culture it also attempts to define. To begin with, the important influence of European writing is registered in several of the essays. There is also a 'four nations' approach to the thorny problem of nationalism, with separate chapters devoted to the short story in Wales, Scotland and Ireland. These discussions demonstrate the ways in which different national traditions permeate 'English' literary culture and also signpost the road to transnationalism. The impact of colonial experience on short fiction is addressed, and the effects of the end of Empire treated at length in chapters that examine the development of postcolonial story traditions around the world, as well as in Britain.

The chapters are grouped according to the following principles: Chapters 1–9 identify the important historical phases up until the end of the Second World War; Chapters 10–14 address the 'four nations' agenda, whilst also identifying the distinctive features of individual national traditions; Chapters 15 and 16 are concerned with the rural/urban division, an important concern in the development of the short story in England; Chapters 17–22 identify the full richness of stories written from the periphery, by writers from a range of marginalized groups and ethnicities; Chapters 23–9 address the exhaustive range of genre fiction in which the short story has excelled; and Chapters 30–5 focus on the formal properties of short fiction and the ways in which modes of transmission have influenced its reputation and development.

The primary function of the chapter divisions is to identify important practitioners and trends; but they also give scope for some 'bringing to bear' of theoretical perspectives on short fiction, which is, indisputably, an under-theorized form. Yet there is also, I hope, something fresh in the overall conception of this volume, with its ambition to establish the literary history of a topic that has not previously received attention on this scale.

Introduction

As a consequence, we sidestep those current debates that call into question the credibility of literary history per se. Fredric Jameson has expressed the view that 'increasing reflexivity' in both critical and creative realms, both of which are now influenced more and more by theoretical concepts, renders literary history ideational, merely, and impossible to carry out in its traditional mode.[1] The status of the short story makes it invulnerable to this new anxiety, to a large extent: it has escaped capture in fully-fledged literary histories, despite numerous attempts to classify its separate components in critical compendia, and has therefore not reached anything like the same degree of critical self-reflexiveness as has the novel.

Despite the fluidity of the publishing world since the nineteenth century, the short story is sometimes perceived to be an essentially static form. This impression has been reinforced by a clear emphasis on formal properties in short story theory, and this has had several negative effects for the reputation of the story as a literary form. Most damaging is the view that the short story can be a formulaic literary genre, with devices – such as the single effect, the moment of revelation, or the surprise ending – sometimes seeming too predictable or uninventive.[2] This compounds the idea that the short story is a minor form, or a training ground for the more serious business of novel writing. Taken as a whole, this History is a correction to these impressions. The exhaustive contextualization of different modes and trends will disprove that persisting notion that there is something static (and so ahistorical) about the formal properties of short fiction. This History, acknowledging and foregrounding the formal and aesthetic specificities of short fiction, is also concerned to trace their evolution.

The work is also an implicit statement about the claims of short fiction among the different literary modes, a challenge to its status as the poor relation, but also an attempt to give defining shape to a tradition that is sometimes perceived as lacking in identity. The discussion of a large number of writers who are known primarily for their stories puts a different complexion on the relative evaluation of the novel and the story: the significant number of short story specialists in the English tradition, writing in a diverse range of styles, underscores its special claims for attention.

The historical weight of evidence in this volume reinforces the idea that the short story proper was a modern literary form, coming to prominence in the nineteenth century, promoted widely by magazine publication. Even so, in a longer literary-historical view, the origins of this modern form can be traced back to much earlier periods. The opening chapter uncovers the origins of printed short fiction in England from Tudor times, showing how some of the features we associate with the short story had their origins in early examples of printed short prose, though without implying a simple 'evolutionary' line. The printed Tudor collection *A Hundred Merry Tales* (1526), a pioneering work in the tradition of the English jest book, demonstrates how various influences were condensed: this volume draws on early storytelling of the late Middle Ages and the Continental Renaissance (Chaucer, Boccaccio). It also anticipates the subversive potential of the Tudor and Elizabethan story collections now best known as jest books, where established class and gender roles – as well as established moral codes – were often challenged or undermined. Something of this ambiguous method, in which the apparent moral of a tale is at odds with the subversiveness of its engaging narrative features – is also apparent in the cony-catching pamphlets of Robert Greene from the 1590s, in which this clash of intentions is deliberately employed. The Elizabethan novella embodies another step forward in the evolution of the short story in the ways it progressed beyond the jests or cony-catching tales, by focusing on a central event or circumstance in a more elaborate manner.

Shorter fiction received another early boost in the Restoration novels (written to be distinct from the longer romance form) from the late seventeenth century, which marked another development in narrative sophistication by virtue of their special interest in setting and character, and – perhaps most importantly – their cultivation of psychological insight. The 'novels' produced around 1700, including the work of Aphra Behn, were a significant staging post in the narrative cultivation of both verisimilitude in the depiction of the world, and in the pursuit of inner realism, features that were further developed in the eighteenth century.

Authors of shorter fiction in the eighteenth century (the focus of Chapter 2) were not striving to develop forms of *technical* complexity, but they did find ways of enhancing their stories by expanding plots and creating stronger characters. This was not an era that cultivated brevity in short fiction, however, since the emphasis was very much on the improving function of fiction as a moral tool with wider social import: the further significant development of the rendering of internal states and the probing of human nature would come later. There were some notable exceptions, however, or at least some innovations that anticipated later developments. For example, the fiction in Eliza Haywood's *Female Spectator* (1744–6) did tend to anatomize the psychology of its protagonists, with a specific focus on the problems and conflicts in women's lives. This focus lent her fiction a specificity that was absent in the work of her male predecessors, who were more concerned with general moral or social issues.

One writer who thought more self-consciously about the form of short fiction was John Hawkesworth, the only eighteenth-century author of short fiction to theorize about it as a distinct species of writing. His theory that a short narrative should be focused on a single incident unusual enough to engage readers and create suspense anticipates later theories about the coherence and shape of a story (most notably, Poe's 'single effect' theory cited above). He retained the conviction that fiction should instruct as well as please; but he recognized that moral instruction would be more effective if rendered implicitly within the events of a story rather than made explicit.

A significant factor in the evolution – and changing fortunes – of the short story has been the publishing history of magazines. One very influential magazine was *The Yellow Book*. Although it ran to just thirteen volumes (April 1894 to July 1897), it remains strongly associated with the short story, and especially with the direction it was to take in the era of High modernism. (Chapter 7 is devoted to the influence of *The Yellow Book* and its culture.) An earlier formative influence on the development of the short story was the Edinburgh print culture of the early nineteenth century – notably *Blackwood's Edinburgh Magazine*, founded in 1817 – which disseminated a distinctive brand of regional Scottish writing rooted in oral traditions. In another example, the new literary magazines in the early nineteenth century created an outlet for a notable development in genre short story writing: the growth of gothic and supernatural short fiction, which flourished through the nineteenth century, leading to the sensational gothic stories of the Victorian era.

The ghost story in England illustrates the porousness of national traditions, since it had myriad influences, notably (but not just) from Ireland and Scotland. Writers were also influenced by European ghost stories dating back to the Middle Ages, and by more recent German authors (such as E. T. A. Hoffmann), as well as by American writers, including Washington Irving and Edgar Allan Poe. The international influence was a significant general trend, in fact. A notable instance is the influence of European – and especially Russian – models on the short story in Ireland, which encouraged the development of a psychological inflection in the Irish story, notably in the work of George Moore, in anticipation of the modernist experiments of James Joyce (see Chapter 10). In the case of the supernatural tale in the nineteenth century, these myriad influences (as Chapter 3 shows) are apt in the sense that supernatural tales have the tendency to interrogate and dissolve notions of identity, by trading on stereotypes of national identity.

The stock figures of gothic and supernatural tales – such as vampires and ghosts – find a central role in short fiction, often revealing a metaphorical function to frame current cultural tensions and anxieties, fears of sexuality, contagion or disease. The vampire figure can also be seen to symbolize a degenerate aristocracy in some instances. In the Victorian era, the ghost story's capacity for social commentary is well illustrated in Elizabeth Gaskell's short fiction, which betrays a gothic dimension. Gaskell's concern with the wielding of power in these tales is given a clear gender inflexion, revealing a point of contact between the gothic short story and the beginnings of the women's movement. In the right hands, the gothic tale could lend itself to relatively sophisticated deliberations about literary form. George Eliot's 'The Lifted Veil' (1859), for example, illustrates the preoccupation with representation in gothic writing: this is a psychological tale that can also be read as an allegory about the role of the author in narrative fiction. Another example of popular writing anticipating the formal concerns of later short story writing is Charles Dickens's well-known story 'The Signal-Man' (1866), an exemplar of the Victorian ghost story. In denying the reader any single interpretation, Dickens's story keeps a number of social topics in view; but it also demonstrates the capacity of the short story to cultivate a resonant ambiguity.

Ghost stories often have their origins in local lore and oral tradition; and, indeed, the influence of the oral story heritage on the modern printed form has been enduring. A notable twentieth century demonstration of this endurance is the category of stories by Anglophone postcolonial writers, where different oral traditions have been hugely important. (As Chapter 22 shows, this is a rich vein of story writing.) In African and Asian societies once subjected to British colonization, the short story has been developed in ways that are significantly shaped by the influence of traditional tale-telling. The legacy of colonialism is a complicated one in this regard, as the taint of imperialism associated with the spread of the English language has been softened and then rendered increasingly inconsequential as English has gained popularity as a lingua franca in the age of globalization. This appropriation has paved the way for the significant enrichment of the short story in English.

In the Anglophone Caribbean, where the legacy of slavery problematizes the lines of cultural continuity, there has been an uneasy, yet productive interaction between local oral traditions and the conventions of the English short story. In other post-imperial sites, in the Americas and in Australasia, indigenous voices have survived, their experiences enshrined in short fiction, which can also comment pertinently on the contemporary context. On the Indian subcontinent, the relationship between the oral and the written has a longer history, drawing on an extensive history of short narrative that has enabled the spoken and the written to coalesce for centuries. The variety of postcolonial short stories embodies a spectrum in the fusion or interaction of oral and written modes: sometimes postcolonial writers extend the range of English conventions by prioritizing the oral and the demotic; in other instances they work more closely with literary conventions, while also altering those conventions by evoking a sense of uncontainable difference.

An earlier, and very different example that illustrates this non-linear process of evolution is the pointed adaptation of oral and traditional story forms by late Victorian and early twentieth-century writers. An appropriation of myth and fable was often a crucial aspect of this phenomenon, as Chapter 5 demonstrates. The fable form, in particular, can reveal modernized satirical potential. The little-read Gilbert Cannan is an excellent example; but T. F. Powys is perhaps the best-known writer of modern fables. In one sense, he is easy to categorize as the writer of quirky religious allegories. At the same time, his fables often serve to ridicule the principles of logic and faith underpinning Western metaphysics.

The potential of the fable to reveal a distinctively – and troubling – modern aesthetic is well illustrated by Rudyard Kipling's *Just So Stories* (1902), which combine elements of both fairy tale and fable in pursuit of a hidden purpose: the stories effectively oust Christian accounts of Creation, whilst also engaging in a humorous and ironic treatment of world myths and religions. Yet fabulistic forms are not always so clear in their moral or topical content, as the work of A. E. Coppard attests: his fiction, to the contrary, can serve to foreground the disjunction between the order imposed by art and the messy contingency of life. In the hands of modernist authors, mythology and religious parable are used as a form of primitivist critique of modernity, productive of a modern form of moral or religious awareness. If some of E. M. Forster's stories hint at this potential, there is a more full-blown attempt to realize it in the fables of D. H. Lawrence, where the rewriting of Christian mythology – as in *The Escaped Cock* – can be challengingly direct.

A feature more commonly associated with modernist writing is also one of the central technical features associated with the short story – the sudden illuminating moment. Yet the idea of the revelation is explored in self-conscious ways that exploit the paradoxical ambiguities that surround the apparent 'epiphany', as it is treated in representative gnomic modernist stories. In some cases, this obfuscation of a simple, single revelation can facilitate a very economical suggestion of the hidden, and perhaps contradictory complexity of personality, as in James Joyce's 'The Dead'; in other cases, a 'non-epiphany' can reveal the social constraints that hinder a character's understanding of him or herself, as in Katherine Mansfield's 'Bliss'. Viewed more broadly, the cultivation of the fragmented perspective has given short story writers purchase on a variety of experiences through the history of modernity. Chapter 9 explores the capacity of short fiction to capture moments of social dissonance and rupture in the short fiction of the two World Wars, showing how the story functions very effectively to capture 'snapshot' views of war experience.

Accounts of the development of the short story, from the nineteenth century through the twentieth century, can frame and condense the experience of modernity in different ways. This economical framing can encompass national experience, too. In the case of the short story in Ireland, key phases in the development of the nation can be read off from the technical and stylistic progression of the short story, which maps on to the transition from colonialism to independence. (Chapters 10 and 11 delineate this process very clearly.) The nineteenth-century tale in Ireland was often implicated in British imperialism, geared to explaining Irish mores to English readers. The origins of an Irish short story tradition are evident in the nineteenth century, but writers were often caught between two stools, celebrating the Irish traditions and communities on one hand, whilst, on the other, pandering to the tastes of an English readership – as in the case of William Carleton. The Irish Literary Revival had an important bearing on the short story in Ireland, reviving and modernizing the folk tradition at the same time. A mood of transition in post-independence Ireland is discernible in the early work of key practitioners Frank O'Connor and Seán O'Faoláin, whose 'apprentice' work of the 1930s anticipated the major contribution they were to make mid-century. There was no greater modernizer than O'Faoláin, whose work as an editor and a writer was instrumental in shaping the Irish short story from the 1940s, giving it greater purchase in its realistic portrayals of contemporary urban and rural life. As modernity gained an increasing hold on Irish life through the second half of the twentieth century, so did a new mood issue in the Irish short story, affecting its forms and techniques. Emerging writers found it possible to be more critical of the Irish state, and moved away from romantic nationalism. A marked tendency in the Irish tradition – for example in the stories of Seán O'Faoláin,

Mary Lavin and Maeve Brennan – was towards more complex psychological treatments.

A transition from depictions of rural to urban life is one of the markers of the march of modernity in the Irish tradition, much as it is in the short story in Scotland, the focus of Chapter 12. This is not a simple linear progression, however, since the depiction of rural isolation can be one of the ways in which Scottish writers negotiate questions of community and belonging. The re-purposing of dialect and orality is another distinctive feature of how Scottish writers interrogate questions of national identity, a feature that also informs arresting experimental forms in the later twentieth century. In this connection the Scottish short story has much in common with the celebrated renaissance of the Scottish novel since the 1980s, especially the dominance of working-class realism: that dominance is just as much a feature of the short story – for example in the work of James Kelman and Agnes Owens.

An element that unites regional and national traditions of short story writing is that they have flourished in difficult social and economic circumstances. This has been especially true of the story in Wales (see Chapter 13), as writers have responded, in different eras, to the consequences of economic collapse. While this capacity seems to chime with that characteristic of the short story identified by Frank O'Connor in his very influential and often cited study – its propensity to treat of the 'submerged population group' – this tendency in the Welsh tradition goes further.[3] Whether presenting politicized anger, or inciting that feeling in readers, short stories from Wales can approach the qualities of social realism that are not often found in regional writing, or the short story.

The dominance of the novel in twentieth-century literary history, coupled with the influence of modernist experimentation, has tended to occlude the reputation of many fine English short story writers (Chapter 14), either because they were not ground-breaking in a technical sense, or because their novels overshadow their achievements in shorter fiction. Graham Greene, for example, wrote many excellent stories, but is primarily known as a novelist. H. E. Bates is, perhaps, the writer whose reputation has suffered most from the dominance of the novel and the prioritizing of technical innovation in accounts of twentieth-century literary history. Bates was not a formal innovator; yet he is strongly associated with a particular mood and style, which can be seen as the translation of European influences – including Maupassant, and especially Chekhov – to an English context.[4] Alongside the lush, romantic style of his rural stories, which evoke and record a passing era in ways that complicate and enrich the nostalgic response, Bates quietly engaged with a host of issues that, with hindsight, can be seen as seminal to the developing twentieth century: the morality of war; the rapidity of class change; evolving social and sexual mores; and, with an expressly formal significance, the increasing importance of middlebrow writing.

Some of the writers associated with this neglected English mood were also proponents of the rural short story (see Chapter 15), a tradition that is often misperceived as an anachronism. In fact, the literary mediation of rural experience serves to frame the challenges of modernity, especially through complex and disjunctive narrative styles, which themselves often embody an ambivalent interrogation of nostalgia. If the rural tradition utilizes specific characteristics of the short story, other distinctive formal features help define a canon of metropolitan writing, focused on London, in the English short story. As Chapter 16 shows, it is the episodic nature of the story that is pertinent here: the short story is well suited to the capture of metropolitan disorientation and to suggesting the connection between isolated moments and the larger throng of city experience. After the Second World War, especially in the 1950s and 1960s, writers from diverse ethnic backgrounds began the task of recasting London as a post-imperial metropolis, with new multicultural energies transforming the urban experience and urban perception.

The short story's capacity to render marginalized experience – or the concerns of Frank O'Connor's 'submerged population groups' – has a relevance not just to life in the British Isles away from the metropolitan centre: it is equally pertinent to the experience of groups marginalized by ethnicity, gender or sexual orientation, or because of experiences of subjugation in relation to the end of Empire. Chapters 17 to 22 examine a series of these contexts, also exploring ways in which the short story can transform the marginal into something affirmative. Strong claims can be made, for example, for a deep affinity between female experience and short fiction, exemplified in the highly accomplished work of the most prominent practitioners in the second half of the twentieth century, such as Nadine Gordimer, Doris Lessing, A. S. Byatt, Margaret Atwood and Alice Munro.

After the Second World War – and especially promoted by second-wave feminism from the 1970s onwards – feminist concerns became increasingly prominent in cultural and political debates, refracted through the lens of dramatic social change: immigration and the end of Empire; the institution of the welfare state; the sexual revolution; and the restructuring of Higher Education, for example. All of these changes had a profound impact on women's opportunities and social roles. The widening of access to universities is very significant, here. In the twenty-first century it has become commonplace to talk of an increasingly dominant link between creative writing courses and the predilections of publishing houses. A different kind of link can be observed a generation earlier, when women's writing became increasingly linked with institutions of learning. A number of significant women short story writers were also intellectuals, including A. S. Byatt, Fay Weldon and Doris Lessing.

In the second half of the twentieth century, the short story lent itself to the expression of many new cultural energies and diasporan experiences. Writers of the Windrush generation are a good example of this. The short stories that contributed to Sam Selvon's *The Lonely Londoners*, for example, sometimes embody a fusion of the calypso and the short story, to produce a new kind of social protest but also a new sense of belonging for the migrant self. If the telling of stories is a form of self-realization, at the heart of multicultural life in Britain, the short story can be seen to have played an important part in that process.

Reading through the lens of postcolonial studies, with reference to the 'settler' nations of New Zealand, Australia, Canada and South Africa, the short story is revealed in Chapter 22 to have been a highly adaptable vehicle for the literary investigation of mutating and emergent identities and nationalities. The episodic treatment of displacement and alienation in Australian short fiction has had a formative bearing on the national culture, for example. Frank Sargeson, in his sketches, proved adept at capturing the New Zealand local vernacular; and Nadine Gordimer, in a remarkable body of short fiction, used the ambiguities and narrative uncertainties that the short story can generate to great effect to register the psychological complexity of white privilege and complicity in apartheid – and then post-apartheid – South Africa. In the postcolonial context, the short story has been used brilliantly to register competing and multiple perspectives, but also to suggest the psychological processes that characterize persistence and adaptability.

In the penultimate group of chapters, formal capacities come to the fore: Chapters 23–9 demonstrate the range of genre fiction in which the short story has excelled. Yet these chapters seek to uncover the contextual factors that allow these genres to flourish. A clear example of how the short story's formal capacities can be directly linked to the wider social context can be found in the detective stories of England's so-called 'Golden Age' of detective fiction, from 1914 to 1945. Of particular note, here, is the conviction of Dorothy L. Sayers that detective writing could perform a moral function through its propensity to provide a social commentary, a view that was instrumental in shoring up the reputation of the genre in the 1920s and 1930s. The association of literary form and society goes beyond the obvious point that the problem-solving plot structure of detective writing – especially pronounced in shorter fiction – supplied a kind of balm for a society needing explanatory narratives of control in the face of unmappable modernity. When the narrative of order restored – rooted in the legacies of late-Victorian and Edwardian mores – began to lose its conviction, or, rather its explanatory force, especially after the Second World War, more 'hard-boiled' tendencies became prominent. Another tendency was to look for deeper explanations for crime – whether psychological or environmental – a trend that has enriched the genre into the twenty-first century. These arguments can also be made in connection with the detective novel; but what is interesting is how the short story concentrates these tendencies.

Another interesting generic point of affinity is that between the development of science fiction and the rise of the short story, both being dependent on magazine culture. This dependence can be said to push both science fiction and the short story towards the middlebrow, so that they present problems for the critical distinction between the 'literary' and the 'popular'. The transgressive impetus of weird writing suggests another distinctive nexus of genre and form. The English weird tradition, associated with the Decadent movement, was from its inception a challenge to the commodification of literature: it was uncompromising in comparison with the easier reading that characterized much of the content of the new mass circulation magazines in the 1880s. Since it is this magazine culture that had a material bearing on the development of the modern short story as a printed form, the weird story stands in an intriguing relationship to that developmental moment, its transgressions and evasions not just a challenge to the literary marketplace, but also, perhaps, an independent check and alternative influence on the short story. Yet that possible influence remains ineffable: the weird remains stubbornly outside the literary mainstream, a marginalized form usually absent in histories of English literature.

Formally experimental short fiction is equally beyond the frame of reference for the English literary mainstream. Indeed, the short story in Britain is not usually associated with the kind of extravagant formal experimentation evident in the work of iconic postmodern writers in the United States, such as John Barth and Donald Barthelme. There are, however, British writers who do push at the limits of the form, such as Samuel Beckett and B. S. Johnson. A less iconoclastic form of self-reflexiveness has perhaps been more prevalent, however, in which form is used in inventive ways to enact content.

There is a long tradition of this kind of self-consciously crafted short story, which suggests that, in the modern era, it has always been creatively self-reflexive. There are also instances of experimentalism being utilized to mount particular social challenges. For example, some women writers, such as Angela Carter, devised new forms of subversion and invention, producing a unique brand of postmodern intertextuality, and metafictional self-consciousness.

The last group of chapters (30–5) focuses on the formal properties of short fiction, embellishing some of the running topics from the earlier essays, and helping to pinpoint ways in which the distinctiveness of the short story sets it clearly apart from the novel, in terms of its aesthetic effects. The propensity of the form to create startling effects by means of a sudden revelation or illuminating moment, for example, establishes an opposite pole in the narrative spectrum to the novel, which hinges on time and causality. There are, however, points where the novel and the short story seem closer, even if they do not converge: the short story cycle and the novella.

It is also important to realize that the evolution of different forms of short fiction – such as the short story cycle – can also be shown to respond to social change. The short story cycle has its roots in a much longer literary tradition, a tradition that includes Homer, Boccaccio and Chaucer. Yet the structural principles of a modern form of short story cycle, emerging in the twentieth century, are distinct. Moreover, it is a format that has grown in popularity. One can speculate that the story cycle – occupying the space between the novel and the short story collection – fills the need of readers for brevity in an increasingly fast-paced and distracting culture, while also supplying the kind of explanatory framework found in the novel.

The ways in which sequences of stories have been utilized for different creative ends is very intriguing. For example, it is possible to detect an increasing prevalence of interconnected story sequences published by British Jewish writers. Work by Gabriel Josipovici, Tamar Yellin and Elena Lappin is notable in this connection, sometimes indicating the desire to transcend the purport of the single story, and to achieve a larger signification, often through narrative framing devices that address forms of displacement or suffering through patterns that, without implying the soothing balm of a falsely imposed order, can serve (at least) to make the traumatic amenable to intelligible analysis and historical memory.

If magazine publication has had a formative influence on the development of the short story over the centuries, short story anthologies have also had a significant bearing, especially in maintaining the reputation of individual writers – sometimes through the repeated selection of individual stories. Although they are often drawn towards more transitory marketable and popular qualities, anthologies have also played a role in shaping short story canons.

Another crucial influence on the perception of what makes a good short story – and so also on the fortunes and forms of the short story – has been the rapid development of university courses in creative writing in British universities from the 1990s onwards. The close relationship between Higher Education and literary publishing has been a longer-term factor in the development of fiction in the United States, but a similar relationship is now discernible in Britain. This has a special influence on the short story, because stories – or shorter fragments of fiction – are very often the focus of creative writing workshops, so students and teachers of fiction writing often hone and reflect on their craft through the medium of the story. One consequence of the creative writing course has been to make writers think more self-consciously about how to avoid the pitfalls of formulaic writing.

Through its history, the short story has revealed affinities with, or adaptability to, new technologies and modes of transmission. For example, the short story has lent itself very well to both large and small screen adaptations, from the silent era onwards. Indeed, there is a significant historical coincidence between the rise of film and the development of the modern short story, which has produced mutual cross-fertilizations of technique, especially concerning the use of point of view, and the kind of 'in medias res' narrative forms that are natural to the short story. Screen adaptations have ranged from the more literal attempts to recapture fully the feel and setting of individual stories, to more radical films in which the perceived 'essence' of a story is the starting point for a film-maker's creativity.

If one speculates about the future of fiction – and especially how fiction might develop in the era of the ebook – it is possible to see the modern short story as well placed for any 'post-book' phase of cultural development, since from its inception it has been adaptable to different modes of transmission, through magazines, pamphlets, radio transmission, and now podcasts and other online modes. To account for the persistence and endurance of the short story, however, it may be enough to observe that, through its special qualities of concentration, it satisfies the never-ending human hunger for narrative.

Introduction

Notes

1. See Fredric Jameson, 'New Literary History after the End of the New', *New Literary History*, 39 (2008), 3, pp. 375–87.
2. This idea of the 'single' and 'preconceived effect' originates from Edgar Allan Poe's review essay of Nathaniel Hawthorne's *Twice-Told Tales*, where he argued that 'in the whole composition there should be no word written, of which the tendency, direct or indirect, is not to the one pre-established design'. See Edgar Allan Poe, 'Review of *Twice-Told Tales*', *Graham's Magazine*, May 1842, reprinted in *Short Story Theories*, ed. Charles E. May (Ohio University Press, 1976), pp. 45–51 (p. 48).
3. Frank O'Connor, *The Lonely Voice: A Study of the Short Story* (London: Macmillan, 1963), pp. 20–1.
4. Bates also published an informed critical study, *The Modern Short Story* (London: Thomas Nelson & Sons, 1941).

I

Early-Modern Diversity: The Origins of English Short Fiction

BARBARA KORTE

This chapter addresses the origins of printed short fiction in England from the Tudor days to the end of the seventeenth century. Any search for the origins of the short story must necessarily acknowledge that early-modern prose fiction precedes the modern short story *and* the modern novel, and that its great diversity makes it impossible to describe the short story's origins in evolutionary terms, as some historians of the genre have tried to do.[1] Nevertheless, the shorter forms of fiction sketched in this chapter cultivated a number of features that anticipated the nature of the short story when it became established in the nineteenth century. The most obvious of these features include the appearance of stories in the medium of print and in the language of prose rather than verse.

William Caxton's edition of Chaucer's *Canterbury Tales* in 1476 marks the transition from late-medieval storytelling to an era when fiction, in short and longer forms, became part of a literary culture that was significantly reorganized by print.[2] By the middle of the sixteenth century, printed books, including collections of short fiction, were 'the primary form in which readers encountered the written word' in a market that made writing of all kinds 'available in hitherto unimaginable quantities' and for 'hitherto unreachable segments of the social world'.[3] *The Canterbury Tales* are told in verse, but print made verse less important as a tool for memorizing stories and so promoted the transition of narrative literature into prose, along with a shift away from the public recitation of stories towards silent reading. The new print market created new audiences beyond the court, but it also incorporated the aristocratic readership. The stigma surrounding print that served to preserve the exclusiveness of some traditional court genres hardly affected prose, and by 1600 as much as 'one-quarter of the books printed in England were prose fiction'.[4] This fiction was written in a variety of modes, long and short, and it reflects, as Paul Salzman argues, 'both the increased reading public and the writers' interest in experiment'.[5] Freedom to experiment was encouraged by the fact that there was no established poetics for prose narratives, and that prose did not enjoy a high level of prestige within the early-modern literary system. As Andrew Hadfield remarks, 'we do not really know that writers themselves knew what they were doing and were basing their efforts on tried and tested models that were commonly understood'.[6] Critical reflection on prose fiction and its possibilities, when it takes place at all, occurs only in the paratexts, the prefaces and dedications, of the books in which this fiction was published. This scarcity of theoretical discussion may well have served ideological purposes. It helped, as Gerd Bayer suggests, to deflect attention from 'a contamination of the larger literary field' through prose fiction, and from the possibilities that an unregulated way of writing had for providing social critique, especially in such contested matters as the relationships between classes and sexes.[7] Few early-modern writers of prose fiction 'seem to have given conscious attention to questions of length'.[8] The trends mentioned above are therefore found in its longer as well as its shorter modes. Nevertheless, prose fiction before 1700 anticipated several of the directions that the later short story would take, just as it preserved the legacy of earlier narrative traditions.

Short pieces of narrative typically survive because they are collected in books. It is through a printed Tudor collection, *A Hundred Merry Tales* (1526), that many early English narratives have been preserved. The enduring popularity of this collection with audiences across the social spectrum is attested to by a reference in Shakespeare's comedy *Much Ado About Nothing* (c.1600) and the fact that its tales were read to Queen Elizabeth as she lay on her deathbed.[9] The *Hundred Merry Tales* were themselves indebted to the storytelling of the late Middle Ages and the Continental Renaissance, including *The Canterbury Tales*, which drew on Boccaccio's *Decameron* (c.1350) and other sources and so preserved comic, romantic and instructive narratives (*fabliaux*, *lais* and *exempla*) that had been circulating, in some instances, since antiquity. The prologue to 'The Miller's Tale' explicitly refers to the many alternatives to a bawdy *fabliau* which Chaucer could offer his audience:

> Those wishing not to hear, pass it by,
> Just turn the page and choose another sort;
> You'll find all kinds of tales, both long and short,
> That touch on genteel things, on history,
> On holiness, and on morality.[10]

Chaucer's tales, printed by Caxton, were not the only sum of older narrative traditions that endured into the era of the *Hundred Merry Tales*. Another landmark is the *Gesta Romanorum*, whose stories were first compiled in England in the late thirteenth century and translated from their original Latin into English in 1473; they were printed by Wynkyn de Worde, Caxton's successor, around 1510. The stories of the *Gesta*, which are 'set arbitrarily and anachronistically in the reign of a Roman emperor', are instructive, and an interpretation appended to each of them 'stresses its value as pious example'.[11] The survival of the *Gesta Romanorum* in Tudor times illustrates, for James Mirollo, that 'storytelling continued to be a prominent feature of Renaissance social life' and was 'virtually a requirement for those who wished to display good manners or needed to employ oratorical skills' (p. 928). Like the *fabliaux*, many medieval *exempla* found their way into those Tudor and Elizabethan story collections now best known as jest books. They lost much of their didacticism in this process, however, and served the reader's merriment more than his or her instruction. As Margaret Schlauch points out, the contents of the jest books 'range from the simplest of jokes based on puns, malapropisms, dialect forms and mispronunciations, to expanded anecdotes and to genuine short tales of a humorous character'.[12] Their humour was often coarse, but the jest books were popular with readers across all social classes, not least because comic stories had a long standing in late-medieval and Renaissance learned culture.

A Hundred Merry Tales was the pioneer of English jest books, and it illustrates several ways in which collections of this type of narrative anticipate the direction taken by narrative fiction in later decades: they are compact, sometimes *very* short stories told with great economy of means. Their central interest is the accessible, entertaining story set around a specific event, and they are enlivened by colloquial dialogue that sometimes even seems 'phonetically transcribed'.[13] Their realism of presentation is combined with social commentary, especially in the form of a gentle satire of contemporary social types: from conmen and craftsmen to hypocritical priests and conceited scholars. The eighth tale, 'Of the scholar that bore his shoes to clouting', directs its irony at an Oxonian whose 'eloquent English and curious terms' make it hard for him to cope with everyday life, for example when he needs to have his shoes repaired. He asks a cobbler to 'set me two triangles and two semicircles upon my subpeditals', and the down-to-earth cobbler clearly has the upper hand on him when he replies: 'Sir, your eloquence passeth mine intelligence but I promise you if ye meddle with me, the clouting of your shoon shall cost you three pence.' This punch line is followed by a lesson in the manner of an *exemplum*: 'By this tale men may learn that it is folly to study to speak eloquently before them that be rude and unlearned.'[14] However, the idea of a moral is not the story's determining feature, and its application is meant to be understood ironically, not as affirming a hierarchy between the learned and the uneducated, but as sympathizing with the quick-witted artisan. The *Hundred Merry Tales* are just as acute with their commentary on the gender order, making the strains of married life and the battle of the sexes one of their favourite themes (which explains the reference in Shakespeare's *Much Ado*). The sixty-sixth tale, 'Of the man that would have the pot stand there as he would', presents a 'young man lately married to a wife' who thinks that it is 'good policy to get the mastery of her in the beginning' and therefore even interferes in her very own sphere of household management. He tells her to take a pot off the fire even though the food is not yet sufficiently cooked, then requests it to be put behind the door, and finally that the wife should put it on the roof – to which she complies after having asked her husband 'to hold the ladder fast for sliding'. The husband is satisfied at last: '"Lo, now standeth the pot there as I would have it"', but this remark finally raises the woman's resistance: 'This wife, hearing that, suddenly poured the hot pottage on his head and said thus: "And now been the pottage there as I would have them."' The interpretation at the end of the tale seems to gloss over this act of subversiveness, but it cannot disguise the woman's triumph: 'By this tale men may see it is no wisdom for a man to attempt a meek woman's patience too far, lest it turn to his own hurt and damage' (pp. 123–4). The *Hundred Merry Tales* have no interest in developing characters, but they point towards the later short story in that they make the most of their shortness, being told in a vivid manner that heads straight towards the climax. Not even the morals can draw the sting out of their stories' tails, for they are obviously mere tags and subvert the instruction they seem to deliver. This was a success formula, and jest books remained popular in England until the seventeenth century.[15] Some of the later ones had central characters such as Howleglass, the Parson of Kalenborowe (both imported from Germany), or Long Meg of Westminster and the Cobbler of Canterbury, lending the books a greater unity and marking their transition to longer narrative forms. This, and their emphasis on the world of the middle classes, combined with realism of speech and circumstance, relates the jest books to the bourgeois fiction of the Elizabethan era, and notably the 'novels' of Thomas Deloney.

Deloney, a weaver, was a popular ballad writer before he turned into an equally popular author of prose narratives for a middle-class audience at a time of flourishing trade. The works of fiction he published between 1597 and 1600, *The Gentle Craft*, *Jack of Newberie* and *Thomas of Reading*, are set in the past but rooted firmly in the realities and desires of late Elizabethan bourgeois life. They celebrate the social success and the values of craftsmen, especially shoemakers and cloth traders, and because they often project an upward mobility it has been observed that their realism is mixed with patterns of chivalric romance 'adapted for a new class anxious to see its newfound respectability and power idealized in the way its superiors continued, more uneasily, to idealize theirs'.[16] However, Deloney's narratives are most obviously connected to traditions of comic and realistic narration, and especially that of the jests. The second part of *The Gentle Craft* announces to the 'Gentle Reader' that he will not find 'pickt words, or choise phrases but a quaint and plaine discourse, best fitting matters of merriment, seeing wee have herein no cause to talke of Courtiers or Scholers'.[17] While focusing on craftsmen and their servants, the social vision of Deloney's narratives is also, however, directed at the national community that formed itself under Elizabeth I and develops, as Cheney notes, a 'view of English prosperity where desires are channelled into fruitful and profitable directions'.[18] Deloney's fiction has been discussed as a precursor of the novel, but the works' episodic character also permits one to read them as interlinked tales, and *The Gentle Craft* (1597) is nothing but a collection of six tales, from saints' legend to jest, constructed around the shoemakers it celebrates. Its best-known story is based on a chronicle and narrates episodes from the life of Simon Eyre, the shoemaker who became a famous mayor of London. It contains elements familiar from jest books, for example when Eyre's clever wife suggests a trick through which he can amass the fortune he needs to become a merchant. This involves impersonating an alderman, whose appearance is detailed from the style of his beard to his 'great seale-ring of gold'.[19] The story also provides occasions for observing and satirizing the foreigners whom late-Elizabethan London attracted in great numbers, while acknowledging that these foreigners also made contributions to English life. One of Eyre's employees, John the Frenchman, is noted for importing a new fashion, namely 'the low cut shoo with the square toe, and the latchet overthwart the instep' (p. 43).

Deloney's narratives are centred on worthy representatives of the aspiring middling classes and their achievements. However, the prosperity of trade and services in Elizabethan England was matched by growing numbers of vagrants, beggars, thieves and conmen that gave rise to fears among the affluent. During the 1560s, the book market responded to such fears with a form of instructive writing that exposed the tricks of criminals and generally expounded the dangers that the underworld posed to the community's wealth and wellbeing. John Awdeley's *Fraternity of Vagabonds* (c.1561) and Thomas Harman's *A Caveat or Warning for Common Cursetors* (1566) adopt an anti-vagrancy policy promoted by the dominant classes that would eventually be inscribed into the strict Elizabethan Poor Laws. They describe types of vagabonds and swindlers, as well as their several tricks, tools and cant, for the benefit of the intended victims. However, usefulness alone does not explain the success of these publications. Their popularity seems to be based on the short tales that accompany the ethnographic descriptions, especially in Harman's *Caveat*, which has 'clear affinities with Tudor jest books'.[20] This affinity threatens to undermine the intention of a 'warning', and the stories in particular portray 'low' life not only in a sensational but also in an entertaining manner.

A deliberate play with this clash of intentions marks the cony-catching pamphlets of Robert Greene that share the contemporary jest book's realistic and satirical manner of writing. They appeared in the 1590s and are almost contemporary with Deloney's narratives about honourable craftsmen, but make a different kind of social commentary. The first of the pamphlets, *A Notable Discovery of Coosnage* (1591), announces in its extended title that it is 'Written for the general benefit of all Gentlemen, Citizens, Aprentises, Countrey Farmers and yeomen, that may hap to fall into the company of such coosening companions', while *The Second Part of Conny-Catching* (also 1592), produced soon after the popular success of the first, blithely advertises 'sundrie pithy and pleasant Tales worthy the reading of all estates'. It also identifies some of its tales explicitly as 'merrye jests'.[21] A good example of this merriness is a story from *The Third Part of Conny-Catching* (1592), in which a 'cunning knave' robs a London merchant of a trunk with precious linen and plate and then even tricks his victim into helping him carry the booty away. The story begins with the explicit suggestion that it should be read as an example: 'Within the Cittie of *London*, dwelleth a worthy man who ... had such a shrewd mischaunce of late by a Conny catcher, as may well serve for an example to others leaste they have the like.' But it then takes a subversive turn when it directs the reader's sympathy less to the victim than to the perpetrator and his struggle with the heavy trunk: 'having it out at the doore, unseene of any neighbour or anybody else, he stood strugling with it to lift it up on the stall, which by reason of the weight trobled him very much'. The thief's predicament becomes even more awkward when the merchant suddenly arrives on the scene, but the thief immediately overcomes his shock and comes up with the idea for his clever trick, which the reader can admire and enjoy. The merchant, by contrast, is presented in the story's moral as a man who has been so involved in the pursuit of his business that he does not even notice when the fruits of this business are carried off.[22] Greene seems to have learned from the best of the jests: his story is witty and skilfully told, zooming in from a panoramic beginning to a lively scene with a surprise ending. Its social sympathies are not with the underclass in the sense of a 'submerged population group', as Frank O'Connor would later write, but it uses the perspective of this class to throw a mildly satirical light on the social inequalities of Elizabethan England.[23]

The Cambridge-educated Greene was one of the first professional writers of prose in England and tried to reach readers of all ranks and tastes. Apart from short cony-catching pamphlets for an audience outside the court, he is also the author of longer pastoral romances written in a more courtly manner, such as *Pandosto* (1588), a source for Shakespeare's *Winter's Tale*. The Elizabethan book market targeted a courtly and educated readership with prose fiction that carried different cultural interests from those that characterized fiction for the middling classes, and that also flaunted its literariness through a consciously heightened style. It included a mode of narrative that can be seen as another significant step in the direction of the short story: the Elizabethan novella, which became popular in the 1560s and 1570s and reached English readers in the form of collections of stories that were translations, or rather free adaptations, of French and Italian sources, including Boccaccio, but also of more recent writers such as Bandello, Cinthio and Marguerite de Navarre.[24] The pioneering publication was William Painter's *The Palace of Pleasure* (two tomes, 1566 and 1567), which was dedicated to a nobleman, the Earl of Warwick, while its address to the reader in the first tome indicates the wider readership that Painter, a Clerk of the Ordinance in the Tower of London, had in mind: 'the Lady, Gentlewoman, or other of the feminine kinde' as well as 'the marchaunt' and 'the yeoman'.[25] So, although Painter's title 'claims to represent courtliness', his collection is actually transgressive and 'offers a shared social experience imagined through the medium of reading the printed book'.[26]

'Novella' translates literally as 'a little new thing', and it is in this sense that Painter used the term in the extended title of his *Palace*, which announced '*pleasaunt Histories and excellent Novelles, selected out of divers good and commendable Authors*'. The address to the reader also refers to 'these newes or Novelles here presented' (p. 10). However, the newness did not lie in the *Palace*'s contents. Before Cervantes' *Novelas ejemplares* (1613, partly translated into

English in 1640), novellas were typically retellings of older stories that sometimes dated back as far as classical antiquity, and their various collections often included versions of the same narratives. The first tome of *The Palace of Pleasure* derives its stories from 'Greeke and Latine Authors', as well as 'Italian, French, and Englishe' ones. It begins with a version of the Rape of Lucrece and ends with a comic story about a 'Doctor of Laws'. Despite using well-known material, Elizabethan adaptors such as Painter, or George Pettie and Barnaby Rich after him, imbued the novella with the 'new courtesy, new philosophy, new civilization' of their time.[27] Their books, like the Continental collections they harvested, offered readers the pleasures of variety with different kinds of stories as well as a wide array of characters, situations and behaviour, and they explored the possibilities of storytelling in the versatile language of prose, so that the novella collections were 'doubtlessly deemed the paradigm of literary diversity'.[28] So what appeared new about the Elizabethan novella, and what points to later developments of the short story, was the way in which it approached its material. It focuses on a central event or circumstance, but in a more elaborate manner than the contemporary jests or cony-catching tales. Its interest in the probability of actions and their circumstances is pronounced, and so is its sense of the dramatic, which might explain the attraction which the novella collections presented as a quarry for contemporary playwrights.[29] The relative length of the novella in comparison to the snappy jest is also due to the flowery style which most writers adopted – Pettie's *A Petite Palace of Pettie his Pleasure* (1576) reached a euphuistic high – as well as their spelling out of didactic messages. Narratorial effusions and stilted speeches retarded the progress of the story and overshadowed what the novella brought to the development of the short story, namely a unified narrative interest combined with an elaborate narrated world. And because the novella was perceived as 'new', it also stimulated the first significant theoretical reflections on (short) fiction.

The dedications and prefaces to novella collections are far more reflective on the genre and its reception than those of other story books.[30] They try to define their readers in a time of expanding audiences, and their comments on female readers in particular have become a matter of debate. While Paul Salzman, for example, finds it 'hard to determine whether we are looking at an actual female readership, or rather at a knowing exchange between men', Melissa Walter claims that 'an axis of gender' was also used 'to recode anxieties about class'.[31] The prefatory materials of the collections also debate the worth of prose fiction in literary as well as moral terms, which can be read as a sign of an anxiety 'that the more the reading public grew, the more literary standards and – by association – social and political order, would be threatened'.[32] The scope of human behaviour which the Elizabethan novellas presented to their male and female readers as matter that was not only pleasant but also 'plausible' could be dubious, and not only where the stories engaged with 'the miseries of rapes and fleshly actions'.[33] For Neil Rhodes, *The Palace of Pleasure* seemed to offer its contemporary readers 'a kaleidoscope of social possibility for modern life' that was transgressive in terms of rank as well as gender norms: 'In many of these stories, women can be seen to be agents in their own lives, whether fortunately or unfortunately, and the effect of the strong undercurrents of illicit sex ... is to lend some legitimacy to the relationships that are illicit only in terms of social difference.'[34] It is understandable why Roger Ascham, a leading educator of his time, was scandalized by the vogue of novellas that Painter's success with the audience unleashed. *The Scholemaster* (1570) complains bitterly about 'fond books, of late translated out of Italian into English, sold in every shop in London' that 'corrupt honest manners'.[35] However, as Salzman remarks, the novella collections themselves expressed concern over their 'potentially harmful effect on the reader', and Painter 'anxiously explains how even the most apparently frivolous and morally suspect elements of his translations have a didactic purpose'.[36]

If transgressive behaviour was most scandalous when it involved women, the story of the 'Duchess of Malfy,' the twenty-third novella in the second tome of *The Palace of Pleasure*, is an apt example.[37] It presents a young widow, the Duchess, who is still 'moved wyth that desyre which pricketh others that be of Flesh and Bone'. She violates decorum not only because she covets a man, but also because that man, Antonio Bologna, is the master of her household and below her family's rank. As is well known from Webster's dramatic treatment of the material, their secret marriage, which yields three children, is punished relentlessly once it is discovered. Even in the novella, Painter points to the tragic curve of the action and compares its stages to acts: 'Beholde the first Acte of this Tragedy, and the provision of the fare which afterwardes sent them bothe to their grave.' However, the narrative's dramatic potential is diminished by the narrator's intrusive commentary, and by long-winded soliloquies in which the Duchess muses over her 'unacquaynted lust' and unequal standards for men and women ('what greater right have Princes to ioyne wyth a simple Gentlewoman, than the Princesse to mary a Gentleman'), while Bologna deliberates the social inappropriateness of the match. A two-page introduction suggests right from the start how virtuous readers are meant to interpret and learn from the scandalous story, and the narrator's authority is boosted by a writing style that is saturated with rhetorical effects and learned allusions:

> Dyonisius the Tyraunt of Scicilia, felt greater payne when hee was expelled his Kyngdome, than Milo did, beinge banished from Rome: for so mutch as the one was a Soveraygne Lorde, the sonne of a Kynge, a Iusticiary on Earth, and the other but a simple Citizen of a Citty, wherein the People had Lawes, and the Lawes of Magistrates were had in reverence. So lykewyse the fall of a high and lofty Tree, maketh greater noyse, than that whych is low and little ... Wherefore it behooveth the Noble, and sutch as have charge of Common wealth, to lyve an honest Lyfe, and beare their port upright, that none have cause to discourse uppon their wicked deedes and naughty life. And above all modesty ought to be kept by Women, whom as their race, Noble birth, aucthority and name, maketh them more famous, even so their vertue, honesty, chastity, and continencie more prayse worthy.

This slow, non-narrative beginning contradicts the modern intuition that a short story is tightly constructed and has an immediate beginning. Its function is, rather, to anchor the story in the tastes, knowledge and norms of a polite Elizabethan readership, and to provide a moral foil (or fig leaf) for the subsequent depiction of the Duchess's sexual longing and her determination to have it fulfilled. The process through which she comes to this decision is rendered in a long oration, which slows the story down yet increases its psychological plausibility. Such plausibility is also created through Painter's eye for non-verbal behaviour, for instance in the scene when the two lovers reveal their feelings to each other: 'The Duchesse ... seeinge hir friend rapt with the passion, and standing still unmooveable through feare, pale and amazed ... knew by that Countenaunce and astonishment of Bologna, that she was perfectly beloved of him.'

Painter's display of learning, his rhetoric and his moral exhortation inflate his *novelle* and distinguish them from later short stories. These elements can be seen to withdraw in manifestations of the novella during the later seventeenth century, while the psychological interest that appears in stories like 'The Duchess of Malfy' increases. First, however, long romances became the new vogue while short fiction stagnated, although the popular chapbooks that included, amongst other material, 'the first prose redactions of several well known stories, such as those of Robin Hood, Guy of Warwick, and Bevis of Hampton', experienced continued demand.[38] Only after the Restoration was shorter fiction revitalized in the hands of literary writers, if usually in longer forms than the modern short story, and once more the impulse came from the Continent. Translations of a new type of *nouvelles* by French writers, such as Paul Scarron and Madame de Lafayette, or the anonymous *Lettres portugaises*, translated as *Five Love Letters from a Nun to a Cavalier* (1678), enjoyed great success, and English writers took up the model. The *nouvelles* or novels, as they were called in English, appealed to a polite readership, but their audience was wider than for the long romances because their relative shortness made them more affordable and more consumable for readers who had less time at their disposal than the aristocracy. First and foremost, however, the Restoration novels were distinguished by a special interest in setting and character. Charles May suggests that, to their contemporary readers, they seemed to observe 'concrete details in the external world' and to study the psychology of their characters.[39]

That the Restoration novels were written in contrast to the longer romance is noted explicitly in prefaces, for example William Congreve's to *Incognita: or, Love and Duty Reconcil'd* (1692). This 'Novel', as the original title designates it, differs from the romance not only in terms of length and the 'more familiar nature' of its characters and action, but also with respect to the structuring of this action. *Incognita* narrates three days of adventures that are caused by mistaken identities amongst two amorous couples. Congreve intended to present these adventures in an imitation of '*Dramatick* Writing', namely 'the Design, Contexture and Result of the Plot', and so to achieve a 'Unity of Contrivance'.[40] However, most of the Restoration novels lack the compactness and unity that Congreve had in mind, and their significance in the development of the short story lies, rather, in their insistence upon verisimilitude, that is, the probability of setting, action and characters' speech, and in their emphasis on psychological insight. It is because of the probability of setting and action that the politician Henry Neville's 'The Isle of Pines' (1668), the account of an imaginary shipwreck and the survivors' settlement and very fruitful reproduction on a remote island, became a European-wide success and was often read as a factual rather than fictional narrative. It has indeed a strong realistic effect, using the fiction of autobiographical narration and being embedded in the context of early global trade. Its detailed descriptions seem to anticipate *Robinson Crusoe*, for example when the narrator describes how he builds a hut: first cutting poles, then digging holes for them, and finally setting them 'at an equal distance, and nailing the broken boards of the Casks, Chests, and Cabins [from the ship], and such like to them, making my door to the Seaward, and having covered the top, with sail-clothes strain'd, and nail'd'.[41]

A concern for verisimilitude is also a strong element in Aphra Behn's novels, and she draws attention to it in her prefaces as well as within the narratives themselves. Since Behn lived by her writing, she was necessarily sensitive to fashions and market demands. It is unsurprising, therefore, that she took up fiction writing, even though few of her narratives are structurally as accomplished as her work for the stage. *Oroonoko; or: The Royal Slave* (1688), now her most famous longer novel, gave her a special opportunity to practise her interest in verisimilitude; it has been acclaimed for the realism with which Behn depicts the colony of Surinam, which she knew from a personal visit in her youth. Behn's *Love-Letters Between a Noble-Man and his Sister* (written 1684), another longish novel, has been named as an example of the 'enormous breakthrough towards psychological realism' that could be achieved in epistolary fiction.[42] The writer's commitment to realism is affirmed even in sensational pieces such as 'The Fair Jilt' (1688), whose title character seduces and manipulates men with great recklessness. The narrator, who proclaims herself to have been an 'Eye-witness' to most of what she tells, assures her readers that she does 'not pretend here to entertain you with a feign'd Story, or any thing piec'd together with *Romantick Accidents*; but every Circumstance, to a Tittle, is Truth'.[43] One of the narrative's most sensational elements is the failed execution of the jilt's husband, who has been condemned to death for trying to poison her sister for her. Behn's circumstantial realism includes such 'tittles' as the 'Sawdust about the place where he was to kneel, to receive the Blood' (p. 44), and the man's account of how he experienced his miraculous survival of the executioner's stroke speaks of an interest in psychological nuance: 'he had no Sense; nay, not even of Pain, so absolutely dead he was with Imagination ... nor did he remember any thing, from the Lifting up of his Hands, to his Fall; and then awaken'd, as out of a Dream; or rather, a Moment's Sleep, without Dream' (p. 47). 'The History of the Nun: or, The Fair Vow Breaker' (1689) is one of those narratives in which Behn focuses on women who experience predicaments in their roles as nuns, daughters, lovers or wives (pp. 205–58). Here, too, readers are granted access to the main character's mind and share her most conflicted moments immediately from her perspective. The story contains many such moments, as the protagonist first breaks her nun's vow to marry the man she loves, and then finds that she has also broken her marriage vow. Believing her first husband, Henault, killed in a battle, she marries the wealthy Villenoys, but then faces the shock of her first husband's return after seven years in Turkish slavery. The woman's dilemma, rendered with urgency, detail and a keen sense for the force of material circumstances in human life, motivates her decision to murder the returnee:

> In one moment, she run over a thousand Thoughts. She finds, by his Return, she is not only expos'd to all the Shame imaginable; to all the Upbraiding, on his part, when he shall know she is marry'd to another; but all the Fury and Rage of *Villenoys*, and the Scorn of the Town, who will look on her as an Adulteress: She sees *Henault* poor, and knew, she must fall from all the Glory and Tranquillity she had for five happy Years triumph'd in; in which time, she had known no Sorrow, or Care, tho' she had endur'd a thousand with *Henault*. She dyes, to think, however, that he should know, she had been so lightly in Love with him, to marry again; and dyes, to think, that *Villenoys* must see her again in the Arms of *Henault*; besides, she could not recall her Love, for Love, like Reputation, once fled, never returns more. (p. 249)

Attention to circumstance and psychology also marks Behn's truly short but lesser known pieces of fiction. 'The Unfortunate Happy Lady: A True History' takes as its point of departure the misfortunes of a young gentlewoman whom her brother tries to cheat out of her inheritance and therefore sends to a brothel (pp. 361–87). 'The Adventure of the Black Lady' narrates the predicament of a young unmarried woman from the country who comes to London because she is pregnant; apart from her personal misery, she faces persecution through parish authorities who do not want to be burdened with the cost of an indigent mother and an illegitimate child (pp. 313–20). Both stories detail settings that would have been familiar to contemporary readers, and they permit glimpses into the protagonists' inner lives. However, most of the short narratives were unpublished at Behn's death and were possibly not finished; their rambling plots suggest that Behn might still have expanded them. Behn's fiction, like that of other Restoration novelists, does not anticipate the modern short story in a direct line. But the 'novels' produced around 1700 were a step forward in terms of the outer and inner realism that the eighteenth century would fully develop.

It was not only fiction, however, that propelled the major tendencies in the writing of short narratives during the sixteenth and seventeenth centuries. Non-fictional writing also left its traces in the development towards greater verisimilitude and formal realism. The prescriptions in Bishop Sprat's *History of the Royal Society* (1667) for a plain style in writing about science and discovery affected the writing of prose fiction before Defoe. The essay and the character sketch – exemplified by Bacon's *Essays* (three editions between 1597 and 1625) and Sir Thomas Overbury's *Characters* (1614) – became influential forms around 1600. Both showed an interest in contemporary reality, its characters and forms of behaviour that mirrored that of the fiction writers, and they demonstrated, above all, the virtues of brevity and a concentration 'on a unified and single idea', as Beachcroft notes.[44] Eventually, fictional stories, essays and character sketches came to co-exist in the magazine, a segment of print culture that would have the greatest impact on the short story next to the book collection. Periodicals did not flourish until the eighteenth century, but their beginnings in England are within the compass of the present chapter: the *Gentleman's Journal* appeared monthly between January 1692 and November 1694, attracting its readers not only with recent news but also with literary pieces. These pieces included stories on modern town life, which Charles Mish characterizes as 'fabliaux for those with some taste and education' that 'necessarily involve some depiction of manners and a realistic viewpoint'.[45]

Printed short fiction published between 1500 and 1700 was in many respects still remote from what came to be understood as the short story in the nineteenth century. The demarcations between longer and shorter forms of fiction were porous and fuzzy, and the formal freedom of prose fiction generated a great diversity of forms. It is precisely this diversity that makes early-modern short fiction, including its medieval legacies, a precursor of the later short story. *Exempla* and *fabliaux*, jests, cony-catching tales, novellas and novels all point towards the later genre, though not in a simple evolutionary line: the Tudor jests demonstrate an instinct for snappy, pointed narration, but the Elizabethan novella, while displaying a sense of unified action, was burdened with learnedness, rhetoric and didacticism, and the Restoration novel, which promoted a new sense of realism, tended to sprawl in length as well as structure. And yet they all cultivated some of the features that converged in the modern short story.

Notes

1. Henry Seidel Canby, *The Short Story in English* (New York: Holt, 1909); T. O. Beachcroft, *The Modest Art: A Survey of the Short Story in English* (London: Oxford University Press, 1968).
2. Edgar Hill Duncan, 'Short Fiction in Medieval English: A Survey', *Studies in Short Fiction*, 9 (1972), pp. 1–28, and 'Short Fiction in Medieval English: II. The Middle English Period', *Studies in Short Fiction*, 11 (1974), pp. 227–41.
3. David Scott Kastan, 'Print, Literary Culture and the Book Trade', in *The Cambridge History of Early Modern English Literature*, ed. David Loewenstein and Janel Mueller (Cambridge University Press, 2002), pp. 81–116 (p. 82).
4. Gary F. Waller, 'British Short Fiction in the Sixteenth and Seventeenth Centuries', in *Critical Survey of Short Fiction*, ed. Frank N. Magill, 7 vols. (Englewood Cliffs, NJ: Salem Press, 1981), II, pp. 483–504 (p. 484).

5. Paul Salzman, *English Prose Fiction 1558–1700: A Critical History* (Oxford: Clarendon Press, 1985), p. 6.
6. Andrew Hadfield, 'Prose Fiction', in *A New Companion to English Renaissance Literature and Culture*, ed. Michael Hattaway, 2 vols. (Chichester: Wiley-Blackwell, 2010), II, pp. 423–36 (p. 423); and Salzman, *English Prose Fiction*, p. 342.
7. Gerd Bayer, 'Early Modern Prose Fiction and the Place of Poetics', *Anglia*, 129 (2011), pp. 362–77 (p. 365).
8. Waller, 'British Short Fiction', p. 483.
9. Linda Woodbridge, 'Jest Books, the Literature of Roguery, and the Vagrant Poor in Renaissance England', *English Literary Renaissance*, 33.2 (2003), pp. 201–10 (p. 206).
10. 'The Miller's Tale', in *The Canterbury Tales by Geoffrey Chaucer*, trans. into modern English by Ronald E. Ecker and Eugene J. Crook (Palatka, FL: Hodge and Braddock, 1993), lines 3176–80.
11. James V. Mirollo, 'Renaissance Short Fiction', in *European Writers: The Middle Ages and the Renaissance*, ed. William T. H. Jackson and George Stade, 14 vols. (New York: Scribner's, 1983), II, pp. 927–56 (p. 932).
12. Margaret Schlauch, 'English Short Fiction in the 15th and 16th Centuries', *Studies in Short Fiction*, 3 (1966), pp. 393–434 (p. 405); see also Ian Munro and Anne Lake Prescott, 'Jest Books', in *The Oxford Handbook of English Prose 1500–1640*, ed. Andrew Hadfield (Oxford University Press, 2013), pp. 343–59.
13. Paul Zall, 'The Natural History of Jestbooks: An Introduction', in *A Hundred Merry Tales and Other English Jestbooks of the Fifteenth and Sixteenth Centuries*, ed. Paul Zall (Lincoln: University of Nebraska Press, 1963), pp. 1–10 (p. 8).
14. *Hundred Merry Tales*, ed. Zall, pp. 72–3. Subsequent page references to this edition are given in parentheses in the text.
15. Charles C. Mish, 'English Short Fiction in the Seventeenth Century', *Studies in Short Fiction*, 6.3 (1969), pp. 233–330 (pp. 259–66).
16. Waller, 'British Short Fiction', p. 496.
17. *The Gentle Craft by Thomas Deloney*, ed. Simon Barker (Aldershot: Ashgate, 2007), p. 73.
18. Donald Cheney, 'Narrative, Romance, and Epic', in *The Cambridge Companion to English Literature, 1500–1600*, ed. Arthur F. Kinney (Cambridge University Press, 1999), pp. 200–19 (p. 212).
19. *The Gentle Craft*, ed. Barker, pp. 42–65 (p. 47).
20. Woodbridge, 'Jest Books', p. 206.
21. *The Life and Complete Works in Prose and Verse of Robert Greene, M.A.*, ed. Alexander B. Grosart, 15 vols. (New York: Russell & Russell, 1964), X, pp. 3, 67.
22. *Prose and Verse of Robert Greene*, ed. Grosart, pp. 182–5.
23. Frank O'Connor, *The Lonely Voice: A Study of the Short Story* (London: Macmillan, 1963), pp. 18–21.

24. Joseph Gibaldi, 'The Renaissance Theory of the Novella', *Canadian Review of Comparative Literature* (1975), pp. 201–27.
25. William Painter, 'To the Reader', in *The Palace of Pleasure*, ed. Joseph Jacobs, 3 vols. (Hildesheim: Olms, 1968), I, pp. 10–14 (p. 12).
26. Melissa Walter, 'Constructing Readers and Reading Communities: Marguerite de Navarre's *Heptaméron* 32 in England', *Renaissance and Reformation*, 27 (2003), pp. 35–59 (p. 45).
27. Canby, *Short Story in English*, p. 107.
28. Gibaldi, 'Renaissance Theory of the Novella', pp. 213–14.
29. Gibaldi, 'Renaissance Theory of the Novella', pp. 215–16.
30. Paul Salzman, 'Placing Tudor Fiction', *Yearbook of English Studies* 38 (2008), pp. 136–49 (p. 137).
31. Salzman, 'Placing Tudor Fiction', p. 147; Walter, 'Constructing Readers', p. 44.
32. Waller, 'British Short Fiction', p. 484.
33. Painter, 'To the Reader', pp. 10, 11.
34. Neil Rhodes, 'Italianate Tales: William Painter and George Pettie', in *The Oxford Handbook of English Prose 1500–1640*, pp. 91–105 (p. 99).
35. Roger Ascham, *The Schoolmaster (1570)*, ed. Lawrence V. Ryan (Ithaca, NY: Cornell University Press, 1967), p. 67.
36. Salzman, 'Placing Tudor Fiction', p. 138.
37. Painter, 'The Duchess of Malfy', *The Palace of Pleasure*, III, pp. 3–43. Subsequent quotations from pp. 3–4, 8, 13, 18, 20.
38. Mish, *English Short Fiction*, p. 316.
39. Charles E. May, 'The Novella', in *Critical Survey of Long Fiction*, ed. Frank E. Magill, 8 vols. (rev. edn Pasadena, CA: Salem Press, 1991), VIII, pp. 3873–9 (p. 3873).
40. 'The Preface to the Reader [to *Incognita*]', in *The Works of William Congreve*, ed. D. F. McKenzie 3 vols. (Oxford University Press, 2011), III, pp. 4–6.
41. Henry Neville, *The Isle of Pines*, cited from the critical text in John Scheckter, *The Isle of Pines, 1668: Henry Neville's Uncertain Utopia* (Aldershot: Ashgate, 2011), p. 19.
42. Waller, 'British Short Fiction', p. 501.
43. Aphra Behn, 'The Fair Jilt, or, The History of Prince Tarquin and Miranda', in *The Works of Aphra Behn*, ed. Janet Todd, 7 vols. (London: Pickering, 1995), III, pp. 1–48 (p. 9). Subsequent page references to this edition are given in parentheses in the text.
44. Beachcroft, *The Modest Art*, p. 78.
45. Mish, *English Short Fiction*, p. 314.

2

Short Prose Narratives of the Eighteenth and Nineteenth Centuries

DONALD J. NEWMAN

In his survey of British short fiction in the early nineteenth century, most of which was first published in periodicals, Tim Killick argues that the perceived lack of imaginative fecundity of the short fiction narratives published between 1800 and 1830 resulted in a large corpus of short fiction being marginalized in the history of the modern short story.[1] The same point can be made about the original short fiction published in the eighteenth century, and there was a good deal of it. Robert D. Mayo catalogued 1,375 titles of fiction at least 5,000 words long that appeared in British periodicals other than newspapers between 1740 and 1815, about half of which were written by British authors, and he emphasizes that his catalogue lists but a tenth of the fiction published in periodicals during that period. Shorter pieces, he reports, enjoyed a 'vast preponderance'.[2] Benjamin Boyce estimates that this remainder could amount to as many as 15,000 to 18,000 pieces.[3] In the beginning of the century, the bulk of this short fiction consisted of 'tiny tales and diminutive sketches', but over the course of the century these tiny tales became the literary groundwork for the tradition that British authors in the middle of the nineteenth century disrupted to create the modern short story, a genre with aesthetic qualities based on narrative brevity that distinguish it from the story that is merely short.[4] This chapter traces the transformation of those tiny tales into full-blown stories.

The beginnings of the modern British short story can be located at the opening of the eighteenth century when innovations in publishing launched fiction on a course of development that steered it towards the modern short story. This is not to say that short fiction did not exist previously, but it is to assert that a variety of circumstances hindered fiction's development. Almost all the short fiction available to English readers was imported. These stories were primarily translations of Roman and Greek authors familiar to the classically educated and classical European authors of interest to those who were, or wanted to be, familiar with Continental literature; French writers of romance who told stories of the sexual escapades of Europe's elite; and, towards the end of the century, fables and exotic tales from the East. Since this literature served its purpose as entertainment, and the only lucrative venue for fiction was the stage, there was no motive to write original short fiction. These narratives were offered in book-length collections, which limited the audience to the nobility and the wealthiest among the middle class, thereby eliminating any incentive to write stories different from those already being published. Even if English authors wanted to publish original fiction, there was, generally speaking, no publication venue for them to insert original short narratives into this relatively stagnant tradition. Only the wealthiest writers had ready access to the press, and they didn't write short fiction narratives, although Peter Motteaux and Aphra Behn, harbingers of an emerging literary impulse, could perhaps be considered exceptions to this generalization. Then there was the general attitude towards fiction, which, regardless of quality, was considered both trivial and a recognized threat to the morality of readers because it could inflame the emotions and encourage immoral behaviour.

The short fiction narratives offered to the reading public – and the reading public itself – might have changed little for decades had not the seventeenth-century tradition been suddenly disrupted by the appearance of the periodical press, a development made possible by the lapse of domestic censorship in 1695. The periodical press gave birth to a new breed of authors, the essay-serialists, and expanded the reading public to include the middle class by offering reading material it could afford. The essay-serialists were typically middle-class men with classical educations and literary aspirations who set themselves up as spokesmen for the Church and arbiters of public morality, personal conduct, right thinking and sometimes taste. Their impulse was reformist and their venue was the single-essay periodical, a half-folio sheet printed on both sides and devoted to an essay on a single topic, usually one that enabled them to promote the interests of established religion and reinforce a traditional Christian-based morality that was being subverted by the spread of mercantilist values and the individualist attitudes promulgated by Enlightenment thought. The structure of the single-essay periodical was predicated upon a fiction. The authors created eidolons who supposedly wrote the essays the public read. They went by such names as the Spectator, the Freethinker, the Plain Dealer, the Midwife, the Grumbler, the Female Spectator, the Old Maid, the Adventurer, the Rambler and hundreds of other equally emblematic names that concealed the identity of the authors and suggested something about their perspectives on society.

These early authors wrote not only to promote public morality but also to improve the manners of a middle class eager to imitate its social betters both socially and economically, thus the single-essay periodical was aimed directly at middle-class readers. The eidolons offered advice on such topics as domestic relations; the nature of true happiness; manners; and a variety of other topics the authors thought would improve readers' lives. Under the heading of vice and folly, they satirized behaviour, tastes and fashions that in their opinions were destroying traditional values and social norms. These topics became the staples of the essay-serialists and the subjects of their fiction for a century.

It was the encounter between middle-class writers and middle-class readers that stimulated the appearance of original short fiction. To make their lectures entertaining as well as instructive, the essay-serialists wove fiction into their essays to illustrate or dramatize their points and provide examples of behaviour to emulate or avoid. They followed the example of Richard Steele, author of *The Tatler* (1709), who recognized that his middle-class audience was more interested in reading about itself than it was about classical heroes and the sexual intrigues of Europe's highborn. It would be better, he wrote in *Tatler* 172, to present readers with 'such adventures as befall persons not exalted above the common level' because the 'ordinary race of men' believe 'nothing can relate to them, that does not happen to such as live and look like themselves'.[5]

It was the effort of the essay-serialists to create fiction that appeared to relate to the actual experiences of living people who looked and lived like their readers that both motivated and sustained the drive to create realistic fiction, fiction that would appeal to middle-class readers. The interest in creating realistic fiction capable of offering pointed social commentary was already stirring in the seventeenth century, for it can be seen in the Theophrastan character sketches of Hall, Earle and Overbury and in some of the short fiction Motteaux published in his *Gentleman's Journal* (1692–4). Men like Motteaux and Ned Ward, author of the *London Spy* (1698–1700), did try to represent the middle class realistically, but their depictions were too distorted by their own class prejudices and sense of superiority to be more than generalized satire holding the middle class up to ridicule. One writer who had no interest in satirizing the middle class was Daniel Defoe, whose early pamphlet 'A True Relation of the Apparition of One Mrs Veal' (1706) was a milestone in the development of realistic fiction and demonstrated how this fiction could be written. This story, which Defoe takes great pains to persuade readers is true, recounts the experience of a middle-class Englishwoman with an English name who discovers that a conversation she had two days earlier in her living room with a friend was actually an encounter with a ghost. The protagonist and the ghost of Mrs Veal are individualized, the setting is an ordinary middle-class home in Canterbury, and the protagonist, Mrs Bargrave, acts the way we would expect anyone to act who has difficulty believing she had just talked to a dead woman. Defoe's example, however, didn't attract any imitators, and except for Defoe's novels, it would not be until Richardson's *Pamela* (1740) that this level of realism would become a common feature of storytelling in print.

In the absence of new fiction narrative forms to draw on, the essay-serialists modernized two old ones, the character sketch and the anecdote, and they appropriated one relatively new one: correspondence to editors. Correspondence usually presented the personal histories of correspondents, real and fictional. It typically took one of two forms, although they were sometimes blended. One was the cautionary tale in which unhappy correspondents offered their experiences to warn readers against making the same mistakes that they had made. In the other, correspondents recounted the circumstances of their lives that had them in a quandary and claimed they were seeking the eidolon's advice or affirmation, which enabled the eidolons to turn their responses into instruction. The character sketches were more often than not satirical, and the anecdote was represented as the personal experience of a correspondent or the eidolon.

The characters in the sketches and narratives were drawn from the upper levels of the middle class, where readers were financially secure enough to be able to devote their energies and resources to personal improvement. Their stories tended to recount the fates of protagonists whose socially unacceptable values or ideas led to imprudent choices and painful consequences. The moral virtues and social defects of the characters were clearly indicated and directly responsible for good or bad effects. The narratives chronicling these effects were necessarily short and without complications or obstacles, as their length was constrained not only by their form but also by a format that restricted the entire piece of writing to about 1,800 words. If a fictional narrative took up most of the essay, there was no room for the author's lecture, and when embedded in a lecture, there wasn't much room left for fiction. Thus little space was available for plot development, dramatization, or dialogue, so the authors offered narrative summary in lieu. Because of the emphasis on moral instruction, the individual experience of the characters was important only to the extent that it was similar to other people's experience and that the experience either affirmed an opinion society desired to be held, or resulted in bad consequences for the protagonists where received opinion was flouted. Enough detail was supplied to suggest that the action occurred in England, usually London.

Usually, these narratives were generalized accounts of what the authors actually witnessed, so the action in them seems realistic enough to modern readers, but, despite touches of individualizing detail, the characters do not convince because they are types rather than individuals, a convention emphasized by their Latinate or emblematic names.

The idea that human beings were unique individuals was alien to writers and readers for most of the eighteenth century. They still viewed human beings through the lens of classical literature, which depicted human nature as static and human beings as a collection of enduring personality types which could be found in any society at any time, whatever alterations might have been made in appearances by changing customs and manners. Thus modern versions of classical types that irritated the authors – fops, coquets, unpleasant wives, women too susceptible to modern ideas, philandering husbands, bad parents, ungrateful children, stupid heirs, pedants and gamblers – parade through this fiction. The essay-serialists believed that specific types were motivated by type-specific personalities, and these determined the depiction of the characters. Thus the experiences represented in the character sketches and narratives were not constructed to represent human experience accurately but to make a point based on attitudes about those types. Judging by the comments of correspondents, however, eighteenth-century readers did consider this early fiction realistic. Steele had to remind readers more than once that his character sketches and anecdotes were not fictionalized portraits of real people. The amount of fiction in the single-essay periodicals varied from author to author, but, in form and subject matter, it varied little for a century.

The exceptions to these generalizations are allegories, dream visions and Eastern tales, all of which often did take up the bulk of the essay. These imaginative forms provided writers with an opportunity to free their imaginations and offer readers some relief from the incessant lecturing, though they were lectures repackaged. Both the allegories and allegorical dream visions, popular with English audiences since the Middle Ages, usually embodied a general moral or offered a social critique by other means. The Eastern tale was still new to English readers, though they had been seeping into the English literary stream since Sir Roger L'Estrange published his translation of *The Fables of Bidpai* in 1692. These were stories about the sultans, caliphs, handsome princes, beautiful daughters and wealthy merchants, often evil, of Egypt, Persia, India and other exotic locales. The plots of these stories comprised events that build to a climax, and the outcome is frequently determined by the interposition of preternatural beings. Often the action is set into motion by a wise genie with the intent of either inculcating wisdom or teaching the protagonist a moral lesson. Many were written by British authors who did their best to imitate the translations, without any real knowledge of the cultures they were writing about. They nearly always focused on general moral issues and mankind's relationship to Providence without offering any direct social commentary on English life. All three of these narrative forms were extremely popular. Even Samuel Johnson and John Hawkesworth wrote them, and they continued to appear in the magazines of the second half of the century.

The development of realistic short fiction was perhaps advanced further by what we might call, anticipating postmodernism, *metafiction*, concerning the fictional surroundings that motivate the creation of fiction narratives and the circumstances in which these narratives are embedded. Metafiction reveals an intriguing dichotomy in the thinking of these early authors about the fiction they were writing. Except for their Eastern tales and allegories, these authors did not think of themselves as creating imaginary characters, situations and actions. When writing their anecdotes and histories of imaginary persons, these early writers did not see themselves as imagining characters and events that didn't exist. Rather, they understood themselves to be generalizing about human nature from what they observed around them. Joseph Addison and Steele, the first and most influential of the essay-serialists, advised readers more than once that they were not creating characters based on real people, and, as Steele said, he would not offer a satirical portrait that did not fit at least a thousand people. In their minds, these writers were providing readers not with fiction but with pictures of real life, which became a prime function of essay-serial fiction.

This is not the case with the eidolons, however, for it appears that the imaginations of the essay-serialists were engaged more intensely with the creation of these characters than they were when creating the ones in their narratives. The eidolons in many cases are far more individualized and realistic than the protagonists in the narratives. The eidolons are given histories, good and bad memories, families, friends and people they disliked for personal reasons. They are characterized by episodes with realistic action and dialogue, and they are further given a third-dimensional existence in the comments of other characters and the correspondence addressed to them. The realistic quality of the eidolons and their experiences provided models showing future writers how to individualize characters, dramatize episodes and create realistic dialogue.

The work of these early essay-serialists is an intriguing chapter in the history of short fiction, for they at once contributed to its development while at the same time hindering its advance. Perhaps the greatest hindrance was the literary authority of Addison and Steele, co-authors of the *Spectator* (1709–11; 1714). They established the generic parameters that determined what kinds of fiction would be written and how it would be used. It was Addison and Steele who first applied to fiction the Roman poet Horace's dictum on poetry – it should instruct as well as delight – and as a consequence fiction and didacticism became inextricably linked. Thus were established the generic conventions governing the writing of short fiction for more than a century: it would reflect the morals and manners of the age, and it would instruct in an entertaining way. The authority of these two London journalists was so influential that as late as 1827, Walter Scott situated his *Chronicles of the Canongate* squarely in the tradition of the *Spectator* and its successor, the *Guardian* (1713), though the only similarity between the works of these three men is that they utilize eidolons. Because these conventions were so firmly inscribed in the minds of authors, they could not think of fiction independently from its functions as illustrative, exemplary, or satirical, a narrow view that discouraged experiments and significant deviations.

Because authors could not conceive of fiction in any other way, there was no theorizing that might have weakened generic conventions or prompted deviations. Narratives, anecdotes, histories, relations, tales and stories were all one to these writers, and at the end of the century a tale could run to more than 40,000 words, though, as Killick has suggested, by the nineteenth century designating a fiction narrative as a 'tale' might have implied some sensitivity to moral imperatives.[6] Since authors were offering portraits of general human nature, they didn't need to think about the aesthetics of short narratives, or even about their different types. That their short narratives are pointed and realistic, however, suggests they had some ideas about how this fiction should be written even though they never articulated them.

The amount of fiction in an essay-serial varied from author to author. Ambrose Phillips's twice-weekly *Free-Thinker*, for instance contains about a dozen essay-length 'Winter-Evening Tales' to entertain young women and stimulate their thinking about philosophy, but most of them were versions of Fenelon's fables. The *Plain Dealer* (1724–1725) of Aaron Hill and

William Bond also published about a dozen essay-length narratives, and in some of them Hill is following Defoe's lead. The eidolon assures readers that one story about a young Catholic man who gives up his title and estate to become a Christian martyr is 'true,' while participants and eyewitnesses attest to the veracity of other stories.

Because of its homogeneity and lack of literary merit, most of the fiction in the essay-serials after mid-century does not warrant scholarly attention. Melvin Watson made an extensive study of essay-serials through the whole century and concluded that they lacked 'not only anything original to say, but any attractive, individual way of saying it'. All they succeeded in doing, he said, was 'being verbose and dull'.[7] But there are three notable exceptions to his generalization: the essay-serials of Eliza Haywood, Samuel Johnson and John Hawkesworth.

These writers were working in the essay-serial tradition, but their fiction registers the influence of the contemporary novel, perhaps because they recognized that they had to compete for readers with the novel and the magazines that began appearing in the 1740s. It appears they recognized that readers, whose taste in fiction was being shaped by the novel, desired longer stories with developed plots. Both Johnson's and Hawkesworth's periodicals, for instance, have many stories offered in two to five instalments to accommodate plots consisting of multiple incidents. But the fiction of all three was significantly different from their predecessors and what was appearing in the other outlets: their fiction explores the mental and emotional states of their protagonists, which added psychological realism to techniques of characterization.

The fiction in Eliza Haywood's *Female Spectator* (1744–6) was the earliest to probe consistently the psychological dimensions of protagonists' actions in periodical fiction. Haywood, a popular novelist in the 1720s whose fiction was highly critical of men and the patriarchal society that gave them leave to treat women as badly as they wanted, was writing to middle-class women and addressed gender-related issues in their lives. Because her fiction depicted specific problems and conflicts in women's lives, her fiction was different from the narratives that dealt with general moral or social issues written by her male predecessors. For the most part, her stories are traditional cautionary tales criticizing individual behaviour and holding up examples for readers to avoid lest they make their lives miserable. But her narratives end up being stories about women who are routinely victimized by men seeking fortunes or sex, and young women victimized by their own sentimental feelings about men and love, feelings shaped by ideas they have absorbed from romance fiction and which have left them vulnerable to the seductive machinations of duplicitous men.

Many of her stories explore the effects of misguided beliefs, feelings and thinking that enable men to victimize women. In their pursuit of marital happiness, her protagonists usually make bad choices, as eighteenth-century protagonists often do, and they suffer as a consequence. To illustrate the motivations behind their bad choices, Haywood creates an intellectual and emotional context for them, thereby enabling readers to understand, for their benefit, the motivations and sentiments behind rash or imprudent actions that court disastrous consequences. Because she was a novelist who had plenty of space to tell her stories, she paid more attention to action and realistic settings than was customary among earlier essay-serialists. Her protagonists, while they tend towards types, are highly individualized, and her female protagonists expanded the range of protagonists available to the authors of periodical fiction. Her stories, however, are reminiscent of those of her predecessors in that she relies on narrative summary, but her summaries are more detailed and thus more dramatic. Almost all her stories could be extracted from the discussions in which they are embedded and published separately as short stories without any loss of meaning.

Haywood's representation of the mental states of her protagonists is an innovation in essay-serial fiction, and she adds another touch of narrative realism: the creation of distance between narrator and character. More than once her narrators indicate they don't know exactly what is in the mind of the protagonists whose stories they are relating. In a story about an obstinate teenager who refuses to obey her father, for instance, the narrator admits to being unsure about what is passing in the protagonist's mind, even though she created the character: "Tis highly probable, that the Knowledge she was born to a Fortune independent of him [her father], went a great Way towards emboldening her to Act in this manner.'[8]

Attention to Haywood's fiction has increased over the last couple of decades, and it has rendered her fiction, including her short fiction, somewhat problematic. The general consensus is that the stories in the *Female Spectator* are intended to guide women, married and single, on how to avoid foolish thoughts and behave to their best advantage in a society where custom, tradition and the law denied them any rights and deprived them of the respect and dignity they are entitled to as human beings. But, depending on her intended audience, some of her stories can be read ironically. Her story of Althea, a paragon of good nature and conjugal love, for example, tells the story of a woman who because of her patience and resilience in the face of the ultimate humiliation inflicted by her philandering husband, reclaims him by agreeing to raise the child he had with another woman. Some readers may have accepted the conventional wisdom that the best way to reclaim an errant husband was to make him aware that no one will love him like his wife, whatever humiliations she must endure, as prudent advice. But others who were conscious of the abuses women experienced were likely to have different attitudes towards events in the story. It is hard to believe that a vigorous critic of men and patriarchal society in the 1720s would expect this story to be taken as serious advice.

Like Haywood, Johnson explores the mental states of victims, although his characters are not victimized by literary conventions or an oppressive society; rather, they are the victims of a society that tells them happiness is a matter of possessions or achievements within their grasp. All they need to be happy, society tells them, is beauty, wealth, a pleasing personality, a scholarly reputation and self-assurance. Johnson's protagonists make life choices based on these promises. This is the 'choice of life', that Carey MacIntosh considers the principal motif in Johnson's periodical fiction. The choice of life is the selection of activities, professions and environments that determine an individual's life course. But those who attempt this choice ultimately discover the vanity of human wishes, as society and chance place too many obstacles in the way of success.[9]

Disillusionment is a related theme that appears frequently in the *Rambler*, where many of the victims also learn too late they are victims of their own self-delusions. Johnson's protagonists overestimate their abilities, their self-knowledge, or their importance in society. Their unrealistic view of themselves and their readiness to believe society's promises leads to bad decisions, belated acquisition of self-knowledge and a more realistic understanding of their position in society. A good number of his stories chronicle the internal process of this acquisition. The story of Eubulus is a good example. He's a young man who through bad decisions lost the financial support of a wealthy uncle and is forced to depend on others for his subsistence. He finally comes to realize the effect this state of dependence was having on him. 'I found the spirit and vigour of liberty every moment sinking in me, and a servile fear of displeasing, stealing by degrees upon all my behaviour, 'til no word, or look, or action, was my own.' Unfortunately, his self-knowledge comes too late to help him, and many other characters suffer the same fate. Thus a good number of Johnson's stories chronicle unintentional and painful journeys of self-discovery. Johnson's fiction, like

Haywood's, relies on narrative summary because he is focused on internal process rather than external action.

Probably the best short fiction to appear during the first two-thirds of the century, from the perspective of contemporary readers, was published by Johnson's one-time friend John Hawkesworth, founder of the *Adventurer* (1752–4). His twice-weekly essay-serial offered readers a considerable quantity of original fiction, most of which was written by Hawkesworth himself, though Johnson was a major contributor. Hawkesworth was the only eighteenth-century author of short fiction to theorize about it as a distinct species of writing. He was as concerned about the moral impact of his fiction on readers as any of his predecessors, but Hawkesworth recognized that writing short narratives was different from writing novels and more difficult than writing mere pictures of life, a belief that suggests he did not think fiction should necessarily be an exact transcription of life. *Adventurer* 4 expounds a theory of narrative unity with an Aristotelian cast. He contends that a short narrative should be focused on a single incident unusual enough to engage readers and create suspense. Events should be logically connected and move rapidly while 'gradually' revealing an 'unforeseen and important event'. He did not abandon the conviction that fiction should instruct as well as please, but he did think the moral would be more effectively communicated, remembered and repeated if it were implicit in the events of the story rather than made explicit.

Much of the fiction in Hawkesworth's *Adventurer* takes up conventional subjects, and, like the stories of Haywood and Johnson, many are counterbalances to the romantic tales of love appearing in other outlets. No relations between men and women, especially marriages, are happy ones, and jealousy, a favourite theme, is often the reason why. But several of his stories further develop the psychological realism of Haywood and Johnson. Whereas Haywood summarizes the thought processes of her protagonists and Johnson generalizes his, Hawkesworth dramatizes the psychological mechanisms that motivate people to act in ways contrary to their physical, mental, or spiritual well-being. The three-part stories of Charlotte and Maria contained in *Adventurers* 54–6 and Flavilla in *Adventurers* 123–5, are two of several stories that probe in detail the feelings and thoughts of characters who court their own misery. Both these stories were reprinted multiple times in later magazines, sometimes in abridged form.

Despite his expressed disdain for the novel, Hawkesworth was clearly influenced by its methods of storytelling. He dramatizes episodes in novelistic fashion: the dialogue in these episodes is often realistic, and the motivations behind the actions of his characters are detailed and realistic enough that they come across as individuals rather than types. In a strategy influenced by Richardson's *Clarissa* (1748), Hawkesworth provides multiple perspectives on the events narrated using first-person accounts from more than one of the characters in a story, though these accounts expand rather than complicate the narrative. Although no less concerned to avoid ambiguity in his stories than any of his contemporaries, he did create one ambiguous ending, though whether by accident or design is impossible to determine. In the story of Charlotte and Maria, Charlotte's husband, jealous of Maria's husband, challenges him to a duel and is killed. Realizing what a terrible thing he has done, Maria's husband flees to France but not before sending her an anguished letter confessing his errors. A few weeks after receiving the letter, Maria learns that her husband was lost overboard during the passage. It is left to readers to decide whether he was washed overboard or committed suicide.

From the time Haywood launched the *Female Spectator*, the essay-serialists faced stiff competition for readers from another vehicle for short fiction, the magazine, which, after Hawkesworth, absorbed the essay-serial as a feature. In 1731, an enterprising publisher named Edward Cave created the *Gentleman's Magazine* (1731–1922), the forerunner of the modern magazine. Cave's magazine collected in one monthly publication of about eighty pages a wide variety of articles on miscellaneous subjects of interest to men, extracts from the columns of other periodicals and a variety of historical information. Cave's magazine is itself not important to the development of short fiction, for it was nearly two decades before *Gentleman's* began publishing original fiction other than what was contained in the extracts it reprinted, which suggests that the belief that fiction was beneath serious readers still prevailed in some quarters. What is important is that Cave's innovation inspired other publishers to think of creating similar publications with content, including fiction, aimed at a general audience of both sexes. Thus was born the general interest magazine, often called a *miscellany* because of its varied content. The publishers of the miscellanies and their editors rightly perceived, as Hawkesworth did, that the reading public had an appetite for stories like those in the novels, and they complied. In its inaugural year the *Town and Country Magazine* (1760–96), for instance, published seventy-two separate pieces of short fiction ranging from short anecdotes to stories of about 8,000 words. In the later years of the century, the miscellanies with the greater circulation and longevity were the ones with the greater range and variety of short fiction.[10]

The fiction in the miscellanies still showed the influence of the essay-serial tradition. Anecdotes, character sketches and personal histories still constituted a significant portion of the fictional content. Many of the stories were still in the 800- or 900- to 1,800-word range, many correspondents still provided cautionary tales for the benefit of readers, and Eastern tales weren't uncommon. Instruction that entertained was still touted as the principle guiding what was published. In an address to the 'fair sex' contained in the inaugural issue of the *Lady's Magazine* (1770–1837), for instance, the editor proudly declared that 'Every branch of literature will be ransacked to please and instruct the mind ... Interesting Stories, Novels, Tales, Romances, intended to confirm chastity and recommend virtue will be inserted every month.'

But the miscellanies also published longer stories that were essentially novels in miniature. Contributors devoted more attention to realistic plotting, dramatization and characterization, which showed that their narratives were influenced by the realistic novels of Richardson and Fielding, French romances, and later the sentimental novels of Henry Mackenzie. Richardson's domestic novels of lust and love encouraged short fiction to bend in the same direction, though, like the essay-serialists, the contributors tended to write stories about the upper middle class. Some miscellanies contained interpolated stories in the manner of Fielding, and some imitated, more briefly of course, the epistolary novels of Mary Colyer and Richardson. The sentimental romances of the French were being satirized as far back as Addison and Steele, but their popularity was increased and their influence intensified by serialization in the early magazines. These literary developments encouraged contributors to write sentimental romance with English characters and settings.

The recognition that to be successful magazines had to cater to readers' desire for entertainment rather than self-improvement began moving short fiction into the realm of entertainment. Third-person narratives disengaged the stories from moral discussion, though a point of some kind was at least implicit in them. Because the sentimental romance and the novel were shaping readers' taste, the miscellanies emphasized stories of love, marriage, gallantry, seduction and rape. Occasionally, stories were modelled on sentimental romance, but more often than not the fiction conformed to moral types: stories of misery and woe occasioned by jealousy, both warranted and unwarranted; adultery; the imprudent choice of a spouse; and naiveté in the ways of men and the world. All the stories either explicitly or implicitly professed to convey a moral. Many titles carried the tag line 'a moral tale', which at least paid lip service to the provision of moral instruction despite the content of the story. But titles such as 'The Careless Lover', 'The Coquet Punished', 'The Way Not to Keep Him: A Tale for Married Ladies', 'The Ungrateful Husband: A Moral Tale' and many others of that ilk give the impression that the stories were intended more to pique readers' prurient interests and entertain them with the pain and tragedy of romantic relationships ruined by rashness, avarice, lust and jealousy, rather than to educate them. The narratives almost always related the consequences of an imprudent action or choice, one that arose out of questionable motives and thus transgressed traditional values or deviated from social norms. Focusing on the disastrous consequences of bad acts or imprudent choices reinforced conventional notions of what constituted a prudent choice in courtship, marriage and gender relations in general. But the miscellanies did provide stories with other subjects. The first issue of the *Town and Country Magazine*, for instance, began a four-part, 8,000-word, story about a young heir of a modest estate who inadvertently fell in with a gang of conmen, much to the detriment of his fortune.

Despite the fact more attention was paid to plot development and characterization, eighteenth-century periodical fiction was not sophisticated. Incidents were more believable than the simplistic narratives at the beginning of the century because the action was motivated by stronger characterization in which action arose from a mental context. Dialogue was more realistic, though in the hands of less skilful writers it could tend towards religious or philosophical declamation. But the stories do not depict human nature as complex. Protagonists and antagonists are seldom presented as having complicated motives. Such inner conflicts as were represented reflected good and bad choices according to contemporary values, and most protagonists opted for the bad ones. The plots are straightforward chains of causes and effects usually arising out of an imprudent choice or act and chronicling its consequences. The virtuous are virtuous, but often they are naïve or terribly misguided in their values or their desires. The villains, usually wealthy men who make seducing women a sport, seldom have any redeeming qualities beyond their polished deportment. The experiences of the protagonists are still common experiences that could offer lessons to others. When the moral was not explicit, it was so implicit that it could not be missed. Nothing was left to readers' imaginations.

Because of their emphasis on instruction the stories themselves lack any complexity. Narrators, whether first- or third-person, are always authoritative figures whose authority to recount or comment on events accurately is never brought into question by a tale's action or characters. Nor is the narrator's understanding of the events being narrated ever called into question by discrepancies between the narrator's understanding of the story and his or her pronouncements upon it. When multiple perspectives on events are presented, they fill in missing details rather than raise questions. These authors never discovered, as did Henry James and his literary contemporaries, 'the art of saying less but meaning more'.[11]

By the last two decades of the century, the venues for short fiction were expanding, and this expansion began breaking down the generic boundaries established early in the century. Publishers began producing magazines that targeted specific segments of the reading public – children, families, heroic artisans, readers interested in travel and adventure – and authors began writing short fiction specifically for these magazines.[12] The protagonists in these stories were still middle class, but not from the fashionable segment of it. But these magazines suggest that authors were perhaps beginning to chafe against the generic boundaries that had been in place so long. The *Sporting Magazine* (1792–1870), for example, was aimed at sportsmen, broadly defined, and featured stories of interest to those who raced horses, hunted, fished and gambled. The fiction in this magazine reveals an interest in experimenting with genres and themes: adultery is not always punished; a dream vision recounted by a horse veterinarian that he is on top of the Temple of Fame despite his being utterly incompetent illustrates the gap between theory and practice rather than offering a moral lesson; and fiction and history are mixed, as when a fictional gambler attends a court hearing presided over by Lord Mansfield.

A new class of protagonist was supplemented by another prose form, the religious tract, which told stories about the moral trials and successes of common folk to simplify an evangelical message for the lower orders. Readers were presented with 'shining examples or wicked failures, usually drawn from the same class as the intended reader', working-class men and women.[13]

This expansion revitalized an old format: the collection. Collections of Eastern tales were still seeping into the literary marketplace, and they were supplemented by collections of folklore and legends. But the demand for short fiction had become high enough to encourage publishers to offer collections of original fiction, and the stories in some of these volumes suggest that short fiction was drifting away from its traditional subjects. The stories of Maria Edgeworth and Walter Scott illustrate this tendency. Edgeworth, who published the first of her two volumes of *Moral Tales* in 1801, wrote her stories to dramatize the principles of education expounded in *Practical Education* (1798), a book she co-wrote with her educator father. Her stories were still aimed at instruction in the guise of entertainment, but they were intended to dramatize the effects of poor moral instruction on children. The stories are told by third-person narrators, and the plots are realistic with detailed dramatization, careful characterization and realistic settings. Realistic plotting and careful attention to setting are obvious features of Scott's *Chronicles of the Canongate* (1827). The two stories in this volume are intended to give readers a realistic sense of the Highland mentality in the wake of the rebellion of 1745, to explain why adjusting to English values after the rebellion was so difficult for them. The stories in both these volumes are essentially novellas, however, and show little development in the sense of the short story as a narrative form distinct from the novel. The first story in Edgeworth's volume, 'Forester', runs to more than 41,000 words, and three of the remaining five stories are well over 20,000 words. The first, and longer, of Scott's two stories, 'The Highland Widow', runs to more than 26,000 words.

By the Victorian era, short fiction had become an industry. Magazines began to appear that specialized in fiction, *Blackwood's Edinburgh Magazine* (1817–1980) and *Fraser's Magazine* (1830–82) being two prime examples. Short fiction was also being commissioned for such presents as gift books, coffee-table books and Christmas annuals. However, despite the prevalence of so much short fiction written by both amateurs and professionals, it would not be until Robert Louis Stevenson began writing that authors began to realize that the short narrative could, as Adrian Hunter says, 'achieve great richness and complexity . . . *as a result of* rather than in spite of, its [the form's] brevity' (his emphasis), an insight necessary for the emergence of the modern short story as a distinct genre.[14] The eighteenth-century authors of fiction were not striving for the kind of richness and complexity in their short fiction that Hunter is talking about. Rather, they tried to make their stories richer and more complex by expanding plots and creating stronger characters, a strategy that ran counter to brevity. It was their function, they believed, to improve their readers and through them their society, not to leave readers pondering the darker recesses of the human heart or the complexity of human nature.

Notes

1. Tim Killick, *British Short Fiction in the Early Nineteenth Century: The Rise of the Tale* (Aldershot: Ashgate, 2008).
2. Robert D. Mayo, *The English Novel in the Magazines, 1740–1815* (Evanston, IL: Northwestern University Press, 1962), pp. 1, 4.
3. Benjamin Boyce, 'English Short Fiction in the Eighteenth Century: A Preliminary View', *Studies in Short Fiction*, 5 (1968), pp. 95–112 (p. 95).
4. Mayo, *The English Novel in the Magazines*, p. 4.
5. Richard Steele, *The Tatler*, Project Gutenberg: Gutenberg ebook 31645, p. 306.
6. Killick, *British Short Fiction*, p. 17.
7. Melvin R. Watson, *Magazine Serials and the Essay Tradition, 1746–1820* (Baton Rouge, LA: Louisiana State University Press, 1956), p. 41.
8. Eliza Haywood, *The Female Spectator*, 7th edn, 4 vols. (London: Printed for H. Gardner, 1771), vol. 1, book 5, p. 219.
9. Carey McIntosh, *The Choice of Life: Samuel Johnson and the World of Fiction* (New Haven, CT: Yale University Press, 1973), pp. 54–5.
10. Mayo, *The English Novel in the Magazines*, p. 220.
11. Adrian Hunter, *The Cambridge Introduction to the Short Story in English* (Cambridge University Press, 2007), p. 2.
12. Mayo, *The English Novel in the Magazines*, pp. 223–4.
13. Killick, *British Short Fiction*, pp. 78–9.
14. Hunter, *Cambridge Introduction*, p. 2.

3
Gothic and Victorian Supernatural Tales

JESSICA COX

In her short story 'Napoleon and the Spectre' (1833), a young Charlotte Brontë parodies the established conventions of the gothic, portraying Napoleon tormented by a hideous spirit. The historical setting for Brontë's story harks back to a period when Napoleon himself functioned as a phantom haunting Europe, and consequently the narrative emphasizes the association between the gothic short story and the broader political landscape in the early nineteenth century, when the spectre of revolution threatened England. The American and French Revolutions (the latter leading to the Napoleonic Wars) were both in living memory. A different kind of revolution, industrialization, brought class unrest, threatening the established order – a threat brought to the fore by the Luddite disturbances of the 1810s. The anxieties provoked by these events contributed to the popularity of the gothic: a genre informed by and in turn informing the social and political climate. Gothic fiction reflects pervasive anxieties about a changing social order, and the language of the gothic is frequently appropriated by cultural and political commentators (most famously in Karl Marx's claim that 'A spectre is haunting Europe').[1] This chapter traces the emergence and development of the gothic short story, examining its role in the literary marketplace as well as its broader cultural and political significance. Over the course of the nineteenth century, the gothic story, with its ability to 'speak to the mysterious fears of our nature, and awaken thrilling horror', became a dominant literary form, and remains perpetually popular, though critically neglected.[2] Taking a broadly chronological approach, I identify the key trends in gothic and supernatural short fiction, from the emergence of the new literary magazines in the early nineteenth century to Victorian sensational gothic stories.[3]

The roots of the literary gothic lie in the Enlightenment and subsequent Romantic backlash beginning in the late eighteenth century. Reacting against the Age of Reason, writers sought to emphasize the fantastical, inexplicable, ghostly and mysterious, evoking tensions between gothic and realism, science and religion, nature and the supernatural, the rational and the irrational, as well as drawing on the anxieties provoked by contemporary events. These tensions are central to gothic fiction, and enable the exploration of other dichotomies: life/death; masculine/feminine; self/society. While gothic stories were produced primarily to entertain readers, like the gothic novel they also reflect a broader social and cultural mind-set, a historical period rife with anxieties about change and progress. With its varied forms, pervasive presence, tendency to provoke distaste in critics, and the terror it sought to elicit from readers, the gothic story functions as a kind of Frankenstein's monster – its presence a constant reminder of something 'other', a perpetual 'haunting' of the nineteenth-century mind.

Romantic Progenies: The Gothic Short Story in the Early Nineteenth Century

In 1816, almost twenty years before Brontë's parody of gothic fiction, a group of English friends, enabled to travel in Europe by a new freedom resulting from the recent conclusion of the Napoleonic Wars, met at the Villa Diodati near Lake Geneva. It was a 'wet, ungenial summer', and they entertained themselves by reading *Fantasmagoriana* (1813) – a collection of German tales translated into French, which told of ghostly brides, supernatural curses, haunted castles and premature deaths.[4] Inspired by these, they began to write their own stories. From that summer emerged Mary Shelley's *Frankenstein* (1818), John Polidori's 'The Vampyre' (1819) and *Ernestus Berchtold; or The Modern Oedipus* (1819), and Byron's unfinished 'Augustus Darvell' (1819). The story of the Villa Diodati and the emerging literary productions provide valuable insights into the gothic and supernatural tales of the nineteenth century: the themes and motifs employed, the genre's influences, its contributors, audience and modes of publication.

By 1816, the gothic tale was a regular feature in literary journals and magazines. European works, such as the tales read at the Villa Diodati, exerted a significant influence on the English short story. If the ghost story became quintessentially English over the course of the nineteenth century, its origins and influences lay elsewhere, in the European ghost stories dating back to the Middle Ages and the later works of German authors such as E. T. A. Hoffmann, as well as American writers including Edgar Allan Poe and Washington Irving, whose particular brand of American gothic was widely read in Britain. British journals included translations of European ghost stories (*Blackwood's Edinburgh Magazine* published a series entitled 'Horæ Germanicæ') and collections of European stories were published in English translation (R. P. Gillie's *German Stories* appeared in 1826). Tim Killick attests to the importance of German work – particularly in relation to the oral tradition of storytelling: 'German writers helped give British authors a new conception of the ways in which traditional oral tales could function when transferred to the unfamiliar medium of the printed page.'[5] Oral tales were similarly important in Scottish and Irish traditions, and these in turn influenced the English gothic tale. Distinguishing between English, Scottish and Irish supernatural tales is problematic, given the extent to which they operated within the wider British literary marketplace. *Blackwood's* was crucial in enhancing the popularity of the gothic and supernatural tale. Although it was edited and published in Scotland, many contributors and readers were from elsewhere. Influential Scottish writers included Walter Scott and James Hogg, while Ireland produced one of the most successful authors in this field in J. Sheridan Le Fanu. Identifying a specifically English tradition, therefore, is not straightforward: the ambiguity that characterizes gothic fiction extends to national identity – in terms of authorship *and* content.

The theme of identity is a strong current in the supernatural tale, which frequently perpetuates stereotypes of national identities and explores issues around the disintegration of identity. This is evident in the works begun at the Villa Diodati. In *Frankenstein*, the theme of fractured identity is (literally) embodied in the figure of the creature, composed from human body parts. Identity haunts nineteenth-century vampire narratives, including Polidori's 'The Vampyre' and Byron's 'Augustus Darvell' (Polidori's story is based on Byron's unfinished narrative). In both, a naïve young gentleman encounters a mysterious aristocrat, and travels Europe with him; the aristocrat suddenly dies, having exacted a promise from the young man to conceal his death. Byron's fragment concludes here. In Polidori's narrative, the aristocrat (Lord Ruthven) reappears in English society, by which point the young gentleman (Aubrey) has connected him with the death of a young woman in Greece, and suspects him of being a vampire. His reappearance enacts a physical and mental toll on the young man (an effect common in gothic tales after encounters with supernatural forces). Shortly before his death, Aubrey learns that his sister is to marry Lord Ruthven, and reveals his secret – but too late: Lord Ruthven disappears, and Aubrey's sister is discovered to have 'glutted the thirst of a VAMPYRE!'[6]

The two narratives introduce the figure of the aristocratic vampire, establishing a stock character of the genre, later epitomized by Stoker's Count Dracula. (In earlier folk tales from Eastern Europe, vampires invariably belong to the peasant classes.) The deceptively respectable appearance of Lord Ruthven and his ability to operate freely in polite society anticipates the sensation fiction of the 1860s and the psychological gothic of the *fin de siècle*, in which the boundaries between monstrosity and civilization appear indistinct. 'The Vampyre' popularized vampire fiction, spawning numerous literary descendants, including the penny-dreadful *Varney the Vampire* (1845–7) (published anonymously, but probably the work of James Malcolm Rymer), Le Fanu's novella *Carmilla* (1871) and Mary Elizabeth Braddon's short story 'Good Lady Ducayne' (1896), as well as *Dracula* (1897). The vampire, along with the ghost, is inextricably associated with the nineteenth-century gothic. Other supernatural figures appear, but their association with the period is less well established. The werewolf, for instance, features in various stories, including Catherine Crowe's 'A Story of a Weir-Wolf' (1846) and several by Victorian fantasy writer George MacDonald.[7] These supernatural figures haunt the peripheries of nineteenth-century fiction, not only through the manner of their representation, but, crucially, through the types of narrative in which they appear: side-lined in the novel, they frequently take centre stage in the short story. Vampires function in a similar way to ghosts: haunting, potentially threatening, signifying a liminal space somewhere between life and death, and representing metaphors for cultural tensions and anxieties. Lord Ruthven symbolizes a degenerate aristocracy, but may also represent (like other literary vampires) promiscuous sexuality, contagion, or disease.

Whereas earlier gothic narratives are frequently set outside Britain's borders, Polidori's story brings the threat closer. Aubrey initially encounters Lord Ruthven in London, although it is in Greece that he first hears 'the tale of the living vampyre' from a superstitious and 'uneducated Greek girl', Ianthe. He is 'incredulous' and attempts 'to laugh her out of such idle and horrible fantasies' (p. 46), but is eventually forced to acknowledge the truth of these tales when confronted with irrefutable evidence in the form of Ianthe's body: 'upon her throat were the marks of teeth having opened the vein' (p. 48). Ruthven's return to England and disappearance at the narrative's conclusion suggests the continued threat. Both the geographical shift from earlier gothic fiction (from distant lands which function as 'other') and Polidori's narrator's initial scepticism represent narrative conventions in the supernatural short story that remain commonplace throughout the century. Ghost stories frequently commence with an assertion of scepticism or outright disbelief by the narrator, paralleling the anticipated scepticism of the reader.

'The Vampyre' appeared in the *New Monthly Magazine* and 'heralded a new phase of modern British fiction in which the opportunist sensationalism of the monthly magazines assumed an unprecedented importance'.[8] The magazine was one of several titles publishing short and serialized fiction for an increasingly literate reading public. These publications offered affordable fiction for readers and an important financial opportunity for writers. One of the most successful was *Blackwood's*, founded in 1817. It became (in)famous for its original stories, which appeared weekly to assuage readers' macabre appetites. By 1838, the formula for the *Blackwood's* tale was sufficiently recognizable for Poe to parody it in his short story 'How to Write a Blackwood Article'. A significant characteristic of many *Blackwood's* stories is an absence of the supernatural: they feature far-fetched plots that stretch the credulity of the reader, but do not insist on the existence of supernatural forces. In John Galt's 'The Buried Alive' (1821), for example, the protagonist suffers a form of paralysis, is declared dead and buried alive. In William Mudford's 'The Iron Shroud' (1830), the narrator is imprisoned in an iron cell, designed to contract gradually until it eventually kills the prisoner. Mudford's story, with its Italian setting, theme of imprisonment and absence of supernatural occurrences, harks back to the gothic novels of Anne Radcliffe and subsequently influenced Poe's 'The Pit and the Pendulum' (1842) and Wilkie Collins's 'A Terribly Strange Bed' (1852). It invokes an oppressive sense of claustrophobia as it moves towards its inevitable conclusion, and emphasizes the quality of some of the *Blackwood's* tales, which, both then and since, have often been dismissed as merely catering to the sensational appetites of a lower class of reader.

Blackwood's dominance in the literary marketplace gave rise to a number of imitators and competitors, and literary annuals offered further opportunities for publishers to capitalize on contemporary reading tastes. Although literary almanacs have a long history, like the magazines they experienced significantly increased popularity in the nineteenth century. Usually published for the Christmas market, they featured work by eminent writers accompanied by detailed illustrations and were another important receptacle for the gothic short story. One of the most popular was *The Keepsake* (1828–57), described in George Eliot's *Middlemarch* (1874) as 'the gorgeous watered-silk publication which marked modern progress at that time'.[9] Later contributors included Dickens ('To Be Read at Dusk' appeared in 1852), while early volumes featured Scott, P. B. Shelley, Wordsworth, Mary Shelley and Coleridge amongst others. Editors were prepared to pay significant sums for contributions and consequently annuals represented another important means of income for writers. The short story, then, frequently served primarily as a source of revenue, rather than an outlet for demonstrating literary skill. While these two aims were not mutually exclusive, the financial benefits to be reaped from the production of short stories goes some way to explain the widely acknowledged lack of literary merit in many of these works. Mary Shelley, in a letter to Leigh Hunt in 1824, states: 'I write bad articles which help to make me miserable [...] It is thus you will make money [...] but I am going to plunge into a novel, and hope that its clear water will wash off the [...] mud of the magazines.'[10] Shelley's assertion hints at a distinction between gothic stories and novels: the latter allowed far more room for development of character and descriptive accounts of events and thus (in some cases at least) leant the form a quality and respectability not always associated with the short story.

The contributions to *The Keepsake* of 1829 provide a flavour of the gothic story at this time. Mary Shelley's 'The Sisters of Albano' and 'Ferdinando Eboli' do not engage with the supernatural (unlike many of her other stories), but contain strong gothic elements.[11] The historical European settings hark back to an earlier gothic tradition. Stock gothic characters appear: the passive female victim, the nun, the villainous double. There is a focus on crime (murder, kidnap, impersonation, robbery), testament to the sensational appetites of readers. The conclusions, though divergent, are broadly representative of the gothic tradition: 'The Sisters of Albano' ends in tragedy, while 'Ferdinando Eboli' provides the familiar romantic conclusion. Echoes of *Frankenstein* are found in the use of frame narrative, and the detailed descriptions of landscape, but these tales lack the sophistication of Shelley's longer works. Some of Shelley's other tales represent higher examples of the form – 'The Mortal Immortal' (*The Keepsake*, 1834), for instance, which Diane Long Hoevler identifies as an important example of Shelley's gothic feminism.[12]

Scott's gothic contributions to the 1829 *Keepsake*, 'My Aunt Margaret's Mirror' and 'The Tapestried Chamber', are more overtly concerned with the supernatural, and notable for their employment of many gothic tropes then in vogue and their simultaneous anticipation of the Victorian ghost story. The historical settings link the narratives to the first wave of gothic writing in the eighteenth century by Matthew Lewis, Anne Radcliffe and their contemporaries. The stock figure of the mysterious foreigner appears (Baptista Damiotti in 'My Aunt Margaret's Mirror'), though the character also anticipates the figure of the mesmerist who was to attract significant interest later in the century. Scott employs the frame narrative that features heavily in gothic fiction (Killick credits Scott with the popularity of the frame narrative[13]). Both stories are prefaced by an account of their oral transmission – a familiar convention in the Victorian ghost story – emphasizing the association between an oral tradition and Scottish literature.[14] Leith Davis and Maureen N. McLane note, 'Oral tradition, humble though it appeared to literate elites, came to acquire a new and unembarrassed status' in the work of Scott and his contemporaries.[15] These allusions indicate the close relationship between Scottish literature and ghost stories, further suggested by the various Scottish precursors to the gothic short story such as Robert Burns's 'Tam O'Shanter' (1791), and by the employment of Scottish settings in many nineteenth-century supernatural tales – the latter reflecting English stereotypes of Scotland as a place where people gave greater credence to superstitions. There are references to the divide between the rational sceptic and the superstitious believer, again anticipating the Victorian ghost story, reflecting an age in which debates over science and religion were brought to the fore. In 'My Aunt Margaret's Mirror', the eponymous aunt instructs her nephew (and effectively the reader) to suspend disbelief: 'All that is indispensable for the enjoyment of the milder feeling of supernatural awe is, that you should be susceptible of the slight shuddering which creeps over you when you hear a tale of terror.'[16] The Victorian ghost story is further anticipated through references to money, wealth and inheritance.[17]

In 'The Tapestried Chamber', the appearance of a malevolent female ghost and her effect on the male protagonist again highlights the narrative's position as an important forerunner to the Victorian ghost story. The ghostly woman represents danger: a consequence of her potential for disruption and men's inability to control her. The result of this encounter with a dangerous femininity is the breakdown of masculine identity. The malevolence of the female spectre and 'manliness' of the male witness are both heavily emphasized. General Richard Browne is a soldier returning from the American Revolutionary War, 'an officer of merit, as well as a gentleman'.[18] The spectre is the ancestor of the General's friend, Lord Woodville, with whom he stays on his journey home. In life, she was guilty of a 'fearful catalogue' of crimes, including 'incest and unnatural murder' (pp. 141–2). She appears in the tapestried chamber where Browne is sleeping, wearing 'the fixed features of a corpse' on which 'were imprinted the traces of the vilest and most hideous passions which had animated her while she lived' (p. 136). She has the effect of entirely unmanning the General: 'all manhood melted from me like wax in the furnace' (p. 137). He faints (an action associated with the passive gothic heroine), and subsequently feels 'ashamed of myself as a man and a soldier' (p. 138). The chamber is subsequently closed, containing though not destroying the disruptive feminine force within. Although the figure of the supernatural, demonic feminine was familiar by this time, the narrative nevertheless establishes a motif that would become commonplace in the Victorian ghost story: the encounter between the female spectre and the rational (masculine) man.[19]

Victorian Hauntings: Dickens and Beyond

Many of these tropes and motifs are evident in Dickens's ghost stories. While *Blackwood's* and *The Keepsake* were becoming increasingly popular, a young Dickens was reading a different type of publication, similarly indicative of the spirit of the age: the *Terrific Register, or, Record of Crimes, Judgments, Providences and Calamities* (1823–5). Though short lived, it heralded a significant development in publishing: the emergence of a distinct market for the poorer reader. Forerunner of the penny dreadful and penny blood, the *Register* provided graphic accounts of crimes, deaths and executions, as well as supernatural occurrences, accompanied by similarly graphic illustrations.[20] Dickens later attested to its appeal, asserting it 'frightened my very wits out of my head, for the small charge of a penny weekly; which considering that there was an illustration to every number, in which there was always a pool of blood, and at least one body, was cheap'.[21] It exerted an influence on Dickens's own fiction: Paul Schlicke suggests the sensational stories of the *Register* 'provided a fertile ground for the imagination that was to create Squeers, Bill Sikes, Quilp, and the self-combusting Krook', while shorter works such as 'The Clock-Case' (*Mr Humphrey's Clock*, 1840) are clearly indebted to Dickens's early sensational reading.[22]

Dickens was instrumental in popularizing the Victorian ghost story – as both editor and author. In 1837, he became editor of *Bentley's Miscellany*. From the outset, ghost stories featured heavily: the first volume includes 'The Marine Ghost', 'The Spectre' and 'Spectre of Tappington' – testament to the continued popularity of the supernatural story, as well as Dickens's own interest in the form. In 1850, he began editing *Household Words*, replaced by *All the Year Round* in 1859. As editor, he was involved in the publication of several important contributions to the genre, including works by Elizabeth Gaskell, Le Fanu and Collins. Supernatural stories sat, as Carol A. Martin points out, somewhat incongruously, alongside 'debunking articles on ghosts and witches which assume an enlightened, modern reader', highlighting Dickens's own scepticism and the tension which existed between 'old' superstitions and progressive (scientific) thinking.[23] However, Dickens recognized the potential for the ghost story as a means of 'illustrating particular states of mind and processes of the imagination', and Dickens's own contributions to the form frequently seek to explore psychological states as much as apparent supernatural occurrences.[24]

One of his most important contributions is 'The Signal-Man' (1866): an example of the Victorian Christmas ghost story, with which Dickens remains closely associated.[25] It appeared in 'Mugby Junction' – a collection of eight stories published in the Christmas edition of *All the Year Round*.[26] Dickens's interest in the psychological ghost story is apparent in the eponymous signalman's conflict between rationality and superstition: his education and professionalism are contrasted with his encounters with the supernatural and his inability to realize its meaning. Critical discussions highlight the story's complexity and ambiguity, but also provide a broader insight into the appeal of the Victorian ghost story – specifically the genre's ability to generate a multitude of possible meanings. Indeed, the story's success lies partly in its refusal to reveal the 'true' meaning of its signs and symbols: the reader, with the signalman himself, repeatedly asks 'What does the spectre mean?'[27] As John Daniel Stahl confirms, it is a story that 'presents a world in which there are signals that have some awful significance, but the signals are confusing and inconclusive'.[28] Jill L. Matus reads the narrative through the lens of trauma theory, and links it to the train crash in which Dickens was involved the previous year.[29] Ewald Mengal proposes it serves to illustrate 'Dickens's fears and apprehensions as to the dehumanizing effects of technological progress on man and the dangers of the Industrial Revolution', while Graeme Tytler suggests it is 'a story about a man evidently suffering from a type of partial insanity'.[30] These varied interpretations emphasize its position as an exemplar of the Victorian ghost story: refusing to lend itself to any single interpretation, 'The Signal-Man', partly enabled by its contemporaneous setting (in contrast to the historical setting of earlier gothic tales), encapsulates an array of social and cultural anxieties.

The ghost story's function as social and cultural discourse is further evident in Gaskell's short fiction. Many of her tales have a gothic dimension, including 'The Old Nurse's Story' (1852), 'The Squire's Story' (1853), 'The Ghost in the Garden Room' (1859) and 'The Grey Woman' (1861), all of which appeared in Dickens's magazines. While Gaskell's novels are diverse, encompassing industrial fiction, realism and elements of sensation fiction, it is in her shorter fiction that she evinces a specific concern with the gothic, emphasizing the potential of the genre for the Victorian woman writer, as well as reflecting a wider trend in the Victorian period. Laura Kranzler observes, 'In Gaskell's Gothic scenarios, it is usually the female characters who are victimized by the males', and notes the narratives' concern with 'exposing the conflict between the powerful and the powerless'.[31] This reading highlights an important parallel between the gothic short story and the concerns of the emerging women's movement: increasingly, the genre provided a significant space for the exploration of gender roles. This is particularly evident in those stories which, like Scott's 'The Tapestried Chamber', portray encounters between men and female spectres: men frequently become unhinged, their masculinity threatened, as a consequence of these confrontations. They behave in a manner associated with the passive, weak woman: crying, fainting and exhibiting a lack of control. In Braddon's 'The Cold Embrace' (*Ralph the Bailiff and Other Tales*, 1862), the protagonist is pursued by the ghost of his wronged lover: unable to enact revenge in life, she does so in death. In Rhoda Broughton's 'The Truth, the Whole Truth, and Nothing but the Truth' (*Temple Bar*, 1868), the male protagonist is literally scared to death. In Charlotte Riddell's 'The Old House in Vauxhall Walk' (*Weird Stories*, 1882), the hero's conquering of the ghosts and solving of the crime is portrayed as a feat of bravery that serves to reunite him with his father (who had previously called him a coward). He intends to prove himself by joining the army, but concludes 'one may as well be picked off by a ghost as a bullet'.[32] Masculinity, its construction and breakdown, is thus central to the Victorian ghost story: ghostly encounters serve to test the 'manliness' of male witnesses and enable an attack on patriarchal structures by otherwise powerless women.

Gaskell's 'The Old Nurse's Story' is similarly concerned with the relationship between the sexes. The 'old nurse' of the title tells the story of the daughters of Lord Furnivall, Maude and Grace, who fall in love with the same man, resulting in a bitter rivalry. Maude secretly marries him and gives birth to a daughter, whom she is forced to conceal from her family. After her husband abandons her, provoked by her sister into revealing the marriage,

Maude and her child are cast out of the ancestral home by her father. In the morning, Maude is found, 'crazy and smiling [...] nursing a dead child'.[33] The house, where Miss Grace (now an elderly spinster) lives, is haunted by the ghosts of her father, sister and niece. When the ghostly scene in which Maude is cast out is played out one evening, Grace collapses and dies. The story is dominated by women, but power is exerted by men. It is also a narrative about the relationship between past and present. Although Gaskell sets the main events of the story in the past, the complex narrative structure links to the narrative present. The story of the sisters is three generations removed from those listening to the tale. However, the listeners are distantly related to the Furnivalls, and their mother and nurse witnessed the ghostly aftermath of the family's breakdown. The suggestion of an inherent connection between past and present is emphasized by Grace's words shortly before her death: 'What is done in youth can never be undone in age!' (p. 32), reinforcing the notion of the past haunting the present and emphasizing the genre's attempts to negotiate (or at least highlight the tensions) between the two.

While Gaskell frequently favours historical backdrops in her short fiction, as the century progressed, events of the supernatural tale were brought increasingly closer to home, enabling a greater engagement with contemporary concerns and anxieties. This change coincides with the emergence of the sensation novel, in which the home becomes the focus of mystery. Many sensation writers also produced supernatural stories, including Wilkie Collins, Braddon, Mrs Henry Wood, Florence Marryat, Broughton and Le Fanu.[34] While many of the leitmotifs of sensation fiction are apparent in these shorter productions, the mid-century ghost story is not merely a condensed form of the sensation novel. Although sensation fiction exhibits a concern with the mysteries of the gothic and employs narrative devices such as dreams and premonitions, there is a shift away from the supernatural, and, when 'ghosts' do appear, there is often a rational explanation.[35] This renunciation of the supernatural enables the sensation genre to bridge the gap between gothic and realist writing. In their shorter fiction, however, sensation writers revel in ghostly occurrences, reflecting a broader trend in nineteenth-century literature. Nonetheless, many central themes and motifs of sensation fiction are evident in these short stories: family secrets, dangerous women, adultery, class relations, crime and madness all feature heavily.

Braddon's gothic tales are a case in point. As with many female sensation writers, she articulates an anxiety about – if not quite a protest against – Victorian women's prescribed roles, the relationship between the sexes, and female (dis)empowerment. These concerns are evident in *Ralph the Bailiff and Other Tales* (1862), which contains several gothic tales. 'Eveline's Visitant' revisits earlier gothic narratives: subtitled 'A Ghost Story' and set in eighteenth-century France, it tells of a woman haunted by the ghost of her husband's cousin – killed by her husband in a duel. 'The Mystery at Fernwood' (first published in *Temple Bar*, 1861) is a prime example of the hybrid gothic-sensation story. Several gothic motifs are employed (the figure of the orphan-heroine, the double, imprisonment), and situated alongside the central tropes of sensation fiction: a contemporary setting, family mystery and the threat of madness. As Eve M. Lynch points out, 'Braddon shows the household haunted by an uncanny influence that turns out to have foundation in the family itself'.[36]

Gender roles are key throughout Braddon's stories, supporting Diana Wallace's contention that 'The Female Gothic is perhaps par excellence the mode within which women writers have been able to explore deep-rooted female fears about women's powerlessness and imprisonment within patriarchy.'[37] However, such explorations are not exclusive to the work of women writers. Throughout his short stories, Collins employs tropes of the gothic to explore a range of social issues. Illegitimacy, a significant concern in his novels, is central to 'The Dead Hand' (*Household Words*, 1857), which in its treatment of the subject anticipates *The Woman in White* (1860) and *No Name* (1862). In 'The Monktons of Wincot Abbey' (*Fraser's Magazine*, 1855; later republished as 'Mad Monkton'), Collins explores the issue of hereditary insanity.[38] It is an important example of the psychological gothic as a consequence of the uncertainty surrounding the supernatural. It was originally intended for *Household Words*, but Dickens refused it because he thought the subject matter unsuitable for his magazine's readership. The narrative opens with an account of the history of the Monkton family's insanity, described as a 'hereditary curse', hinting at the blurred line between the supernatural and psychological disorder.[39] Alfred Monkton, the last of the Monktons, becomes obsessed with discovering the missing body of his uncle, who has been killed in a duel. Alfred is urged on by a vision of his uncle's ghost, and an old family prophecy which claims the Monkton line will end when one of its own lies 'Graveless under open sky' (p. 671). The body is eventually discovered, unburied, but lost during a shipwreck on the journey to England. Alfred subsequently develops brain fever and dies, fulfilling the prophecy. The narrator of the story attributes events to Alfred's inherited malady, and 'strange coincidences'

(p. 676), but an element of uncertainty prevails, marking the tension between the rational and the supernatural.

Collins's narrative deliberately creates uncertainty, refusing to dismiss entirely the possibility of a world oblivious to progress and reason. Similar tensions are evoked in the opening to 'The Dream Woman' (*The Frozen Deep and Other Stories*, 1874), in which the multiple narrators highlight divisions between rationality and superstition: the gothic story is framed within the narrative of a rational narrator, Percy Fairbank, who introduces the supernatural narrative of Francis Raven.[40] Significantly, while Fairbank is a gentleman, Raven is a servant, thus the divide between rationality and superstition is construed partly in relation to class identity. Raven is disturbed one night by a vision of a woman trying to kill him with a knife. A year later, he meets and is 'bewitched' by the woman from his vision, aptly named Alicia Warlock, whom he subsequently marries. The marriage breaks down, and the pair separate. Through a series of convoluted events, his wife discovers him and kills him, as foretold by his vision. As Catherine Peters suggests, the story expresses 'a barely suppressed anxiety about the dangers of marriage', a key theme in Collins's writing and in sensation fiction more generally.[41] It presents the (stock) figure of the beautiful but dangerous feminine, anticipating Braddon's Lady Audley. The murder scene represents an inversion of the traditional power balance: the male is rendered passive and silent, the victim of an aggressive and violent woman, who reflects tensions and anxieties surrounding the figure of the Victorian woman.

Similar anxieties are evident in George Eliot's 'The Lifted Veil' (*Blackwood's*, 1859). It tells the story of Latimer, who develops the ability to read minds and experiences prophetic visions. It is a psychological tale, concerned with exploring the effects of this 'double consciousness'.[42] Latimer becomes obsessed by his brother's fiancée, Bertha, whose mind he cannot access, and, despite a vision in which he witnesses her cruelty, marries her following his brother's death. Following their union he finds himself able to read her thoughts, including her desire that he might kill himself. When Bertha's maid falls ill, an old friend of Latimer's, Charles Meunier, asks permission to conduct an experiment just after her death, involving temporarily reanimating the corpse. Performed without the maid's consent, this suggests the dangerous power of the scientist (echoing *Frankenstein* and anticipating *Jekyll and Hyde* (1886)), as well as the powerlessness of the lower-class woman. Brought back to life for a few moments, the maid announces Bertha's intention to poison Latimer. The scenes in which these events are conveyed lend the narrative its credentials as a work of horror fiction, while

Eliot's engagement with the subject of clairvoyance reflects contemporary interests. The narrative remains ambiguous regarding the veracity of these events. Narrated in the first person, it leaves open the possibility that these psychic experiences are the consequence of Latimer's mental state. This typically gothic ambiguity enables it to be read as a commentary on artistic practice. Gothic writing insistently concerns itself with representation, and the manner in which narratives are imparted to the reader is central to their potential meanings. Critical readings of 'The Lifted Veil' suggest its allegorical status – in this instance, as an allegory 'of the workings of fictional narrative itself', a 'self-conscious fiction', in which 'Latimer's access to others' minds mimics authorial omniscience'.[43]

These stories highlight the burgeoning interest in dreams, visions and altered states of mind, which took on increasing significance in the middle of the nineteenth century, coinciding with developing interest in psychology. Fictional dreams often represent the hinterland between the natural and the supernatural: a state in which reality appears distorted. Broughton's 'Behold, it was a Dream' and 'Poor Pretty Bobby' (both *Temple Bar*, 1872), and Charlotte Riddell's 'Hertford O'Donnell's Warning' (*London Society*, 1867), 'The Old House in Vauxhall Walk' and 'Sandy the Tinker' (*Weird Stories*, 1882) all employ dreams as key plot devices, while also engaging with other prevalent social concerns. In 'Behold, it was a Dream', a strong distinction is drawn between the English and 'other' races – in this instance, the Irish, reflecting broader attitudes, particularly during the years of the Home Rule debates. Describing the murderer who appears in a vision, the protagonist states, 'I felt sure he was Irish';[44] her friend subsequently protests, 'there is such a family likeness between all Irishmen' (p. 699). The English labourers, with their 'honest bovine English faces' (p. 710), are contrasted with the Irish labourers, who all have 'the same look of debased, squalid cunning' (p.722). There are class issues at work here, with the murderer a working man, playing on contemporary middle-class anxieties, and reflecting a key concern of sensation fiction.

Le Fanu's fiction is similarly concerned with visions and altered states of mind. An important figure within the sub-genre of Irish gothic, he exerted significant influence on what is now construed as the quintessentially English supernatural story. Several of his early works appeared in the *Dublin University Magazine*, but he published widely in London based magazines, including *Temple Bar* and *All the Year Round*. He achieved significant popularity in Ireland and Britain, and his work influenced later gothic writers. Traditional gothic conventions are evident in his stories: historically or geographically distant settings (in contradistinction to the fiction of other sensation writers), stereotypical heroines, castles, clergymen and priests (as well as vampires). Rational explanations for apparently supernatural events remain a possibility in much of his writing, marking his contribution to the psychological gothic. His best-known collection, *In a Glass Darkly* (1872), consists of five tales, including his vampire novella *Carmilla* and the short story 'Green Tea' – the latter, a significant example of the psychological gothic, contains echoes of Eliot's 'The Lifted Veil' and draws on well-established gothic conventions (the frame narrative, historic setting, figure of the clergyman, ghostly apparition), as well as anticipating late Victorian gothic fiction. The story is narrated by Dr Martin Hesselius, a German physician who represents the voice of scientific reason. Reverend Jennings is tormented by the apparition of a monkey, which gradually grows more agitated, and urges Jennings to self-destruction. Having detailed his experience to Hesselius, Jennings commits suicide. The narrative encourages the reader to consider a rational explanation for Jennings's experience: no one other than Jennings sees the monkey, suggesting hallucination, and the first doctor consulted diagnoses a problem with the optic nerves. Jennings, influenced by his reading of Swedenborg, believes he is terrorized by some form of evil spirit, but Hesselius disputes this, and points to his excessive consumption of green tea as a possible explanation.

The spectre of the monkey serves as a useful symbol, highlighting the gothic's ambiguous nature, and enabling multiple interpretations. The apparition may represent Jennings's religious doubt, or the tension between superstition and reason, religion and science. In light of Darwinian debates current at the time, the form the apparition takes is obviously significant. An alternative reading posits the monkey as a visual symbol of repressed homosexual desires.[45] As Eve Sedgwick observes, 'the Gothic was the first ... form in England to have close, relatively visible links to male homosexuality'.[46] Le Fanu's narrative anticipates *Dr Jekyll and Mr Hyde*, which also hints at the possibility of suppressed homosexual desire.[47] Indeed, the similarities between these two works – the role of science, the appearance of a simian-like creature (Hyde is repeatedly described in these terms), the hidden meanings suggested by narrative symbols – establish 'Green Tea' as an important intertext for Stevenson's work.

'Green Tea' thus offers a narrative bridge linking the gothic tales of the early nineteenth century, the sensation stories of the mid-Victorian period, and later *fin de siècle* narratives. The tropes that characterize the stories read and produced by the residents of the Villa Diodati in 1816 are still in evidence, but the features of the psychological gothic, which would culminate in the later works of Henry James, Robert Louis Stevenson and their contemporaries, are also apparent. The ghost story's potential for engaging with contemporary social and cultural anxieties is clearly evident. 'Green Tea', then, stands as a seminal example of the form. These anxieties continue to attract the attention of short story writers for the remainder of the century, though tensions around empire and race become increasingly prevalent, reinforcing the genre's social and historical significance. At the end of the century, cultural critics such as Max Nordau employed the language of the gothic to articulate apprehensions about the state of society. The gothic short story, through its haunting of the nineteenth-century literary landscape, succeeds (in spite – or indeed because – of its status as popular fiction) in articulating, often through its ambiguities and silences, the anxieties which pervaded the cultural and national conscience.

Notes

1. Karl Marx and Frederick Engels, *The Communist Manifesto* (London: Verso, 2012), p. 33.
2. Mary Shelley, Preface to 1831 edition, *Frankenstein*, ed. Judith Baxter (Cambridge University Press, 1998), p. 10.
3. I use the term 'gothic' to refer to those works that adopt the broader conventions of gothic writing. Not all gothic stories contain supernatural elements, while not all supernatural stories feature ghosts, so there are subtle distinctions between the three categories I refer to throughout the chapter: gothic, supernatural and ghost stories.
4. Mary Shelley, *Frankenstein*, ed. J. Paul Hunter (New York: Norton, 2012), p. 166.
5. Tim Killick, *British Short Fiction in the Early Nineteenth Century: The Rise of the Tale* (Aldershot: Ashgate, 2008), p. 13.
6. John Polidori, *The Vampyre: A Tale; and Ernestus Berchtold, or, The Modern Oedipus*, ed. D. L. Macdonald and Kathleen Scherf (Peterborough, Ontario: Broadview, 2008), p. 59. All quotations are from this edition, with page numbers given in parentheses in the text.
7. See Alexis Easley and Shannon Scott, eds., *Terrifying Transformations: An Anthology of Victorian Werewolf Fiction* (Kansas City: Valancourt Books, 2013).
8. Robert Morrison and Chris Baldick, Introduction to *The Vampyre and Other Tales of the Macabre* (Oxford University Press, 1997), p. xii.
9. George Eliot, *Middlemarch*, ed. Gregory Maertz (Peterborough, Ontario: Broadview, 2004), p. 235.
10. *The Letters of Mary Wollstonecraft Shelley*, ed. Betty T. Bennett (Baltimore: Johns Hopkins University Press, 1980), p. 412.

11. Between 1828 and 1838, Shelley contributed at least fourteen stories to *The Keepsake*. See *The Cambridge Bibliography of English Literature, Volume IV: 1800–1900*, ed. Joanne Shattock (Cambridge University Press, 1999), pp. 1063–72.
12. Diane Long Hoevler, 'Mary Shelley and Gothic Feminism: The Case of "The Mortal Immortal"', in *Iconoclastic Departures: Mary Shelley After 'Frankenstein'*, ed. Syndy M. Conger *et al.* (Madison: Fairleigh Dickinson University Press, 1997), pp. 150–63.
13. British Short Fiction, pp. 126–7.
14. See Charlotte Riddell's 'Sandy the Tinker' (1882) and Henry James's 'The Turn of the Screw' (1898).
15. 'Orality and Public Poetry', in *The Edinburgh History of Scottish Literature, Volume II: Enlightenment Britain and Empire*, ed. Ian Brown (Edinburgh University Press, 2007), p. 127.
16. Walter Scott, 'My Aunt Margaret's Mirror', in *The Keepsake*, ed. Frederic Mansel Reynolds (London: Hurst, Chance and Co., 1829), p. 11.
17. See Andrew Smith, *The Ghost Story, 1840–1920: A Cultural History* (Manchester University Press, 2012).
18. Walter Scott, 'The Tapestried Chamber', in *The Keepsake*, ed. Reynolds, p. 124.
19. Examples from gothic fiction include Matilda in Matthew Lewis's *The Monk* (1796).
20. The 1825 volume includes 'Well-Authenticated Account of Spectres' and 'Horrible Execution of a Bohemian Jew' along with images of disembowelment, impaling, and stabbings.
21. Quoted in John Forster, *The Life of Charles Dickens, Volume 1: 1812–1842* (Leipzig: Tauchnitz, 1872), p. 101.
22. *The Oxford Companion to Charles Dickens* (Oxford University Press, 2011), p. 450.
23. Carol A. Martin, 'Gaskell's Ghosts: Truths in Disguise', *Studies in the Novel*, 21 (1989), 1, p. 28.
24. Charles Dickens to Elizabeth Gaskell (25 November 1851), in *The Letters of Charles Dickens*, ed. Kathleen Tillotson *et al.* (Oxford: Clarendon, 1988), VI, p. 546.
25. Dickens's other notable contributions include the novella *The Haunted Man and the Ghost's Bargain* (1848) and 'To Be Read at Dusk' (*The Keepsake*, 1852).
26. Four of these stories were authored by Dickens, with the remaining four by Andrew Halliday, Charles Alston Collins, Hesba Stretton and Amelia B. Edwards.
27. *Mugby Junction* (London: Chapman and Hall, 1866), p. 105.
28. John Daniel Stahl, 'The Source and Significance of the Revenant in Dickens's "The Signal Man"', *Dickens Studies Newsletter*, 11 (1980), p. 101.

29. Jill L. Matus, 'Trauma, Memory, and Railway Disaster: The Dickensian Connection', *Victorian Studies*, 43:3 (Spring 2001), p. 414.
30. Ewald Mengal, 'The Structure and Meaning of Dickens's "The Signalman"', *Studies in Short Fiction*, 20:4 (Fall 1983), p. 271; Graeme Tytler, 'Dickens's "The Signalman"', *Explicator*, 53:1 (Fall 1994), p. 26.
31. Introduction to Elizabeth Gaskell, *Gothic Tales* (London: Penguin, 2000), p. xi.
32. *Weird Stories* (Brighton: Victorian Secrets, 2009), p. 110.
33. Gaskell, *Gothic Tales*, p. 28.
34. Like Dickens, Braddon, Wood and Marryat also edited magazines that published many supernatural and gothic tales – *Belgravia*, *The Argosy* and *London Society* respectively.
35. See Collins's *Armadale* (1866), and Wood's *The Shadow of Ashlydyat* (1863), *Verner's Pride* (1863) and *Anne Hereford* (1868).
36. Eve M. Lynch, 'Spectral Politics: M. E. Braddon and the Spirits of Social Reform', in *Beyond Sensation: Mary Elizabeth Braddon in Context*, ed. Marlene Tromp, Pamela K. Gilbery and Aeron Haynie (Albany: State University of New York Press, 2000), p. 242.
37. Diana Wallace, 'Uncanny Stories: The Ghost Story as Female Gothic', *Gothic Studies*, 6 (2004), 1, p. 57.
38. The story is also of interest for its representation of Catholicism.
39. *Fraser's Magazine* (July–Dec. 1855), p. 488.
40. The story is an expanded version of 'The Ostler', which appeared in the Christmas number of *Household Words* for 1855.
41. Catherine Peters, *The King of Inventors: A Life of Wilkie Collins* (London: Secker and Warburg, 1991), p. 155.
42. *Blackwood's Edinburgh Magazine* (July–Dec. 1859), p. 35.
43. Jill Galvan, 'The Narrator as Medium in George Eliot's "The Lifted Veil"', *Victorian Studies*, 48 (2006), 2, p. 240.
44. *Twilight Stories*, ed. Emma Liggins (Brighton: Victorian Secrets, 2009), p. 675.
45. See André L. DeCuir, 'Homosexuality at the Closet Threshold in Joseph Sheridan Le Fanu's "Green Tea"', in *Mapping Male Sexuality: Nineteenth-Century England*, ed. Jay Losey and William Dean Brewer (Cranbury: Associate University Presses, 2000), pp. 198–214.
46. Eve Sedgwick, *Between Men: English Literature and Male Homosocial Desire* (New York: Columbia University Press, 1985), p. 91. In *Carmilla*, Le Fanu explores the possibility of lesbian desire.
47. See Elaine Showalter, *Sexual Anarchy: Gender and Culture at the Fin De Siècle* (London: Bloomsbury, 1991), p. 107.

4

The Victorian Potboiler: Novelists Writing Short Stories

SOPHIE GILMARTIN

In May of 1897, the greatly prolific, and sometimes great, author and critic Margaret Oliphant wrote 'A Preface: On the Ebb Tide' describing 'the strange discovery which a man makes when he finds himself carried away by the retiring waters, no longer coming in upon the top of the wave, but going out'.[1] 1897 was Queen Victoria's jubilee year, and the coincidence of those celebrations for an aged monarch with the ebbing of the century, made for a cultural moment of reflection and a retrospective gaze over the long Victorian era.

In her own career, Oliphant had always been a canny and reliable author in touch with the cultural moment and the publishing market, so in her writing of an 'ebb tide' she was yet again in tune with her readership. But for Oliphant this was as much a personal 'strange discovery' of ending as it was cultural: she died just over a month after her preface was published, but even in this preface to a book of short stories she was not writing about death itself, but – to her mind – the more difficult ending of a career. She contemplates the artist's realization that the public is no longer interested in his or her work, even though he or she still feels a vigorous creativity. In fact 'On the Ebb Tide' introduces her book of short stories *The Ways of Life* (1897) that republished 'Mr Sandford' (1888) and 'The Wonderful History of Mr Robert Dalyell' (1892). In each of these stories, the artist outlives the acclaim and respect of his public.

After she died the critics wrote of Oliphant that she had not outlived her relevance or become simply a voice of the past, and that her reputation would survive. Perhaps they were being kind, because it has to be admitted that Oliphant's work did not, unlike that of Anthony Trollope, to whom she was often compared, survive the modernist rejection of the Victorian three-decker novel, the 'potboiler,' and what was deemed to be the stuffy morality and heavy detail of plot and description in the novel and short fiction. The tide of Oliphant's literary fortunes is now coming in, and some of her novels are back in print and receiving scholarly and popular attention. But Oliphant is just one recent example of a 'forgotten' Victorian writer who is in the process of being rediscovered (like Gaskell and Braddon before her). These rediscoveries and reprintings are usually of the long novels. This chapter will focus on the yet more deeply forgotten short stories of some of these writers, as well as stories by enduringly popular Victorian novelists such as Charles Dickens and Trollope, whose novels never quite sank into the oblivion effected by modernist and postmodernist attitudes.[2]

It is telling that Oliphant wrote of her own literary ebb tide in that 1897 preface to short stories. It is in the short story form that the fault lines of the great divide between Victorianism and modernism can be seen very clearly, although – as much recent scholarship exploring this divide has determined – there is more continuity than was deemed to be the case in the earlier twentieth century. The form and definition of the short story became a rallying point in the 1880s and 1890s for those writers and readers who sought to distance themselves artistically from what they regarded as the amorphous Victorian short story that novelists wrote simply to keep the pot boiling while a long novel was in preparation or on the back burner. The 1890s in particular saw much debate over the definition and parameters of the short story and experimentation with its form. As with Margaret Oliphant's, most Victorian short stories were first written for the periodical market, which burgeoned in the 1840s and 1850s after the 'taxes on knowledge' were abolished (the first of these taxes went in 1836 and the last in 1855). Consequently, there was a huge market for short stories, which were interleaved with the latest serialized novel in the periodicals, from the point in 1836 when 'the newspaper tax fell from 4d. to 1d., thereby setting the stage for a 70 percent increase in press circulation over the next seven years'.[3]

Underlining their close narrative relationship to the novel, many 'short' stories were serialized: Dickens's own editorial edicts for the short fiction he would publish in his periodicals, as Deborah Thomas has noted, were that it be told by someone (linking it to oral tradition) and that it be of no greater length than could be accommodated in four instalments or fewer.[4]

In 1901, the American critic Brander Matthews anathematized such loose definitions of the short story: in his view the British publishing 'machine' which promoted the three-volume novel had killed the short story form in

Britain. The British short story was merely periodical padding to the thick mattress of the serialized three-decker novel:

> Now, the British short story, as the machine makes it and as we see it in most British magazines, is only a little British Novel. It is thus the exact artistic opposite of the American Short-story, of which ... the chief characteristics are originality, ingenuity, compression, and not infrequently, a touch of fantasy.[5]

Edgar Allan Poe both pre-empted and influenced such formal notions of the short story genre in his review essay of Nathaniel Hawthorne's 'Twice-Told Tales' (1841) and in his essay, 'The Philosophy of Composition' (1846). His emphasis on works that can be 'read at one sitting' and on the effect 'derivable from unity of impression', foregrounds generic features that were much discussed in the British literary culture of the 1890s.[6] Impression, compression, and the inclusion of detail and description only when they are essential to the action or meaning are all qualities that were returned to and unevenly employed by Henry James, R. L. Stevenson, Rudyard Kipling and Oscar Wilde, among others.

Poe's contemporary, Charles Dickens, and other novelists from midcentury into the 1880s were known for an expansive style encouraged by the capaciousness of the three-decker novel. Nevertheless, Dickens, Gaskell, Trollope, Oliphant, Wilkie Collins and Thomas Hardy, among others, all wrote stories that could be read in an evening. In the work of Dickens, Gaskell and Hardy especially, many stories have a framed narrator, still carrying that feel of oral tradition seen earlier in the century in the tales of James Hogg, Walter Scott and Maria Edgeworth. Many are told by the fire on a winter evening, and often traditionally at Christmas (the title of the 1852 Christmas Number of Dickens's journal *Household Words* was 'A Round of Stories by the Christmas Fire').[7] The supernatural story was a popular nineteenth-century Christmas tradition, very much encouraged by these extra or expanded 'Christmas Numbers' in many periodicals. Several of these stories are discussed in Chapter 3 of this volume, including Dickens's 'The Signal-Man' (from the 1866 multi-authored Christmas Number of *Household Words*) and Gaskell's 'The Old Nurse's Story' (from the 1852 Christmas number, mentioned above). Aiming for commercial success, Henry James adopted the popular form of the Christmas ghost story told around the fire in his opening to the supernatural tale 'The Turn of the Screw' (1898): 'The story had held us, round the fire, sufficiently breathless, but except the obvious remark that it was gruesome, as, on Christmas Eve in an old house, a strange tale should essentially be, I remember no comment uttered ...'[8]

Dickens's 'Barbox Brothers' and 'Barbox Brothers and Co.' are the first two short stories in the Christmas number of 1866 entitled *Mugby Junction*. As was usual with the Christmas numbers, the collection of stories was authored by several writers; in this case four of the stories were by Dickens and then there was one each from Andrew Halliday, Charles Collins, Hesba Stretton and Amelia Edwards, although there is a possibility of shared authorship with some of the tales that is difficult to ascertain because they were published anonymously (as were the majority of periodical stories, articles and novels in the Victorian period). All the tales are connected to the railway station and junction at Mugby. Each story is short enough to be read, as Poe exhorted, 'at a single sitting', and each has a discrete 'unity of impression'; nevertheless all are connected into a larger multi-plotted whole, however tenuously, through the many railway connections and lines that meet and disperse at Mugby. If Victorian literature was ruled by the multi-plot novel, these stories are an odd inverse to that dominant form: they seem to take apart the multi-plot structure, dividing it into discrete elements, and revealing disconnection between stories and characters as much as the unavoidable connections, for good or ill, that novelists such as Dickens, George Eliot and Trollope famously vaunt in their novels.

Mugby Junction opens in the least leisurely style possible: there are no novelistic introductions of scene or description. Instead there are staccato phrases, as a man with a through ticket decides, on a random and sudden whim, to halt his journey at Mugby.

The guard moves rapidly to get his luggage off the train in the three minutes before the train must leave. Then 'Lamp waved. Signal lights ahead already changing. Shriek from engine. Train gone.'[9] Impression and compression are certainly to the fore at the opening of this short story. Dickens also foregoes the more traditional framed narrator, evocative of the oral tale. Of the anonymous traveller, we are told: 'He spoke to himself. There was no one else to speak to. Perhaps, though, had there been anyone else to speak to, he would have preferred to speak to himself' (pp. 3–4). (Perhaps there are shades here of Herman Melville's 1853 short story 'Bartleby, the Scrivener: A Story of Wall Street', in which the clerk Bartleby responds to work demands with depressed disassociation in his repeated phrase, 'I would prefer not to'.) Walking the platform, driven by the wind and rain at 3 o'clock 'of a tempestuous morning!' the man says to himself, 'it signifies nothing to me to what quarter I turn my face' (p. 4). The sparse language, the inscrutability of the traveller, the non-place that is the railway junction, all indicate distinctively modern short story features. Experimentation with the short story form in the 1890s is critically regarded as a forerunner of the modernist short story, but there are few *fin-de-siècle* stories that could match this opening by Dickens for its proto-modernist alienation and defamiliarization.

Yet Dickens does not sustain this disconnectedness. At first the man is only known to the reader as 'Barbox Brothers', the title of the firm he directed most of his life, but this impersonality is gradually undermined as the man develops connections with the people of Mugby and its junction. In the second story, 'Barbox Brothers and Co.', he extends his stay in Mugby, in order to ponder which railway line he should take to put his past unhappy life behind him. But every journey out leads to ever-expanding lines of connection, and to stories: of the woman he loved, of the man who betrayed him, of forgiveness, or, in other words, to a 'typical' sentimental Victorian story. In these two stories, Dickens uses the railway junction's web of lines, and the man who arrives seemingly from nowhere, to underline the idea that stories are inescapable and connected. One line intersects, leads to, or parallels another. But the collection of stories as a whole tends to work against the coincidences and meetings of the multi-plotted novel, to create a sense of separate characters living in their own worlds.

The man named Barbox Brothers eventually follows one of the railway lines on foot into the country to immerse himself in village life. But the clamour and rush of city life is never far off when the railway junction is at the bottom of the hill. Dickens's ambivalence here about the choice between the country and city, a choice made in the endings of so many of his novels, is part of a larger phenomenon which affects the short story form in the nineteenth century. The persistent movement of people from rural areas to the cities over the period meant that by 1851 the census of that year revealed that for the first time in history more people lived in the cities than the countryside. For many in the city, and especially those who were removed by a generation or two from village life, the harshness and penury of agricultural labour and lack of opportunity in the countryside (especially during the agricultural depression of the 'Hungry '40s') were forgotten and replaced by a nostalgia for the beauties of landscape, nature and the intimate, knowable community of the village. This nostalgia can be seen across the arts; in painting, poetry, the novel and the short story, but it was the short story or tale, and its affinities with the oral tradition of the countryside and the past, that filled an increasingly urbanized population's need for the rural, regional and ancestral. The cultural impact of a changing demographic in Britain included the popularity of the short story genre of the regional, provincial or, in the case of Wales, Ireland and Scotland, the national tale. These stories were profoundly rooted in local place and often related, at least in part, in local dialect.

Far from the bustle of the railway junction is the scene of Mary Russell Mitford's *Our Village* (1832), subtitled, 'Sketches of Rural Life, Characters and Scenery'.[10] Mitford, whose place in the rural tradition is treated more explicitly in Chapter 15, associates the regional with the short story genre and its 'unities': 'Even in books I like a confined locality, and so do the critics when they talk of unities.' Rather than train or stage-coach she takes a slower pace: 'Will you walk with me through our village, courteous reader?' (p. 2). Mitford's friend and correspondent Elizabeth Barrett Browning wrote to her in July of 1837, admiring the stories of *Our Village* (which were written between 1824 and 1832, and mostly published in the *Lady's Magazine*), noting their 'power of bringing from the surface of things that freshness of beauty, which others search for in the profundities of nature. While others lose their breath in diving, you are gathering pearls on the shore – and scarcely stooping to do so.'[11] Far from being an underhand compliment, calling Mitford's work superficial ('the surface of things'), Elizabeth Barrett Browning's observations fall in with a growing artistic and literary sensibility in the nineteenth century that turned from the subjectivity of Romantic lyric poetry to the 'objectivity' of vernacular language and dialect, of empirical observation and detail. In poetry, both Alfred Tennyson and Elizabeth Barrett's future husband, Robert Browning, would be important exponents of this trend.[12] In the short story and novel, domestic realism answered this turn to the objective 'surface of things', to the observation of daily life.

Mitford's stories are local, found close at hand 'on the shore', and the first-person narrator speaks with unaffected ease, guiding the reader on a diurnal round of an intimately known rural space and community. Indeed, the role of the narrator is a key feature of the nineteenth-century regional story because 'he' or 'she' underlies its connections with the oral tale, mimicking that old traditional genre which Walter Benjamin so lovingly considers in his essay 'The Storyteller' (1936). For Benjamin, the best stories come from an 'intimate interpenetration' of two types of tellers, who are combined for him in 'the artisan class': in this class was 'combined the lore of faraway places, such as a much-travelled man brings home, with the lore of the past, as it best reveals itself to the natives of a place'.[13] This type of storyteller may have come from afar, but is often a returned native who knows his homeland or region; he is able to have enough distance to relate the stories that his listeners know, but perhaps need to be told afresh, with another accreted layer of meaning that answers to their moment in time and place. Benjamin's construct has many permutations in the nineteenth-century regional tale. For example, in Robert Louis Stevenson's supernatural tale 'Thrawn Janet', the story is introduced by a traveller who is only peripherally connected to the region, but who 'speaks' southern English. A Victorian urban or southern reader may have been lulled by the frame narrator into thinking that he will have a guide through this culturally unfamiliar Scottish tale of possession and the devil. But Stevenson disappoints this expectation and the narration moves over to a man in the inn, who tells the story in strong and uncompromising Scots dialect. There is no 'translation' of culture, theme or language in this framed story, and this contributes much to its powerful otherness. Framed narration; the diegetic narrator; the narrator who is barely there or who disappears: these stances are all employed in the regional or national tale of the period and are crucial to its meaning and reception. James Hogg's Scottish tales early in the century; George Eliot's *Scenes of Clerical Life* (1857); Elizabeth Gaskell's *Cranford* (1853); Margaret Oliphant's collections *Chronicles of Carlingford* (1862–65) and *Neighbours on the Green* (1889); most of Thomas Hardy's short stories, but especially *Wessex Tales* (1888); Arthur Quiller Couch's Cornish stories of the late nineteenth century: these and others demonstrate how the Victorian reader continued to be fascinated by the regional tale across the century. In all these collections of stories the narrator has a distinctive role as guide and voice in the space of the tale.

All three 'scenes' of Eliot's *Scenes of Clerical Life* take place twenty-five to thirty years before the time of publication, so before Victoria came to the throne, just before the Great Reform Bill and before the wide spread of the railways. Late in the century, Hardy would set many of his novels and short stories at least thirty years before the time of writing. The quarter-century to thirty years span gave a temporal and spatial distance for these writers, taking them back to stories overheard in childhood, and to their childhood homes, to the oral and the regional. Certainly in the third of Eliot's *Scenes*, 'Janet's Repentance', the narrator seems to be a returned native, writing of what he had seen twenty-five years ago when he tells us that 'some of us had just assumed coat-tails'.[14] While the male intradiegetic narrator gives credence to the detailed descriptions of mundane life in the town and village – Milby and

Shepperton – of these stories, he slips out of his partial vision into omniscience throughout the story. In fact, Eliot's narrator takes the reader erratically high and low, far and near in focalization. At one moment he is a boy watching the beautiful heroine of the tale, at another he takes a bird's eye moral viewpoint over the people of Milby, only to come down again as he observes the young and much-tried Evangelical minister struggle through the town: 'But I am not poised at that lofty height. I am on the level and in the press with him, as he struggles his way along the stony road, through the crowd of unloving fellow-men!' (p. 229).

Again, the male narrator turns from proximity to the lofty height of omniscience to describe Janet's innermost thoughts, as she hides her alcoholism and her husband's physical brutality under a veneer of respectability in her home on Orchard Street. (Oliphant, Eliot, Gaskell and Hardy often give street names and map out the village or town of their stories.) We forget the presence of the narrator, as he cannot have witnessed the dramatic and sinister episode which takes place at night in the house: the drunken husband confronts Janet, who knows she will be beaten: '"What, you been drinking again have you? I'll beat you into your senses." He laid his hand with a firm grip on her shoulder, turned her around, and pushed her slowly before him along the passage and through the dining-room door which stood open on their left hand.' The narrator 'sees' for us the portrait of Janet's mother on the wall, whom he imagines seeing the brutal scene below her: Janet, 'standing stupidly unmoved in her great beauty, while the heavy arm is lifted to strike her. The blow falls – another – and another. Surely the mother hears that cry – "O Robert! Pity! Pity!"' (p. 199). While the theatrical language and blocking of this scene is reminiscent of Victorian stage melodrama, this fact does not lessen its raw immediacy and shocking nature. The narrator presents it in the present tense, thereby placing the reader close to the action.

The story was first published in *Blackwood's Edinburgh Magazine* in 1857, at the height of the sensation novel's popularity. *Blackwood's* was famous for its publication of sensational stories. Indeed, Edgar Allan Poe had written parodic instructions of 'How to Write a Blackwood Article' (1838), which include the gothic editor's plan to have a female aspiring writer drowned or savaged by dogs. But Eliot is not a 'sensation' writer, and here she is able to deploy her narrator/s at two removes: the narrator is hardly present and the boy he was at the time of the action could not have seen or known what was happening in the house on Orchard Street; instead he imagines the anguish of the mother in the portrait witnessing the beating inflicted on her daughter.

These deflections do not make the scene less painful, but focus the reader's attention on the psychological cruelty and damage rather than on sensational blood and gore. Similarly, the narrator never allows the reader a glimpse of Janet when she is drunk. We see her feverish self-loathing the morning after, and also her desperate desire for drink in her long recovery from alcoholism. To depict a middle-class lady drunk and out of control would be too disturbing, it seems. But in this early work of hers, Eliot deals with subject matter that is rarely handled in nineteenth-century literature. There are plenty of examples of drunken lower-class women and men, and of middle- and upper-class drunken men, but she crosses lines of class and gender to portray a heroine who is a middle-class alcoholic.

Liggins, Maunder and Robbins conjecture whether or not a comparison of longer and shorter works by individual authors could reveal that 'short stories offered writers more freedom of expression, or the opportunity to examine – or experiment with – topics felt to be unsuitable for the Victorian novel'.[15] While this question needs and warrants full scholarly investigation, certainly several of the writers considered in this chapter use subject matter that is not taken up in their novels, and cross boundaries which the censorious Mrs Grundy or, more tangibly, Mudie's Circulating Library would carefully police in the novels. (Mudie's bought advance copies of novels from publishers, when they had finished their run in the periodical and were then published, usually as a three-volume novel; short stories would have escaped some censorship, as Mudie's was far less interested in ordering collections of short stories.) While Eliot does not shy away from very difficult subject matter, such as infanticide in *Adam Bede*, one could argue that Hetty is lower class and to many middle-class Victorians that makes criminal and immoral behaviour if not acceptable, then at least expected, and cordoned off from the middle and upper classes. Many writers, such as George Gissing and Hardy, in both their novels and their short stories, question this blind prejudice, but it is nevertheless the case that much Victorian literature reflects the conviction that promiscuity, intemperance, wife-beating and even infanticide are the province of the 'lower orders'. Eliot's 'Janet's Repentance' is in this sense a more experimental and disturbing tale than the narratives of her novels. The manipulation of the narrator, who mimics an oral story, helps her to tell it the way she does.

Elizabeth Gaskell's 'The Well of Pen-Morfa' (1850) is a fascinating example of a 'regional' tale that is in fact a national tale, as the narrator tells us it is set in '*Welsh* Wales'.[16] The Welsh language surrounds the narrator, who is a visitor to Pen-Morfa, so the tales she tells have been told, or translated, to her, doubling the power of the oral in this story. The Celtic remoteness of the setting is associated for many Victorian readers with supernatural tales; to their minds, these 'primitive' cultures still hold on to their superstitions. The Scottish short stories of James Hogg in the early nineteenth century and of R. L. Stevenson's Scottish and South Sea tales late in the century play brilliantly with these expectations for an urban English readership. But Gaskell turns from the uncanny doubling and otherness of these tales to tell a story in which the 'other' is replaced by a young woman with mental disability. This woman is feared and ostracized by her community, but is profoundly humanized over the course of the tale. The young and beautiful Nest is rejected by her fiancé after a fall at the well of Pen-Morfa leaves her crippled. Her grief and bitterness cause her to reject her mother's love and comfort, and only when her mother dies and an old Methodist preacher speaks with her is she gradually able to turn from herself to care for others. She takes into her home the 'crazy' Mary Williams, who has been boarded by the parish to a man who beats and starves her. Mary is described as 'savage': her 'eyes glare like a wild beast' and the villagers believe that one day Nest 'will be found murdered'.[17] However, Nest is strong enough to bear with Mary's violent fits, and to help calm her. Mary grows to love Nest, and to be happy and docile with her. Yet, Gaskell writes,

> there were times when Mary was overpowered by the glooms and fancies of her disordered brain. Fearful times! No one knew how fearful. On those days, Nest warned the little children who loved to come and play around her, that they must not visit the house. The signal was a piece of white linen hung out of a side window. (p. 141)

We cannot know what Nest endures and Mary suffers behind closed doors, because Nest never lets anyone see and never seeks help; to do so would risk Mary being taken away from her, and 'she knew what hard curses and blows, what starvation and misery, would await the poor creature' (p. 141). This short story is unusual in its setting of a 'foreign' culture within Britain, but its use of the traditionally gothic or supernatural Celtic 'fringe' tells a story which is more grounded in realism – even domestic realism – and which humanizes a mentally disabled woman. Gaskell does this without sentimentalizing Mary or prettifying Nest's life with her. While the women grew to love each other, Mary is not miraculously 'cured' of her occasional outbreaks into violence. Unlike Dickens, with the evil Quilp (*The Old Curiosity Shop*), the crippled Tiny Tim, Jenny Wren and Sloppy (*Our Mutual Friend*), Gaskell eschews her editor's tendency to portray the physically or mentally disabled as fantastic creatures, who are either evil or almost impossibly good. In this story, she experiments in the short story genre with the creation of a doubled layer of 'orality' (in its spoken translation from the Welsh) and in its translation of a gothic setting and the gothic other to domestic realism. Generically and in its subject matter the story is both experimental and groundbreaking.

The famous adage attributed variously to Dickens, Wilkie Collins and Charles Reade, 'Make them laugh, make them cry, make them wait' was hardly experimental or groundbreaking. It was a strategy that sold periodicals while it ignored Poe's 'unity of effect' and impression. However, these novelists' clever use of the novel's periodical instalment left their readers eager if not desperate to purchase the next segment, and this strategy lent itself especially to the abrupt plot changes and surprises of the sensation novel. Although many sensation stories were long enough to be published in more than one instalment, they did not have the luxury of three-decker space for the creation of atmosphere and drawn-out mystery. Yet in 'The Dead Secret', 'The Dreaded Guest' and 'The Unholy Wish' – three short stories by Collins, Mary Elizabeth Braddon and Ellen Wood respectively – the short form took advantage of the fast pace of sensation fiction to create sudden shocks. 'Sensation' stories filled the popular weekly and fortnightly magazines, and their subject matter mimicked that of the news items and court reports in the newspapers: murder, theft, adultery and bigamy were, it seems, ever-fascinating to a Victorian readership, and especially so in literature at the height of the sensation genre in the 1850s and 60s. While Wilkie Collins's 1868 novel *The Moonstone* is often credited as the first detective novel, his short story, 'Brother Owen's Story of Anne Rodway' (1856) hails the early, if not the first, arrival of the female detective. Sensation stories move widely and indiscriminately over class and gender boundaries and the short form emphasizes the tensions and conflict across these relations of the upper and lower classes, and between men and women. Collins's Anne Rodway writes in the first instalment of her diary:

> The clergyman said in his sermon last Sunday evening that all things were ordered for the best, and we are all put into the stations in life that are properest for us. I suppose he was right, being a very clever gentleman who fills the church to crowding; but I think I should have understood him better if I had not been very hungry at the time, in consequence of my own station in life being nothing but plain needlewoman.[18]

The story is completely focalized through the working-class Anne, who takes on the murder investigation after her beloved friend and lodging house companion is killed. The dreary lives and hard labour of these women in a teeming city lodging house is full of subtle commentary on class inequality, while at the same time it is a swift-moving and exciting detective story.

One of the most popular crimes in the sensation register was bigamy. The difficulty of divorce before the Matrimonial Causes Act of 1857 (and indeed after that Act) and then the widespread news reportage over the judgments of Sir Cresswell Cresswell (the matrimonial court's first judge) increased the public's appetite for stories of marital breakdown, and especially of the most sensational kind such as spouse murder and bigamy. Earlier in the nineteenth century, gothic novels and short stories were often centred on supernatural or psychic doubling and the doppelgänger. In sensation stories, the doubling of the bigamous marriage and the double role played by the bigamist convert the gothic double into realist, contemporary fiction. So many of the same anxieties and questions arise from the masks and doubles of the bigamist as arose from the mysterious gothic doppelgänger: the fragmentation of the self; the inscrutability of the other; the destabilization of identity and of the familiar. One of the numerous sensation stories with a bigamy plot is 'A Marriage Tragedy' (1858), which is also an early detective story by Wilkie Collins.[19]

Margaret Oliphant's stories treat often 'sensational' themes in a quiet, non-sensational manner. Oliphant was a staunch defender of the sanctity of marriage, and critical of campaigns for divorce and women's custody rights. Indeed, many readers until recently would have known her mainly for her attack on Thomas Hardy's *Jude the Obscure* in her review article, 'The Anti-Marriage League' (1896). However, Oliphant must be credited for a far more complex understanding of marriage and its discontents, as two of her bigamy-plot stories demonstrate. 'The Two Mrs Scudamores' (1871–2) opens with the widowhood of the wealthy wife and mother, Mrs Scudamore, in deep mourning on a beautiful summer's day in her country estate. Surrounded by her children, she cannot mourn her husband's death properly: he 'had not been a good husband. During all the earlier years of her married life he had neglected her; more than this, he had outraged her in the way women feel most deeply'.[20] Finally left alone she cannot help but feel 'a faint, exquisite sense of deliverance . . . her struggle was over' (p. 5). Peace is shattered shortly after, however, by the arrival of another Mrs Scudamore, married many years before to the late husband. Her arrival means that the woman who has reared the late husband's children is nothing but a mistress, and her children illegitimate. Neither in this story, nor in the later 'Queen Eleanor and Fair Rosamond' (1886) – another story of a bigamous marriage – does Oliphant indulge in the obvious opportunities for dramatic confrontation between these rival women: in the earlier story, the two Mrs Scudamores decide to live together on the family estate and to hide from the children their illegitimacy; in the late story, the wife meets the young mistress who believes herself married to the husband, but in sorrow for the young woman's 'blighted' life, refrains from confrontation or revelation; she simply leaves. Oliphant transforms sensation into quiet devastation.

As Oliphant's fame was based on her many triple-decker novels, her short stories risk being dismissed as the detritus of an enormous volume of work produced under financial pressure, even as hack work. But many of her stories are tightly written and progressive, if not experimental in content, and some have affinities with the 'New Woman' stories being published in journals dedicated to new ideas of the short story form at the turn of the century. A case in point is a late short story by Oliphant, 'A Story of a Wedding Tour' (1894). The story concerns a timid and clever young woman, married off to a wealthy man she hardly knows; after very little time on the wedding tour in France, she knows him too well, as a brutish sensualist who cares nothing for her. Her own 'exquisite sense of deliverance' occurs as the train stops at a station and the husband, stretching his legs on the platform, fails to get back to the train in time. In the carriage alone she experiences 'a mingled sensation of excitement and terror and tremulous delight which words could not tell!'[21] Janey makes a bid for escape, and catches a stopping train along the coast, alighting randomly at a little town by the sea where she settles, unknown to the world.

Although Oliphant's story ends more ambivalently, the exhilarating freedom and independence that Janey experiences on the local train into the French countryside is very closely allied to the rushes at freedom that occur in many New Woman short stories. These stories, written in the 1880s and 1890s found publication in new periodicals, some of which rejected the serialized novel and dedicated themselves to the new aesthetic demands of the short story genre. Brander Matthews made the distinction in 1885 between the 'Short-story' with a capital S, and the 'story which is merely short'. The latter types are 'merely amplified anecdotes or else incidents which might have been used in a novel just as well as not'.[22] 'New Woman' stories were sometimes experimental in form as well as controversial in subject matter, and they found their place in new journals in the late nineteenth century that were dedicated to short fiction. *The Yellow Book* stands out as the short-lived (1894-7) great journal of aestheticism, which specialized in innovations of the short story, but other journals of the 1880s and 1890s, *The Strand, The Idler, Black and White* and *The Graphic* all embraced the short story form rather than the serialized novel.

Women writers such as Ella D'Arcy, George Egerton, Sarah Grand and Vernon Lee experimented with questions of gender and genre through the short story form, as did George Moore, Oscar Wilde, Grant Allen, Gissing and Henry James. New Woman short stories often associate women's independence with a freedom of movement: like Janey in Oliphant's 'Story of a Wedding Tour' who takes a train to escape her husband, women travel on the early London underground, on omnibuses and trains and further afield by ship to the British colonies.

Thomas Hardy's short story 'The Melancholy Hussar' (1889), though hardly a New Woman short story, gives a sense through contrast of the great strides that the New Woman needs to take. Phyllis lives on a remote part of the downs with her father, meeting few people. But she gets to know a homesick German soldier camped with the English regiment nearby: 'The spot at the bottom of the garden where she had been accustomed to climb the wall to meet Matthaus, was the only inch of English ground in which she took any interest.'[23] Over time her small steps there have trodden down the grass and left tracks. She grasps her one chance for escape and love, but loses courage, and when he is shot for desertion she is once again confined. As in Charlotte Perkins Gilman's 'The Yellow Wallpaper' (1892), in which the heroine is found creeping around the papered walls of the room where she is incarcerated, Phyllis's tentative steps across the garden to the wall render the New Woman's journeys out by train, bus or stride painfully and urgently necessary.

Voyages out to the corners of the globe were a fact of nineteenth-century family life. Most families across the class divides had a family member or friend who had emigrated: after the agricultural depression of the 'Hungry '40s' – to the gold rush in California and Australia; to India and Africa – whether as soldiers, farmers or convicts. Anthony Trollope, whose son had emigrated to Australia, wrote several stories set in former or current British colonies. In fact his fiction about foreign travel and settlement is concentrated in the short stories more than his novels. His story 'The Journey to Panama' (1861) is a moving story of a friendship made on board a ship between a young woman emigrating to Peru to be married and a young widower on his way to California. It does not end with the closure of marriage for the fellow travellers, although they have fallen in love, nor in marriage between the woman and her affianced in Peru. Coming down to breakfast after his early morning writing, Trollope once announced to assembled house guests, 'I have just been making my twenty-seventh proposal of marriage.'[24] But Trollope avoids the expected closure in this short story written for the family magazine *Victoria Regia*. Hardy's judgement that marriage 'was almost *de rigueur* in an English magazine at the time of writing [1879]' does not hold true in Trollope's tale.[25] The short story form and the liminal setting of a ship's voyage provided some release from the conventionalities, both for the writer and his characters.

Towards the end of her career, Margaret Oliphant admitted to some weariness with the marriage plot in fiction. While late nineteenth-century writers (such as Hardy) complained that they were not allowed the freedom to write of passion and desire freely, Oliphant felt it 'would be more reasonable if they complained of the monotonous demand for a love-story which crushes out of court all the rest of life'. She singles out Rudyard Kipling's short stories as providing new sustenance for narrative: 'Romance itself, they say, is gone, which is an assertion strenuously contradicted by the most powerful of our young writers, Mr Rudyard Kipling, who replies to it in very energetic tones, that, Here is a steam-engine, which is Romance incarnate, the great poetry of form and purpose.'[26]

Kipling brought with him from India 'a blast of reputation' as Oliphant writes, based upon his *Plain Tales from the Hills* (1888). The colonial tale in the hands of Kipling, Trollope, Joseph Conrad and Stevenson, among others, deals with men, action and harsh life, but, to varying degrees between these authors, women take part in that harsh life as well. This topic, which is treated in more detail in Chapter 6, reveals a dramatic re-envisioning of the Victorian love plot: Kipling's 'The Courting of Dinah Shadd', for example, is couched in promiscuity, swearing, drink, bloodshed and one of the longest, nastiest curses in Victorian literature. This is hardly the usual treatment of the Victorian love plot, and it is hardly surprising that Kipling's tales of life at the limits of British rules and conventions were the most popular stories of the late Victorian period.

Notes

1. Margaret Oliphant, 'A Preface: On the Ebb Tide', in Joanne Shattock and Elisabeth Jay, eds., *The Selected Works of Margaret Oliphant*, part III, vol. XI: 'Novellas and Shorter Fiction, Essays on Life-Writing and History, Essays on

European Literature and Culture', ed. Muireann O'Cinneide (London: Pickering and Chatto, 2013), p. 319. First published in *The Ways of Life* (London: Smith, Elder and Co., 1897), pp. 1–20.
2. In the case of Trollope's novels, there has been critical neglect through much of the twentieth century, especially in Britain, but the novels were always popular and in print.
3. James Secord, *Victorian Sensation: The Extraordinary Publication, Reception and Secret Authorship of Vestiges of the Natural History of Creation* (University of Chicago Press, 2000), p. 33. See also, Martin Hewitt, *The Dawn of the Cheap Press in Victorian Britain: The End of the 'Taxes on Knowledge', 1849–1869* (London: Bloomsbury, 2013).
4. Deborah Thomas, *Dickens and the Short Story* (Philadelphia: University of Pennsylvania Press, 1982), p. 4.
5. Brander Matthews, *The Philosophy of the Short Story* (New York: Longmans, Green and Co., 1902), p. 24.
6. Edgar Allan Poe, 'The Philosophy of Composition', in *The Complete Works of Edgar Allan Poe*, ed. James A. Harrison, 17 vols. (New York, 1902), *Volume XIV: Essays and Miscellanies*, p. 196. This essay was originally published in *Graham's Magazine*, April 1846. Harrison's edition of *The Complete Works* is available online at www.eapoe.org/works/harrison/jahinfo.htm (accessed 18 July 2015).
7. Thomas, *Dickens and the Short Story*, p. 143.
8. Henry James, 'The Turn of the Screw', in *'The Aspern Papers' and 'The Turn of the Screw'*, ed. and with an introduction by Anthony Curtis (London: Penguin Books, 1984), p. 145. www.gutenberg.org/files/209/209-h/209-h.htm (accessed 20 July 2015) (para. 1)
9. Charles Dickens, 'Barbox Brothers', in *Mugby Junction*, with a foreword by Robert Macfarlane (London: Hesperus Classics, 2005), p. 3.
10. Mary Russell Mitford, *Our Village* (London: Bell and Daldy, 1871). The first series appeared in book form in 1824.
11. Letter from Elizabeth Barrett Browning to Mary Russell Mitford, 17 July 1837, in *The Letters of Elizabeth Barrett Browning to Mary Russell Mitford 1836–1854*, ed. Meredith B. Raymond and Mary Rose Sullivan, 3 vols. (Waco, Texas: Armstrong Browning Library of Baylor University, The Browning Institute, Wedgestone Press and Wellesley College, 1983), I, p. 38.
12. See, for example Robert Browning's 'Essay on Shelley' (1852) reprinted in *Robert Browning: The Major Works including Courtship Correspondence*, ed. Adam Roberts with an introduction by Daniel Karlin (Oxford University Press, 2005), pp. 574–90.
13. Walter Benjamin, 'The Storyteller' (1936), in *Illuminations*, ed. Hannah Arendt, trans. Harry Zorn (London: Pimlico, 1999), p. 84.
14. George Eliot, 'Janet's Repentance', in *Scenes of Clerical Life* (Oxford University Press, 1988), p. 201.

15. Emma Liggins, Andrew Maunder and Ruth Robbins, *The British Short Story* (Basingstoke: Palgrave Macmillan, 2011), p. 29.
16. Elizabeth Gaskell, 'The Well of Pen-Morfa', in *The Moorland Cottage and Other Tales*, ed. Suzanne Lewis (Oxford University Press, 1995), p. 123. First published in *Household Words*, 2, 16 and 23 November 1850.
17. Gaskell, 'The Well of Pen-Morfa', p. 139.
18. Wilkie Collins, 'Brother Owen's Story of Anne Rodway', in *The Queen of Hearts* (London: Hurst and Blackett Publishers, 1859), pp. 206–7. (Originally published in *Household Words*, 19–26 July 1856.) https://archive.org/stream/02690469.4962.emory.edu/02690469_4962#page/n213/mode/2up (accessed 18 June 2016), p. 1.
19. This story was republished by the Sensation Press in 2000 under the title 'The Fatal Marriage', but attributed mistakenly to Mary Elizabeth Braddon. As the editor Chris Willis explains, 'as "The Fatal Marriage" was taken from an American copy, it now seems clear that the earlier version of Collins's story was widely published in America, and that many pirate editions renamed the story and attributed it to Braddon for sales purposes'. Mary Elizabeth Braddon, *The Fatal Marriage and Other Stories*, ed. Chris Willis (Hastings: Sensation Press, 2000), 'Addendum' inserted between pp. 18 and 19.
20. Margaret Oliphant, 'The Two Mrs Scudamores', in part III, vol. IX of *The Selected Works of Margaret Oliphant*, p. 4.
21. Margaret Oliphant, 'A Story of a Wedding Tour', in part III, vol. IX of *The Selected Works of Margaret Oliphant*, p. 257.
22. Matthews, *Philosophy of the Short Story*, p. 24.
23. Thomas Hardy, 'The Melancholy Hussar of the German Legion', in *Wessex Tales* (London: Macmillan, 1971), p. 63.
24. Quoted in Victoria Glendinning, *Trollope* (London: Hutchinson, 1992), p. 341.
25. Thomas Hardy, endnote to his story 'The Distracted Preacher', in *Wessex Tales*, p. 286.
26. Margaret Oliphant, 'Preface: On the Ebb Tide', in part III, vol. IX of *The Selected Works of Margaret Oliphant*, p. 321.

5

Fable, Myth and Folk Tale: The Writing of Oral and Traditional Story Forms

ANDREW HARRISON

Oral and traditional story forms – from fable, myth, fairy tale and folk tale to religious parable – underwrote the nature and purpose of the short story from its earliest incarnations, offering powerful narrative models for authors to imitate, pastiche and subvert. The most obvious common feature of these forms is their didacticism: fables, myths, fairy tales, folk tales and parables are recounted and retold in order to instil specific moral and/or religious values, and to record cultural practices, passing on the wisdom of the ages while reinforcing a collective sense of identity among members of a given community, nation or religious group. Influential studies of the generic structures of oral and traditional written narratives by Vladimir Propp, Joseph Campbell and Northrop Frye reveal archetypal patterns which reflect certain universal aspects of human experience, but they also acknowledge how these structures are transformed across periods and cultures, registering both subtle and sweeping shifts in the nature of individual and social experience.[1] Inflections in the use of the earlier forms in a particular national literature can tell us a great deal about changes in attitudes to the coherence of community identity and beliefs, especially during periods of marked historical change.

In this chapter, I will explore how late Victorian and early twentieth-century practitioners of the English short story adapted oral and traditional story forms to address their own historical situations. In doing so, I take for granted the pervasive influence on these writers of the Bible stories; of John Bunyan's religious allegory *The Pilgrim's Progress* (1678); of Greek and Roman mythology; of key transcriptions of oral tales such as Charles Perrault's *Histoires ou contes du temps passé* (1697) (*Tales and Stories of the Past with Morals*), Jacob and Wilhelm Grimm's *Kinder- und Hausmärchen* (1812) (known in English as *Grimm's Fairy Tales*) and Andrew Lang's twelve *Fairy Book* compilations of fairy tales (1889–1910); of *Aesop's Fables* and the fables of

La Fontaine; of Hans Christian Andersen's fairy tales; and of written texts structured around a series of connected oral narratives, like *Arabian Nights* (first translated into English from Arabic in 1706), Giovanni Boccaccio's *Decamerone* (completed in 1353, but not translated into English, as *The Decameron*, until 1886) and Geoffrey Chaucer's *Canterbury Tales*.

In the English tradition, Thomas Hardy is the figure most closely associated with the traditional form of the folk tale. Adrian Hunter has suggested that Hardy was drawn to the pre-modern qualities of the short story, wishing to 'preserve and revitalize the form's attachment to oral, communal taletelling traditions – traditions he believed were rapidly vanishing in an urbanized, print-literate culture'.[2] His first collection, *Wessex Tales* (1888), originally contained five historical narratives drawing closely on West Country folklore and superstition, dealing with deeply taboo topics such as criminality, illicit desire and supernatural forces. In 'The Distracted Preacher', a young replacement preacher in a coastal parish is attracted to his mysterious landlady, who turns out to be involved in the smuggling of spirits from French ships. A grim sense of fatalism is felt in 'The Three Strangers', in which a disguised escaped convict, his executioner and the convict's brother come to disturb a christening party in an isolated and exposed shepherd's cottage. 'Fellow-Townsmen' and 'Interlopers at the Knap' are both concerned with thwarted love. Coincidence and romantic betrayal play a central role in the most striking tale in the collection. In 'The Withered Arm', a jilted and ruined milkmaid named Rhoda Brook dreams that Gertrude Lodge, the beautiful young wife of her former lover, is crushing her in her bed, and she strikes out by grabbing the girl's left arm. The dream appears to have come true when Gertrude's left arm swiftly withers in a manner inexplicable to her doctor. Gertrude is directed to visit a 'knowing man', Conjuror Trendle, who informs her that her ailment is caused by the actions of an enemy. In the tragic finale, Gertrude's marriage deteriorates and she seeks out Conjuror Trendle once more, who tells her that the only cure for her arm is to 'turn the blood' by touching it against the still-warm neck of a hanged man. She attends the county jail and manages to carry out the order, only to find that the hanged man is her husband's illegitimate son by Rhoda Brook, who had been unjustly executed for arson; Gertrude's blood is turned but the shock revelation brings on her death.

Two brief historical tales set at the turn of the nineteenth century and originally published in Hardy's third collection of stories, *Life's Little Ironies* (1894) – 'A Tradition of Eighteen Hundred and Four' and 'The Melancholy

Hussar of the German Legion' – were moved in 1912 to the Wessex Edition of *Wessex Tales*, while 'An Imaginative Woman' (which Hardy added to *Wessex Tales* in 1896) was transferred to the later collection. These changes had the effect of distinguishing the modern atmosphere of *Life's Little Ironies* from the traditionalism of the earlier volume. A number of the stories in *Life's Little Ironies* ('An Imaginative Woman', 'The Son's Veto', 'For Conscience' Sake' and 'A Tragedy of Two Ambitions') hinge upon the open conflict between moral duty and the desire for personal fulfilment. The lengthy, ten-part concluding tale, entitled 'A Few Crusted Characters', is modern in a different sense; its markedly self-reflexive use of oral narrative and the folk tale form shows how an elegiac quality in Hardy's writing can combine with a more ironic and critical understanding of nostalgia as a negative quality of modernity. In this tale, several inhabitants of a Wessex village named Longpuddle tell a series of connected narratives about their home during a shared journey on public transport for the benefit of a fellow passenger who had left the area with his family in childhood and is now thinking of returning to see out the remainder of his days. What emerges is a piecemeal oral history of the people of Longpuddle and its outlying districts, recording some of the changes in manners and customs that have occurred during the period of the man's absence. Yet, the pathos implicit in the story's central device of the homeward journey is offset by a feeling of unheeding relentlessness in the nine oral narratives. The storytellers seem motivated not by sensitivity to the needs and feelings of their addressee but by a powerful compulsion to re-tell episodes of Longpuddle history and folklore in order to ward off ritualistically the ghostly displacement to which their interlocutor is condemned. So much has changed both within and outside Longpuddle since the man's departure that he finds himself a foreigner there, sadly measuring what he sees around him against his childhood memories and realizing the extent of his rootlessness. His idealization of his rural youth and the older villagers' desire to keep their village intact prevent both him and them from inhabiting Longpuddle in the unthinking manner of earlier generations. In the bluntly anti-climactic ending, we are informed that he disappears after a few days and is never seen in the area again.

Like Hardy, Robert Louis Stevenson engaged with and transformed the traditional qualities of oral narrative. In *The Merry Men and Other Tales and Fables* (1887), Stevenson adheres quite closely to the conventional structures of the folk tale and fable. In 'Thrawn Janet', an aged inset narrator speaking in a broad Scots dialect recounts the folkloric tale of a hell-fire Scottish preacher in 1712 who ignores the protests of his parishioners by marrying a woman who turns out to be a witch in league with the Devil. In contrast, 'Will o'the Mill' is an understated but touching fable in which an otherworldly orphan living on a mountain-top between two powerful and conflicting kingdoms comes to believe that travel and marriage would merely detract from the reflective peace of mind he cultivates by dwelling in the abstract on love and the condition of Man; he lives out his uneventful life in comparative ease and happily agrees to accompany the figure of Death when it comes to fetch him. The story is imbued with the sceptical atmosphere and insight of Voltaire's *Candide* and Samuel Johnson's *Rasselas* (both 1759), but it deliberately avoids their reliance on satire and adventure.

Stevenson was aware that in the modern fable 'the moral tends to become more indeterminate and large'; he noted that for writers of his generation the fable had begun 'to take rank with all other forms of creative literature, as something too ambitious, in spite of its miniature dimensions, to be resumed in any succinct formula without the loss of all that is deepest and most suggestive in it'.[3] In *Fables* (1896), he directly foregrounds and problematizes the moralizing function of the form. The opening piece, entitled 'The Persons of the Tale', consists of a conversation between the central characters of his own best-selling novel *Treasure Island* (1883), in which each lays claim to the author's respect and sympathy: Stevenson is content simply to present the clash of views, implying that moral sense must be actively sought by each reader, since there is no single authorial line to uncover. The fables that follow undermine the impulse to draw simple moral distinctions by emphasizing the perverse aspects of human nature. Two of the pieces actually include a moral postscript in verse form. 'The House of Eld' concerns the quest of a young boy to rid himself and his fellow villagers of the painful fetters which they wear on their right legs through the power of superstition; the boy slays the being which holds them in thrall to the fetters, only to find that the members of his community have taken to wearing a fresh fetter on the left leg. The hero has only succeeded in killing his parents and uncle through his actions, and in giving rise to a new set of false beliefs. In 'Something In It', a missionary comes to realize that he was wrong to dismiss outright the beliefs of the native people he lives among, but his mind swiftly adjusts itself to the situation and he goes on treating them as servants all the same. Stevenson's fables are neither wholly impersonal nor unequivocally satirical: they combine a compassionate understanding of human weakness with a sardonic appreciation of the narrow-mindedness and cruelty to which it can lead.

By contrast, the satirical potential of the fable form is blatantly accentuated in Gilbert Cannan's *Windmills: A Book of Fables* (1915). This volume is dedicated to D. H. Lawrence; its epigraph is taken from Swift's *A Tale of a Tub* (1704), and the four tales in the volume are strongly influenced by *Gulliver's Travels* (1726), Defoe's *Robinson Crusoe* (1719) and William Morris's *News from Nowhere* (1890). Cannan presents a thinly veiled fantasy world in which Fatland (England) is at war with Fatterland (Germany). The opening fables, 'Samways Island' and 'Ultimus', concern themselves with George Samways, the founder and first castaway inhabitant of a moving island, and his son Ultimus, who, together with a Fatterland philosopher named Ignatz Siebenhaar, negotiate and comment upon the barbarity and prejudice of a world which is in a constant state of conflict from the splendid isolation of their neutral island home. At the conclusion of 'Ultimus', the son and Siebenhaar destroy Bondon (London) in a fit of disgust and then broker a deal to end the war, disarming the warring nations by driving their island through the separate fleets of warships. The two remaining fables have different satirical targets. In 'Gynecologia', an American citizen is shipwrecked in the Fatland of the future and discovers to his horror that women have seized power and subjected men to the same state of dependency and abject servitude which they had earlier rebelled against. The final tale, 'Out of Work', concerns an embittered and impoverished citizen of Fatland who strikes up a friendship with the Devil (Mr Nicodemus) and makes it his life's ambition to redress his deep-seated grievance against God (Jah) only to discover that the deity is not jealous or unjust but a sympathetic Blakean figure firmly committed to both passion and imagination. The exigency of the fable form in approaching topics too sensitive or controversial for a more straightforward wartime treatment is clear in the critical depiction of patriotism in the stories, and in their reflection of anxieties about changes in gender roles and religious faith, but the sharpness of the satire is adversely affected by the extent of the allusiveness.

T. F. Powys's *Fables* (1929) contains a much stronger and more distinctive engagement with the fable form than we find in either Stevenson or Cannan. Like Hardy, Powys was a Dorset writer greatly preoccupied with the impact of social change on the identity and values of isolated rural communities. However, while Hardy mourned the loss of a historical community identity, Powys willingly embraced it, opening up established forms of oral narrative to the altered belief systems and contested moral outlook of modern times. As Clare Hanson has noted, Powys is 'a religious allegorist, writing in the tradition of Chaucer and Bunyan', but his unorthodox and protean religious vision can seem at times pagan and pantheistic;[4] where the fables of Aesop and La Fontaine had used anthropomorphism to draw out specific moral lessons, prioritizing human over animal life in accordance with established Christian tradition, Powys's nineteen fables employ speaking objects to de-centre the human world and to question its values. In 'The Clout and the Pan', two domestic objects discuss the behaviour of a married couple, causing us to question the links between fidelity and love; in 'The Bucket and the Rope' the items which a young farmer used to commit suicide after discovering his wife's infidelity try to piece together the mystery of his actions, and their false reasoning forces us to confront the difficulties involved in reconciling natural desire with the Christian belief in monogamy. The eighth fable, 'The Stone and Mr Thomas', consists of a combative dialogue between the mortal remains of the eponymous Mr Thomas and his headstone, in which each lays claim to prominence over the other. The stone argues that its time-resisting qualities lend it an importance not shared by the perishable body, while Mr Thomas's skull counters with the claim that inanimate objects are self-evidently lower in the order of things than Man. The fable ends with the skull facing the indignity of being wheeled away and pounded into dust, mistaken for a drunkard who drowned in a horse-pond.

One obvious purpose of Powys's fables is to poke fun at the overweening forms of logic and faith underpinning Western metaphysics. In two of the fables he invokes Plato and Bishop Berkeley in decidedly unflattering terms.[5] The formal qualities of individual fables, and the connections between them, serve to expose awkward flaws in logic and cohesion; they make us aware that Western beliefs and scales of value are tied in to particular reading practices. By inhibiting our unthinking consumption of his fables, Powys de-naturalizes the set of assumptions which the traditional form inculcates, undermining its prioritization of age and experience, rationality, spirit, loyalty and selflessness in favour of an ironic and at times grotesque acceptance of youth, irrationality and the seven mortal sins. Unlike Hardy, Powys adopts an irreverent approach to death and the loss of faith and collective memory, taking wicked pleasure in displacing the joyless self-importance and spiritual solemnity of a limited, anthropocentric view. In its place, he offers the vision of a deeply sensual world of Creation that does not conform to the demands of human logic or morality. In responding sensitively to the tonal complexities of the fables we are conditioned to overturn our stock response to instances of injustice and immorality, moving from complacent outrage to puzzled nonchalance and a wry, sardonic appreciation of things as they are.

The Victorian preoccupation with – and reinvention of – the fairy tale form satisfied a comparable desire to recover ancient forms of wisdom obscured by the logic of commerce, industry and 'progress'. As Marina Warner has noted, 'utopian ambitions beat strongly in the heart of fairy tale', allowing authors to 'challenge received ideas and raise questions into the minds of their audience'.[6] In John Ruskin's fairy tale *The King of the Golden River, or The Black Brothers: A Legend of Stiria* (1850), a traditional quest narrative involving a contest between three brothers (two of them evil and greedy, the other selfless but downtrodden) resolves itself into a celebration of compassion and charity, qualities directly opposed to the opportunistic values of the economic individualist. William Thackeray and George MacDonald used the form more or less explicitly to question the period's compensatory obsession with childhood innocence. Thackeray's *The Rose and the Ring* (1855) adopts an ironic tone which mockingly undercuts the assumption that children are immune to adult wiles: its bathetic plot stresses the need for a belief in magic to be replaced by a healthy adjustment to a complex and fallen reality. MacDonald's adult fairy tales, including 'The Light Princess' and 'The Shadows', first published in his novel *Adela Cathcart* (1864), and 'The Golden Key' from *Dealings with the Fairies* (1867), immerse their readers in a fantasy world that dissolves the porous boundaries between innocence and gullibility, scepticism and calculated self-interest. Charles Dickens's fairy tale 'The Magic Fishbone' (first serialized in 1868) engages good-humouredly with stock figures like the King and Queen and the fairy godmother; it concludes with a wise child, Alicia, being rewarded for her resourceful use of the eponymous magic fishbone through marriage to a Prince named Certainpersonio. Christina Rossetti included two moralistic fairy tales ('Nick' and 'Hero. A Metamorphosis') in *Commonplace and Other Stories* (1870); in both, a dissatisfied protagonist is granted the power of transformation by fairies but learns to value the life that has been left behind. In contrast, the five fairy tales in Oscar Wilde's *The Happy Prince and Other Tales* (1888) defy moral closure, modulating with disconcerting ease between tragic and comic registers, and between fantasy and realism. While Ruskin and Rossetti affirm the timeless values of a pre-modern world, Thackeray, MacDonald, Dickens and Wilde exploit the full expressive range and variability of direct address in the fairy story to challenge the complacency of readers and provoke a reflective re-engagement with the form.

Ford Madox Ford wrote three book-length fairy tales early in his career: *The Brown Owl* (1891), *The Feather* (1892) and *The Queen Who Flew* (1894). The books reflect both conservative and experimental features of the

Victorian fairy tale: they reproduce stock characters and situations, but they are also teasingly self-reflexive in their use of word play and incorporation of autobiographical references. *Christina's Fairy Book* (1906), containing nine fairy stories and seven poems, is more blandly traditional. The stories were written by Ford for his two daughters. In the prefatory note, he expresses a desire to spare them from the wolves and demons that haunted his own imagination as a child; he deliberately sets out to entertain, amuse and reassure children rather than frighten them. For example, in 'Mary and Matty and Lob' and 'Bingel and Bengel' he presents a knowable world of right and wrong in which kind actions are rewarded and cruel actions meet with mild rebuke.

Rudyard Kipling's *Just So Stories* (1902) are rather more unsettling tales for children which blend fairy tale and fable features to account for the more inexplicable aspects of the animal kingdom and cultural history, answering troubling questions such as 'How the Whale Got his Throat', 'How the Leopard Got his Spots' and 'How the Alphabet was Made'. The most distinctive feature of the tales is their reliance on an abrupt form of direct address: the narrator mockingly cajoles the reader, underlining the absurdity of the events described by accentuating and repeating simple rhetorical phrases and apparently unimportant details. However, the tales have an ulterior purpose: through their shifting forms (drawing on a rich blend of American Indian, Indian, African, Australian, Egyptian and Arabic oral traditions), their combination of prose and poetry, and their assault on hierarchies of logic and faith, they simultaneously dislodge more straitlaced written Christian accounts of Creation while implicitly subjecting competing world myths and religions to humour and irony.

The disconcerting nature of direct spoken address is central to the complex tonal effects achieved in the tales of A. E. Coppard. In *The Modern Short Story: A Critical Survey* (1941), H. E. Bates highlights Coppard's interest in the oral roots of the short story form and his desire to 'see tales once more told as if in the marketplace, in the inn, at the street corner'.[7] Several of Coppard's stories open with familiar fairy-tale formulations, only to disorientate the reader with an idiosyncratic blend of realistic, fantastic, religious and visionary elements. 'The King of the World' and 'The Princess of Kingdom Gone', from the collection *Adam and Eve and Pinch Me* (1921), are deeply enigmatic stories which eschew moral or logical closure in order to dwell on the more tangible pleasures of fairy-tale diction and poetic archaism. In the former, a young Assyrian captain in the eighth century BC stumbles upon the lost shrine of the defunct god Namu-Sarkkon and falls in love with the reanimated form of his most beautiful devotee, who then proceeds to absorb him into the shrine in her place. In the latter, a young princess falls in love with a red-haired poet whose tree releases crimson flower petals into the river where she bathes; the youth refuses to marry, and dies, so the princess grieves for him, building an elaborate shrine in his honour, but time passes and in due course the shrine is stolen and the princess returns to her former habits, catching her hair in a tree as she leaves her bathing place. Both pieces seem calculated to expose the disjunction between our love of familiar art forms like the fairy tale and the unpredictable waywardness of life itself. In 'The Bogey Man', from the volume *The Field of Mustard* (1926), a girl steals a small box in which to house her sick godmother's pearls, only to find that it is the home of an evil imp in the service of the devil, which proceeds to prey on her life, tempting and finally ensnaring her with the promise of beauty, riches and eternal life. The moral of the story is far from clear since there is no obvious link between the girl's crime and the penance that the imp exacts. The conflict between the orderliness of art and the messiness of life is self-reflexively foregrounded in a later fable entitled 'Speaking Likenesses', collected in *Ninepenny Flute* (1937). In this tale, an attorney-at-law appropriates an old book and a whistle from among the possessions of a deceased man before the sale of his estate; the story resolves itself into a bitter argument between the life-like images in the book, which the attorney frames and puts on the wall, and a plant which grows from the discarded pea in the whistle. In an abrupt ending, the man pulls up and discards the plant, but leaves the faded illustrations in place.

Walter de la Mare is another author who was preoccupied with both the form and language of traditional oral narratives. In *Broomsticks* (1925) he collected his own conventionally oriented fairy tales, a number of which reflect regional folk influences. In 'The Three Sleeping Boys of Warwickshire', a brutal employer witnesses the spirits of his three mistreated chimney sweeps joyfully escaping his home at night-time and schemes to prevent their return to the house, believing that the boys will thus attain eternal youth and be bonded in servitude to him; instead, they enter a state of catalepsy which is only broken accidentally by a sympathetic museum worker responsible for overseeing their upkeep as items on public display. In 'The Thief', a wealthy London criminal lives a lonely and paranoid life until an unwonted act of kindness to a blind man sets in motion a chain of events that leads to his discovery of a magic egg and his marriage to a devoted and kind-hearted scullery-maid who enjoys great good luck after his death. De la Mare's commitment to the traditional fairy story is made clear in 'Dick and the Beanstalk', from *The Lord Fish* (1933). In this homage to the old English tale 'Jack and the Beanstalk', a farmer's son from Gloucestershire who is obsessed with fairy tales comes across Jack's cottage and the gnarled old beanstalk up which he climbed to reach the land of the Giants; Dick re-traces Jack's steps and is involved in similar adventures, returning with a giant named Grackel, who proves to be so greedy and stupid that Dick plots to have him return home and then burns the vine, but not before he has plundered some valuables from the giant and his wife, and stored up several dry bean seeds for future use.

Through their rewriting and transformation of traditional oral narrative, practitioners of the modern short story acknowledge the power of their source material while also signalling their departure from the assumptions and consensual values enshrined in the forms of the folk tale, fable and fairy tale. As Ann Martin notes in her study of fairy tale allusions in modernist writings, it is the omnipresence of oral narratives and their variant forms in any given culture that underwrites their potential to 'reflect the instability and the variability that is the experience of modernity'.[8] In a number of the stories discussed above, an original form is inhabited with a degree of irony, and altered from within to express the author's vision of an uprooted or amoral world. Mythology and religious parable are drawn upon and transformed in similar ways in the writings of modernist authors, allowing them the scope either to critique the shallowness of modern life by measuring it against the grand narratives of Western culture, or to envision a modern form of moral or religious awareness by re-conceiving the narratives from within the changed circumstances and frames of reference of contemporary society.

Two early short stories by E. M. Forster, 'The Story of a Panic' and 'The Road from Colonus', published in his first collection, *The Celestial Omnibus* (1911), shine a harsh analytical light on the English middle classes by pitting their repressive Christian values, prejudice and class consciousness against the older forms of religion and myth which persist in the landscapes and peoples of Italy and Greece. In 'The Story of a Panic', a chronically unimaginative Englishman recounts a visit which he and his family had made to Ravello on the Amalfi coast of southern Italy eight years earlier, in the course of which he and a small band of fellow English tourists experienced an inexplicable feeling of fear while out on a picnic in the woods. The implication is that a sullen fourteen-year-old English boy named Eustace becomes possessed by the spirit of Pan. In the tragic denouement, the narrator arranges for the boy to be captured by his friend, an Italian waiter, who later dies in helping to free him. 'The Road from Colonus' traces the experiences of an aged Englishman who travels through Greece with his daughter and a group of English Hellenophiles to see Olympia. En route they stop to rest by a country inn, where the man discovers a hollow plane tree through which spring water flows. The tree has become a makeshift shrine replete with votive offerings. It is so startling that he steps inside it, experiencing a strong determination to stay at the inn. The group forcibly drags him away on a mule, fighting off the angry children of the Greek family who stood to gain from his custom. The final section of the story sees the man back at home in a foggy English suburbia, discovering that the tree had fallen down onto the inn on the very night of their visit, killing the entire family.

The key to both stories is in their titles. The comical pun on 'Panic' in 'The Story of a Panic' identifies the bathetic device at the heart of the narrative, by which the supernatural theme of Eustace's possession by the spirit of Pan gives way to a social satire on the priggish panic and terror of the narrator, who is less exercised by the teenager's embodiment of a pre-Christian deity than by his unseemly fraternizing with the Italian waiter, his disobedience and his refusal to maintain decorum and keep up appearances as an English gentleman should. In 'The Road from Colonus', we are told that the Hellenophiles call the old man 'Oedipus' and his devoted daughter 'Antigone', so that the inn becomes a surrogate 'Colonus': 'Antigone and Oedipus. Of course you must stop at Colonus!'[9] The title again highlights the bathetic implications of these jocular comparisons, since the road from Colonus that the modern tourists feel compelled to take proves to be a symbolic retreat from an ancient Greek world of shrines, fate and tragedy to an English bourgeois existence based around flower bulbs, faulty plumbing and letters of complaint to one's landlord. The stories are truly tragic in their suggestion that the ancient cultures of Italy and Greece retain the capacity to connect us to feelings of religious awe, but do not do so because of our inability to escape the materialistic and sentimental modern mindset.

In contrast to Forster, D. H. Lawrence sought to discover the different forms in which religious consciousness (both Christian and pre-Christian) continues to underwrite modern experience. In the mid-1920s, Lawrence wrote a number of short stories with fable-like titles and openings that satirize those features of modernity which he found most irksome; the majority of these were collected in *The Woman Who Rode Away and Other Stories* (1928). For example, 'The Rocking-Horse Winner', 'The Woman Who

Rode Away' and 'The Man Who Loved Islands' target materialism, the deathliness of Western capitalism and the insanity of modern individualism respectively. Like Katherine Mansfield in her archly titled 'A Suburban Fairy Tale', from the collection *Something Childish* (1924), Lawrence uses the traditional oral form to de-naturalize the habits and attitudes of his modern characters, exposing their egotism and greed. Yet, Lawrence's longer-term project involved an attempt to imagine an alternative religious mode of life that might revivify a culture devoid of values. For Lawrence, this meant reactivating biblical and mythological narratives through a process of subversive or re-accenting allusion so as to recover the vital symbolic and emotional truths they contain from behind a wall of moral doctrine. The titles of several of his early short stories – 'The Old Adam' (1911), 'New Eve and Old Adam' (1913) and 'Samson and Delilah' (1916) – reveal how central this process was to his writing from the outset. It was in his late work, however, following his protracted imaginative engagement with the religious practices of North American Indians and the Etruscans, that he attempted his fullest and most explicit articulation of a modern religious consciousness through his re-telling of Christ's resurrection.

In *The Escaped Cock* (1929), which was first published in England as *The Man Who Died* (1931), Lawrence sets out to describe Christ's resurrection in the flesh, to provide a corrective to Christian accounts, which he felt had concentrated too exclusively on the Ascension. Like Powys in *Fables*, Lawrence attempts to articulate a sensual awareness of the physical world through a synthesis of Christian and pagan worldviews; it is significant that both men wrote non-fictional works of biblical criticism as accompaniments to (or commentaries on) these fictional projects.[10] While Powys uses his innovative engagement with the fable form to shift the focus from human morality to the tangible and tactile world of animals and objects, Lawrence literalizes biblical narrative in order to explore Christ's physical suffering as a man who has outlived his mission and must discover a new sense of being and self-responsibility through earthly vocation and sexual relationship. In Lawrence's story, the Christ figure has not actually died on the cross; he has been taken down too early, so that his emergence from the tomb on the third day is a physical rather than a spiritual re-awakening. In the first part of the story, the Man finds shelter with a peasant and his wife near Jerusalem. It is through his careful observation of the hosts' bound game-cock that he discovers a life-force in Nature based on pride and self-sufficiency to offset the humility and servitude of his former public role as Saviour. He buys the cock from the peasant and wanders away, determined to 'return to men' in the guise of a physician.[11] The second part of *The Escaped Cock* is set on the Mediterranean coast of Lebanon and follows the gradual and painful sexual awakening of the Man through his relationship with a Priestess of Isis. The Man impregnates the Priestess before escaping in a boat to avoid being apprehended once again by a Roman overseer and his slave.

By opening the story with the bird instead of the Man, Lawrence deliberately combines fable and religious parable, creating a hybrid narrative that subverts both the moral simplicity and spiritual portentousness of the earlier forms. This effectively prevents readers from abstracting a stable message from the two very different parts of the story: the significance of the gamecock and its relationship to the Man's awakening is *experienced* through the different kinds of language (biblical, pagan and secular) which it employs, and it is inseparable from them, so that any précis will seem a travesty of the complex layers of meaning and implication which it opens up. Michael Bell has argued that Lawrence's writings are 'mythopoeic' precisely because they contain in their narrative medium this heuristic awareness that one must experience a state of being in order to understand it.[12] Where Powys had employed impersonal and detached forms of logic in his fables to unpick the claims of rationalistic and moral discourse, Lawrence does not even offer the consolation of a consistently subversive position; instead, he immerses his readers in an echo-chamber of different registers and forces them to discover a fresh orientation.

It is noteworthy that writers in the native tradition are centrally troubled by the links between aesthetic form and communal, moral or religious values, since, as Stephen Benson has shown, a later generation of postmodernist writers, including Italo Calvino, John Barth and Robert Coover, has seemed more preoccupied with 'a self-contained, overtly fictional environment' and with the potential that oral and traditional story forms provide for fabrication or playful intertextuality.[13] The impulse in the English short story to rewrite traditional forms of oral narrative in order to gain a purchase on contemporary moral and religious experience is forcefully evident in Angela Carter's *The Bloody Chamber and Other Stories* (1979), in which the sexual sadism latent in fairy tales is explored through an affirmative feminist lens, but it has also persisted in writings where the adaptation is less obvious and more implicit.

The short stories of William Sansom, Alan Sillitoe and Graham Swift are particularly interesting in this respect. Sansom's tales combine the clarity and concentration of the fable with enigmatic or uncanny endings that upset the expectation of simple moral closure or straightforward existential insight.

In several of his better-known short stories, working-class characters leading ordinary lives suddenly face extraordinary situations which expose the grotesque reality lying beneath the comforting world of habit and ritual. For example, in 'The Wall', from his first collection *Fireman Flower and Other Stories* (1944), three fire-fighters survive the collapse of a burning wall by the mere chance of being framed by an oblong window space; in 'Among the Dahlias', the title story of a 1957 volume of tales, a fireplace salesman walks through an empty zoo and is confronted by an escaped lion, only for the animal to turn away from him with an expression of distaste at the very instant when he expects death. In these stories, the characters' inexplicable survival leaves readers uncertain of the external forces that govern the worlds they inhabit. In 'The Vertical Ladder', from *Something Terrible, Something Lovely* (1948), a youth who wishes to impress a young girl accepts a challenge to scale a rusty gasometer using an old and worn iron ladder clamped to its side, only to find himself terrified by the height and cut adrift by male friends who take away the wooden step ladders he used to get to the lowest rung; the tale ends with him reaching the top but not knowing why he is there or what he can do.

Sillitoe and Swift have also exploited the open form of the ambivalent fable in their short fiction. In the title story of Sillitoe's *The Loneliness of the Long-Distance Runner* (1959), a young petty thief incarcerated in a borstal agrees to compete in that institution's All-England Blue Ribbon Prize Cup for Long-Distance Cross-Country Running. Training for it affords him a rare opportunity for self-reflection, but at the event itself he deliberately falters when in a winning position close to the finishing line, embracing failure as the only form of rebellion against institutional control. We are left to ponder the nature and extent of his freedom and autonomy as a disaffected character on the criminal margins of society.

Freedom and control are also the issues at stake in the title story of Swift's first collection, *Learning to Swim and Other Stories* (1982), which explores the marital alienation of a couple through their conflicting attitudes to their young son during a family holiday in Cornwall. The significantly named Mrs Singleton wishes to prolong the son's reliance on her as a compensation for her lack of erotic satisfaction with her husband, while Mr Singleton is mechanically driven to create a son in his own image. The story ends with the boy overwhelmed by the choice between them, swimming away from his father and out to sea in an equivocal gesture which seems at once affirmative and suicidal. In 'First on the Scene', from Swift's second collection, *England and Other Stories* (2014), a widowed man who enjoys speaking to his dead wife during regular solitary walks in the countryside comes across the lifeless body of a young woman at the side of a path. After feeling inexplicable anger and briefly considering walking away from it, he decides to contact the police, accepting that he is in some way implicated in her death. The final line of the story – 'What a terrible thing it can be just to be on this earth' – is an ambiguous moral of questionable origin, attributable either to the character or the narrator, or both.[14]

The disconcerting elusiveness of these thoroughly modern fables reflects the deracination of characters who desire to find meaning in life but instead experience scepticism, physical horror, conflict and moral emptiness. The real interest of the tales emerges through their formal experimentalism; they take their place in a strong line of English short stories that invoke a traditional story form in order to measure the distance travelled from its familiar and cohesive structures to the strange and alienating experiences of modernity.

Notes

1. See Vladimir Propp, *Morphology of the Folktale* (1928), trans. Laurence Scott, 2nd edition (Austin, TX: University of Texas Press, 1968); Joseph Campbell, *The Hero with a Thousand Faces* (1949), 2nd edn (Princeton University Press, 1968); Northrop Frye, *Anatomy of Criticism: Four Essays* (Princeton University Press, 1957). In the Preface to *The Hero with a Thousand Faces*, p. viii, Campbell says: 'There are of course differences between the numerous mythologies and religions of mankind, but this is a book about the similarities.'
2. Adrian Hunter, *The Cambridge Introduction to the Short Story in English* (Cambridge University Press, 2007), p. 15.
3. Robert Louis Stevenson, *Lay Morals and Other Papers* (London: Chatto and Windus, 1911), p. 167.
4. Clare Hanson, *Short Stories and Short Fictions, 1880–1980* (Basingstoke: Macmillan, 1985), p. 104.
5. T. F. Powys, *Fables* (New York: The Viking Press, 1929), p. 8 and p. 70.
6. Marina Warner, *From the Beast to the Blonde: Fairy Tales and their Tellers* (London: Chatto and Windus, 1994), p. 411.
7. H. E. Bates, *The Modern Short Story: A Critical Survey* (London: Thomas Nelson and Sons Ltd, 1941), p. 135.
8. Ann Martin, *Red Riding Hood and the Wolf in Bed: Modernism's Fairy Tales* (University of Toronto Press, 2006), p. 12.
9. E. M. Forster, *The Celestial Omnibus* (London: Sidgwick and Jackson, 1911), p. 151.
10. Lawrence wrote a study of the New Testament Book of Revelation between November 1929 and January 1930; it was published posthumously as *Apocalypse* (1931). Powys published *An Interpretation of Genesis* in 1929.

11. D. H. Lawrence, *The Virgin and the Gipsy and Other Stories*, ed. Michael Herbert, Bethan Jones and Lindeth Vasey (Cambridge University Press, 2005), p. 138.
12. See Michael Bell, *Literature, Modernism and Myth: Belief and Responsibility in the Twentieth Century* (Cambridge University Press, 1997), pp. 93–4.
13. Stephen Benson, *Cycles of Influence: Fiction, Folktale, Theory* (Detroit, MI: Wayne State University Press, 2003), p. 17.
14. Graham Swift, *England and Other Stories* (London: Simon and Schuster, 2014), p. 255.

6

The Colonial Short Story, Adventure and the Exotic

ROBERT HAMPSON

In his essay on 'The Short Story', W. Somerset Maugham describes two very different pleasures that reading fiction offers its readers: the pleasure of 'recognition' and the pleasure of 'strangeness and novelty'.[1] The 'exotic story' offers the latter pleasure: 'it is a release from the monotony of existence to be absorbed for a while in a world of hazard and perilous adventure' (p. 175). He identifies Kipling as 'the first to blaze the trail through this new-found region': 'in his discovery of what is called the exotic story he opened a new and fruitful field to writing' (pp. 157, 156). In fact, if the 'exotic story' – or, more accurately, the colonial short story – was initiated by Kipling, it was to reach its final flowering with Maugham.

Exotic Stories

Early in 1890, Sampson Low published Rudyard Kipling's *Soldiers Three* in an edition of 7,000 copies. Although this was Kipling's introduction in book form to the general reading public in Britain, he had been publishing short stories for a number of years in India, and his work was not unknown even in English literary circles. Indeed, when he had arrived in London towards the end of 1889, his reputation as a writer of short stories preceded him. Sidney Low, the editor of the conservative daily newspaper *The St James's Gazette*, had read (and been impressed by) the Indian Library edition of *Soldiers Three*, and Andrew Lang had praised two of the other Indian Library volumes, *In Black and White* and *Under the Deodars*, in the *Saturday Review*.[2] As Andrew Lycett notes, Lang – together with W. E. Henley and Edmund Gosse – had been promoting the work of Robert Louis Stevenson and Rider Haggard as part of a consciously masculinist agenda.[3] Kipling, with his stories about British soldiers in India, looked like a new recruit for the campaign and for the promotion of Britain's imperial role.

Whether Kipling was the first person to write an 'exotic story', as Maugham suggests, is debatable. Nevertheless, because of the quantity, quality and high profile of his work, Kipling's fiction would seem to offer the epitome of the colonial short story. However, he was clearly not writing adventure romances of the kind written by Haggard. *King Solomon's Mines*, Haggard's imperialist response to *Treasure Island*, is a quest romance in which a trio of European adventurers discovers an unknown African country, intervenes in its politics, and comes away with immense riches. Even a story like 'The Man Who Would Be King', about two Englishmen who establish themselves as rulers in north-eastern Afghanistan, which bears some superficial similarities, is far from being an adventure romance: Dravot and Carnehan are loafers and confidence tricksters with none of the heroism and stature of Haggard's Sir Henry Curtis; and the story is full of uncertainties and ambiguities. As John McBratney suggests, it can be read as supporting the actions of 'strong men' who act independently, but also as a warning against imperial over-reaching and decline: as Carnehan observes, 'This business is our Fifty-Seven.'[4] More generally, Kipling's short stories about Peshwari horse-dealers, rural policemen, Punjabi money-lenders, Bihari miners, not to mention his stories about missionaries and Anglo-Indian hill-station infidelities, are hardly adventure stories at all. And, if the work seemed 'exotic' to metropolitan readers – Lang, in a review of *Plain Tales from the Hills*, welcomed the volume as 'an addition to the new exotic literature' – that apparent exoticism concealed a more complex position-taking.[5]

In 1885, Kipling had published some of his stories for the first time in *Quartette*, work by the Kipling family published as a Christmas supplement to the Lahore *Civil and Military Gazette*, for which he worked as assistant editor.[6] In this secure, familiar context Kipling published 'The Phantom Rickshaw', a story of guilt, haunting and mental breakdown, and 'The Strange Ride of Morrowbie Jukes', a nightmare of powerlessness and colonial reversal. After a change of editor in 1886, he started publishing his sketches and stories on a regular basis in the *Gazette*. Thirty-two of these 'turnovers', short stories of around 2,000 words, were collected (with eight new tales) as *Plain Tales from the Hills* and published in 1888. Nine of these stories were about army life; twenty-four related to Anglo-Indian society, including four involving Mrs Hauksbee's interventions in hill-station social life and two involving Strickland, an intelligent police-officer who 'held the extraordinary theory that a policeman in India should try to know as much about the native as the natives themselves', a theory which has 'done him no good in the eyes of the Indian Government'.[7] When Kipling moved from Lahore to Allahabad in 1887, he was given the job of editing the *Pioneer*'s weekly supplement, *The Week's News*, and he wrote for it at least one story per week. In 1888, A. H. Wheeler, the publisher of the *Pioneer*, had the idea of producing cheap reprints for railway reading. Five of the first six volumes of Wheeler's Indian Railway Library were collections of stories by Kipling, most of which had already appeared in the pages of *The Week's News*: *Soldiers Three*, *In Black and White*, *Under the Deodars*, *Wee Willie Winkie* and *The Phantom Rickshaw*.[8]

This history is relevant for an understanding of Kipling's position as a writer of colonial short stories. As David Sergeant has convincingly demonstrated, Kipling 'would overhaul his narrative technique in response to changes in location and readership, political context and biographical circumstances'.[9] The first major change was produced by the shift from writing for the British community in the Punjab to writing for an India-wide British readership. In Lahore, Kipling's stories were read by the small colonial community to which he belonged.[10] This was, as Sergeant observes, an 'intensely tribal readership', and his stories not only provided them with 'consolatory Anglo-Indian spaces', but also represented a very specific Anglo-Indian ideology in which 'unillusioned pragmatists with practical experience' had to confront the absurdities of a distant colonial government (pp. 26–7, 34, 37).[11] In this context, Strickland, like Kipling's narrator, can be seen to embody the 'illusion of mastery and knowledge that justifies English hegemony'.[12] When Kipling moved to Allahabad, the capital of the United Provinces, he not only moved to a newspaper physically and politically closer to the colonial central government, but he was also writing for a British readership dispersed across India. Stories such as 'The Gate of the Hundred Sorrows' (with its vivid evocation of the effects of opium) now acquired frame-narratives to distance them from the author. The first volume published by the Indian Library was *Soldiers Three*. Kipling's stories about Privates Learoyd, Ortheris and Mulvaney introduced a new world to his Anglo-Indian readership. As David Sergeant notes: 'The military were crucial to British power, but the common soldier was too distanced from other sections of society; these stories humanized him for a civilian readership'.[13] Charles Carrington puts this more bluntly: the private soldiers of the British army were drawn from 'the unemployed or unemployable'; as a result, 'the soldiery formed a caste apart and a caste of untouchables'.[14] Kipling confirms this: in his own words, his 'Three

Musketeers' were 'in no sense refined, nor to be admitted to the outer door-mats of decent folk'.[15] The Yorkshireman Learoyd, the Londoner Ortheris and the Irishman Mulvaney were thus as exotic to Kipling's original readers as the various indigenous and colonial inhabitants of the sub-continent were to his later readers.

When Kipling's colonial stories were republished in Britain, he had to make numerous minor revisions to re-shape them for a different readership. One obvious change related to the liberal, unglossed use of Hindi in the original versions. As Lang put it, 'the general reader is much averse to the study of Indian matters, and is baffled by *jhairuns* and *khitmatgars*, and the rest of it'.[16] Less obviously, Kipling also had to confront in London a very different ethos from that of colonial India. *The Times* (25 March 1890) dedicated a leading article to his work. This praised his representation of 'various aspects of native life' and hailed him as 'the discoverer, as far as India is concerned, of "Tommy Atkins" as a hero of realistic romance'. It also mentioned his treatment of 'that unfortunate result of our settlement in India, the Eurasian', and his familiarity with 'Simla life'.[17] This last proved the least transportable of Kipling's subjects: what had been, in Lahore, the extension of Punjab Club tales into print for a local audience familiar with some of the originals had already looked uncomfortably like making public that close community's dirty washing when the tales reached a wider colonial audience.[18] Back in Britain, hill-station flirtations and political intrigues seemed, at best, small scale and unattractive; at worst, these stories amounted to what Margaret Oliphant described as 'distasteful visions of something odious'.[19]

On the other hand, Kipling's stories of 'native life' were welcomed for providing British domestic readers with 'glimpses of the secret life of India'.[20] As Henry James put it, 'he is wonderful about India, and India has not been "done"'.[21] Here, the young Kipling's air of 'knowing his way about life' paid off: James praised Kipling's evocation of India – its 'heat and colour and danger and dust', but also the 'curious glimpses of custom and superstition' (p. 165); Lang praised his 'knowledge of things little known – the dreams of opium smokers, the ideas of private soldiers, the passion of pathans and wild Border tribes'.[22] A later essay by Lang even considered the difference between their first publication in India, where the 'subjects, no doubt, seemed so familiar' as against their British publication, where 'the strangeness, the colour, the variety, the perfume of the East' stood out and where the stories fed a recently acquired 'taste for the exotic'.[23] The earlier article in *The Times* had already summed up this aspect of Kipling's fiction: these stories 'appear to lift the veil from a state of society so immeasurably distant from our own and to offer us glimpses of unknown depths and gulfs of human existence'.[24]

Kipling's stories of soldiers' life (and the Irishman, Mulvaney, in particular) were similarly well received from the start.[25] The article in *The Times* had picked up on Kipling's representation of 'the dull hard work' of the soldiery: 'their few comforts, their dreary, enforced leisure, and their almost irresistible temptations for getting into mischief'. Even Oliphant praised 'the great Mulvaney and his comrades', while Henry James described the group of stories devoted to 'the common soldier' as 'brilliant'.[26] It is perhaps significant that, once settled in London, Kipling began to write a series of new stories about his 'Three Musketeers': 'The Incarnation of Krishna Mulvaney', 'The Courting of Dinah Shadd', 'On Greenhow Hill' and 'Love o' Women'. With these, and his *Barrack-Room Ballads* (1890), Kipling struck a less problematic vein for the contemporary metropolitan reader.

Kipling's colonial short stories were thus colonial short stories in two different senses: they were, in their first showings, stories written for colonists by one of their own, drawing on shared linguistic understanding and shared (or, at least, overlapping) experiences; when they were republished for a domestic readership, they acquired the added interest of revealing an unknown world. In addition, Kipling had both the advantage and the disadvantage of not knowing the rules of the domestic world. This produced a negative response to the hill-station stories, but it also meant that he had a freedom denied to metropolitan writers conscious of what 'the public' would allow. As J. M. Barrie put it, 'Kipling has done what we are to understand they [metropolitan writers] could do if they dared.'[27] Barrie also notes another kind of freedom, which was granted to Kipling by the readers' uncertainty about some of his subject matter: 'There is something wrong, they feel, and they have a notion that they could put their finger on it if the stories were English rather than Indian' (p. 84). In addition, as Kaori Nagai has shown, Kipling's colonial short stories themselves changed radically once he moved to England. Nagai notes that the oppressive hot weather and the monsoons disappear (since they might undermine the picture of an efficient and disciplined Raj) and the narrator becomes more all-knowing in the stories written after Kipling's return to England.[28] Thus, she argues, whereas he plays the role of witness or reporter in the stories of *Soldiers Three*, in a later story such as 'The Incarnation of Krishna Mulvaney', the narrator is privy to the private conversation between the colonel and his adjutant, while in 'The Courting of Dinah Shadd', the story of Mulvaney's courtship begins with a panoramic overview of the British army in India: 'Thirty thousand troops had, by the wisdom of the Government of India, been turned loose over a few thousand square miles of country'.[29]

Nagai also draws attention to Mulvaney in relation to 'the impossible position of the Irish within the Raj'. Where P. J. Keating discussed Mulvaney, Learoyd and Ortheris as working-class characters, Nagai foregrounds Mulvaney's Irishness and Kipling's 'mystification of Mulvaney's pre-army life' which serves to cover up 'the hard reality of Ireland'.[30] She notes, for example, how both Ortheris and Learoyd experience 'homesickness', in 'The Madness of Private Ortheris' and 'On Greenhow Hill', but the concept of 'home' is avoided (as more problematic) in relation to Mulvaney. Not only would it involve an imaginative return to a troubled Ireland, but it would raise the issue of 'home' in the context of political demands for 'Home Rule'. 'The Mutiny of the Mavericks', which Kipling wrote in London, is particularly revealing here. In this story, Kipling relates how a North American Fenian organization sends the Irish-American Mulcahy to stir up the 'Mavericks', an Irish regiment in India, but the planned mutiny is thwarted by the Irish soldiers. Kipling's Irish soldiers in India, like the old Indian soldier encountered by the lama in *Kim*, affirm their loyalty to the Empire. In Kipling's fiction, the independence struggles in both countries are countered and contained by voluntary assertions of loyalty.

Ethnographers of a Vanishing Culture

On the publication of his first novel, *Almayer's Folly* (1895), Conrad was hailed as having 'annexed' Borneo for fiction, and it was predicted that he might become 'the Kipling of the Malay Archipelago'.[31] Conrad continued to mine this vein in some of his early short fiction: a slight tale, 'The Lagoon' was finished in 1896; a more substantial story, 'Karain' was completed in 1897. However, not all reviewers were as positive about the exotic setting of Conrad's work. An unsigned review in *World* (15 May 1895) described *Almayer's Folly* as 'a dreary record of the still more dreary existence of a solitary Dutchman doomed to vegetate in a small village in Borneo' (p. 51); an unsigned review in the American journal, *Nation* (17 October 1895) was similarly disenchanted with exotic locations: 'We have become inured to tiresome fiction supposed to be descriptive of outlandish places, but a feeling of resentment smoulders' (p. 60). It should also be said that Conrad was not the only person to be writing what might be called colonial short stories in English about Malaysia. Two colonial administrators, Sir Frank Swettenham and Sir Hugh Clifford, were also in the field.

Swettenham arrived in Singapore in 1871 at the age of twenty and was to spend the next thirty-four years in the administration of the Malay States. In 1895 he published his *Malay Sketches*.[32] Although he describes Malaya as the 'land of the pirate and the *amok*', his concern is not with adventure but with the ethnographic task of recording manners and customs. His 'sketches' are conscious attempts at salvage anthropology, offering a detailed description of a culture before it vanishes. Thus the volume begins with 'The Real Malay', in which the experienced colonial administrator offers advice to other colonizers. Subsequent sketches, such as 'The Tiger' and 'A Fishing Picnic', tell stories, but they aim to present a typical experience rather than a specific incident. Of the other sketches, 'The Murder of the Hawker' presents the story of a murder in order to reveal 'the state of feeling in a real Malay *kampong*' (p. 29); 'Amok' similarly presents a specific incident of *amok* in order to discuss the phenomenon more generally; while 'The Story of Mat Aris' is another crime-report, this time used to explain the nature of the Malay jungle. With 'The Eternal Feminine', the story of a Malay woman's attempt to prevent the murder of her European partner, 'The Noon of Night' and 'A Malay Romance', Swettenham begins to turn what are clearly true stories into short fictions.

His colleague, Hugh Clifford, arrived in Malaya in 1883 at the age of seventeen. Like Swettenham, he lived an adventurous life as a colonial administrator, and, like Swettenham, he was very attached to the Malay culture which it was his job to displace. *In Court and Kampong* (1897), a collection of nineteen tales and sketches, begins with two chapters, 'The East Coast' and 'The People of the East Coast', which are purely descriptive as their titles suggest; the subsequent short stories (for example, 'The Experience of Raja Haji Hamid') are clearly modelled on Kipling's Indian tales.[33] The stories and sketches in this volume are all about Malays and Malay life – 'The Were-Tiger', for example, is told to illustrate Malay cultural beliefs, while 'The Amok of Dato Kaya Biji Dera' addresses European misunderstandings of *amok*. The Preface makes clear Clifford's sense not only that the Malay Peninsula 'is but little more than a name to most dwellers in Europe' but also that 'the east Coast and the remote interior' (of which he writes) are 'almost as completely unknown' even 'in the Peninsula itself' (p. vii). Most of these stories and sketches were first published in Singapore in a volume called *East Coast Etchings* (1896). Like Kipling, Clifford wrote for a colonial audience before he wrote for the domestic audience, but, unlike Kipling's, the stories he published were 'exotic' for both readerships.

This was the context in which Conrad's early short stories appeared. The first of his colonial short stories was 'An Outpost of Progress', written in July 1896 and published in *Cosmopolis* a year later. This was the lighter part of the 'loot' he had brought back from the Congo. Often read simply as a darkly sardonic account of the deterioration of two European colonists at an upriver trading station, it effectively counterpoints their story with that of the Sierra Leonean Henry Price as he successfully negotiates between the various cultures of the Congo. Carlier and Kayerts, their names chosen to reflect the two cultures of Belgium, far from being adventurers, are two ineffectual individuals, totally reliant on the local people for their survival. Their inadequacies are set against the 'high-flown language' of a newspaper article about 'the sacredness of the civilising work', which they discover on the station.[34] When the station is visited by slavers from the coast, it is Henry Price and his Angolan wife, not the Europeans, who find a way to resolve the crisis. Conrad's representation of Price and of a variety of different African cultures in this story shows the error of those who, like Chinua Achebe, insist on reading the Marlow of 'Heart of Darkness' as Conrad's mouthpiece.[35]

In August 1896, Conrad wrote 'The Lagoon', which was published in the *Cornhill* in January 1897. The story begins with the arrival of a 'white man' at the riverine house of a Malay, but it is the Malay, Arsat, who is named and individuated, not the European, and it is Arsat who tells his story. Arsat tells how he betrayed his brother for the sake of the woman he loved. The story has an ethnographic basis, but is not told for the sake of displaying that knowledge: the hostile attitude of the Malays towards Arsat, as a man who has repaired a ruined house and made it his home, is part of the story's engagement with the seen and the unseen. Also, as this suggests, the story presents the Malay perspective on Europeans and each other, as well as the European's attitude towards the Malays. Similarly, in 'Karain', which Conrad wrote in February 1897, although the European gun-runners who visit Karain are more fully individuated, it is Karain who tells his story. Again, this is a story about the betrayal of a male friend to save a woman and the burden of guilt that follows. More than 'The Lagoon', this is a story about 'the exotic', but it is an exotic world that is presented as such through the partial memory of its European primary narrator. Karain's account of his travels through the archipelago includes his contact with cultures (like the Hindu statues of an earlier empire) that are equally exotic to him. And the story's climax, which involves the recognition of a bond between Karain and the white men, underwrites that bond by insisting on the equivalence between the charm Karain seeks and the 'charms and talismans' of white men.[36] Where Rider

Haggard, in *King Solomon's Mines*, presented the triumph of European science over African superstition in the strategic use of an eclipse, Conrad draws on a Frazerian understanding of the survival of 'magical' ways of thinking in European culture to prevent any such assumption of superiority. Instead, Conrad pushes further the concern with the seen and the unseen introduced in 'The Lagoon' to produce an exploration of different cultures and different versions of reality, which leaves the comparison of European and Malay worlds unresolved.

Where Conrad does bring in a sense of adventure is in his sea stories, which are only by implication colonial stories. In 'Youth' (written in May 1898), for example, which was Marlow's first outing as a storyteller, he recounts his first voyage to 'the East'. It is a story of gales, delays, collisions, fire in the hold and, finally, abandoning ship. It is, as Marlow remembers himself thinking, 'the deuce of an adventure', but it is also the case that this sense of adventure is precisely represented as the younger Marlow's romantic feeling.[37] 'Typhoon' (written between December 1900 and January 1901) similarly presents contrasting viewpoints on its story of a ship caught by a typhoon in the South China Sea: from the literal Captain MacWhirr and the imaginative young mate, Jukes. 'The End of the Tether' (1902), with its impressionistic and topographical descriptions of Singapore, is the most colonial of these stories. However, the world it presents is neither exotic nor adventurous. Captain Whalley's adventures are all in the past in the era of sail; he now commands a steamship which follows its 'monotonous huckster's round up and down the Straits' (p. 166). The problems he confronts are those of ageing, making a living, and providing for his unluckily married daughter in Australia. Conrad's maritime world might, nevertheless, seem the equivalent of Kipling's stories about soldiers: bringing an exotic unknown world to the eyes of metropolitan readers. However, Conrad's sea-fictions were regularly criticized for lacking adventure. For example, the anonymous reviewer in the *Daily Mail* described *The Nigger of the 'Narcissus'* as 'no tale, but merely an account of the uneventful voyage of the *Narcissus* from Bombay to the Thames': 'There is no plot, no villainy, no heroism, and, apart from a storm and the death and burial, no incident.'[38] It is clear that the reviewer expected a proper story to have a hero, a villain and some romantic involvement with women: a storm that turns the ship onto its side, a near-mutiny and the slow death of a crew member do not count.

Conrad's younger contemporary, Somerset Maugham, wrote a number of short stories about colonial life in the South Pacific, Hong Kong and Malaysia from the First World War into the 1920s. In his essay on 'The Short Story',

Maugham defined the 'exotic story' as 'set in some country little known to the majority of readers', but also, more precisely, as dealing with 'the reactions upon the white man of his sojourn in an alien land and the effect which contact with peoples of another race and colour has upon him'.[39] Maugham's stories are primarily stories about the European colonists – planters, administrators, missionaries and their wives; very rarely is the focus on inter-racial encounter as such, although this often provides the context. An early story, 'Mackintosh', deals with the antipathy between two colonial administrators, Walker and Mackintosh, on a Samoan island. The cultural clash between them develops into monomaniacal hatred and ends in the violent death of both men. This is the European part of 'An Outpost of Progress' translated to Stevenson's Pacific. At the same time, Walker's outsmarting of the villagers who refuse to work for the low wages he offers presents the kind of trick which would have been celebrated in a Kipling story, but here is the direct cause of his death. Another Samoan story, 'Rain', like Kipling's 'The Judgment of Dungara', deals with the discomfiture of missionaries – but this victory over Christianity comes at the hands of another European not, as in Kipling's story, through the local priest using his local knowledge. In 'Rain', the Davidsons are proud that they have 'practically eradicated' local dress in their district, the 'lava-lava' replaced by 'the Mother Hubbard' for women and 'trousers and singlets' for men.[40] Mrs Davidson boasts that 'no-one has danced in our district for eight years' (p. 76). Their strict opposition to anything joyful or pleasurable is countered and ultimately circumvented in the tale by Miss Thompson, a prostitute from Honolulu, who shares their temporary accommodation when they are delayed on a journey. In the course of the narrative, Maugham shows the political power of the missionaries and depicts Davidson twice using this power to try and ruin the life of an individual of whom he disapproves. Davidson's undoing through his self-righteous wrath, his ruthless desire for punishment, and his own sexual desires complete the story's critical presentation of missionaries.

As these stories suggest, there is a sense of belatedness about Maugham's colonial fiction. In 1926, Maugham published *The Casuarina Tree*, a set of six stories set in the Malay Peninsula and Borneo. In his Preface he describes his subjects as the English planters and administrators who came 'after the pioneers who had opened these lands to Western civilisation' and would, in turn, be replaced by 'a more varied, but less adventurous, generation' (p. 117). These are not stories of pioneering adventures, but rather the small change of colonial life. Maugham's stories recall Kipling's stories of colonial life in Simla, but on the smaller scale and with the greater isolation of Malay stations and plantations. In 'Before the Party', as the Skinner family get ready for Canon Heywood's garden party, Maugham gradually reveals the truth behind the daughter's marriage to a planter: the story of his alcoholism and her murder of him contrasting comically with the family's concern for 'good form'. In 'P & O', a planter returning home to Ireland after twenty-five years in the Federated Malay States dies before landfall as a result of the curse placed upon him by the Malay woman he has left behind, while Mrs Hamlyn comes to terms with the fact that her husband of twenty years has left her for another woman. In 'The Letter', by contrast, Mrs Joyce kills her lover, because he is leaving her for a Chinese woman. 'The Outstation', in a variation on the theme of 'Mackintosh', recounts the fatal outcome of the cultural clash between the gentlemanly Resident, Mr Warburton, and his ungentlemanly, colonial-born assistant, Mr Cooper. In 'The Yellow Streak', Izzart, the son of an engineer in the Government Service, who has been given the job of accompanying a mining engineer into the interior, fails at a critical moment, when their boat is caught by the tidal current of a bore. This story of momentary cowardice, which is linked to Izzart's Malay 'blood' – his dark complexion is not the result of a Spanish grandmother, as he claims, but a half-Malay mother – is the counter-version of Kipling's 'His Chance in Life', where Michele D'Cruze triumphs in a crisis, quelling a rebellious mob, because of the 'drop of White blood' in his make-up.[41]

There is belatedness in another sense, too. In Maugham's 'Before the Party', Skinner quotes Kipling ('What can they know of England who only England know'), while the dipsomaniac Harold explains his shakes by referring to 'the strain it puts upon a man to be an empire builder' (p. 136). In neither case is the source given: Kipling has become part of the conventional knowledge. This is confirmed in a later story, 'Virtue', where one character describes Morton, the protagonist, as 'Rather the Kipling type, you know ... Empire-builder and all that sort of thing'.[42] In 'The Short Story', Maugham observed that Kipling 'not only created characters; he moulded men': 'there were men scattered about the outlying parts of the Empire who would never have been just what they were except for him' (p. 156). Not only has Maugham learnt from Kipling's stories; but the people whose stories he tells have been shaped by Kipling as well. Conrad's work is also a point of reference. In 'The Force of Circumstance', Doris had met Guy at a seaside hotel in England, while he was on home leave. When she returns with him to Sembulu, where he is a second-generation colonial administrator, she discovers that he has a Malay lover and three children, who refuse to leave quietly. She reflects, on remembering her arrival, 'of course she had read novels about the Malay Archipelago and she had formed an impression of a sombre land with great ominous rivers and a silent, impenetrable jungle'.[43] The choice of adjectives suggests that she had read Conrad's early Malay novels, *Almayer's Folly* and *An Outcast of the Islands*. Neil MacAdam, in the story of that name, had also read his Conrad before arriving: 'He knew his Conrad almost by heart and he was expecting a land of brooding mystery. He was not prepared for the blue milky sky ... Neil had no feeling of being shut in, nor, in that radiant morning, of gloom, but of space and freedom.'[44] Another later story, 'Flotsam and Jetsam', depicts another unhappy marriage, that of Norman Grange and his wife, Vesta. She had been an actress with a touring company and had met him in Singapore. She tells Skelton, a sick anthropologist who stays with them briefly: 'They talk of the romance of the East. They can have it. I'd rather be a dresser in a provincial theatre.'[45] Maugham is revisiting here the territory that Conrad explored with Lena and Mrs Schomberg in *Victory* and with Anne in 'Because of the Dollars': the lives of European women in the East. At the end of this story, we are told that Vesta 'would have given anything to get away' but the reality is: 'She had to stay – or starve; and Norman had to keep her – or hang' (p. 85). In 'P & O', Mrs Hamlyn had reflected more benignly on what she lost through separating from her husband: 'the settled establishment and the assured position, the ample means and the support of a recognized background' (p. 169). While these small colonial communities are striated with affairs and infidelities, Maugham depicts not just the more sensational outcomes but also the lives of quiet desperation and what is at stake for the men and women involved.

Skelton, in 'Flotsam and Jetsam', had described himself as wanting to study 'the manners and customs of tribes that haven't had any contact with civilisation' (p. 71), and, in a sense, that is what he encounters with the Granges. Grange is a second-generation rubber planter. The story opens with his brusque treatment of his wife and her unhappiness with life on the plantation. The story within the story is a tale of adultery and murder: Vesta's passionate love for their neighbour, Jack Carr, and Jack's death at her husband's hands. The initial crack in her relationship with her husband derives from her sense that 'There had always been something about Norman that she hadn't quite been able to get to the bottom of' (p. 82). Jack provides the explanation: 'it was because he was country-born; even though he hadn't a drop of native blood in his veins, something of the country had gone to the making of him so that he wasn't white really; he had an Eastern streak in him' (p. 83). In his Malay short stories, Maugham has become the ethnographer of a vanishing culture – not that of the native peoples of the Peninsula and Archipelago, but that of the European colonists, the 'exiled lives' for whom the casuarina tree is Maugham's symbol. This colonial ethnography records not only their manners and customs in Malaysia, but also their difficult relationship with England. Morton, in 'Virtue', is a district officer in the archipelago. His bungalow is described with a taxonomic, ethnographic eye:

> It was furnished in the impersonal fashion that characterised the dwellings of government officials who were moved here and there at little notice according to the exigencies of the service. There were native hats as ornaments on the walls, and the horns of animals, blow-pipes, and spears. In the bookshelf were detective novels and old magazines. (p. 153)

The story focuses, however, on his visit to London, and his unexpected experience of displacement: 'It was great to come home but you couldn't live there any more, and sometimes you thought of your bungalow overlooking the river and your tours of the district' (p. 156). It is not just a question of attachment to place: the visiting colonials find they 'had nothing in common with the acquaintances they made': 'They were more lonely than in the jungle' (p. 156). At the same time, as in 'Flotsam and Jetsam', the story avoids any romanticization of the colonial life. When the married woman with whom Morton gets involved wants to follow him to Malaysia, the story rejects her romantic assumptions about the East: 'people thought the East was free and easy; it wasn't; it was more suburban than Clapham' (p. 180). Morton thinks how the European women out there would turn their noses up at her.

Graham Greene's colonial short stories can be seen as the tail-end of this tradition. *Twenty-One Stories*, published in 1954, included two colonial stories among a collection predominantly based in southern England. 'A Chance for Mr Lever' (1936) begins like a classic colonial short story: the rice, the camp-bed and mosquito net, the mud wall, the thatched pointed roofs quickly establish the African setting, and there is even a quest, Mr Lever's search for Davidson. Lever, however, is not a heroic adventurer (in the mould of Haggard's Sir Henry Curtis): he is an elderly commercial traveller, who lost his job in the Depression, gambling on one last, desperate deal. The Liberian forest through which he travels is no Conradian jungle, but rather 'an endless back-garden of tangled weeds', the tedious setting for a journey through abjection; and Davidson is a poor substitute for Kurtz.[46] 'The Blue Film'

(1954), the story of an elderly married couple visiting an unnamed eastern city, marks the end of the road: here the colonial administrator has given way to the tourist, the 'exotic' has become routinized (the wife mentions 'The reclining Buddha, the emerald Buddha, the floating markets' like items in a checklist), and 'adventure' is similarly commodified: smoking opium, Japanese strip-tease, prostitutes and blue movies.

Liberating the Colonial Consciousness

In July 1904, George Russell asked Joyce if he could write a short story for his journal the *Irish Homestead*.[47] In *Dubliners*, the resulting volume, Joyce was concerned not just to depict the symptoms of paralysis in Dublin, but also to analyse its causes in the colonial domination of England and the power of the Roman Catholic Church. As Stephen Dedalus was to say in *Ulysses*: 'I am a servant of two masters ... an English and an Italian.'[48] The first task was the mental struggle to liberate that colonized consciousness.

'After The Race' is Joyce's clearest engagement with the colonized consciousness. It begins with the spectators at Inchicore watching a motor-race: 'through this channel of poverty and inaction the Continent sped its wealth and industry'.[49] After this initial view of what Joyce precisely and cuttingly terms 'the gratefully oppressed' (p. 378), the story focuses on the occupants of a particular car: Ségouin, the owner of the car, is 'in good humour because he had unexpectedly received some orders in advance'; Rivière is 'in good humour because he was to be appointed manager' of Ségouin's new 'motor establishment' in Paris; the Hungarian hanger-on, Villona, is 'in good humour because he had had a very satisfactory luncheon'; the Irishman, Jimmy Doyle, is 'too excited to be genuinely happy' (p. 378). Joyce makes clear how each of the occupants of the car has a solid, material basis for their happiness, except for the Irishman. The story explores further Jimmy's cast of mind as an instance of colonial mentality. Jimmy's father 'had begun life as an advanced Nationalist' but had 'modified his views early' (p. 378). He had made his money as a butcher, and his 'modified views' no doubt helped him to gain 'some of the police contracts' (p. 378). This social and political realignment has continued with Jimmy. Thus, Jimmy was sent to England to be educated 'in a big Catholic college', but then studied law at 'Dublin University', the Protestant Trinity College, and has spent a term at Cambridge 'to see a little life' (pp. 378–9). This 'seeing life' aligns him with the Inchicore 'sightseers': in both cases there is a purely spectacular engagement. And this spectacular engagement comes at a price. At Cambridge, 'His father, remonstrative, but covertly proud of the excess, had paid his bills.' These bills were 'within the limits of reasonable recklessness', and his father is covertly proud to pay them because they show that his son can afford to live like an English gentleman (p. 379). Part of Jimmy's pleasure in the events immediately after the race is that 'he has been seen by many of his friends ... in the company of these Continentals' (p. 379). While Jimmy is lost in these spectacular pleasures, the story keeps a clear eye on the money. Jimmy is 'about to stake the greater part of his substance' on Ségouin's business, while 'Ségouin had managed to give the impression that it was by a favour of friendship the mite of Irish money was to be included in the capital of the concern' (pp. 379–80). As Vincent Cheng says, this is 'a story about foreigners who come to Ireland to exploit it and take its money', but it is also about the colonized mentality that allows this to happen. This is made clear in the card game with which the story concludes: Jimmy is fleeced of his money by the Continentals, but, while he is being cheated, he is 'grateful for the experience, enjoying the excitement and privilege of their company'.[50]

'Ivy Day in the Committee Room' is also relevant here. The commemoration of the lost leader, Charles Parnell, which gives the story its title, also provides the measure of the political decay of post-Parnellite Ireland as evidenced by the exchanges in Tierney's committee room among the canvassers for the municipal elections. The story's nationalist pre-occupation is expressed through its concern with 'dependence and independence, colonizer and colonized, Home Rule and the British Monarchy'.[51] At the same time, the story offers the picture of a blocked nationalist project and its replacement by a mesh of political compromises. The various ways in which Joyce anatomizes the colonized consciousness under specific historical conditions adds another dimension to the importance of *Dubliners* in the history of the short story.

Notes

1. W. Somerset Maugham, 'The Short Story', in *Points of View* (London: Heinemann, 1958), pp. 142–88 (pp. 174–5).
2. Lang had already reviewed Kipling's *Departmental Ditties* in his monthly piece in *Longman's Magazine* in October 1886, while an anonymous review of *Plain Tales from the Hills* had been published in the *Saturday Review* (9 June 1888).

3. Andrew Lycett, *Rudyard Kipling* (London: Weidenfeld and Nicolson, 1959), p. 185.
4. John McBratney, 'India and Empire', in Harold Booth, ed., *The Cambridge Companion to Rudyard Kipling* (Cambridge University Press, 2011), pp. 23–36 (p. 27). Rudyard Kipling, 'The Man Who Would be King', in *Wee Willie Winkie, Under The Deodars, The Phantom Rickshaw and Other Stories* (London: Macmillan, 1969), pp. 238–9.
5. Andrew Lang, unsigned review, *Daily News* (2 November 1889). See Roger Lancelyn Green, ed., *Kipling: The Critical Heritage* (London: Routledge & Kegan Paul, 1971), pp. 47–50 (p. 49).
6. This supplement was written by Kipling, his mother, father and sister, hence the title.
7. Rudyard Kipling, 'Miss Youghal's Sais', in *Plain Tales from the Hills* (Harmondsworth: Penguin Books, 1987), p. 51.
8. The second volume, Kipling's *The Story of the Gadsbys*, was a short novel, of eight episodes, written in dialogue. 'Black Jack' in *Soldiers Three* and 'On the City Wall' in *In Black and White* had no magazine publication and appeared for the first time in the collection.
9. David Sergeant, *Kipling's Art of Fiction, 1884–1901* (Oxford University Press, 2013), p. 5.
10. As Kipling records, the centre of his world in Lahore was the Punjab Club, where he would be 'told every evening of the faults of that day's issue' (*Something of Myself* (Harmondsworth: Penguin Books, 1992), p. 58).
11. The knowing tone of the reference to Strickland's reputation with the Indian Government (cited above) is evidence of this close, collusive relationship with his original readers.
12. Jan Montefiore, *Rudyard Kipling* (Tavistock: Northcote House, 2007), p. 20.
13. Sergeant, *Kipling's Art of Fiction*, p. 57.
14. Charles Carrington, *Rudyard Kipling: His Life and Work* (1955) (Harmondsworth: Penguin Books, 1986), p. 145.
15. Rudyard Kipling, 'The Incarnation of Krishna Mulvaney', in *Life's Handicap* (London: Macmillan, 1911), p. 1. Edmond Gosse, in his 1891 essay on Kipling, observes that army officers are 'of ourselves': 'they marry our sisters and our daughters; and they lay down the law about India after dinner'; but the private soldier is unknown to 'us' (Green, ed., *Kipling: The Critical Heritage*, p. 110).
16. Green, ed., *Kipling: The Critical Heritage*, p. 48.
17. *Ibid.*, p. 51.
18. Carrington identifies the originals for Mrs Hauksbee and Captain Gadsby (*Rudyard Kipling: His Life and Work*, pp. 135, 138), and proposes sources for a number of Kipling's army tales (p. 144), which Kipling might have heard as soldiers' yarns.

19. Margaret Oliphant, anonymous review of *Plain Tales* in *Blackwood's Magazine* (November 1891), in Green, ed., *Kipling: The Critical Heritage*, p. 135.
20. Edmund Gosse, 'Rudyard Kipling', *Century Magazine* (October 1891); Green, ed., *Kipling: The Critical Heritage*, pp. 105–24 (p. 116).
21. Henry James, Introduction to *Mine Own People* (1891), in Green, ed., *Kipling: The Critical Heritage*, pp. 159–67 (p. 162).
22. Green, ed., *Kipling: The Critical Heritage*, p. 48.
23. Andrew Lang, *Essays in Little* (1891), in Green, ed., *Kipling: The Critical Heritage*, pp. 70–5 (p. 71).
24. Green, ed., *Kipling: The Critical Heritage*, p. 51.
25. The first review of *Plain Tales* singled out four army stories and the character of Mulvaney for praise. See Green, ed., *Kipling: The Critical Heritage*, p. 37.
26. Green, ed., *Kipling: The Critical Heritage*, pp. 52, 135 and 165.
27. J. M. Barrie, 'Mr Kipling's Stories', *Contemporary Review* (March, 1891). See Green, ed., *Kipling: The Critical Heritage*, pp. 78–87 (p. 78).
28. Kaori Nagai, *Empire of Analogies: Kipling, India and Ireland* (Cork University Press, 2006), p. 45.
29. Kipling, *Life's Handicap*, p. 38.
30. Nagai, *Empire of Analogies*, pp. 11 and 15; P. J. Keating, *The Working Classes in Victorian Fiction* (London: Routledge & Kegan Paul, 1971). The chronology of Mulvaney's career indicates that he was born during the Great Famine and grew up in its aftermath.
31. Arthur Waugh in his 'London Letter', *Critic* (11 May 1895); unsigned review, *Spectator* (19 October 1895). See Norman Sherry, ed., *Conrad: The Critical Heritage* (London: Routledge & Kegan Paul, 1973), pp. 50, 61. Subsequent reviews quoted are from this volume.
32. Frank Swettenham, *Malay Sketches* (London: John Lane, 1895). Swettenham's subsequent volumes included *Unaddressed Letters* (1898), *The Real Malay* (1899) and *Also And Perhaps* (1912).
33. Hugh Clifford, *In Court and Kampong, Being Tales and Sketches of Native Life in the Malay Peninsula* (London: Grant Richards, 1897).
34. Joseph Conrad, *Tales of Unrest* (London: J. M. Dent, 1923), p. 94.
35. Chinua Achebe, 'An Image of Africa: Racism in Conrad's *Heart of Darkness*', *The Massachussetts Review*, 18 (1977), pp. 782–94. For a fuller, more detailed reading, see Robert Hampson, '"An Outpost of Progress": The Case of Henry Price', in *Conrad in Africa: New Essays on 'Heart of Darkness'*, ed. Attie de Lange and Gail Fincham (Boulder, CO: Conrad: Eastern and Western Perspectives, 2001), pp. 211–30.
36. Conrad, *Tales of Unrest*, p. 48.
37. Joseph Conrad, *'Youth'*, *'Heart of Darkness'*, *and 'The End of the Tether'* (London: J. M. Dent, 1923), p. 12. Subsequent quotations and page numbers are from this edition.

38. Unsigned review, *Daily Mail* (7 December 1897), in Sherry, ed., *Conrad: The Critical Heritage*, p. 83.
39. Maugham, 'The Short Story', p. 156.
40. W. Somerset Maugham, 'Rain' in *Short Stories* (London: Vintage Books, 1998), pp. 73–115 (pp. 77–8). Subsequent page references to this edition are given in parentheses in the text.
41. Rudyard Kipling, 'His Chance in Life', in *Plain Tales from the Hills*, p. 94.
42. W. Somerset Maugham, *Collected Short Stories* (Harmondsworth: Penguin, 1963), II, p. 166.
43. *Collected Short Stories*, vol. II, p. 46.
44. W. Somerset Maugham, 'Neil MacAdam', in *Far Eastern Tales* (London: Mandarin, 1993), pp. 184–239 (p. 190). As this suggests, Maugham was very critical of Conrad's work.
45. Maugham, *Collected Short Stories*, vol. II, p. 77. Subsequent page references to this edition are given in parentheses in the text.
46. Graham Greene, *Twenty-One Stories* (London: Vintage Books, 2009), pp. 142–57 (p. 151).
47. Richard Ellmann, *James Joyce* (Oxford University Press, 1982), p. 163. As Andrew Gibson points out, if this is true, Joyce's response was 'remote from Russell's Anglo-Irish agenda'. See *The Strong Spirit* (Oxford University Press, 2013), p. 36.
48. James Joyce, *Ulysses* (London: Bodley Head, 1986), p. 17. He adds 'And a third there is … who wants me for odd jobs.' For Joyce's negotiation of the political demands of Ireland, see Andrew Gibson, *Joyce's Revenge* (Oxford University Press, 2002).
49. James Joyce, *Dubliners*, in Harry Levin, ed., *The Essential James Joyce* (Harmondsworth: Penguin, 1963), p. 378.
50. Vincent Cheng, *Joyce, Race and Empire* (Cambridge University Press, 1995), pp. 104, 109.
51. Gibson, *The Strong Spirit*, p. 46.

7

The *Yellow Book* Circle and the Culture of the Literary Magazine

WINNIE CHAN

Few literary endeavours lend their names to an era. For many critics – then and now – *The Yellow Book* defined the 1890s, a decade whose influence persisted well into the twentieth century, through formal, thematic and discursive innovations that anticipated modernism. (The journal's influence is registered in several essays in this History; yet it is also worthy of a separate treatment, to convey a sense of its formative role in the development of the modern short story.) While art editor Aubrey Beardsley's striking line-block illustrations remain as noteworthy as they were once notorious, the short-lived quarterly made its most lasting literary contributions through its promotion of the short story, a genre its authors redesigned to exploit and to expand the divide between the aesthetic and the commercial. Today, even the most specialized scholar of the Victorian period would be hard pressed to name any one of the stories published in *The Yellow Book*'s thirteen volumes from April 1894 to July 1897; but its association with the form has put beyond question its influence on not only the short story, but also literary magazines and the creative culture they sought to transform.

No history of the short story seems to be complete without some mention of *The Yellow Book*. Before short story collections emerged in the 1890s, the short story form was shaped in and by its periodical environments. Because a 'short story is always printed as part of a larger whole, either a collection of short stories or a magazine, which is a collection of various kinds of texts', as Mary Louise Pratt observes, 'individual short stories are usually read as part of a larger reading experience'.[1] From its inception the enemy of philistinism, *The Yellow Book* made an unlikely environment for cultivating such a popular, yet minor and ephemeral form. It was one that 'for much of the nineteenth century attracted little critical attention', with the result that, Harold Orel reasons, 'many Victorian authors regarded it with suspicion, as a diversion from more profitable novels and plays; even when prospering periodicals paid them decent wages for short stories that pleased readers, authors usually neglected to collect them and reprint them in hard covers'.[2] Before long, the three-decker novel had run its course: readers and writers were looking for something new. Addressing, perhaps even constructing, an elite bohemian readership, *The Yellow Book* insisted on distinguishing the short story for its sophistication and complexity.

While *The Yellow Book* was not the first or the last British periodical to claim an association with the form, it established a reputation for doing so. As bold as any of its literary experiments was its capacity to promote the myth of its experimentalism. Like the 'little magazines' it would influence to help fashion modernism into being, *The Yellow Book* made a reputation for opposing commercialism while championing the aesthetic experimentation of hitherto unknown writers. In reality, the journal was partly involved in changing perceptions, as it manufactured prestige for a form that had previously been regarded as entertainment.

The *fin de siècle* had introduced aestheticism, a movement that, before it was engulfed in the moral panic of the Wilde trials, championed art for its own sake. In its literary contents as in its visual art, *The Yellow Book* aligned itself with aestheticism through an exaggerated, ostentatious preoccupation with technique and an equally exaggerated, ostentatious aloofness from the market. In doing so, the quarterly negotiated its position in relation to emerging mass culture (and its literary manifestation in mass-circulation magazines) by striking a posture that was as retrograde as it was *avant garde*. Though it published writing by W. B. Yeats, H. G. Wells, Henry James, Edmund Gosse, Kenneth Grahame, George Gissing, John Buchan and Arnold Bennett – among other writers who would go on to command enduring reputations of varying distinction – *The Yellow Book* functioned as a vehicle for the now-forgotten authors who published with The Bodley Head. This groundbreaking periodical was thus a publisher's organ in the conventionally Victorian fashion that the *Cornhill* (1860–1975) was for George Murray Smith or *Macmillan's* (1859–1907) and *Cassell's* (1853–1932) were for their respective houses. Though its coterie consisted of Bodley Head authors, *The Yellow Book* had recognizable precedents in coterie productions such as the Pre-Raphaelite *Germ* (1850) and the *Century Guild Hobby Horse* (1884–94); yet, as the organ of a publishing house, it was not as anti-commercial as these predecessors or the little magazines it would influence.

Nevertheless, it was aggressively promoted as a break with convention, its stylish prospectus a manifesto for 'an Illustrated Magazine which shall be beautiful as a piece of bookmaking, modern and distinguished in its letterpress and its pictures, and withal popular in the better sense of the word'.[3] In the most literal sense of the word, however, short fiction – if not 'the' short story redefined by *The Yellow Book* – was already popular. By April 1894, when *The Yellow Book* debuted, nearly all periodicals were publishing short fiction. For a new generation of the allegedly literate created by recent, 'universal' educational reforms, the grubby weekly *Tit-Bits* (1881–1984), comprising fiction, humour, and news snipped from elsewhere, made a publishing magnate of George Newnes, whose instantaneous success with *The Strand* (1891–1951), an illustrated monthly that limited its fiction to short stories (including Arthur Conan Doyle's stories of Sherlock Holmes), spawned numerous imitators. Newnes was not the first to develop a strong identification for his magazines with particular kinds of short fiction, either. Without illustrations, short fiction had already established such a distinct association with monthlies such as *Blackwood's* (1817–1980) that Edgar Allan Poe – no casual observer of literary periodicals or short fiction – satirized its tales of gothic horror in both a parodic story and an essay claiming to describe 'How to Write a Blackwood Article'.[4] Still, the short fiction that occupied odd spaces in British periodicals, not to mention gift books and annuals, of the time posed little challenge to the three-volume novel that dominated British fiction.

By the 1880s, however, short stories had become so popular that even the new illustrated weekly newspapers favoured them over serials, though their frequent publication made them an ideal medium for serializing fiction. While the more established *Illustrated London News* (1842–1901) and the *Graphic* (1869–1932) continued to serialize novels as they introduced short stories, the state-of-the-art *Black and White* (1891–1912) made good on its advertisements of a 'complete short story (illustrated)' in each number, and the *Sketch* (1893–1959) offered a short story each week under the heading, 'A Novel in a Nutshell'. No matter their frequency or readership, British periodicals abounded with short fiction, which could be found in magazines for even the most esoteric interests, ranging from badminton to theosophy. Numerous new periodicals appeared, advertising their association with 'stories' in their titles. *Short Stories* (1890–1903), for example, billed itself as 'A Magazine of Select Fiction'.

For *The Yellow Book*, however, short stories were an editorial necessity. As a quarterly, it could not have sustained a readership for a serial over such a long interval. It aspired to the prestige of the *Edinburgh Review* (1802–1929) and the *Quarterly Review* (1809–1967), among other quarterlies whose high standards, intellectual heft and uncompromising discussions of important ideas made them British institutions. Where magazines were *magasins* of literary goods seeking to entertain, reviews, by contrast, proposed to instruct their readers. Their critical essays, book reviews and social commentary, like their occasional fiction and poetry, were, if not short, then self-contained. Though a quarterly, however, *The Yellow Book* was not a review *per se*. It did review literary currents in order to situate itself within them, but these infrequent essays were as often satiric as they were serious, and short stories supplanted them as its fortunes faltered.

Until then, *The Yellow Book* made a feature of its own non-commercialism. Appropriating the quarterly's non-commercialism as part of a marketing strategy, its prospectus emphasized that 'The Yellow Book will contain no advertisement other than publishers' lists', which in the early numbers included all of the Bodley Head's smartest competitors.[5] Yellow and a book, *The Yellow Book* set itself apart from even its most august periodical precedents. Moreover, though its subtitle billed it as 'An Illustrated Quarterly', what its first number's table of contents calls 'Pictures' make no pretence of illustrating its 'Letterpress'. Seeking to correct the convention established by popular illustrated magazines that made images ancillary to words, the *Yellow Book* made both words and images autonomous, to the point of reversing the imbalance by privileging illustrations with better paper, title pages and tissue guards. Not only did the 'Art' not serve as an aid to interpreting the 'Literature', but – sold unopened and requiring readers to cut open the pages in order to gain access to their contents – the magazine as physical object imitated the past to resist the process of its consumption.

Looking to the old to make it new, *The Yellow Book* reflected the cultural aspirations of its publisher, The Bodley Head, which exploited and created literary fashions that included its own mythology. Founded in 1887 by Elkin Mathews and John Lane to trade in antiquarian books, it began to publish stylish and (now) representative *fin-de-siècle* works in 1893. *The Yellow Book* was a commercial concern that created a diversion from its commercialism by asserting its literary value, as measured in the creative latitude it appeared to afford writers of short stories. Even its price, fixed at five shillings, one shilling less than the stalwart quarterly reviews but significantly more than the sixpenny illustrated monthlies, signalled its position, negotiating the yawning chasm between the Victorian past and the modernist future, mass culture and high art. The minute calculations that pursuing this aspiration demanded can be seen in the prominence *The Yellow Book* assigned to established men of letters such as Edmund Gosse, Arthur Waugh and Richard Garnett.

In this negotiation between commerce and art, Henry James occupies a definitive if not constitutive role. Author at the time of ten novels that included *The Portrait of a Lady* (1881) and *The Bostonians* (1885–6), James found his work increasingly difficult to market to a public that found it obscure. The accelerated transactions of periodical publishing exaggerated this problem, as did the failure of his only play, *Guy Domville* (1895). *The Yellow Book* would capitalize on James's unique combination of unpopularity and eminence to advertise its own aloofness from the market. Appropriately, each of the three long tales James would publish in *The Yellow Book* recounts the struggles of a literary artist against the market. The psychological realism, minimal action and relative compression of these tales would achieve their full expression in *The Wings of the Dove* (1902) and *The Golden Bowl* (1904), the challenging masterpieces of his mature period.

With contradictory connotations – respectability, difficulty and unpopularity – James's work embodied a potent fusion for *The Yellow Book* to appropriate. For this reason, the formal properties of his fiction at the time were just as valuable as his reputation. At the front of the first volume, 'The Death of the Lion' literally sets the tone for the quarterly's fiction. At nearly 15,000 words, its conspicuous length disrupts the standard to which other periodicals had habituated readers (5,000 to 7,000 words) – just enough to be read in a sitting. The prospectus's warning that 'complete stories will sometimes run to a considerable length in themselves' implied that the conventional word count would be yet another of 'the limitations of the old-fashioned periodical' that *The Yellow Book* would defy.[6] Authors' correspondence, memoirs and even the entrepreneurial how-to-write manuals cited this as evidence of its liberating allegiance to literary Art. The first *Yellow Book*'s prose fiction ranges from an unremarkable 4,000 words to James's maximum, but most stories in fact run the typical length, just as they would in subsequent issues. At 24,000 words, 'The Coxon Fund', which closes the second issue, would be *The Yellow Book*'s longest item in any genre. Both tales appear in James's *Terminations* (1895), a quartet of metafictions that expose a *fin-de-siècle* literary culture in which periodicals tied to immediate sale are seen as necessarily inimical to Art.

The relationship of the unappreciated genius struggling against the degradations of the emerging mass market – famously satirized in George Gissing's *New Grub Street* (1891) – became a prominent theme in *The Yellow Book*, almost a story sub-genre. Every member of its supposed 'school' contributed at least one such story. Literary editor Henry Harland published many, which he would complement via the masked diatribes of 'the Yellow Dwarf'. This theme became such a fixture that contributors would parody it within the same pages. After three years' ostentatious, exaggerated devotion 'to what in English must be called the "short story"', the protagonist of 'A Chef-d'Oeuvre' wills himself to die after finding his self-declared masterpiece rejected by a benighted editor.[7] Written by Reginald Turner, one of Oscar Wilde's circle, and published towards the end of the quarterly's three-year print run, this portrait of the artist of the short story as a victim of periodical publishing might be regarded as an allegory for *The Yellow Book* itself.

Literary editor Henry Harland, whose closest collaborators at the time remembered him decades after his death in 1905 as something of a living parody of James, was also an American expatriate.[8] Harland had a flair for reinvention and self-promotion. Having professed himself an acolyte of James, Harland – through his editing, editorializing and lionizing – amplified James's influence. Before Harland arrived in London in 1889, he had, until exposed as a fraud by a journalist, enjoyed modest success in the States as 'Sidney Luska', publishing sensational novels on Jewish themes, novels he attempted (and failed) to suppress during *The Yellow Book* years. He also claimed aristocratic English ancestry, and for some years after his death his wife Aline styled herself 'Lady Harland' in correspondence. Not until *The Yellow Book* had expired would he achieve broad popularity, and not through short stories, but novels heavily perfumed with the incense of Catholic subjects, most notably *The Cardinal's Snuff-Box* (1900).

Until then, each of the thirteen *Yellow Books* included one of Harland's own stories, which The Bodley Head repackaged as *Grey Roses* (1895) and *Comedies and Errors* (1898). These oscillated between witty tales of artistic life in the Parisian Latin Quarter and, as James observed in an obligatory review praising the latter volume, witty romances 'all whimsical and picturesque, of palace secrets, rulers and pretenders and ministers of bewilderingly light comedy, in undiscoverable Balkan states, Bohemias of the seaboard, where queens have platonic friendships with professional English, though not American, humourists'.[9] As the editor of one *Yellow Book* retrospective compilation explains, justifying his own selections, 'Henry Harland has been placed high up [in the table of contents] because that is where he generally put himself'.[10] Under pseudonyms, Harland is believed to have published two additional stories whose darker themes do not luxuriate in cosmopolitan wit.[11]

Under Harland's editorship, *The Yellow Book* insisted on its cosmopolitanism. Its Continental literary associations manifested themselves in two stories untranslated from the French, by Anatole France and the Serbian Prince

Bojidar Karageorgevich; by contrast, English translations by *Yellow Book* regulars accompanied a smattering of poems in French, in the manner of recent French Symbolists. This practice was amplified in such competing periodicals as *Cosmopolis* (1896–8), subtitled *An International Monthly Review* and published in English, French, German and later Russian by T. Fisher Unwin, a rival to The Bodley Head. Yet *The Yellow Book* also exaggerated its own cosmopolitanism. One way it did so was by questioning the taste of the British reading public in its denunciations of popular short fiction. As *The Yellow Book*'s fortunes faltered, Harland's 'Yellow Dwarf' persona functioned to drum up publicity, and also to shame the 'imbecile ... Anglo-Saxon Public' for favouring inferior periodicals, and their standardization of the short story. While he savaged George du Maurier and Marie Corelli for their sensationally successful novels, he saved his most vicious diatribes for Arthur Conan Doyle, L. T. Meade and others who made long careers and large fortunes from a short and minor form of prose fiction. Britain abounds with 'nice people who have read Mr Conan Doyle! And ... nice people who do not read Mr James!'[12] His fury would not subside with *The Yellow Book*. When a fourteenth *Yellow Book* would have appeared but failed to do so in July 1897, Harland unleashed a diatribe on 'the Average Man' in an essay nominally 'Concerning the Short Story', his only signed, public remarks on a form that defined – and was defined by – the literary contents of his now-defunct magazine.

Harland was not *The Yellow Book*'s sole champion of the short story. Lena Milman, best known then and now as a translator of Tolstoy and Dostoevsky, laments the 'contempt for the short story prevalent in England, but unknown elsewhere' because 'we are too apt to regard the short story as a cartoon for a possible novel'. In an essay on 'Mr Henry James', she cites as a national characteristic the resistance to the 'beautiful suggestion' of 'passing emotions, those elusive impressions' that she claims only the short story is capable of preserving.[13] In an earlier *Yellow Book*, Hubert Crackanthorpe had already challenged the British penchant for 'Reticence in Fiction', and the British failure to recognize that 'fiction has taken her place among the arts'.[14] By the time he was writing in *The Yellow Book*, his *Wreckage* (1893) was already recognized as 'one of the sensations of the period', and as editor of the *Albemarle* (1892), a monthly review that did not survive a year, he had an ideal vantage point of the literary market. It should be recognized that impatience with the British reading public was neither original nor unique to *The Yellow Book*. Distinguishing the short story 'as a medium for the exercise of the finer art', Frederick Wedmore, who published with

The Bodley Head but never in *The Yellow Book*, echoed Milman's sentiments about the British preference for the 'novel in a nutshell'.[15] This impression of the form was so entrenched that the *Sketch*, an illustrated newspaper that had begun publication in 1893, continued to print its weekly short story under the heading of 'A Novel in a Nutshell' well into the twentieth century.

Given this tendency, unfavourable comparisons with French sophistication are predictable; and, as technologies of production and distribution extended readerships beyond national boundaries, the United States emerged as an equally important rival and example. A typically invidious comparison was that of Robert Barr, longtime co-editor of the illustrated monthly *Idler* and a regular contributor to *The Strand*, who complained in 1897 that 'the English reader of short stories ... insists upon being fed with a spoon. He wants all the goods in the shop window ticketed with the price in plain figures. I think the reader should use a little intellect in reading a story, just as the author is supposed to use a great deal in the writing of it'.[16] Barr, a Canadian, had begun his career in the United States, where a longer tradition of periodical publishing had accustomed readers to short stories and thus to their suggestion by omission. It was this tradition that Harland brought with him to London in 1889, a tradition that could not help informing his work on *The Yellow Book*. Indeed, James complemented this kind of cosmopolitanism. Consistent with his contemporaries in and outside *The Yellow Book*, James's unappreciated geniuses are British, unappreciated to death by a public of British publishers, reviewers and readers.

After James, George Egerton may have been the most valuable contributor to the inaugural *Yellow Book*'s literary contents. As an Irish writer whose life on three continents explicitly informs her fiction, Egerton embodied the cosmopolitanism to which *The Yellow Book* aspired, but she was much more important for her notoriety as a New Woman. Four months before *The Yellow Book* made its debut, her book of short stories, *Keynotes* (1893), scandalized literary London with its frank treatment of female sexual desire and, naturally, stimulated an immediate sensation. In part because of the publication of *Keynotes* late in the previous year, 1894 was the year of the New Woman, an appellation brought to controversial notice by Sarah Grand in a newspaper debate only a month before *The Yellow Book*'s debut.[17] Already notorious for *The Heavenly Twins* (1893), Grand would collect six 'Stories from Life' that she had previously published in the *Pall Mall Magazine*, the *Temple Bar*, and other magazines into *Our Manifold Nature* (1894). Like Grand's novels, and the pioneering series of vignettes that comprise Olive Schreiner's *The Story of an African Farm* (1883) (originally published under the pseudonym

'Ralph Iron'), Egerton's *Keynotes* continues to be recognized among the most important *fin-de-siècle* texts by women. As if to underscore its modernness, every one of its nine stories is narrated in the present tense. The stories' repetitive style, together with their essentialist assumptions about 'eternal womanhood', made them easy targets for parody, as *Punch* demonstrated in 'She-Notes' by 'Borgia Smudgiton, with Japanese Fan de Siècle Illustrations by Mortharthurio Whiskersly' (Aubrey Beardsley had supplied the illustrations for the cover of Egerton's *Keynotes*).[18] That Egerton had attracted such notice by the quintessentially Victorian *Punch* indicates the magnitude of the mainstream anxiety that her stories, in form and content, had engendered.

Inevitably, The Bodley Head capitalized on Egerton's notoriety. *Keynotes* was such a sensation that it launched a series that includes Egerton's *Discords* (1894) among its nineteen volumes of short stories and fourteen novels, a proportion that indicates the short story's role in The Bodley Head's fortunes. Published in book form unlike rival periodicals, *The Yellow Book* and this 'Keynotes' series share many obvious bibliographical similarities, including book lists and bold title-page designs by Beardsley. The series prominently included Egerton's two short story collections; she also contributed two short stories to *The Yellow Book*. Dispensing with both the overt femininity and the present-tense narration that had made *Keynotes* so notable, each of these metafictional contributions to *The Yellow Book* laments a perceived masterpiece that never made its way to paper. The first of these, 'A Lost Masterpiece' ironically shares a subject with 'The Death of the Lion', in which a masterpiece is lost by hapless aristocrats and their underlings who care only for connections not to the master's genius but to his fame. At the height of her own fame, Egerton's sketch is a dramatic monologue narrated by a man in town for 'business', who pompously revels in and then curses the loss of his 'darling brain-child', an 'embryo of genius' and 'dainty elusive birthling' to a stranger whose crime is to be an aesthetically displeasing woman in public.[19] Fusing misogyny with maternity in the creative process, the story subverts the myth of tortured male genius exalted in stories by James and others. Still, Egerton's continuing value to *The Yellow Book* is apparent from a sketch of her as number 3 in a series of 'Bodley Heads' in the April 1895 *Yellow Book*: in words and pictures, The Bodley Head found innovative ways to deploy Egerton's fame to advertise its own associations with the New Woman and the short story.

While the Keynotes series varied greatly in subject matter, and most of its volumes were in fact written by men, it is persistently identified with the

New Woman. Excluding Milman's translation of Dostoevsky's *Poor Folk* (Keynotes 3), thirteen of the thirty-three volumes are by women. Among these, Evelyn Sharp, Netta Syrett and Victoria Cross(e) contributed short stories to *The Yellow Book* as well as a first novel to Keynotes. Both Sharp and Syrett got their big breaks with multiple stories in *The Yellow Book* while employed as schoolteachers. As Keynotes 13 and 21, Sharp's *At the Relton Arms* (1895) and Syrett's *Nobody's Fault* (1896) began long, prolific novel-writing careers for both women, which for Sharp combined writing for children with her work as a prominent suffragist. As 'Victoria Cross', Annie Sophie Cory contributed to *The Yellow Book* the supposedly racy 'Theodora' before creating a greater sensation for Keynotes as 'Victoria Crosse' with *Consummation*, which The Bodley Head retitled *The Woman Who Didn't* (1895) and marketed as a rejoinder to Grant Allen's *The Woman Who Did* (1895), whose title refers to its protagonist, an intellectually and sexually liberated woman who, though pregnant, refuses on principle to marry. While Allen published short fiction in virtually all the popular periodicals of the day – as he lay dying in 1899, it was Arthur Conan Doyle who finished his last story for *The Strand* – his stories never appeared in *The Yellow Book*, though his controversial best-seller was Keynotes 8. The sensation it caused prompted The Bodley Head to enlist him as one of only four authors to publish two volumes in the series. Apart from Egerton, the other two are also men: the horror pioneer Arthur Machen and the fabulist M. P. Shiel. Although most of these authors contributed novels, and the men generally did not share Allen's overt support of feminism, Keynotes, like *The Yellow Book*, seemed to yoke aestheticism and the New Woman together, through the medium of the short story.

Apart from its association with the New Woman, *The Yellow Book* lacked the political engagement of its predecessors (among the quarterlies it imitated) and its successors (among the little magazines it influenced). Even now, critical opinion remains divided about *The Yellow Book*'s proto-feminist commitments. While Sally Ledger and Linda Hughes maintain the autonomy the quarterly gave women writers, Laurel Brake concludes that its sexual politics were on the whole misogynistic.[20] What is beyond dispute is that the quarterly provided a significant platform for women's writing. Volume 10 (July 1896) may have been the only *Yellow Book* to which female and male writers contributed in equal numbers; but several others, especially the later issues, came close.

If James and Egerton exemplify the extremes of respectability and sensationalism in the balance *The Yellow Book* attempted to strike, the tormented-genius plot and the marriage-problem plot associated with each of them characterized the quarterly's fiction in a less oppositional contrast. Long or short, marriage-problem plots radically challenged the convention of the Victorian novel that ends in a wedding, simply by depicting what happens after the happily-ever-after ending. Denied the right to earn their own livings, middle-class women were forced into marriages that could prove miserable for both spouses. In Edwardian novels, the marriage-problem plot would become synonymous with the New Woman novel, but *The Yellow Book* made a convention of it in shorter forms. Some stories, such as Crackanthorpe's 'The Haseltons' and H. B. Marriott Watson's 'The Dead Wall', quite literally marry the marriage-problem plot to the tormented-genius plot. So does Ella D'Arcy's 'Irremediable', which appeared in the first *Yellow Book*. In this story, a promising writer weds a coarse and manipulative – but sexually irresistible – woman, who ruins his life. Scoffing at his 'rubbishing stories', she is a misogynistic caricature of the harpy whose negligent housekeeping exacerbates her illiterate, incurious mind.[21] In her capacity as the *Yellow Book*'s sub-editor, and by association with her friends Sharp and Syrett, D'Arcy is often classified as a New Woman; but stories like 'Irremediable' reveal a more ambivalent attitude.

No writer was more closely associated with the Decadent movement than Oscar Wilde, The Bodley Head's most famous author. The English translation of his one-act play *Salomé* (1894) bore illustrations by Aubrey Beardsley – as did the Keynotes series – that shocked with their ambiguous yet explicit eroticism. From the planning stages, Beardsley and Harland had agreed to exclude Wilde from *The Yellow Book*, which nonetheless capitalized upon the association as long as it could. After all, its yellow clothbound cover was modelled after French railway novels and reminiscent of the 'poisonous' yellow book that corrupts the protagonist of *The Picture of Dorian Gray*. However, the same association nearly ended *The Yellow Book* when Wilde was arrested for sodomy on 6 April 1895, days before the fifth *Yellow Book* was supposed to hit the stands. As numerous newspapers reported, he was clutching a yellow book. Though it was a French novel and not *The Yellow Book*, the damage was done.

In the aftermath of Wilde's arrest, Lane – feeling the pressure of public opinion – sacked Beardsley, who was strongly associated with Wilde, and Beardsley promptly took over the *Savoy* with Arthur Symons, the English proponent of French Symbolism whose 'Stella Maris', a lyric addressed to a prostitute, had appeared in the first *Yellow Book* the previous year. Universally regarded as superior to *The Yellow Book*, the *Savoy*'s notoriety accelerated its quarterly frequency to monthly, but it expired before *The Yellow Book*, having survived for only eight issues in 1896. It did not limit its prose fiction to short stories, serializing Beardsley's illustrated 'Romantic Novel', *Under the Hill*, in addition to poems by Yeats and Symons and essays by George Bernard Shaw and Edmund Gosse, as well as short stories by Ernest Dowson and Frederick Wedmore. Published by Leonard Smithers, known for erotica and curiosities including one (perhaps apocryphal) volume bound in human skin, the *Savoy* was more properly a little magazine doomed never to expand its reach beyond a decadent coterie, which had all but evaporated after the Wilde scandal.

If *The Yellow Book* had a literary coterie, it was an incestuous one – as, effectively, The Bodley Head's house journal – and its fortunes dwindled precipitously as its shock-value faded. Not long before the magazine's last edition, *The Times* yawned that 'principle upon which THE YELLOW BOOK is edited would seem to be that at intervals of every three months a section of the reading public is seized with a craving for fresh work by Mr Henry Harland, Miss Ella D'Arcy, and others of the little school of writers whom the Bodley Head has brought into notice'.[22] This description had some basis in truth. As the Yellow Dwarf, Harland promoted not only James's *Terminations*, but also D'Arcy's *Monochromes* and his own *Grey Roses*, stories from *The Yellow Book* and other periodicals conveniently converted into Keynotes 12 and 10 in 1895.

Beyond this coterie, there was a looser 'little school' associated with *The Yellow Book*, which included many professional writers who contributed to competing periodicals, which some of them edited. In 1892 alone, Crackanthorpe had edited the short-lived *Albemarle*, while William Sharp (whose poems in *The Yellow Book* are ascribed to 'Fiona McLeod') edited the even shorter-lived *Pagan Review*, neither of which survived the year. *Fin-de-siècle* London was a lively environment for periodical publication, which made cross-pollination inevitable. Richard Le Gallienne, a reader for The Bodley Head whose 'Prose Fancies' appeared in almost every *Yellow Book*, contributed to a bewildering range of periodicals, including the *Westminster Gazette* and *Realm*, as well as the general-interest *Nineteenth Century*, when he was not reviewing his cronies' books as 'Logroller' for the *Star* and other magazines. And Harland, for all of his public snobbery, contributed to many of the popular periodicals he considered 'miles below the YB standard' stories indistinguishable from those he ran in *The Yellow Book*.[23]

The identity and coherence of *The Yellow Book* was also targeted by rival publications. Situating itself against *Yellow Book*'s perceived decadence, the *New Review* (1889–97) recruited the respected, influential William Ernest Henley to bring his 'regatta' of young writers to bolster English realism in 1895. This new *New Review* published *The Nigger of the 'Narcissus'* by Joseph Conrad, whose 'The Idiots' appeared the same year in the *Savoy*, in addition to such contributors to *The Yellow Book* as H. G. Wells, Arthur Waugh, and even Beardsley, whose essay about advertising billboards appeared in the *New Review* at the height of *The Yellow Book*'s initial sensation.

Time seems to have gilded *The Yellow Book*, especially for those who had achieved massive commercial success after passing through its pages only once. Collecting his stories, H. G. Wells praised 'the generous opportunities of the *Yellow Book*' for launching his career as a serious writer when it published 'A Slip Under the Microscope' in 1896.[24] Likewise fondly recalling his 'Yellerbocky days', Arnold Bennett claims it was not until *The Yellow Book* published his 'A Letter Home' in 1895 that 'I saw that I could *write*'. Clarifying his italics, Bennett describes how publishing 'this jewel, this caviare-to-the-general', where he published it, had transformed him into an artist: 'I had just discovered that I could write – and when I use the term "write" here, I use it in the special sense, to be appreciated only by those elect who can themselves "write", and difficult of comprehension by all others'.[25] Already appreciated by the elect as difficult of comprehension, Henry James agreed. He had privately condemned *The Yellow Book* to his brother William for 'the horrid aspect and company of the whole publication', but did not take long to change his mind.[26] Not only did he oblige 'the worshipful Harland' with two more stories and an essay, but in the preface to the volume of his 1908 New York Edition that includes all three of the stories he published in *The Yellow Book*, James pronounced it 'the sweetest aid to inspiration ever snatched by a poor scribbler from editorial lips', because it 'offered licence that, on the spot, opened up the millennium to the short story'.[27] James's association of the form with Harland confirms the recollections of Ella D'Arcy and Ethel Colburn Mayne, the quarterly's sub-editors, as well as Richard Le Gallienne, The Bodley Head's reader, whose memoirs coalesce in anecdotes of Harland 'excitedly propounding the *dernier mot* on the build of the short story or the art of prose'.[28]

James recalled the short story being the 'object of almost extravagant dissertation' in the 1890s. *The Yellow Book*, invoked in his review of Harland's stories, was central to this extravagant dissertation, which (paradoxically) informed mainstream recognition of the form's rarified poetics.

As Robert Scholes and Clifford Wulfman declare in the online Modernist Journals Project, 'modernism began in the magazines'.[29] For serializing Joyce's *Ulysses* (1918–20), among its many achievements, the avant-garde American *Little Review* (1914–22) is one of modernism's most important magazines, and its founder, Margaret Anderson, cited *The Yellow Book* among its chief influences: 'look at the "Yellow Book." You can look at it on the library shelves of almost any book lover, richly bound, and rated among his more precious possessions'.[30] The *English Review* (1908–13) was conceived by Ford Madox Hueffer as 'an *aube de siècle* Yellow Book';[31] similarly, John Middleton Murry had founded *Rhythm* (1911–13), later the *Blue Review* (1913), as 'the *Yellow Book* for the modern movement'.[32] *Rhythm*, the first journal in Britain to publish a print by Picasso, also published short stories by D. H. Lawrence and Katherine Mansfield, who became Murry's spouse as well as his assistant editor. Concentrating on the theory of rhythm in the arts, it was a precursor to the Vorticists, who published two issues of *BLAST* (1914–15) with The Bodley Head before perishing in the outbreak of the First World War. The Bodley Head also published the even more esoteric *Form* (1916–22), and both magazines included advertisements for issues of the dormant *Yellow Book*. As Sean Latham and Robert Scholes have influentially reminded scholars of periodicals, 'The rise of cultural studies enables us to see this distinction [between art and commerce] as artificial, since high literature, art, and advertising have mingled in periodicals from the earliest years, and major authors have been published in magazines little and big'.[33] For those who wrote, edited and published little magazines, however, this distinction defined modernism.

Unlike their precursor, none of these little magazines restricted themselves to short stories, which were nevertheless crucial to the 'aesthetic of difficulty' that, according to Adrian Hunter, made the form so amenable to modernist poetics.[34] *The Yellow Book* may have ceased publication in 1897, but its legacy has endured: no study of the short story form, of the period, or of literary periodicals can fail to mention the vivid quarterly. (*The Yellow Book* continues to thrive as the digital cornerstone of *The Yellow Nineties Online*, a scholarly archive in 'homage to the innovative publishing spirit of the 1890s'.[35]) Declaring the decade 'the yellow nineties', Holbrook Jackson pronounced *The Yellow Book* 'newness *in excelsis*: novelty naked and unashamed. People were puzzled and shocked and delighted, and yellow became the colour of the hour, the symbol of the time-spirit. It was associated with all that was *bizarre* and queer in art and life, with all that was outrageously modern.'[36] If anything, the 1890s were even more colourful, with absinthe and aniline dyes tinting gazes and gauzy frocks green and mauve in the causes of Decadence and mass production. *The Yellow Book* encompassed both apparent extremes, setting an example for modernist media and art, whose literary epitome was the short story. By 1937 Elizabeth Bowen could claim, introducing the *Faber Book of Modern Stories*, that 'within the last fifteen years, the non-commercial or free short story – that is to say, the story unsuitable, not meant to be suitable, for the popular, well-paying magazines, and free, therefore, not to conform with so-called popular taste – has found a wider opening: it has come to have an eclectic vogue'.[37] Always at the mercy of the environments in which it is published, the short story had always been eclectic, but it took *The Yellow Book* to bring it into vogue. In so doing, it may well have been what its prospectus had dared to claim: 'the most interesting, unusual, and most important publication of its kind that has ever been undertaken'.[38]

Notes

1. Mary Louise Pratt, 'The Long and the Short of It', in *The New Short Story Theories*, ed. Charles E. May (Athens, OH: Ohio University Press, 1994), pp. 91–113 (pp. 103–4).
2. Harold Orel, *The Victorian Short Story* (Cambridge University Press, 1986), p. ix.
3. 'Announcement', quoted in Katherine Lyon Mix, *A Study in Yellow: 'The Yellow Book' and Its Contributors* (Lawrence, KS: University of Kansas Press, 1960), pp. 77–9 (pp. 77–8).
4. 'How to Write a Blackwood Article' was published in 1838 in the *American Museum of Science, Literature and the Arts* with 'The Psyche Zenobia', which was retitled in subsequent republications and now most frequently anthologized as 'A Predicament'. See *Complete Stories and Poems of Edgar Allan Poe* (New York: Doubleday, 1966), pp. 320–7, 327–34.
5. 'Announcement', quoted in Mix, *A Study in Yellow*, p. 79.
6. Ibid., p. 78.
7. Reginald Turner, 'A Chef-d'Oeuvre', *The Yellow Book*, 11 (October 1896), pp. 237–47 (p. 242).
8. See Ella D'Arcy, '*Yellow Book* Celebrities', *ELT: English Literature in Transition, 1880–1920*, 27.1 (1994), pp. 33–7 (p. 36); and Richard Le Gallienne, *The Romantic '90s* (New York: Doubleday, Page & Co., 1925), p. 228.
9. Henry James, 'The Story-Teller at Large: Mr Henry Harland', *Fortnightly Review*, 69 (April 1898), pp. 650–4 (p. 654).
10. Norman Denny, 'Selector's Note', *The 'Yellow Book': A Selection* (London: The Bodley Head, 1949) n. pag.

11. Mix speculates that Harland contributed additional stories as 'Robert Shews' and 'Samuel Mathewson Scott'. See *A Study in Yellow*, p. 230.
12. 'The Yellow Dwarf', 'A Birthday Letter', *The Yellow Book*, 9 (April 1896), pp. 11–22; 'Dogs, Cats, Books, and the Average Man', *The Yellow Book*, 10 (July 1896), pp. 11–23.
13. Lena Milman, 'Mr Henry James', *The Yellow Book*, 7 (October 1895), p. 71–83. (p. 72).
14. Hubert Crackanthorpe, 'Reticence in Fiction: Some Roundabout Remarks', *The Yellow Book*, 2 (July 1894), pp. 259–69 (p. 268).
15. Frederick Wedmore, 'The Short Story', *The Nineteenth Century*, 43 (1898), pp. 406–16 (pp. 406, 407).
16. Robert Barr, 'How to Write a Short Story (Symposium)', *Bookman*, 36 (October 1897), pp. 369–72 (p. 371).
17. Sarah Grand, 'A New Aspect of the Woman Question', *The North American Review* 158.448 (1894), pp. 270–6.
18. 'She-', *Punch, or the London Charivari*, 10 March 1894, p. 109.
19. George Egerton, 'A Lost Masterpiece: A City Mood, Aug. '93', *The Yellow Book*, 1 (April 1894), pp. 189–96.
20. Sally Ledger, 'Wilde Women and the *Yellow Book*: The Sexual Politics of Aestheticism and Decadence', *ELT: English Literature in Transition, 1880–1920*, 50.1 (2007), pp. 5–26; Linda K. Hughes, 'Women Poets and Contested Spaces in the *Yellow Book*', *SEL: Studies in English Literature, 1500–1900*, 44.4 (2004), pp. 849–72; and Laurel Brake, 'Endgames: The Politics of *The Yellow Book* or, Decadence, Gender and the New Journalism', *Essays and Studies*, 48 (1995), pp. 38–64.
21. Ella D'Arcy, 'Irremediable', *The Yellow Book*, 1 (April 1894), pp. 87–110 (p. 104).
22. 'Short Notices', *The Times*, January 29 1897, 14B.
23. Henry Harland to John Lane, 22 October, 1895, Texas. Quoted in Winnie Chan, *The Economy of the Short Story in British Periodicals of the 1890s* (London: Routledge, 2007), p. 67.
24. H. G. Wells, Introduction, *'The Country of the Blind' and Other Stories* (London: Thomas Nelson and Sons, 1913), pp. iii–ix (p. v).
25. Arnold Bennett, *The Truth about an Author* (New York: George H. Doran Co., 1911), pp. 65, 62.
26. Letter to William James, 28 May 1894, *The Letters of Henry James*, ed. Percy Lubbock (New York: Scribner, 1920), pp. 216–17.
27. Henry James, *The Art of Fiction* (Boston: Northeastern University Press, 1984), p. 219.
28. Le Gallienne, *The Romantic '90s*. See also Ella D'Arcy, 'Yellow Book Celebrities', *ELT: English Literature in Transition, 1880–1920*, 27.1 (1994), pp. 33–7.
29. Robert Scholes and Clifford Wulfman, 'Modernism in the Magazines – The Case of Visual Art', in *Modernism in the Magazines: An Introduction*

(New Haven: Yale University Press, 2010), quoted in 'About the MJP Slogan', *Modernist Journals Project*, www.modjourn.org (accessed 31 May 2015).
30. Margaret C. Anderson, *My Thirty Years' War* (London: Knopf, 1930), p. 40.
31. Ford Madox Ford, *Thus to Revisit: Some Reminiscences by Ford Madox Hueffer* (New York: E. P. Dutton, 1921), p. 48.
32. John Middleton Murry, *Between Two Worlds: An Autobiography* (London: Jonathan Cape, 1935), p. 275.
33. Sean Latham and Robert Scholes, 'The Rise of Periodical Studies', *PMLA*, 121.2 (2006), pp. 517–31 (p. 519).
34. Adrian Hunter, 'The Short Story and the Difficulty of Modernism', in *Modernism, Postmodernism, and the Short Story in English*, ed. Jorge Sacido (Amsterdam: Rodopi, 2012), pp. 29–46 (p. 29).
35. Lorraine Janzen Kooistra and Dennis Denisoff, 'Introduction to the Yellow Nineties', in *The Yellow Nineties Online*, 2012 (accessed 30 May 2015).
36. Holbrook Jackson, *The Eighteen Nineties* (London: Penguin, 1913), p. 46.
37. Elizabeth Bowen, 'Introduction: The Short Story', in *The Faber Book of Modern Stories*, ed. Elizabeth Bowen (London: Faber, 1937), p. 13.
38. 'Announcement', quoted in Mix, *A Study in Yellow*, pp. 78–9.

8

The Modernist Short Story: Fractured Perspectives

CLAIRE DREWERY

The literary term 'epiphany', in its original inception in James Joyce's draft-novel *Stephen Hero* (c.1901–6), has become synonymous in critical accounts of modernism with the moment of transcendent insight, intensity of experience or revelation. In a literary movement in which a prevalent aesthetic aim was the representation of a reality beyond appearances and below material surfaces, the significant moment came to epitomize the endeavour to capture, however fleetingly, the 'truth' of subjective experience. It is noteworthy, however, that the version of Joyce's novel published in 1916 as *A Portrait of the Artist as a Young Man* drops any overt reference to the epiphany, and its depiction is frequently problematized by elliptical, fragmented language. The revelatory moment, this chapter will claim, may thus be interpreted in terms of tension and contradiction as opposed to conveying a transcendent insight.

Whilst the epiphany first receives its name in *Stephen Hero*, it was to become a structural and aesthetic marker of modernism in general and of the short story form in particular. The moment of epiphany around which modernist short stories have traditionally been seen to pivot is closely associated with the oblique, experimental narrative styles that were distinct from the rich, descriptive canvas of Victorian realism. As modernist writers began to privilege impressionistic, ambiguous depictions of subjective consciousness over the didacticism, materialism and omniscient narration of literary realism, the breakdown of the serialized Victorian novel was superseded by an increased dissemination of short fiction through the literary magazines in which it was frequently published. The emergence of new periodicals such as *The Yellow Book, The New Age, The Savoy* and *The Dome* promoted the short story form, as well as various modernist movements, by publishing the work of authors whose work they viewed as avant-garde and experimental. *The New Age*, for instance, published the work of H. G. Wells and G. B. Shaw, as well as several examples of Katherine Mansfield's early work. It also had feminist affiliations with magazines such as *The Freewoman* (1911–12), *The New Freewoman* (1913) and *The Egoist* (1914–19), which later superseded *The Freewoman* and was presided over by Rebecca West and later Ezra Pound.

Despite the apparent symbiosis emerging in the period between modernism, the epiphanic trope and the brevity of the short story form, however, the notion of the epiphany as an aesthetic of *dis*unity is gaining in critical currency. Dominic Head, for instance, identifies a 'non-epiphany principle' in Joyce's stories and José María Díaz similarly notes that canonical modernism 'abounds in failed, missed or truncated epiphanies'.[1] Díaz has further questioned the pervasive critical view of the modernist text as a mimesis of an 'inherently fragmented' modernity, suggesting, conversely, that modern experience is 'overwhelmingly unified and oppressively self-coherent' (p. 51). This apparent dichotomy is continually negotiated and on occasion exploited through the aesthetic of the epiphany, which typically encapsulates a tension between surface impressions comprising material, corporeal experience and the 'reality' defined by Joyce's Stephen Dedalus as a 'sudden spiritual manifestation': a unity of form capable of revealing cosmic, universal truths.[2]

The modernist short story writers I discuss – James Joyce, May Sinclair, Virginia Woolf, Katherine Mansfield and Wyndham Lewis – share similar aesthetic aims in rejecting traditional notions of subjective reality, but their work conveys widely differing attitudes to formal innovation. The stories of the canonical modernists Joyce and Woolf, for instance, typically work against Edgar Allan Poe's definition of the 'ideal' attributes of short fiction in his review of Nathaniel Hawthorne's *Twice-Told Tales* (1837): brevity of form and a sense of closure. Their writing does, however, uphold Poe's view that a chief aim of literature should be 'the development of all points of thought or expression which have their basis in Truth', and their stories further appear to embrace 'the unity of effect or impression' he favours in the short story form.[3]

For Woolf, the importance of unity as an aesthetic aim in her short fiction is noted in a diary entry of January 1920 in which she envisaged her two stories 'Kew Gardens' and 'An Unwritten Novel' 'taking hands and dancing in unity'. To this end, although she is unable to predict the precise form the unity will take, she sees 'immense possibilities' in the short story.[4] Woolf's experimentation with modernist narrative forms was further made possible by a cultural and aesthetic shift in the early twentieth century, enabling new perspectives on truth, reality and literary representations of individual consciousness. In her 1924 essay 'Mr Bennett and Mrs Brown', she claimed that changes in human character and relations 'in or about December 1910' brought about a corresponding shift in 'religion, conduct, politics, and literature'.[5] That Woolf places this shift to coincide with Roger Fry's first Post-Impressionist art exhibition is illustrative of a wider dialogue in the period between the fracturing of traditional assumptions about social and subjective identity, and their representations in literature and art.

Like Woolf, the modernist author May Sinclair endeavoured to formulate aesthetic techniques through which the subjective experience of reality might be represented. Now largely forgotten, Sinclair was a best-selling author of her day whose versatile literary output, including criticism, philosophy, poetry and experimental fiction, now frequently falls between the established categories of literary modernism. In terms of her contribution to dominant modernist paradigms she is perhaps best remembered for recasting the psychological novel as 'stream of consciousness' narrative, a term she adopted from William James's *Principles of Psychology* in a 1918 review of Dorothy Richardson's *Pilgrimage*.[6]

Yet Sinclair's representations of what she termed the 'ultimate reality' or 'Absolute' were also influenced by early twentieth century shifts in philosophical and scientific discourses. In *A Defence of Idealism* (1917), a study opposing the New Realist school of philosophical thought which rejected metaphysical interpretations of reality, Sinclair asserts that 'there is no sort of necessity to go out and look for multiplicity and change if you have got them all around you. I want to know what, if anything, lies behind or at the bottom of multiplicity and change.'[7] This goal, through which Sinclair believed a spiritual reality might be articulated, was conceivably informed by her interest in Freudian theories of sublimation – most notably '"Civilized" Sexual Morality and Modern Nervous Illness' (1908), 'On Narcissism' (1914) and *The Ego and the Id* (1923) – which in Freud's definition involved the deflection of 'sexual instinctual forces away from their sexual aim to higher cultural aims'.[8]

The writing of Katherine Mansfield, who unusually worked solely within the short story form, is less formally experimental than that of Woolf or Joyce but her epiphanies are nonetheless elusive in their satirical depiction of the subtle social discourses governing individual consciousness. Such an interrogation is again made possible through an epochal shift in humanist beliefs about subjective construction following thinkers like Marx and Freud, who theorized humans as constructs of social, historical and economic discourses or as motivated by unconscious drives and desires. Mansfield's work, I shall argue, can be viewed in this context as a radical challenge to traditional, humanist conceptions of a core or essence of being.

Of the five writers, Wyndham Lewis most overtly embraces the anti-epiphany as an aesthetic of discontinuity in his collection *The Wild Body* (1927), which privileges grotesque, abject bodies over spiritual insight and revels in an ironic recognition of the failure of that insight. Lewis's anti-epiphanies are conceivably informed by his view of an over-simplified dichotomy between mind and matter, as indicated in his chapter on Woolf in *Men Without Art* (1934), in which he suggests that her spiritual values are much the same as the materialism she opposes in Wells, Galsworthy and Bennett, 'only with a more strongly marked subjective flavouring'.[9]

A consideration of the short fiction of these writers reveals that, despite the marked differences in their approach to the revelatory moment, their anti-epiphanies have in common not only a renegotiation of traditional ideas about subjective construction but also a sexual encoding behind their apparent revelations. Sinclair's sublimative aesthetic implies one such connection, whilst Mansfield's 'Bliss' challenges essentialist beliefs about human subjectivity through Bertha Young's painful negotiations with her own half-acknowledged bisexuality. Similarly, unacknowledged or frustrated sexuality is a recurring theme in Joyce's and Woolf's anti-epiphanies, whilst depictions of revelatory insights in both Joyce and Lewis are frequently voyeuristic.

The close association between the epiphanic moment and sexuality also finds an explanation in Adam Parkes's 1996 study *Modernism and the Theater of Censorship*, in which he explores how, in a culture of censorship following the trials of Oscar Wilde, sexual content in literature was rigorously suppressed. The contemporary periodicals and presses that served as an important site for the publication of modernist short fiction found themselves significantly constrained by this censorship. The premises of *The Yellow Book*, for instance, were vandalized in the aftermath of Wilde's conviction for acts of gross indecency, despite the fact that he never wrote for the periodical. *The Little Review*, confiscated in 1917 because of Wyndham Lewis's story 'Cantleman's Spring-Mate', was further prosecuted in 1921 for the publication of *Ulysses*. (The Woolfs' Hogarth Press had earlier declined to publish the novel to avoid the risk of an obscenity charge.)

The elusive representation of the modernist epiphanic moment may, then, be reread in the light of Parkes's claim that whether openly or covertly, the writers of the period challenged the censorious conditions under which they wrote.[10] Within this social, historical and literary context, the incidence in which the moment of transcendent recognition first receives the name of epiphany is illuminating. In *Stephen Hero*, the protagonist identifies the term when he overhears a broken, fragmented conversation:

> The Young Lady – (drawling discreetly) ... O, yes ... I was ... at the ... cha ... pel. ...
> The Young Gentleman-(inaudibly) ... I ... (again inaudibly) ... I ...
> The Young Lady – (softly) ... O ... but you're ... ver ... ry ... wick ... ed. .... (p. 216).

This enigmatic, elliptical exchange inspires Stephen's definition of the 'sudden spiritual manifestation' which prompts him to collect 'a book of epiphanies' (p. 216). The passage is, however, ironic in the sense that its elliptical structure makes unambiguous interpretation impossible. The fragmented sentences enable the reader merely to infer a conspiratorial, mildly flirtatious tone which is suggestive of an element of voyeurism on the part of Stephen.

From the original explication of the epiphany through the transcendent moments in *A Portrait of the Artist as a Young Man* and also *Dubliners*, the short story sequence Joyce published two years previously in 1914, there is a clear association between the epiphany and sexuality. This in turn is associated with a conflict between corporeality and spirituality in which Stephen's intense spiritual experiences are continually undercut by the discourse of the physical body and sexual desire. Such representations of the epiphany recur throughout 'The Dead', the last short story in *Dubliners*, in which the protagonist Gabriel Conroy experiences a consistent failure in communication and consequently misreads the motivations of those around him. His efforts to articulate an after-dinner speech, significantly taking place on or close to the feast of the epiphany, are disastrous, and he ultimately misreads what he believes is his wife's mutual desire for him with the consequence that his entire sense of identity is destabilized.

The symbolism in this story reveals the irony behind its numerous epiphanies. The name of Lily, who inspires a minor revelation anticipating Gabriel's recognition of his social and sexual inadequacy, in Renaissance art frequently symbolizes the Virgin's purity at the Annunciation.[11] Lily's cynical observation – ironic in this context – that 'The men that is now is only all palaver and what they can get out of you' (p. 178) is discomfiting to Gabriel to the extent that he loses his communicative power. No longer able to find words to deliver his speech to an audience whose 'grade of culture' he perceives differs from his own, he grapples unsuccessfully with quotations from Browning, Shakespeare and The Melodies before becoming convinced that the speech 'was a mistake from first to last, an utter failure' (p. 179).[12]

Gabriel's failure of communication anticipates his mistaken belief at the end of the story that his wife Gretta comes to him 'of her own accord. Perhaps her thoughts had been running with his' (p. 219). His subsequent realization that she has been comparing him in her mind with her former lover, Michael Furey, inspires the penultimate epiphany in which he sees himself as 'a ludicrous figure [...] a nervous well-meaning sentimentalist, orating to vulgarians and idealising his own clownish lusts, the pitiable fatuous fellow he had caught a glimpse of in the mirror' (p. 221). Metaphors of light punctuate the narrative at intervals leading up to this revelation, ironically serving to accentuate the *lack* of illumination Gabriel experiences through his sequence of epiphanies. The 'tender fires of stars' which 'broke upon and illuminated' the memory of his secret life with Gretta give way later in the story to the 'guttering candle' carried by the porter upon return to their hotel room. Finally, following the revelation of his own ludicrousness, Gabriel turns his back to the light lest Gretta sees 'the shame that burned upon his forehead' (pp. 217, 221).

In the closing words of the story the snow, 'general all over Ireland [...] faintly falling, like the descent of the last end, upon all the living and the dead', implies an epiphany for 'all Ireland', with the metaphors of snow as well as the dead denoting spiritual paralysis, sexual and social failure (p. 225). Thomas Dilworth has pointed out that in the context of the feast of the epiphany, a derivation from the ancient Roman fertility ritual of Saturnalia, the etymological connection between the name 'Conroy' and the Gaelic for 'King' has a particular symbolic resonance. In European fertility religions, Dilworth notes, 'the intercourse of the king with his consort consequently corresponds to rain, which is the cosmic intercourse of sky with earth'.[13] In this context, Gabriel's failure to achieve sexual intercourse has a potent and humorous irony. His epiphany for 'all Ireland' is exposed merely as a revelation of impotence and inertia, and his sense of identity consequently flickers and wavers like the guttering candle: 'His soul had approached that region where dwell the vast hosts of the dead. He was conscious of, but could not apprehend, their wayward and flickering existence. His own identity was fading out into a grey impalpable world: the solid world itself was dissolving and dwindling' (p. 224). The fact that Gabriel cannot fully apprehend the dissolving of this ephemeral, indistinct social and individual existence means the reader has no more access to this elusive spiritual realm than he does.

The solid, material world is no more substantial than the states of consciousness denoting Gabriel's disintegrating sense of self, revealed through a series of anti-epiphanies which are self-negating and finally convey less the revelation of a spiritual reality behind surface appearances than instances in which the reader and protagonist become aware of irresolvable conflicts of identity.

For May Sinclair, the aim towards a textual representation of reality is reminiscent of the Joycean epiphany in that it, too, focuses on sexuality, albeit in Sinclair's work this is filtered through an aesthetic of sublimation. As opposed to Joyce's representations of inertia and frustration in his anti-epiphanies, however, Sinclair's sublimative aesthetic amounts to a metaphysical quest in which 'the end goal . . . has been mainly one ultimate principle: the assumption of an underlying truth'.[14] Throughout her 1923 short story sequence of *Uncanny Stories* – indebted for its title to Freud's 1919 essay *The Uncanny* – there are numerous examples of sublimation as a quasi-mystical state. The hauntings in the stories are frequently manifestations of repressed sexuality, or represent extremes of success or failure in the reunion with what Sinclair, drawing on philosophical Idealism, variously termed the Absolute, ultimate reality, unity and God.

In the story 'If the Dead Knew', Wilfred Hollyer is prevented from marrying because of his financial dependence upon his mother. Reasoning that by the time he and his fiancée Effie could marry they would be 'old; too old to feel, to care passionately', he summons a will that is 'indestructible, for it was a form of his desire for Effie', which breaks loose and gets through to his mother in order to kill her.[15] He is later tormented by guilt over his own sexual impulses, and consequently a confrontation with his mother's apparition occurs when he assumes she knows 'she had died because, secretly, he had wished her dead' (p. 185).

Freud's essay on *The Uncanny* is illuminating in the context of this 'haunting' for its detailed etymological explication of *heimlich*, a word encompassing the double meaning of familiar or homely and also something secret or hidden. Its contrast, *Das Unheimliche*, denotes 'everything that was intended to remain secret, hidden away, and has come into the open'.[16] Whilst apparently oppositional, the two terms thus overlap in meaning, *unheimlich* becoming 'eerily familiar' in terms of its inadvertent revelation of what is hidden from the self and others. Sinclair's story remains ambiguous as to whether its 'ghost' resides within Wilfred's psyche as a metaphor for his guilty conscience, or is a manifestation of the return of the repressed arising from a failure of sublimation. What is evident, however, is that whatever form the haunting takes, it involves the 'frightening element' of the Freudian uncanny: 'something that has been repressed and has now returned.'[17]

The fact that the haunting is framed within two instances of piano-playing – for Sinclair a recurring symbol of artistic and sexual expression – supports a twofold Freudian interpretation in the light of both sublimation and the uncanny. Whilst the story is told primarily from the perspective of Wilfred, the opening lines focus on Effie's intensely sexual response to Wilfred's church-organ recital:

> her heart swelled; her whole body listened, with hurried senses desiring the climax, the crash of sound. [. . .] she loved his playing hands, his rocking body, his superb, excited gesture [. . .] The climax had come. The voluntary fell from its height and died in a long cadence, thinned out, a trickling, trembling diminuendo. It was all over.
> The young girl released her breath in a long, trembling sigh. (p. 163)

The narrative perspective in this passage is couched in overtly sexual, corporeal language and is clearly descriptive of a physical climax. Effie, however, is able to sublimate her passionate libido into the music. This sublimative power, the story implies, enables the possession of the mystic insight through which Effie eventually reconciles Wilfred with his mother's spirit. Significantly, this is achieved through a second interlude of piano-playing when Effie persuades Wilfred to return to the feared drawing room, scene of the phantom's visit, and play Mrs Hollyer's favourite music. This results in a second 'supreme manifestation' of his mother's spirit who offers Wilfred forgiveness and peace (p. 188).

Whilst Effie and Wilfred are married by this point in the story, Effie's mystic insight is nonetheless made possible through her capacity for sublimation and self-sacrifice. Her response to Wilfred's confidence of his inability to marry her during his mother's lifetime is simply 'I can wait' (p. 166). Moreover, there is no further reference to the marriage within the story. The need to consummate physical desire is removed by the device of sublimation, and despite the explicit language through which Effie's sexuality is articulated, the physical body is absent from what is primarily a spiritual experience articulated through her consciousness.

For Virginia Woolf also, the failure she acknowledges in her essay 'Professions for Women' to solve the dilemma of telling the truth of her experiences 'about the body, about the passions', underpins her anti-epiphanies.[18] As in Sinclair's work there is an omission of the physical body from the revelations Woolf termed 'moments of being', which have in common with those of Joyce and Sinclair their basis in sexuality as well as the obfuscation of the revelations they appear to convey. As Krystyna Colburn has noted, lesbian sexuality in Woolf's short fiction is frequently articulated through Terry Castle's concept of the apparitional spinster; 'her single state underlined by the title "Miss"; an intense sexuality in the use of sound; traditionally lesbian floral and jewel imagery'. According to Colburn, these are particularly noteworthy features of Woolf's 1906 short story 'The Mysterious Case of Miss V'.[19]

There is a ghostly quality to the language in this story, in which the protagonist is referred to continually as a shadow and is ephemeral and elusive. When Miss V disappears from the text, the narrator initially fails to notice, observing only that 'when [. . .] she ceased to haunt my path, I knew vaguely that something was missing'.[20] The epiphany occurs when the narrator wakes at dawn and cries aloud: 'Mary V. Mary V!!' (p. 31). The eventual realization that Miss V 'had been ill for two months; she had died yesterday morning, at the very hour when I had called her name' suggests an impassioned connection between the two women which remains elusive throughout the text (p. 32). The epiphany fails because it reveals what is missing, not what is attainable.

If this story is read as a lesbian text it suggests that, as Annette Oxindine has noted, 'Sapphic vision' has in common with the epiphany 'the quality of not being directly translatable into language'.[21] Like 'The Mysterious Case of Miss V', in which a search for the language to convey a missing 'shadow' proves fruitless, Woolf's most explicitly lesbian story 'Moments of Being: Slater's Pins Have No Points' also relates to the search for a missing object which symbolizes an inability to articulate sexuality openly. For most of the duration of the story, Fanny Wilmot's eyes are cast onto the floor as she searches for a lost pin. The reader is never made aware of whether Fanny's desire for Julia Craye is reciprocated, although Fanny's repeated question to herself at the beginning of the story: 'what use had [Julia] of pins?' metaphorically suggests that her sexuality is impossible to pin down as Julia gives no outward recognition of lesbian desire (p. 215).

From the point where 'the rose fell out of Fanny Wilmot's dress, and Fanny stooped . . . to look for the pin on the floor', there are constant interjections of her 'looking for the pin' which had held the flower to her dress (p. 215). The significance of the pin and flowers as symbols of female desire is discernible when Julia 'picked up the carnation which had fallen on the floor, while Fanny searched for the pin. She crushed it . . . she had her hands on it; she pressed it; but she did not possess it, enjoy it, not altogether' (p. 217). When viewed from the perspective of Fanny, this metaphor is ambiguous as to whether it indicates Julia's latent lesbianism or Fanny's own interpretation of Julia's perceived desire.

The moment of epiphany occurs at the point in the story where Fanny finds the pin and looks at Julia as she sits holding the carnation, surprising her 'in a moment of ecstasy' which, like the Joycean epiphany, cannot be accessed linguistically. Fanny muses, 'It seemed in its bareness and intensity the effluence of her spirit, something she had made which surrounded her, which was her' (p. 220). Like the epiphany in 'The Mysterious Case of Miss V', this suggests unspoken communication between the two women which could be read as a real or imagined moment of spiritual ecstasy. The 'revelation', remaining beyond the confines of the text, results in a scene between Fanny and Julia which is couched in language sufficiently ambiguous to allow for a real or imagined scenario:

> She saw Julia open her arms; saw her blaze; saw her kindle. Out of the night she burnt like a dead white star. Julia kissed her. Julia possessed her. 'Slater's pins have no points', Miss Craye said, laughing queerly and relaxing her arms, as Fanny Wilmot pinned the flower to her breast with trembling fingers. (p. 214)

There are striking similarities between this passage and a scenario in Katherine Mansfield's 'Bliss', in which an imagined intense spiritual and sexual connection between Bertha Young and Pearl Fulton later gives way to an ambiguously worded scene, from which Bertha infers her husband is having an affair with Pearl.[22] In both stories, the words 'she saw' serve to convey these scenes through the perspectives of protagonists who witness events unfold but whose powers of observation are limited. Moreover, it is unclear whether Fanny pins the flower to her own breast or Julia's, which in the light of the symbolic resonance between flowers and lesbian desire is a significant omission. Thus Woolf's apparently overt story about Sapphism ironically remains elusive on the subject of lesbian sexuality. Like Sinclair's *Uncanny Stories*, desire resides within the realm of consciousness, as opposed to the physical body, accessible through a revelatory moment that reveals only ambiguity.

In 'Bliss', lesbian desire is also a key theme through which irony, satire, pathos and humour gradually unmask the protagonist's illusions about her sexuality as social constructs. The device of the anti-epiphany subtly exposes the discourses which censored issues of sexuality in contemporary literature and upheld those identities socially deemed 'natural'; the 'other' of which, as Judith Butler shows in her much later theoretical work, *Bodies That Matter*, culminated in the pejoration of the 'queer'.[23] Mansfield's story emphasizes how Bertha Young's re-enactment of artificial, pre-ordained identities in relation to both her gender and her class undermines Victorian realist modes of representation, the assumption of naturalness and essentialist notions of the fixity of gender.

That Bertha is performing in accordance with such discourses is clear not only from her inability to recognize and articulate her own desires, but also because of the lack of any available language through which to do so. As with the anti-epiphanies depicted in the stories of Joyce and Woolf, the numerous revelatory insights ostensibly offered by 'Bliss' – including the elusive source of the ecstasy itself – are inaccessible linguistically. As Bertha oscillates between a powerful erotic connection with her friend Pearl Fulton and her first ever feelings of desire for her husband, she experiences a sense of euphoria which she is unable to express or even interpret. She therefore accounts for it by itemizing the things that, according to the conventions of femininity, thirty-year-old females were expected to desire: a husband, a family and a domestic life (p. 96).

Throughout the narrative, Bertha's strong identification with various symbols is illustrative of her struggle to articulate a sexuality she can neither fully comprehend nor acknowledge. The central image in 'Bliss' is the 'tall, slender pear tree in fullest, richest bloom' standing against the garden wall 'as though becalmed against the jade-green sky' (p. 96). Bertha immediately identifies with this object as a 'symbol of her own life', yet the tree merely represents the constraints under which she lives (p. 96). The wide open blooms of a fertile, flowering fruit tree equally symbolize both fertility and domesticity and the space of an enclosed domestic garden signifies cultivated, middle-class femininity.

The mutual, erotic connection Bertha believes she shares with Pearl and the profound epiphanic moment the two share beside the tree, 'caught in that circle of unearthly light, understanding each other perfectly, creatures of another world', is ultimately ironic (p. 102). Despite Bertha's conviction that she has guessed Pearl's mood 'exactly' and 'instantly', the illusion is destroyed with the revelation that Pearl's attraction is directed not towards her, but her husband (p. 101). A further irony is that the pear tree is a treacherous, duplicitous image. Initially, Bertha's 'bliss' is associated in her mind with the tree and appears to represent new sexual possibilities. The connections she makes between herself and the tree's 'wide open blossoms', together with the observation that her 'petals rustled softly into the hall' as she moves to greet her dinner-party guests are implicitly sexual images (p. 96). However, normalizing discourses begin to reassert themselves when two shifts take place which dismantle Bertha's illusions and restore her to the role of the middle-class female to which she so carefully categorizes herself at the beginning of the story.

The first, following Bertha's moment of insight with Pearl in the garden, occurs when she experiences sexual desire for Harry. The second – the penultimate epiphany in the story – exposes her shared sexual attraction with Pearl as imaginary and hints at the possibility of an affair between her husband and Pearl. In this scene, witnessed by Bertha and interpreted by her via a series of gestures rather than speech, Harry's 'lips said: "I adore you," and Miss Fulton laid her moonbeam fingers on his cheeks and smiled her sleepy smile. Harry [...] whispered: "Tomorrow", and with her eyelids Miss Fulton said: "Yes"' (p. 105).

The ambiguous, metaphorical language representing Bertha's perception allows for the possibilities of the affair being real, imaginary or misconstrued. This ambiguity remains unresolved and the closing words of the story leave Bertha poised on a note of pessimism and stagnation: 'But the pear tree was as lovely as ever and as full of flower and as still' (p. 105). The last word of the narrative is revealing, as whilst the connection between the anti-epiphany and frustrated or unrealized sexuality in Mansfield's story is reminiscent of both Joyce and Woolf, in 'Bliss' Bertha's stasis implicitly satirizes a society whose narrow strictures on sexuality leave her no available position from which to speak. In this sense, Mansfield's anti-epiphanies have a closer affinity with those depicted in the short fiction of Dorothy Richardson.

Three of Richardson's stories: 'Death' (1924), 'Ordeal' (1930) and 'Tryst' (1941) are structured around brief epiphanies offering each of the women protagonists a respite from their lives of domestic responsibility as dictated by their heterosexual status. Each story is resolved differently. Having reflected upon the social constraints governing her life, the first unnamed protagonist is released from these only by means of her own death. The story of 'Ordeal' remains ambiguous as to whether or not the main character, Fan, will recover from a major operation as she succumbs to anaesthesia at the end of the story. She does, however, consider her sojourn within the nursing home to be 'the first holiday of her adult life'.[24] In 'Tryst', the woman protagonist experiences the merest glimpse of what a life outside her socially dictated identity might be like, but must re-constrict her newly 'elastically expanded being' (p. 59) in order to return home from a solitary walk and resume her roles as a wife and mother.

The conclusions of Richardson's stories and Mansfield's 'Bliss' might be viewed as upholding the dominant contemporary discourse of heterosexuality. In each of the four stories, however, the epiphanies remain beyond linguistic reach. They may thus equally be read as satires of the *lack* of discourse available through which the characters might envisage or negotiate identities distinct from those imposed by their sexuality, or in the case of Mansfield's Bertha, to understand and articulate her bisexuality. In the context of modernist short fiction, in which a lack of illumination typifies the anti-epiphany, the subversive interpretation is more persuasive than the conformist one.

In his short story collection *The Wild Body*, Wyndham Lewis similarly adopts a satirical style but, unlike the authors previously discussed, he privileges neither the modernist inner consciousness nor the epiphany. As Head has noted, *The Wild Body* is historically significant because it represents a 'systematic application' of Vorticism to the short story form in which Ker-Orr, the narrator of the volume, represents the centre of the vortex.[25] In these stories, Lewis depicts corporeal and conscious experience through satirizing the literary text and the human body as abject. The stories recounted by the narrator, Ker-Orr, amount to a series of encounters with various characters that appear to undermine their own meaning. The essay 'Inferior Religions', which appears within the volume as a manifesto for *The Wild Body*, juxtaposes 'the fascinating imbecility of the creaking men machines' with laughter, 'the brain-body's snort of exultation' which is 'all that remains physical in the flash of thought'.[26]

The metaphor of eyes and blindness is central to the story of 'Bestre', which, like the stories of Mansfield and Woolf, focuses on a lack of ability to see. In 'Bestre', however, blindness evokes satirical laughter because the eponymous protagonist is 'jocose; he will beset you with mocking thoughts as the blindfold man is danced round in a game of blind man's buff' (p. 81). Described in 'Inferior Religions' as the 'eternal watchdog', Bestre uses his eyes as weapons to attack numerous manifestations of 'the enemy' (p. 150). The ammunition for this weapon is drawn, in Ker-Orr's description, 'from all the most skunk-like provender, the most ugly mucins, fungoid glands, of his physique. Excrement as well as sputum would be shot from this luminous hole, with the same certainty in its unsavoury appulsion' (p. 83).

In this passage the physical body is abject; a revulsion Julia Kristeva theorizes as emanating from the bodily waste residing on the borders of human existence. As Kristeva argues, 'these body fluids, this defilement, this shit are what life withstands, hardly and with difficulty, on the part of death'. More violent than 'uncanniness', moreover, abjection 'is elaborated through a failure to recognize its kin; nothing is familiar, not even the shadow of a memory'.[27] In 'Bestre', it is thus ironic when Ker-Orr loses his status as a detached observer of *The Wild Body* in his failure to recognize himself in Bestre's persona. Seeing 'an odiously grinning face' peering into his window, Ker-Orr initially fails to realize that 'It was I who was the intruder [...] I myself who was guilty of peering into somebody else's window: this was hidden from me in the first moment of consciousness about the odious brown person of Bestre' (p. 76).

The depiction of eyes, watching and a disassociation between 'I' and an abject 'other' here involves a combination of the abject and the Freudian uncanny. Freud's literary critique of E. T. A. Hoffmann's story of 'The Sandman', a mythical apparition who tears out children's eyes, relates anxiety of the uncanny to fear of losing one's eyes; a fear which many children retain into adult life. Freud concludes that 'anxiety about one's eyes, the fear of going blind, is quite often a substitute for the fear of castration'.[28] A similar implication is also evident in Lewis's story from Ker-Orr's observation that that the principles of Bestre's strategy 'are possibly the possession of his libido' (p. 88). Moreover, the return of what has been forgotten by means of repression or sublimation thus conceivably relates to Ker-Orr's failure to recognize Bestre as an entity within himself. The realist principle of omniscient narration, as well as its pretensions to convey an authentic textual representation of reality, is also mocked through the obscure distinction between Bestre and Ker-Orr, who describes the subject of his story as omnipresent, all-seeing and all-powerful:

> He watched you being born, and has watched you ever since. Don't be too sure that he did not play some part in planting the little seed from which you grew into such a big, fine (many withering exclamation marks) boy (or girl). He will be in at your finish too. But he is in no hurry about that. [...] Meanwhile he laughs at you. He finds you a little funny. Yes! I am still looking! (p. 77)

Like the anti-epiphanies in the stories of Mansfield and Woolf, which are obscured by ambiguous pronoun use and an implied lack of vision on the part of their protagonists, the source of the 'I' at the end of this passage is again elusive. It is unclear who or what is being observed, given that Ker-Orr, too, is a watcher who bears witness to the subtleties of Bestre's 'warlike ambush' and is 'perpetually entertained' by the spectacle (p. 78). When Ker-Orr's ultimate moment of self-recognition is further obfuscated by the fact that he is 'prevented from turning my eye upon myself', his condition as a 'detached' observer is undermined (p. 84). In his own moment of self-discovery, which he ironically believes few people achieve 'so thoroughly, so early in life and so quickly', he merely recognizes 'more and more the beauty of Bestre' (p. 84).

Unlike the anti-epiphanies discussed thus far, the moment of self-discovery in 'Bestre' is overt in its lack of revelation. Ker-Orr recognizes beauty within the abject form of Bestre, but here again the lack of boundaries between 'I' and the other obscures the distinction between watcher and watched. Moreover, in the light of the voyeurism which pervades the story and is reminiscent of Stephen Dedalus's original epiphany, Ker-Orr's anti-epiphany may be read in the wider significance of art as a satire of modernism itself. His recognition of the beauty of abject bodies conceivably relates to the physical bodies of himself and Bestre, as well as the wider textual corpus of *The Wild Body*. Abjection in this context recalls a modernist aesthetic described by Ezra Pound as the 'cult of ugliness'.[29] Elaborating on notions of beauty in 'Inferior Religions', Lewis states that beauty is 'an immense predilection, a perfect conviction of the desirability of a certain thing [. . .] we can aim at no universality of form, for what we see is not the reality' (p. 155). In 'Bestre' the notion of a universality of form is, then, continually subverted; the reality conveyed is merely a relentless metaphorical game of blind man's buff indulged in between Bestre, Ker-Orr and, ultimately, the reader.

The fracturing of traditional perspectives on subjective construction, as well as pre-twentieth century conceptions of material and spiritual realities, thus characterizes the representation of the anti-epiphany in the short fiction of Lewis, as well as that of Joyce, Woolf, Sinclair and Mansfield. The fragmented, elliptical language of the anti-epiphany conveyed in the work of all five writers enabled them to experiment with subversive depictions of social and sexual identity, to resist the constraints of contemporary literary censorship and to challenge rigid and exclusionary subjective, cultural and aesthetic categories. Their implicit satires of literary production and dissemination are also revealed through revelatory moments that, ironically, obscure the 'realities' they profess to reveal. Thus, as Lewis's Ker-Orr's narration appears to suggest, the eyes of Bestre are also the eyes of the modernist artist: 'looking at the reality with a professional eye, so to speak: with a professional liar's' (p. 88). Likewise, the anti-epiphanies conveyed in the work of these most prominent modernist short story writers obscure the 'truth' they appear to convey and thus bear within themselves their own negation. Linguistically elusive, they yield no transcendent insight, nor do they pose a solution to the nineteenth-century myth of unity. Conversely, they illustrate merely the absence of a solution.

Notes

1. Dominic Head, *The Modernist Short Story: A Study in Theory and Practice* (Cambridge University Press, 1992), pp. 37–8; José María Díaz, 'Allegory and Fragmentation in Lewis's *The Wild Body* and Barnes's *A Book*', in *Modernism, Postmodernism and the Short Story in English*, ed. Joge Sacido (New York: Rodopi, 2012), pp. 47–76 (pp. 47–8).
2. James Joyce, *Stephen Hero: Part of the First Draft of A Portrait of the Artist as a Young Man*, edited and introduced by T. Spencer (London: Cape, 1944), p. 216. All subsequent quotations and page references in this chapter refer to this edition.
3. Edgar Allan Poe, 'Review of *Twice Told Tales*', in *The New Short Story Theories*, ed. Charles May (Athens: Ohio University Press, 1994), pp. 59–64 (pp. 60–2).
4. Virginia Woolf, *The Diary of Virginia Woolf, Volume II: 1920–1924*, ed. Anne Olivier Bell (London: The Hogarth Press, 1978), p. 14.
5. Virginia Woolf, 'Mr Bennett and Mrs Brown', in *Virginia Woolf: A Woman's Essays*, ed. Rachel Bowlby (London: Penguin, 1992), pp. 69–87 (pp. 70–1).
6. May Sinclair, 'The Novels of Dorothy Richardson', in *The Gender of Modernism: A Critical Anthology*, ed. Bonnie Kime Scott (Bloomington: Indiana University Press, 1990), pp. 442–8 (p. 443).
7. May Sinclair, *A Defence of Idealism: Some Questions and Conclusions* (London: Macmillan, 1917), p. 306.
8. Sigmund Freud, '"Civilized" Sexual Morality and Modern Nervousness', in *The Standard Edition of the Complete Psychological Works of Sigmund Freud*, translated by James Strachey (London: Hogarth 1956–74), vol. IX, p. 193.
9. Wyndham Lewis, *Men Without Art* (London: Cassell, 1934), pp. 158, 161.
10. Adam Parkes, *Modernism and the Theater of Censorship* (New York: Oxford University Press, 1996), p. vii.
11. James Joyce, *Dubliners* (London: Penguin, 2000), pp. 305–6. All subsequent quotations and page references in this chapter refer to this edition.
12. Thomas Moore's *The Irish Melodies* are lyrics to a series of Irish folk tunes published in ten volumes between 1808 and 1834.
13. Thomas Dilworth, 'Sex and Politics in "The Dead"', *James Joyce Quarterly*, 23 (1986), 2, pp. 157–71 (pp. 164–5).
14. May Sinclair, *The New Idealism* (London: Macmillan, 1922), p. 332.
15. May Sinclair, *Uncanny Stories* (London: Hutchinson, 1923), pp. 169, 178. Subsequent page references to this edition are given in parentheses in the text.

16. Sigmund Freud, *The Uncanny*, trans. David McLintock (London: Penguin, 2003), p. 132.
17. Freud, *The Uncanny*, p. 147.
18. Virginia Woolf, 'Professions for Women', in *A Room of One's Own/Three Guineas*, ed. Michèle Barrett (London: Penguin, 1993), pp. 356–61 (p. 359).
19. Krystyna Colburn, 'The Lesbian Intertext of Woolf's Short Fiction', in *Trespassing Boundaries: Virginia Woolf's Short Fiction*, ed. Kathryn N. Benzel and Ruth Hoberman (Basingstoke: Palgrave Macmillan, 2004), pp. 63–80 (pp. 64–5).
20. Virginia Woolf, *The Complete Shorter Fiction of Virginia Woolf*, ed. Susan Dick (Orlando: Harcourt, 1985), p. 31. All quotations from Woolf's stories in this chapter are from this edition, with subsequent page numbers given in parentheses in the text.
21. Annette Oxindine, 'Sexing the Epiphany in "Moments of Being"', Woolf's Nice Little Story about Sapphism', *Journal of the Short Story in English*, 31 (1998), pp. 51–61 (p. 55).
22. Katherine Mansfield, *The Collected Stories of Katherine Mansfield* (London: Penguin, 2007), p. 105. All quotations from Mansfield's stories in this chapter are from this edition, with subsequent page numbers given in parentheses in the text.
23. Judith Butler, *Bodies that Matter: On the Discursive Limits of 'Sex'* (London: Routledge, 1993), p. 234.
24. Dorothy Richardson, *Journey to Paradise*, ed. Trudi Tate (London: Virago, 1989), p. 73. All quotations are from this edition, with subsequent page numbers given in parentheses in the text.
25. Head, *The Modernist Short Story*, pp. 139–40.
26. Wyndham Lewis, *The Wild Body* (London: Penguin, 2004), pp. 149, 153. All quotations are from this edition, with subsequent page numbers given in parentheses in the text.
27. Julia Kristeva, *Powers of Horror: An Essay on Abjection* (New York: Columbia University Press, 1982), pp. 3, 5.
28. Freud, *The Uncanny*, p. 139.
29. Ezra Pound, *Literary Essays of Ezra Pound*, ed. T. S. Eliot (New York: New Directions, 1935), p. 45.

9
War Stories: The Short Story in the First and Second World Wars

ANN-MARIE EINHAUS

As a result of two wars, H. E. Bates claimed, the modern short story of his time was better than it had been ever before.[1] Short story writer and anthologist Dan Davin felt that the short story 'proved to be one of the hardiest blooms to survive in a time of devastation and weeds'.[2] But why is the short story such a useful medium to writers in wartime? The particular conditions of publishing in wartime, from paper shortages to editorial constraints, seem to encourage the publication of short fiction in periodicals over the individual publication of long novels.[3] The short story has also been described as a medium that 'lends itself to the representation of experience fragmented by war'.[4] Its brevity, its ability to capture snapshot views of life at war, and particularly its modernist, fragmented incarnation have been regarded as ideal means of expression in wartime, responding quickly to events, whether traumatic or mundane, without having to offer a panoramic overview. Compared to the larger-scale explorations of war novels and memoirs, the war story's 'strength is its affinity to the experience of the mere moment, which goes hand in hand with a special closeness to its moment of publication and reception'.[5] A time-strapped and anxious reading public may have turned to short stories because they 'could at least be read quickly, in a single sitting', offered 'the satisfaction of immediate closure', and did not require the same 'lengthy emotional investment' as novels.[6] These qualities were not obviously new: they were pre-existing features that had made the short story popular with an increasingly literate British public before 1914. When the First World War broke out, the short story was an established (if notoriously ill-defined) form that happened to work particularly well within a wartime context of readers' limited time, constant physical or emotional disruption, paper shortages and fragmented experience. These ostensible handicaps for the literary market in general all served to make the short prose form 'an inescapable element of the wartime literary field' and blackouts and the dangers of leaving the house after dark owing to lack of street lighting in both wars meant that 'Reading – like knitting – flourished on the Home Front.'[7]

While 'the' short story of either the First or the Second World War does not exist, short stories for this precise reason – the absence of a 'typical' kind of story – illustrate the great diversity of responses to both wars. They throw into relief the ability of short fiction to take advantage of the wartime publishing scene and illustrate the continuity of experience linking both wars in manifold ways. Rather than attempting to capture an elusive essence of war stories, it is more fruitful to talk about tendencies and themes prevalent during the First World War, inter-war period and the Second World War, and work with examples of how even short stories one might think advance 'typical' views can be surprisingly nuanced. One distinction, however, is broadly useful: responses to the two world wars in British short fiction are roughly split between short prose that is *about* the war and its effects, and stories that *incorporate* the war into other, often pre-existing narrative or aesthetic concerns. Either kind of war story contributes to one of the most important social functions of literature, namely the enabling of readers to employ fictional narrative frameworks against which to 'read' their own experience of war. As Elizabeth Bowen observed in 1945 in the preface to her collection *The Demon Lover and Other Stories*, stories could fulfil the same crucial function of coping with traumatic experience as material objects:

> People whose homes had been blown up went to infinite lengths to assemble bits of themselves – broken ornaments, odd shoes, torn scraps of the curtains that had hung in a room – from the wreckage. In the same way, they assembled and checked themselves from stories and poems, from their memories, from one another's talk.[8]

Stories that incorporate the war can range from a magazine romance tale in which the heroine happens to be a munitionette to modernist sketches such as Virginia Woolf's 'The Mark on the Wall', in which the war for the most part appears in the background, fleetingly visible behind the narrator's stream-of-consciousness until it is interrupted by another character's observation, at the close of the story, that 'it's no good buying newspapers ... Nothing ever happens. Curse this war; God damn this war!'[9] Stories that address the war specifically also do so in a wide variety of ways, from scrutiny of the conduct of war in particular locations or service branches – as in Mary

Borden's nursing sketches in *The Forbidden Zone* – to its psychological consequences, such as Katherine Mansfield's exploration of grief in 'The Fly'.

Besides benefiting from similar practical and financial constraints in both wars, short stories – like novels and poetry – acknowledged political and emotional links between the two conflicts. As Victoria Stewart has noted, many literary texts written during the Second World War consider both wars 'in tandem', and while 'the First World War is not the principal focus of the action' as a general rule, it 'is used as a means of attempting to grasp the import of a new, and in many respects very different, war'.[10] Whether read as a study of psychological disintegration or as a ghost story, Bowen's story 'The Demon Lover' addresses the link between the two wars. Its main protagonist is a middle-aged wife and mother who, having returned to her temporarily abandoned London home during the Blitz to collect some belongings, finds herself confronted with a spectre from the past, her former fiancé, who was supposedly killed in the First World War. Engulfed by war once more, the protagonist has forced upon her the realisation that 'The years have gone by at once slowly and fast', and that, in many ways, 'nothing has changed'.[11] However, not all short stories portray links between the two wars as exclusively negative. The 'Great' War repeatedly crops up in the stories of Mollie Panter-Downes as a yardstick of home-front experience, as in 'Meeting at the Pringles'', first published in January 1940. For a committee of respectable village ladies, the prospect of voluntary work making bandages and other medical supplies is an altogether pleasant resumption of duties last carried out in 1914–18:

> 'Of course it's nonsense!' Mrs Carver was shouting into the telephone. 'I said to Mrs Peters that you'd never find a perfectly antiseptic room in any village. "In the last war," I said to her —'
> 'But my heart's right there!' roared the voices of the potential customers in whose service the ladies were being so busy and happy – happier, as a matter of fact, than they had been for the last twenty-one years.[12]

The outbreak of a new war offers these women an opportunity for useful activity and allows them to claim past experience of voluntary war work as grounds for authority on the subject of surgical supplies. Knowledge about the 'last war' also becomes crucial for the older generation in Arthur Calder-Marshall's 'Before the War', set in 1939. In this story, a father maimed and permanently hospitalized in the First World War finally bonds with his son when the younger man realizes that he is about to run the same risk as his father. Previously, the son had tried his best to forget, but his own approaching army service effects a fundamental change. Talking to an orderly, himself a veteran, at his father's nursing home who complains that 'most people want to forget we exist at all', the son is overcome by a sense of guilt. Asking his father about his experiences, he finds himself 'for the first time in [his] life seeing him as the man of his eyes instead of the mutilation of his flesh', as veteran and future combatant bond over shared fears and desires, however briefly.[13]

Although the First World War is regarded as a mere forerunner to the 'total war' of 1939–45, its short stories show just how deeply war penetrated into the everyday lives of British civilians. Comic stories can be as revealing of the deep impact of war as serious short fiction: Blanche Wills Chandler's 'Zepp Proof' (1917) bears testimony to the terror inspired by the first air raids on the civilian population in England, foreshadowing the effect of the Blitz.[14] The story's narrator is a soldier home on leave with 'nerves', who has been invited, along with a friend, to recuperate at the house of a kindly elderly gentleman. Their host, however, is terrified of zeppelin attacks to such an extent that he forces his guests to sleep in the cellar and prompts them to dig an air-raid shelter in his garden. Allowing for a somewhat transparent endeavour to make light of the new phenomenon of shell-shock, Chandler's comic tale illustrates war's incursions into civilian life at the time. But air raids or naval bombardments were not the only impact of war on the civilian sphere. Far more pervasive was the effect of propaganda and (self-) censorship. Since many papers and publishers took the decision to aid the war effort by carefully selecting material fit for publication in wartime and prominent literary figures pledged their support to the nation's cause, writers of short fiction also rushed to the colours.[15] One of the most frequently cited patriotic stories was Arthur Machen's 'The Bowmen', which sparked a widespread belief in divine intervention during the retreat of Mons.[16] In Machen's tale, the ghosts of English bowmen from the battle of Agincourt, summoned inadvertently by a tired and desperate soldier, come to the aid of the retreating British Expeditionary Force. Machen's story represents a particularly successful bid to spin an unsettling military mishap into a more positive story for worried readers at home and was picked up widely by the media at the time.

While Machen's story retains a certain wry humour – the soldier who summons the spirit of the bowmen of Agincourt does so by quoting a Latin motto encountered before the war on the crockery of a new-fangled vegetarian restaurant in London – and focuses on the military side of war, other short stories demonstrate the darker sides of propaganda.

Along the lines of the now notorious Bryce report (Report of the Committee on Alleged German Outrages) of 1915, Rudyard Kipling's 'Swept and Garnished' is a grisly tale in which an elderly German housewife is confronted with the ghosts of killed and mutilated Belgian children. Kipling leaves it open to interpretation whether these represent a fever dream or a real supernatural encounter, but, whether real or imaginary, the young victims lend powerful fictional weight to rumours of German atrocities. The omnipresence of propaganda is also illustrated by Arthur Conan Doyle's decision to revive one of his most popular magazine characters, Sherlock Holmes. Published in *The Strand Magazine* and *Collier's Weekly* in September 1917, 'His Last Bow' sees Holmes turn from private investigator to counter-espionage agent and successfully take a dangerous German agent out of action just before the outbreak of war. This story was by no means Conan Doyle's only propagandist effort, however, and his patriotic and often cautionary tales appeared regularly in best-selling fiction magazines. 'The Prisoner's Defence', in which a stalwart British army captain finds himself on trial for shooting his fiancée when he discovers she is a German spy, is but one further example.[17]

A preoccupation with espionage is a feature of First World War stories that continued and developed throughout the inter-war years. This feature was intensified by the outbreak of the next war, but was manifest in variously modified forms. The issue of secrecy and anti-espionage propaganda is humorously picked up in Bowen's 'Careless Talk'. Seemingly bent on impressing a bombed-out friend visiting from out of town, where she is experiencing the more mundane aspects of wartime life by keeping hens and accommodating evacuees, Bowen's group of wartime Londoners speak in nothing so much as hints and riddles, perpetually steering the dinner conversation into dead ends:

> 'Which reminds me. Edward sent you his love.'
> 'Oh, how *is* Edward?' Joanna said. 'What is he doing?'
> 'Well, I'm not strictly supposed to say. By the way, Eric, I asked Joanna, and she doesn't know where the Stones *or* the Hickneys are.'[18]

Requests for information are made and immediately declined or dismissed, and communication between friends has deteriorated to a farcical competition of who is inside and who outside the real action, while Joanna, the only one of the four to have lost her home to the Blitz, is barred from joining the non-conversation at every turn. Bowen here and elsewhere captures the impact of renewed total war on civilians in the Second World War, struggling with its physical manifestations of destruction and evacuation on the one hand, and its unreality and insecurity on the other.

Short fiction also served to give expression to the oppressed and marginalized, particularly in the inter-war period, when writers and readers alike had to come to terms with changes brought about by the war. This included greater freedom to write about previously taboo subjects, as Bates noted in *The Modern Short Story* (1941):

> Writers, after the Great War of 1914–18, found themselves less fettered than at any time in history. They had suddenly a free pass to say and see and do and describe anything they wanted. No subject was now barred to a writer, to the last limit of physical experience.
>
> To the short-story writer, therefore, perhaps even more than to the novelist, a world of immense new possibilities was opened up. (p. 133)

While Bates was most likely thinking of new sexual licentiousness, this new freedom also extended to questioning the situation of those oppressed on the grounds of gender or nationality. Two of Radclyffe Hall's stories about the First World War, first collected in *Miss Ogilvy Finds Herself* (1934), look back at the war as a period of temporary liberation as well as persecution. In the title story, Miss Ogilvy, to all intents and purposes a man born in a woman's body, briefly experiences freedom and happiness as the leader of an ambulance unit on the Western Front, only to be thrust back into a life of repression upon her return. In 'Fräulein Schwartz', an elderly German spinster is stranded in London when war breaks out. Living in a lodging house and alone in the world except for her cat, Karl-Heinrich, she is increasingly isolated as a result of mounting anti-German sentiment, and when the housemaid's boyfriend is killed at the front, the housemaid poisons Fräulein Schwartz's cat. Devastated by the loss of her only friend, Fräulein Schwartz drowns herself in the Thames. In Hall's story, women are shown to be particularly vulnerable to wartime discrimination and persecution – Fräulein Schwartz, unlike male Germans in Britain, is not interned as an enemy alien during the war, but her isolation is the more complete because she lacks even the comfort of fellow sufferers. A similar sense of isolation and persecution is described in Jean Rhys's 'I Spy a Stranger', set during the Second World War. Rhys's story puts paid to nostalgia about wartime solidarity in its portrayal of the vicious hounding of a middle-aged refugee, a British woman who had lived in Germany until the outbreak of war. Her perceived difference from the small-town population leads to threatening anonymous letters and visits from the police, and even her down-to-earth cousin in whose house she had found temporary refuge has to observe to her sister, reflecting on the actions of her neighbours and her own husband, 'Sometimes I wonder if she wasn't a bit right – if there isn't a very nasty spirit about.'[19]

Inter-war short stories naturally also contemplated the male experience of the war in diverse ways. Combat was described in varying amounts of detail in popular tales for adults and particularly young readers, and in modernist experimental fiction such as Herbert Read's ironically titled 'Killed in Action', a story included in *Naked Warriors* (1919), in which the protagonist reaches breaking point and commits suicide when he fails to be killed in battle. However, in a market for stories largely centred on civilian readers, combat was only one aspect of war among many addressed by short story writers. W. Somerset Maugham's Ashenden stories are based on the author's experiences of working for the secret service during the war, and constitute an early example of (semi-) professional spy fiction. Maugham's emphasis throughout is on the moral quandaries involved in counter-espionage, as in 'Giulia Lazzari', in which Ashenden has to coerce an ageing Italian dancer into betraying her lover, Chandra, an Indian agent working for Germany. Chandra kills himself rather than fall into English hands, and Ashenden is left puzzling over Giulia Lazzari's enigmatic character, which combines great affection for her dead lover with enough mercenary instinct to demand the return of an expensive present she had made him.

A wider range of stories reflect on the situation of the army veteran returned from the war and faced with adjusting to peacetime reality. In 'Sapper' H. C. McNeile's chauvinist tale 'The Man Who Would Not Play Cards', an officer returned from the Middle East finds his young wife in love with another man, 'an effeminate clothes-peg' with manicured hands and immaculate clothes.[20] The manly veteran succeeds in winning back his wife by exposing his would-be competitor as a fraud who has no interest in marriage. By contrast, Richard Aldington's 'The Case of Lieutenant Hall' – part of Aldington's embittered and thoroughly disillusioned collection, *Roads to Glory* (1930) – counters 'Sapper's' portrayal of the successful, empowered veteran with that of a deeply damaged man ravaged by guilt and depression, and driven to suicide by his memories of killing an innocent German and the atmosphere of rejection and poverty into which he returns. Composed as a series of diary entries, Aldington's story documents Hall's creeping mental and emotional decline, from the Armistice through a prolonged stint in post-war Belgium prior to being demobilized, to his 'demobbed' life in London.

Aldington's portrayal exemplifies the influential perspective of the well-educated, idealistic and disillusioned veteran who served in a junior officer role and experienced the war as a profound challenge to his liberal ideals. Crucially, however, stories such as 'The Case of Lieutenant Hall' are, though ostensibly about the First World War, really more concerned with the inter-war world and often say more about the 1920s and early 1930s than about the war itself. D. H. Lawrence's 'England, My England' is an interesting example of shifting perspectives, as this story exists in two strikingly different versions penned during and after the war, and thus illustrates changes between wartime and inter-war expression. The first, much shorter version of the story appeared in the *English Review* in October 1915, the second, extended version was collected in *England, My England and Other Stories* in 1921. Both versions follow the same basic plot: they outline the disintegrating marriage of a temperamentally ill-matched couple before the war, and the husband's enlistment and death at the front. However, while the earlier version looks in detail at the male protagonist's training and frontline experience, which culminates in his killing three enemy soldiers and being killed and mutilated in turn, the later version shifts emphasis away from army life and combat experience and explores the couple's troubled relationship in greater depth. In the inter-war version of 'England, My England', the war thus becomes part of a larger narrative of psychological disintegration rather than an immediate focal point.

Once the Second World War was underway, writers such as Alun Lewis began to record their war experience while still in training, and captured aptly the transitional period between being a civilian and being a combatant that had already been the subject of writers in the previous war. As Lewis himself put it in the 'Author's Note' to *The Last Inspection*, all but five of the stories in that collection

> are, if you like, studies of a 'hang-over.' Death in battle, death on a large scale, and all the attendant finalities and terrors – these are outside. They are the bread and water of our comrades overseas [. . .] The only deaths in these stories are from air raids and accidents; the main motif is the rootless life of soldiers having no enemy, and always, somehow, under a shadow.[21]

This shadow of war finds poignant expression in stories about soldiers stuck in training or on home duty, waiting and faced with the task of being reinvented, as the narrator of 'Lance-Jack' explains: 'In the Army you begin again. All you were seems to have vanished.'[22] And yet Lewis's soldiers also struggle with close ties to home and the fear for, or grief over, loved ones at present in greater danger than themselves. H. E. Bates's wartime short fiction is unusual in that it was officially commissioned. Bates was attached to the Royal Air Force at Oakington 'as a morale-boosting short-story writer – officially a flight lieutenant to public relations, Air Ministry', in which capacity he wrote and published a number of stories under the pseudonym 'Flying Officer X'.[23] No fewer than three of these were later anthologized in Dan Davin's *Short Stories from the Second World War* (1982). Bates's stories strike a balance between offering lively accounts of the reality of war in a branch of the military that had been imbued with a greater glamour than others from its beginnings in the First World War, and subtle reassurance for an anxious civilian audience. Bates's fictional(ized) aerodrome is a place of international collaboration, courage and fierce, personal dedication in the face of a shared enemy. The two main protagonists in 'There's Something in the Air', young English flying ace Anderson and his older Czech comrade Auerbach, each exemplify particular virtues of the airman: keenness and youthful energy in Anderson's case, patience and persistence in Auerbach's, highlighting the successful collaboration of Britons and their Allies. Understatement is the order of the day in an environment where the bland phrase 'good show' serves among the airmen to convey everything that, in Bates's view, press and general public can have no access to, 'something that could be read nowhere except in their eyes and expressed in no language but their own'.[24] His stories implicitly lay claim to bridging this gap between the fighter pilot and the woman in the street.

Short stories about war share with all other short fiction the handicap of relative ephemerality. Published in transitory media – magazines, newspapers, annual 'best of' collections – most stories disappeared from view quickly and thoroughly. The problem of ephemerality affected popular fiction more than 'literary' (particularly modernist) short fiction, but was certainly not limited to commercial fiction. Mainstream and avant-garde short stories alike relied for longevity on re-publication in anthologies, and war story anthologies have played an important part in perpetuating certain kinds of war stories over others, and in both shaping and illustrating how both wars are remembered through fiction. Market-driven, commercial anthologies in particular make an effort to stay close to the pulse of their time. In order to sell, they have to include stories (and authors) likely to appeal to a wide readership, and through their selection more often than not reveal the taste of this readership at the time of publication. Anthologies of war stories during the First World War unsurprisingly prioritized stories of patriotic sacrifice, most of which have gone out of fashion and are no more heard of today.

Some anthologies adopted a narrow focus on particular kinds of experience, such as naval or aerial warfare, a trend that continued after the war ended. Moreover, the 'stories' in these wartime anthologies are almost always real or fictional eyewitness accounts rather than genuine short stories in the literary sense of the word, as their editors inevitably emphasize the veracity and authenticity of the material included.

Although the taste for 'real' war stories continued after 1918, many inter-war anthologies began to collect short stories proper from among the rich crop of stories published during the war years and beyond. The most extensive and influential of these inter-war literary anthologies was Captain James H. C. Minchin's international anthology *Great Short Stories of the War: England, France, Germany, America* (1930). Minchin's selection set the tone for an understanding of First World War short fiction as fundamentally disillusioned and largely centred on fellow feeling and shared suffering between combatants of the major Western nations involved in the war. When Minchin observed in his prefatory note that 'much that has been written recently about the War is for the hour only and will cease to be; but much remains which will form the real history, imaginative and actual, of the greatest human experience' (p. e), he aptly reflected on the process of selecting what is to be remembered and what forgotten that is mirrored in the fate of the authors he included.[25] His collection is painstakingly balanced in terms of its four different national perspectives and includes some of the most poignant stories written about the war, including – as an opening tale – John Galsworthy's civilian war story 'Defeat'. Some of the authors included by Minchin subsequently featured regularly in the selections of other editors, first and foremost Richard Aldington, Henri Barbusse, C. E. Montague, E. M. Remarque and H. M. Tomlinson, but also popular authors like naval writer 'Bartimeus' (Lewis Anselm da Costa Ricci) or 'Sapper'. Joseph Conrad's 'The Tale' and W. Somerset Maugham's 'The Traitor' are another two stories first anthologized as 'war stories' in this volume that were picked up by a number of later editors. Many others, however, like Stacy Aumonier or Frederick Britten Austin, are now largely forgotten. Subsequent editors also cultivated a trend already emerging in Minchin's anthology, namely the inclusion of excerpts from longer works of prose (fiction or memoir) alongside genuine short fiction. This practice is taken to its extreme in two commercial war story anthologies of the 1990s, Hayden McAllister's *War Stories* and Jörg Hensgen's *The Vintage Book of War Stories*, which came with an introduction by Sebastian Faulks, himself a successful novelist with best-selling historical novels on both world wars, rather than a short story writer.[26] Both McAllister's and Hensgen's anthologies include virtually no genuine short stories and rely instead on excerpts from novels such as Elizabeth Bowen's *The Heat of the Day* (1949) or Robert Harris's *Enigma* (1995). Where McAllister's anthology offers a wider spread of stories from different conflicts, Hensgen's betrays a strong bias in favour of Second World War writing.

Collections with a more academic focus tend to place greater emphasis than purely commercial anthologies on the recovery of neglected material. This emphasis is visible in one of the best-known modern scholarly anthologies of First World War stories, Trudi Tate's *Women, Men and the Great War: An Anthology of Stories* (1995). Tate's decision to include stories written in English by an international range of authors means that a broad base of styles and experiences are represented, from William Faulkner, H. D., Ernest Hemingway and Edith Wharton to British and Commonwealth modernists like Katherine Mansfield, D. H. Lawrence, Virginia Woolf, Wyndham Lewis and Mary Butts. Tate chose to also include more traditional, popular writers like Rudyard Kipling and W. S. Maugham in a bid to represent the diverse short story market at the time. However, like other anthologies of the 1990s, Tate's collection pre-dates attempts to include writing by non-white colonial authors. This may in part be due to the fact that the process of recovering women's war writing was still in full swing, visible in other anthologies, such as Agnès Cardinal's impressive *Women's Writing on the First World War* (1999). Tate's anthology, however, remains the only genuine short story anthology of this period, as Cardinal's anthology, Margaret R. Higonnet's *Lines of Fire: Women Writers of World War I* (1999) and Angela K. Smith's *Women's Writing of the First World War* (2000) all include only a relatively small proportion of genuine short fiction. The 2000s saw the publication of two further anthologies specifically of First World War short stories, the *Penguin Book of First World War Stories* (Barbara Korte and Ann-Marie Einhaus, 2007) and Andrew Maunder's *British Literature of World War I: The Short Story and the Novella* (2011), the first volume in a series dedicated to recovering popular, mainstream writing about the war. While there are more attempts at including material dealing with frontlines other than the Western Front and the home front, however, these volumes equally do not stretch to covering colonial contributions beyond the white ANZAC narrative.

The Second World War also sparked a number of similar 'true story' eyewitness account collections and specialized naval or flying anthologies. Anthologies of Second World War short stories proper, however, are as few and far between as their First World War counterparts. The majority of Second World War anthologies include only some short stories alongside a larger proportion of excerpts from longer prose texts, letters and poetry, including Ronald Blythe's repeatedly reprinted *The Components of the Scene: An Anthology of the Prose and Poetry of the Second World War* (1966) and Robert Hewison's *Under Siege: Literary Life in London 1939–1945* (1977). While many commercial or educational anthologies of war stories include a proportion of Second World War material, this more often than not takes the form of excerpts from longer prose works, and collections of actual short fiction dealing with the war are rare. Two anthologies of Second World War short stories stand out, however: Dan Davin's *Short Stories from the Second World War* (1982) and Anne Boston's *Wave Me Goodbye: Stories of the Second World War* (1988). The majority of stories in Davin's anthology are by or about the combatant experience of war, although Davin strove to cover 'as many aspects as possible of the British at war in the years 1939 to 1945' and chastised earlier editors who had excluded home front stories as 'fastidious'.[27] It is perhaps understandable that Davin's selection was strongly informed by his own experience as a veteran writer, and no coincidence that he echoes Minchin in noting that many short stories of the Second World War had 'faded like the cheap paper of the little magazines in which they were printed, or like the photographs in old wartime albums, meaningful only to those who shared the experience they recall and incapable of transmitting it to those who did not' (p. xiv). However, the anthology also includes some stories – such as Graham Greene's 'Men at Work', William Sansom's 'The Wall' and Elizabeth Bowen's 'Mysterious Kôr' – which reflect the quintessential non-combatant experience of wartime London that has become such an intrinsic part of the war's cultural memory. A theme connecting many of the combatant and non-combatant stories in the collection is that of unreality coupled with the struggle to remember accurately after the fact. The mildly Kafkaesque world of Greene's Ministry of Propaganda, Sansom's firefighter recalling a collapsing wall seemingly suspended in mid-air, Bowen's moonlit metropolis made alien by war compare easily to Roald Dahl's RAF story 'A Piece of Cake', in which the narrator wakes from a strange fever dream to the nightmarish reality of severe facial injury, or to the sense of being outside oneself felt by the narrator of H. R. Savage's 'Night Attack'. In the face of traumatic experience, confident recall is frequently replaced by conjecture: while small, random details are burnt into the memory of the stories' narrators – the exact shape, size and make-up of a metal derrick in 'The Wall', the face of a middle-aged airman in 'A Piece of Cake' – their grasp of the hard facts is hazy and manifests itself in cautious, self-doubting expression. 'I suppose we took off from Fouka and flew towards Mersah, and I suppose we flew at about eight hundred feet', says Dahl's RAF pilot, echoed by Sansom's firefighter, who states, 'I suppose we were worn down and shivering. [...] I suppose we were drenched.'[28]

Anne Boston's Virago anthology, by contrast, explores the civilian experience of war beyond the metropolis and counters Davin's male-dominated selection with a deliberate female bias. Boston's sense of mission is to carve out a place for female war experience in particular, although many of the stories included, though written by women, adopt a male perspective. Her other declared aim, however, is to challenge reductive stereotypes of the 'official brave face of women at war' that have become a staple of the war's depiction in the popular imagination.[29] Rose Macaulay's autobiographically informed 'Miss Anstruther's Letters' is a case in point, as it is only one of several stories collected in *Wave Me Goodbye* that subtly undermines sentimental ideas about the so-called Blitz spirit. Having lost her flat and most of her possessions in a bombing raid, the eponymous Miss Anstruther is heartbroken solely over the loss of her dead lover's letters:

> 'Have you lost *all* your own?' the basement tenant asked, thinking about her motoring cups, and how she must get at them before the demolition men did, for they were silver.
> 'Everything,' Miss Anstruther answered. 'Everything. They don't matter.' [...] What she looked for was not there; it was ashes, it was no more.[30]

Although Miss Anstruther no longer cares, she is being victimized not simply by the destruction wreaked by German bomber planes, but by her own countrymen: the demolition men feared by her neighbour, who systematically loot bombed-out buildings and deprive desperate former inhabitants of even the last few possessions they have left. Nevertheless, Boston's anthology does not just focus on the darker aspects of civilian war experience; it also includes light-hearted popular stories of the magazine variety that would have made up the bulk of wartime reading for many British readers at the time. Most notable among these is Margery Sharp's short comic romance tale, 'Night Engagement', in which a young woman on the look-out for a suitable husband makes the most of a night spent trapped in a London basement with an eligible young railway clerk and emerges engaged, much to the delight of her enterprising mother. Boston's selection also includes reflections on the aftermath of war, most notably in the closing story of *Wave Me Goodbye*, Elizabeth Taylor's post-war story 'Gravement Endommagé':

> Across the street, which once had been narrow and now was open to the sky, a nun went slowly, carrying bread under her arm. The wind plucked her veil. A thin cat followed her. They picked their way across the rubble. The cat stopped once and lifted a paw, licked it carefully, and put it back into the grit. The faint sound of trowel on stone rang out, desultory, hopeless, a frail weapon against so convincing a destruction. That piteous tap, tap turned him away from the window. He could not bear the futility of the sound, or the thought of the monstrous task ahead, and now feared, more than all he could imagine, the sight of his wife hurrying back down the street, frowning, the picture-postcards in her hands.[31]

Which war is being referred to here? The setting is somewhere in France, but the time could be either post-1918 or post-1945. This ambiguity is not coincidental in 'Gravement Endommagé', which links the destruction of both world wars and the emotional as well as physical damage they leave behind explicitly as well as implicitly. The sense of futility felt by the protagonist, a veteran of both wars, is particular to the aftermath of the Second World War, however, and its pervasive sense that total war is not a once-in-a-lifetime occurrence, but something repetitive, unavoidable. Taylor also links the task of physical rebuilding with the potentially even more monumental (and possibly futile) task of rebuilding relationships damaged in the war: the protagonist finds himself estranged from his wife, whose very character has been affected by her anxious wartime exile in the English countryside, and whose love and trust he seems to have lost.

Scholarly and revisionist anthologists of war stories from either war are faced with the same need to balance the desire to reflect the diverse experience of war as fully as possible with the desire to select stories that, as Dan Davin put it, 'merited inclusion by [their] own literary right'.[32] Both of these aims are ultimately subjective, and it is perhaps impossible to do equal justice to both at the same time. Since so many war stories are geared particularly towards an 'in-group' of readers with the relevant experience of the war, their very nature is likely to clash with the notion of lasting literary value. This circumstance at least in part explains the conspicuous lack of canonization enjoyed by most short stories of the First and Second World War. Those stories that survive tend to be the ones that are either felt to encapsulate best a particular experience of these wars as they are popularly remembered – the Western Front trenches, the Blitz, desert warfare – or are in some way felt to transcend the experience of one war in particular and speak to some fundamental human condition. In their very elusiveness and frequent obscurity, short stories about either war thus offer a fitting analogy to the cultural memory of war. As a highly diverse, often contradictory body of texts drawn from all walks of life and a wide range of different experiences, war stories are subject to the same selective processes – re-arrangement and rewriting to suit particular needs – as are memories of either the First or the Second World War.

Notes

1. H. E. Bates, *The Modern Short Story: A Critical Survey* (1941) (Boston: The Writer, 1965), pp. 222–3.
2. Dan Davin, 'Introduction', in *Short Stories from the Second World War* (Oxford University Press, 1982), pp. i–xiv (p. ix).
3. See Rod Mengham, 'British Fiction of the War', in *The Cambridge Companion to the Literature of World War II*, ed. Marina MacKay (Cambridge University Press, 2009), pp. 26–42 (p. 26).
4. Richard Greaves, 'Responses to War: 1914–1918 and 1939–1945', in *A Companion to the British and Irish Short Story*, ed. David Malcolm and Cheryl Alexander Malcolm (Oxford: Wiley-Blackwell, 2008), pp. 35–50 (p. 49).
5. Barbara Korte and Ann-Marie Einhaus, 'Short-Term Memories: The First World War in British Short Stories, 1914–1939', *Literature & History*, 18.1 (2009), pp. 54–67 (p. 55).
6. Andrew Maunder, *British Literature of World War I, Volume 1: The Short Story and the Novella* (London: Chatto & Pickering, 2011), p. xv.
7. Maunder, *British Literature of World War I*, pp. xxxiii; xli.
8. Elizabeth Bowen, *The Mulberry Tree: Writings of Elizabeth Bowen*, ed. Hermione Lee (London: Virago, 1986), p. 97.
9. Virginia Woolf, 'The Mark on the Wall', in *Women, Men and the Great War: An Anthology of Stories*, ed. Trudi Tate (Manchester University Press, 1995), pp. 160–6 (p. 166).
10. Victoria Stewart, 'The Last War: The Legacy of the First World War in 1940s British Fiction', in *British Popular Culture and the First World War*, ed. Jessica Meyer (Leiden: Brill, 2008), pp. 259–81 (p. 260).
11. Elizabeth Bowen, 'The Demon Lover', in *The Collected Stories of Elizabeth Bowen*, intro. by Angus Wilson (London: Jonathan Cape, 1980), pp. 661–6 (p. 662).
12. Mollie Panter-Downes, 'Meeting at the Pringles'', in *Good Evening, Mrs Craven: The Wartime Stories of Mollie Panter-Downes* (London: Persephone, 1999), pp. 7–13 (pp. 12–13).
13. Arthur Calder-Marshall, 'Before the War', in *English Story: First Series*, ed. Woodrow and Susan Wyatt (London: Collins, 1941), pp. 113–26 (pp. 117; 124–5).

14. Blanche Wills Chandler, 'Zepp Proof', in *Tommies Two* (London: Sampson Low, 1917), pp. 34–7.
15. See e.g. Jane Potter, 'For Country, Conscience and Commerce: Publishers and Publishing, 1914–18', in *Publishing in the First World War: Essays in Book History*, ed. Mary Hammond and Shafquat Towheed (Basingstoke: Palgrave Macmillan, 2007), pp. 11–26.
16. First published in the *Evening News* on 29 September 1914, this story was subsequently published in a short collection of war tales entitled *The Angels of Mons: The Bowmen and Other Legends of the War* (1915).
17. 'The Prisoner's Defence' appeared in *The Strand Magazine* in February 1916.
18. Elizabeth Bowen, 'Careless Talk', in *The Collected Stories of Elizabeth Bowen*, pp. 667–70 (p. 669).
19. Jean Rhys, 'I Spy a Stranger', in *Wave Me Goodbye: Stories of the Second World War*, ed. Anne Boston (London: Virago, 1988), pp. 85–97 (p. 94).
20. 'Sapper' [H. C. MacNeile], 'The Man Who Would Not Play Cards', *Strand Magazine*, 59.354 (June 1920), 541–49 (p. 545).
21. Alun Lewis, *The Last Inspection* (London: Allen & Unwin, 1942), p. 5.
22. Alun Lewis, 'Lance-Jack', in *The Last Inspection* (London: Allen & Unwin, 1942), pp. 69–78 (p. 70).
23. Robert Lusty, 'Bates, Herbert Ernest (1905–1974)', Rev. Clare L. Taylor, in *Oxford Dictionary of National Biography*, ed. H. C. G. Matthew and Brian Harrison (Oxford University Press, 2004). Online edn ed. Lawrence Goldman. Oct. 2009, www.oxforddnb.com/view/article/30796 (accessed 25 July 2014).
24. H. E. Bates, 'No Trouble at All', in *Short Stories from the Second World War*, ed. Dan Davin, pp. 93–8 (p. 98).
25. Minchin's anthology was published in the United Kingdom by Eyre & Spottiswoode with an introduction by Edmund Blunden (1930), and in the United States by Harper Brothers (with the modified title *Best Short Stories of the War*) introduced by H. M. Tomlinson (1931).
26. Hayden McAllister, *War Stories* (London: Octopus, 1997); Jörg Hensgen, *The Vintage Book of War Stories* (London: Vintage, 1999).
27. Davin, 'Introduction', in *Short Stories from the Second World War*, pp. i, x.
28. Roald Dahl, 'A Piece of Cake', pp. 40–51 (p. 42); William Sansom, 'The Wall', pp. 20–3 (p. 20), both in *Short Stories from the Second World War*, ed. Davin.
29. Anne Boston, 'Introduction', in *Wave Me Goodbye: Stories of the Second World War* (London: Virago, 1988), pp. ix–xviii (p. ix).
30. Rose Macaulay, 'Miss Anstruther's Letters', in *Wave Me Goodbye: Stories of the Second World War*, ed. Anne Boston, pp. 40–7 (p. 41).
31. Elizabeth Taylor, 'Gravement Endommagé', in *Wave Me Goodbye: Stories of the Second World War*, ed. Anne Boston, pp. 260–6 (p. 264).
32. Davin, ed., *Short Stories from the Second World War*, p. i.

10

The Short Story in Ireland to 1945: A National Literature

HEATHER INGMAN

The Nineteenth-Century Tale

Any account of the Irish short story would be incomplete without some reference to its predecessor, the nineteenth-century tale. The 1800 Act of Union stimulated English interest in this part of their empire and depictions of Irish life and customs, collections of folklore and travelogues, often presented in quasi-fictional form, became immensely popular in the first decades of the nineteenth century. However, just as the Irish state had still to come into being, so the Irish short story had yet to stabilize as a genre. 'Tale' in the nineteenth century could mean anything from a brief sketch, anecdote or fable to a novella or even a three-volume novel. Much of the short fiction in this period was used for extra-literary purposes as Protestant and Catholic writers were propelled by their anxiety to defend and explain the Irish to the English and to record the beliefs and habits of Irish peasant life before they vanished forever. Under pressure from the turbulent times in Ireland, the realistic framework of the fiction often collapsed into gothic or melodrama, sentimentality or didactics.

In the first decades of the nineteenth century Anglo-Irish writers like Maria Edgeworth and Anna Hall published tales designed to instruct English readers in an understanding of the Irish way of life, essential if the Anglo-Irish were to govern Ireland effectively. Their didactic, though lively, tales were thus implicated in the imperial project. Other writers from the Protestant tradition, such as Thomas Crofton Croker (*Fairy Tales and Legends of the South of Ireland*, 1825) and Samuel Lover (*Legends and Stories of Ireland*, 1832), drew on oral storytelling and Irish folklore for the amusement of their English readers. Lover aimed to reproduce the lively tones of an Irish storyteller but undermined this by framing it with the voice of an educated, highly condescending narrator.

Catholic writers John and Michael Banim took exception to these portrayals of the Irish peasant as buffoon. In their *Tales of the O'Hara Family* (first series, 1825) they aimed for serious portraits of contemporary rural hardship and thereby came nearer to bringing a national literature into being. As the successive Irish famines took hold, the Banims' tales grew darker and more conflicted as the authors strove to present the nobility of the Irish peasant without alienating their English readers. Advances the brothers made in the art of characterization and maintaining tension in their tales were undercut by the pressure of the times, which impelled them to break off their storytelling to lament the suffering in the Irish countryside. The middle-class Catholic writer Gerald Griffin likewise sought to present his country in a favourable light to an English readership but he was also conscious of inheriting a specifically Irish literary tradition, paying homage in *Tales of the Munster Festivals* (1827) to Maria Edgeworth and the Banim brothers as his predecessors in the form. A story like 'The Knight of the Sheep' displays Griffin's gifts for structure, characterization and a psychological intensity that nudges the nineteenth-century tale towards the modern short story.

The fracturing of the short fictional form under pressure from Ireland's turbulent times is seen most clearly in William Carleton's *Traits and Stories of the Irish Peasantry* (1830). Carleton's tales capture Irish identity at a moment of transition, providing the most vivid portrait in Irish literature of pre-famine Ireland, its hedge schools and chapels, its weddings and wakes, at the same time as illustrating how such a culture was becoming unsustainable in the modern world. Born into a bilingual peasant family in County Tyrone, Carleton was closer to the lives he was describing than Griffin or the Banims and he had a direct link back through his father's storytelling and his mother's songs to the Gaelic culture that was even now passing away. He received his education in various hedge schools and rose to become the first major Irish Catholic writer in English. The pressing circumstances of Irish life meant, however, that non-literary matters often took precedence over the literary in Carleton's writing. In his preface to the 1842 edition of his tales he positioned himself, as Griffin had done, as inheritor of an Irish literary tradition, citing such predecessors as Maria Edgeworth, Anna Hall, John Banim and Griffin himself. The larger part of his preface was taken up, however, not with establishing an Irish literary tradition, but with his defence of the nobility of the Irish peasant, and it is evident from contemporary reviews in the *Dublin University Magazine* and the *Dublin University Review* that what readers looked for in his tales was not Carleton's handling of the short narrative form but a portrait of their country.[1]

Carleton's increasing success as a writer distanced him from the peasant community into which he had been born: as Declan Kiberd has described it, Carleton became a sort of middleman between the peasants he understood so well and the English audience for which he was writing.[2] The strain of this dual aim, to make known the world of the Irish peasant and to impress the English reader, shows in his writing. Although his stories are full of authentic details, strong characterizations and lively dialogue, his eye to an English audience meant that as much as his predecessors he could not let a story tell itself but felt obliged to intervene and explain things to the reader. Barbara Hayley has studied Carleton's transformation, under pressure to comment on Irish circumstances, from the oral storytelling techniques of his early stories towards an omniscient narrator and standard English. Carleton's constant revisions between editions of his tales, listed in detail by Hayley, reveal his uncertainty about his aims.[3] His concern to document his stories as factual and authentic accounts of life in the Irish countryside meant that by the 1842 edition the original tales were often swamped by footnotes and commentary. Carleton chose to sacrifice spontaneity and lively storytelling to the felt need to comment on Ireland.

If the short fiction of Catholic writers reflected the chaos following the dissolution of a way of life and a language, Anglo-Irish writers, for all their belief in their hereditary right to rule Ireland, were also left shaken by events. The post-Famine era saw the rise of Fenianism and expansion of the Catholic Church's influence, while in England a Whig government rejected an identity of interests with the Anglo-Irish landlords. The 1869 Act disestablishing the Church of Ireland and the 1870 Land Act giving rights to tenants were widely interpreted as marking the end of the Ascendancy. Sheridan Le Fanu's collection, *In a Glass Darkly* (1872), draws on the gothic to express Anglo-Irish guilt and anxiety in a series of tales that portray minds on the brink of collapse. Like Edgar Allan Poe, Le Fanu uses the tale to portray psychological states of mind and his tightly structured stories may, like Poe's work, be seen as forerunners of the modern short story.

Also contributing to the shaping of the modern short story were the Anglo-Irish writers Edith Somerville and Violet Martin, who wrote under the pseudonym of Somerville and Ross. On the surface their *Irish R.M.* stories (*Some Experiences of an Irish R. M.*, 1899, *Further Experiences of an Irish R. M.*, 1908, and *In Mr Knox's Country*, 1915), drawing on Irish folk beliefs and portraying obtuse Protestant landlords and wily Catholic tenants, may be regarded as extending the nineteenth-century tale. The difference is that now, as with Anthony Trollope's two Irish stories from the 1860s,

'The O'Conors of Castle Conor, County Mayo' and 'Father Giles of Ballymoy', it is the naïve English visitor to Ireland who is the chief object of satire. A recent critical study has emphasized the alertness of Somerville and Ross to contemporary artistic developments and linked their stories to European traditions of pantomime, carnival and harlequinade.[4] This, together with an emphasis on the tight formal structure of their stories, their sharp ear for dialogue and a consistent narrative voice, gives a markedly more modern reading of their stories.

For much of the nineteenth century the story form was under pressure from external events. Nevertheless, as the century wore on, Irish writers began to pay attention to structure, tension and psychological development in a way that intermittently foreshadowed the short story of the twentieth century.

The Irish Literary Revival

At the turn of the century the Irish Literary Revival, part of a general move to strengthen Irish identity after the devastating famines of the nineteenth century, inspired antiquarians and collectors of folklore like Douglas Hyde and William Larminie to retrieve authentic folk tales from oral sources.[5] Although the short story is generally held to be a modern form, in Ireland this judgement has been complicated by the long-perceived relationship with the tradition of oral storytelling. Commentators on the Irish short story remain divided as to how much the modern form owes to the oral tradition. Donna Wong has argued that the relationship between the literary short story and the tradition of oral storytelling in Ireland accounts for the centrality of the genre in the Irish canon.[6] Other scholars, such as Elizabeth Fine, have drawn a clear distinction between the copious and dramatic art of the storyteller and the tautness of the modern short story, arguing that to write down oral material is irrevocably to alter it.[7]

Writers of the Irish Literary Revival participated in the effort to rescue the folk tale from its nineteenth-century accretions: inspired by long holidays spent in his mother's native Sligo, W. B. Yeats edited two books of fairy and folk tales and in 1893 published *The Celtic Twilight: Men and Women, Dhouls and Fairies*. Despite its stated desire to retrieve an ancient culture, however, the impetus behind the Irish Literary Revival was essentially a modernizing one: Yeats and his colleagues in the revivalist movement (Lady Gregory, J. M. Synge, James Stephens) were intent on reshaping the Celtic past to suit their own vision of Ireland. Yeats used folk themes to explain and justify his belief in the spiritual qualities of the Irish landscape and peasantry and to develop his occult and aesthetic interests. As early as 1902 he was complaining that tellers of folk tales 'did not think sufficiently about the shape of the poem and the story'.[8] His unease is demonstrated in his introduction to *Representative Irish Tales* (1891), his influential selection of short fiction by Carleton, Griffin, Croker, Lover, the Banim brothers and others, where he lays stress on the fact that, with a few exceptions, these tales are limited by their lack of artistry. In Yeats we see a tension between the demands of the Irish Revival and the quest for artistic form that has implications for our understanding of the development of the Irish short story.

Yeats's knowledge of modern literary developments was deepened by his frequentation of London's *avant garde* literary circles, especially the Rhymers Club. Despite its name the latter took an interest in short fiction, reflecting the fact that, on the international scene, the short story was very much the modern artistic form of the 1890s. Irish periodicals such as the *Irish Homestead* (1895–1923), the *Irish Review* (1911–14) and, later, the *Irish Statesman* (1919–30) played an influential role in the development of the modern Irish short story, publishing work by writers associated with the Revival and thereby providing a new readership for short fiction. A new type of story was developing, one less concerned with a remarkable incident or a plot recounted by an omniscient narrator but focusing rather on mood and psychological exploration. Irish writers were influenced by the psychological realism of Flaubert and Maupassant, by Ibsen's naturalism, and by the newly translated Russian authors, Tolstoy, Turgenev and Chekhov. There is thus a tension in this period between the impulse towards the past and the local inspired by the Gaelic Revival and modern literary trends, often influenced by foreign models.

Yeats was less interested in the technical innovations of the short story than in the work of Oscar Wilde who made occasional appearances at the Rhymers Club and whose reputation as an author dated from the publication of *The Happy Prince and Other Tales* in 1888. Wilde had been brought into direct contact with the world of the Irish-speaking peasants in the late 1870s when he accompanied his father to the west of Ireland and recent critical writing on Wilde's fairy stories has emphasized their links with Irish folklore.[9] Critics have connected Wilde's choice of the stylized form of the fairy tale with his nationalist sympathies and with his subversive critique of Victorian society from the point of view of the marginalized and dispossessed.[10] It has been argued that Wilde's fairy tales may be interpreted as criticizing British imperialism from the perspective of the colonized Irish, portrayed in the tales as children ruled by wrong-headed giants and princes.[11] Less didactically than Maria Edgeworth, Wilde used children's stories to convey to the English reader a message about Ireland. Readings such as these draw Wilde's fairy tales close to Yeats's alliance of mysticism and nationalism in his collection *The Secret Rose* (1897). The dominant theme of both *The Happy Prince* and Wilde's later collection of stories, *A House of Pomegranates* (1891), namely the conflict between society's materialism and the spiritual and artistic life, is one that also preoccupied Yeats.

Yeats used his short fiction first and foremost to transmit his occult and nationalist vision. His stories belong to his formative years as an artist and were part of a process by which he was elaborating his quest for enlightenment and exploring the tension between the material world and the world of the occult imagination. The chronological ordering of the stories in *The Secret Rose* emphasizes the continuing conflict between the spiritual and the material world through different historical periods and gives the collection a unity of design almost unknown in Irish story collections until Joyce's *Dubliners*. Unity is also provided by the tight geographical focus on the west of Ireland but, despite drawing on Irish folklore, Yeats was not addressing a popular audience in this collection. Rather he was writing in a polished, Paterian style for an intellectual elite whom he hoped would understand and profit by the esoteric and occult meanings in his stories. In *The Secret Rose* Yeats moved the folklore tradition away from its oral and popular roots into the realms of the literary and the occult. The stories reflect Yeats's range of influence, from Joachim of Fiore to William Blake and Joris-Karl Huysmans. Early reviewers of the collection, accustomed to the heavily plotted stories of Stevenson and Kipling, castigated Yeats's stories for having too little plot and relying instead on mood and atmosphere. Mood and atmosphere are, however, precisely the qualities that were to become characteristic of the modernist short story and it is at moments like these one spies the overlap between writing of the Irish Revival and the modernist movement.

Modernism

The New Woman writer George Egerton was, like Wilde and Yeats, initially allied to London's decadent and aesthetic literary circles and she published her first short story, 'A Lost Masterpiece', in the first volume of *The Yellow Book* (1894). Her stories, some of which are set in Ireland, fitted in well with that periodical's emphasis on psychological intensity and formal innovation.

Born Mary Chavelita Dunne, Egerton spent part of her childhood in Ireland and it was there that she worked on her first two collections of stories, *Keynotes* published in 1893 to immediate acclaim, and *Discords* published a year later. New Woman writers, it has been observed, were especially attracted to short fiction because it freed them from the traditional plots of the Victorian novel and made possible the formal innovation necessary for exploring the new subject of women's consciousness.[12] Gender themes outweigh nationalism in Egerton's work as she explores women's inner lives, arguing that women should enjoy the same sexual freedoms as men. Her stories draw on the subversive qualities inherent in the form to do away with conventions of plot, linearity and discursive explanation in favour of dreams, symbolism and stream-of-consciousness. In them it is possible to discern an emerging modernist aesthetic.

Egerton was greatly influenced by Scandinavian writers such as Strindberg and Ibsen and it is arguable that the Irish short story was shaped in this period, not by the indigenous folk tradition, but by foreign writers like Turgenev, Chekhov, Flaubert and Maupassant. From these authors Irish short story writers learned irony, brevity and the importance of attention to style and to sentence rhythm. Chekhov's reliance on mood, feeling and tone to achieve unity in his stories was influential. Irish writers were influenced too by the movement away from authorial comment, by Flaubert's free indirect style presenting events through the consciousness of his characters and by Chekhov's depictions of an experience encountered rather than explained. The turn of the century debates on the aesthetics of the short story were no doubt a factor in attracting James Joyce, a writer unusually alert to international developments, to the form. Joyce believed that Yeats was on the wrong track with his obsession with folk themes but he praised Yeats's occult stories for being 'Russian' and, by a telling coincidence, it was the Russian quality of *Dubliners* (1914) that Yeats was later to admire.[13]

The tension between the local and the foreign, the past and modernity in this period is exemplified in George Moore's groundbreaking collection, *The Untilled Field* (1903). After a lengthy residence abroad Moore returned to Dublin in 1901 determined to contribute to the Gaelic Revival and it was suggested to him that if he wanted to write stories about the west of Ireland peasantry Turgenev's *Sketches from a Hunter's Album* (1852) would be a suitable model.[14] The social context of Turgenev's *Sketches*, a collection of observations about the suffering and exploitation of the Russian serfs narrated by a compassionate and intelligent landowner, had particular resonance for Irish readers. Moore's openness to international artistic developments attracted him to Turgenev's manner of proceeding through implication and evocation. Though Moore's stories present a rural Irish parish that seems unchanged since Carleton's tales, his literary techniques, inspired by Flaubert as well as by Turgenev, move his stories into the modern period. Through a remarkable intertwining of the local and the foreign, the modern short story was born in Ireland.

Carefully controlled stories like 'Exile', 'Homesickness', 'The Window' and 'The Wedding Gown' move adeptly between the outer and inner lives of the characters in a technique Moore borrowed from Flaubert rather than from Turgenev. As 'Exile' unfolds, through dialogue between Pat and his sons with the minimum of authorial comment, the reader has to interpret the subtext of a conversation where what is left unsaid is often more important than what is voiced. 'Homesickness' vividly encapsulates the tension between modernity and the past, the international and the local, in the contrast it draws between American urban life and Irish rural life. In its mixture of external details (the Irish landscape) and psychological states of mind (the landscape alters according to Bryden's mood), 'Homesickness' is a Chekhovian story transplanted to Ireland. Moreover, like many of Chekhov's stories, it opens out in the end into a reflection on the universal longing for happiness, its evocation of the human condition as one of exile and loneliness foreshadowing Frank O'Connor's definition of the short story as representing 'the lonely voice'.[15] Moore's portrait of the exile's eternal restlessness was to influence many later Irish short story writers.

Yet *The Untilled Field* also displays unevenness in its handling of the short story form. The collection does not confine itself to Irish rural life but takes in the urban poor, as well as city-dwelling bohemians and artists. In three of the stories – 'Alms-Giving', 'The Wild Goose' and 'Fugitives' – Moore was unable to resist the impulse to didacticism, rendering them stylistically very different from the rest. In 'The Wild Goose' Ned Carmady becomes a mouthpiece for Moore's disillusionment with Ireland and his deepening anti-clericalism. Echoes of the oral tradition in stories such as 'A Play-House in the Waste' and 'Julia Cahill's Curse' reveal a local influence that disrupts the claims of *The Untilled Field* to be regarded as a unified collection of modern short stories. Rather, the collection may be seen as a transitional volume, employing some traditional techniques while at the same time developing the sophistication of the Irish short story form through psychological insight, concision, allusiveness and understatement. A story like 'So on He Fares' perfectly illustrates the blend of old and new in Moore's work. It is at once a psychological study of a child's awareness of his rejection by his mother and a folk tale in which the boy is saved from drowning by a bargeman, finds a substitute mother and embarks on a quest for adventure. It may be that it was such lingering traces of the folk tale, together with the didacticism of stories like 'The Wild Goose' and 'Fugitives', which led James Joyce to speak critically of *The Untilled Field*, calling it 'very dull and flat indeed: and ill-written'.[16]

Dubliners was an innovation in the development of the Irish short story: never before had there been such an artistically unified collection, nor one that so clearly broke with the Gaelic tradition of storytelling. Joyce himself, in a letter to his brother Stanislaus in 1905 outlining the pattern of his book, signalled the thematic and stylistic originality of *Dubliners*. It was to consist of stories about childhood followed by stories about, respectively, adolescence, maturity and public life, all set in the context of life in Dublin, a city that, he explained to his English publisher, Grant Richards, with more enthusiasm than accuracy, 'I do not think any writer has yet presented to the world'.[17]

From Joyce's description, readers might expect to find a collection of short stories depicting in realist fashion the life of Dublin's citizens at the turn of the century. In one sense they would be right. *Dubliners* is deeply embedded in the historical fabric of Dublin: 'Araby' refers to a bazaar held in Dublin in 1894, 'A Mother' incorporates a concert that took place in 1904. In the Dubliners' wanderings around the city, they are shadowed by monuments of the British colonial administration. Writing, like Moore, against the romantic nationalism of the Celtic Revival, and influenced by Ibsen's social realism, Joyce portrays the reality of living in a decaying, defeated colonial backwater. One of his stated aims in *Dubliners* was to encourage his fellow Irish to relinquish Revivalist writers' idealizations about Ireland and see the truth of themselves in his 'nicely polished looking-glass'.[18] The opening three stories of childhood reveal a world that offers so little to the young narrator that he is constantly seeking ways to escape and yet that world gradually closes in on him until all his dreams of escape end in frustration. The boy's realization of the extent to which he has become implicated in the corrupt ideologies of the adult world marks the end of childhood. Henceforth the stories are told in the third person, for their older protagonists have already become trapped by Dublin's paralysis. The long shadow of colonial exploitation is evident in the desperate stratagems of both men and women to cope with Dublin's depressed economic climate and the corruption of the city's politics, culture and religion by material self-interest. In the final story,

'The Dead', Joyce attempted to make amends for the bleakness of his earlier stories by depicting the city's tradition for generous hospitality.

Dubliners is very far from being confined to a realist text, however. Joyce extends Moore's method of operating through suggestion and implication, using ellipses, hiatuses and silences in a way that obliges the reader to become an essential part of the equation in order to complete the story's meaning: the figure of the *gnomon* meaning, amongst other things, an incomplete parallelogram, which fascinates the boy in the opening story, 'The Sisters', has been taken by many readers to be an organizing motif for the whole collection. The subject becomes decentred in a manner characteristic of modernism, or even postmodernism, and the gaps in the discourse demand that the reader work to supply the meaning of the incomplete parallelogram: another meaning of gnomon is judge or interpreter. This participation of the reader in constructing the meaning of the text marks Joyce's break with the didacticism of nineteenth-century short fiction. Using free indirect style borrowed, like Moore's, from Flaubert, Joyce enters directly into the thoughts of his characters but extends this technique in stories like 'Clay' to produce a narrator who is unreliable and a text that is unstable. In the first three stories the narrators' limitations arise from their youth. These stories signal that suspension rather than closure is to be the keynote of the collection and they point forward to Joyce's final masterpiece, 'The Dead', where the uncertainty becomes metaphysical.

In *Dubliners* Joyce transformed the Irish short story through his adaptation of tone, style and form to the character of his protagonists, his use of patterning, epiphany and symbols, his intertextuality and his 'writerly' texts that compel the reader's active participation in determining meaning. The irony is that, ignoring the implications of Joyce's modernist experiments, the Irish short story of the following decades turned back on itself and attempted to pin down the realism that had largely eluded it in the nineteenth century.

Post-Independence Ireland

As the energies sparked by the Literary Revival and by the 1916 Rising and the War of Independence faded in the more repressive and provincial atmosphere of the 1920s and 1930s, the short story in this period in the hands of writers like Frank O'Connor, Seán O'Faoláin and Liam O'Flaherty reflected a realistic awareness of the limitations of the Irish nation as embodied in the Irish state. Yeatsian romanticism, useful for inspiring a revolution, no longer seemed adequate to portray the realities of Irish life. In the post-independence era, as in the nineteenth century, the pressing circumstances of Ireland had its consequences for the short fiction form. The land, nationalism and religion were the topics Daniel Corkery deemed suitable for a genuinely Irish literature. For other writers, the civil war, censorship, a puritanical religion and the narrowly defined nationalism that marked the newly independent state, were all deeply disillusioning: the banning for alleged obscenity of *The Tailor and Ansty* (1942), Tim Buckley's traditional Irish tales collected by Eric Cross, is only one example of the repressive atmosphere of these years. Despite the fact that the short story was developing into the characteristic Irish prose form, several writers were not to reach full maturity as artists until after these decades and what most strikes the reader is the transitional nature of the Irish short story of this period, both in theme and style.

An example of this is Seumas O'Kelly's masterpiece, 'The Weaver's Grave', published posthumously in 1919 and republished in 1922 by Dublin's Talbot Press with illustrations by Jack Yeats. The tragi-comic tone, earthy dialect and length of 'The Weaver's Grave' recall the nineteenth-century tale, but the elderly *seanchaí* (storytellers), Meehaul and Cahir, know that they possess skills no longer needed in the modern world. Despite echoes of the oral tradition, this is not a peasant story; instead it is narrated in standard English for an educated and literate readership. At the end the focus shifts from storytelling to modernist stream-of-consciousness, entering into the thoughts of Hehir's young widow as she realizes she is falling in love. What seems like a tale of peasant life ends on a modernist epiphany, perhaps one of the reasons why Joyce admired this story.

Also transitional are the stories of Daniel Corkery. Corkery was mentor to both Frank O'Connor and Seán O'Faoláin and, despite the propaganda for Irish nationalism in his non-fiction, his best stories bear witness to the stresses of an emergent Irish nation unsure of the way forward and of how much of the past to jettison. In his finest collection, *The Stormy Hills* (1929), stories like 'The Emptied Sack' and 'Carrig-an-Afrinn' depict the psychological and emotional price of progress. While the former ends on stasis with the furze-gatherer's lament over the modern furnace that has put him out of business, the latter's conclusion is equally poised between past and present: Michael Hodnett's endeavours to raise his family in the world may have exhausted his energies and those of his older children, but they have produced a model farm and a younger generation with energy and ambition. Many of Corkery's stories draw on the oral tradition but employ an educated narrator to introduce and explain the settings and it has been argued that Corkery's stories seek not so much to reproduce oral techniques as to combine them with modern literary forms.[19] Stories like 'Nightfall', tightly narrated, in standard English, by someone slightly distanced from the community he describes, and 'The Awakening', which ends on a moment of epiphany for the youthful protagonist, illustrate Corkery's move towards the modern short story.

At first sight the stories of Liam O'Flaherty seem to belong to an older tradition of storytelling. O'Flaherty grew up on the Aran islands in an Irish-speaking community where the oral tradition was still very much alive, and its influence is evident in O'Flaherty's three major collections published during the 1920s: *Spring Sowing* (1924), *The Tent* (1926) and *The Mountain Tavern and Other Stories* (1929). Many of the stories in *Spring Sowing* and *The Tent* are seemingly timeless, lyrical evocations of nature, the animals and the peasants among whom O'Flaherty spent his childhood. Some of his stories are plotless sketches, word pictures of nature's energy ('A Wave') or the primitive struggle for life ('The Rockfish'). Others portray brief moments of sympathy between humans and animals, as in 'The Cow's Death', one of O'Flaherty's personal favourites, where the farmer's wife empathizes with the cow's grief for her dead calf. Several, like 'The Blackbird', are animal fables in the manner of La Fontaine, with animals taking on human traits. Yet change is evident even in these rural communities and stories such as 'The Caress' abandon the mythic in favour of social realism, reminding us that from an early age O'Flaherty was educated outside his community and became influenced by the portrayal of peasant life in Maupassant and Gorky, as well as by the naturalism of writers like Zola and Jack London. This influence is most clearly seen in *The Mountain Tavern and Other Stories* published at the end of a decade during which O'Flaherty had become disillusioned by the stifling of intellectual and artistic life in Ireland and where the picture of peasant life is bleaker and more critical than in the earlier collections.

The writers who arguably did most to shape the Irish short story mid-century, Frank O'Connor and Seán O'Faoláin, published their first collections in the 1930s. Frank O'Connor's *Guests of the Nation* (1931) and *Bones of Contention* (1936) are apprentice volumes in which traces of the oral tradition, and an emphasis, like Corkery's, on the community rather than the individual, make these stories uncharacteristic of his later style. Influenced by Chekhov, O'Connor began to formulate his view of the short story as a tightly controlled form focused on a single situation that provokes a crisis. O'Connor's earliest stories, however, reflect his preoccupation with the speaking voice and his efforts to recreate in the modern short story the human warmth and vigour of oral storytelling. In *Guests of the Nation* stories such as 'The Late Henry Conran' are related almost entirely through dialogue in a way that is uncharacteristic of the later O'Connor. 'September Dawn', portraying the emotional state of a republican gunman on the run, is more typical of the mature O'Connor.

The title story, 'Guests of the Nation', one of O'Connor's best-known stories, centres on what was to become an important theme in his work, namely the juxtaposition of the public political world with the private world of ordinary human ties. Set during the war of independence, 'Guests of the Nation' reveals how far O'Connor had travelled from Corkery's influence, in both style and subject matter, romantic nationalism being replaced by an ironic realism that becomes transmuted at the end into tragedy. The story exemplifies several traits that were to become characteristic of the modern short story: precision of language, economy and careful attention to tone, imagery and structure. The focus on a moment of crisis in the narrator's life makes this a paradigmatic O'Connor story, though in his later work the turning point would be conveyed more subtly, through the narrative itself. The ending opens out onto a wider alienation for the narrator as the deaths of the two Englishmen make him realize how easily home and human affections can be betrayed. In *Bones of Contention* stories such as 'The Majesty of the Law' and 'In the Train', pitting individuals against the community, private morality against public law, mark a development towards O'Connor's later style. The controlled narrative perspective of 'In the Train' moves from a picture of the closed, materialistic, prejudiced village environment that has provoked Helena's crime to focus on Helena herself. It illustrates O'Connor's shift from stories based around traditional communities to the modern short story centred, like Joyce's writing, on the alienated individual.

Seán O'Faoláin's stories in his first collection, *Midsummer Night Madness* (1932), are more extended than those of O'Connor and nudge the short story more firmly towards modernist techniques of irony, indirection and probing the inner consciousness of the characters. The title story, 'Midsummer Night Madness' is shaped, not by external events such as the burning down of the Big House, but by the narrator's partial consciousness and a skilful exploration of the gunmen's psychology. The speaking voice of oral tradition becomes transformed into the perspectivalism of the modernist narrator. Other modernist traits in this collection include the musical counterpointing and inconclusiveness of 'Fugue' and the intermittent use of stream-of-consciousness in 'The Small Lady'. Such modernist traces point forward to O'Faoláin's next collection, *A Purse of Coppers* (1937), where the fractured dialogues of stories like 'Admiring the Scenery' and 'A Broken World' oblige the reader to supply the meaning.

Their willingness to critique post-independence Ireland lends O'Faoláin's stories particular historical importance. Many of the stories in *Midsummer Night Madness*, based on his own experiences of fighting on the republican side, depict his disillusionment with violence and with republican politics. The final story, 'The Patriot', portrays the dehumanizing effect of violence and marks a clear break with the past as abstract love of Ireland is replaced by the warmth of a human relationship. In 'Midsummer Night Madness' Henn's marriage with Gypsy, however incongruous, suggests a Yeatsian alliance of Anglo-Irish and peasant, and their flight to Paris indicates the direction O'Faoláin believed Ireland should turn to renew its cultural and literary life: the stories in *Midsummer Night Madness* are as much about current debates on the nature and direction of Irish society in the 1930s as they are about the revolutionary fighting.

A Purse of Coppers also contains penetrating analyses of the chaos and diminishment of life in post-revolutionary Ireland. Several stories focus specifically on women's entrapment in the family home, a theme that contributes to the modernity of the collection: 'A Meeting', with its tragic insight into the retreat into domesticity of Irish women who had previously participated in the struggle for independence, anticipates later writing by Irish women. O'Faoláin's work as a short story writer complemented his influential role as editor of *The Bell* (1940–6), in which he lambasted Ireland's isolationism, provincialism and dominance by the Catholic Church. Editorship of *The Bell* gave O'Faoláin the chance to publish other writers and he spent time helping younger writers revise their work, turning this aspect of his editorship into what amounted virtually to a creative writing course on the short story. Through his comments on the short story form in *The Bell* and by his selection of authors, O'Faoláin shaped the Irish short story of this period towards realistic portrayals of contemporary urban and rural life.

Transnationalism

At the same time it should not be forgotten that other Irish writers of the period were working more centrally in the modernist mode. Samuel

Beckett's *More Pricks than Kicks* (1934) is a series of ten interlocking stories recounting the life of Belacqua from student to corpse. The use of interlinked stories may recall oral storytelling, but Beckett moved his stories away from folk tradition by announcing his adherence to the European masters: Belacqua is named after Dante's indolent Florentine lutemaker, who appears in the fourth canto of *Purgatory*. As this echo of Dante suggests, *More Pricks Than Kicks* is written in a self-consciously literary style replete with literary allusions. Nevertheless, these stories are recognizably Irish for, bucking the trend of the Irish short story of the period, one of the masters Beckett follows is Joyce. Joycean attention is paid to the precise locations of Belacqua's wanderings around Dublin as Beckett continues, through parodic imitation, Joyce's satire of provincial Dublin life. Like Stephen Dedalus, Belacqua desperately wants to break free of the structures in which he has been raised. The difference from *Dubliners* lies in the noticeably Protestant colouring of Beckett's stories. Despite the apprentice nature of these stories many deal with recognizably Beckettian themes: 'Dante and the Lobster', for instance, is a tragi-comic meditation on pain opening out into a general disquisition on suffering. Beckett is already depicting a profounder, more universal, sense of alienation and isolation than can be found in the stories of O'Connor and O'Faoláin.

Elizabeth Bowen began her writing career in the 1920s and her short stories prolonged into this period the nineteenth-century Anglo-Irish preoccupation with the supernatural and with what could not be expressed out loud, using these themes now to suggest the unease and insecurities that lay beneath modern life. Many of her stories are set in countries other than Ireland but 'The Back Drawing-Room' (1926) and 'Her Table Spread' (1930) take as their subject the situation of the Anglo-Irish after the war of independence. The former introduces a familiar Bowen theme, the rootlessness of the dispossessed: the Barran family have become living ghosts who haunt their Big House, Kilbarran, burnt down by the rebels two years previously. The dissolution of Anglo-Irish identity, signalled in the nineteenth century by Sheridan Le Fanu, has now become a reality. In 'Her Table Spread', the statuesque, deluded Anglo-Irish heiress, who relies on the English to save her but is disappointed, sums up in her person the hopeless political situation of the Anglo-Irish.

Bowen's modernist style came into its own during the Second World War as a means of expressing the fragmented, heightened feelings of those years, particularly on the part of the Anglo-Irish community torn between their Irish identity and their traditional loyalties to England. Such a conflict is portrayed in 'Sunday Afternoon' (1941), where the stylized civilities of the Anglo-Irish in neutral Ireland are contrasted with the breakdown in language and identity experienced by those living through the Blitz in London. Stories such as 'Summer Night', 'Unwelcome Idea' and 'A Love Story, 1939' published in *Look At All Those Roses* (1941), convey something of the claustrophobia and restlessness experienced by many Irish during the war owing to their country's isolation from the rest of the world. 'The Happy Autumn Fields' (1944) is characteristic of Bowen's war writing in its use of ghost themes and the uncanny to juxtapose nineteenth-century Anglo-Ireland with bombed out London, presenting both as places of instability and insecurity. Unlike the stories of their Catholic contemporaries, which focus on recognizably Irish themes and only intermittently reveal traces of modernist influence, the stories of Bowen and Beckett, both writers from the Protestant minority, transcend national boundaries in themes and style.

Notes

1. See, for example, *Dublin University Magazine*, 4 (September 1834), p. 303 and *Dublin University Magazine*, 17 (January 1841), p. 66.
2. Declan Kiberd, *Irish Classics* (London: Granta, 2001), p. 273.
3. Barbara Hayley, *Carleton's 'Traits and Stories' and the Nineteenth-Century Anglo-Irish Tradition* (Gerrards Cross: Colin Smythe, 1983).
4. Julie Ann Stevens, *The Irish Scene in Somerville and Ross* (Dublin: Irish Academic Press, 2007).
5. See Georges Zimmermann, *The Irish Storyteller* (Dublin: Four Courts Press, 2001), pp. 273-427.
6. Donna Wong, 'Literature and the Oral Tradition', in *The Cambridge History of Irish Literature, Volume 1: To 1890*, ed. Margaret Kelleher and Philip O'Leary (Cambridge University Press, 2006), pp. 668-9.
7. Elizabeth Fine, *The Folklore Text: From Performance to Print* (Bloomington and Indianapolis: The Indiana University Press, 1994).
8. W. B. Yeats, *Writings on Irish Folklore, Legend and Myth*, ed. Robert Welch (Harmondsworth: Penguin, 1993), p. 329.
9. Richard Pine, *The Thief of Reason: Oscar Wilde and Modern Ireland* (Dublin: Gill and Macmillan, 1995).
10. See, for example, Neil Sammell, *Wilde Style: The Plays and Prose of Oscar Wilde* (Harlow: Pearson, 2000) and Jarlath Killeen, *The Fairy Tales of Oscar Wilde* (Burlington: Ashgate Press, 2007).
11. Jarlath Killeen, 'Diaspora, Empire, and the Religious Geography of Victorian Social relations in Wilde's Fairy Tales', in *New Voices in Irish Criticism*, ed. P. J. Mathews (Dublin: Four Courts Press, 2000), pp. 183-9.

12. Elaine Showalter, ed., *Daughters of Decadence: Women Writers of the Fin de Siècle* (London: Virago, 1993), pp. viii–ix.
13. R. F. Foster, 'The Gift of Adaptability: Yeats, Joyce and Modern Ireland', in *That Island Never Found: Essays and Poems for Terence Brown*, ed. Nicholas Allen and Eve Patten (Dublin: Four Courts Press, 2007), p. 58.
14. See George Moore, *Hail and Farewell: Salve* (London: William Heinemann, 1947), pp. 107–31.
15. Frank O'Connor, *The Lonely Voice: A Study of the Short Story* (1963) (Cork: Cork City Council, 2003).
16. A 1905 letter from Joyce to his brother Stanislaus, quoted in James Carens, 'In Quest of a New Impulse: George Moore's *The Untilled Field* and James Joyce's *Dubliners*', in *The Irish Short Story: A Critical History*, ed. James Kilroy (Boston: Twayne, 1984), p. 66.
17. Richard Ellmann, *James Joyce* (Oxford University Press, 1959), p. 216.
18. A 1906 letter to Grant Richards, quoted in Ellmann, *James Joyce*, p. 230.
19. Daniel Corkery, *The Stones and Other Stories*, ed. Paul Delaney (Cork: Mercier Press, 2003), p. 9.

11

The Short Story in Ireland since 1945: A Modernizing Tradition

HEATHER INGMAN

The Irish Short Story Mid-Century

Two writers, Frank O'Connor and Seán O'Faoláin, played an important part in establishing the short story as the quintessential Irish literary form in the middle of the twentieth century. The previous chapter highlighted O'Faoláin's influential role as editor of *The Bell* (1940–6), which gave him the opportunity both through his comments on the short story form and through publishing such authors as Frank O'Connor, Bryan MacMahon, James Plunkett, Mary Lavin, Sam Hanna Bell, Mary Beckett and Michael McLaverty, to mould the Irish short story of this period. O'Faoláin's views on what the modern short story should be were incorporated into his study, *The Short Story* (1948), where he endeavoured to distinguish the modern short story from the loosely structured tale of oral tradition by associating the short story with concision, irony and open-endedness and stressing that the modern short story differed from the tale or anecdote in being chiefly 'an adventure of the mind'.[1] In his view, the modern short story achieved its best effects through suggestion and implication: the influence of Chekhov on the Irish short story was still much in evidence.

O'Faoláin's own stories from this period, in *Teresa and Other Stories* (1947) and *The Finest Stories* (1957), display an uneven application of his theories of what the modern short story should be doing: rather than focusing on psychological exploration, many of them are taken up by satirizing aspects of Irish life. Frank O'Connor described Irish literature in these years as being 'diverted' by the realities of Irish life, and stories such as 'The Man Who Invented Sin' express O'Faoláin's barely contained resentment against the claustrophobic nature of Irish life and the role of the Catholic Church in hampering individual fulfilment.[2] The comedy of a story such as 'Unholy Living and Half Dying' does not disguise the fact that mid-century Ireland is as much a place of stagnation and paralysis as it was in the stories of Moore and Joyce. In 'Lady Lucifer', three representatives of the intelligentsia, a priest, a bank clerk and a doctor, debate whether they should stay in a country where so many lead lives of quiet despair.

In O'Faoláin's finest stories of the period social commentary is subordinate to psychological exploration of states of mind. 'A Letter', a Chekhovian story of a teacher isolated in a rural area and torn between love of the Irish landscape and the feeling that life is passing her by, is a carefully controlled mood piece reflecting not only O'Faoláin's ambivalence towards Ireland but also his view that the modern short story should focus on interiority. 'Lovers of the Lake' explores the psychological cost of the conflict between tradition and modernity as Jenny, one of the lovers of the title, alternates between her residual religious belief and sexual desire for her married lover. O'Faoláin's lengthy psychological probing of Jenny's state of mind and detailed depiction of the changing moods of the two lovers combine to mark 'Lovers of the Lake' as a technically skilled, emotionally intense modern short story.

Frank O'Connor's trenchant criticisms of Irish life led to his unofficial blacklisting during the Second World War and as a consequence he spent most of the 1950s outside Ireland, in the United States, where his career flourished. Traces of the oral storytelling tradition of his native Cork are still present in *Crab Apple Jelly* (1944): 'The Grand Vizier's Daughters' features a storytelling uncle while several stories, such as 'The Long Road to Ummera', 'The Cheapjack' and 'The Luceys', have openings that suggest a story arising out of a community. Unlike the storyteller of the oral tradition, however, these narrators, unreliable and often limited in their point of view, cannot be straightforwardly equated with O'Connor's own voice. The evolution in O'Connor's understanding of the short story form during these years was influenced, not only by his study of French and Russian authors, but also by his connection with the *New Yorker* magazine, which encouraged him to move away from reliance on oral storytelling techniques into a more complex literary story suited to his new reading public.[3] Though he never entirely abandoned his attempt to incorporate the speaking voice of oral tradition into the modern short story, O'Connor reduced or ironized the role of the narrator and focused on character, producing story cycles centred on particular figures, such as Father Fogarty and Larry Delaney.

O'Connor was not alone in securing a 'first reading agreement' with the *New Yorker*. Other Irish writers, including Brian Friel, Mary Lavin and, later,

Edna O'Brien, Benedict Kiely and William Trevor were published regularly there and it could be argued that the editorial policies of the *New Yorker* during this period affected the shape of the Irish short story. The magazine required stories of around 4,000 words, setting, mood and character were all-important, experimentation was frowned upon, there had to be a certain amount of dialogue and the preferred tone was understated irony.[4] It was a formula that suited O'Connor's treatment of the short story as an epiphany in the realist mode focusing on a turning point in an individual's life, sometimes tragic, sometimes humorous, as in 'My Oedipus Complex'. His stories deepened as a consequence of his association with the *New Yorker* and, in turn, his complex narrative voice expanded the range of that magazine's fiction, dealing as his stories did with failed marriages, infidelity, prostitution and illegitimacy.

International influences – French, Russian, American – are felt in O'Connor's much-cited study, *The Lonely Voice*, published in 1962 after his return to Ireland. Here, prompted partly by personal disillusionment with post-independence Ireland, O'Connor identified loneliness as a distinguishing theme of the modern short story and argued that, whereas the novel generally deals with societies, the short story portrays marginal or isolated individuals and what he termed 'submerged population groups'.[5] His argument that the short story prospers at times of social upheaval and was therefore more suited than the novel to portraying Irish life has been endlessly cited and did much to establish the short story as the pre-eminent Irish literary form in this period. His own work (between 1944 and 1969 he published eight major collections) deals sympathetically with the isolation of priests in rural communities in the Father Fogarty stories, the marginalization of the elderly ('The Long Road to Ummera'), the loneliness of those affected by the shift from rural to urban life ('Uprooted') and those who in increasing numbers in this period chose emigration ('Darcy in the Land of Youth'). At a time when the Catholic Church was emphasizing the evils of sexuality outside marriage, children born out of wedlock also suffered social exclusion, and stories such as 'The Babes in the Wood' and 'The Weeping Children' are heartbreaking portrayals of children farmed out to indifferent carers. Religious and class differences are frequently depicted as obstacles to romance in O'Connor's stories of the provincial middle classes ('Legal Aid', 'My First Protestant', 'The Cheat' and 'The Corkerys') and sexual repression also plays its part in hindering the development of mature relationships ('The Mad Lomasneys', 'The Cheapjack', 'The Sorcerer's Apprentice', 'Judas'). Despite their often light-hearted tone, these stories link thwarted love with the characters' oppressive social circumstances in a way that underpins O'Connor's central theme of human loneliness. In the best of his stories, such as 'The Long Road to Ummera' or 'The Mass Island', the endings achieve a haunting transcendence that will reappear in the work of John McGahern.

O'Connor's themes are echoed in other writers of the period. Liam O'Flaherty in *Two Lovely Beasts and Other Stories* (1948) moves away from his earlier lyrical descriptions of life in the Irish countryside to emphasize the loneliness, poverty and sexual frustration of its inhabitants. Materialism is a prominent theme in the stories of Mary Lavin, who began her writing career in the 1940s, publishing four collections in this decade alone. Many of her stories feature a Catholic middle class so consumed by the need to earn a living that the death of the heart ensues. The theme encompasses both urban stories like 'The Little Prince' and 'The Becker Wives' and those that have a rural setting, such as 'Lilacs' and 'The Widow's Son'. As in O'Connor's stories, oppressive structures of class ('A Gentle Soul') or religion ('The Convert') are obstacles to love.

Lavin's gender, which caused O'Connor such confusion in *The Lonely Voice* on account of the domestic and apolitical nature of her work, led to an emphasis on themes that would be taken up by later Irish women writers. These include female sexuality ('Sunday Brings Sunday,' 'Sarah'), repression of the body ('The Nun's Mother', 'Chamois Gloves'), the portrayal of often fraught mother–daughter relationships ('The Will', 'A Cup of Tea'), as well as her stories of widowhood published in the 1960s ('In the Middle of the Fields', 'In a Café', 'Happiness'). Lavin herself highlighted gender differences in 'A Story with a Pattern' (1945), where she signals her intention of abandoning the well-made short story packed with incident for a looser structure, more suited to probing beneath the surface and exploring states of mind, and defends this view of the short story against a male interrogator who urges her to get more plot into her work. Lavin later famously defined the short story as 'an arrow in flight' having no definite beginning or end, being a revelation of life's unpredictability rather than an explanation.[6] Lavin's employment of modernist indeterminacy contrasts with O'Connor's rejection of modernist techniques in *The Lonely Voice* and may account for some of his hostility to her work.[7]

Women's lives feature prominently in the stories of Maeve Brennan, another Irish writer closely associated with the *New Yorker*. Born in Dublin, Brennan moved to the United States when she was seventeen and thereafter, like Joyce in exile, endlessly recreated the constricting world of the Dublin in which she had grown up. Her stories depicting her childhood home in Ranelagh began to appear in the *New Yorker* in the 1950s. She followed these with a series of stories about the Derdon and Bagot families, describing unhappy wives trapped in unfulfilled marriages, tyrannized over by neglectful husbands on whom they are financially dependent and living in dark, cramped Dublin houses suggestive of the emotional oppression of their lives. In six stories published between 1953 and 1956 in the *New Yorker* Brennan takes up the theme of the Irish emigrant, a dominant theme in the Irish short story of this period, portraying the wealthy inhabitants of Herbert's Retreat through the often sardonic eyes of their Irish maids. Their alienation from the social performances of their employers reflects the author's own increasing dislocation both from America and from the country of her birth.[8]

Brennan's stories, like many Irish stories in this period, were written to appeal to an international readership. Some Irish writers, however, continued the nineteenth-century practice of using the short story to portray regional customs: Sam Hanna Bell's stories in *Summer Loanen and Other Stories* (1943) are set mainly in rural Northern Ireland and, as the title indicates, they make use of local dialect. Michael McLaverty's first two collections, *The White Mare* (1943) and *The Game Cock* (1947), portray daily life in rural Northern Ireland, Rathlin Island and the slums of Belfast. Fidelity to the local was McLaverty's advice to Irish short story writers: 'Be artists of the normal. It is the normal that survives, and it comes from exploring the resources of your own people and your environment – no matter how small the latter is, if it is deeply pondered the resultant work will overleap its boundaries.'[9] It was advice that John McGahern was to take to heart. Bryan MacMahon's collection, *The Lion-Tamer and Other Stories* (1948), set in a precise locality (Listowel, County Kerry) and rooted in the tradition of Irish storytelling, combines this regional emphasis with a series of reflections on the storyteller's role. MacMahon saw storytelling as necessary to the life of a community and a vital part of the educational process that would drive the Irish nation forward. Before turning to the theatre, Brian Friel published two story collections, *The Saucer of Larks* (1962) and *The Gold in the Sea* (1966), set against the background of small town life in the north west of Ireland, where the importance of fantasy in sustaining everyday life in these impoverished rural communities is evident.

Notwithstanding these examples, what is most marked in this period is the intrusion of the modern world into Irish traditional life. In portraying the material constraints and restrictions of Irish life, the short story of this period reveals a generation of writers moving away from romantic nationalism and becoming more critical of the state than the previous generation had the freedom to be. Whereas O'Connor continued to write stories focused on an emotional turning point that changes the life or perception of a character, the drive of the Irish short story in the hands of writers like Seán O'Faoláin, Mary Lavin and Maeve Brennan was towards greater sophistication and psychological complexity.

Transformations: 1968–89

The more favourable economic circumstances in Ireland following Seán Lemass's election as Taoiseach in 1959 fostered a general air of renewal and self-confidence in the country, turned the tide of emigration and gave a boost to indigenous publishing houses. From 1968 'The New Irish Writing' pages of *The Irish Press*, edited by David Marcus, did much to promote the Irish short story and encourage emerging Irish writers. Nationalist and Catholic discourses began to lose some of their power as the process of revisionism got under way and a younger, more cosmopolitan generation became open to influences outside Ireland. These changes are reflected in Seán O'Faoláin's collections, *I Remember! I Remember!* (1961) and *The Heat of the Sun* (1966), which often feature the Irish abroad in Europe and the United States ('One Night in Turin', 'The Planets of the Years'). However, some of these stories ('A Shadow, Silent as a Cloud', 'A Touch of Autumn in the Air') reveal an uneasiness about the cost of progress characteristic of the Irish short story of this period, reflecting contemporary debates in the country at large over whether Ireland's distinctive culture, traditions and language were being too quickly sacrificed to the desire to modernize.[10]

One of the most widely noticed of these new voices was Edna O'Brien, whose first collection, *The Love Object*, was published in 1968. Many of her stories feature women routinely brutalized and crushed, not only by their men folk, but also by the constraints of the patriarchal society in which they live. Though an often ambivalent figure for Irish feminism, O'Brien introduced a new note into the Irish short story by dealing frankly with such themes as female sexuality ('The Love Object') and lesbianism ('The Mouth of the Cave'). In her later collection, *A Scandalous Woman* (1974), the title story is a bleak and forceful presentation of the sacrifice of a lively young girl, Eily, to social respectability. 'The House of My Dreams', from the same collection, highlights the oppressive religious and social ideologies governing Irish women's lives when the narrator's unmarried sister is banished to a Magdalene laundry to have her baby. The mother–daughter relationship, so often regarded in feminist theory as crucial to female identity, is a central theme in O'Brien's work from the martyr mother figure seen through the eyes of her young daughter ('A Rug') to the more ambivalent presentation of the rural Catholic mother in stories such as 'Cords' and 'A Rose in the Heart of New York' (*Mrs Reinhardt*, 1978). The daughter's sophisticated, cosmopolitan life becomes a source of conflict and misunderstanding that leaves the relationship unhealed even in the late story 'My Two Mothers' (*Saints and Sinners*, 2011).

With O'Brien, Joyce's influence starts to be felt in a more consistent way in the Irish short story and it has been argued that many of her stories reveal a writing back to Joyce from a gendered perspective.[11] In 'Irish Revel' (*The Love Object*) imagery and narrative irony undermine the protagonist's romantic illusions while in 'The Love Object' O'Brien extends Joyce's method by recounting everything from inside her heroine's mind, without authorial commentary. In 'Over' (*A Scandalous Woman*), she experiments with the second person, utilizing a stream of consciousness about a love affair gone wrong that is directly addressed by the woman to her ex-lover. Extra-literary considerations, such as the focus on her appearance, lifestyle and her supposedly scandalous material, have often hindered proper discussion of O'Brien's writing, but her work displays a serious attempt to break new ground in the Irish short story, both thematically and stylistically.

Transformations in Irish life and the shift from rural to urban living affect fathers and sons in John McGahern's work as much as they do mothers and daughters in O'Brien's short stories. In 'Wheels' (*Nightlines*, 1971) the failed father–son relationship is set in the wider context of the Irish nation: just as the educated, urban son hopes for a rapprochement with his farmer father that will never take place, so life in Ireland after independence has been a matter of waiting for 'the rich whole that never came but that all the preparations promised'.[12] Paralysis is a major theme of McGahern's 1970s collections, *Nightlines* and *Getting Through* (1978), covering both professional life (time-serving teachers in 'The Recruiting Officer', unsuccessful artists in 'The Beginning of an Idea' and 'Swallows') and personal (failed love affairs and sexuality gone awry in 'Doorways', 'Along the Edges', 'My Love, My Umbrella' and 'Peaches'). However, the central focus of McGahern's stories is not so much social analysis as the consciousness of the private, disillusioned, more or less stoical, individual treated, in the manner of Flaubert and Chekhov, in an objective, non-judgemental style. His stories extend Joyce's use of symbolism, epiphany and formal patterning in a way that obliges the reader to work to achieve the meaning that eludes his narrators.[13]

Indicating his debt to Proust, McGahern once remarked: 'One of my favourite definitions of art is that it abolishes time and establishes memory.'[14] 'The Wine Breath' (*Getting Through*), in which the priest transcends time through an effort of the imagination, marks a shift in the presentation of time as repetitive and entrapping that points forward to McGahern's *High Ground* (1985). In this collection the theme of paralysis gives way to that of social change and the sense of society's shifting structures is apparent in the autobiographical coming of age story 'Oldfashioned' as well as in 'Eddie Mac' and 'The Conversion of William Kirkwood', where the decline of an Anglo-Irish family becomes a symbol for the perceived loss of moral and cultural values in late twentieth-century Ireland. In 'Gold Watch', the father's anguish at his loss of status in modern Ireland contrasts with the son's acceptance of change as an inevitable part of life, while in 'The High Ground' and 'Crossing the Line' the youthful narrator observes the failings of an older generation of teachers, knowing he must carve out a path different from theirs. 'Like All Other Men' portrays characters living with the remnants of a lost faith, situating McGahern in a line of post-Catholic Irish writers stretching back to Joyce.[15] In *High Ground* there are broader perspectives, a moral concern and a sense of communal life that will find its full flowering in the late story, 'The Country Funeral' (*The Collected Stories*, 1992). In stories like these, the themes of time, memory and imagination so characteristic of the Irish short story in this period receive their most sophisticated articulation.

With eleven collections appearing between 1967 and 2007, William Trevor is regarded as one of the finest practitioners in the genre. As in McGahern's writing, imagination is a central theme in his work. In stories such as 'The Raising of Elvira Tremlett' (*Lovers of Their Time*, 1978), protagonists fashion a compensatory version of reality to help them cope with everyday life. In others, such as 'An Evening with John Joe Dempsey' (*The Ballroom of Romance*, 1972), one of a series of Trevor stories portraying small-town Ireland as a place where sexuality goes wrong in early childhood and can never be put right because of the silence of Irish society surrounding the subject, the protagonist's imaginative life is entrapping and narcissistic. Joyce's influence is evident both thematically and stylistically: 'The Ballroom of Romance', one of Trevor's best-known stories, invokes the Joycean theme of paralysis in its description of an evening entertainment that ends in anti-climax and constriction that mirrors the wider social scene. A characteristic Trevor short story exhibits careful construction involving complex time shifts, a delicate balance between lyricism and irony, and a flexible but precise narrative voice capable of moving in a sentence from objective-sounding narration to subjective. His interest in form and patterning, which has been related to his early work as a sculptor, extends even to the shape of a collection: the stories in *A Bit on the Side* (2004) are united by things or people left behind, while *Cheating at Canasta* (2007) is structured around different forms of deceit and betrayal.[16]

In his stories of the Northern Irish Troubles, such as 'The Distant Past' (*Angels at the Ritz*, 1975), 'Attracta' and 'Another Christmas' (*Lovers of Their Time*, 1978), Trevor's dual focus as an Irishman from the Protestant tradition living in England enables him to trace the impact of the Northern Irish situation on the Irish in England and on the Anglo-Irish in the Republic: as ancient tribal loyalties resurface, both these groups, marginalized in their respective communities, come to be perceived as a threat. Trevor employs the form to explore moral problems centred on tolerance, forgiveness and reconciliation, often going back into the past to uncover the historical roots of the violence. His emphasis is always on the personal as a way of understanding the conflict, portraying not only the impact of the Troubles on the lives of ordinary people, but also, as in 'Beyond the Pale' and 'Autumn Sunshine' (*Beyond the Pale*, 1981), stressing the individual's moral responsibility to understand the world beyond the private self. In an age of theory and abstraction, Trevor's stories return us to small details of everyday life, humanist values and ethical choices.

Many of Trevor's stories are set outside Ireland, reflecting a growing international dimension to the Irish short story in this period. During the 1970s and 1980s an emerging generation of writers such as John Banville (*Long Lankin*, 1970), Neil Jordan (*Night in Tunisia*, 1976), Aidan Higgins (*Asylum and Other Stories*, 1978), Desmond Hogan (*The Diamonds at the Bottom of the Sea*, 1979) and Dermot Healy (*Banished Misfortune*, 1982) published collections that embody a new sense of risk-taking in speaking of sexual matters, together with an openness to revisionism, formal experimentation and international influences: Hogan's characters read Hesse and Kerouac, and the lyrical style of his stories reflects the fluidity of their lives as they move between Ireland, Europe and the United States, while American jazz features in stories by Banville, Hogan, Jordan and Healy.

Pope John Paul II's visit to Ireland in 1979 strengthened Catholic opinion against divorce, homosexuality and abortion. Economic recession and high unemployment reinforced conservative attitudes during this period and short stories by Irish women frequently protest against the legal and ideological constraints on women's lives. Maeve Kelly's collection, *A Life of Her Own* (1976), with its echo of Woolf and its portrayal of the daily crushing of women's aspirations, reflects the struggles of the Irish feminist movement in the 1970s. Ita Daly's *The Lady with the Red Shoes* (1980) depicts Irish women deeply entangled in the masculinist values of their society and their often fruitless attempts to break free, while Evelyn Conlon's first collection, *My Head is Opening* (1987), highlights women's issues around motherhood and the social unacceptability of unmarried mothers. Other notable collections include Val Mulkerns's *An Idle Woman* (1980), a series of satirical portraits of Irish life, Clare Boylan's *A Nail on the Head* (1983) and *Concerning Virgins* (1989), containing witty insights into Irish women's attempts to forge new identities for themselves, and *Dublin 4* (1982) by the popular writer, Maeve Binchy, exposing the hypocrisy that lay beneath the supposed liberalism of Dublin's professional classes. Leland Bardwell's *Different Kinds of Love* (1987) focuses on such topics as domestic violence, child abuse and incest not previously much represented in the Irish short story, while the end of the decade saw the publication of Mary Dorcey's impassioned and stylistically experimental collection, *A Noise from the Woodshed* (1989), giving a voice to those defined as marginal in the life of the Irish nation: battered wives, the elderly and, above all in this collection, lesbians. The noise from the woodshed turns out to be the sound of lovemaking between two women.

Northern Ireland

Not all short stories by Northern Irish writers during this period are concerned with the Troubles: Robert Harbinson's collections, *Tattoo Lily* (1961) and *The Far World* (1962), are wry evocations of pre-Troubles life in Northern Ireland, full of details about rural customs and beliefs, while the harshness of life in rural Northern Ireland is the focus of Patrick Boyle's *The Port Wine Stain* (1983). John Montague's 'The Cry' (*The Death of a Chieftain and Other Stories*, 1964), is prescient about the reluctance of the Northern Irish to confront the growing problems of sectarianism. In the 1970s and 80s, sectarian violence became the subject of most short fiction set in Northern Ireland, leading one commentator to claim that: 'No issue has been treated so extensively and so probingly in the modern Irish story as the Troubles.'[17] As in the case of William Trevor, stories about the Troubles attracted international interest and Troubles anthologies, such as David Marcus's *Tears of the Shamrock* (1972) and Michael

Parker's *The Hurt World: Short Stories of the Troubles* (1995), aimed to explain the historical roots of the conflict to an international readership.

The prevalence of short stories on the Troubles has been linked to its association as a form with ellipsis, reticence and occluded voices that evade dominant discourses.[18] Although there is something to be said for this argument, the work of Omagh-born Benedict Kiely is perhaps an anomaly in the period in that he rejects Irish writers' preference for understated irony in favour of the oral storytelling tradition, employing in his stories Irish sayings, anecdotes, digressions, verbal playfulness, that nevertheless conceal a careful structuring purpose and a sophisticated range of literary reference. As the sectarian violence increased, Kiely's tone changed from the humorous, at times bawdy, tone of 'A Ball of Malt and Madame Butterfly' (*A Ball of Malt and Madame Butterfly*, 1973), to the darker tone of 'Bluebell Meadow' (*A Cow in the House*, 1978), a Romeo and Juliet story of love thwarted by the growing sectarianism in Northern Ireland. 'Proxopera' (1977) uses the Troubles to stimulate general reflections on life and death, incorporating the copiousness of the oral storytelling tradition with the chaotic stream-of-consciousness of the elderly Mr Binchey as he is forced into carrying a bomb while his family is held to ransom. The fact that 'Proxopera' should properly be classed as a novella on account of its length indicates the difficulty writers faced in attempting to confine exploration of the moral and psychological effects of acts of terrorism to the limits of a short story. Eugene McCabe similarly drew on the resources of the novella for the concluding story in his 1976 trilogy – 'Cancer', 'Heritage' and 'Victims' – portraying the effect of the Troubles on people living close to the border. 'Victims' brings together characters from the previous two stories and, by exploring the network of relations in a single community and letting this stand as a microcosm for life in Northern Ireland, McCabe exposes deep-seated religious and national divisions.

The Troubles became a prominent theme in Bernard MacLaverty's 1980s collections, *A Time to Dance* (1982) and *The Great Profundo* (1987). As in stories by John McGahern, MacLaverty's 'Some Surrender' employs the father–son relationship as a metaphor for the wider political situation, in this case that of an Ulster Protestant family living through the Troubles. Like the fathers in McGahern's stories, Roy's father feels a stranger in his own country, seeing his life's work, in the form of flats he designed, in the process of being demolished and Ulster's Protestant identity compromised by a British government that seems to favour the other side. 'The Daily Woman' presents a female angle on the Troubles, painting a bleak picture of a young working-class woman's struggle to survive everyday life in Belfast.

The daily battle to cope with the Troubles features prominently in women's stories on Northern Ireland where, as in MacLaverty's 'The Daily Woman', the violence in the streets is shown as spilling into the home: Brenda Murphy's 'A Social Call' (1988) links male violence in the home with paramilitary activities outdoors while Fiona Barr's 'The Wall-Reader' (1985) shows the effects on one family of intimidation outside the home. 'The Wall-Reader' was one of a series of stories published in Ruth Hooley's anthology, *The Female Line: Northern Ireland Women Writers* (1985), exploring the impact of the Troubles on women's lives. The difficulties internment created for families are portrayed in Frances Molloy's posthumous collection, *Women Are the Scourge of the Earth* (1998), while Anne Devlin's 'Naming the Names' (*The Way-Paver*, 1986) is one of the few stories of this period that attempts to explore the mind of a female Irish Republican Army (IRA) activist. Mary Beckett's collection, *A Belfast Woman* (1980), employs the realist mode to portray the inner lives of ordinary women struggling to make meaningful lives for themselves in a sectarian society and, while the choice of the realist mode by women writing on Northern Ireland has been criticized as unadventurous, within the realist mode writers like Beckett attempt to demythologize the ideologies behind the conflict.[19]

1990 Onwards: Postmodernism, Postfeminism, Postnationalism

The 1990 election of Mary Robinson, a feminist and civil rights lawyer, as Ireland's first female President ushered in a modernizing agenda: divorce, contraception and homosexuality would all be legalized in the following years. From the late 1990s, the rapid growth as Ireland entered the global economy, the so-called Celtic Tiger years, gave rise to a period of urbanization and secularization during which Ireland displayed national self-confidence and cultural sophistication to match its economic optimism. This optimism continued until 2007, when a severe recession halted Ireland's economic growth. Nevertheless, the country would not return to traditional values: a referendum in 2015 wrote the right of same sex couples to civil marriage into the Constitution.

An increasingly liberal society encouraged Irish women writers to move beyond the angry feminist voice of the 1970s and 1980s and explore the changing nature of femininity and the instability of female identity in a playful, postmodernist style. Anne Enright's witty deconstruction of myths around femininity and marriage in *The Portable Virgin* (1991) was widely acclaimed by Irish commentators as 'a real departure in women's fiction in this country'.[20] 'Fatgirl Terrestrial' is a convincing exploration of why educated and successful women feel under pressure to conform to society's expectations of femininity, while in Enright's title story the narrator, who endeavours to fit into the feminine ideal by dyeing her hair blonde, finds ironically that 'the new fake me', conforming to a female stereotype, 'looks twice as real as the old'.[21] In her second collection, *Taking Pictures* (2008), Enright continues her edgy exploration of contemporary life but stories like 'Honey' and 'Little Sister' demonstrate an advance on her earlier collection by combining stylistic subtlety with emotional depth.[22]

Éilís Ní Dhuibhne's first collections, *Blood and Water* (1988) and *Eating Women is not Recommended* (1991), are more overtly feminist than the later *The Pale Gold of Alaska* (2000), where she employs the voice of a detached, omniscient storyteller to give an overview of changes in Irish society ('The Truth about Married Love'), portray cultural differences between Irish and Americans ('The Day Elvis Presley Died'), or draw parallels between the colonization of nature and the colonization of women ('The Pale Gold of Alaska'). The quality of Ní Dhuibhne's spare, ironic prose probing her characters' fractured states of mind lifts her stories above any tendency to reportage and her constant experiments with the short story form, with unreliable narrators, non-linear plots, complex ironies and lack of closure align her with postmodernism. Though written in a deceptively transparent style, her stories often require a range of intertextual knowledge on the part of her readers: 'Oleander' turns on surprises that are chiefly aesthetic, such as the heroine's discovery of her preference for the stories of Henry James over those of Richard Ford. In stories like 'Midwife to the Fairies' (*Blood and Water*) and 'The Mermaid Legend' (*Eating Women is not Recommended*) Ní Dhuibhne draws on her expertise in folklore to move away from the symbolic realism of John McGahern into a postmodern, metafictional world, inhabiting the borders between fantasy and reality. '*The Inland Ice*' *and Other Stories* (1997) extends this by interweaving a retelling of a traditional Irish folk tale, 'The Search for the Lost Husband', with contemporary stories of women's disillusionment in love.[23]

Feminist and lesbian rewritings of fairy tales are the focus of Emma Donoghue's *Kissing the Witch* (1997), while her second collection, *The Woman Who Gave Birth to Rabbits* (2002), portrays women from various historical periods battling against patriarchal society to secure their independence. Some of these stories have a specifically Irish dimension: 'Night Vision' on the blind Donegal poet, Frances Brown, and 'Words for Things' on Mary Wollstonecraft's period as a governess in Ireland. The historical notes at the end of each story underpin the authenticity of these tales and anchor them in the feminist project of recovering women's history.

Mothers emerge from their traditional role of self-sacrificing domestic martyrs in Colm Tóibín's first collection, *Mothers and Sons* (2006), which presents a variety of new twists on the old Irish theme of the mother–son relationship. Far from idealizing their sons, these mothers are often sceptical about them: in 'The Name of the Game', Nancy refuses to sacrifice her future to that of her son, in whom she sees many traits of his authoritarian father. Tóibín employs an austere, understated style to probe dysfunctional family relationships and the darker side of life in contemporary Ireland. 'Three Friends' portrays the hedonism ushered in by Ireland's increased prosperity while 'A Priest in the Family' reflects the fall in status of the Catholic Church after revelations of sexual abuse of children. Tóibín's later collection, *The Empty Family* (2010), reprises some of these topics but focuses also on gay love in Ireland and abroad and the search for identity against a background of failed relationships and a secular, post-nationalist Ireland.

A fresh theme entered the Irish short story as growing prosperity transformed Ireland in the late 1990s from a country of emigrants into one that attracted increasing numbers of foreign immigrants. Irish writers turned back to the past to examine the immigration experience in earlier decades. Several of the stories in Hugo Hamilton's collection, *Dublin Where the Palm Trees Grow* (1996), are recounted through the eyes of a German-Irish boy growing up in Ireland during the 1960s. In Colum McCann's 'A Basket Full of Wallpaper' (*Fishing the Sloe-Black River*, 1994), Osobe, a Japanese man who has relocated to Ireland after the Second World War, comes up against Irish racist attitudes that do not dissolve until after his death, when the community finally recognizes all he has done for them over the years by employing their young men in his painting business.

By contrast with the transformation of social mores in the Republic, stories set in Northern Ireland continued to record the polarization of national and religious identity: in Briege Duffaud's *Nothing Like Beirut* (1994), Irish emigrants return home to find that despite superficial changes people's attitudes have not altered, while entrenched sectarian attitudes are the subject of several stories in Bernard MacLaverty's fifth collection, *Matters of*

Life and Death (2006). In *Everything in this Country Must* (2000), Colum McCann's two stories and a novella set against the background of the Troubles, ellipsis, symbolism and understatement are employed in the manner of John McGahern to portray the physical and emotional stress of living through the Troubles.[24]

McGahern's influence is also felt in Claire Keegan's *Walk the Blue Fields* (2007), with its evocation of life in an Irish countryside seemingly untouched by the Celtic Tiger. The title story places the same emphasis as McGahern on the ritualistic life of the community, though it makes more use of interior monologue and many of the stories draw on folkloric supernaturalism to defamiliarize the familiar. Keegan has been described as 'reinventing rural Ireland'[25] and stories like 'Men and Women' from her earlier collection, *Antarctica* (1999), record the shifting of the balance of power between husband and wife, even in conservative rural families. Like William Trevor, Keegan creates stories that are simultaneously up to date and timeless.

In the 1990s and beyond, Irish short story writers displayed a readiness to tackle current topics (immigration, child abuse, national identity, received gender roles, women's history), as well as a willingness to experiment with language and complex, non-linear narratives. Intertextual references ranged widely, as in William Wall's *No Paradiso* (2006), and the Irish short story of this period often demanded a sophisticated and knowledgeable readership. During the Celtic Tiger years increasing globalization meant that the Irish short story was as likely to be set in Bucharest or Boston as Dublin: in Philip Ó Ceallaigh's *Notes from a Turkish Whorehouse* (2006), a series of tales of down-and-outs set in Turkey, Romania and the United States, Ireland scarcely features. Emigration, often voluntary in contrast with earlier generations, is a prominent theme in the collections of Éilís Ní Dhuibhne, Colum McCann, Colm Tóibín and Claire Keegan. In Emma Donoghue's *Astray* (2012) the topic is given a historical twist, the collection spanning four centuries of travel.

The economic recession brought a more inward-looking focus, with writers returning to recognizably Irish subject matter and settings. Collections by Kevin Barry (*There Are Little Kingdoms*, 2007 and *Dark Lies the Island*, 2012) and Colin Barrett (*Young Skins*, 2013) provide new and dark variations on the theme of small town Ireland depicting a society that has lost its moral compass. Christine Dwyer Hickey (*The House on Parkgate Street and Other Dublin Stories*, 2013) returns to Joycean territory, exploring Dublin city in different periods, often through the eyes of a child, while Mary

Costello (*The China Factory*, 2012) evokes both traditional Irish rural life and unfulfilled suburban marriages. With young writers continuing to bring a variety of perspectives and formal invention to the genre, the centrality of the short story to the Irish literary canon looks assured for some time to come.

Notes

1. Seán O'Faoláin, *The Short Story* (Cork: The Mercier Press, 1948), p. 213.
2. Frank O'Connor, *The Backward Look: A Survey of Irish Literature* (London: Macmillan, 1967), p. 227.
3. James Alexander, 'Frank O'Connor in The New Yorker, 1945–1967', *Éire-Ireland*, 30 (1995), 1, pp. 130–44.
4. See Ben Yagoda, *About Town: The 'New Yorker' and The World It Made* (London: Duckworth, 2000).
5. Frank O'Connor, *The Lonely Voice: A Study of the Short Story* (Cork: Cork City Council, 2003), p. 4.
6. Leah Levenson, *The Four Seasons of Mary Lavin* (Dublin: Marino Books, 1998), p. 54.
7. See Anne Fogarty, 'Discontinuities: Tales from Bective Bridge and the Modernist Short Story', in *Mary Lavin*, ed. Elke D'hoker (Dublin: Irish Academic Press, 2013), pp. 49–64.
8. For further details of Brennan's life and work see Angela Bourke, *Maeve Brennan: Homesick at the 'New Yorker'* (London: Jonathan Cape, 2004).
9. Michael McLaverty, *In Quiet Places: The Uncollected Stories, Letters and Critical Prose of Michael McLaverty*, ed. Sophia Hillan King (Dublin: Poolbeg, 1989), p. 165.
10. See Terence Brown, *Ireland: A Social and Cultural History 1922–2002* (London: Harper Perennial, 2004), pp. 254–96.
11. Rebecca Pelan, 'Reflections on a Connemara Dietrich', in *Edna O'Brien: New Critical Perspectives*, ed. K. Laing, S. Mooney and M. O'Connor (Dublin: Carysfort Press, 2006), pp. 12–37. For further details of O'Brien's reworking of Joyce, see Rachel Jane Lynch, '"A Land of Strange, Throttled, Sacrificial Women": Domestic Violence in the Short Fiction of Edna O'Brien', *The Canadian Journal of Irish Studies*, 22 (1999), 2, pp. 37–48.
12. John McGahern, *Collected Stories* (London: Faber & Faber, 1992), p. 11.
13. See Bertrand Cardin, 'Figures of Silence: Ellipses and Eclipses in John McGahern's Collected Stories', *Journal of the Short Story in English*, 40 (2003), 1, pp. 57–67.
14. Quoted in Eamon Maher, *John McGahern: From the Local to the Universal* (Dublin: The Liffey Press, 2003), p. 146.
15. Eamon Grennan, '"Only What Happens": Mulling Over McGahern', *Irish University Review*, 35 (2005), 1, p. 17.

16. Paul Delaney and Michael Parker, 'Introduction', in *William Trevor: Revaluations*, ed. Paul Delaney and Michael Parker (Manchester University Press, 2013), p. 3.
17. Michael Storey, *Representing the Troubles in Irish Short Fiction* (Washington: The Catholic University of America Press, 2004), p. 1.
18. Ronan McDonald, 'Strategies of Silence: Colonial Strains in Short Stories of the Troubles', *The Yearbook of English Studies*, 35 (2005), pp. 249–63.
19. Eve Patten, 'Women and Fiction 1985–1990', *Krino*, 8–9 (1990), pp. 1–7.
20. *Irish Times*, 2 March 1991, p. 37.
21. Anne Enright, *The Portable Virgin* (London: Vintage, 2002), p. 87.
22. For the evolution of Enright's style in these two collections, see Elke D'hoker, 'Distorting Mirrors and Unsettling Snapshots: Anne Enright's Short Fiction', in *Anne Enright*, ed. Claire Bracken and Susan Cahill (Dublin: Irish Academic Press, 2011), pp. 33–50.
23. For an examination of how the two narrative forms intertwine, see Anne Fogarty, '"What Matters But the Good of the Story?": Femininity and Desire in Éilís Ní Dhuibhne's *The Inland Ice and Other Stories*', in *Éilís Ní Dhuibhne: Perspectives*, ed. Rebecca Pelan (Galway: Arlen House, 2009), pp. 69–85.
24. For discussions of McCann's stories, see Eóin Flannery, 'Troubling Bodies: Suffering, Resistance and Hope in Colum McCann's "Troubles" Short Fiction', *Irish Review*, 40/41 (2009), pp. 33–51 and Catherine Mari, 'Tell-Tale Ellipsis in Colum McCann's *Everything in this Country Must*', *Journal of the Short Story in English*, 40 (2003), pp. 47–56.
25. Mary Fitzgerald-Hoyt, 'Claire Keegan's New Rural Ireland: Torching the Thatched Cottage', in *The Irish Short Story: Traditions and Trends*, ed. Elke D'hoker and Stephanie Eggermont (Bern: Peter Lang, 2015), pp. 279–96.

12

The Short Story in Scotland: From Oral Tale to Dialectal Style

TIMOTHY C. BAKER

While Walter Allen labels Walter Scott's 'The Two Drovers', from *Chronicles of the Canongate* (1827), the 'first modern English short story', Scott's texts emerged in an Edinburgh print culture in which the short story was rapidly achieving prominence as a literary form.[1] The founding of *Blackwood's Edinburgh Magazine* in 1817 was crucial not only for the development of the terror tale, but also for regional fiction, often explicitly connected to oral traditions. The short fiction published in *Blackwood's* frequently combined correspondence, journalism, historical enquiry and narrative; Scott's description of his *Tales of My Landlord* series as a collection of 'Tales, illustrative of ancient Scottish manners, and of the Traditions of their Respective Districts' could also serve for much of the fiction published in the magazine. *Blackwood's* was one of the first periodicals to pay writers of fiction at the same rate as its essayists and reviewers, and by 1820 fiction made up roughly one-fifth of its annual contents. William Blackwood published tales by writers such as Thomas De Quincy, John Wilson and William Maginn, as well as Scott himself. Most influentially for the development of the short story in Scotland, Blackwood also published tales and serialized novels by James Hogg and John Galt. Many of these writers used *Blackwood's* and its competitor journals as places to experiment with genre, often drawing explicitly on nonfiction published alongside their tales, as well as taking advantage of the magazine's reputation for self-reflexive commentary on authorial identity and narrative form.

Hogg's four collections of tales focused on the Scottish Borders and Galt's series of 'Tales of the West' set in Ayrshire and Glasgow, many of which were in part serialized in *Blackwood's*, use a miscellany form to present a series of first-person fictional memoirs with a specific regional identity. Their texts explore the interconnections of fiction and nonfiction, as well as poetry and prose in the case of Hogg, and highlight the relation between reportage and storytelling. Hogg frequently exploits his dual position as a representative of unlettered, rural identity in his guise as 'The Ettrick Shepherd' in the magazine's series of satirical sketches *Noctes Ambrosianae* and as a member of Edinburgh's literary establishment: Hogg is presented as an authentic countryman who has infiltrated the urban intellectual sphere. Many of Hogg's stories, notably those collected in *The Shepherd's Calendar* (1829), employ rural settings, privileging communal identity and integrating the observational and the supernatural. Hogg's stories are especially notable in their use of Scots and emphasis on oral style, and narrative perspective is frequently foregrounded. 'An Old Soldier's Tale', from *Winter Evening Tales* (1820), for instance, begins:

> 'Ye didna use to be sae hard-hearted wi' me, goodwife,' said Andrew Gemble to old Margaret, as he rested his meal-pocks on the corner of the table: 'If ye'll let me bide a' night I'll tell you a tale.'[2]

While Margaret complains about the story's 'cursing and swearing', Andrew insists that she either '"let [him] tell it in [his] ain way, gudewife, or else want it"' (p. 100). The importance of the tale lies not solely in its narrative, but in its fidelity to an individual voice. Unlike Allan Cunningham's collection of *Traditional Tales of the English and Scottish Peasantry* (1822), which similarly had some of its origins in *Blackwood's* serialization, Hogg positions his stories not simply as products of a larger oral tradition, but often as the work of an individual storyteller.

At the same time, however, Hogg also highlights the communal context in which many of these stories are told. 'The Barber of Duncow – A Real Ghost Story', published in *Fraser's Magazine* in 1831, depicts a family of tinkers exchanging ghost stories until their conversation, and the tale itself, is ended by the possible appearance of a real ghost. Other stories are explicitly directed to a local audience familiar with particular settings and customs. Like many of the texts in *Blackwood's*, Hogg's stories are often conversational and intimate; equal importance is given to the tale itself, its manner of telling, and its presumed audience. Whether framed as oral tales, series of letters, or simply as first-person reminiscences, Hogg's stories consistently complicate the relationship between author and reader.

The relation between framing narratives and the tales themselves is also integral to Scott's stories. Although Scott's stories are often reprinted divorced from their original contexts, their meaning is frequently contingent on that context. The story 'Wandering Willie's Tale' from *Redgauntlet* (1824) appears, if printed independently of the novel, to be simply a Scots-language tale of the supernatural, much like some of Hogg's texts. In the novel, however, it appears in the middle of a letter from Darsie Latimer to Alan Fairford, and is marked as an act of writing as much as speech. Latimer introduces the story with the line 'I will not spare you a syllable of it, although it be of the longest; so I make a dash – and begin.'[3] The dash, much like the story's offset title in Gothic script, indicates that the story is simultaneously a work of oral and print cultures. Similarly, the dialogic relationship between the three stories in *Chronicles of the Canongate* can be seen only when they are read not just together, but also in relation to the framing narrative of Chrystal Croftangry. For both Scott and Hogg, the short story functions simultaneously as an independent narrative and as an element in a much wider network of textual conversations. Likewise, the short story is not simply a transcription, real or imagined, of an oral or traditional tale, but provides an opportunity to foreground and problematize the relationship between speech and writing.

Despite the great success of Hogg, Scott and other Edinburgh writers, the Scottish short story, like the novel, largely fell into decline after the early 1830s. When it was resuscitated as a form several decades later, the story appeared in three distinct forms: stories of the supernatural, stories of rural nostalgia and stories of the larger world. Both George MacDonald and Margaret Oliphant were highly prolific writers of novels, equally employing English and Scottish settings and often focusing on religious disputes. Several of MacDonald's most famous fairy tales and short stories, including 'The Light Princess', appeared within the larger narrative of *Adela Cathcart* (1864), while others such as 'The Golden Key' were published in the collection *Dealing with Fairies* (1867). Although written mainly for children, MacDonald's fairy tales often function as complex allegories, heavily indebted to German Romanticism. Later stories such as 'The Carasoyn' (1871), which begins in a pastoral Scottish setting before introducing cruel fairies, are often grimly ironic as they detail the power of internal and external evil. Oliphant similarly makes use of older forms, especially the ghost story, in her own tales. Unlike her novels, which were often written out of financial necessity, Oliphant claimed that her stories could be written only out of direct inspiration. While the stories that make up her 'Little Pilgrim' series are uncomplicated religious allegories, some of her 'Tales of the Seen and the Unseen' are far more sophisticated, blending the natural and supernatural in surprising and complex ways.

Oliphant's most important contribution to the short story is 'The Library Window', published in *Blackwood's* in 1896. The unnamed narrator has been sent to St Rule's (a thinly disguised St Andrews), where, looked after by various elderly relatives, she sees, with increasing detail, the figure of a solitary writer in a window opposite. Even as she learns that the window does not in fact look onto a room, the writer figure functions as a reflection of herself and her own anxieties about artistic creation. Oliphant uses the story not only to explore the gradations between the seen and unseen, but also to trace the development of the individual imagination. The room behind the window, and the writer in it, vanishes when the narrator attempts to speak of them to other people, and she is left with the realization that 'the dreadful thing was that there was nothing, nothing to look for, nothing to hide from – only the silence and the light'.[4] Like Hogg and Scott, Oliphant uses the form of the short story to reflect on the relation between writing and speaking, and similarly emphasizes the way the form navigates between the individual and the communal.

Like Oliphant, J. M. Barrie uses the supernatural as a way to depict the writing self, notably in his novella *Farewell Miss Julie Logan* (published in book form in 1932, but based on sketches published in 1890). His fame as a short story writer, however, rests on his collections focused on rural life, including *Auld Licht Idylls* (1888) and *A Window in Thrums* (1889). Alongside S. R. Crockett's *The Stickit Minister* (1893) and Ian Maclaren's (John Watson) *Beside the Bonnie Brier Bush* (1894), these works inaugurated the oft-derided 'Kailyard' school of Scottish literature. While exceedingly popular, and indeed the first texts to which the term 'best-seller' was applied in its modern sense, these stories are often castigated by their detractors as presenting a falsely nostalgic and sentimental portrait of a Scotland locked in a rural past. The unnamed narrator of *A Window in Thrums*, however, is quick to argue that the community presented in his stories is irrecoverable. At the same time that he argues that the reader 'must not come in a contemptuous mood', he also notes the 'many changes' that have taken place in the past decades.[5] The stories themselves often present an idealized vision of Scotland, however, arguably in order to appeal to an emigrant readership. While in many ways Barrie replicates the regional specificity of Hogg's and Galt's stories, as well as their structural interconnections, his use of an idyllic historical setting results in arguably less challenging narratives. The gentle nostalgia of Barrie's work is a direct influence on Neil Munro's popular stories about Para Handy, captain of a Clyde steamboat, in collections such as *The Vital Spark* (1906), but his early stories have had little other resonance in the twentieth century.

Robert Louis Stevenson's stories of both British and South Sea island life, in contrast, are nothing if not challenging. As well as famous long stories and novellas including *The Strange Case of Dr Jekyll and Mr Hyde* (1886) and *The Ebb-Tide* (1884), Stevenson's most notable collections include *New Arabian Nights* (1882) and *The Merry Men and Other Tales* (1887). 'Thrawn Janet', his first Scottish-set story and one of his own favourites, initially appears to be a familiar historical tale of religion and superstition. Like Scott's 'Wandering Willie's Tale', however, it is complicated by its framing. A brief prologue in English introduces the 'atmosphere of terror' surrounding the Reverend Murdoch Soulis, the explanation for which is told in Scots by 'one of the older folk [warming] into courage over his third tumbler'.[6] The story grows more fantastical and preposterous as it goes, leading the reader to question how many tumblers the narrator has had, and to reflect on the potential fictitiousness of the tale. As with the various manuscripts and letters that form *Dr Jekyll and Mr Hyde*, Stevenson draws the reader's attention to the degree to which any tale is always and necessarily mediated by its form and manner of presentation.

Over the next decades, however, Stevenson's greatest influence on the Scottish short story came from his tales of the South Sea islands. 'The Bottle Imp', collected in *Island Nights' Entertainments* (1893), like some of his later fables, retells a local island story, and was simultaneously targeted at a Samoan and British readership. Longer stories from the same collection, such as 'The Beach of Falesá', depict Europeans on the fringes of empire, both geographically and morally adrift. Throughout these stories Stevenson combines a fidelity to individual voices and dialects with more sweeping stories of adventure. Most influentially, Stevenson's island stories depict not contained or localized cultures, as in Barrie's or even Hogg's stories, but rather a persistent clash of cultures. As *The Ebb-Tide* famously opens: 'Throughout the island world of the Pacific, scattered men of many European races and from almost every grade of society carry activity and disseminate disease.'[7] In such stories Stevenson maintains the setting and action of adventure romance, but positions it as inherently damaging.

Stevenson's two closest followers were similarly based outside Scotland for most of their careers. Although best known for the Sherlock Holmes stories, Arthur Conan Doyle began his career as a historical novelist and short story writer, explicitly emulating Stevenson. His two collections of stories set in Napoleonic Europe, *The Exploits of Brigadier Gerard* (1896) and *The Adventures of Gerard* (1903), both originally published in *The Strand*, combine humour and derring-do in a style reminiscent of Stevenson's earlier work. Other stories, such as the marvellous supernatural tale 'The Horror of the Heights', use found manuscripts to report disastrous scientific experiments, much like *Dr Jekyll and Mr Hyde*. Doyle was an astonishingly prolific writer of short stories; while the Professor Challenger series of scientific romances and the Brigadier Gerard series deserve rediscovery, his many tales of boxing are perhaps best forgotten.[8] Stevenson's other great descendent, R. B. Cunninghame Graham, emulates the later novellas. Cunninghame Graham's stories are set in North and South America, Africa and throughout Europe, as well as in Scotland, and combine detailed descriptions of various places and customs with a morally complex worldview. Admired by his contemporaries if largely forgotten now, Cunninghame Graham's best stories can be seen as important forerunners of the work of both Ernest Hemingway and Paul Bowles. The wide variety of settings for the popular supernatural tales of Saki (H. H. Munro), born to Scottish parents in Burma, can also be seen as representing the internationalization of Scottish adventure romance.

John Buchan's stories bear the clear influence of both Stevenson and Conan Doyle; indeed, Buchan produced a collected edition of the latter's non-Holmes stories. Although Buchan worked in a variety of genres, his most successful short fiction is set largely in Scotland. While the stories collected in *Grey Weather* (1899) are often simple vignettes of rural Scottish life, those in *The Watcher by the Threshold* (1902) combine romance and horror with pastoral realism in surprising and disconcerting ways. The long story 'Fountainblue', for instance, begins with a romantic castle and 'once upon a time', suggesting MacDonald's fairy tales, but ends with a moment of self-revelation when the protagonist forsakes his 'romantic boyhood' in recognition of the power of death and 'the cosmic order of nature'.[9] Later stories, such as the remarkable 'Skule Skerry' from *The Runagates Club* (1928), combine a matter-of-fact narration with an almost existential terror.

Although Buchan, Conan Doyle and Cunninghame Graham were arguably the most successful writers of short stories in their generation, the early decades of the twentieth century also saw a return to the story as a markedly regional form. The most important innovations were in the Northeast, especially in the use of Doric dialect. William Alexander's *Sketches of Life Among My Ain Folk* (1882), is innovative in its use of regionally specific dialogue, although less so in theme and structure. The liveliness of his Doric speech is often offset by a formal and heavy-handed English narration. Similarly, Lorna Moon's *Doorways in Drumorty* (1926), written when its author had emigrated to Hollywood to work as a screenwriter, combines a sentimental and nostalgic perspective on local communities with a Scots-inflected vocabulary. While the stories themselves are indebted to Kailyard notions of morality and tradition, Moon's dialogue is often sophisticated. Like Moon, Violet Jacob published a single collection during her lifetime, with another collection released posthumously; her stories display arguably the best ear for local dialects since Hogg. The title of *Tales of My Own Country* (1922) echoes Alexander's collection; Jacob is similarly attentive to the rhythms and sounds of Northeast speech. Set predominantly in Angus, her stories frequently depict the relation between a regional community and an outside visitor. They often combine painterly descriptions of a particular landscape with a more musical approach to language; one of her best stories, 'The Fiddler', uses the historical figure of Neil Gow to chart how music can both bind a community and change individual fortunes. While Jacob's work largely limits Scots to dialogue, Lewis Grassic Gibbon's most notable stories use Scots throughout. Although he published a number of adventure romance tales under his birth-name, James Leslie Mitchell, Gibbon's greatest success was with his tales of Northeast life published under his better-known pseudonym. 'Smeddum', his most anthologized story (originally published in the miscellany *Scottish Scene* (1934), co-authored with Hugh MacDiarmid), uses the same language for both narration and dialogue, distinguished only by the use of italics:

> And Meg heard the news and went into Stonehive, driving her sholtie, and stopped at the shop. And some in the shop knew who she was and minded the things she had done long syne to other bit bairns of hers that went wrong; and they waited with their breaths held up with delight. But all that Meg did was to nod to Kath, *Ay, well, then, it's you – Ay, mother, just that – Two pounds of syrup and see that it's good.*[10]

Although Gibbon uses Scots terms sparingly, his persistent use of anaphora and second-person narration blur the lines between oral and written, as well as Scots and English.

Similar linguistic experiments can be found in West Coast writers. The stories in Edward Gaitens's *Growing Up* (1942), later incorporated into his novel *Dance of the Apprentices* (1948), are among the first to use Glaswegian dialect. Robert McLellan's *Linmill Stories* (1990) comprises stories broadcast on the radio in the early 1960s. While McLellan's work is, like Barrie's, set in a rural past and is often nostalgic, he is one of the few twentieth-century writers to work entirely in literary Scots, rather than restricting it to dialogue.

His stories often resemble prose-poetry, and his language is closer to MacDiarmid's early poems than any contemporary writers of fiction. The stories are attuned to the rhythm of the seasons, as in his description of spring in Clydeside at the opening of 'The Falls Brae':

> The flourish cam afore the fullyery was thick, and through the trees ye could still mak oot the parks risin ahint them frae the holms by the watter-side, covered wi raws o groset and curran busses, and rasp canes and strawberry beds, rennin this wey in ae plot, and that in anither, aye wi the lie o the grun, sae that aa was pitten to the best use, and there was haurdly a neuk or crannie that didna grow its share.[11]

Ian Hamilton Finlay's stories of West-Coast shepherds and fishermen, collected in *The Sea-Bed* (1958), are written mainly in Standard English, but employ a similarly poetic vocabulary. Both writers give equal attention to the land and its people; the narratives are as likely to be based in the shifting appearance of the landscape as in social interaction.

Mid-century writers frequently used the short story as a place to experiment with genre. Neil M. Gunn's second collection, *The White Hour* (1950), for instance, ranges from rural idyll to supernatural and scientific horror. Naomi Mitchison's stories, produced over a long career, range from antiquity and pre-history to apocalyptic futures. Her work is often explicitly political; she presents a variety of cultures and periods in a contemporary idiom in order simultaneously to treat them seriously in themselves and to demonstrate their social relevance. Most influentially, her novella *Beyond This Limit* (1935), published with illustrations by Wyndham Lewis, introduces a vein of domestic surrealism that can also be seen in the stories of Muriel Spark and Elspeth Davie. Spark's early work often employs African settings; her first published story, 'The Seraph and the Zambesi' (winner of a 1951 open competition in *The Observer*), features a protagonist familiar from Charles Baudelaire who appears in 1946 Rhodesia, as well as an enormous Seraph. Both supernatural elements are presented without commentary. Other early stories hinge on a reversal of cliché or reader expectations. The opening of 'The Portobello Road', for instance, reads: 'One day in my young youth at high summer, lolling with my lovely companions upon a haystack, I found a needle.'[12] The narrator, herself known as Needle, was murdered five years before the story begins; her death is reported as '"Needle" is found: in haystack!' (p. 19). Needle's apparent nonchalance over her death provides much of the story's humour; like the flying saucers in 'Miss Pinkerton's Apocalypse', the success of Spark's use of the fantastic and surreal lies in her refusal to explain or contextualize.

Davie's stories, meanwhile, are largely set in middle-class Edinburgh or unnamed British locations. Davie was not only Spark's contemporary and childhood neighbour but was also launched by the *Observer* competition; her work similarly presents an eccentric, if more sympathetic, perspective on domestic foibles. In Davie's stories, however, escape from the confines of quotidian life is found not through geographical remove but sensory experience. In 'The Colour' the protagonist finds his need for a colour television fulfilled by a brilliant sunset; 'The Concerto', meanwhile, juxtaposes the story of a disturbance at a concert with a detailed description of the music being played. Davie's work combines a stern Presbyterian morality with a focus on everyday ritual: in her stories the smelling of books, the buying of newspapers and the eating of eggs are presented as life-altering interactions. Her stories are largely conversational: many of them present a dialogue between two or more people as a way of highlighting the nuances in small incidents. In 'The Snow Heart' from her second collection, *The High Tide Talker* (1976), for instance, an unnamed woman and man, both visiting their children in hospital over a long period, reflect on a heart shape that has been trampled into the snow on the hospital grounds. Over their conversations the man comes to believe that the heart is not an act of vandalism, as he had thought, but simply '"a not unfriendly shape"'.[13] The characters' focus on the apparently trivial is ultimately more revealing than more direct conversation might be. Although not as consistently remarkable as Davie, Dorothy K. Haynes is similarly underrepresented in recent criticism. Her best stories often use supernatural motifs to comment on girls and women at the fringes of society. 'Dorothy Dean', for instance, centres on a lonely child whose only comfort is an imp born of her imagination. Jessie Kesson's more realistic, often autobiographical stories similarly focus on women and children who are to some extent outcasts, usually because of poverty. All three writers use the story form to highlight the separation between familiar locations and individual imagination.

Many of Spark's stories suggest the extent to which the local community is inherently hostile to individual freedom. This aspect is also found in her contemporary Fred Urquhart. Urquhart demonstrates a wide range in his many stories, from rural traditions of the Northeast to London office life. His second collection, *The Clouds are Big with Mercy* (1946) is notable for its relatively rare focus on the effects of the Second World War. His long story 'Namiętność: or The Laundry Girl and the Pole', like a number of his later stories, details a romance between a working-class Scottish girl and a Polish soldier stationed in the town. Although the soldiers are initially viewed with suspicion, the local residents soon realize that '"they look just the same as oor ain sodgers [. . .]. Except that they've got Poland in red on their shoothers"'.[14] Throughout the collection Urquhart explores the way the war both disturbs and acts as a catalyst for individual relationships, as well as the way it changes the relation between the individual and the community. A far more mythic perspective on the war can be seen in Eric Linklater's 'The Goose Girl', from *Sealskin Trousers* (1947), which juxtaposes the trauma of a returning soldier with a fairy-tale structure. The soldier's experiences in Italy alienate him from the community, and even watching a swan he sees 'the heavy tread of German infantry'; the consolations of both traditional rural life and narrative are no longer available.[15]

Jacob's and Urquhart's interest in the relation between the individual and the community resurfaces in two authors associated with islands, Iain Crichton Smith, from Lewis, and George Mackay Brown, from Orkney. Smith's work often positions island villages as stable communities that cannot be sustained in the modern world. Many of his stories, for instance, focus on an intruder who destabilizes a local community. In 'The Existence of the Hermit', a story Smith reworked several times, the community – voiced in first-person plural – comes to realize that 'the very fact of [the hermit's] existence was a disturbance to the village even though he never talked to us, in fact, precisely because he never talked to us'.[16] In the widely anthologized 'An American Sky' from *The Black and the Red* (1973), similarly, an island native returns home after some years in America, and finds that he is no longer part of the town he left. While Smith wrote in a variety of genres, ranging from ghost stories to a series of Flann O'Brien-esque comic tales featuring the semi-autobiographical Murdo Macrae, much of his best work is infused with a prevailing melancholy for a sense of place and a shared culture of storytelling that are no longer possible. Although the vast majority of Smith's fiction was published in English, his work often looks back to a Gaelic culture that cannot fully be integrated with the modern world.

For Brown, on the other hand, the island community is a continually renewing source of stories. Set largely in Orkney, Brown's stories range from swashbuckling historical romance to allegorical fairy tales to haunting ghost stories such as the well-known 'Andrina'. Many of his stories, however, illustrate the centrality of storytelling to communal life. In 'Five Green Waves' from his first collection, *A Calendar of Love* (1967), a young boy has episodic encounters with schoolteachers, sailors, tinkers, crofters and gravediggers, as well as an imagined interlude in Spain. The story is not dependent on linear narrative, instead highlighting the relationship between imagination and experience. The narrative arc is centred on the progression between the first and last sentences, each of which is given its own paragraph: 'Time was lines and circles and squares' and 'Time was skulls and butterflies and guitars'.[17] The boy, by listening to the stories told around him, is able to construct an imagined and poetic community that is not available through individual experience. While this poetic tendency is also presented as destructive in stories such as 'The Eye of the Hurricane', throughout Brown's work the writer or poet is able to create community by collecting and juxtaposing separate stories. Although both Brown and Smith remain better known as poets, their short fiction presents a strong argument for the short story as the best form with which to examine the relation between individuals and communities.

This relationship appears in a different light in the Glasgow-set stories of Alan Spence and James Kelman, as well as the earlier work of George Friel. The title story of Spence's *Its Colours They are Fine* (1977) showcases the insularity of Glaswegian sectarian culture. Like many of Spence's stories, as well as contemporary works by Brian McCabe and Ronald Frame, it is characterized by its depiction of a sometimes brutal working-class environment with a repressive emphasis on masculinity, as well as by the use of local dialect. As one character introduces the importance of the Orange Walk: "'Look, wumman, this is a Protestant country. [...] An if a Marshal in the Ludge canny walk the streets in is ain regalia, ah'll fuckin chuck it.'"[18] Spence's stories avoid moral judgement in favour of a complex portrayal of a community based in close observation, and emphasize the kindnesses as well as the difficulties of their characters. Kelman's stories depict an even more insular world. Kelman writes in English, Scots and a mixture of the two; many of his stories are presented as the first-person monologues of characters who are unable to communicate their unhappiness; the stories replicate the rhythms of both speech and thought. The title story of *Not Not While the Giro* (1983), for instance, records the fragmented thoughts of a narrator intent on removing himself from the social world:

> Something must be done. A decisive course of action. Tramping around pubs in the offchance of bumping into wealthy acquaintances is a depressing affair. And as far as I remember none of mine are wealthy and even then it is never a doddle to beg from acquaintances – hard enough with friends. Of which I no longer have.[19]

At both sentence and narrative levels, Kelman's stories are often static and abrupt; moments of epiphany or change are rare. Few of his stories feature a traditional plot; instead they have open beginnings and endings that suggest little resolution. Likewise, in many of Kelman's stories there is no linguistic distinction between narrative and dialogue, and neither author nor narrator provides contextualization or explanation. Kelman restricts his settings largely to dole offices, betting shops and pubs, as well as flats and hostels. Throughout his work, Kelman's protagonists occupy themselves with systems and rituals in place of social or narrative progression. Although his work has often been contextualized in relation to Thatcherism and the dismantling of the welfare state, the politics of the stories themselves are almost entirely locally determined and restricted to the needs of particular individuals.

While the restricted view of Kelman's stories, as well as his coarse vocabulary, has been subject to criticism, his stories inaugurate an approach to working-class realism that has become dominant in Scottish writing since the 1980s. Kelman has argued extensively that his work demonstrates the validity of his own working-class community, and does not require explanation or defence; instead, close observation is itself a form of realism. As Alasdair Gray writes in the cover blurb for *Lean Tales* (1985), an anthology featuring his own work alongside stories by Kelman and Agnes Owens, all three authors 'write as if poverty is normal, but poverty is no more their theme than a fixed income is Jane Austen's'. Gray's work is often more fanciful than Kelman's. Both in length and genre, his stories are widely varied, incorporating autobiography, myth, parable, domestic realism and fantasy, as well as Gray's own illustrations. His most influential story, 'Five Letters from an Eastern Empire' from *Unlikely Stories, Mostly* (1983), details the rise and fall of a corrupt empire from the perspective of a court poet. As he laments the destruction he sees around him, the poet is consoled by being told:

> 'You are able to bring your father, mother and city to life and death again in a tragedy, a tragedy the whole nation will read. Remember that the world is one vast graveyard of defunct cities, all destroyed by the shifting of markets they could not control, and all compressed by literature into a handful of poems.'[20]

Here, as elsewhere, Gray argues for a connection between the work of art and national identity. Although they treat many of the same themes and settings, Gray's work is far more expansive than Kelman's. His use of typographic and generic innovations often serves to make his stories more hopeful, and perhaps more universally appealing, than those of many of his contemporaries.

Owens's stories are far closer to Spence and Kelman than Gray. Her first published story, 'Arabella', is one of her few to use any elements of the fantastic; the tale of an impoverished witch, of sorts, it is closest to Dorothy Haynes's tales of outcast women. The story begins with the arresting lines: 'Arabella pushed the pram up the steep path to her cottage. It was hard going since the four dogs inside were a considerable weight.'[21] Although the stories that followed are more grounded in social realism, this twist on readerly expectations is repeated in many of her stories. Whether focusing on the horrific or the banal, Owens leavens her work with surprising humour. Owens's first volume, *Gentlemen of the West* (1984), presents a series of separate stories in the shape of a novel, and is an early example of experimentation with the borders of the novel and the story collection that became common in the 1980s and 1990s. Gray's *Something Leather* (1990), Brown's *Time in a Red Coat* (1984), Irvine Welsh's *Trainspotting* (1993) and, most unusually, Kelman's *Translated Accounts* (2001) were all marketed as novels, but can equally be read as collections or story cycles. Kelman's text is a series of first-person stories from an unnamed country presumably under military rule, all of which have been translated, perhaps inaccurately, into a rudimentary English: 'Let us clear matters here. I did work as was necessary. Work that I did, I can say she did not approve. She said so, that it had no importance in this world that we share, she said this to me. Meanings. She said of meanings, no meanings.'[22] At times the testimonies are further garbled by faulty computer transmission: '```¿FoocumentforwhichdeptˏifanyNBoocumentifwe may do so if wemaysppeaknocurfewanycurfewwhatforthatevening' (p. 19). Kelman's innovative approach forces the reader to question the nature of storytelling itself, as well as the extent to which a story can have meaning if it is not told in its original language. While much of *Trainspotting*'s success may be due to its exuberant portrayal of a hedonistic lifestyle, meanwhile, like Kelman Welsh presents working-class language as being as valid as more traditional ways of writing.

The extraordinary popularity of *Trainspotting*, combined with the continued influence of Kelman's work and Kevin Williamson's notable anthology *Children of Albion Rovers* (1996), represent a preponderance of regionally focused, dialect-driven collections distinguished by their gritty realism. Laura Hird's *Nail and Other Stories* (1997), Duncan McLean's *Bucket of Tongues* (1992), Suhayl Saadi's *The Burning Mirror* (2000) and, more recently, Neil Butler's *The Roost* (2011) showcase Edinburgh, the Northeast, Glasgow and Shetland respectively in ways reminiscent of Welsh's Edinburgh. Bill Duncan's more light-hearted *The Smiling School for Calvinists* (2001) similarly provides a showcase for a highly phonetic representation of Dundonian speech. 'Baather wi a Snake', for instance, opens: 'The wife's mither had an affy baather wi a snake last week. Ehh. She still bides doon the stairs fae us an she's daein no bad fur her age but eh thocht it wiz the end [. . .].'[23] In many of these authors' stories, meaning and narrative are consistently intertwined with the flow of vernacular language.

In sharp contrast to the emphasis on working-class masculinity found in Welsh and Kelman, many contemporary Scottish women writers have in different ways developed Spark's domestic surrealism. Shena Mackay's stories are often macabre and are characterized by abrupt shifts in perspective. The title story of *Dreams of Dead Women's Handbags* (1987) explores a writer's fear of death through a series of images of handbags filled with seashells and other jetsam; 'The Most Beautiful Dress in the World' frames a murderous imagination in relation to a hideous dress that carries 'a whiff of the grave, of black lips of earth and churning worms'.[24] The stories in Janice Galloway's first collection, *Blood* (1991), similarly intermingle the grotesque and the everyday, although Galloway's images are far more fragmentary than Mackay's ornate sentences. Galloway's inventive use of spacing and capitalization, among other textual features, draws attention to characters whose lives resist traditional narrative form. 'Breaking Through' is reminiscent of both Owens and Haynes in its description of the self-immolation of an old woman; the title story likewise uses gothic imagery to convey the horror of a young girl's visit to the dentist, resulting in a unique coming-of-age story. Like some of Kelman's work, Galloway's stories often combine postmodern techniques with social realism; particularly in her second collection *Where You Find It* (1996), however, her work is distinguished by an emphasis on emotional effect, whether comic or horrific.

While Mackay's stories are frequently set in southern England and Galloway's in western Scotland, Candia McWilliam's display an interest in the relation between north and south. *Wait Till I Tell You* (1997), like the work of many of her contemporaries, focuses on submerged population groups, from the elderly to a woman who 'lives on the step of the bank and eats soap'.[25] Like her contemporaries Dilys Rose and Jackie Kay, McWilliam's work combines an interest in the individual longing for love and acceptance with a questioning of the importance of national and cultural identity. A. L. Kennedy's stories similarly focus on the disenfranchised and lonely. The stories in her first collection, *Night Geometry and the Garscadden Trains* (1990), combine domestic realism with touches of the surreal in a manner reminiscent of Galloway's early work. Although her stories frequently employ linear narratives, Kennedy also makes inventive use of new forms. 'The Mouseboks Family Dictionary' in *Now That You're Back* (1994) is a Kafkaesque satire told in dictionary entries, ending: '**what you deserve:** A random but always negative quality. **where it gets you:** Nowhere at all.'[26] Kennedy is also attentive to all aspects of love, from the imaginative to the erotic; 'Sympathy', from *What Becomes* (2009), tells the story of a sexual encounter entirely in dialogue.

The tension between stories of isolated individuals and depictions of national and regional communities indicates the extent to which the Scottish story has become increasingly cosmopolitan and international. Two of the most influential contemporary practitioners of the short story in Scotland were born elsewhere: Bernard MacLaverty, from Belfast, and the Dutch-born Michel Faber both combine Scottish settings with an international idiom. Although Faber is best known for his experiments with genre, he also displays an eye for domestic detail that aligns him with writers like Kennedy and McWilliam. 'Vanilla-Bright Like Eminem', from *The Fahrenheit Twins* (2005), crystallizes the past and future of a man's life as he sits with his family on a train in Inverness, experiencing the happiest moment of his life, his son's trendy haircut 'making everything worthwhile, shining so bright it leaves a pattern on your retina when you close your eyes'.[27] MacLaverty's stories focus on family and community connections in both Scotland and Northern Ireland. Like John Burnside and James Robertson, these writers largely eschew formal experimentation and use of dialect to focus on questions of genre and cultural or familial belonging.

Finally, the work of Angus Peter Campbell and Ali Smith represents a return to some of the experimental approaches found in Romantic-era Scotland. Both authors are as influenced by the fanciful postmodernism of Jorge Luis Borges and Italo Calvino as they are by a Scottish tradition. Campbell works primarily in Gaelic, but also writes in English; his *Invisible Islands* (2006) details an imagined Scottish archipelago where each island has a different approach to language and narrative, whether in the case of a deserted island continually reinvented by visitors' stories or an island whose inhabitants speak only in the present indicative. In Campbell's work, stories and places are interdependent and self-renewing. Smith's work is often self-reflexive; her deceptively simple lexicon and frequent use of the second person create an intimacy between storyteller and audience. 'The Universal Story', from *The Whole Story* (2003) tells seven distinct stories in eleven pages, each of which interrupts the previous one, and which are connected by elements as diverse as a common housefly and a used copy of *The Great*

Gatsby. Smith's playful approach to titles indicates her approach; the title story of *The First Person* (2008) is preceded by 'The Third Person' and 'The Second Person', all of which are presented in, and complicate ideas of, their chosen voice. Smith's and Campbell's work, alongside that of their many contemporaries, demonstrates the extent to which the short story continues to be a vibrant and experimental form in Scotland.

Notes

1. Walter Allen, *The Short Story in English* (Oxford: Clarendon, 1981), p. 9.
2. James Hogg, *Winter Evening Tales*, ed. Ian Duncan (Edinburgh University Press, 2004), p. 98.
3. Walter Scott, *Redgauntlet*, ed. G. A. M. Wood with David Hewitt (Edinburgh University Press, 1997), p. 86.
4. Margaret Oliphant, *A Beleaguered City and Other Tales of the Seen and the Unseen*, ed. Jenni Calder (Edinburgh: Canongate Classics, 2000), p. 401.
5. J. M. Barrie, *A Window in Thrums* (Edinburgh: Saltire Society, 2005), pp. 1, 4.
6. Robert Louis Stevenson, *Weir of Hermiston and Other Stories*, ed. Paul Binding (London: Penguin, 1979), p. 206.
7. Robert Louis Stevenson, *South Sea Tales*, ed. Roslyn Jolly (Oxford University Press, 1996), p. 123.
8. The six-volume edition of Doyle's selected stories published by John Murray in 1922 is divided into *Tales of Adventure and Medical Life*, *Tales of Long Ago*, *Tales of Pirates and Blue Water*, *Tales of Terror and Mystery*, *Tales of the Ring and the Camp* and *Tales of Terror and Mystery*.
9. John Buchan, *The Watcher by the Threshold: Shorter Scottish Fiction*, ed. Andrew Lownie (Edinburgh: Canongate Classics, 1997), p. 305.
10. Lewis Grassic Gibbon, *Smeddum: A Lewis Grassic Gibbon Anthology*, ed. Valentina Bold (Edinburgh: Canongate Classics, 2001), p. 44.
11. Robert McLellan, *Linmill Stories* (Edinburgh: Canongate Classics, 1990), p. 201.
12. Muriel Spark, *The Collected Stories* (London: Penguin, 1994), p. 1.
13. Elspeth Davie, *The Man Who Wanted to Smell Books and Other Stories* (Edinburgh: Canongate Classics, 2001), p. 70.
14. Fred Urquhart, *The Clouds are Big with Mercy* (Glasgow: Kennedy & Boyd, 2011), pp. 12–13.
15. Eric Linklater, *Sealskin Trousers and Other Stories* (London: Rupert Hart-Davis, 1947), p. 10.
16. Iain Crichton Smith, *The Red Door: The Complete English Stories 1949–76*, ed. Kevin MacNeil (Edinburgh: Birlinn, 2001), p. 444.
17. George Mackay Brown, *A Calendar of Love and Other Stories* (London: John Murray, 2000), pp. 41, 60.

18. Alan Spence, *Its Colours They are Fine* (London: Phoenix, 1996), p. 80.
19. James Kelman, *Not Not While the Giro* (Edinburgh: Polygon, 2007), p. 206.
20. Alasdair Gray, *Every Short Story, 1951–2012* (Edinburgh: Canongate, 2012), pp. 119–20.
21. Agnes Owens, *The Complete Short Stories* (Edinburgh: Polygon, 2008), p. 1.
22. James Kelman, *Translated Accounts* (London: Secker & Warburg, 2001), p. 68.
23. Bill Duncan, *The Smiling School for Calvinists* (London: Bloomsbury, 2001), p. 43.
24. Shena Mackay, *The Atmospheric Railway: New and Selected Stories* (London: Vintage, 2010), p. 162.
25. Candia McWilliam, *Wait Till I Tell You* (London: Bloomsbury, 1997), p. 161.
26. A. L. Kennedy, *Now That You're Back* (London: Vintage, 1994), p. 124.
27. Michel Faber, *The Fahrenheit Twins* (Edinburgh: Canongate, 2006), p. 230.

13
The Short Story in Wales: Cultivated Regionalism

JANE AARON

Wales in its entirety is not the 'region' to which this chapter heading refers. 'The term "region" usually designates a patch of geography, the borders of which do not correspond to the borders of an individual country', as Wendy Griswold puts it in her recent study of literary regionalism.[1] Cairns Craig has pointed out in relation to Scotland that it is only from the centralized perspective of the English literary tradition that all Scottish regional fictions, dealing as they do with a diversity of Scottish geographical 'patches', can be seen as the product of one region, and the same is true also of Wales.[2] Welsh short stories frequently manifest many of the features which Griswold lists as characteristic of regional writing: they too tend to focus on the representation of particularized Welsh locations, and on the nature of the human experience forged within those places by their specific history. Since at least the middle of the nineteenth century, however, regions in north, south, east and west Wales have differed markedly from one another as shifting patterns of agrarian blight, industrial development, population migrations and economic depression affected their communities. Anthologists have frequently drawn attention to the fact that Welsh short stories portray 'not one Wales, but many'.[3] Alun Richards introducing his Penguin anthologies stressed the distinguishing importance of 'the varied backgrounds against which the stories are set', and in his 1993 collection went so far as to 'arrange them accordingly rather than in any chronological order'.[4] More recently, other anthologists have chosen to focus on one region alone; Dewi Roberts' *Heartland* (2005), for example, confines itself to tales from north-western Wales, while Lewis Davies's *Urban Welsh* (2005) focuses predominantly on urban south Wales.[5]

Another feature of the Welsh short story is, however, frequently referred to by its anthologists as a characteristic element, common across its regional diversities. Introducing his Faber collection in 1959, George Ewart Evans sees the genre as having 'flowered during a period of acute social stress'. The communities depicted, whether labouring on the green hilltops of Cardiganshire, the slate mountains of Gwynedd, or underground in the coal pits of Glamorganshire, all inspired short story writing during otherwise disastrous epochs in their history, when they faced economic collapse. 'During times of tension the average social construction is at a higher level than usual', claims Evans: 'The writers [. . .] respond quickly to the altered vibrations in society [. . .] they become the peaks in the new consciousness.'[6] That consciousness is essentially 'rebellious', according to Gwyn Jones;[7] it 'assaults' the 'cyclical economic processes' to which each geographical patch in turn fell 'victim', claims Alun Richards in his 1993 Penguin collection.[8] Introducing the latest addition to the stable of Welsh short story anthologies, the two-volume *Story* (2014) in the Library of Wales series of republished classics, its editor Dai Smith also stresses the radicalism of many of the stories, their tone sometimes raised to a 'scream' of protest, at other times bitter and sardonic.[9] Such expressions of politicized discontent are not, however, expected of the regional short story, which characteristically features those 'submerged population groups' that Frank O'Connor saw as typical of the genre.[10] 'Submerged' in economic terms the characters in these Welsh stories may be, but to an unusual extent they protest against their dispossession. In other stories, in which the protagonists do not themselves protest but appear numbed by their predicaments, their silence and apparent acquiescence are likely to arouse the reader to yet greater discomfiture on their behalf: the accumulative effect of the detailing of their underprivilege creates anger at the social circumstances in which they have their being. Arguably then, in effect if not in form, Welsh short fictions share attributes with the genre of social realism to a greater extent than is usual in regional fiction.

A sardonic anger at the social and cultural conditions in which he had himself been reared in rural Cardiganshire is certainly the predominant note in the short stories of Caradoc Evans (1878–1945), who is frequently credited with fathering the modern Welsh short story in English. In the introduction to his 1956 anthology, Gwyn Jones constructed a strongly gendered saga of the genre's birth in which Evans's tales of 'greed, lust and hypocrisy among the peasantry of West Wales' destroyed 'the sentimental dynasties of Allen Raine', ushering in the new era.[11] Since the 1970s and the onset of the critical move to rehabilitate neglected women writers, Allen Raine (Anne Beynon Puddicombe, 1836–1908), who shared Evans's rural west Wales geographical 'patch', has been defended from accusations of sentimentality, however; in

1979 Sally Jones argued that though the romance plot of her longer fictions could distort the realism of her writing, Raine's 'sober, precise' depiction of the Cardiganshire peasantry mark her out as an acute social observer.[12] The best amongst her short stories are characteristically austere and bleak; in the ironically entitled 'Home, Sweet Home' (1908), for example, an old woman perishes of exposure as she attempts to escape incarceration by her son in the local workhouse.[13] But in the middle of the twentieth century, Gwyn Jones's saga was largely accepted: Glyn Jones in his influential *The Dragon Has Two Tongues* (1968) refers to Evans as 'the man who Professor Gwyn Jones has taught us to regard as the first of the modern Anglo-Welsh'.[14]

On its publication in 1915, Caradoc Evans's *My People* roused outrage in Wales; its abrasively concentrated satiric style, based according to Evans on a combination of the prose rhythms of the Old Testament, with its magisterial brevity, and the suggestive allusiveness of the popular music hall artistes of his day, proved an effective weapon with which to scourge his compatriots.[15] In his tales lives are devastated with shockingly stark abruptness and very little or no recorded emotional effect. In 'Be This Her Memorial', for example, a pauper parishioner eats rats and dies of starvation in the attempt to save enough of her scant pennies to buy a gift for a pastor who treats her with contempt. Though the reforms Evans's stories most obviously solicit relate to the autocratic and corrupt nonconformist chapel culture, as he saw it, the injustice which they speak against most persuasively, perhaps, is the physical impoverishment of lives trapped in agrarian depression, which leaves his villagers incapable of responding humanely to the recurring disasters which befall them. Their average income was so low in the 1870s, at the time in which these stories were set, that whereas the tax collected for income per head in England stood at £15.7, in Cardiganshire it was nearly half that, at £8.4 per head, compared with £12 in Wales generally.[16] Most of Evans's villagers are struggling to survive, their deprivation rendered more devastating by their universal belief that poverty is God's punishment upon them for their sins. In 'The Way of the Earth', for example, a small farmer and his wife toil to scrape together enough pennies from their meagre acres to win back for themselves a place in Zion, after having been excommunicated from chapel membership when their only child was born before their marriage. In age, after losing their savings in the attempt to save their pregnant daughter from similar disgrace, they await death in stark penury.

The modern Welsh-language short story, on the other hand, developed not in rural Wales but in a north-west Wales still dominated by a failing slate industry: according to Kate Roberts, Richard Hughes Williams (1878–1919), also known by his pseudonym Dic Tryfan, was 'the pioneer of the short story in Welsh as we know it today'.[17] Under the influence of the late nineteenth-century Russian and French short story writers he admired, Williams developed an austere style, largely restricted to dialogue, with which to represent the communities of the slate quarries in which he himself had worked in his youth. The first anthology of Welsh short stories, published by Faber in 1937, included in translation his 'Siôn William', in which a gang of slate-quarry workers discuss the fact that the day's rain means they'll be taking home no pay. Siôn William, the oldest amongst them, is in fact already starving, but such is his taciturn pride that it is only from his neighbour that his fellow workers discover the next day that he has been forced to commit himself to the workhouse. The story ends apparently very abruptly, with Guto Jones, one of Siôn's co-workers, 'looking down at his sleeve' when he hears the news.[18] His glance refers back to the one occasion on the previous day when the older man had reached out from his self-imposed isolation, touching Guto's sleeve as he offered him a slate-cutting tool he would not himself be using again. Spare as it is, the style of Richard William Hughes's stories effectively arouses readers' outrage at the exigencies of the struggle for existence in the slate-quarrying industry, which dominated the economic life of north-west Wales during his lifetime.

Kate Roberts (1891–1985), also, like Dic Tryfan, a north-Walian quarryman's child whose purpose in writing was to give expression to 'the experiences of the people among whom I was raised', furthered the development of the modernist Welsh-language short story, and became its most appreciated practitioner.[19] Whereas Dic Tryfan focuses predominantly on depicting the male world of work, her tales add female perspectives. In 'The Condemned' (1937), the story she apparently considered her best, a quarryman, whose energies and health have been exhausted by his labours, learns from his doctor that he is a doomed man. At home during his last months of life, he traverses a spectrum of awareness, from grief and shock at the loss of his work identity to an intense appreciation of his wife and the loving care she expresses through the minutiae of her daily domestic toil. But the years of extreme gender-segregated labour have left them too much strangers to one another to break the pattern of restraint and speak of their regained intimacy. By means of these glimpses into the inner lives of her characters Kate Roberts protests against the emotional as well as material impoverishment brought about by the customary patterns of life in their communities.

As a young schoolteacher, Kate Roberts had moved south to find work in the coalfield, and many of her later stories reflect the life of that region as it in turn faced economic depression. In 'Protest March' (1949), for example, the wife of an embittered unemployed miner in the 1930s still has enough political hope to join a United Front march against the Means Test, only to be disillusioned by the sight of her local Labour MP's wife flaunting a fur coat in the face of the rest of the semi-starved procession.[20] But in 1915, when Kate Roberts first left Gwynedd, the promise of the 'black gold' still lured workers made redundant as the northern slate quarries closed and agrarian depression depopulated the rural west. In the 1881 Census, industrial Glamorganshire's population was recorded as 518,383; by 1911 its numbers had more than doubled, to 1,130,668, nearly half of the total population of Wales. During its boom years, the coalfield also attracted immigrant workers from outside Wales, of course, creating linguistically diverse communities in which many parents gave up on the struggle to rear their children as Welsh speakers, unsupported as they were at the time by an almost entirely English-language education system. Within the metal-works townships and pit villages there were, however, few opportunities for employment for men or women other than in the production of raw materials. The sociologist Graham Day points out that 'while Wales was virtually the only producer of tinplate and sheet steel in Britain, only 11% of the former and 4% of the latter were processed for finished products within Wales'. Consequently 'no self-sustaining industrial base' was developed in a country in which the mines and steel furnaces were usually controlled by external investment, with the profits 'creamed off and realized elsewhere'.[21] For those who left the land to cram into the packed terraced houses which mushroomed under the shadow of the pits, there was therefore little prospect of escape for themselves or their children from dependence on underground labour, with its concomitant threat of sudden death from rock fall, explosion, coal-gas or flooding, or of slower death from silicosis. By the 1930s and 1940s, the majority of Wales's most productive short story writers, authors like Rhys Davies (1901–78), Glyn Jones (1905–95), Gwyn Jones (1907–99), George Ewart Evans (1909–88) and Gwyn Thomas (1913–81), reared in the coalfield and writing in English, were recording their remembrance of the price of coal.

In his short story 'The Pit' (1945) Gwyn Jones, for example, portrays a man trapped underground in an old pit who becomes traumatized by his awareness of the unnatural sacrifice the mine would have demanded during its working days: 'With frightful vividness he thought of the piled-up hillside above him. Four hundred feet of unbroken rock under which to creep and creep till your lantern gave out and you were part of the dark for ever.'[22] A native of New Tredegar, Gwyn Jones was the son of a miner; through education he escaped the darkness of the pit himself, but the manner in which his father and his colleagues earned their living marks many of his fictions. Glyn Jones from Merthyr was the son of a postman, not a collier, but his experience of the Depression in south Wales, which he described as 'more agonizing [...] even than the Second World War', and his recollection of the colliers' maimed lives resonate in his surreal symbolist fantasy 'The Kiss' (1937).[23] A dead miner lying 'deep in the coalfield [...] stirred out of his first death' and rose again to the surface, where he delighted in the simple realities of life, longing 'to see the bodies of men and women moving once again with passionate or even commonplace movements as the restless urgency used them'.[24] But the first person he encounters is his brother, whose hand has been mangled and shattered into pulp, presumably also through a pit accident. He helps his brother home; their mother who 'recognized the dead voice of her son' is agitated when he asks to see his brother's wound; she cannot bear to see their wounded lives uncovered. But 'don't be afraid of an action for healing' her son tells her, as he reverently unwinds the bloodied cloth: exposure is necessary if the healing of the wrong is to begin (p. 46).

The stories of Rhys Davies, the son of a Tonypandy grocer, also characteristically feature lives shadowed by the pit. In the tellingly entitled 'The Pits are on the Top' (1942) a young couple on a bus journey overhear their fellow passengers discussing a recent death from silicosis and referring to the ubiquity of the disease in the neighbourhood. As they leave the bus, the girl, haunted by her foreboding that her lover, with his bad cough, has not escaped the collier's disease, sees the other passengers nod to each other knowingly, and recognizes that nod as a prediction of his likely death. The terrible acceptance on the part of her fellow passengers of early death as inevitable, as part of the price of coal, embitters her more at that moment than the likely death itself. During the Depression years, the colliers and their communities struggled to overcome that confounding sense of doomed helplessness. In Merthyr, 69.1 per cent of the population was unemployed in 1939, and, in neighbouring Dowlais, 73.4 per cent: at least 430,000 people emigrated from Wales, and the coalfield became a 'problem' area.[25] The solidarity of the community that remained is evinced by the fact that often, in Rhys Davies's stories, at least, it is the Valleys' women, toiling to maintain a healthy workforce in the insanitary terraces, who most often express defiant protest. In 'Period Piece' (1958), set during the Depression, an irate woman bursts without knocking into the office of a colliery's general manager, and insists that he accompany her to view the hanging body of her husband Griff, an unemployed miner who has just committed suicide. Unable to withstand the force of her anger, the manager does so and witnesses her berating the corpse in her unappeasable fury at being thus deserted with her children: she 'knew Griff had been too gentle a chap altogether, and she could not forgive him that he had not her savage defiance'.[26]

Her defiance reflects the changes at the time transforming the political face of industrial Wales. In the 1900 General Election, Keir Hardie in Merthyr won the first Westminster seat for what was then the Independent Labour Party; by the 1945 General Election, twenty-seven of Wales's thirty-five parliamentary seats were held by socialist candidates. The south Wales author who most effectively fictionalized socialist theories, illustrating the manner in which the 'tradition of all the dead generations weighs like a nightmare on the brain of the living'[27] was, arguably, Gwyn Thomas, the youngest of twelve children of an unemployed miner. The common theme of his 1946 collection *Where Did I Put my Pity? Folk Tales from the Modern Welsh* is the difficulty of protesting in the face of social injustices to which a community has become so habitualized that its deprivation seems 'natural'. 'We weep often to see in those around us, young and old, the cramped passivity of the seat they had in the womb', says the narrator of 'Dust in the Lonely Wind'.[28] But the collier Milton Nicholas, sent by his trade union to college, has, since his return to the valleys, 'been spreading more light than the gasworks with much less smell and cost' (p. 146). In his classes at the Miners' Institute, Milton 'thaws and astonishes' the awakening consciousness of his students with his analyses of the class and capitalist system, though the narrator, habitualized to servitude, finds it difficult to sustain an active faith in the possibility of a socialist rebirth: 'When Milton and I try to talk, the long-dead and the unborn mouth at each other through glass', he says (p. 192). Similarly in 'Simeon' a pit village landowner tyrannizes a population which experiences itself as bound to subordination by the labour of generations. 'There had been so many slaves in my family we got more pliable from father to son', says his servant Ben (p. 112). But this taught patience is eroded when Ben learns the dark secrets of Simeon's household: two of his daughters have been raped by their father and have had children by him. When Eleanor, Simeon's third daughter who as yet knows nothing of her father's crimes, returns to the house from which her older sister had sent her away for safety, and Ben realizes that she too is now endangered, he determines to kill Simeon, but finds that 'my limbs were frozen [. . .] I still couldn't move' (pp. 138–9). It is Eleanor herself, not as indoctrinated in the ways of subservience as the other members of the household, who succeeds in killing her father, simply by holding in front of herself a knife onto which the momentum of his incestuous passion dashes him. Following Marx, Gwyn Thomas suggests with some optimism at the close of such modern 'folk tales' that should oppressed communities but withdraw their collaboration and stand firm, the capitalist system would be toppled by the momentum of its own deregulated greed.

Marxist educationalists also have a key role to play in George Ewart Evans's fictions. Reared in the coalfield, Evans was later to find fame as a pioneer of oral history, but in his youth he published a number of short stories in magazines such as *Life and Letters Today* and Keidrych Rhys's *Wales*. In 'Ben Knowledge' (1949) the unemployed colliers of Llwyncelyn meet on the mountains above the village on Sunday mornings to discuss political theory: 'A crowd of the boys used to gather up there under the sheep-wall and they'd talk and argue the sun out of the sky.'[29] Jim Adams, their leader, is according to Ewart Evans's biographer, a fictional portrayal of the Communist collier Jim Adlam, 'a well-informed critical unemployed miner of acute political insight'.[30] Adams, in Evans's story, manages to refute Berkeley's Idealism by reference to a hefty infant that one of the colliers has carried up the mountain in a shawl twisted Welsh-mam fashion about his chest. Tales such as these capture the unique geography of the south Wales industrial region, in which the shanty-town terraces crossed the hillsides, with their front doors opening on to the pit, while their back alleys fringed the mountains. They also successfully evoke the continuing intellectual and political vitality of the Valleys' communities during the Depression years, notwithstanding the ravages caused by unemployment.

Another Marxist teacher, one of Ogmore Vale's socialist activists, was the father of short story writer Dorothy Edwards (1903–34), but she chose to locate most of her fictions not in the coalfield but amidst middle-class households over the border, describing her sojourns in England as 'pilgrimages' in which she hoped to 'track' down the 'hereditary enemies' of her own class and region, and dissect 'the English spirit'.[31] One of her few stories not set in England but on the Welsh border, 'The Conquered' (1926), portrays a young Welsh heiress, Gwyneth, so enamoured of the 'charming Romans' who have left their traces in the neighbourhood, and of the British royalty, one of whom once visited her home, that she can only identify with the songs and spirit of imperial conquerors. Yet according to the logic of the story she herself and her lost Welshness are the conquered, for all the elegance and confidence with which she initially charms the story's narrator.

Edwards's 'The Conquered' serves as a prototype for many subsequent narratives increasingly concerned with border locations and the phenomenon of border identity. To be of the border also entails loss – the erosion in particular of Welsh rural identity – in the fictions of Geraint Goodwin (1903–41), who left his native Welsh border county of Montgomeryshire for London in 1923. His tales characteristically feature protagonists who yearn to unify lives torn, physically and psychically, between Wales and England but cannot do so. In 'The White Farm' (1937) the Welsh wife of an Englishman persuades him to take her back on a visit to the farm where her grandparents reared her and, once there, is overwhelmed by the sensation that this 'was where she belonged. She let it all possess her, gave herself up to it, as to a lover. She had gone away from herself, far, far away. Now she was – only now she was.'[32] But the border crossing is only temporary, and leave for England she must. Similarly, in Goodwin's 'The Lost Land' (1938) a Welshman estranged from his kin after an unfortunate marriage feels he has lost his anchor now that he is tied to the 'sullen humid life' of a border town and cannot return to the family farm on the 'old mountains [...] the lost land that was and would for ever be' (pp. 187–8). In 'Janet Ifan's Donkey' (1937) the 'land of lost content' has never been acquired in the first instance by an English magistrate in a border town who falls in love with a Welsh woman, but loses her when his incapacity to respond humanely to the Welsh peasantry brought before the bar of his court becomes all too clear to his fiancée. As Katie Gramich suggests, 'the border for Goodwin is a negative territory, a limbo world where there can be no belonging, no authentic being'.[33]

The more positive possibilities inherent in a hybrid border identity are explored by Margiad Evans (1909–58), born Peggy Eileen Whistler in Uxbridge, who moved to live on the Wales–England border in 1938. When readers assumed from her pseudonym that she was Welsh, they were soon corrected. 'I'm *not* Welsh: I never posed as Welsh [...] *I am the border* – a very different thing', she tells Gwyn Jones in 1946.[34] In her *Autobiography* (1943) Evans presents a border identity as one in which, released from any single ethnic identity, a subject can relate wholly and with particular intensity to her chosen 'patch of geography'. 'My country, my *body*, why must I die and leave you, why was I born away from you, why am I not your native spirit?' she cries, addressing the landscape around her high hillside cottage above Llangarron in the Wye valley: 'My brain and body survive, because I can look out upon the hills [. . .] I can *be* the field, the trees – the movement of the branches in the breeze is like my own blood going through and round my life-centre – the earth is the lung by which I breathe – the earth is my greater flesh.'[35] Why women in particular should value such elemental freedom is suggested in her story 'Mrs Pike's Eldorado' (1948), in which the twice-married Mrs Pike migrates from the border to the coalfield only to find her existence at each stage nothing but an endless round of lonely domestic toil. After escaping back to the border country she pronounces to her sister 'possibly the only passionate reference to her life she ever made': 'Maria! Don't tha feel ... it be just as if summat was stolen from you everyd'y? We don't never get the day as we do see rising. No, never. We do see it over there with the sun rising and then summat else do seem to slip in, like, and that un be what we do get.'[36] Throughout Evans's writings a note of feminist protest is dominant, as her characters experience early twentieth-century women's lack of control over their lives within conventional gender-segregated societies. Amongst the short stories in which Evans most memorably imagines the possibility of escape from such patterns is 'The Old Woman and the Wind' (1944), whose protagonist, living alone in a hilltop cottage, chooses the elements as her companions rather than the society of the villagers below. 'I bain't got the *use* of a lot of people and voices', the old woman explains to the wind; 'I've worked with people, not loved them, and now I be done with work I do want to be shut of 'em'.[37]

Margiad Evans was a poet as well as a novelist and short story writer and in her poetry she frequently explores themes similar to those that preoccupy the characters in her short stories. Over-riding themes, worked through in both verse and prose, also feature extensively in the writings of Dylan Thomas (1914–53) and Alun Lewis (1915–44), both primarily known as poets. At every stage in his short career Dylan Thomas published short stories that interrelate with his verse. According to Annis Pratt, his early pre-war short stories in particular 'can be taken as part of the symbolic universe of both the early and later poetry'; they are 'much more a unity with the poetry' than his later tales, she suggests.[38] In 1934, when his first verse collection, *18 Poems*, was published, Thomas inscribed in his 'Red Notebook' the story 'The Visitor', in which a dying man receives a visitor who takes him to the valley of death and reveals it to be resplendent with life: 'He saw [. . .] how the flowers shot out of the dead, and the blades and the roots were doubled in their power under the stride of the spilt blood.'[39] The connections between 'The Visitor' and such poems as 'And death shall have no dominion' and 'The force that through green fuse' are evident enough: death has no dominion because the corpse decays in readiness to 'hammer through daisies'. 'It is my aim as an artist [. . .] to prove beyond doubt to myself that the flesh that covers me is the flesh that covers the sun, that the blood in my lungs is the blood that goes up and down in a tree', Thomas proclaimed in 1934, and he seeks at this prewar stage to do so in his stories as much as in his verse.[40] In 'The Burning Baby' (1934) a cremated infant lights up the hills with the energy of its combustion, and in the 1936 story 'The School for Witches', a coven of witches dancing on the hilltops above the diseased village of Cathmarw (Dead Cat) whirl cyclically with such galvanized intensity that they draw all passers-by into their circle and 'dance the metamorphoses of the dusts of Cathmarw', unloosing 'the spellbound [. . .] human skeleton'.[41]

Such tales may seem far removed from regionalism, but in a sense they represent the opposite side of the same coin; the poetic imagination here turns away from the decaying communities of the Depression, and imagines for all life an orgiastic release of its trapped energies. Similarly, though in a more sombre vein, the stories for which Alun Lewis is today best remembered echo the existentialist themes of his verse. In his poem 'The Jungle' the 'cultures of the west' are seen as exhausted by economic depression and war; the jaundiced Second World War soldiers resting by a jungle pool 'Prefer the instinctive rightness of the poised / Pied kingfisher deep darting for a fish / To all the banal rectitude of states.'[42] Lewis's story 'The Orange Grove' (1948) continues to explore the same theme: here a British officer lost in the Indian countryside chooses finally to give up his struggle to conform with the regimental requirements of his post and joins a passing troop of nomads. 'Stumbling up the track in the half-light among the ragged garish gipsies, he gradually lost the stiff self-consciousness with which he had first approached them' and merges with a freer mode of living, remembering that once in past eras, 'Life had been nothing worth recording beyond the movements of people like these.'[43] These are amongst Lewis's last writings, penned just before his 'accidental' death in 1944, on active service in Burma, now believed to be suicide. For those Welsh writers who outlived the war years, however, renewed hope for a better future for their communities, particularly those of the industrialized south, seemed promised by the Labour landslide of the 1945 General Election, the nationalization of the coal industry in 1947 and the development, under Aneurin Bevan, of the National Health Service. A decade later, though, the drowning of the village of Capel Celyn in the Tryweryn valley by Liverpool Corporation, the latest in a long succession of valleys drowned in Wales's middle and border counties to provide water for the English midlands, aroused prolonged though fruitless opposition throughout Wales, and led to further strongly regionalized fictions.

Roland Mathias (1915–2007), also best known as a poet, was born in Ffynnon Fawr, a farm fringing what was later to become the Talybont reservoir in the border county of Breconshire. In a story entitled 'Ffynnon Fawr' (1956), Rendel Morgan returns to his family homestead from Australia, to which his parents had emigrated in his childhood, only to find the reservoir covering the old road to the farm and lapping at its walls, entering with him as he opens its front door. After one disturbed night, Rendel flees: 'He was too timid for Ffynnon Fawr, too timid to make a future where the generations cried out on him in their sleep.' Unprepared for this aspect of his inheritance Rendel lets it go rather than take up the struggle, though 'what he had been and was not and now could never be clutched at him'.[44] More of a fight is put up to save another Welsh homestead in 'Dinas' (1968) by Emyr Humphreys, reared in Flintshire on the north-east border. Threatened in this case by demolition to make room for caravan parks, Dinas is saved by its dying owner's decision not to bequeath it to his son, who he knows will sell it to the highest bidder, but to entrust it at a token price to his nurse, an 'extremist' according to the son, who 'has a deep affection for the place'.[45] Nurse Jones represents those activists within the movement to save the Welsh language whose non-violent grassroots campaigns had a profound effect upon Wales as a whole throughout the last four decades of the twentieth century.

Welsh-language activism received short shrift, however, from some Rhondda writers like Ron Berry (1920–97) and Alun Richards (1929–2004) who, as the coalpits continued to close throughout the 1960s and 1970s, resented the expenditure of scarce resources on a language they had already lost. At the same time their own regional loyalties remained deeply embedded; in Richards's 'The Scandalous Thoughts of Elmyra Mouth' (1973), for example, Elmyra stoutly resists her husband's attempts to move her from the valleys to Cardiff, Wales's capital since 1955, when he gets a job there as a technician in the BBC studios: 'She was a valley girl, was she not? [...] So when Davie'd proposed moving to Cardiff as it would cut down on his travelling time, she had a cryptic and typical answer. "Travel you bugger," she said flatly. "You'll not move me an inch!"'[46] Regional communities under threat developing a sharp sense of their distinctive identity and struggling to preserve that distinctiveness is a typical pattern in Welsh political consciousness-raising according to Raymond Williams, but in the

1970s it worked to alienate one half of Wales from the other and led to the debacle of the 1979 Devolution referendum.[47] The dire consequences of not having voted for at least a measure of devolution in 1979 were, however, most effectively brought home to the Welsh population at large by the pit closures that preceded and followed the Miners' Strike of 1984–5, and the Welsh-language Society's active involvement in that struggle, as part of their pledge to campaign for the survival of all Welsh communities, dissipated much of the old antagonism. When Levi Jones, in Ron Berry's 'Natives' (1982), proclaims to his audience of unemployed colliers 'But listen, the best human stuff comes from roots, from inheritance. Put bluntly, a man can't, he *can't* renege on the way he's made, his birth-given packet. Where people don't belong, that's where they go doo-lally. Therefore, boys, culture, civilization, these are ours until Upper Coed-coch becomes totally extinct', he is speaking for every Welsh region, whatever its language.[48]

Since the 1990s the multi-ethnic community of Cardiff's docklands, with its long history dating from the 1880s, has also finally found reflection in short fictions. Leonora Brito first came to prominence when her story 'Moonbeam Kisses' – on its narrator's upbringing in a Catholic orphanage where she is labelled 'half-caste' and yet expected to know that God made her – won the Rhys Davies Short Story Prize in 1991. In her 1995 collection *dat's love*, Brito fictionalized episodes from the past history of the docklands, such as the occasion in 1955 when the ship in which Churchill ceremoniously visited the new capital broke an old sea-lock; he called upon the inhabitants of Tiger Bay to save the day by clearing the debris, summoning them 'to toil, sweat' as a 'test of our national character'.[49] His imperial rhetoric, evocative of World War years, now rings hollow in the ears of some of its hearers, however; ironically entitled 'Digging for Victory' the story is a subtle critique of imperial exploitation. Another notorious historical event from the 1950s is fictionalized in Sean Burke's 'The Trials of Mahmood Mattan' (2004), on the trial and wrongful execution on scant evidence of Mattan, a Somali, for the murder of a docklands shopkeeper. Earlier Mattan had alienated his community and the white authorities by marrying and having children with a white woman from the Valleys. Realizing that Mattan 'had been arrested for marrying rather than murdering a white woman', his friend, the narrator, tries to succour aid in his defence, but his activities only lead to further revelations of overt and hidden racism amongst the white community.[50]

Sean Burke, himself a Cardiffian of Irish extraction, has suggested that in recent fictions Cardiff is emerging as yet another distinct Welsh 'region', marked in this case by its cosmopolitan multiculturalism.[51] Post-industrial fictions from the Valleys have also reflected that area's long-standing Irish, Jewish and Italian communities, dating from the era of peak immigration to the coalfields. In 'Jigsaw' (2005) by Rachel Trezise, born in the Rhondda in 1978, a Valley girl is shocked when her father intervenes to prevent her growing friendship with the son of the local Italian café owner on the grounds that 'they're not like us'.[52] Initially she acquiesces, and marries her father's choice of suitor, only to realize subsequently that neither she nor her generation share the patriarch's narrow values or can live as a community within them: the ethnic hybridity of the community in which she was reared is part and parcel of its meaning and history. The attachment to the region remains, however: Trezise, whose short story collection *Fresh Apples* won the inaugural Dylan Thomas Prize for writers under thirty in 2006, has located most of her fictions to date in the Rhondda and is as much a cultivator of regionalism as any of her inter-war predecessors. Regional literature is currently flourishing across the globe, according to such critics as Wendy Griswold. Places which have long cultivated a cultural understanding of their changing history and social connectedness, and told their distinctive story, generation after generation, presenting it as patterned in the local terrain – such places accrue meaning, and in the current era of globalization and proliferating information technologies readers hunger for such embedded meaning, says Griswold. If she is right, the Welsh short story looks set to prosper in the twenty-first century.

Notes

1. Wendy Griswold, *Regionalism and the Reading Class* (University of Chicago Press, 2008), p. 12.
2. Cairns Craig, 'Scotland and the Regional Novel', in *The Regional Novel in Britain and Ireland, 1880–1990*, ed. K. D. M. Snell (Cambridge University Press, 1998), p. 221.
3. Gwyn Jones, ed., *Welsh Short Stories* (London: Oxford University Press, 1956), p. xi.
4. Alun Richards, ed., *New Penguin Book of Welsh Short Stories* (Harmondsworth: Penguin, 1993), p. xi.
5. Dewi Roberts, ed., *Heartland: Short Stories from North-Western Wales* (Llanrwst: Gwasg Carreg Gwalch, 2005); Lewis Davies, ed., *Urban Welsh* (Cardigan: Parthian, 2005).
6. George Ewart Evans, ed., *Welsh Short Stories* (London: Faber, 1959), pp. 9–10.

7. Jones, ed., *Welsh Short Stories*, p. xiii.
8. Richards, *New Penguin Book of Welsh Short Stories*, pp. x–xi.
9. Dai Smith, 'Introduction', *Story II: The Library of Wales Short Story Anthology* (Cardigan: Parthian, 2014), pp. ix–x.
10. Frank O'Connor, *The Lonely Voice: A Study of the Short Story* (London: Macmillan, 1963), pp. 20–1.
11. Jones, ed., *Welsh Short Stories*, p. x.
12. Sally Jones, *Allen Raine* (Cardiff: University of Wales Press, 1979), p. 31.
13. Allen Raine, in *A View across the Valley: Short Stories by Women from Wales, c. 1850–1950*, ed. Jane Aaron (Dinas Powys: Honno, 1999), pp. 45–58.
14. Glyn Jones, *The Dragon Has Two Tongues: Essays on Anglo-Welsh Writers and Writing* (London: J. M. Dent, 1968), p. 55.
15. Caradoc Evans, 'Self Portrait', *Wales* (1944), p. 3.
16. See W. J. Rees, 'Inequalities: Caradoc Evans and D. J. Williams', *Planet*, 81 (1990), p. 77.
17. Kate Roberts, 'Richard Hughes Williams', *Taliesin*, 5 (1962), p. 65.
18. Richard H. Williams, 'Siôn William', trans. Ll. Wyn Griffith, in *Welsh Short Stories: An Anthology* (London: Faber, 1937), p. 415.
19. Saunders Lewis interviewing Kate Roberts, 'The Craft of the Short Story' [1947], trans. John Phillips and Ned Thomas, *Planet*, 51 (1985), pp. 43.
20. Kate Roberts, 'Protest March', trans. Joseph Clancy, in *The World of Kate Roberts: Selected Stories 1925–1981* (Philadelphia: Temple University Press, 1991), pp. 111–15.
21. Graham Day, 'The Sociology of Wales', in *The Welsh and their Country*, ed. I. Hume and W. T. R. Pryce (Llandysul: Gomer Press, 1986), pp. 163–4.
22. Gwyn Jones, *Collected Stories* (Cardiff: University of Wales Press, 1998), p. 21.
23. Glyn Jones, *The Dragon Has Two Tongues*, p. 32.
24. Glyn Jones, *The Collected Stories of Glyn Jones*, ed. Tony Brown (Cardiff: University of Wales Press, 1999), pp. 41, 45.
25. Gwyn A. Williams, *When Was Wales?* (Harmondsworth: Penguin, 1985), pp. 252–3.
26. Rhys Davies, *Collected Stories* ed. Meic Stephens (Llandysul: Gomer Press, 1998), pp. iii, 404.
27. Karl Marx, 'The Eighteenth Brumaire of Louis Bonaparte' (1852), in Karl Marx and Friedrich Engels, *Selected Works* (London: Lawrence & Wishart, 1968), p. 96.
28. Gwyn Thomas, *Where Did I Put my Pity? Folk Tales from the Modern Welsh* (London: Progress Publishing, 1946), p. 148.
29. George Ewart Evans, *Let Dogs Delight* (London: Faber, 1975), p. 29.
30. Gareth Williams, *George Ewart Evans* (Cardiff: University of Wales Press, 1991), p. 17.

31. See Dorothy Edwards's letters quoted in Claire Flay, *Dorothy Edwards* (Cardiff: University of Wales Press, 2011), p. 80.
32. Geraint Goodwin, *The Collected Stories of Geraint Goodwin*, ed. Sam Adams and Roland Mathias (Tenby: H. G. Walters, 1976), p. 109.
33. Katie Gramich, '"Those Blue Remembered Hills": Gender in Twentieth-Century Welsh Border Writing by Men', in Jane Aaron, Henrice Altink and Chris Weedon, eds., *Gendering Border Studies* (Cardiff: University of Wales Press, 2010), p. 151.
34. Margiad Evans to Gwyn Jones, January 1946, quoted in Ceridwen Lloyd Morgan, *Margiad Evans* (Bridgend: Seren, 1998), p. 32.
35. Margiad Evans, *Autobiography* (1943; London: Calder and Boyars, 1974), pp. 93, 108.
36. Margiad Evans, *The Old and the Young* (1948; Bridgend: Seren, 1998), p. 184.
37. Evans, *The Old and the Young*, p. 43.
38. Annis Pratt, *Dylan Thomas' Early Prose: A Study in Creative Mythology* (University of Pittsburgh Press, 1970), pp. xi and 32.
39. Dylan Thomas, *Collected Stories*, ed. Walford Davies (London: Dent, 1984), p. 30.
40. Dylan Thomas to Trevor Hughes, January 1934, *The Collected Letters of Dylan Thomas*, ed. Paul Ferris (London: Dent, 1985), pp. 89–90.
41. Thomas, *Collected Stories*, pp. 72–3.
42. Alun Lewis, *Selected Poems of Alun Lewis*, ed. Jeremy Hooker and Gweno Lewis (London: Unwin, 1987), p. 98.
43. Alun Lewis, *Collected Stories*, ed. Cary Archard (Bridgend: Seren, 1990), p. 224.
44. Roland Mathias, *The Collected Short Stories of Roland Mathias* ed. Sam Adams (Cardiff: University of Wales Press, 2001), p. 141.
45. Emyr Humphreys, *Natives* (London: Secker & Warburg, 1968), pp. 193 and 200.
46. Alun Richards, *Selected Stories* (Bridgend: Seren, 1995), p. 305.
47. Raymond Williams, 'The Importance of Community', in *Resources of Hope* (London: Verso, 1989), p. 115.
48. Ron Berry, *Collected Stories*, ed. Simon Baker (Llandysul: Gomer Press, 2000), p. 77.
49. Leonora Brito, *dat's love* (Bridgend: Seren Books, 1995), p. 71.
50. Sean Burke, 'The Trials of Mahmood Mattan', in *Wales Half Welsh*, ed. John Williams (London: Bloomsbury, 2004), p. 20.
51. Sean Burke interviewed by Mark Jenkins, 'From Barthes to Butetown', *New Welsh Review*, 58 (2002), 24.
52. Rachel Trezise, *Fresh Apples* (Cardigan: Parthian, 2005), p. 150.

14
The Understated Art, English Style

DEAN BALDWIN

The writers discussed in this chapter form a unique group in the history of modern British fiction. Most were born during the rise of high modernism and came to maturity during its flourishing decade, the 1920s, yet, with a few exceptions, they have seldom been included in discussions of modernism, or in considerations of the 'Auden generation'. If anything, they might be called second generation modernists, for their stories – influenced by the stark realism of Maupassant, the open-ended poetics of Chekhov and the sexual politics of D. H. Lawrence – often seemed unconventional to magazine editors and contemporary readers. Nevertheless, they embodied in many ways the fears of some high modernists, springing as they did from the lower middle classes, educated not in public schools and universities but in the newly created grammar schools, earning their living by their pens. Except for Lawrence and Graham Greene, the writers discussed here were not intellectuals; they had no overriding theories of politics, economics and sociology, though inevitably their stories touch on these issues. With a few exceptions, they resembled E. M. Forster's Leonard Bast – struggling to move upwards culturally by locating themselves between the extremes of popular genres (mystery, adventure and romance) and the experiments of *The Yellow Book*, *Ulysses* and *Mrs Dalloway*.

As most of these writers came to maturity between the World Wars, they reacted to the mass murder of the First World War by focusing on the individual, but, unlike the modernists, they found much of their inspiration among the people of the small towns and farms outside London. Jed Esty argues that the 'metropolitan modernists' (T. S. Eliot, Virginia Woolf, Forster) turned away from internationalism, fragmentation and the city in the 1930s to focus on an inward-looking, non-imperial England.[1] Following Esty's lead, we might postulate that the writers discussed here also focused inwardly on individuals at the margins of society, as Frank O'Connor's theory of the story claims. Like the modernists, they often delved into their characters' internal lives and found complex, unstable characters, but the traditional omniscient or first person, or occasionally the free-indirect, points of view – not stream of consciousness – were the staples of their narrative repertoire. If their stories lack plot in the traditional sense, they nonetheless often have a strong narrative thrust. Forced to live by their pens and rely heavily on middlebrow magazines as their publishing outlets, they rejected the elitism of modernism and actively sought to cultivate, stimulate and challenge their middle-class readers.

With rare exceptions, the writers covered in this chapter have been slighted by literary historians. They belong to a group rarely included in the syllabi of courses in modern British fiction, which includes such writers as Charlotte Mew, L. P. Hartley, E. F. Benson, Stacy Aumonier, A. E. Coppard, Elspeth Davie, Rhys Davies, H. E. Bates, V. S. Pritchett, Fred Urquhart, Sylvia Townsend Warner, Alan Sillitoe, Angus Wilson, William Sansom and Eric Linklater. D. H. Lawrence slips uneasily into the modernist fold, as does Graham Greene; Angus Wilson and Alan Sillitoe have affinities with the 'angry young men', and Julian Barnes can be claimed as a postmodernist. But between Charlotte Mew and Julian Barnes lies a great, largely unexplored middle ground of accomplished writers whose achievements in the short story have rarely been fully appreciated but here, one hopes, will receive something of their due.

Charlotte Mew (1869–1928) exemplifies many of the characteristics outlined above: a tragic figure on the outskirts of literary society, known today, if at all, as a poet but little studied despite high praise in some quarters. Only eighteen of her stories are extant, and of these only half are considered significant; yet she exemplifies qualities that many better-known writers exhibit – a restless experimentation, sharp realism, vivid characters and themes of loneliness, moral ambiguity and a quest for knowledge and identity. 'Passed', published first in *The Yellow Book* in 1894, is an ambitious, experimental account of a young middle-class woman's encounter with poverty, death and prostitution. The first-person narrator relates her experiences in nightmarish, almost hallucinatory prose that at the time associated Mew with the avant-garde. Later stories are more straightforwardly realistic but no less powerful. Chief among them is 'The China Bowl', set in a remote fishing village where David Paris's mother and bride duel for his trust and affection. Rich in local detail and dialect, the story shows Mew's unflinching insight into its characters and offers no guidance to readers looking for simple right and wrong. It is doubtful that Mew's Hardyesque pessimism influenced subsequent writers, as her output was too small and her reputation too slight by the time of her suicide, but hindsight credits her with anticipating trends that characterized those who followed.

If Mew's influence was slight, that of D. H. Lawrence was profound. In *The Modern Short Story*, H. E. Bates credits him with influencing all the important writers born between 1900 and 1910 because he turned his and thus their attention to ordinary people and problems in real, local settings.[2] The problems Lawrence highlighted are famously those of class, power and sex, and there is no way to settle here whether he deserves his reputation as a misogynist for advocating a 'male mystique' that asserts the rights of dominant males over 'weaker' females. The battle between the sexes is, however, just one of the dichotomies that structure his stories. Human versus machine, authority versus freedom, body versus intellect, married couples versus the outside world and contentment versus agitation are also recurring conflicts, vividly brought to life in the stories for which he is justly famous: 'The Prussian Officer', 'Daughters of the Vicar', 'Odour of Chrysanthemums', 'Tickets, Please', 'The Blind Man', 'The Horse Dealer's Daughter' and many others.

Despite his inclusion in this chapter, Lawrence's prose cannot easily be characterized as 'understated', especially in the novels. Yet those who consider his novelistic style over-wrought find a more straightforward mode of expression in such stories as 'The Man Who Loved Islands' or 'Rawdon's Roof'. Nevertheless, especially when he attempts to delve into complex emotional states, his vocabulary tends towards the extreme. Words like 'soul', 'blood', 'hate', 'passionate', 'naked', 'dumb' and 'stricken' pepper his analyses as he struggles to convey emotional extremes and internal conflict. Readers of short stories were mystified, even repelled, by his insistence on exposing what was generally considered 'morbid' in human nature. From a later perspective, however, Lawrence's explorations of the complex emotions of his characters were liberating to authors and readers.

Lawrence may also have influenced those who followed in another way. Educated at a local grammar school and a provincial university, he scratched and clawed his way into literary circles by sheer originality, barely touching the hem of Bloomsbury, perhaps showing others that talent could overcome the restrictions of class. His strong connection with the countryside expressed in lyrical descriptions and lush atmospherics would resonate with Bates, Rhys Davies and A. E. Coppard, to name just a few, as would his emphasis on the essential driving force of sex. These writers and others, like Lawrence, may have incurred opposition and neglect *because* of their roots in the working class – that dark, unknown, threatening and potentially revolutionary underbelly of conventional Britain.

Roughly contemporaneous with Mew and Lawrence were two writers who commented on Britain's social scene: E. F. Benson (1867–1940) and Stacy Aumonier (1887–1928). Benson never achieved the popularity or public affection of P. G. Wodehouse (1881–1975), but his satires of the upper classes cover some of the same ground – social climbing, snobbery and eccentricity. Benson's bright, glittering style is well suited to satirical thrusts at the likes of socialite Amy Bodham, whose pursuit of the titled and famous often ends in comic disappointment, but that same style and approach can sometimes result in stories portraying the cruel side of snobbery, such as 'The Puce Silk', or of prudery, as in 'A Breath of Scandal'. Benson's reputation is not high today, but his stories are worth exploring for what they say about the pettiness and hypocrisy of Edwardian England and the social structure that would be undermined by the First World War. Stacy Aumonier sometimes ventured into satire, but his style is much less sparkling and brittle than Benson's and his tone is more serious. Highly regarded by contemporary critics for such stories as 'Overheard' and 'The Friends', Aumonier can sympathetically portray exploited or down-on-their-luck characters like an overworked waitress or a delusional, alcoholic salesman, members of the working and lower middle classes whose lives were a mystery to middle-class Britons. 'Where Was Wych Street' pokes fun at men of all classes who elevate their dim recollections into 'facts' over which they quarrel with absurd assurance. Aumonier aspired to literary seriousness, but touching as some of his stories can be, they often lack depth; and he all too often adopts Kipling's superior, know-it-all tone, which can be irritating. Despite their weaknesses and current critical neglect, Benson and Aumonier deserve credit for adapting the short story to the tastes of ordinary readers and using the form to raise the social consciousness of their readers.

Mystery and detective stories, despite their relegation to popular entertainment until relatively recently, are significant for exposing and in most cases allaying the anxieties of readers concerned about crime. Many critics argue that Dorothy L. Sayers (1893–1957) raised the quality of detective fiction to that of art, particularly in her novels. Her most famous detective, Lord Peter Wimsey, is regarded by some readers as an epitome of the British aristocracy, by others as a parody of the same. Sayers's polished style, ingenious plots and erudition raise her stories well above the common level. Certainly they reflect a class-conscious society longing to return to the status quo of pre-First World War society. Her other protagonist,

Montague Egg, a wine and spirits salesman, represents the striving lower middle class, more at home with the wisdom of the *Salesman's Handbook* than with Wimsey's esoteric culture. Many of her best stories, however, feature neither detective. 'Nebuchadnezzar', for example, turns a charades-like parlour game into a psychological study of guilt; 'The Inspiration of Mr Budd' features a struggling barber frustrated by a lack of capital who ingeniously helps arrest a fleeing murderer and thereby reaps a handsome reward. 'Bloody Sacrifice' is a taut, beautifully paced study of a moral dilemma in which neither the protagonist nor the reader knows for certain whether the protagonist is responsible for a man's death. Whatever one's attitude towards the mystery/detective genre, Sayers must be regarded as showing subsequent authors that crime fiction need not be relegated to second-rate status.

As already intimated, H. E. Bates (1905–74) is the natural heir of Thomas Hardy and Lawrence, seasoned with the Continental influences of Maupassant and Chekhov. A fair criticism of Bates – and of many others discussed in this chapter – is that he broke no new literary ground. Nevertheless, within the confines of the form as he found and adapted it, he produced a body of short fiction rivalled by few before or since. Like Lawrence, he began by delving into the characters and topography of his native Northamptonshire. *Day's End and Other Stories* (1928) empathizes with obscure, thwarted lives, most notably in 'The Baker's Wife', 'The Shepherd', 'The Fuel-Gatherers' and 'The Idiot'. Already in these stories we note intense natural descriptions, uncanny exploitation of atmosphere, and sympathetic yet complex depictions of 'simple' characters. From the outset, too, Bates showed a dual consciousness: on the one hand, a fierce naturalism – cool, objective, deterministic – and, on the other, a lush romantic streak evident in loving depictions of nature and a sympathy for the underdog, the exploited and the unlucky.

Seven Tales and Alexander (1929) contained Bates's first unqualified success, the 'Alexander' of the book's title. Like many of Bates's previous and subsequent stories, it is written in a lushly romantic style from the point of view of a child. Framed by a morning drive to and an evening's drive from a fruit-picking expedition, the narrative records a twelve-year-old boy's impressions of the day's events, including the awakening of sexual desire and his puzzled encounter with a human snake who invades his Edenic paradise. Bates is fully in control of his materials, presenting the experience as equally mythic and real, conveying the boy's innocence and prefiguring his awakening to experience. It is richly atmospheric, radiating layers of meaning belied by its simple style and deceptively innocent point of view.

During the 'low dishonest decade' of the 1930s, Bates and many of his short story writing peers paid little overt attention to politics, preferring to deal with political questions indirectly by highlighting poverty, oppressive working conditions and class prejudice through the lives of ordinary working people. 'The Hessian Prisoner' and 'The Black Boxer', for example, sympathetically portray a First World War German prisoner of war, and a Negro boxer nearing the end of his career.

The Woman Who Had Imagination (1934) demonstrates Bates's continuing growth and maturation, particularly in the title story. Following the same organizational pattern as 'Alexander', it focuses on a bored, sarcastic teenager named Henry, who accompanies his father's choir to a choral competition at a manor house. Once again we enjoy the rich natural descriptions and the mythic sunrise-to-sunset structure, but the dialogue is sharper, the character sketches more penetrating and the whole even more tightly structured than 'Alexander'. The ending contains a jarring revelation that works perfectly to explain the story's central mystery and to put into perspective Henry's petulant brooding.

Cut and Come Again (1935) contains stories in a variety of modes, from the humorous ('The Irishman'), to the realistic ('Cut and Come Again'), to the uncompromisingly naturalistic ('The Mill'). The title story provides an intriguing contrast with Lawrence. Dramatizing an argument between two country newlyweds, it traces their quarrel and reconciliation objectively, without any of Lawrence's commentary or insistence on masculine superiority. 'The Mill' is one of Bates's unqualified masterpieces, in which a simple country girl (Alice) is emotionally bullied by her father, then hired to nurse an invalid woman and cook for her husband, who sexually exploits her and gets her pregnant. Here, Bates's mastery of atmosphere emphasizes the cold, impersonal, desolate world of the mill, which itself symbolizes the automaton-like way in which Alice drifts and the mechanical indifference and coldness with which she is treated first by her father, then by her employers. Objectivity, atmosphere, sympathy and a touch of nostalgia combine in 'The Pink Cart,' seen through the eyes of an adolescent boy who looks on as his grandfather renews a friendship with a family of gypsies whose daughter is dying of tuberculosis. Here, the weather is fittingly cold and harsh, echoing the grasping selfishness of the dying girl's mother, contrasting with the grandfather's hospitality, the warmth of a fire roasting potatoes and the girl's delight in a friendly cat. Balancing these contrasting elements in a tightly unified, moving story shows the hand of a master.

Something Short and Sweet (1937) is an uneven collection, with some stories (such as 'The Captain' and 'Mr Livingstone') taking on new subjects, but the collection as a whole dwells repetitiously on themes of sexual repression, despite the success of two fine stories, 'The Kimono' and 'Breeze Anstey'. 'The Kimono' is noteworthy for its unabashed sensuality and its sympathetic portrayal of an unashamedly sexual woman. 'Breeze Anstey' resembles Lawrence's 'The Fox'. Bates's account is unusually frank in its discussion of heterosexual love-making and in portraying Breeze's awakening to lesbian desire. Two Uncle Silas stories prefigure another new direction, resulting in a collection of comic anecdotes, *My Uncle Silas* (1939), a collection that delighted many readers with its depictions of the rascally Silas and his amorous and mischievous adventures; but it perhaps damaged Bates's reputation as a serious writer.

The outbreak of the Second World War changed directions yet again for Bates, as he was brought into the Royal Air Force specifically to write stories about the pilots who battled the Blitz and bombed Germany. The stories appeared first in the *News Chronicle* under the pseudonym 'Flying Officer X' and were later collected into *The Greatest People in the World* (1942) and *How Sleep the Brave* (1943). The stories, like the men they portray, are understated, even laconic, but their realistic portrayal of the humour, stoicism, diffidence and bravery of the pilots, navigators and gunners of the RAF were hugely popular and made Bates a household name when his identity was revealed. Given the circumstances of their production, stories that might have descended into propaganda rise occasionally to the level of art, as in 'How Sleep the Brave' and 'The Young Man from Kalgoorie'. War also produced the grimly naturalistic *The Cruise of the Breadwinner* (1946), a realistic depiction of a boy's awakening to the horrors of war.

The commercial success of Bates's war novel, *Fair Stood the Wind for France* (1944), combined with the dwindling market for short stories as magazines lost readership and circulation to radio and television, turned Bates's attention increasingly to novels, though his production of short stories never ceased. The content of these post-war stories remained much the same – rich natural description, suggestive atmosphere and a frequent focus on childhood or other marginalized characters – but there are new notes: a shift in location from Northamptonshire to Kent; from England to Europe and even the Far East; an increased emphasis on adult characters; and a tendency to favour novellas – among which are many of Bates's finest creations. *The Daffodil Sky* (1955) shows also a shifting social concern. 'Country Society' satirizes the character types of a village; 'The Evolution of Saxby' portrays a husband who wants nothing more than to settle in a house and tend a garden, but his wife 'flips' one house for another and another, trading financial gain for a genuine home. Rural stories retain their atmospheric richness and thematic import, but there is a new note in 'The Common Denominator', where the cool efficiency of a National Health nurse is contrasted with the warm care two sisters give their dying man-servant.

During the last twenty years of his life, Bates focused increasingly on novels, novellas, nature writing and his autobiography. His literary reputation was damaged again by the popular series of comic novels about the Larkin family and its exploits. Sadly, with too many readers and critics, that is where it has remained, whereas Bates should be remembered for his lasting contributions to the short story and the novella – complex characters, vivid natural description, the artistic exploitation of atmosphere and a genuine human sympathy for people of all ages, classes and conditions. His stories chronicle, often indirectly but nevertheless effectively, the transition of England from a rural to an urban country, from sexual repression to frankness, through two world wars and into a late twentieth-century culture that inhabitants in the early years of the century would hardly have recognized.

Graham Greene (1904–91) was as ambivalent about the short story as Bates was enthusiastic. At one point, he dismissed his stories as 'scraps', only to recant later and acknowledge their value and integrity. Indeed, some critics and readers regard his stories, as others do those of Lawrence, as better conveying his thematic ideas – an imperfect, fallen world, decay, moral ambiguity, even nihilism – more clearly and forcefully than his novels. A case in point is 'A Chance for Mr Lever' (1936), in which a salesman chasing a client in a disease-ridden, chaotic jungle comes to see the futility of strict honesty and forges documents that could make him rich – if he can return home alive. 'The Basement Room' (1935), is one of Greene's best-known stories because of its film version, 'The Fallen Idol' (1948). The story traces young Philip's disillusion about his idol, Mr Baines, as the boy learns about adultery, deception and murder. Perhaps most disturbing is 'The Destructors' (1954), in which a gang of boys inflicts creative destruction on a house built by Wren that somehow survived the blitz, and reduces it to a pile of rubble. Later stories, such as 'May We Borrow Your Husband?' (1962), are lighter in tone but nonetheless deeply sceptical about innocence and fidelity, whereas 'Under the Garden' (1963) combines recollections of childhood, dreams and fantasy into an *Alice in Wonderland*-like nightmare, the import of which is the necessity of resisting any status quo. Greene's pessimism and scepticism fit well into the post-Second World War era of dashed hopes and radical disillusionment with human kind and the killing machines it builds despite the efforts of religion and morality. Greene will probably always be considered a novelist who incidentally wrote stories, but, as the forty stories in the collected edition attest, his short stories deserve much more attention and credit than they have received.

V. S. Pritchett (1900–97) epitomizes the rise from obscurity shared by so many of his contemporaries. Born into a lower middle-class household to a father whose failures in business were exceeded only by his delusional optimism, Pritchett left school at fifteen to work in a leather factory and educated himself through voracious reading and sheer determination, publishing his first novel in 1929 and his first collection of stories, *The Spanish Virgin and Other Stories*, in 1930. Like Bates, he is valued primarily for his short stories, which focus almost exclusively on lower middle-class men and women who, like Pritchett's father, live as much by their delusions as by the often sombre reality of their lives. Pritchett's approach, however, is ironic and comic, not political or judgmental, but inevitably the realities of his subjects' lives create a picture of a submerged class in Britain's social hierarchy. Although he eventually disowned all the stories in his first collection, 'Greek Theatre Tragedy' and 'The White Rabbit' point in the direction Pritchett's stories would take. His first unqualified success, however, is 'Sense of Humour', a richly complex study of its narrator, a travelling salesman (Arthur), his girlfriend (Muriel) and his girlfriend's persistent admirer (Colin). Though the phrase 'a sense of humour' recurs frequently, particularly with reference to Muriel, the story's thematic focus is on the blatant materialism of Arthur and Muriel. Muriel chooses Arthur over Colin in part because Arthur drives a car, Colin a motorcycle; and Arthur can offer Muriel stockings and other goods at a substantial discount. Despite being rejected, Colin follows Muriel and Arthur wherever they go, which results in his death in a gruesome accident. The story's power emanates from its combination of traditional plot, trenchant dialogue, situational and verbal ironies and psychological realism, particularly in the ways Arthur and Muriel disguise their material ambitions and sexual longings behind a veneer of respectability and pragmatism. They represent the England of the post-Second World War years – morally jaded by another war of mass slaughter, deprived of consumer goods by Britain's war debt and need to export, and increasingly focused on getting ahead in the new welfare state.

Pritchett's ability to portray characters as both unpleasant and sympathetic is the hallmark of his next collection, *It May Never Happen and Other Stories* (1945). 'Pocock Passes', for example, presents two obese and alcohol-soaked loners who find solace in one another because of their similarities; yet ultimately, the story suggests, similarity is neither knowledge nor sympathy: Pocock dies as unknown and unknowable to his friend Rogers as both are to the omniscient narrator and reader, as neither experiences an epiphany or revelation.

'The Sailor' makes an instructive comparison with 'Pocock Passes', another story of two men living on intimate terms, but in this case of very different temperaments though drawn together by mutual need and a desire to avoid temptation. The narrator is imaginative and messy; Thompson, the sailor, scrupulously clean and organized except in his own untidy room, suggesting that his outward discipline is merely a superficial remnant of his navy past. Gradually, Thompson succumbs to temptation, primarily drink and the company of villagers who fleece him, but also to the Colonel's daughter, to whom the narrator is also drawn. Temptation/abstinence/sin, city and country, intention and realization, appearance and reality, loneliness and community, self-knowledge and self-deception are the opposites out of which Pritchett concocts his unity. At the beginning of the story, the narrator bumps into the sailor when the latter is looking for Whitechapel. The story ends with the sailor once again in search of his elusive, perhaps unattainable, goal – the fate of all wanderers on this earth, implying that what both men seek, an orderly world free of temptation, is equally unattainable. 'The Saint' is autobiographical insofar as it relates to Pritchett's upbringing as a Christian Scientist and in its depiction of Pritchett's struggle with organized religion – one shared by many of his contemporaries. Like the sailor, who succumbs to temptation even while professing to shun it, the saint (Mr Timberlake) demonstrates that he knows nothing about evil by pretending that the realities of the world do not exist. Religious images – especially those equating Mr Timberlake with a cracked idol and a gilded statue – compete with the image of the ape, and the ape wins. The boy comes to understand that denying the existence of evil only affirms the reality of the ape in all the urges of the id.

These stories show all the characteristics of Pritchett's mature short fiction: characters who struggle with some weight or burden made vivid by revealing dialogue and actions; precise, suggestive descriptions of place and characters; dramatic episodes that reveal how characters fail to deal with the burdens they bear. The result is often tragi-comic, for failure can evoke both mirth and sadness, distance and sympathy. Behind and around these characters and their situations is a society that makes everything more difficult by expecting behaviour to conform to norms that individuals cannot live up to. If there is an overriding conflict in Pritchett's stories (as in short stories generally) it is between the unique individual and the pressures of society.

These pressures and the characters who struggle with them appear in Pritchett's next collection, *When My Girl Comes Home and Other Stories* (1961). Pritchett's rather small output of stories since *It May Never Happen* was the result of the diminished market for them because of the collapse of magazines and his consequent turning to criticism and non-fiction. The most ambitious and original work in this collection is the title story, set just after the Second World War in a London neighbourhood awaiting the return of Hilda, thought by everyone to have endured years as a prisoner in a Japanese camp. Astonishingly, the Hilda who appears is anything but the emaciated wreck they envisioned; she is, in fact, in perfect health, beautifully dressed and prosperous. The narrator is a young man only tangentially related to the main characters, and his mode is the most experimental Pritchett ever attempted. The story emerges in brief scenes and snatches of dialogue that the narrator himself only partially understands as people talk around or over each other. As the narrator begins to grasp the situation, he organizes these impressions into patches of coherent narration. The effect of this method is dramatic and immediate, as if the narrator were recording impressions and dialogue directly, so that we puzzle over them as he did. What emerges is not only a fascinating picture of exploded expectations and slowly unravelling mystery but also a gradual unveiling of war as corruption. (A similar theme is explored in 'The Satisfactory'.) Nearly everyone is shown to have participated in some 'fiddle', whether it was Bill Williams learning how to manipulate the Japanese guards while a prisoner, Hilda's exploitation of her sexuality in two advantageous marriages to foreigners or the revelation that nearly everyone on Hincham Street fudged ration coupons, purchased things on the black market or avoided military service by self-inflicted injuries or false medical reports. The goal of combatants and civilians in any war is survival, and Hilda is the ultimate survivor but also the catalyst for revelations about how civilians survive – and some even prosper – by skirting the rules and bending the law. The one exception is Hilda's mother, who worked extra jobs and saved every penny in anticipation of her daughter's needs, only to learn that her daughter had no need of her sacrifice. The story is not, however, a condemnation of anyone's activities, except perhaps those of Bill Williams, who blatantly steals everything Hilda owns. Rather, the dramatic distance achieved by Pritchett's narrative stance minimizes the urge to judge or condemn: once again we see the strategies by which people cope with one another, with the expectations of society, with love and sex, with their own inadequacies and self-delusions.

'The Wheelbarrow', like 'The Saint', 'The Sailor' and other stories, features two characters who in many respects are direct opposites or, more accurately – like yin and yang – complements of each other. Robert Evans is a revivalist preacher and reformed sinner, brisk, decisive, yet materialistic, acquisitive and sexually alert. Miss Freshwater's niece (the only name she is given) has rejected religion (as has most of England), her past and her family, and needs Evans's decisiveness to help her clear out her late aunt's house so it can be sold. On one level, the story satirizes religion, in part by portraying Evans as sexually attracted to Miss Freshwater's niece and materialistic in his covetousness for the green wheelbarrow that she eventually gives him. But it is also a story about family and the pull of the past. Evans credits thoughts of his family with saving him while he was trapped in a coal mine; for the niece, family is a burden to be shed, a collection of memories that, like the furniture left in the house, must be discarded. Yet, just as he rejected his licentious life and became 'reborn,' so she, through his help and the clearing out of the house, comes to terms with family, divorce and the pull of the past. Moreover, his flirtations revive her sense of herself as a desirable woman. At a more abstract level, the story suggests that England's religious past lingers in the tension between the decline of religion as a public force and as an active element, filling a need in the lives of some.

Pritchett's comic genius and light touch attack the social hierarchy in a series of three stories stitched together under the title *The Key to My Heart* (1963). As in 'Passing the Ball' (1950), here he glances at the sexual peccadillos of the upper classes and additionally wonders at the centuries-old habit of merchants admiring aristocrats because they *don't* pay their bills. A more serious, even touching view of the class and economic divide is 'The Cage Birds' from *Blind Love and Other Stories* (1969), in which a wealthy woman invites her poorer sister for an annual visit to pick through her last year's wardrobe for clothes she might want. As children they were poor; now the rich sister, Elsie (who calls herself Augusta), is caged by her wealth, as two robberies have prompted her husband to put bars on the door and windows, and further caged by the lies she tells the succession of men who support her.

Grace is caged by a skinflint husband and years of meanly pinching pennies, economizing until miserliness has become a substitute for life and love. Trying on one of her sister's beautiful dresses transforms her momentarily into someone glamorous, but habit triumphs. She will sell all the dresses. In their different ways, the sisters have sacrificed affection, family and honesty for their contrasting versions of materialism. The story is in some ways an updated version of 'Sense of Humour' but is also connected to another story in the collection, 'The Skeleton', a portrait of a miserly octogenarian whose only pleasures in life are his collection of paintings by Flitestone and victory over real and imaginary enemies. It takes a visit by Gloria, a woman from his past hoping to sell Flitestone's letters, to make him realize that he has not won any victories, that his ascetic, self-absorbed, loveless life has left him a skeleton. In part a commentary on the ugly side of aesthetic acquisition, in part a study of age and its discontents, 'The Skeleton' is vintage Pritchett.

Pritchett's powers of observation and construction waned not a bit with age. All the stories in his last two collections, *On The Edge of the Cliff* (1980) and *A Careless Widow* (1989) are worthy additions to the canon, but the most admired among them is 'On the Edge of the Cliff'. Like many of these later stories, it focuses on the elderly, in this case Harry, a seventy-five-year-old widower and his twenty-five-year-old lover, Rowena. Harry knows that he is no match for a lover her own age and thus treats the affair as a game, one with fixed boundaries and rules. A real shock to him and Rowena occurs when he encounters Daisy Pyke, a friend from the distant past, now in her fifties, who has taken a lover many years younger than herself. Their disbelief when they learn that Stephen is Daisy's lover, not her son, reflects the general attitude that an older man is entitled to a young lover, but an older woman is not. Beyond this theme are the issues of time, youth and age, death and the ways in which the elderly fend off fears of dying – in Harry's case by plunging naked into the frigid waters of the Atlantic. It is a complex, many-layered story narrated with Pritchett's unique blend of compassion and irony.

Pritchett's approach to story writing seems almost *sui generis*. There are echoes of Chekhov, but Pritchett's handling of materials is unique. Notable as much for what is omitted as for what is included, his stories are models of economy, directness and simplicity, yet alive with overtones and suggestions. Several readings are often necessary to catch the subtleties of his characters, their situations and the ways in which they cope. The comedy is subtle, modulated, always respectful, never vicious. Highly unusual is Pritchett's use of figurative language, as these few examples will show: 'The furniture might have come out of old-fashioned hotels and had the helpless look of objects too large, ill-met commercially and too gregarious'; '[She] walked down the road in the strong shade of the firs and the broad shade of the oak trees, whose leaves hardened with populous contentment'; 'Old Mrs Draper made one of her fundamental utterances again, one of her growls from the belly of the history of human indignation'; 'London was cabbaged with greenery . . . The place was a fate, a blunder of small hopes and admired defeats'; 'They sat in silence for a long time but he gazed at the rising floor of eventless water'.[3] Like his approach to character and structure, Pritchett's use of language is fresh and original without being flashy or obviously experimental.

By the 1950s, the literary landscape had changed to reflect the grim realities of post-Second World War England, with its lingering class divisions despite legislative attempts at social levelling (the National Health, heavy death duties on the rich), lack of housing and jobs, economic austerity and a general feeling that the old order was passing away. Short story writers who clearly reflected these changes include Angus Wilson (1913–91) and Alan Sillitoe (1928–2010). Wilson's first two collections, *The Wrong Set and Other Stories* (1949) and *Such Darling Dodos and Other Stories* (1950) caught the new spirit of the times through satire, some of the stories looking back to the 1930s, others being set in contemporary times. Much of their satire derives from conflicts that arise within apparently normal families or other social groups whose internal divisions lead to misunderstandings and quarrels. The opening interior monologue of 'The Wrong Set', for instance, establishes a bitchy tone in the central consciousness that is perfectly in keeping with the class and economic jealousies, sexual intrigues and antisemitism that provide the background for a conflict over who is in 'the wrong set' and who (if anyone) is in 'the right set'. Wilson's complex objectivity contrasts sharply with Sillitoe's obvious sympathies with the working classes, most famously dramatized in 'The Loneliness of the Long Distance Runner' and continued in many of the stories in *The Ragman's Daughter and Other Stories* (1963). Wilson and Sillitoe, along with Graham Greene, Kingsley Amis (1922–95), Ruth Prawer Jhabvala (1927–2013), Doris Lessing (1919–2014) and John Wain (1925–94) clearly set English fiction in new thematic directions, even as their styles remained primarily in the vein of social realism. All have contributed significantly to the short story canon and kept the genre alive and vital despite the dearth of magazines that until the 1950s kept the short story at the centre of literary culture.

The Understated Art, English Style

Julian Barnes (1946–), like V. S. Pritchett, writes in a variety of styles about ordinary people, but his thematic concerns are very different. As in his novel *Flaubert's Parrot* (1984), he often meditates on the postmodern ideas of the uncertainty of knowledge, the problem of historical understanding, the unknowability of people (including oneself) and the mystery of God's existence. *Cross Channel* (1996) tackles the instability of history in 'Evermore' and 'Tunnel'. In 'Evermore,' Miss Moss cherishes the memory of her brother Samuel, killed near the end of the First World War and buried in a French graveyard. She has visited his resting place faithfully for many years and noted the gradual diminution of interest in the war, a slighting of its historical importance, a lack of respect for its monuments, in part because the Second World War has eclipsed it in contemporary minds. She envisions a time when the graveyards will be ploughed under, the monuments forgotten or destroyed, the war effectively erased not just from living memory but also from its emotional significance, reduced to words in books. For her the tragedy is epitomized in 'evermore', which she believes should be two words, 'ever more,' meaning 'For all future time'.[4]

'Tunnel' echoes the historical themes of 'Evermore' and even refers to the concern about erasing the memories and cemeteries of the First World War, but the tone is lighter, even droll; reversing history, Barnes projects himself forward to 2015, as a sixty-nine-year-old taking Eurostar to France and reflecting on his past, imagining lives for his fellow passengers, and contemplating his own ageing. There is even a postmodern metafictional nod at the end, inviting readers to re-read the collection with its last story in mind.

The major themes of *Cross Channel* recur in *The Lemon Table* (2004). In 'The Things You Know', two widows meet for breakfast and the discussion turns to their late husbands, each woman extolling the virtues of her departed spouse. Interior monologues reveal, however, that each knows (or believes she does) something damning about the other's husband. 'Appetite' focuses on a wife's visits to her husband in hospital, who is suffering from dementia. She entertains him by reading recipes that bring back memories and reveal his idiosyncratic insistence that all measurements be exact, not 'two or three tablespoons' but one or the other. He emerges as prim, exacting, even moral; but momentary outbursts of filthy language reveal a layer of aggression and sexual perversion hitherto unsuspected, leaving the wife to wonder who her real husband is.

Four of the stories in *Pulse* (2011) explore the theme of uncertainty in dialogues, discussions over the dinner-party table in which the characters argue from positions of insufficient or uncertain knowledge. In interesting departures from this idea, 'The Limner' and 'Harmony' deal with truth in art. The limner is Wadsworth, a deaf itinerant painter, who ekes out a living painting the petit bourgeois. The conflict between artist and subject over the truth of a portrait suggests that art may penetrate surfaces to reveal both to the subject and to posterity what the subject may not be willing to recognize about himself. It is also a story about power: the power of the subject to grant or withhold payment and the power of the artist to reveal what the subject wants hidden. Barnes highlights the tension artists of whatever type experience in a capitalist economy in which the curator, the editor, the producer or the director determines the value of an artist's creativity and insight. 'Harmony' is set in the eighteenth century and employs some of that period's conventions, for example by naming the protagonist M–. The story works at two levels, one being the attempts of Dr M– (presumably the historical Dr Franz Mesmer) to cure the blindness of Marie Theresia (Maria Theresia von Paradis, an actual patient of Mesmer's) by the application of magnets and psychological counselling. Marie Theresia's blindness, however, is an asset to the family, as she is considered a piano prodigy. As her condition improves, the family fears a loss of the income she provides, halts the treatments, and conspires to have M– exposed as a charlatan. Thus, the story comments not only on popular resistance to new ideas, but also on the process of finding scientific truth, for, as the narrator points out, Mesmer's real discovery may have been the efficacy of psychology, not the power of magnets.

The English short story as represented by the authors discussed above may certainly be described as 'understated', but this does not mean, nor should it be taken to imply, that it is therefore without influence or impact. The short story, like other art forms, reflects, comments on and often challenges the assumptions, prejudices, politics, manners, mores and class conflicts of society at large, primarily by offering insights into people and situations that other art forms often neglect. Yet the aesthetics of compression and suggestion focus and concentrate social commentary and psychological insights, and that is the particular legacy of the writers considered here.

Notes

1. Jed Esty, *A Shrinking Island: Modernism and National Culture in England* (Princeton University Press, 2004), pp. 162–226.
2. H. E. Bates, *The Modern Short Story: A Critical Survey* (London: Michael Joseph, 1941), p. 203.

3. All quotations are from V. S. Pritchett, *Complete Collected Stories* (London: Random House, 1990): 'The Wheelbarrow', pp. 412, 426; 'When My Girl Comes Home', p. 447; 'The Cage Birds', p. 698; and 'On the Edge of the Cliff', p. 965.
4. Julian Barnes, *Cross Channel* (London: Jonathan Cape, 1996), p. 100.

15

The Rural Tradition in the English Short Story

DOMINIC HEAD

This chapter is specifically concerned with an English tradition of rural writing, developing in tandem with the short story as a distinctly modern form, from the nineteenth century onwards. As other chapters in this History attest, rural experience is also prominent in short fiction across the full geographical range of the four nations – for example, as a way of framing ideas about national identity or social hardship – in Scottish, Welsh and Irish writing. Rural experience can focus key points of social history in England, too; yet the tradition is distinctive in that conventions (and expectations) of aesthetic appreciation concerning the countryside are often made to jar with rural reality, in intense episodes written against the (sometimes unspoken) background contexts of imperialism and international conflict, where uncertainty about Englishness – or a homogenizing Britishness – can explain the macro context for the micro event. It would be misleading to claim that there is a *necessary* or *compelling* connection between rural experience and the fragmented and episodic form of the modern short story; yet the literary mediation of rural experience serves to frame the challenges of modernity, especially through complex and disjunctive narrative styles, which themselves often embody an ambivalent interrogation of nostalgia. In this respect, the English rural short story, especially in the twentieth century, can be seen to bear the impress of modernity's influence on literary creativity.

Mary Russell Mitford was an early innovator in the rural story. She is best known for *Our Village* (1824–32), which was originally issued in five separate volumes. Because the pieces that make up *Our Village* do not really harness the narrative capacities of short fiction, they now read as sketches rather than stories, or 'a series of snapshots of rural life', as Tim Killick has it.[1] However, they represent a noteworthy landmark in the development of the short story form, first appearing in the decade that, for Killick, 'saw the beginning of short fiction's emergence as a distinct and challenging form of literature' (p. 2). They are still more significant in the emerging tradition of the rural short story, playing an important role in defining its niche in English literary history. Mitford acknowledged her debt to Jane Austen in the treatment of 'gentle country life', but recognized the 'lower' social focus of her own writing, as well as its propensity to 'sentiment' rather than 'humour' (p. 2). This succinctly locates two of the defining features of the rural short story tradition through to the twentieth century: an inclusive portrait of social strata (even if there is sometimes a tendency to deal in 'types'), and a celebratory – often nostalgic – treatment of its subject. What follows from this social purview is a seminal historical role for the rural tradition, a role that is now often overlooked. As Killick points out, '*Our Village* continues the role that pastoral literature had historically played in Britain reinforcing belief structures that asserted the centrality of the morality and functionality of the countryside to the ethical and economic fabric of the nation' (p. 4). To trace the development of the rural short story is also to trace a progressive interrogation and movement beyond such literary conventions and the social stability they might imply. An important point of comparison and contrast between the enduring tradition of pastoral literature and the specific forms of rural short fiction that built into a separate tradition from the nineteenth-century onwards is suggested in Kristin Brady's account of Thomas Hardy's short stories, which serves to place Hardy on the cusp of change. With reference to *Wessex Tales* (1888; expanded in 1896 and 1912),[2] Brady suggests that Hardy was concerned to present Wessex 'as a symbol', and that his 'strategy of subordinating realistic details to a symbolic pattern' puts the collection 'firmly in the tradition of pastoral', especially where pastoral poetry exploits the contrast between the real world and the poet's imagined (and often idealized) world.[3]

Part of Hardy's achievement in *Wessex Tales* is to record a fading moment of cultural history, by capturing something of the customs, beliefs and oral tradition of rural Dorset. The superstition that the flesh of a hanged man can restore health ('The Withered Arm') is the best-known example; but the depiction of a community thriving on smuggling and illegal liquor ('The Distracted Preacher') may have greater historical importance. The historical and folkloristic dimension of Hardy's tales contributes strongly to that 'symbolic' aspect of Wessex, a region of the imagination from which more universal ideas can be implied.

There is, however, also a more tangible resonance in Hardy's backward look. Most of the stories were written in the 1880s, a time of agricultural depression.[4] Their historical setting, 'forty to seventy years earlier', embraces a previous period of agricultural depression and unrest, so there is a distinct historical echo that serves to underscore the contemporaneous resonance of farming in crisis. There is, then, a duality in *Wessex Tales*: there is the dimension of historical fiction, and the celebratory recording of a fading culture, with its folklore and oral tradition; and, simultaneously, there is a more urgent political impulse rooted in a current social crisis. This kind of dualism, which is typical of the rural short story, also generates a complex nostalgia, a self-conscious double-vision, in which the reader's desire to escape into the past is disrupted.

The ironic contrast in pastoral literature between the real world and the poet's imagined world is often complicated in its effects. Following William Empson, Brady considers how 'the pastoral contrast' involves a complication of 'the simple'. This leads to a kind of dialectical process by which various contrasts – 'rural versus urban, regional versus non-regional, past versus present' – encourage the reader to reassess his or her own world by comparing it to the 'fully realized world' of the text, which is not idealized, but just 'as fraught with suffering and difficulty' as the world we know.[5] This encounter involves a reversal of expectations predicated upon the deployment of pastoral codes, because Hardy 'exploits the tension in the discrepancy between historical Dorset and the reader's presumed simplistic image of it'. Trading on 'the reader's nostalgic impulse for a glimpse of the rural past', Hardy is then able to present the rural image from an unexpected perspective. The desire for a straightforward nostalgic escape is 'undermined and replaced' by 'immediate emotional engagement in the events of the stories themselves'. Withdrawal becomes, instead, identification; which, in turn, generates recognition and fresh understanding for the reader vis à vis the world he or she knows (p. 5).

Something of this process applies to all good rural fiction, which is very often realistic in orientation, although often set in the past. The opposition that generates the recognition is then rooted in the contrast between the past and the present. Another aspect that complicates any presumed quaintness surrounding Hardy's tales is that they were written at a time of 'great technological change'. This is reflected in the collection's pervasive mood of anxiety, whether generated by 'real or imagined threats to a community and its survival through time').[6] The threat of the urban is another common rural theme, evoked strongly in 'The Three Strangers' in the contrast between Timothy Summers and the man appointed to hang him. Summers, sentenced to death for stealing a sheep to feed his starving family, epitomizes the desperation of rural poverty; the hangman epitomizes urban indifference. This evocation of the rural, as a response to modernity – whether conceived as a corrective to the urban emphasis of the modern world, or a more emphatic critique of modernity – is a pervasive factor in the rural short story through the twentieth century, giving rise to a set of literary effects of which Hardy has been an influential progenitor.

Mary E. Mann (1848–1929) was a Norfolk writer, famous for her rural village stories first collected as *The Fields of Dulditch* (1902), and then brought together more comprehensively as *The Complete Tales of Dulditch* in 2008. For champions of regional writing, Mann's stories surpass those of more canonical authors. D. J. Taylor, for example, considers her rural stories to be 'as good as anything by Thomas Hardy, George Gissing, George Moore or any other English writer at work in the last decade of the nineteenth century'.[7] Mann's most famous story is 'Little Brother', a brief but horrifying episode about a woman, already the mother of twelve, who has a still-born baby. Left to herself to recover, she cannot attend to her other children, who amuse themselves by playing with their new 'little brother' as if he were a doll. When 'the desecrated body' is returned to its makeshift bier, the mother is unmoved by the discovery of the use to which the baby's corpse has been put: 'Other folkes' child'en have a toy, now and then, to kape 'em out o' mischief. My little uns han't. He've kep' 'em quiet for hours, the po'r baby have; and I'll lay a crown they han't done no harm to their little brother.'[8] For Taylor, such moments in Mann offer 'paralysing glimpses of human elementals that are sometimes terrifying in their refusal to accept the moral conventions of Victorian story-telling' (p. 5). The reader's sense of paralysis, or helplessness, in the face of a poverty that robs people of their dignity is heightened by the flouting of convention and the consequent shock of the uncompromising manner of Mann's presentation.

Mann's depiction of poverty is often manifested in a preoccupation with material things. In 'Blue Beads', for example, a dying woman's precious beads are coveted by Alice, her 'fifteen-year-old maid-of-all-work' (p. 250), on whom the sick 'poor mistress' is dependent, knowing that she may not be able to replace her maid (p. 251). The mistress associates the blue beads with her girlhood, and intends to be buried in them, so much do they seem to enshrine her identity (and status). But Alice takes the beads to wear to church, without permission, and attracts the attention of a boy, 'Sheep-face' who agrees to 'walk with' her (p. 254), only to choose another girl to walk with on the following Sunday, when Alice's mistress has taken to wearing her beads, sensible of Alice's dishonesty. The mistress can win back Alice's favour only by agreeing to bequeath the beads to her, and Alice contrives to poison the dying old woman so she can expedite the bequest and wear the blue beads the following Sunday to entice Sheep-face back.

This vignette of desperate dependency, covetousness and immorality is made to speak to a wider situation of poverty, embodied in the class that Alice represents: her grandfather was hanged for murder, as was her cousin, who had murdered a boy for 'his clo'es ... and his boots', which he sold 'for sixpence'. The mistress is horrified at this tale – 'And he was hanged? Hanged for sixpence?' – but the placid Alice understands the pragmatism, and 'serenely' replies: 'He wanted the sixpence' (p. 252). One of Mann's best tales of extreme rural poverty is 'Wolf-Charlie'. The protagonist's nickname is explained 'by reason of the famished look in his melancholy eyes, of the way in which the skin of his lips, drawn tightly over his gums, exposes his great yellow teeth; by reason of the leanness of his flanks, the shaggy, unkempt hair about his head and face, the half fierce, half frightened expression' (p. 96). Driven to the workhouse one harsh winter, Wolf-Charlie falls ill, but recovers and emerges the following spring with the woman who had nursed him back to health, 'a middle-aged woman, with a red and foolish face', encumbered by 'a wooden leg and six children' (p. 99). They live in 'a tumble-down cottage', one of a derelict pair, the other inhabited by Wolf-Charlie's bedridden grandmother (p. 96). The eldest child, thirteen-year-old Beatrice, is deputed to look after the grandmother next door, and, in a similar dyad of desperate mutual dependency to 'Blue Beads', steals food from the old lady every night: grandmother sees what is happening, but remains silent out of a 'spirit of prudence' as she is 'entirely at the mercy of this abominable child', who yet leaves her enough to prevent starvation, and to allow the arrangement to endure (p. 101). In summarizing the desperate situation of Wolf-Charlie and his brood, the narrator ponders how ignorance of anything better might be their salvation: 'perhaps, never having had enough to eat, Wolf-Charlie does not understand how bad it is to be hungry ... perhaps their lot, if one could see from the inside, as it were, is a happy one after all' (p. 104). This rhetorical device, the surmise the reader will clearly reject, is as close as Mann comes to proselytizing: her chief method is to show, and let her accounts speak for themselves.

Mann's own social position established her as an intermediary. She married a gentleman farmer when she was twenty-three, but the couple's fortunes were badly hit by the agricultural depression of the 1880s: writing became, for her, an economic necessity.[9] She and her husband were intimately involved with the community she wrote about, which makes her an insider by knowledge, empathy and location, even if she was an outsider, by class and education, to those facing the full hardship of rural existence. The problem of the intellectual and/or urban outsider, often prominent in rural and pastoral writing – to the point of becoming the central theme in some cases – is simply not present in Mann's short stories. This is what lends them their sense of immediacy and pathos.

The Westmoreland novelist Constance Holme (1880–1955) was one of the best-known regional writers in her day. Her career is interesting here in that her social focus changed emphatically, from the upper- and middle-class worlds of her earlier novels, to the 'humbler social level' that she explores in her last five novels.[10] Although not her best, her last book, the short story collection *The Wisdom of the Simple and Other Stories* (1937), is noteworthy in that it encompasses the full social range of her rural fiction. From a publishing point of view it was also significant in that its first publication was in the 'Oxford World's Classics' series, a highly unusual accolade for a living author, which underscores Holme's status in the interwar period. Although some of the 'simple' folk depicted in the collection are clownish, rather than wise, native wit is sufficiently celebrated to justify Holme's title. An example of the 'wisdom' she proposes to be intrinsic to the rural community is found in 'Second Wind', where a young land agent, Hardistry, exasperated by the mercurial nature of his employer, is persuaded against handing in his notice by 'old Jammie', the keeper on neighbouring land.[11] Jammie, like the story's narrator, recognizes that Hardistry's potentially self-destructive impatience is a disease of youth, stemming from a disposition based on 'permanently-fixed ideas on almost every subject' (p. 94); what he must learn is the humility that is also self-preservation, so that – like Jammie before him – he can get his 'second wind' (p. 96). *The Wisdom of the Simple* was a notable publishing event, rather than a landmark in the development of the short story. Yet it also has a topical and historical significance, condensing as it does the major interwar rural themes: social change; agricultural depression; and the negative impact of the First World War, where the rural was usually a symbol of stability threatened by the machine of war. Not every interwar short story writer saw beneficence in rurality, however. An exception to the rule is 'Speed the Plough' (1923), a First World War story by Mary Butts (1890–1937), which subverts the idea of rural and agricultural work as a form of convalescence. The story concerns a soldier recovering from experiences at the front, rendered so as to capture his hazy, trance-like state, which is characterized by sensuous perceptions of women and an idealized sense of their delicate clothing. What seem to be the subconscious fears of a lame soldier, however, finally point in a different direction, as the soldier appears to resume his work as a costumier, fitting a selfish young woman for a dress.

In Sussex novelist Sheila Kaye-Smith's best-known work, *Joanna Godden* (1926), the career of the feisty eponymous protagonist reveals a complex exploration of rural society, her determination to succeed as a yeoman farmer finally defeated by gender roles. That rich social purview is beyond the scope of Kaye-Smith's shorter fiction, but Joanna Godden does make some interesting appearances in her stories, notably 'Joanna Godden's Joy Ride' (from *Faithful Stranger and Other Stories*, 1938). This is a simple narrative, yet it offers a snapshot of interwar rural life on the cusp of modernity. Godden lunches by chance with a well-to-do captain of industry when his car breaks down. She accepts a lift home from town on market day, and, her interest in the driver displaced by the intoxication of the machine, she is left in a state of strange exhilaration by her first ride in an 'ortomebeely': she wears a 'triumphant smile upon her lips', even though her whole body is shaking after the experience, with a 'curious dinning noise in her head'.[12] It is a short episode that encapsulates the idea that the machine world is having a dehumanizing and destabilizing impact on the rural.

The two most noteworthy twentieth-century English writers of rural stories are H. E. Bates (1905–74) and A. E. Coppard (1878–1957).[13] Coppard, like Hardy before him, can be seen to have forged another bridge between the folk tradition and a modernizing world-view. In the foreword to the edition of his collected tales for the American market, Coppard articulated his strong sense of the short story as a form quite distinct from the novel: the story is 'an ancient art originating in the folk tale' with a dynamic that endures in the era of the printed story.[14] Like the folk tale, the successful 'modern short story' emulates 'that ancient tradition of being spoken to you'. Its other distinctive feature, for Coppard, was a principle of composition, the principle that 'unity, verisimilitude, and completeness of contour are best obtained by plotting your story through the mind or consciousness of only one of your characters' (p. viii).

Coppard epitomizes that side of rural story writing that has its roots in the oral or ballad tradition, with a focus on human passions, sometimes thwarted, sometimes tragic in their consequences. Yet there is also a modern challenge to sexual mores in Coppard's work – rather than the more enduring, or static treatment of human nature associated with the folk tradition – and this sense of developing an oral tradition is clear in one of his finest stories, 'Dusky Ruth', from the collection *Adam and Eve and Pinch Me*

(1921). In many ways this is an exemplary rural story. The opening description of 'a country town' in the Cotswolds, on 'an April day, chilly and wet', establishes an intimate connection between mood and description, the upland road scene 'void of human affairs', the occasional appearance of fauna a 'mitigation of the living loneliness'.[15] This is the scene traversed by the unnamed narrator making his way to a lonely country inn where he will spend the night, the setting for his mysterious sensual encounter with the barmaid. Finding themselves alone in the smoking-room at the end of the night, they kiss and caress each other in a spontaneous understanding, and then have a strange, unconsummated liaison in her room, lying together 'innocent as children, for an hour' (p. 95). The barmaid remains inscrutable, refusing to reveal her name, so the traveller calls her 'Dusky Ruth', establishing a private connection. His restraint is a response to 'her strange sorrow', and the story seems to be a moment of tenderness and care for unspoken sadness. A second reading of the story suggests a more explicit explanation for 'Ruth's' misery: the traveller's eye is caught (twice) by an article in the local paper concerning 'the execution of a local felon, one Timothy Bridger, who had murdered an infant in some shameful circumstances' (p. 89). The first mention seems just to contribute to the mood of repressed passions; the second mention of 'the miscreant Bridger' (p. 93) makes the reference more insistent. Is 'Ruth' concealing her identity because she is connected to Bridger? Was the murdered infant hers? It is left to the reader to make the inference that might explain the 'tears, salt and strange and disturbing' that she sheds at the prospect of intimacy.

Doris Lessing's account of the 'steadily flowing stream in English writing ... quiet, low in key' to which Coppard belongs is perceptive and instructive.[16] For Lessing, this stream – 'full of nature and the countryside' (p. viii) – includes the stories of H. E. Bates, but not Hardy, who is distinguished sharply from Coppard: 'sorrow and rebellion rage in Hardy; nothing of the kind in Coppard, who doesn't believe in tragedy'. Without the tragic vision, Coppard's is 'a sparrow's-eye view, sharp, wry, surviving, and not one that can quarrel with the savage economies of the field or the hedgerow' (p. viii). 'The Higgler', from Coppard's *Fishmonger's Fiddle* (1925), illustrates Lessing's distinction between Hardy and Coppard: the material would lend itself to tragic treatment, but becomes wry and ironic in Coppard's depiction of the rural economy. Harvey Witlow, the higgler of this story (a pedlar, chiefly of dairy and poultry), struggling to make a living in the interwar depression, has the chance to marry the beautiful but enigmatic Mary Sadgrove, whose widowed mother, a prosperous farm owner, seems keen to push the marriage. The story makes good use of Coppard's principle of the restricted perspective, confining itself to Witlow's understanding of events. Suspicious of Mrs Sadgrove's motives – this would be a union beyond his station – Witlow marries his sweetheart Sophy instead. After the death of Mrs Sadgrove he discovers that it was the daughter, Mary, who had wanted the marriage, and realizes that he had 'thrown away a love' and 'a fortune too!' (p. 30). But this is not a tragic tale of thwarted passion: the story ends with Witlow apparently planning to become Mary's bailiff, the keen bargaining instinct of the higgler bringing him closer to prosperity. 'The Watercress Girl', from the same collection, is another rural tragedy transmuted in a wry treatment of country passions and manners. A girl, abandoned by her lover by whom she has an 'early born' baby that dies (p. 508), throws acid in the face of her rival; but the original lovers are finally reunited by the bond produced by thoughts of the child they might have had. Yet the rival remains disfigured and unmarriageable. It is a harsh world of passion and competition, but treated with wry detachment.

The title story of *The Field of Mustard* (1926) typifies Coppard's method: the element of bucolic description is suggestive of languor and solitude, but the human drama reveals contempt for social convention as well as hardship. The story opens with 'three sere disvirgined women' – a callous, utilitarian categorization that the story debunks – gathering kindling wood. Two of them share stories of their sexual adventures, discovering that, dissatisfied with their husbands, they both had had affairs with the same roguish gamekeeper. The story suggests a thwarted mutual attraction between them, conveyed in the closing pathetic fallacy: 'the lovely earth seemed to sigh in grief at some calamity all unknown to men' (p. 496).

Coppard was one of the writers cited by H. E. Bates as an influence on his work, drawing attention to the fact that Coppard had made him realize the cinematic qualities of the short story.[17] Bates's stories are certainly visual in their quality, especially in their description of rural scenes. 'Harvest', for example (from *Day's End and Other Stories* (1928)), is typical of Bates in its presentation of a figure in the landscape, in this case a pregnant mother soon to give birth to her fifth child, watching her children fill a basket with apples, blackberries and mushrooms, reflecting on her domestic burden, and her fear of labour. The idyllic setting, where she had played with her children in the summer, becomes ambivalent in the autumn twilight. The obvious reading – that she is, psychologically, out of sympathy with the fecundity of the rural scene – is balanced and enriched by the evocation of the natural life cycle, and the decay implicit in autumn. 'Harvest' illustrates the more straightforward, poetic treatment of rural setting in Bates – no less affecting for that – which evolves into a more nuanced kind of pathetic fallacy in his richest work. For example, a related kind of ambivalence, premised on natural bounty, pervades the longer and more complicated 'Alexander', the most memorable piece in *Seven Tales and Alexander* (1929).[18] Rooted in first-hand experience, the story concerns a boy, twelve-year-old Alexander, on a day's fruit-picking trip with his grandfather. It is a skilfully realized account of a boy's heightened impressions and interactions with the world, on the cusp of manhood, and a central aspect of the story is how an oppositional morality – and a straightforward symbolism – must be improved upon in the struggle for a more mature understanding of events and circumstances. The character Alexander also appears in the later story 'The White Pony' (1939), another tale of a boy fumbling towards maturity, where the elliptical qualities of the short story serve Bates's purpose very well. Alexander is instrumental in a plot to catch some gypsies stealing hens, and when a gun goes off in the melee his terrified pony breaks out of his stall, and runs himself to injury or exhaustion and has to be put down the following day.[19] The apparently straightforward moral, about the self-destructive nature of power and ownership, is complicated by the more powerful theme of appearance and reality, the subtleties of motive that the boy is learning to read.

Some of Bates's most memorable stories have a simple and enduring appeal. 'The Gleaner' (1932) is an affecting sketch about a 'very old' woman gleaning in an autumn field from noon until dusk. She is 'the last of the gleaners, the last survivor of an ancient race'. Her strength almost fails her at the end of the day, heaving her heavy sack, but on her journey home her tears of frustration dry to salt on her lips, 'the salt of her own body, the salt of the earth'. The familiar Batesian ambiguity about rural life is condensed into the powerful image of this ancient, who 'looks more than ever eternal, an earth figure'. It is simultaneously a record of agricultural history (and hardship), and a paean for a simpler life now gone, but which still embodies 'ageless and primitive' human interaction with the earth.[20] 'The Cowslip Field' (1959) is another of Bates's simplest and best stories, about a young boy picking cowslips in a meadow with a dwarfish and unattractive young woman, Pacey. His questions reveal his innocence – he asks her if she will grow any more, and if she has many suitors – but he is also able to see her true beauty, invisible to the adult world. It is a vignette of beautiful simplicity, a true rural idyll.

More commonplace in Bates's *oeuvre* is the exploration of social tensions. 'The Mower', from *The Black Boxer* (1932), is typically Batesian in its ambivalent treatment of the rural scene. Pondo is the expert mower, whose help a farming couple depend upon to get their meadow cut, when he can be enticed away from the beer in 'The Dragon'. Pondo is skilled in his handling of his scythe; he is also skilled in seduction, toying with the affections of the wife, who is clearly under his spell, and ready for a sexual encounter. The story creates the unified atmosphere typical of Bates, heavy with the various intoxications of June heat, the scents of summer, the replete meadow, beer and sexual desire. 'The Mill' (1935), discussed more fully in the previous chapter, is a fine study of hardship and decay, its atmosphere well integrated with its theme and characterization. In particular, the disused mill, with its waterlogged fabric, is the perfect setting for this story of claustrophobic brutality. A similar theme, treated in a way that is more recognizably Batesian, occurs in 'The Good Corn' (1955), where the sadness of a childless couple is overcome when they take on a stolid young woman to help on their farm, and then adopt her child, sired by the husband. In this story it is the bounty of nature that is emphasized.

One of Bates's most famous creations was the character Uncle Silas, a rural reprobate and a comic invention designed to ridicule and challenge convention. Bates published two collections of Uncle Silas stories, *My Uncle Silas* (1939) and *Sugar for the Horse* (1957). As with much of Bates's fiction, the impression of a rural community – especially its pinched narrowness – is a side effect of these stories. The main achievement is the personality of Silas, who emerges as a new folk anti-hero of English rural fiction, trading on the English enthusiasm for puncturing pretension. These are not technically innovative stories, but they are deft in their use of voice and point of view. The Silas stories are told by Silas's great nephew, and there are some stories, such as 'The Wedding' (1934), in which Silas is observed externally: in this case the focus is on his drunken antics at his son's wedding, culminating in a singing duet with the bride, which is felt to be improper. More commonly, Silas is telling a yarn about his adventures, which the boy is recounting, so that Silas is the narrator within a frame tale, as in 'Queenie White' (1957), the story of the time Silas did 'a bunk' to the coast for a fortnight with a married woman. The flouting of convention epitomizes the philosophy of Silas: 'Mek the most on it while you can.'[21]

In 'The Grass God' (1951) Bates offers a snapshot of the changing rural society in the aftermath of the Second World War. The protagonist is a landlord and landowner, who pursued a policy of land acquisition, after his more cautious father died in the interwar slump. He now lives with his estranged wife in a converted farmhouse, the big house on his estate, taken over by the military during the war, now in a state of decay. He conducts a summer-long affair with a young woman returning to the area, their trysts occurring in the dilapidated house. For him, it is the imagined start of a new love; for her it is just a summer fling. The protagonist is cruel and careless of his wife and his employees, and gets his just come-uppance. But this is also a tale about social change: the protagonist is not the ideal good landlord of traditional rural society, but rather a single-minded economist, with an obsession for grass cultivation. At the end of the story, the hot summer has killed the grass, a comment on the protagonist's failings; but the story is also a comment on the changing countryside, no longer peopled by workers, but by sundry retired folk who have no need of a landlord's patronage.

Two of Bates's stories from the 1950s illustrate very well his eye for a compelling story situation, but also how the specific context of English rural history – in this case concerning the changing post-war world – supplies a precise atmosphere that anchors his analysis of human relations. 'The Daffodil Sky' concerns the return of a convicted killer, having served his time for the manslaughter of a rival in love, to the house of his former lover, Cora Whitehead, who had been pregnant when he last saw her. The mother is out on shift work, but the man finds himself in a situation of mutual attraction with her daughter, who has the mother's flirtatious characteristics, and who produces a strange temporal dislocation for a character seeking lost time. Of course, the possibility that she might also be his daughter adds another layer of discomfort and complexity. The mood of lost time, however, is predicated on the man's dream of owning his own smallholding – he and Cora had planned to marry and pool their resources – and it is this 'dream of a piece of orchard land' that generalizes the sense of loss. The canker of his jealousy seems to blend with the world of night-shifts, roaring trains and the 'jumping, yellow fires' of the pin-table that has transformed the atmosphere of the local pub. As the man and Cora's (his?) daughter walk off for their drink, a storm has passed, and he sees something calm in 'the rain-washed daffodil sky'.[22] This recalls the time when he had first met Cora, after a day when he had been gathering daffodils to sell, and hints at the benediction of memory, the rural dream, in a situation that seems to hold little future promise.

Another story that maps a moment of post-war social change, and one in which Bates uses symbols in an arresting way, is 'Now Sleeps the Crimson Petal' (1958). In this story a butcher's wife, Mrs Corbett, finds herself drawn into a strange bond with the flamboyant man, Lafarge, who has bought the local big house, and is restoring it, only to be alienated by his friends, the gossipy and pseudo-intellectual crowd invited to his house-warming party. Her wartime anti-gas cape symbolizes the post-war social transition in the countryside. She believes the cape saved her life in a bomb blast in the war, but stops wearing it when Lafarge criticizes her style. She pulls the cape back on at the story's end, however, when she has realized that Lafarge and his crowd do not take her seriously, and that she is a misfit in that company: she buries her face in the cape, 'as into a shroud'. In its initial life-saving capacity, the cape 'might have been her shroud', so it now seems to fulfil this function, in the symbolic death of Mrs Corbett's self-esteem.[23] This also marks the death of a stable community, with defined roles and places.

The East Anglian author Ronald Blythe (1922–) occupies a similar, if less prominent position in the history of the rural story. Best known for his non-fiction, including *Akenfield: Portrait of an English Village* (1969), Blythe also wrote short stories that embody the last phases of traditional village life, based on a local rural economy, the Church and the patronage of the land-owning classes. Most of the stories collected in *The Stories of Ronald Blythe* (1985) were originally published from the 1950s through to the 1970s; yet Blythe claimed that 'these stories belong mainly to the first years of my writing life, when I seemed to be reading and writing and thinking about short stories much of the time'.[24] From the perspective of literary (and social) history, this locates Blythe at an important point of change: the stories pervaded by childhood and youthful memories evoke the interwar period; yet in other stories he also offers a perspective from the fast-fading traditional village England in the second half of the twentieth century.

'The Windfall' seems written to endorse the proverbial idea, 'good things come to he who waits'. Toby Kettle is the boy-narrator who recounts the day when he and his uncle tramped across ripe corn fields, on a hot August day, to the house of a relative, known simply as 'Aunt', who has just died. As they pass her apple orchard, Toby recollects how 'Aunt used to take me into this orchard and poke about in the rank grass with her polished cane' to retrieve a fallen apple, usually half eaten by wasps (p. 184). Aunt would polish the good side on her skirts, and present it to him as a treat, but would never *pick* one for him, even though she had more apples than she 'could ever eat, sell or want' (p. 185). Arriving at her house, Toby and his uncle are confronted with other relatives laying claim to Aunt's best household items. Partly to escape this scene, but also fearful of having to pay his last respects to Aunt laid out in her coffin, Toby retreats to the apple orchard, and, finding the trees 'roped' with apples in glorious weather, he reaches out to pick one from her 'precious permain tree'. At the last moment he resists temptation, reasoning that to take the apple would put him in the company of the other avaricious relatives (p. 187). Returning to the house, he is overtaken by the Parson, hurrying to Aunt's house to read the short will she has left in his care, and in which she bequeaths all of her belongings, including the house and the orchard, to Toby (p. 188). The apparently trite moral of the story, and its title-pun, can obscure the story's virtues, especially the way it evokes rural rhythms and conventions, and instinctive prudence (always making use of the windfalls). Blythe is also careful to divert us from the moral. On the journey, Toby has been preoccupied with Aunt's name, 'Minta', which is always omitted when she is referred to. When the will is read, Toby is most impressed, not by his inheritance, but by the discovery that Aunt's full name is 'Araminta' (p. 188). There is a suggestion that the boy, too young to understand the significance of the bequest, is beginning to respond to Aunt as a person, and to think about the set roles that comprise rural identity.

In 'The Right Day to Kill a Pike', Blythe treats the persistence of rural folklore and superstition. This is another story involving Toby and his uncle, on an eerily still February day, when the uncle decides that they will have to kill a pike to usher in the spring. This apparently primitivist 'sacrifice' (p. 159) appears to work, as there are hints of spring in the air as they return from their challenging fishing expedition, the pike having been extraordinarily elusive (p. 162). It is not so much an unfettered celebration of rural primitivism – the housekeeper dismissively discards the pike when they return (p. 163) – but rather a quiet celebration of seasonal change and human dependence upon it.

If 'The Windfall' and 'The Right Day to Kill a Pike' offer a record of fading rural habits, the social moment of rural change is captured more precisely in one of Blythe's best stories, 'The Shadows of the Living', the action of which is set in 1970. The story is presented in the third person, but chiefly from the perspective of Colonel Robert Faulkner, owner of Springwaters Hall, who is losing motivation for his estate duties, following 'a slight coronary' the previous year (p. 102). He is weary of 'all the rooms and acres and farms': he feels he could 'heave the house and its contents into the lap of the National Trust', but that he could not divest himself of 'his duties' (p. 93). The greatest burden and antagonism for him is the Church (in which there is a 'Faulkner chapel'), and when a new incumbent is appointed – Rector Deenman – he feels immense hostility towards him, seeing him as his 'quarry' (p. 107). For his part, Deenman identifies in Faulkner someone he must 'bring . . . back to

God' (p. 100). This mutual and seemingly instinctive antagonism is revealed to have a supernatural dimension (and explanation), however: a sixteenth-century parson with an almost identical name (John Daneman) was burnt to death on the village green, the warrant that sent Daneman to the stake having been signed by one of Faulkner's ancestors (p. 108). Deenman and Faulkner re-live, or are inhabited by, their past shadows; and when Faulkner goes to find Deenman on Guy Fawkes night – ostensibly to bring him to the ceremonial lighting of the bonfire, but in the manner of an executioner fetching a condemned man – there is perhaps little surprise for the reader, given the supernatural 'logic' of the tale, that Deenman has died whilst saying his prayers (p. 110).

In 'The Shadows of the Living', Blythe pushes through the eerie tale of historical repetition to suggest an inverse parallel: it is the enervation and exhaustion of Faulkner that makes him so resentful of Deenman's piety. The superstitious order of the sixteenth century has given way to a world of fading faith, both in terms of religious conviction and social duty. In this sense, Faulkner is 'killing' the traditional rural society through the clergyman who is at the heart of this structure. As in the best supernatural short stories, Blythe is more interested in hidden social anxieties than he is in ghosts.

It is hard to see the rural English short story thriving in the twenty-first century, a point illustrated by Louis de Bernières's (1954–) short story cycle *Notwithstanding* (2009), which is both a lament for the passing of rural village England and a coda to the tradition traced in this essay. Based on the Surrey village where de Bernières grew up in the 1960s and 1970s, the stories of fictionalized 'Notwithstanding' continue the convention of celebrating the English rural eccentric – epitomized in H. E. Bates's Uncle Silas – but do so to show how behaviour beyond a notional social norm now helps define the anachronism of the self-contained rural community. In 'Obadiah Oak, Mrs Griffiths and the Carol Singers', the transition is pinpointed in the character of Obadiah, known as Jack, who is the 'village's last peasant', and who 'reeks of six decades of neglected hygiene'.[25] Jack is now 'considered a "character" ... but newcomers avoid him if they can' (p. 9). In the 'Afterword', de Bernières shows how his Surrey village is representative of the erosion of rural communities, now pervaded by (sub)urban habits and behaviour. His upbringing occurred 'many years past the era of rural idyll', itself a myth, since 'the centuries of "idyll" were ... a period of ignorance, disease, servitude, bone-numbing cold, relentless hard work, perinatal death, and extreme penury' (p. 267). And yet, de Bernières still looks back on the location of his upbringing as 'a rural idyll':

the 'old social structure had gone', but 'the countryside was still intact' (p. 271). What redeems and enriches this nostalgic vision, however, is not the resilience of verdant England, but the social values of rurality that *Notwithstanding* memorializes. Set against the typical village families, who now 'often live in complete isolation from each other ... getting in their cars to go and see their friends elsewhere' (p. 268), is the abiding image of the boy Robert in 'The Girt Pike', who is commissioned by young, vivacious Mrs Rendall to catch the eponymous fish in her pond. A year after this heroic episode, Mrs Rendall dies of cancer, and the heartbroken Robert writes a thank-you letter to her, folds it up in a tobacco tin, and buries it in the 'upturned clay' of her fresh grave. He uses the fishing reel she had bought him as a present for the rest of his life, and each time he passes the churchyard, he wonders if his tobacco tin and message have rotted away, and 'would feel all over again his long-standing sorrow' (p. 45). This is a memorial for the enduring connection between person and place, a connection that is not always comfortable, but which was the lynchpin of the traditional communities that featured in the tradition of the rural story.

Notes

1. Tim Killick, 'Mary Russell Mitford and the Topography of Short Fiction', *Journal of the Short Story in English* (online), 43 (Autumn 2004), http://jsse.revue.org/index396.html, p. 2 (accessed 1 June 2013).
2. The final (1912) version of *Wessex Tales*, which is the version used here, contains seven tales. The 1888 edition had contained just five stories; in 1896 Hardy added a sixth, and for 1912 he removed one and added two more. See Kathryn R. King's 'Note on the Text', in Thomas Hardy, *Wessex Tales*, ed. Kathryn R. King (Oxford University Press, 1991), pp. xxi–xxiv (p. xxi).
3. Kristin Brady, *The Short Stories of Thomas Hardy* (London: Macmillan, 1982), p. 4.
4. The worst years of this phase of depression were 1879–96. See Richard Perren, *Agriculture in Depression, 1870–1940* (Cambridge University Press, 1995).
5. Brady, *Short Stories of Thomas Hardy*, pp. 4–5. See William Empson, *Some Versions of Pastoral* (London: Chatto & Windus, 1935).
6. King, 'Note on the Text', pp. xi and xvii.
7. D. J. Taylor, 'Foreword', in Mary E. Mann, *The Complete Tales of Dulditch* (Dereham: Larks Press, n.d. [2008]), p. 5.
8. Mann, *The Complete Tales of Dulditch*, p. 141. Subsequent page references refer to this edition and are given in parentheses in the text.
9. See Patience Tomlinson's 'Introduction' to *The Complete Tales of Dulditch*, pp. 11–18 (pp. 12–13).

10. Philip Gardner, 'Constance Holme', *Oxford DNB* (online: www.oxforddnb.com).
11. Constance Holme, *The Wisdom of the Simple and Other Stories* (1937; rep. London: Oxford University Press, 1950), p. 92. Subsequent page references to this edition are given in parentheses in the text.
12. Sheila Kaye-Smith, *Faithful Stranger and Other Stories* (1938; rep. Bath: Lythway Press, 1973), p. 314.
13. Frank O'Connor considered Coppard to be a 'master of the English Short Story'. See *The Lonely Voice: A Study of the Short Story* (London: Macmillan, 1963), p. 170.
14. A. E. Coppard, 'Foreword', in *The Collected Tales of A. E. Coppard* (New York: Alfred Knopf, 1951), p. vii.
15. Coppard, *The Collected Tales*, p. 87. All quotations from Coppard's tales are from this edition, with subsequent page numbers given in parentheses in the text.
16. Doris Lessing, 'Introduction' to Coppard's *Selected Stories* (London: Jonathan Cape, 1972), pp. vii–xii (p. vii).
17. H. E. Bates, *The World in Ripeness* (London: Michael Joseph, 1972), pp. 124–5.
18. This story, along with a few more of Bates's excellent rural stories – including 'The Mill', 'The Pink Cart' and 'Breeze Anstey' – are discussed by Dean Baldwin in the previous chapter in a different context, and so receive only passing mention here.
19. 'Gypsies' is the term Bates uses. Travellers are often treated more sympathetically in his fiction, as in the story 'The Pink Cart' (1933), which coveys the insecurity and uncertainty of a gypsy couple and their consumptive daughter.
20. H. E. Bates, *The Woman Who Had Imagination* (London: Jonathan Cape, 1934), pp. 49, 52, 55.
21. H. E. Bates, *Sugar for the Horse* (London: Michael Joseph, 1957), pp. 28 and 35.
22. H. E. Bates, *The Daffodil Sky* (London: Michael Joseph, 1955), pp. 40, 27 and 48.
23. H. E. Bates, *Now Sleeps the Crimson Petal and Other Stories* (London: Michael Joseph, 1961), pp. 71 and 48.
24. 'Introduction' to *The Stories of Ronald Blyth* (1985; rep. London: Methuen, 1986), p. ix. Subsequent quotations are from this edition, with page numbers given in parentheses in the text.
25. Louis de Bernières, *Notwithstanding* (London: Harvill Secker, 2009), p. 9. Subsequent page numbers are given in parentheses in the text.

16

Metropolitan Modernity: Stories of London

NEAL ALEXANDER

Stories of London constitute a significant strand within the literature of London, and of urban modernity generally. Their significance has been obscured, however, by a persistent critical fascination with the London novel. There are grounds for such fascination in the fact that the history of London's growth into a world city and the rise of the novel as a literary form are closely intertwined.[1] 'The English novel itself can be said to have grown out of the streets, stews and rookeries of outcast proletarian and criminal London', argues Ken Worpole, pointing to a tradition that stretches from Daniel Defoe to Iain Sinclair.[2] Moreover, it is widely assumed that the novel's capaciousness and discursive flexibility make it the most suitable form for depicting the size, diversity and complex social life of the modern metropolis. However, there are limits even to the novel's comprehensiveness. Between 1800 and 1900 the population of London grew rapidly from 1 million to 4.5 million inhabitants, and the immense physical expansion of the city made it increasingly 'difficult to envisage the whole'.[3] Consequently, one of the most widely noted features of London's cultural image is the city's capacity to overwhelm any attempt to represent it in its totality. In *The Soul of London* (1905), for instance, Ford Madox Ford remarks upon the impossibility of 'having an impression, a remembered bird's-eye-view of London as a whole'.[4] The city comes into focus for the observer only through partial glimpses and personal impressions, its larger life registered fleetingly as a 'background' that cannot be encompassed.[5] It is in this respect that the short story form, with its limited scope and narrative intensity, has something important to offer the literature of London. For, whilst individual stories may achieve varying degrees of formal resolution, they can powerfully convey the fragmentary, disorienting character of metropolitan experience by isolating particular moments or places within a larger, ungraspable whole. Even where they appear to offer their readers representative images of the city, stories of London implicitly acknowledge its incomprehensibility through their own formal circumscription.

The origins of the London short story lie in the 1830s and are closely related to the explosive growth of English periodical culture during the Victorian period. By the time of Victoria's death in 1901, more than 2,500 newspapers were published annually in Britain and Ireland, and over one fifth of the total appeared in London.[6] Indeed, the titles of some of the more prominent periodicals emphasize their close relationship with the metropolis and its thriving print culture: *London*; *London Journal*; *London Magazine*; *London Monthly Magazine*; *London Penny Journal*; *London Review*; *Cornhill Magazine*; *The Strand Magazine*; *Illustrated London News*. The main drivers of this publishing phenomenon were the creation of a mass reading public during the first half of the nineteenth century and the mechanization of printing methods, which made it possible to meet rising demand with weekly numbers.[7] Most newspapers and journals included short fictions alongside opinion pieces, light-hearted essays and reviews, whilst a host of penny magazines – 'penny dreadfuls' – satisfied the public's appetite for lurid tales of crime and gothic horror by writers like G. W. M. Reynolds, author of *The Mysteries of London* (1844–56). Reynolds's text, which was loosely modelled on Eugène Sue's *Les Mystères de Paris* (1843), appeared in weekly instalments and exemplifies 'a new consciousness of the city as inexplicable and impenetrable', which was to become an important component of many stories of London.[8] By the 1880s the short story had begun to crystallize as a distinct generic category, its popularity ensured by a large urban readership; and it is in the last decades of the nineteenth century that stories of London begin to proliferate. Nonetheless, several pioneering examples can be identified in the preceding half-century.

Perhaps the most iconic early story of London is Edgar Allan Poe's 'The Man of the Crowd', which appeared in both *The Casket* and *Burton's Gentleman's Magazine* in December 1839. Anticipating Reynolds, Poe's tale conceives of the city's modernity as a mystery to be explored and anatomized, although it admits no ultimate solution. At the outset, Poe's narrator is convalescing after an unspecified illness and spends his time watching the 'tumultuous sea' of London's crowds from the window of a coffee shop on The Strand.[9] Absorbed in his contemplation of this ever-changing urban scene, he becomes a physiognomist of the crowd, distinguishing between the different ranks of clerk, identifying gamblers, dandies, pedlars and prostitutes by their looks or dress or manner of walking. In this way, he seeks to impose some measure of order upon the disturbing and fascinating spectacle of the city streets, which clearly influences his 'peculiar state of mind' (p. 87). Already in Poe the city is associated with alterations in the psychology and mental life of its modern citizens. The crux of the story is reached when the narrator catches sight of 'a decrepit old man' and is arrested by 'the absolute idiosyncrasy' of his expression, a face that he cannot read but which excites 'a craving desire to keep the man in view – to know more of him' (p. 88). He abandons his role as a detached voyeur and crosses over into the public world of London's streets, following the old man on his peregrinations like a shadow or double. Throughout the night, the man of the crowd frantically seeks out the company of strangers in one quarter of the city after another, leading the narrator from London's grand thoroughfares to its impoverished underworlds and back again. Finally, when he can follow no more, the narrator confronts the old man face to face but receives no glimmer of notice or recognition. His conclusion is that the man of the crowd is not a man at all but rather an embodiment of urban modernity itself, 'the type and the genius of deep crime' (p. 91). Taking up this phrase, Walter Benjamin aptly describes Poe's tale as 'something like an X-ray of a detective story', stripping the nascent genre back to its basic elements: the pursuer, the crowd and the enigmatic individual who haunts the city's public spaces.[10]

Although best known as a novelist, Charles Dickens is also an important progenitor of the London short story, and has probably had a more enduring influence on subsequent writers in this tradition even than Poe. Throughout his career, Dickens published dozens of supernatural tales, Christmas stories, impressionistic sketches and dramatic monologues, many of them in *Household Words* and *All the Year Round*, the weekly journals he edited consecutively between 1850 and 1870.[11] The everyday life of London and its citizens provides the focus for his otherwise miscellaneous *Sketches by Boz* (1939), which is divided into four sections – 'sketches', 'scenes', 'characters' and 'tales' – as though on a sliding scale of fictiveness. What is distinctive about Dickens's short fictions, however, is their protean variety and hybrid forms, which frequently merge elements of fictional and non-fiction genres. For instance, although it is designated a 'tale', 'The Drunkard's Death' closely resembles a moralistic essay in many respects; whereas the descriptive scene-setting of 'Meditations in Monmouth Street' rapidly evolves into a surreal fantasia of animated second-hand clothes in London's 'burial-place of the fashions'.[12] Throughout, Dickens's depictions of London's streets and shops, theatres and cab stands are inflected by the moods, prejudices and imaginative disposition of his roving character-narrator, Boz. In 'Our Next-door

Neighbour', he wonders what house doors and knockers might reveal about the characters of those who live behind them; and in 'Shops and Their Tenants', exclaims: 'What inexhaustible food for speculation, do the streets of London afford!' (pp. 58, 80). Frequently, Boz is to be found speculating on the ways in which London shapes, and sometimes deforms, the lives of its citizens. 'Thoughts about People' reflects upon the conditions of anonymity and alienation in which many individual Londoners exist, signalling a sympathetic identification with socially marginal figures. This identification is also present in 'Shabby-genteel People', which describes a submerged population group that seems 'to belong as exclusively to London as its own smoke, or the dingy bricks and mortar' (pp. 303–4). As this example illustrates, in Dickens's stories character and environment are mutually defining, so that people and the places they inhabit are often near-indistinguishable.

Dickens's imaginative 'commitment to London' is further evident in the short texts – neither essays nor stories – collected in *The Uncommercial Traveller* (1861), though here the keynote is more consistently nostalgic or melancholic.[13] Dickens's narratorial persona is another indefatigable wanderer with a fascination for London's forgotten corners: City churches and churchyards, for instance, or those 'shy neighbourhoods' where donkeys live upstairs. Frequently, Dickens is drawn to those times of day or year in which the city reveals some unfamiliar aspect of itself or is transformed into an alien landscape. In 'Arcadian London', he describes a city temporarily abandoned by its citizens as they holiday by the sea, its empty streets reverting to 'wilderness' and pastoral simplicity for six glorious weeks.[14] The tone becomes much darker and more explicitly fictive in 'Night Walks', as its insomniac narrator imagines spectral suicides by the banks of the Thames and conjures a vision of the 'enormous hosts of dead' repopulating the city streets (p. 140). By comparison with these acutely observant and inventive sketches, more conventional 'tales' such as 'The Boarding House' or 'Passage in the Life of Mr Watkins Tottle' can seem awkward and flat-footed, as though Dickens were attempting to condense enough material for a novel into the limited space available.

Dickens and Poe both introduce the gothic tropes of haunting and doubling that will recur frequently in stories of London by authors such as Elizabeth Bowen, Muriel Spark, Iain Sinclair and Will Self. The most widely influential example of London gothic in the nineteenth century, however, is Robert Louis Stevenson's novella, *The Strange Case of Dr Jekyll and Mr Hyde* (1886). London's streets, squares and buildings serve as something more than a mere backdrop to Stevenson's psychological thriller, for the city itself is associated with doubleness and secret identities, its civilized milieu of middle-class professionalism existing in close proximity with its disorderly underworlds of pleasure and vice. Initially, a stark class geography is revealed, as when Mr Utterson pursues Hyde to his lodgings and apprehends working-class Soho as 'like a district of some city in a nightmare'.[15] Yet, the text itself tends to cut across and complicate such socio-spatial prejudices by showing how the various districts and quarters of the city are liable to overlap or merge with one another. In this respect, it is symbolically significant that Dr Jekyll's home in 'a square of ancient, handsome houses' should adjoin, at its rear, the 'sinister block of building' from which Hyde is seen coming and going (pp. 40, 30). In this way, the story creates an architectural link not only between the two men but also between the very different spheres of London life in which they have their social being. This disturbing confusion of spaces and identities is further compounded by the fog that envelops Stevenson's city, blurring its outlines and making any sure orientation impossible: 'The fog still slept on the wing above the drowned city, where the lamps glimmered like carbuncles; and through the muffle and smother of these fallen clouds, the procession of the town's life was still rolling in through the great arteries with a sound as of a mighty wind' (pp. 53–4). Fog partially obscures Hyde's crimes and allows him to evade capture, though it also seems to place London itself in some twilit realm between life and death: it is a 'drowned city', but one that roars with vitality. This roar or hum is present throughout Stevenson's tale as a kind of ground bass, reinforcing the text's metaphorical correlation between urban environments and unconscious drives or desires.

The narrative form of *Dr Jekyll and Mr Hyde* – an assemblage of testimonies and letters – recalls the generic conventions of gothic fiction, though its taut plotting and focus on mysterious crimes are derived from the urban detective story. After Poe, one of the earliest pioneers of this thoroughly modern genre was Wilkie Collins, whose *The Moonstone* (1868) has been called the first English detective novel. Collins was also a prolific writer of short stories, many of them detective fictions, including several set in London. For instance, 'The Diary of Anne Rodway' predates *The Moonstone* by more than a decade and features perhaps the first female amateur detective in English fiction. When her friend, Mary, is injured in the street and ultimately dies, Anne is convinced that she has been murdered and determines to track her killer down by descending into the seedy underworlds of 'this cruel city'.[16] The story, which begins as a rather mawkish tale of sisterly affection, gradually develops into a tense murder mystery in which Collins's deft manipulation of the diary format sustains the reader's interest. Collins's interests in formal experimentation and generic hybrids are also evident in two other London stories. In 'The Biter Bit', he rewrites the now-familiar conventions of the police procedural as comic farce, unfolding his narrative through a series of letters between officers of widely differing ranks, outlooks and levels of competence. And in the much later story 'Who Killed Zebedee?', he reinvigorates the classic whodunnit by relaying its details via the death-bed confession of a former member of the London police. What is striking about Collins's urban detective stories is his ability to adapt or subvert the conventions of a genre that was still in the early stages of its development.

Influenced by Poe and Dickens, Collins was in turn an important influence upon the author of the most famous series of urban detective stories, Arthur Conan Doyle. Doyle's Sherlock Holmes is a quintessentially metropolitan figure, entirely at home in London's fog-bound streets and capable of moving fluently between its high-class society and criminal quarters. Of course, Holmes's attachment to London is bound up with his role as a sleuth, for the city is essentially a place of mystery and hidden vices. In 'A Case of Identity', he imagines being able to 'hover over this great city', removing the roofs of houses in order to 'peep in at the queer things which are going on' in secret.[17] Because this fantasy of panoptic dominance is unachievable, Holmes must use his powers of logic and observation to penetrate the city's 'endless labyrinth of gas-lit streets' (p. 62). There are clearly moral overtones to the mastering drive that Holmes embodies in so many of the stories. Indeed, as Raymond Williams observes, in detective fiction 'the opaque complexity of modern city life is represented by crime', and the role of the detective is to render some of that threatening complexity soluble.[18] And yet, if Holmes pits his intelligence against the sinful, criminal city, he also identifies with it. In 'The Resident Patient', Watson says of his friend: 'He loved to lie in the very centre of five millions of people, with his filaments stretching out and running through them, responsive to every little rumour or suspicion of unsolved crime' (p. 416). Although this image depicts Holmes as an unsleeping surveillant presence within the city, the story also underlines his 'love' of London and profound enjoyment of its 'ever-changing kaleidoscope of life' (p. 418). Holmes is as much a product of London as are the criminals he pursues. Although his scientific rationality and impersonal detachment appear to set him apart from the common run of humankind (whose representative is Watson), they are also defining characteristics of the metropolitan individual, as described in Georg Simmel's 1903 essay, 'The Metropolis and Mental Life'. According to Simmel, the mental life of the metropolis is 'essentially intellectualistic' and the city-dweller typically adopts an attitude of indifference or abstraction in his or her dealings with others.[19] It is not difficult to recognize Holmes in this description, though it is also worth noting the way in which he alternates between periods of intense, obsessive interest and cocaine-induced ennui both within and between stories.

In spite of Holmes's famous ability to see 'what others overlook', Doyle's stories have their own socio-geographical blind spots (p. 30). As Franco Moretti points out, the 'epicentre' of Doyle's criminal London is the West End; in only one story, 'The Man with the Twisted Lip', does Holmes venture further east than the City.[20] This topographical lacuna is all the more striking given the interest that other writers of the 1890s show in representing working-class communities in the East End. During the second half of the nineteenth century, the living conditions and moral character of the urban poor became a subject of fascination for middle-class commentators. The most extensive and important reports, Henry Mayhew's *London Labour and the London Poor* (1851–62) and Charles Booth's *Life and Labour of the People in London* (1889–1903), both spawned many imitators. Although Booth demonstrated that slums and poverty were fairly evenly spread across London, popular novelists and story writers tended to present the East End as the deepest abyss, 'an unknown land of destitution, immorality and disease'.[21] In doing so, they often combined a mode of ethnographic realism with fantastic projections of social anxieties, viewing the East End as a space of disturbing 'otherness' that conflated class and ethnic differences. For instance, in George Gissing's 1893 story, 'Fleet-Footed Hester', the Hackney-born heroine is described as follows: 'She looked what she was, a noble savage. Her speech was the speech of Hackney, but on her lips it lost its excessive meanness, and became a fit expression of an elementary, not a degraded, mind.'[22] Linguistic and class differences are clearly entwined here with imperialist conceptions of racial development, nobility and degeneracy. Gissing's impulse to exoticize the East End is part of a larger pattern in fiction of the 1890s, and is shared by several writers who themselves originate from the Far East of London. In the introductory 'Proem' to his *Children of the Ghetto* (1892), Israel Zangwill describes London's East End Jewish community, centred on Petticoat Lane, as a world apart, through which 'the rose of romance blows yet a little longer in the raw air of English reality'.[23] Even more explicitly Orientalist in tenor and outlook is Thomas Burke's *Limehouse*

Nights (1916), which depicts the lives of Chinese immigrants in London's docklands and foregrounds the perceived threats of inter-racial sex and miscegenation in many individual stories.

The most sustained and influential treatment of the East End in the short story form is Arthur Morrison's *Tales of Mean Streets* (1894). Morrison's flinty, dispassionate tales depict moments in the lives of the East End's slum-dwellers, striking workers and criminal underclass. The collection's title foregrounds its preoccupations with the hardships and cruelties peculiar to urban environments. In 'Lizerunt', for instance, Morrison's eponymous heroine is not a noble savage but simply an eighteen-year-old girl from Stepney who works in a pickle factory and is 'something of a beauty'.[24] By the end of the story, Lizer has lost her looks and figure to years of hard work and is forced into prostitution by her abusive, wastrel husband. What is distinctive about Morrison's stories, however, is not their subject matter but the manner in which they depict the harsh realities of working-class lives. His observant, ironic naturalism contrasts sharply with the sensationalism and sentimentalism of many contemporary writers on the East End, and Morrison stubbornly refuses to explain the actions and behaviour of the characters he depicts.[25] In 'On the Stairs', a medical assistant gives Mrs Manders five shillings to buy medicine for her dying son, but the mother keeps the money to pay for a more 'respectable' funeral (p. 109). Crucially, Morrison denies the reader access either to Mrs Manders's thought processes or the room of the dying man; in fact, the narratorial perspective of the story is confined to the semi-public, communal space of the stairwell. In this way, important aspects of the private lives of his East End characters remain inscrutable or mysterious to the middle-class reader. Indeed, Morrison's largely plotless tales can be seen as anticipating the modernist short story's interest in elliptical, enigmatic and unresolved narratives.

As Malcolm Bradbury observes, early twentieth-century London has an ambiguous reputation as both 'the obvious centre of English-language Modernist activity' and 'one of the dullest and most deadening of capital cities'.[26] Nonetheless, a new consciousness of the intensity and ephemerality of modern urban experience is arguably crucial in the development of the modernist short story, with its emphasis on fragmented impressions and characteristically open forms, and is particularly evident in the London stories of Virginia Woolf. For example, in Woolf's most famous story, 'The Mark on the Wall', her narrator finds an analogy for 'the rapidity of life' and her own flux of consciousness in London's public transport system: 'Why, if one wants to compare life to anything, one must liken it to being blown through the Tube at fifty miles an hour – landing at the other end without a single hairpin in one's hair.'[27] Modern life is emphatically urban in character according to this striking analogy, and Woolf's story depends for its effects upon a similar tension between order and chaos, narrative structure and random associations to that which is found in metropolitan centres such as London. In another experimental short fiction, 'Kew Gardens', Woolf juxtaposes a series of fragmentary human dramas with microcosmic impressions of the non-human life of a west London park, before drawing back at the story's end and situating the park and its inhabitants within the larger macrocosm of the city itself:

> But there was no silence; all the time the motor omnibuses were turning their wheels and changing their gear; like a vast nest of Chinese boxes all of wrought steel turning ceaselessly one within another the city murmured; on the top of which the voices cried aloud and the petals of myriads of flowers flashed their colours into the air. (p. 89)

This description of the form of the city as a nest of Chinese boxes clearly also applies, self-reflexively, to the story in which it appears, for 'Kew Gardens' co-ordinates between a wide variety of inter-related scales and perspectives, worlds-within-worlds. Similarly, London's incessant murmur of sounds and voices provides a model for the multi-accentual character and 'all-embracing impetus' of Woolf's prose style, which restlessly seeks to reveal the connections between people, places and things.[28]

Although her creative and personal relationships with the city were more fleeting than Woolf's, the New Zealand-born Katherine Mansfield also produced several modernist stories of London during the 1920s. But whereas Woolf's London is characterized by colour and movement and irrepressible vitality, the urban scenes of Mansfield's stories are typically dull and deadening, if not actively hostile towards her emotionally vulnerable characters. In 'Pictures', a failed actress and singer, Ada Moss, endures poverty, hunger and the threat of eviction from her rented top-floor room in Bloomsbury. The story follows her wanderings through London's streets in search of work and romance, employing interior monologue to reveal the ways in which she maintains a fragile sense of self through cinematic fantasies: 'I might just have a stroke of luck ... A dark handsome gentleman in a fur coat comes in with a friend, and sits at my table, perhaps.'[29] Set against such wishful imaginings is the cold impersonality of the city, which repeatedly confronts Miss Moss with reflected images of herself that she does not want to recognize and seems to conspire in her eventual slide towards prostitution. Andrew Bennett remarks that vagrancy is a common condition for many of Mansfield's characters, who are often 'in transit, on the move' or 'people with no fixed abode'.[30] This is certainly the case with Ada Moss and is also true, in a different sense, of Ma Parker in 'Life of Ma Parker'. An elderly woman who has recently buried her beloved grandson, Ma Parker reflects on her 'hard life' and pent-up grief as she cleans the rooms of an idle 'literary gentleman' (pp. 303, 301). Using free indirect style to alternate between the perspectives of individual characters, Mansfield both exposes the gentleman's class-bound insensitivity and provides the grounds of an empathetic identification with Ma Parker through a sequence of embedded analepses. However, the story's conclusion also makes it clear that Ma Parker's suffering is enhanced and perpetuated by the fact that she has nowhere she can go to cry and thereby ease her feelings: 'She couldn't sit on a bench anywhere; people would come asking her questions. [. . .] If she sat on some steps a policeman would speak to her. [. . .] There was nowhere' (pp. 308, 309). Ma Parker's impossible situation is compounded by her class position but also indicates a more general existential condition that Mansfield's London stories adumbrate: as a place in which to live, the city is isolating and constraining, an environment of privation and inexpressible misery.

Although she is often regarded as more marginal and more middlebrow than either Mansfield or Woolf, Elizabeth Bowen is another important theorist and practitioner of the modernist short story. Particularly significant are her fictions of wartime London, which search for ways of articulating the mix of excitement and shattering loss that characterized life in the blitzed city. In her essay 'The Short Story in England', Bowen suggests that the short story is 'the ideal *prose* medium for wartime writing' because of its responsiveness to 'the discontinuities of life', and recalls her sense that wartime London 'teemed' 'with untold but tellable stories'.[31] If Bowen's emphasis upon formal and thematic 'discontinuities' indicates her debt to modernism, then this is also combined with a more conventional desire to tell stories. What is distinctive about her stories of wartime London is their facility for rendering the spaces of the city uncanny, at once strange and familiar, exposed and mysterious. For example, 'In the Square' opens by describing an empty square of bomb-damaged houses on a July evening, presenting it self-consciously as an 'extinct scene' that has 'the appearance of belonging to some ages ago'.[32] Often, Bowen's London streets, squares and houses seem to have been blasted out of time's continuum, existing in a time between times. When Mrs Drover returns briefly to her bomb-damaged house in Kensington in 'The Demon Lover', she is unsettled by the 'hollowness' of what had formerly been her home, for it has the 'air of being a cracked cup from which memory, with its reassuring power, had either evaporated or leaked away' (p. 664). Similarly, in the opening pages of 'Mysterious Kôr', the moonlit streets of London are transformed into an eerie, alien landscape – 'shallow, cratered, extinct' – and have become conflated in the minds of the main characters with the ruined, forsaken city of Rider Haggard's *She* (1887) (p. 728). As the two young lovers, Pepita and Arthur, wander the empty streets, they experience wartime London simultaneously as an eroticized space, a 'ghost city' and a kind of utopian terrain for the projection of individual and collective fantasies (p. 738). The status of the real is called into question in 'Mysterious Kôr', which illustrates Julian Wolfreys's point that Bowen's fiction is chiefly preoccupied with 'the psychic and phantasmagoric aspects of the city'.[33] Yet, Bowen's wartime stories are also acutely responsive to the strange materiality of London, its resistance to as well as its stimulus for the creative imagination.

With the rapid dissolution of Britain's empire in the decades immediately following the Second World War, London was reconfigured as a post-imperial metropolis, its new multiracial and multicultural reality created by burgeoning immigration from its former colonies. As John Clement Ball observes, cities have always been 'places of mixture, of the commingling of differences', though this role was newly foregrounded in post-war London.[34] In the short story form, London's status as a transnational space of cultural encounters is deftly rendered by Sam Selvon, who had himself emigrated from Trinidad in 1950. Selvon's collection, *Ways of Sunlight* (1957), was published just one year after his novel, *The Lonely Londoners*, and similarly deals with the attempts of its West Indian characters to make a home for themselves in a strange and sometimes inhospitable urban environment. *Ways of Sunlight* is divided into two parts, 'Trinidad' and 'London', as if formally reflecting the split or doubled identities of the main characters in its individual stories, who each straddle a series of geographical, cultural and racial divides. All but one of the London stories employ Selvon's characteristic third-person narrative voice, which blends standard English with Trinidadian dialect and refuses to mark itself off from the language of his characters. Thematically, they deal with patterns of work and worklessness ('Working the Transport', 'Eraser's Dilemma', 'Basement Lullaby'), interracial relationships ('Waiting for Aunty to Cough', 'If Winter Comes') and the resourcefulness of immigrants in response to prejudice or hardship ('Calypso in London', 'Obeah in the Grove'). Several characters appear in more than one story, and seem to know one another, thereby gesturing to a fragile sense of community amid displacement. Moreover, a characteristic feature of these stories is to include moments when the narrator addresses the reader directly, assuming a common knowledge of the people and places he describes: 'If you are one of the hustlers on Route 12 I don't know how you could fail to notice Eraser, he such a cheerful conductor.'[35] London is the shared context for these stories, uniting narrator, reader and characters in spite of their manifold differences.

Another important strand in post-war stories of London concerns the projection of dystopian or post-apocalyptic futures for the city. Particularly significant in this regard are several early stories by J. G. Ballard, which extrapolate from contemporary trends in urban development and population growth to imagine their possible consequences for human societies. In his 1957 story, 'The Concentration City', Ballard describes Franz's attempts to escape from the vast megalopolis in which he lives, a quest 'to find the City's end' which is driven by his desire for 'free space'.[36] Ultimately, Franz's journey only returns him to where he started from, the official explanation being that the city is without either origin or bounds; it is as inescapable as time itself. In another story, 'Billennium', Ballard turns his attention to the related problem of urban overcrowding, describing a city of thirty million inhabitants who endure extremely cramped living conditions and almost no private space. Neither of these stories mentions London by name, though the British metropolis is certainly one model among others for Ballard's composite urban dystopias. The ruined city of Ian McEwan's 'Two Fragments: March 199–' is explicitly identified as London, but it is an unsettling version of the capital transformed by some unspecified disaster. The Thames is drying up and rumours of poison in the water supply drive the city's more resourceful inhabitants to collect rainwater when they can. McEwan's two fragmentary narratives follow a father's efforts to care for his young daughter under such conditions and 'make a future' for them both whilst simultaneously indulging his desire to remember the lost city of the past.[37] A further example of this fictional impulse to imagine London's possible futures is Angela Carter's story, 'Elegy for a Freelance', which is narrated retrospectively by a female revolutionary and concerns events just prior to the fall of the capital. The London Carter's narrator describes is a decadent, whorish city and she recalls her fantasies of its destruction whilst walking the nocturnal streets: 'It hardly seemed possible the city could survive that summer [. . .] The night would part, like two halves of a dark shell, and spill explosions.'[38]

However, the narrator remains evasive about London's post-revolutionary present and her chronicle of the city's last days implies a lingering attachment to the past that she claims to repudiate.

Since the early 1990s, writers have increasingly explored London's hidden histories and spaces, or sought to trace its psychogeographical contours. The key figure in this respect is Iain Sinclair, whose restless, divagating, obsessive narratives seek both to tap the occluded energies of the metropolis and to chronicle its late twentieth-century decline. Sinclair is usually thought of as a novelist, but his prose texts have always been difficult to categorize, combining fictional and non-fictional elements in narratives that are often highly episodic or structurally fragmented. Two books in particular can be regarded as contributing to the tradition of London stories: *Downriver* (1991) and *Slow Chocolate Autopsy* (1997), on which he collaborated with the graphic artist Dave McKean. The subtitle of *Downriver* is 'A Narrative in Twelve Tales', indicating its close resemblance to a short story cycle, and Brian Baker comments that the text's disjunctive form 'resists totality'.[39] Each of the twelve 'tales' in *Downriver* responds more or less directly to the effects of Thatcherism and capitalist redevelopment upon the metropolis, especially its East End boroughs and riverside. For instance, in 'Horse Spittle (*The Eros of Maps*)' Sinclair's writer-narrator remarks caustically: 'It was an accepted natural law that any piece of ground overlooking a puddle of water – river, canal, sewer, or open-plan cesspit – would be a golden handshake for a speculative builder.'[40] 'Art of the State (*The Silvertown Memorial*)' presents a memorably grotesque sketch of Margaret Thatcher herself as 'the Widow'; and in 'The Isle of Doges (*Vat City plc*)' Canary Wharf figures as a shrine to both free-market economics and ritual human sacrifice. *Slow Chocolate Autopsy* also consists of twelve loosely connected tales, though it is even more generically diverse than *Downriver*, melding aspects of the novel, short story and graphic fiction. Many, but not all, of the stories feature the protagonist Norton, a 'jaded scribbler' whose motivating desire is 'to be free of London, all the trash of history'.[41] Norton is clearly Sinclair's alter-ego, and his wanderings through time and space take him from the Deptford pub in which Christopher Marlowe was stabbed to the ganglands of the Kray twins. What all of the stories in the book share, however, is Sinclair's or Norton's urgent drive to transcribe 'the trivia of the real'.[42]

If Sinclair is the contemporary laureate of the East End's mean streets, Hanif Kureishi might be said to perform a similar role for the leafy boulevards and bohemian quarters of West London, particularly in the stories that make up *Love in a Blue Time* (1997) and *Midnight All Day* (1999). The protagonists of

Kureishi's London stories are often middle-class men entering middle age, who struggle to reconcile themselves to the perceived loss of freedom that comes with marriage and parental responsibilities. In 'In a Blue Time', Roy, a producer of music videos and commercials, is afflicted with sensations of 'vertigo' at the thought of his impending fatherhood and clings to 'the delinquent dream of his adolescence', a dream that is closely linked to the city's status as a place of pleasure and desire.[43] Indeed, in another story, 'Nightlight', London is imagined as a libidinous space of free love and anonymous sex: 'A city of love vampires, turning from person to person, hunting the one who will make the difference' (p. 142). Desire is a fundamental theme in many of Kureishi's stories, almost a principle of life – 'he knew that without desire there was nothing' – but it is also a destructive force in the personal lives of his characters.[44] In a number of stories Kureishi departs from his predominant focus upon West London's affluent milieux to consider a more socially diverse and fractured urban community. For instance, in 'With Your Tongue down my Throat', which is largely set on a council estate, Nina views 'the honeyed London for the rich' with a mixture of longing and resentment from across a stark class divide.[45] Kureishi's most successful story, and one of the few that deals explicitly with issues of race and cultural difference, is 'My Son the Fanatic' from *Love in a Blue Time*, which centres on Parvez, a taxi driver, and his attempts to understand his teenage son's attraction to Islamic fundamentalism. To Ali, his father has compromised his identity as a Muslim by becoming 'too implicated in Western civilisation', whereas the liberal and irreligious Parvez has 'to check that they were still in London' as he listens to his son talk (pp. 125, 126). For Parvez, London embodies a postcolonial dream of freedom and opportunity, one that no longer seems viable to a younger generation of the city's British Asian communities.

Although it has long been overshadowed by the London novel, the London short story has evolved over more than a century and half into a fugitive but tenacious tradition of its own, as this chapter has shown. It can also be regarded as a significant strand within the larger history of the English short story as a literary form, not least because so many important practitioners of the short story – from Poe and Stevenson to Mansfield and Bowen – have written stories of London. Moreover, this is a living tradition: London continues to generate fascinating stories of itself in the first decades of the twenty-first century, often by writers who are also novelists. In Michael Moorcock's *London Bone* (2001), the city's layered histories are excavated in a manner that combines nostalgia with scepticism and satire; and in the short fiction of Will Self London is a seemingly inexhaustible source of all that is grotesque, bizarre and compelling about the human condition. One of the most recent stories of London is Zadie Smith's *The Embassy of Cambodia* (2013), which explores migrant experience, modern slavery and the problem of human suffering in a uniquely deft and light-handed manner. The title of Smith's story derives from an urban improbability: the Cambodian Embassy happens to be located in a suburban villa in Willesden, north London. Like all the best stories of London, then, *The Embassy of Cambodia* takes as its premise the city's potential for surprise and the unexpected, whilst also foregrounding its capacity to bring together the cosmopolitan and the stubbornly local within the same shifting frame.

Notes

1. Ian Watt, *The Rise of the Novel: Studies in Defoe, Richardson and Fielding* (London: Chatto & Windus, 1957), pp. 184–7.
2. Ken Worpole, 'Mother to Legend (or Going Underground): The London Novel', in *Peripheral Visions: Images of Nationhood in Contemporary British Fiction*, ed. Ian A. Bell (Cardiff: University of Wales Press, 1995), p. 182.
3. Roy Porter, *London: A Social History* (London: Hamish Hamilton, 1994), p. 226.
4. Ford Madox Ford, *The Soul of London* (1905; London: J. M. Dent, 1995), p. 15.
5. *Ibid.*, p. 11.
6. Harold Orel, *The Victorian Short Story: Development and Triumph of a Literary Genre* (Cambridge University Press, 1986), pp. 186–7.
7. *Ibid.*, p. 184.
8. Trefor Thomas, 'G. W. M. Reynolds's *The Mysteries of London*: An Introduction', in G. W. M. Reynolds, *The Mysteries of London*, ed. Trefor Thomas (Keele University Press, 1996), p. ix.
9. Edgar Allan Poe, *Selected Tales*, ed. David Van Leer (Oxford University Press, 1998), p. 84. Subsequent page references are given in parentheses in the text.
10. Walter Benjamin, *The Writer of Modern Life: Essays on Charles Baudelaire*, ed. Michael W. Jennings, trans., Howard Eiland *et al.* (Cambridge, MA: The Belknap Press, 2006), p. 79.
11. See Deborah A. Thomas, *Dickens and the Short Story* (London: Batsford, 1982).
12. Charles Dickens, *Sketches by Boz*, ed. Dennis Walder (1839; London: Penguin, 1995), p. 98. Subsequent page references are given in parentheses in the text.
13. Jeremy Tambling, *Going Astray: Dickens and London* (London: Pearson, 2009), p. 39.
14. Charles Dickens, *The Uncommercial Traveller* (1861; London: Mandarin, 1991), p. 170. Subsequent page references are given in parentheses in the text.

15. Robert Louis Stevenson, *Dr Jekyll and Mr Hyde and Other Stories*, ed. Jenni Calder (Harmondsworth: Penguin, 1979), p. 48. Subsequent page references are given in parentheses in the text.
16. Wilkie Collins, *Mad Monkton and Other Stories*, ed. Norman Page (Oxford University Press, 1994), p. 129.
17. Arthur Conan Doyle, *'The Adventures of Sherlock Holmes' and 'The Memoirs of Sherlock Holmes'*, ed. Ed Glinert (1892/1894; London: Penguin, 2001), p. 27. All quotations are from this edition, with subsequent page references given in parentheses in the text.
18. Raymond Williams, *The Country and the City* (London: Chatto & Windus, 1973), p. 227.
19. Georg Simmel, 'The Metropolis and Mental Life', in *The Blackwell City Reader*, ed. Gary Bridge and Sophie Watson (Oxford: Blackwell, 2002), p. 12.
20. Franco Moretti, *Atlas of the European Novel 1800–1900* (London: Verso, 1998), p. 134.
21. Stephen Inwood, *A History of London* (Basingstoke: Macmillan, 1998), p. 501.
22. George Gissing, *The Day of Silence and Other Stories*, ed. Pierre Coustillas (London: J. M. Dent, 1993), p. 26.
23. Israel Zangwill, *Children of the Ghetto: A Study of a Peculiar People* (1892; Black Apollo Press, 2004), p. 13.
24. Arthur Morrison, *Tales of Mean Streets* (1894; Chicago: Academy Publishers, 1997), p. 13.
25. Adrian Hunter, 'Arthur Morrison and the Tyranny of Sentimental Charity', *English Literature in Transition, 1880–1920*, 56 (2013), 3, pp. 292–312 (p. 294).
26. Malcolm Bradbury, 'London 1890–1920', in *Modernism 1890–1930*, ed. Malcolm Bradbury and James Macfarlane (Harmondsworth: Penguin, 1991), p. 172.
27. Virginia Woolf, *A Haunted House: The Complete Shorter Fiction*, ed. Susan Dick (London: Vintage, 2003), p. 78. Subsequent page references are given in parentheses in the text.
28. Dominic Head, *The Modernist Short Story: A Study in Theory and Practice* (Cambridge University Press, 1992), p. 99.
29. Katherine Mansfield, *The Collected Stories* (Harmondsworth: Penguin, 1981), p. 127. Subsequent page references are given in parentheses in the text.
30. Andrew Bennett, *Katherine Mansfield* (Tavistock: Northcote House, 2004), p. 33.
31. Elizabeth Bowen, *People, Places, Things: Essays*, ed. Allan Hepburn (Edinburgh University Press, 2008), pp. 314, 315.
32. Elizabeth Bowen, *Collected Stories* (London: Vintage, 1999), p. 609. Subsequent page references are given in parentheses in the text.
33. Julian Wolfreys, *Writing London: Volume 2: Materiality, Memory, Spectrality* (Basingstoke: Palgrave Macmillan, 2004), p. 59.

34. John Clement Ball, 'Immigration and Postwar London Literature', in Lawrence Manley, ed., *The Cambridge Companion to the Literature of London* (Cambridge University Press, 2011), p. 223.
35. Sam Selvon, *Ways of Sunlight* (1957; London: Longman, 1979), p. 146.
36. J. G. Ballard, *The Complete Short Stories* (London: Flamingo, 2001), p. 33.
37. Ian McEwan, *In Between the Sheets* (1978; London: Vintage, 1997), p. 50.
38. Angela Carter, *Fireworks* (1974; London: Virago, 1988), p. 105.
39. Brian Baker, *Iain Sinclair* (Manchester University Press, 2007), p. 85.
40. Iain Sinclair, *Downriver (Or, The Vessels of Wrath): A Narrative in Twelve Tales* (London: Paladin, 1991), p. 76.
41. Iain Sinclair with Dave McKean, *Slow Chocolate Autopsy: Incidents from the Notorious Career of Norton, Prisoner of London* (London: Phoenix, 1997), pp. 6, 10.
42. *Ibid.*, p. 54.
43. Hanif Kureishi, *Love in a Blue Time* (London: Faber & Faber, 1997), pp. 13, 38.
44. Hanif Kureishi, *Midnight All Day* (London: Faber & Faber, 1999), p. 204.
45. Kureishi, *Love in a Blue Time*, p. 72.

17

Gender and Genre: Short Fiction, Feminism and Female Experience

SABINE COELSCH-FOISNER

When the Canadian writer Alice Munro was awarded the Nobel Prize in 2013, the jury's express appraisal of a woman short story writer brought to wider public attention both the vitality of the genre at the turn of the millennium and the outstanding tradition of prize-winning women practitioners of the art: Nadine Gordimer, Doris Lessing and Alice Munro are all Nobel Prize winners; A. S. Byatt, Margaret Atwood and Gordimer have each won the Booker Prize. Their work suggests deeper ties between female experience and short fiction. As for the post-Second World War era, which forms the historical focus of this chapter, these ties need to be explored in terms of the short story's modernist legacy, its material conditions and affinities with second-wave feminism, as well as its connection with postmodern ethics and aesthetics. The central topics for this discussion are: the concern with continuities and discontinuities in the histories of individuals, cultures and nations; the probing into power structures; and the interest in alternative identities, lifestyles and modes of expression.

These issues will be brought together in this chapter, which shows how the short story has answered and shaped a feminine consciousness both within and beyond the feminist frameworks of the 1970s and 1980s. While feminism has provided groundbreaking ideas for the study of women's writing, its political agendas were often met with reservations by the writers themselves, who feared essentialist traps and new forms of discrimination. Significantly, Nadine Gordimer, who approved of the modernist ideal of the 'androgynous' writer, objected to being shortlisted for the 1998 Orange Prize on the grounds of its recognition of women writers only.

This chapter concentrates on women short story writers who came to maturity in the decades after the Second World War: Jean Rhys (Ella Williams, 1890–1979), Elizabeth Coles Taylor (1912–1975), Doris

Lessing (1919–2013), Nadine Gordimer (1923–2014), Alice Munro (1931–), Fay Weldon (1931–), A. S. Byatt (1936–), Margaret Atwood (1939–), Angela Carter (1940–92) and Marina Warner (1946–). Coming from different cultural backgrounds and witnessing the watersheds in European and colonial history from different corners in the world, theirs were divided feelings of alienation and submission, empathy, rage and revolt. Although the overall work of these writers traverses most of the twentieth century, they are far from forming a coherent generation. Rhys, Taylor, Lessing and Gordimer form the older group. Their early publishing careers still overlap with the modernist pioneers of the genre. Rhys was born only two years after Katherine Mansfield, but published her first volume, *The Left Bank and Other Stories* (1927), at a time when Mansfield's reputation was already established with *In a German Pension* (1911), *Bliss and Other Stories* (1920) and *The Garden-Party* (1922). By contrast, Taylor's and Lessing's first volumes were published in the 1950s, Gordimer's *Face to Face* in 1949; and while Rhys and Taylor died in the 1970s, Lessing and Gordimer continued writing short fiction for almost four more decades, their later careers overlapping with those of Munro, Weldon, Byatt, Atwood and Carter.

Despite such different publishing histories, these writers share the consciousness of their age, or to use Gordimer's phrase were 'selected' by it, and brought to the short story pungent insights into twentieth-century history, a profound humanitarian interest, bold wit and social criticism, as well as violent transgressions and liberating fantasies.[1]

The modernist emphasis on the writer's autonomy, which coincided with the cause of women's liberation and encouraged technical experiment, forms a major legacy of twentieth-century short fiction. Apart from Virginia Woolf (1882–1941) and Katherine Mansfield (1888–1923), most of the short story writers of the early decades died in the 1970s: Elizabeth Bowen in 1973, Frances Bellerby and Elizabeth Taylor in 1975, Sylvia Townsend Warner in 1978, Jean Rhys in 1979. In these years, there was a resurgence of feminist questions, fuelled by the profound changes of British society after the Second World War, notably the institution of the welfare state and women's changing roles in society, public debates about sexuality, the reorganisation of universities, constitutional independence of the colonies, and the rise of youth, popular, immigrant and working-class cultures. While Woolf's feminism grew out of elitist notions about art being the proper environment for the artist, whose main task was to fulfil his or her vocation (characteristically reflected in the *Künstlerroman*), 1970s feminism gained momentum from the social aims of the post-Second World War period and its democratic understanding of culture as the 'whole way of life'. Given women's improved access to higher education, writing became increasingly linked with institutions of learning, which were now considered the proper environment for the writer: Byatt, Warner, Weldon and Lessing were/are academics; Munro worked as a librarian and ran a bookshop; so did Taylor; Atwood is a leading member of many literary networks; Gordimer was awarded fifteen honorary degrees and, like Munro, lectured widely.

Ideologically rooted in centre-margin debates, second-wave feminism became discursively connected with minority issues, proclaiming at the core of its programme subversion and protest, polyphony and heteroglossia, Menippean satire and the recovery of laughter and the abject. A decisive element was its radical politics of the body, whose biological difference was connected with modes of thinking and writing (*écriture féminine*). Second-wave feminism was overtly political and rebellious, anxious to dismantle (patriarchal) power structures, to combat discrimination and revise canons by 'writing back'.

These features are variously prominent in the short fiction explored here; but such features also link the short story with other modes of writing: Carol Ann Duffy's confessional story poems and dramatized fairy tales; Jenny Joseph's satirical fables in verse; Etel Adnan's cosmic-philosophical aphorisms; Warner's mythological criticism; Gordimer's anti-apartheid lectures; and Atwood's ecocritical essays. Arguably, most women discussed in this chapter have gained more attention for their novels and were already established writers when their short story collections appeared with major publishers like Vintage, Penguin, Faber and Bloomsbury. Still, despite the postmodern predilection for the (long) novel, short fiction offered women writers new opportunities for exploring hitherto repressed areas of experience, such as violence, wickedness, sexuality and transgender, magic and strangeness. (This capacity was notable in the 1960s, a decade when short story critics deplored the genre's low esteem.) In this respect, the female intersects with the colonial, as Rhys, Lessing, Gordimer, Munro and Atwood suggest in some of postmodernity's most disturbingly germane visions of humanity.

The 'double process' which Gordimer perceives as the crux of writing, the 'excessive preoccupation and identification with the lives of others, and at the same time a monstrous detachment' ('Introduction', p. 4), is apt to circumscribe the postcolonial imagination. Rhys was born in the West Indies and, at the age of sixteen, left Dominica. She spent the years after the First World War in Paris and after 1928 in England, never abandoning her emotional ties with the Caribbean. Lessing was born in Persia, spent her childhood in Southern Rhodesia (now Zimbabwe), and in 1949 moved to London, where she started publishing. For both writers, the politics of gender are inseparable from the politics of race, and their multi-cultural backgrounds alerted them to social pressures, whilst filling them with an insurmountable sense of exile: suffering alienation in England, they, perhaps more tragically, felt severed from their non-European roots. Rhys's 'I Used to Live Here Once' (1976) conveys a Blakean feeling of lost innocence, as she revisits her former home in Dominica. Each tree evokes happy memories, but the children playing in the garden flee from the intruder: 'That was the first time she knew.'[2] Lessing deplores her limited understanding as a white writer, who can merely re-tell 'a story that you are told by others' about Africa's loss of dignity, self-respect and tolerance under the impact of colonization.[3] Her authorial voice repeatedly reminds the reader of the white settlers' exclusion from the 'ancient wisdom of leaf and soil and season' ('No Witchcraft for Sale', 1951).[4]

For both Rhys and Lessing, traditional forms of fiction were inadequate to encompass their divided lives. The single, coherent voice becomes double or multiple, split or de-centred, a prime example being Lessing's fractured diary *The Golden Notebook* (1962), which reflects a woman writer's crisis over her socially compartmentalized roles as woman, lover, writer and political activist. She had already challenged some of the conventions of realism in her African stories, collected in *This Was the Old Chief's Country* (1951) and *The Sun Between Their Feet (African Stories*, 1964), which bear a unique testimony to the mind's struggle to contain the injustices that assault it.

What Africa had taught Lessing was, above all, 'the atrophy of the imagination that prevents us from seeing ourselves in every creature that breathes under the sun', and the awareness that 'man is a small creature, among other creatures, in a large landscape'.[5] Calling for responsibility towards Africa's tribal life threatened by technological progress, these stories convey a deeply humanitarian message: 'we have to lose the arrogance that is the white man's burden, to stop feeling superior, and this is only just beginning to happen now' (p. 10).

'No Witchcraft for Sale' tells the story of the moving relationship between Teddy, a white child, and the native cook, Gideon. When a tree-snake spits in the boy's eyes, Gideon saves him from blindness with a herb, but refuses to share his wisdom with a group of scientists pressing around him 'like a circle of yelping dogs' (p. 41) and, instead, leads them astray in the bush. Told from the white observer's perspective, Lessing's voice criticizes the colonials' complacency and their tacit acceptance of social inequality. In 'Little Tembi' (1951), Jane McCluster runs a clinic on her husband's farm and nurses a native baby, little Tembi, back to health. When she has children of her own, the social rift widens and little Tembi begins to vie for her attention by stealing. 'Little Tembi' enshrines the impenetrable secrets of Africa, its stark presence and haunting mystery for the non-indigenous population. The scene where Tembi, convicted of theft, returns to the village and secretly watches Jane, who desperately appeals to his moral sense, strikes a note of tragic failure. Empathy is all Lessing can hold against the deep-seated racial prejudice and the blatant misunderstandings (on either side), for love and fear simply co-exist in this divided country. Lessing was thirty when she left South Africa. Its impact on her consciousness was informed by a young woman's concern with marriage, raising a family and work.

Like Lessing, Nadine Gordimer remembers how her 'femaleness' provided a 'form of communion' with the African people ('Introduction', p. 3). Given the individual's exposure to the unknown, such moments of understanding carry epiphanic weight. When attacked by a black man, a white girl undergoes absolute horror. After the police investigation, however, she wonders why she had not left her handbag to the man. This brings into sudden relief the morally ambivalent subtext of the title: 'Is There Nowhere Else Where We Can Meet?' (1951). Drawing on her own experience, Gordimer never allows the narrator to control a scene, but relies on the revelatory force of small incidents. Again, empathy is a prevalent feeling, but characters are prone to err, since they extrapolate from their own situation. By balancing or shifting perspectives, the narrator strips away their convictions and unveils the ironic limitations of Western knowledge and, more universally, of human understanding. In 'The Soft Voice of the Serpent' (1951), the young man who recovers his health after losing a leg and is wheeled into the garden by his wife all at once feels in communion with a one-legged locust: 'he knew exactly what the creature felt. Of course he knew that feeling! That absolute certainty that the leg was there [...] He *knew* ... '.[6] However, the invalid locust is not trapped in immobility like him, but spreads its wings and flies away. In 'The African Magician' (first published in *The New Yorker*, 1961) a moment's gesture suffices to expose the insurmountable clash of religious, economic and social attitudes of cultures violently forced into contact. Annoyed by the badly performed tricks of an African magician, the white spectators demand a demonstration of African magic. Reluctantly, the magician calls out a young woman from the audience and leaves the onlookers baffled when her body bends to his commands.

Born near Johannesburg of Jewish descent, Gordimer lived all her life in South Africa and became one of the foremost anti-apartheid writers and activists, helping Mandela edit his famous speech 'I Am Prepared To Die' during his trial in 1964. She joined the African National Congress and became a member of South Africa's Anti-Censorship Action Group, opposing all forms of discrimination and state control of information. Gordimer dedicated her entire life to the cause of equal rights, and in her stories moves beyond personal experience: all of humanity is potentially caught in a mesh of betrayal and persecution, like Mr Van As, the cartage contractor in 'The Last Kiss' (1960), who rises to fortune when gold is discovered in a coal-mining village. Eventually he falls into disrepute and is even accused of kissing a young girl on a train. The closing image of a bleeding statue exquisitely captures Gordimer's warm humanity and reaches beyond its immediate political significance to convey an epic understanding of man's vulnerability and the transitoriness of social values: 'It was as if the town's only statue, a shabby thing of an obscure general on a horse, standing in a dusty park and scrawled over by urchins, were to have been observed, bleeding' (p. 188). Such sympathy lies at the heart of the short story, which Gordimer defines as 'a concept that the writer can "hold", fully realized, in his imagination, at one time.' ('Introduction', p. 7).

While Gordimer's stories trace the changing attitudes of South African society (reflected in her changing use of 'African', 'native', 'black', in the creation of black narrators in the 1980s and 1990s, and in an 'increasing sophistication'), the central impression of all Rhys's work is distance, both geographical and psychological.[7] Culturally displaced, she is at once haunted by memories of the West Indies and acutely sensitive to women's subordination. Written between the 1920s and the 1970s and published in four volumes with a forty-year break – *Left Bank and Other Stories* (1927), *Tigers Are Better-Looking* (1968), *Sleep it Off Lady* (1976), *Let Them Call It Jazz* (1995) – Rhys's stories evince a psychobiographical consciousness torn between the postcolonial and the cosmopolitan. Her Caribbean memories convey intense moments of joy, like the 'warm, velvety, sweet-smelling night' she remembers in 'Mixing Cocktails' (1927) (p. 38). Rife with sense-impressions vividly captured in an imagist diary style, her early stories differ in tone from her late work, where spontaneity collides with official history. In 'Heat' (1976), the public British account of the outbreak of the Mont Pelée volcano contrasts with her own memory of natives superstitiously blaming the island's wicked mores for the catastrophe.

Rhys's voice characteristically oscillates between observer and participant perspectives, foregrounding female characters who are exposed to raw brutality and confirm her awareness that 'women have been rather badly treated'.[8] Through these destitute and abandoned women, who often appear irrationally narcissistic, she traces her own experience from innocent girlhood and adolescence to adult life and late middle age. Superbly detached in tone, her portraits of social outcasts point the way from modernist estrangement (in the manner of Mansfield's marginalized heroines) to postmodern self-alienation. Showing little zest for life, Rhys's heroines combine a Byronic sense of exile with futile wandering. Their aim is survival rather than protest, as she explained: 'They're always standing by the river but they never jump' (Cantwell, p. 26). 'Good-bye Marcus, Good-bye Rose' (1976) deals with Captain Cardew's passes at twelve-year old Phoebe. Selina Davis, the West Indian immigrant from 'Let Them Call It Jazz' (1968), and Liliane in 'The Whistling Bird' (1987) suffer from the hardships encountered in a hostile culture, and in 'Rapunzel, Rapunzel' (1976), set in a convalescent home, a men's barber cuts off an elderly patient's silver hair to gain profit. Like many of Rhys's abused women, she dies. Her death is barely noticed.

In this climate of ruthless patriarchal-capitalist exploitation, Rhys's heroines develop an admirable indifference. Aged over seventy, Miss Verney in 'Sleep it Off Lady' (1976) is on the brink of despair about a dilapidated shed, but quickly recovers her emotional poise: 'But crying relieved her and she soon felt quite cheerful again. It was ridiculous to brood, she told herself' (p. 377). She dies after a fall, because her cries are ignored by passers-by, and a neighbouring girl simply tells her to 'sleep it off', thinking she is drunk. In a way reminiscent of Stevie Smith's poem 'Not Waving but Drowning', Rhys's heroine acquires an almost tragic posture as she accepts her destiny – without winning the reader's sympathies. Autobiographical motivation links these postcolonial voices with Elizabeth Taylor and Alice Munro. Yet, where Rhys identifies with her characters, Taylor creates personae, whose social masks she strips off with quick touches, and Munro stretches the mimetic by confronting her lifelike characters with lust and crime.

Taylor's four collections – *Hester Lilly and Other Stories* (1954), *The Blush and Other Stories* (1958), *A Dedicated Man and Other Stories* (1965) and *The Devastating Boys* (1972) – bridge the post-war ideology of domesticity and the subversive ethos of the 1970s and 1980s. Concentrating on human relationships and small incidents from everyday life, her stories comply with conventions of social-psychological fiction and with post-war notions of women's writing. As a result, her unpretentious, miniature mode was either favourably compared with Jane Austen (she, too, was educated at the Abbey School in Reading) or, like many mid-twentieth-century women's voices, criticized as genteel and parochial.

However, within the narrow compass of family relations, friends and children, recalling the minimal plots of Sylvia Townsend Warner's stories, Taylor delights in disrupting social patterns and, with utmost economy, exposes devastating moments in a character's life, carefully balancing compassion and wit. The tenor of her stories is self-deceit and a 'yearning disappointment' ('The Blush', 1958), as in 'Perhaps a Family Failing' (1958), where Beryl's romance is ruined during a calamitous wedding night.[9] From her first to her last stories, written when Taylor was dying from cancer, the sexes occupy different spheres: men are commonly absent or about to disappear; women are almost uniformly unhappy, whatever their social background. The narrator tends to escape from self through dialogue, focalization and shifts of perspective, *showing* women in their discontent: 'I am rather like a ghost, unobserved; and *they* are the real ones at that moment.'[10]

Taylor captures the essence of a situation through minutely observed gestures and details that function as objective correlatives in conspicuously symbolic settings: a trapped butterfly; Mrs Allen's fat spaniel; a dead wasp that was 'fantastic and frightening, like a Japanese mask'; or the 'boring little garden [...] full of colourless hydrangeas and snails and tongue ferns'.[11] With such deft expressionistic 'strokes of reality, highlights, dashes of colour', Taylor, who meant to become a painter, 'sets her scenes', conveying what she admired most in Virginia Woolf: 'the vividness and importance of every minute, the significance of every action'.[12]

Taylor's imagist method affords the reader acute insights into human psychology. In 'Better Not' (first published in *The Adelphi*, 1944), Helen's despair over her husband's departure looms in the allusive title, and a few telegram-like remarks suffice to reveal her profound grief: 'Another day gone. A sense of achievement in this. Going cheerfully towards the grave'.[13] Occasionally, such subdued discomfort breaks forth in violent action, as when Dosie in 'Oasis of Gaiety' (first published in *The New Yorker*, 1951), bored with her mother's fashionable society, mischievously pushes the latter's favourite garden gnome into the pond. In genuinely existentialist scenarios, Taylor's female protagonists prove life's victims rather than agents, undergoing crises without gaining self-awareness. As in Rhys, the sense of an uncaring god is strong, whilst the piercing dramatic ironies recall Mansfield's gift for disclosing the unsaid.

Indebted to modernist technique, Taylor expanded the mode of manners through multiple perspectives and a wider class-range, often compromising irreconcilable attitudes, as in 'The Blush' (in *Dangerous Calm*): facing up to being childless, Mrs Allen, nonetheless depreciates her housekeeper's pregnancy: 'Poor woman, she thought again and again with bitter animosity' (p. 58). A sudden insight crushes her pretence, since her husband obviously plays a key role in this domestic disaster. These are minor events but not minor issues.

Although Taylor's characters fail to address social ills, their persistent malaise harbours a great potential for subversion, and her voice's peculiar mixture of cruelty and sympathy presses home a greater need for understanding. Such is the feminist legacy of Taylor's stories: alienation is an issue of gender inequality rather than of social milieu. As this leads her to question the complicity of realist fiction with the social order, scepticism and the vituperative power of language are, more fundamentally, Taylor's legacy to the postmodern feminist short story.

Equally reticent and concerned with character and setting, Munro pushes psychological realism into abject realms of madness, guilt and shame. Born in 1931 in Wingham, southwestern Ontario, she started writing in her teens and, from the beginning of the 1950s, published stories in various magazines. Like Taylor, Munro captures epiphanic incidents that raise grave existential questions, but insists less on women's disappointments. Her only novel, *Lives of Girls and Women* (1971), is a *Bildungsroman* composed of interlinking stories about Del Jordan's growth as a writer. It is typical of her *oeuvre* in tracing the moral pressures and incompatible life ambitions faced by young girls on the threshold of adolescence.

'Walker Brothers Cowboy' (1968) is told by a girl who accompanies her father, 'a peddler knocking at backwoods kitchens', on his visits to farms and learns about a former mistress of his.[14] In 'Wild Swans' from *The Beggar Maid* (first published in 1978 under the title *Who Do You Think You Are?*), the obsessive warnings of Rose's stepmother, Flo, will not save young Rose. On her first train journey to Toronto, she is seduced by a United Church minister and responds to the 'stranger's hand' between her thighs. In a vortex of metaphors, Munro links the flying landscape to the girl's erotic sensations: 'Invasion, and welcome, and sunlight flashing far and wide on the lake water; miles of bare orchards stirring round Burlington' (p. 122).

Munro's impressionistic technique conveys a superb sense of authenticity. Scrutinizing her characters with unabashed honesty, she discloses the tension between their outer composure and the hushed-up failures typical of small-town respectability. Margaret Atwood succinctly characterizes Munro's 'Sowesto': 'an area of considerable interest, but also of considerable psychic murkishness and oddity'.[15] In the title story of Munro's first collection, *Dance of the Happy Shades* (1968), the girl-narrator remembers her annual piano recital at the home of Miss Marsalles, her spinsterish music teacher, when a group of handicapped children – 'little – little idiots for that's what they are' (p. 24) – join in the performance. Among them is a girl who exhibits real talent. The story's revelation concerns less her ability than the audience's feeling of it being 'out of place', and Miss Marsalles's admirable generosity in the midst of such prejudice.

Constructing characters from multiple angles is an outstanding merit of Munro's storytelling. Set in the nineteenth century, 'A Wilderness Station' (1994) traces Annie McKillop's life-journey from an orphanage via an arranged marriage to prison and, finally, to a respectable household as a seamstress. Annie's biography unfolds like a crime story told in interlinking letters that reveal different aspects of a murder. When Annie's husband, Simon, is killed by his brother, George, she escapes to Walley gaol and is accepted on grounds of insanity for falsely confessing to the murder herself. By fracturing her story, Munro allows superstitions and nightmares to control her characters' actions, whilst calling into doubt the official truths of law and medicine. In different I-narratives, the reader is offered different accounts, fraught with male prejudice and degeneration hypotheses about the female body, its clinical propensity to hysteria and its amenability to economic and sexual exploitation. Eventually, Annie is given a voice in two letters to her former female companion in the orphanage, in which she reveals her down-to-earth practicality and resilience, embodying what Atwood considers to be the central symbol for Canada: survival.

Munro's regionalism avoids nostalgia as it foregrounds the terrors and generational dilemmas of small-town life, perpetuating a vital tradition in women's writing from the eighteenth century to the present: 'the part of the country where I come from is absolutely Gothic'.[16] The oppressor is not uniformly male: often an archetypal gothic mother suppresses female experience, like Mrs Netterfield in 'Dear Life' (2012), a previous owner who haunts Munro's family home. The incident suggests how, historically, the gothic keeps alive the past while exploiting the fallibility of memories, and how, psychologically, it offers a safety valve for fears and suffered wrongs. Its inherent subversions, its interest in the forbidden, macabre and preternatural, and its focus on domestic horror and invasions have secured the gothic a privileged role in the feminine imagination, which filtered into the short story through Elizabeth Bowen's wartime collections *Look at All Those Roses* (1941) and *The Demon Lover* (1945), with their haunted locales and symbolic encounters between a demolished past and a dismal present. Especially with the advent of second-wave feminism and its protest against male dominance, women's incarcerated lives were readily perceived as proto-gothic scenarios. Moreover, the fragmentary aesthetic of the gothic, its elusiveness and loose ends, are conducive to the brevity of the genre, as early practitioners such as Edgar Allan Poe and Henry James have shown. Particularly sensitive to life's gaps and stoppages, late-twentieth-century women's short fiction has championed the postmodern gothic revival, questioning power hierarchies and dismantling publicly constructed identities in favour of more fluid selves. Fay Weldon, Angela Carter and Jeanette Winterson have all reclaimed repressed desires, and, by eroding biological and cultural boundaries, destabilized Western concepts of identity.

Weldon is among the most prolific and committed feminist writers of the post-war era. In over thirty novels, filmscripts, plays, librettos and short stories, she traces women's changing roles in the twentieth century from domestic to increasingly wider social responsibilities. Her grasp of topical issues hits the nerve of the age – ranging from consumerism to political corruption, from medical ethics and nuclear war to lifestyle and the wellness-boom (*The Spa Decameron*, 2007). Weldon publicly denounces the worldwide discrimination against women as 'appalling'.[17] Waging war on the constraints imposed on them in patriarchal society, she also depicts women as self-pitying, envious and vicious, and accuses them of collusion in their subjugation. Relationships commonly lack emotional commitment, and marital breakdown constitutes a central interest in her stories from *Watching Me, Watching You* (1981) to *Nothing to Wear & Nothing to Hide* (2002). Weldon's shrewd exposure of flawed patterns of behaviour, customs and family rituals serves the diagnosis of social ills rather than any particular policy: 'I put things too strongly, or over the top or Gothic or a little more to the bizarre. But they're usually only normal situations taken to an extreme so that the reader has to react.'[18] Despite postmodern digressions and addenda, Weldon's work shows a tendency towards resolution, ensured by her commenting and counselling narrators: 'It never does to ask men what the matter is because they either refuse to say or don't know, or offer the wrong answer.'[19] In moral fables, parables and cautionary tales, she sees her characters through everyday crises, giving practical advice like a coach, while also hushing up their little lies and ruses instead of pointing a moral finger at them. In 'Who

Goes Where? A Christmas Tale', Adrienne behaves like a spoilt child, but eventually learns to accept her husband's children by his previous marriage. It is this note of shared experience, coupled with an immense readiness to understand even mean and irrational behaviour, that accounts for Weldon's extraordinary success.

Weldon's call for 'invention' circumscribes a prevalent current in post-modern women's fiction: A. S. Byatt, Marina Warner, Angela Carter and Margaret Atwood all portray empowered heroines who shed their roles as victims and perform their dark and demonic natures by reclaiming non-mimetic modes. This has brought to women's fiction new female casts embodying the abject: old hags, freaks and vampires, she-devils, sirens and beasts of prey. Emma Tennant's work features witches (*Wild Nights*, 1979); Susan Hill portrays ghosts who impinge on the living (*The Woman in Black*, 1983; *The Mist in the Mirror*, 1992); and Carter's most celebrated stories involve shape-shifters and werewolves. More than any other writer in the gothic-subversive vein, Carter invents untrammelled fantasies about sex and power, charged with Menippean parody and exaggeration, and set either in the circus or in subterranean, secluded spaces inspired by the eerie topographies of (pre-)Romantic gothic.

Having translated *The Fairy Tales of Charles Perrault* (1977) and edited *The Virago Book of Fairy Tales* (London, 1990–2), Carter was intimately familiar with Western mythology, which she considered a 'vast repository of outmoded lies'.[20] Unlike early feminists, who blamed fairy tales for perpetuating these lies, she welcomed them as moulds for attacking hypocrisy and redressing those 'false universals' and 'consolatory nonsenses' of mythic versions of women.[21] Through carnival and paradox, Carter deconstructs familiar gender images and releases the spiteful Other from patriarchy's dungeons, attics and torture chambers. Symptomatically, her protagonists break the stigma attached to femininity and enact their (terrible) sexual power, thus deconstructing the symbolic in favour of the semiotic – the boundless, polyphonous potential of the pre-verbal imagination. The result is a blending of genre conventions – gothic, romance, opera, realism, pornography, adventure story – and a distinctive, 'highly wrought' prose, which Salman Rushdie considers more effective in the stories than in her novels.[22] Hyperbolic avalanches of attributes, associative word-chains and metamorphic play create atmospheres of sensuous delirium or abysmal danger, as this example attests: 'They will be like shadows, they will be like wraiths, grey members of a congregation of nightmare; hark!'[23]

Carter reclaims the night and, in typical double-voiced discourse, violates her readers' expectations. 'The Werewolf' and 'The Company of Wolves' (both 1979) are retellings of the story of Little Red Riding Hood, who in the former prospers after slashing off the wolf's paw and in the latter adopts the beast's carnivorous sexuality and 'sleeps in granny's bed, between the paws of the tender wolf' (p. 220). The title story of *The Bloody Chamber* (1979) is based on the fairy tale of Bluebeard – a favourite in feminist rewrites – and reshaped under the impression of Carter's reading of the Marquis de Sade.[24] It is told by a seventeen-year-old bride, who disobeys her husband's command not to enter a locked room in his castle. What she discovers is a torture chamber containing the embalmed remains of the Marquis's previous three wives. Stock gothic properties and intertextual allusions to prime scenarios of entrapment (Tennyson's 'The Lady of Shalott') and sexual violence (Browning's 'My Last Duchess') foreshadow her ineluctable fate, which is, however, prevented by maternal love. For such myriad subversions to resonate, Carter wanted her stories to be read as multiple allegories, 'on as many levels as you can comfortably cope with at the time'.[25]

Duplicity is a recurrent motif in Carter's fiction, underlying mistaken identities, role-switching and disguise, which in *Nothing Sacred* (1982) she describes as 'a relaxation from one's own personality and the discovery of maybe unsuspected new selves'.[26] This explains the feminist interest in metamorphosis, for which writers are indebted both to Ovid's epic and to a vivid tradition of fairy tales, a prime example being Marina Warner's seminal study *Fantastic Metamorphoses, Other Worlds: Ways of Telling the Self* (2002). In *Wonder Tales* (1994), bringing together fairy tales by seventeenth- and eighteenth-century women storytellers, in her novels and in her two collections of short stories, *Mermaids in the Basement* (1993) and *Murderers I Have Known and Other Stories* (2002), Warner's aim is to re-tell myths in terms of lived experience.

A. S. Byatt and Margaret Atwood share this practice of mythopoetic 'revisioning' (to use Adrienne Rich's term) or 'reformulating' (in Carter's words) and, by self-consciously referring to the act of storytelling, they defamiliarize the familiar. In her early novels, beginning with *The Game* (1967), Byatt draws on her struggle for an academic career in post-war Britain. Observing that 'women, once they got over the age of 45, began to be persecuted by groups of people', she became interested in the body as the locus of marginalization and (self-) loathing and, in an effort to 'accommodate the strange', turned to the short story.[27]

From her first collection, *Sugar and Other Stories* (1987), to *Little Black Book of Stories* (2003), Byatt presents women across cultures as victims of ageism. 'The Dried Witch' (1987) is an oriental story about a middle-aged peasant woman who becomes a jinx and cures people with magic potions. When a death occurs, she is found guilty and sentenced to death by drying in the sun. Her final stream of consciousness is a singular achievement in the art of storytelling, tracing the mind's separation from the scorched body: 'On the third day, she was two. Her mind stood outside herself, looking down on the shrivelling flesh, with its blues and umbers, on the cracked face, the snarling mouth, the bared, dry-bone teeth [...] The eddies of heat from the burning swirled out across the muddy ground and took her with them, away from the strapped and cracking thing, away.'[28]

In Byatt's stories, the carcass is a radical subversion of the body beautiful, normatively constructed as sexually attractive, fecund and maternal. Thus the anorectic art student in 'The Chinese Lobster' from *The Matisse Stories* (1993) recovers the social taboos of filth, stench, faeces and blood to counter the repressive iconography of female sexuality embodied by Matisse's nudes. Her bandaged body violates her instructor's gaze and carnivalizes capitalist politics of monitoring and modifying the body. In a similar effort, symbolizing the curse of 'The Lady of Shalott', Susannah in 'Medusa's Ankles' (1993) violently destroys the mirror in a hair-salon.

In non-mimetic or exotic environments, Byatt's heroines often experience the generosity of a lover (sometimes otherworldly). In 'A Stone Woman' (2003), the protagonist undergoes a metamorphosis into stone, but is redeemed by a sculptor through whom she finds freedom as a mythical stone troll. The title story of *The Djinn in the Nightingale's Eye: Five Fairy Stories* (1994) is a therapeutic fantasy about Dr Gillian Perholt, a middle-aged narratologist who opens a Turkish flask and through the love of a djinn recovers her self-image. Drawing on the pythonesses, abbesses and sibyls who 'revealed mysteries', Byatt's stories self-consciously reflect their role as vehicles for reconceiving female experience. In a feminist context, the aesthetic of telling and re-telling stories is a transformative and, therefore, innately political process – 'a kind of rather gleeful, slightly surreal constant twisting of the given so that it looks completely different and you're completely bewildered'.[29]

Margaret Atwood is among the most versatile and experimental twentieth-century authors, writing poetry, novels and short fiction, apart from being a distinguished critic and member of many literary institutions. Her earliest collection, *Dancing Girls* (1977), was followed by *Bluebeard's Egg* (1983), *Murder* in the Dark (1983) and *Wilderness Tips* (1991). In *Good Bones and Simple Murders* (1994), *Moral Disorder* (2006) and *Curious Pursuits: Occasional Writing 1970–2005* (2005), she combines the story with the prose poem and the essay.

Atwood draws together the most decisively innovative short story strands in the 1970s and 1980s: postmodernism, feminism and postcolonialism – in her case Canadian nationalism. As she argues: 'Canada shares with all of the New World ex-colonies, and with others such as Australia and New Zealand, the historically recent experience of a collision between a landscape and a language and social history not at first indigenous to it, with each side altering the other'.[30] This collision operates on different levels and connects major topics in her work, such as power hierarchies and double standards, ecological concerns, human rights and identities in conflict. Atwood dismantles established patterns of thought and behaviour, gender stereotypes, social organizations, as well as conventions of language and genre. Hers is a deep-seated distrust of fixities. 'But who gives it? And to whom is it given?' she asks in 'Giving Birth' from *Dancing Girls*, twisting the metaphor out of its meaning: 'Certainly it doesn't feel like giving, which implies a flow, a gentle handing over, no coercion. But there is scant gentleness here, it's too strenuous, the belly like a knotted fist, squeezing.'[31]

'Giving Birth' is symbolically charged with the womb's primordial darkness, the act of creation and the discrepancy between surfaces and invisible existences. The labour room, in particular, 'this dark place', is a prime locus of the feminine uncanny, where identity ceases and language gives way to screams, and where duality pervades – in the hallucinating mind, the division of bodies at birth and the double perspective of narrator and protagonist. Atwood typically destroys the illusion of the story as she addresses the reader and comments on its constructedness: 'Now she's having her nap and I am writing this story' (p. 227).

In *Good Bones and Simple Murders* (1994) metafiction is central: 'Simple Murder' is about putting together a murder story from motifs, evidence and explanations; 'Women's Novels' and 'Happy Endings' (both originally published in 1983) delineate structuralist permutations of marriage; and in 'There Was Once' (1992), the ingredients of a fairy tale are deconstructed in a storytelling situation, where the narrator and the listener totally reshape the given material, exposing its flawed ethnic and ethical undertones, until the story is fit for the here and now. Unexpected shifts and sharp repartee are hallmarks of Atwood's stories in which she explores situations that throw up crises – sexual betrayal ('Under Glass', 1977), disintegrating relationships

('The Grave of the Famous Poet', 1977), the breakdown of communication between men and women and the arrangements they make to stay together. In *Moral Disorder* (2006), Atwood employs third-person narration, whilst no longer disavowing connections with her own biography. 'Entities' is about Lillie, a concentration-camp survivor who falls victim to Alzheimer's, and 'My Last Duchess' deals with a high-school student decoding the meaning of Browning's classic. For Atwood, social relevance is the touchstone of the writer's art, with stories forming an interface between language and reality.

Feminine experience in the immediate post-war era was bound up with the disjuncture between woman as artist and the roles available to her. Spurred by the social exigencies of their historical condition, writers explored ways of actively confronting injustice and correcting patriarchal constructions of femininity and the female body. Death and suicide loom as large in their work as metamorphic fantasies of self-discovery and regeneration. Indebted to their modernist precursors for enlarging the short story's experiential range through daring technique, these writers carried further many of their concerns into a postmodern climate of subversion and invention, bringing to the short story intertextuality, self-referentiality and metafictional commentary. Caustic wit, irony and irreverent humour suggest a new sense of authority and social bonding. Even where writers do not subscribe to feminist politics, fairness and equal opportunities, minorities' rights, a respect for the Other, and the intrinsic worth of the individual are shared aims.

In these respects, the short story coincides with strategies and concerns in poetry and the novel, but the short form, while unsuited to containing a particular programme or worldview, renders more vividly experiences underlying these concerns – flashlights of despair and defeat, animosity and self-hatred, anger, power, joy and triumphant liberation. Given such intense, often celebratory, moments, women's short fiction after the Second World War recaptures earlier moments of unity – of experience rather than effect, and epiphany – adapting the disruptive aesthetics of the genre to a feminist ethics of self-assertion via duality and discord. With postmodern voices speaking *from* the grave, *from* the margin, *from* the site of the abject, *from* dark, otherworldly and magic realms, *from* the bloody chamber and the cultural Other, rather than *about* them, the modernist short story – it seems – has come full circle, ready for the first answers to Virginia Woolf's question 'What is a woman?' By shifting the focus from the psychology of harm to its socio-historical and ethical-ontological implications, these voices appear to straddle yet another boundary, evincing a feminine consciousness on the brink of the post-postmodern.

Notes

1. Nadine Gordimer, 'Introduction' to *Selected Stories* (1975; London: Bloomsbury, 2000), pp. 1–7 (p. 7). All quotations from Gordimer's stories are from this edition, with subsequent page references given in parentheses in the text.
2. Jean Rhys, 'I Used to Live Here Once', in *The Collected Short Stories* (New York and London: Norton, 1987), pp. 387–8 (p. 388). All quotations from Rhys's stories are from this edition, with subsequent page references given in parentheses in the text.
3. Doris Lessing, 'Preface for the 1973 Collection', in *Collected African Stories, Volume I: This Was the Old Chief's Country* (London: Flamingo, 2003), pp. 10–11 (p. 11).
4. Doris Lessing, *This Was The Old Chief's Country*, pp. 35–42 (p. 38).
5. *This Was the Old Chief's Country*, p. 8. Subsequent page references are given in parentheses in the text.
6. *Selected Stories*, pp. 13–18; p. 16.
7. Dominic Head, *Nadine Gordimer* (Cambridge University Press, 1994), pp. 161–81 (pp. 173–4; 181).
8. Mary Cantwell, 'A Conversation with Jean Rhys', in *Critical Perspectives on Jean Rhys*, ed. Pierrette M. Frickey (Washington, DC: Three Continents Press, 1990), pp. 21–34 (p. 25).
9. *Dangerous Calm: The Selected Stories of Elizabeth Taylor*, ed. Lynn Knight (London: Virago, 1995; 2011), pp. 53–61 (p. 61).
10. Elizabeth Taylor, 'Setting a Scene', first published in the *Cornhill Magazine* (no. 1045, Autumn 1965), in *Elizabeth Taylor: A Centenary Celebration*, ed. N. H. Reeve (Newcastle upon Tyne: Cambridge Scholars Publishing, 2012), pp. 69–72 (p. 70).
11. Elizabeth Taylor, 'Better Not', in *A Centenary Celebration*, ed. Reeve, pp. 21–3 (pp. 22–3).
12. Elizabeth Taylor, 'Choosing Details that Count', *Writer*, 83 (1970), 1, pp. 15–16 (p. 15); 'Letter to Virginia Woolf', 15 Oct. 1932, in *A Centenary Celebration*, ed. Reeve, p. 97.
13. *A Centenary Celebration*, ed. Reeve, p. 22.
14. Alice Munro, 'Walker Brothers Cowboy', in *Selected Stories* (New York: Alfred A. Knopf, 1996), pp. 3–15 (p. 5). All quotations from Munro's stories are from this edition, with subsequent page references given in parentheses in the text.
15. Margaret Atwood, 'Alice Munro: An Appreciation', *The Guardian*, 11 October 2008, p. 2.

16. Quoted in Graeme Gibson, 'Alice Munro', in *Eleven Canadian Novelists* (Toronto: Anansi, 1973), pp. 237–64 (p. 248).
17. Mara Reisman, 'An Interview with Fay Weldon', in *Modern Language Studies*, 37 (2008), 2, pp. 32–49 (p. 42).
18. Craig Gholson, 'Fay Weldon', in *BOMB*, 30 (Winter 1989/1990), pp. 44–7 (p. 46).
19. Fay Weldon, 'Who Goes Where?', in *Moon over Minneapolis* (Harmondsworth: Penguin, 1991), pp. 95–103 (pp. 99–100).
20. Peter Childs, 'Angela Carter: The Demythologizing Business', in *Contemporary Novelists: British Fiction Since 1970* (Basingstoke: Palgrave Macmillan, 2005), pp. 100–22 (p. 119).
21. Marina Warner, 'Chamber of Secrets: The Sorcery of Angela Carter', *The Paris Review*, 17 October 2012 (www.theparisreview.org/blog/2012/10/17/chamber-of-secrets-the-sorcery-of-angela-carter).
22. Warner, 'Chamber of Secrets'; Salman Rushdie, 'Introduction' to Angela Carter, *Burning Your Boats: Collected Short Stories* (London: Vintage, 1996), pp. ix–xiv (pp. ix–x).
23. Angela Carter, 'The Company of Wolves', in *Burning Your Boats*, pp. 212–20 (p. 212). Subsequent page references are given in parentheses in the text.
24. Angela Carter, *The Sadeian Woman: An Exercise in Cultural History* (1978; London: Virago, 1979).
25. John Haffenden, 'An Interview with Angela Carter', in *Novelists in Interview*, ed. John Haffenden (London: Methuen, 1985), pp. 76–96 (p. 86).
26. Angela Carter, *Nothing Sacred: Selected Writings* (London: Virago, 1982), pp. 86–7.
27. Jean-Louis Chevalier, 'Entretien avec A. S. Byatt', in *JSSE: Proceedings of the Conference on The English Short Story Since 1946*, 22 (1994), pp. 11–28 (p. 14; p. 13).
28. A. S. Byatt, 'The Dried Witch', in *Sugar and Other Stories* (1987; London: Penguin, 1988), pp. 85–111 (pp. 110–11).
29. 'Antonia S. Byatt in Interview with Boyd Tonkin', *Anglistik*, 10:2 (Sept. 1999), pp. 15–26 (p. 20).
30. Margaret Atwood, 'Introduction' to *The Oxford Book of Canadian Short Stories in English*, selected by Margaret Atwood and Robert Weaver (Oxford University Press, 1986), pp. xiii–xix (p. xv).
31. Margaret Atwood, *Dancing Girls and Other Stories* (New York: Simon and Schuster, 1977), pp. 225–40 (p. 225).

18

Queer Short Stories: An Inverted History

BRETT JOSEF GRUBISIC AND CARELLIN BROOKS

In 2013 LGBT History Month Scotland, a website project administered by LGBT Youth Scotland and partially funded by the Scottish government, posted a submissions call for *Out There*, an anthology in which Scottish authors who self-identify as lesbian, gay, bisexual, transgender or intersex would explore the nation's social and sexual landscape. The call stated that in addition to posting select pieces online, the anthology would be published by Glasgow's Freight Books, whose sister publication, *Gutter*, devoted a 2012 issue to LGBT stories.

From the vantage point of 2015, a special issue and an anthology focused on LGBT writing does not represent groundbreaking news. That status quo, however, is in itself noteworthy. When Lillian Faderman and Stuart Timmons remark that 'changes in gay life over the past half-century have been astonishing', they refer to widespread societal developments (in the European Union and North America especially) related to the heightened agency and social status of sexual minorities that began in the late 1960s.[1] These changes are all the more striking in light of earlier periods. Ellis's 1897 summation – 'I realized that in England, more than in any other country, the law and public opinion combine to place a heavy burden and a severe social stigma on the manifestations of an instinct which to these persons who possess it frequently appeared natural and normal' (p. 59) – stands in marked contrast to Tom Warner's 2002 description of the 'historically unprecedented' accomplishments of Anglo-American activists during the twentieth century's final decades: they rejected 'the quasi-human role in which gays, lesbians and bisexuals had been cast throughout history, a role that forced them to hide their sexual orientation, to disguise themselves, and to lead double lives filled with fear, isolation, and self-loathing'.[2]

Burdensome conditions took various forms. Faderman illustrates one effect of categorization: 'As an undergraduate in college I was an English major, but the only time I learned about a lesbian book was in an Abnormal Psych class, where [Radclyffe Hall's 1928 novel] *The Well of Loneliness* was mentioned.'[3] Similarly, Terry Castle remarks on Jeanette Howard Foster, whose *Sex Variant Women in Literature* was 'issued privately and at her own expense in 1956, at a time when no reputable publisher would touch the subject of female homosexuality'; as an undergraduate in the early 1970s, Castle located Foster's book 'hidden away in a special, non-circulating, "Triple X-rated" stack behind the front desk'.[4] Though Martin Duberman comments on the absence of a public historical record of homosexuality before the 1970s, other historians cite increased antipathy. Alan Bray identifies mass arrests and executions that 'violently repressed' homosexuality, stating that 'on whatever scale [homosexuality] was viewed its visibility would be curtailed'.[5] Likewise, Randolph Trumbach labels the eighteenth century sodomite subclass in England a 'despised minority' subject to 'physical violence' and H. G. Cocks states that same-sex 'desire was criminalized in new ways and policed more vigilantly than ever' in the nineteenth century despite a handful of intellectuals making minor inroads into Victorian prejudices.[6]

Given the trajectory charted by historians of sexual minorities – from 'nothing but oppression and isolation, opprobrium and closetry' with concomitant efforts at survival, resistance and agency, to visibility in the form of a multi-faceted reader/author demographic and an equally diverse literary infrastructure of LGBT publishers, bookstores, journals and websites – it is unsurprising that Mark Mitchell and David Leavitt conclude that the vast majority 'of "gay" texts known today were written after the Great War; and the majority of these after the Stonewall riots; and, as if literary history were a series of Chinese boxes, the vast majority of these after the advent (in the West) of the human immunodeficiency virus' in the early 1980s.[7]

This contemporary plenitude can be confirmed by a glance at any multinational bookseller's website. Alongside scores of anthology titles, English, Irish and Scottish prose anthologies such as Joseph Mills's *Borderline* (2001), Joanne Winning's *The Crazy Jig* (1992) Toni Davidson's *And Thus Will I Freely Sing* (1989) and Mark Hemry's *Chasing Danny Boy* (1999) appear under 'Gay and Lesbian Literature Anthologies'. From Nicola Griffith and Stephen Pagel's Bending the Landscape genre series (queer fantasy, science fiction, horror) and G. Abel-Watters's *People Your Mother Warned You About* (2012) (stories of admonition by lesbian and gay authors), to Michael Harth's *Eros at Large* (2013) (gay male tales of desire) and Tom Léger and Riley MacLeod's *The Collection* (2012) (transgender short fiction), the myriad perspectives these volumes put into circulation attest not only to the complexity of queer experience but to the ongoing push to represent its thematic and aesthetic breadth.

Before this period of relative discursive plenitude, homosexuality remained a profoundly taboo subject. In *A Problem of Modern Ethics* (1891) John Addington Symonds described common belief as dictating that a male loving his own sex must be regarded as despicable, vicious and incapable of human sentiments. Long associated with sexual sin and social dissolution, its ignominiousness can be gauged through the condemnations expressed by eminent nineteenth-century figures: in 1803, Samuel Taylor Coleridge defined male–male love as 'that very worst of all possible vices' and during his closing statement at Oscar Wilde's second trial in 1895, Justice Wills castigated the felon (newly convicted of gross indecency): 'One has to put stern restraint upon oneself to prevent oneself from describing in language I ought not to use the sentiments which must arise in the breast of every man who has a spark of decent feeling in him, and who has heard of details of these two terrible trials.'[8]

Considering what Jeffrey Weeks calls the grey intellectual climate for homosexual discourse and related subjects that threatened the moral consensus, and what Joseph Cady, surveying nineteenth-century literary production, defines as an identity fettered by the 'long-standing cultural claim that same-sex desire was "unspeakable"', the non-visibility of both homosexuals and their literature can scarcely register as surprising.[9] To simplify, a contemporary reader searching for a 'lesbian story' published around 1864 (the year Karl Heinrich Ulrichs coined the word 'homosexual') or a 'gay story' in 1885 (when the Labouchère Amendment of the British Criminal Law Act made all male homosexual acts imprisonable offences) would not readily obtain one, especially if their expectation matched Marilyn R. Farwell's definition – 'I argue that the lesbian narrative is not necessarily a story by a lesbian about lesbians but rather a plot that affirms a place for lesbian subjectivity, that narrative space where both lesbian characters and other female characters can be active, desiring agents.'[10]

Despite the hostile milieu, however, scholars have made persuasive claims for the steady growth of a discreet homosexual literature throughout this period. Speaking broadly, Weeks observes that the 'tightening grip of the law, and the force of public disapproval which it stimulated, was beginning to create a community of knowledge, if not of life and feeling, among male homosexuals'. For evidence, he refers to Symonds's fin-de-siècle claim that a vast subterranean literature on homosexuality little known to general readers existed for those who knew where to search. Mitchell and Leavitt likewise contend that since the eighteenth century, men who were 'sexually attracted to other men – sodomites, pederasts, urnings, Uranians, similsexualists, queers' have constituted a distinct reading class and have displayed an 'astonishing tenacity in locating those poems, stories, novels, essays, and even individual sentences in which references to homosexual experience might be found'.[11]

Cady observes that blanketing prohibitions resulted in two general patterns: homosexual writing – including letters, journals, fiction, poetry and drama – that remained unpublished or printed for private circulation only; and, when released publicly, literature whose homosexual 'content was substantially camouflaged or buffered'. As such, James Gifford notes, the gay writing published between 1830 and 1920 and after 'often presents us with a mysterious text, because we are not sure how to read it . . . It offers an opening, we suppose, to certain sympathetic readers, men "in the know".'[12] Gifford implies that during this period a proto-international gay male literature was forming, and cites 'Out in the Sun' (1913), an American-authored short story published by an Italy-based English vanity press, to illustrate that homosexuals seeking to write themselves into history faced mores that largely disallowed sexual otherness 'a platform for open discourse' (p. 8).

One consequence of the norm that predates the normalization of homosexuality in Western culture was authorial ingenuity at embedding queerness in print. Besides foreign, private and vanity presses, scholars list genre subversion – 'no matter which genre was chosen, it had to be modified, to allow for a different kind of expression', as Gifford puts it (p. 12) – as well as an encoded homosexual theme, mood, or aesthetic within a work, with masked and highly ambiguous results. Gifford discerns at least six discursive sites available to homosexual writers that range from portrayals of athleticism and fraternity to modes of aesthetics (posture, style, wit). Works with ambiguities featured suggestive markers that hinted at or touched on queerness while simultaneously letting readers 'know the limits of socially acceptable male homosocial desire' (p. 27).

Moreover, contrary to the assertions of Brian Reade ('it is true to say that homosexual literature [over the 1850–1900 period] for all practical purposes is male homosexual literature' and Monique Wittig ('Male homosexual literature has a past, it has a present. The lesbians, for their part, are silent – just as all women are as woman at all levels'), literary historians discern a rich, if similarly indirect, tradition for lesbianism.[13] As with Emma Donoghue, the research leads scholars to assorted representations of women who felt passion for women, though again with the caveat of reading between the lines, or modifying contemporary expectations so that they include cryptic references or homoaffectional expression. Lillian Faderman asserts that veiling was a commonplace strategy to sidestep censorious social edicts, as was masking via 'perfunctorily changing the gender' of characters, or 'encoding' subject matter.[14] Faderman argues that Victorian literary representations of socially condoned romantic friendships between women were 'love relationships in every sense except perhaps genital' (p. 16). Surveying assorted texts, Faderman observes fluctuating attitudes that include the lesbian figure as exotic, fashionable, taboo, innocent and evil. She lists numerous serialized stories appearing in publications on both sides of the Atlantic before concluding that before the rise of lesbian-feminism, lesbian writers of popular literature generally depicted one of two types: the lesbian as a sickie or as a martyr (p. 392). Moreover, Faderman discerns an epochal break in lesbian imagery before and after 1920. With the popularization of medical models of sexuality, the lesbian character, she argues, would have 'been rushed off to a psychoanalyst to undergo treatment for her mental malady, or she would have ended her fictional existence broken in half by a tree, justly punished by nature ... for her transgression'.[15] But a decade or two earlier, 'homoaffectional expression between women was far less restricted'; permissible behaviour included 'caressing, holding, exchanges of endearments and expressions of intense emotional commitment to each other' (p. 801). These relationships were regarded as unthreatening because society understood that the woman would give up her female love 'with the advent of a suitable male,' and that as an identity 'the lesbian' was virtually non-existent (p. 801). If depicted as lesbian, the figure would be expected to conform to a medical model (a masculine type, subject to scanty menstruation and pelvic disorders, or 'more or less hysterical or insane' (p. 802)).

Encoded, disguised, ambiguous, implicit and reformulated, these literary portrayals of homosexuality (generally, and within short stories in particular) offered distinct reading audiences dissimilar experiences: for one reader, a story's plot or characters would not incite moral outrage or obscenity proceedings because of its protective veil of indirectness; and for readers attracted to the same sex who constituted a criminalized subclass demographic, the author encrypting her text in order to register an outlawed identity semi-publicly allowed queerness to be simultaneously discerned while remaining virtually undetected.

Characteristically published in magazines, newspapers and literary journals before being collected in book form, the following stories did not generally amass widespread attention for promoting or even hinting at indecent situations, characters, or themes: Reverend Edwin Emanuel Bradford's 'Boris Orloff' (1893); John Francis Bloxam's 'The Priest and the Acolyte' (1894); Charles Warren Stoddart's 'Pearl Hunting in the Pomotous' (in *South-Sea Idyls* (1873)); and Wilde's fairy tales (collected in *The Happy Prince and Other Tales* (1888) and *A House of Pomegranates* (1891)), in which John-Charles Duffy discerns 'five "answers" to anti-homosexual Victorian discourses' in the form of devoted friendships, non-reproductive sex, aestheticism, *paiderastia* and the 'unblessed, unnatural, unnameable'.[16] Other examples include Wilde's 'The Portrait of Mr W.H.' (1889); Count Stanislaus Eric Stenbock's *Studies of Death: Romantic Tales* (seven stories, including 'The True Story of a Vampire' (1894)); Frederick Rolfe's (Baron Corvo) 'In Praise of Billy B.' (1897) and 'Stories Toto Told Me' (1895); Charles Kenneth Scott-Moncrieff's 'Evensong and Morwe Song' (1908); D. H. Lawrence's 'The Prussian Officer' (whose strong homosexual component is noted by Mitchell and Leavitt; Faderman argues that Lawrence's *The Fox*, serialized in 1922, is a story that 'teaches that lesbians must be either killed or captured');[17] Charlotte Mew's 'Passed' (1894), which Kate Flint interprets as a story 'in which the style is directly ... related to the expression – or the problematics of the expression – of a queer consciousness';[18] and Joseph Sheridan Le Fanu's 'Carmilla' (1871–2). Furthermore, the transnational periodical economy enabled foreign-authored short fiction – ranging from Jeanette Lee's 'The Cat and the King' (1919), Catherine Wells's 'The Beautiful House' (1912), O. Henry's 'The Last Leaf' (1906) and Gertrude Stein's 'Miss Furr and Miss Skeene' (1922), to Thomas Bailey Aldrich's 'Marjorie Daw' (1873), Jack London's 'The White Silence' (1899), Guy de Maupassant's 'Paul's Mistress' (1880) and Henry James's 'The Author of Beltraffio' (1884), 'The Pupil' (1891) and 'The Great Good Place' (1900), which Mitchell and Leavitt view as indicative of the author's rarely explicit homosexual content – to appear in English periodicals.

Evidently regarded by publishers as meritorious, such stories raised no subsequent controversy. Bret Harte's work serves as a useful illustration.

Hugely popular, the well-paid author was known for sentimental regionalism and adventure tales of the Wild West. One typical story, 'Uncle Jim and Uncle Billy,' appeared in the *Illustrated London News* (1897) during the American's residency in England. Ostensibly an account of close fraternity, Axel Nissen interprets it as a tale (one of many California-set tales about 'men without women' that Harte wrote between 1862 and 1895) highlighting 'male romantic friendship' and the 'romantic tradition of love between men'. In Nissen's reading Harte constructs 'an alternative, same-sex domesticity that problematizes and subverts the essentialism of Victorian domesticity's gender roles and norms'.[19]

In *Coming Out* Weeks references key societal contexts for British sexual minorities over a significant portion of the twentieth century with a sampling from England's popular press. Titled 'Evil Men,' one 1952 *Sunday Pictorial* article aimed to end a purported conspiracy of silence about the anarchic impact of homosexuality. A decade later the same mass-circulation newspaper printed 'How to Spot a Homo'. Between them, the 'Report of the Wolfenden Committee' (1957) in England recommended a progressive law modification for male homosexuals. Concerned about potential ramifications, its authors added a caveat: the proposed reform 'should not be interpreted as . . . a general licence to adult homosexuals to behave as they please'.[20]

For *Between the Acts*, moreover, Weeks and Kevin Porter collected reminiscences by homosexual men (born between 1892 and 1921) who were eyewitnesses to the era that stretched from the passing of the prohibitive Labouchère Amendment, notoriously known as a 'blackmailer's charter', to the Sexual Offences Act (1967), which partially decriminalized male homosexual activities. Weeks and Porter's introduction charts an overall 'triumph of individual courage and endurance' despite odds established by limiting forms of social regulation that enacted 'the privileging of heterosexuality and the denial of homosexuality'. In their view an aspect of that triumph was 'a small body of writing', from sexology research to poetry, which provided a vocabulary for homosexual men to understand and define themselves.[21]

From Wilde's conviction to obscenity trials for literary works by Hall, Lawrence, James Joyce, Henry Miller, Lawrence Durrell, A. T. Fitzroy (Rose Allatini's pseudonym) and Cyril Connolly, however, the twentieth century did not begin (nor reach a mid-point) in a manner that was auspicious to literary depictions of putatively obscene sexual congress or queer identities. As a result of these and other social prohibitions, writers addressing homosexuality often continued to adopt protective encoding tactics and what Robert Phillips, editor of *The Stories of Denton Welch*, describes as Welch's 'Proustian Albertine strategy' – changing the 'sex of the protagonist from male to female'.[22] Also Proustian in style, Welch's *Brave and Cruel and Other Stories* appeared in 1948, the year of his death (at age thirty-three). Highly mannered early short fiction by Ronald Firbank, such as 'A Study in Temperament' (1905) and 'A Study in Opal' (1907), reads as influenced by British Aestheticism generally and Wilde in particular. Reviewers of a homosocial later work, the fifty-one-page 'Santal' (1921), nonetheless noted its dandyism, attention to style and (in a 1955 review) the author's 'discomforting sexual maladjustments', a view echoed in key reviews of Stephen Spender's story collection, *The Burning Cactus* (1936).[23] That sensibility (as well as read-between-the-lines quality) is apparent too in the prodigious output of L. P. Hartley. His story collections, such as *The Travelling Grave* (1948) and *The White Wand* (1954), range in genre from horror and supernatural to comedy of manners. Appearing sporadically, Christopher Isherwood's stories, including 'An Evening at the Bay' (1933), 'The Nowaks' (1936) and 'A Berlin Diary (Autumn 1930)' (1937), offer glimpses of urban culture characterized by the intermingling of heterosexual and homosexual.

Acts of private circulation and withholding writing from publication also remained in practice. E. M. Forster's novel *Maurice* and the short pieces in *The Life to Come and Other Stories* appeared posthumously (in the early 1970s). Forster's assessment of these works varied: in a diary entry from 1922 he called writing them 'positively dangerous to my career as a novelist'; he wrote that he burned all of his 'indecent writings or as many as the fire will take'.[24] He also showed them to other writers, including Isherwood and T. E. Lawrence (p. xiii). The sexual dalliances of 'Arthur Snatchfold' (1928), 'What Does it Matter' (c. 1930s) and 'The Obelisk' (1939), are set in circumstances ranging from fraught to comically satiric, and Forster's stories oscillate between gentle protests against the consequences of homosexual acts and paeans to the potential transcendence at the core of sexual experience.

The evocation of lesbians as monstrous, doomed or 'more or less hysterical or insane' continued as normative too, to the point that, in introducing her 'philosophical disquisition on the subject of the female variant', Ann Aldrich – the pen name of Marijane Meaker – included a story-sized excerpt from *The Price of Salt*, a novel that Patricia Highsmith published under the pseudonym Claire Morgan after her regular publisher rejected it.[25] Appearing when 'dozens of novels of male and female homosexuality ... wound matters up with sleeping pills, murder, imprisonment, unbelievable self-reconversion, or the corpse in the swimming pool', this 1952 novel's happy ending caught Aldrich's eye.[26] Surveying fiction portraying lesbians, Bonnie Zimmerman supports the view held by Aldrich, stating that typical mid-century plots in English-language works 'either doomed [lesbian characters] to a cycle of unhappy love affairs or redeemed them through heterosexual marriage'.[27]

Similarly, tactful ambiguity stayed relatively commonplace. If the eroticism of Edith Ellis's 'Dolores' (1909), in which 'two women kissed in silence, their eyes lowered before the sorrow they had caught in each other's faces' draws attention with its rarity, with its echo of Edward Carpenter's *Ioläus: An Anthology of Friendship* (1917), editor Patrick Anderson and Alistair Sutherland's *Eros: An Anthology of Male Friendship* (1961) suggests an ongoing preference for euphemistic or veiled public terminology.[28] Short fiction by Radclyffe Hall ('Miss Ogilvy Finds Herself', 1934), Djuna Barnes ('A Little Girl Tells a Story to a Lady' and 'Cassation', 1929), Thomas Burke ('The Pash', 1926), Ivy Compton-Burnett (whose work, Jane Rule claims, 'stands at the asexual extreme of lesbian sensibility'), Elizabeth Bowen ('The Jungle', 1929, 'The Apple Tree', 1934, and 'The Demon Lover', 1944), H. E. Bates ('Breeze Anstey', 1937), Katherine Mansfield ('Leves Amores', written in 1907, 'Bains Turc', 1911, and 'Bliss', 1918), which Gillian Hanscombe labels as not 'a story about lesbians, but ... a story about lesbianism', Henry Handel Richardson (the pseudonym of Ethel Richardson) ('The Bathe' and 'Two Hanged Women', 1934) and Virginia Woolf's 'little Sapphist story', 'Slater's Pins Have No Points' (1928), feature content and sensibilities identifiable as homoerotic and homosocial, or otherwise imbued with homosexual themes.[29]

Still other stories, especially those by women, remain the subject of continuing critical argument. Their innate ambiguity or indirectness hinders simple or certain interpretation. For example, did Elizabeth Bowen, in 'The Demon Lover', intend the tale of a woman (haunted by memories of a female friend's death, saved by another woman's friendship and restored to her heterosexual marriage) to be read in terms of erotic same-sex attraction as well as friendship? Did D. H. Lawrence depict a weird and decidedly anxious parable about same-sex 'courtship' in 'The Prussian Officer' (1914)? Certainly his 'Rupert and Gerald', arguably not a short story at all (the characters reappear in *Women in Love*, in far more circumscribed form), depicts frank same-sex desire: 'All the time, he recognized that, although he was always drawn to women, feeling more at home with a woman than with a man, yet it was for men that he felt the hot, flushing, roused attraction which a man is supposed to feel for the other sex.' This unvarnished tale, thought to have been written around 1916, remained unpublished until 1994.[30]

In the second half of the twentieth century depictions of unequivocally homosexual characters and social formations began to gain traction. For instance, Daphne du Maurier's 'Ganymede' (1959) is a *Death in Venice*-style account of a tourist enraptured by a waiter in the Piazzo San Marco. In 'May We Borrow Your Husband?' (1967), Graham Greene recounts a newlywed groom's deliberate seduction by a couple of male interior decorators, along with the bride's uncomprehending distress. In the same collection, 'Chagrin in Three Parts' features a narrator eavesdropping on a scene of seduction between a pair of wine-besotted women.

Gay writers' works also mirrored their historical period more generally, in particular with the popularization of Freudianism. Angus Wilson, whose short story collection *The Wrong Set* appeared in 1949 (followed by *Such Darling Dodos* in 1950), addressed the question of the smothering mother-figure from whom the young man wishes to free himself, only to be left bereft by her death ('Mother's Sense of Fun') and a paterfamilias, steered straight by his wife, whose eye begins to rove upon the arrival of a handsome young male exchange student ('Et Dona Ferentes'). In this latter story, Wilson's protagonist muses on the 'old feeling of twenty years ago, the old sensual pattern' that arises at the sight of Sven's 'brown chest where the line of his shirt lay open almost to his stomach'.[31] In the titular story a piano player informs the club's owner that 'surely you know Terry's a pansy' only to have him reply without rancour, 'That gets 'em all ways' (p. 105).

Internationally influential, Tennessee Williams exhibits ambivalence about homosexuality, especially in *Hard Candy* (1954), where homoeroticism is 'always linked to death'.[32] Noel Coward's stories span a range of camp but undeclared characters in earlier periods, as when the male main character of 'Star Quality' (1951), a playwright, defines his distaste for his director's assistant thus: 'You make it fairly obvious that you don't care for women.'[33] Later characterization becomes more frank, however. The narrator of 'Me and the Girls' (1964), for example, describes himself as 'queer' (p. 469). By 1978, William Trevor's titular character in 'Torridge' can expose the hypocrisy along with the homosexual affairs at the public school that other male characters believe they left behind with their boyhoods. Invited to a get-together with three former pupils and their families, Torridge stands out as a figure of sophistication: "'I'm what they call queer", he explains to the children. "I perform sexual acts with men".'[34] His audience reacts with outrage, but Torridge remains unmoved by their disgust.

Although the historical liberation of sexual minorities is popularly thought of as having been sparked off in mid-1969 with an unwarranted police raid and subsequent rioting in front of the Stonewall Inn in New York City, such a belief overlooks a series of incremental nation-centric changes (like amendments to the legal standing of homosexuals, the founding of activist homophile organizations and the creation of lesbian and gay periodicals) that predated those summer protests. Even granting that galvanizing event a global watershed status, there was no corresponding literary moment. In short, the literature of sexual minorities did not suddenly blossom over a single season around 1970. Its growth was fitful, especially outside the United States.

Nonetheless, although typically 'very polemical', occasional liberation-era anthologies from lesbian-feminist presses – for example, Barbara Grier and Coletta Reid's *The Lesbians Home Journal* (1976) and Judith Grahn's *True to Life Adventure Stories* (1978) – put into circulation narratives that diverged markedly from the typical 'hysterical or insane' portraiture of preceding decades. Most scholarly analyses of post-Stonewall queer literature foreground non-fiction and novels and mention short stories in passing.[35] However, a tenuous internationalism began to emerge. In an early lesbian and gay fiction anthology, *The Other Persuasion* (1977), US editor Seymour Kleinburg selected English authors (including Isherwood, Hall, Lawrence, Greene and Forster) as well as Americans, while Anglo-Canadian editor Ian Young's *On the Line* (1981) focused on US gay male authors.

The burgeoning market throughout the 1970s of quasi-lesbian erotic short fiction published in *Playboy* and competitors such as *Mayfair* and *Men Only* introduced (an admittedly ersatz version of) female homoeroticism to mainstream culture on a mass scale. For gay men, meanwhile, the 'one-handed' erotic short fiction of early pornographic magazines (such as *Quorum*, *Spartacus* and *Jeffrey* in Britain and *Mandate* in North America) served both utilitarian and political purposes.[36]

Conforming with Reed Woodhouse's survey of post-Second World War gay male fiction and its overall taxonomy of a 'basic polarity' between portrayals of gay assimilation into mainstream mores and modes of sovereign gay identity (p. 6), Les Brookes views Stonewall as pivotal in gay self-awareness, though not an absolute break from past themes, and post-Stonewall literature as reflecting a 'conflict between assimilationism and radicalism: between a fundamental acceptance of social and sexual norms and an outright rejection of them'.[37] While noting similarities (such as the thematic predominance of self-discovery, or coming out), Paulina Palmer's survey of literary productions of the same period pays less attention to Stonewall and instead asserts the centrality of the Women's Movement, lesbian-feminism and the growth of independent activist publishers.[38] Regarding lesbian material, Zimmerman states that over two hundred English language novels, memoirs and short story collections were published between 1969 and 1989 and that the vast majority were published by alternative presses and 'advertised through lesbian networks, sold in women's bookstores, and reviewed in lesbian, gay, and feminist newspapers', pointing to the cross-border maturation of a formerly non-hegemonic and invisible subculture.[39] To Zimmerman, the crucial motif within that body of work, stories included, was the creation of a myth of origins that enabled lesbians to self-identify and comprehend a historical community.

Short story anthologies of sexual minority writing appeared in larger numbers in the 1980s and reached an apex in the 1990s. The stories collected in this way might be valued as much for their representational qualities as for their literary excellence. Of note here are: the US-centric but internationally-marketed 'Men on Men', 'Women on Women' and 'Flesh and the Word' series that began in 1986; the *Faber Book of Gay Short Fiction* (1996); P. P. Hartnett's *The Gay Times Book of Short Stories* series (2000–2); and English editor Richard Canning's 'Between Men' series (2007–9), which features English authors Patrick Gale (author of *Dangerous Pleasures*, 1996), Alan Hollinghurst and Shaun Levin (author of *A Year of Two Summers*, 2005), among predominantly US authors. Because readers experienced relatively few reflections of their lived realities in other mainstream media during that era, depictions of the circumstances of sexual minorities, including family, romance and differences in class served important social functions beyond the sheer novelty of uncoded or unambiguous visibility.

Following the publication of his story collection *Lantern Lecture* (1981), Adam Mars-Jones anthologized writers in *Mae West is Dead* (1983), which collected lesbian and gay stories in relatively equal number but did not focus exclusively on the United Kingdom. While Mars-Jones refers only in passing to AIDS, 'the 1982 epidemic of panic and sexual fear', he later meditated upon the crisis facing gay males and men sexually involved with other men.[40] *The Darker Proof: Stories from a Crisis* (1987), by Mars-Jones and Edmund

White, contained six stories, four by Mars-Jones and two by White. They displayed assorted responses, from the gallows humour Mars-Jones described as necessary to break through his block in writing about the topic ('Slim'), through denial and sudden realization ('A Small Spade'). Mars-Jones, in introducing a 1992 collection of his own stories on the subject, asserted that 'the big issue [of AIDS] and the little form [of the short story] had a paradoxical affinity'.[41]

The first anthology of lesbian-feminist short stories in the United Kingdom was Lilian Mohin and Sheila Shulman's *The Reach* (1984). Although just one of its contributors used a pseudonym, in a subsequent anthology, Mohin and Anna Livia's *The Pied Piper* (1989), three opted to, citing fears regarding their employment: a controversial amendment to the Local Government Act of 1988 that forbade the teaching or publishing of material thought to promote homosexuality, Section 28 (repealed a dozen years later) contributed to a retributive social atmosphere for activism related to public homosexuality.

By the time of *The Pied Piper* its editors already understood the conventional scope of such an anthology: 'Here we have the "expected themes" of coming out, "bar" stories, countering anti-lesbianism, recovering lesbian history.'[42] They describe their project, in addition, as 'fashioning ... lesbian culture' (p. x). Contributors express a preoccupation with links to the previously unknown, and magic realism is present in the titular story, where the Pied Piper turns out to be a lonely, time-travelling magical lesbian. In others, like Patricia Duncker's 'James Miranda Barry 1795–1865', women disguise themselves as men to obtain a better social status. In this collection, continuing preoccupations arise with the hidden and subterfuge. As editor of a later collection stated, lesbian short stories, written in an era of incomplete disclosure and societal repercussion, commonly reflect the 'importance of what is unsaid or cannot be said between women'.[43]

Perhaps as a consequence of the paucity of pre-twentieth century lesbian representation, writers re-imagine the past. 'The Secret of Sorrerby Rise', published by Frances Gapper in 1991, parodies Victorian melodrama. Commissioned for a 1993 anthology, Emma Donoghue's 'Words for Things' itemizes the dawning vocabulary of a fourteen-year-old girl in 1786: 'Tommie was when women kissed and pressed each other to their hearts, it said so in a dirty poem on the top shelf of the cabinet. Tribad was the same only worse.'[44] Other characters perpetuate a culture of concealment by not declaring their emotional states or desires. The reticence leads to re-enactments of the lesbian unhappy ending so familiar from *The Well of*

Loneliness and lesbian pulp fiction. But as Sara Ahmed notes in *The Promise of Happiness*, this spectre might in fact lead to societal critique by leaving open the possibility that the character's unhappiness, rather than being solely individuated, results from heteronormativity.[45] In addition to anthologies of lesbian literary fiction from English publishers (like *Everyday Matters 2* (1984) and *In and Out of Time* (1990)), there were also collections of lesbian science fiction (*The Needle on Full* (1985)), feminist supernatural fiction (*What Did Miss Darrington See?* (1989)) and love or eros (*Incidents Involving Warmth* (1988) and *Girls Next Door* (1985)). These all appeared during the late 1980s and early 1990s, alongside short fiction volumes by Livia, Barbara Burford, J. E. Hardy, Mary Dorcey, Cherry Potts and Caroline Natzler.

Generally, the anthologies have had overwhelmingly Anglo-Saxon contributors. There are, for example, no biographically identified writers of colour in *Mae West is Dead*, and *The Penguin Book of Lesbian Short Stories* (1993) contains one piece by a self-identified African-American writer, Jewelle Gomez. Likewise, in the *Diva Book of Short Stories* (2000), a single contributor, Jackie Kay, is readily identifiable as black. Although at least three women of colour contributed stories to *The Pied Piper*, only Maud Sulter's 'Blackwomansong' overtly references black characters. Appearing in late 2014, however, *Black and Gay in the UK* (edited by John R. Gordon and Rikki Beadle-Blair) features short fiction, poetry and essays.

As the simple catch-all of 'gay and/or lesbian writing' grew indistinct, geography also inspired the editors of story collections. The first Scottish-themed gay and lesbian anthology, *And Thus Will I Freely Sing* (1989), was followed by *The Crazy Jig* (1992). The editor, Joanne Winning, expresses satisfaction that *Jig* includes black Scottish voices, and Iona McGregor's introduction lauds the balance of male and female writers. Preoccupied as ever with the perennial question of taxonomy, McGregor poses familiar questions: 'Is it any longer possible to define or circumscribe gay writing? Must gay writers assert their identity in order to avoid being deconstructed into the heterosexual majority?'[46] Featuring Scottish authors, *Borderline* (2001) continued to broaden the content of gay and lesbian anthologies, the 'borderline' defined not by author sexuality per se – gay-themed excerpts from writers such as Irvine Welsh are included – but by geography. In this 'determinedly broad picture of Scottish writing [t]here are gay characters, perspectives, themes and – or maybe that should be "but" – there is a whole lot more'.[47] Topics include sadomasochism, abuse, bar pickups, religion and coming out; mythology and science fiction genres, among others, are represented.

Helen Sandler, editor of the *Diva Book of Short Stories* (2000), describes the stories in this 'Britdyke' anthology as 'Modern Lesbian ... a way of weaving a story without sticking to a single thread, of letting the thoughts wander into wordplay or a witty aside without losing the plot. It's a use of the vernacular which looks casual but isn't.'[48] Limited to authors under twenty-five, Hartnett's *The Next Wave* (2002) includes transgendered writers. 'Bloke', by a writer identified only as 'Geezer', describes the main character's travails as a female-to-male transsexual. In 'Girl', the narrator is attracted to a transvestite, and their dalliance partakes in gender fluidity. As with *Diva* the anthology includes author photographs, indicating the distance between these anthologies and the pseudonyms of *The Pied Piper*.

Any discussion of contemporary short fiction is inseparable from reference to the general literary market. The undoubtable fact of best-selling, literary prize-winning and publicly queer-identified authors whose publications span novels, poetry and short fiction – ranging in the United Kingdom from Carol Ann Duffy, Jackie Kay, Ali Smith, Sarah Waters and Jeanette Winterson to Peter Ackroyd, Paul Bailey, Neil Bartlett, Alan Hollinghurst and Jamie O'Neill – suggests a wholly positive outcome to the political activism of earlier generations. Then again, contrary assertions (such as Justin Gowers's that the publishing industry in Britain remains indifferent to promoting the work of sexual minorities and that readers are more 'likely to discover exciting new gay writers in the blogosphere, or in queer literary magazines like *Chroma*, than on a publisher's list') imply an ongoing resistance to the worldview of sexual minorities unless it is accompanied by impressive sales figures.[49]

If nothing else, however, the perspectival breadth of literature written by and about sexual minorities spins a tale of diverse origins, politics and forms as well as a multiplicity of ongoing purposes. For example, in the preface of *Out There* (2014), a volume of thirty-two contributors 'who consider themselves LGBT and Scottish by birth, residence, inclination or formation', editor Zoë Strachan anchors the anthology in a personal context.[50] Strachan also places the volume within a broader political framework related to same-sex marriage in Scotland and, larger still, the urgent need for equal rights and freedom from persecution worldwide. *Out There* ends with contributor statements. Val McDermid's statement – 'My sexuality is important to my writing. But so is being a woman, being a mother, being Scottish and having a political consciousness' (p. 286) – echoes that of Jackie Kay, who writes:

'I suppose that everything I am influences my writing in some way – being black, being a mother, a daughter, a lesbian' (p. 282). Christopher Whyte, however, introduces a distinctly politicized motivation: 'The oppression I grew up with [in Glasgow] meant taboo after taboo had to be broken' (p. 292). The collective point of view diffused through *Out There*, and in scores of previous anthologies, and short story collections (including Ronald Frame's *Watching Mrs Gordon*, 1987, V. G. Lee's *As You Step Outside*, 2008, Ali Smith's *Free Love and Other Stories*, 1995, or Colm Tóibín's *The Empty Family*, 2010) evokes a complexity and irreducibility common to literature in general.

Notes

1. Lillian Faderman and Stuart Timmons, *Gay L.A.: A History of Sexual Outlaws, Power Politics, and Lipstick Lesbians* (New York: Basic Books, 2006), p. 347.
2. Tom Warner, *Never Going Back: A History of Queer Activism in Canada* (University of Toronto Press, 2002), p. 3.
3. Lillian Faderman, ed., *Chloe Plus Olivia: An Anthology of Lesbian Literature from the Seventeenth Century to the Present* (New York: Viking, 1994), p. vii.
4. Terry Castle, ed., *The Literature of Lesbianism: A Historical Anthology from Ariosto to Stonewall* (New York: Columbia, 2003), p. xix.
5. Alan Bray, *Homosexuality in Renaissance England* (London: Gay Men's Press, 1982), pp. 99, 78.
6. Randolph Trumbach, 'Modern Sodomy: The Origins of Homosexuality, 1700–1800', in *A Gay History of England: Love and Sex Between Men Since the Middle Ages*, ed. Matt Cook (Oxford: Greenwood, 2007), pp. 77–106 (pp. 77, 78); H. G. Cocks, 'Secrets, Crimes and Diseases, 1800–1914', in *A Gay History of England*, ed. Cook, pp. 107–44 (p. 107).
7. Martin Baumi Duberman, *About Time: Exploring the Gay Past* (New York: Meridian, 1991), p. 453; Mark Mitchell and David Leavitt, eds., *The Penguin Book of Gay Short Stories* (New York: Penguin, 1994), p. xvi.
8. Joseph Cady, 'English Literature: Nineteenth Century', in *The Gay and Lesbian Literary Heritage*, ed. Claude J. Summers (New York: Henry Holt, 1995), pp. 240–50 (p. 241); Michael S. Foldy, *The Trials of Oscar Wilde: Deviance, Morality, and Late-Victorian Society* (New Haven: Yale University Press, 1997), p. 46.
9. Jeffrey Weeks, *Coming Out: Homosexual Politics in Britain from the Nineteenth Century to the Present* (London: Quartet Books, 1990), p. 48; Cady, 'English Literature: Nineteenth Century', p. 247.

10. Marilyn R. Farwell, 'The Lesbian Narrative: "The Pursuit of the Inedible by the Unspeakable"', in *Professions of Desire: Lesbian and Gay Studies in Literature*, ed. George E. Haggerty and Bonnie Zimmerman (New York: MLA, 1995), pp. 156–68 (p. 157).
11. Weeks, *Coming Out*, p. 22; Mitchell and Leavitt, *Penguin Book of Gay Short Stories*, p. xiv.
12. Cady, 'English Literature: Nineteenth Century', p. 247; James Gifford, ed., *Glances Backward: An Anthology of American Homosexual Writing, 1830–1920* (Peterborough: Broadview, 2007), p. xx.
13. Brian Reade, ed., *Sexual Heretics: Male Homosexuality in English Literature from 1850 to 1900* (New York: Coward-McCann, 1971), p. 2; Wittig quoted in Diana Collecott, 'What is Not Said: A Study in Textual Inversion', in *Sexual Sameness: Textual Differences in Lesbian and Gay Writing*, ed. Joseph Bristow (London: Routledge, 1992), pp. 91–110 (p. 92).
14. Lillian Faderman, *Surpassing the Love of Men* (New York: Quill, 1981), p. 392.
15. Lillian Faderman, 'Lesbian Magazine Fiction in the Early Twentieth Century', *Journal of Popular Culture*, 11 (1978), 4, pp. 800–17 (p. 800).
16. John-Charles Duffy, 'Gay-Related Themes in the Fairy Tales of Oscar Wilde', *Victorian Literature and Culture*, 29 (2001), 1, pp. 327–49 (pp. 329, 340).
17. Faderman, 'Lesbian Magazine Fiction in the Early Twentieth Century', p. 811.
18. Kate Flint, 'The "Hour of Pink Twilight": Lesbian Poetics and Queer Encounters in the Fin-de-Siècle Streets', *Victorian Studies*, 51 (2009), 4, pp. 687–712 (p. 705).
19. Axel Nissen, 'The Queer Short Story', in *The Art of Brevity: Excursions in Short Fiction Theory and Analysis*, ed. Per Winther, Jakob Lothe and Hans H. Skei (Columbia, SC: University of South Carolina Press, 2004), pp. 181–90 (pp. 186, 188, 198).
20. Quoted in Weeks, *Coming Out*, p. 165.
21. Jeffrey Weeks and Kevin Porter, eds., *Between the Acts: Lives of Homosexual Men 1885–1967* (London: Rivers Oram, 1998), pp. 1, 3, 4.
22. Robert Phillips, ed., *The Stories of Denton Welch* (New York: E. P. Dutton, 1985), p. xii.
23. Steven Moore, *Ronald Firbank: An Annotated Bibliography of Secondary Materials 1905–1995* (Champaign, IL: Dalkey Archive Press, 1996), p. 8.
24. E. M. Forster, *The Life to Come and Other Stories* (London: Edward Arnold, 1972), p. xii.
25. Lillian Faderman, 'Lesbian Magazine Fiction in the Early Twentieth Century', p. 802; Terry Castle, ed., *The Literature of Lesbianism*, p. 1025.
26. Ann Aldrich, ed., *Carol in a Thousand Cities* (Greenwich, CT: Gold Medal Books, 1960), pp. 101–2.

27. Bonnie Zimmerman *The Safe Sea of Women: Lesbian Fiction 1969–1989* (Boston: Beacon Press, 1990), p. 9.
28. Jo-Ann Wallace, 'The Case of Edith Ellis', in *Modernist Sexualities*, ed. Hugh Stevens and Caroline Howlett (Manchester University Press, 2000), pp. 13–40 (p. 21).
29. Jane Rule, *Lesbian Images* (Garden City, NY: Doubleday, 1975), p. 105; Gillian Hanscombe, 'Katherine Mansfield's Pear Tree', in *What Lesbians Do in Books*, ed. Elaine Hobby and Chris White (London: The Women's Press, 1991), pp. 111–33 (p. 113); Erin Douglas, 'Queering Flowers, Queering Pleasures in Virginia Woolf's "Slater's Pins Have No Points"', *Virginia Woolf Miscellany*, 82 (2012), pp. 13–15.
30. Alberto Manguel and Craig Stephenson, eds., *Meanwhile, In Another Part of the Forest: Gay Stories from Alice Munro to Yukio Mishima* (Toronto: A. A. Knopf, 1994), pp. 572, 559.
31. Angus Wilson, *The Wrong Set* (London: Secker and Warburg, 1949), pp. 217, 214.
32. John M. Clum, 'Williams, Tennessee (1911–1983)', GLBTQ.glbtq.com/litera ture/williams_t.html (accessed 26 Aug. 2014).
33. *The Collected Stories of Noël Coward* (New York: Dutton, 1983), p. 349.
34. Manguel and Stephenson, eds., *Meanwhile, in Another Part of the Forest*, p. 404.
35. Faderman, ed., *Chloe Plus Olivia*, p. 51.
36. Reed Woodhouse, *Unlimited Embrace: A Canon of Gay Fiction, 1945–1995* (Amherst: University of Massachusetts Press, 1998), p. 304.
37. Les Brookes, *Gay Male Fiction Since Stonewall: Ideology, Conflict, and Aesthetics* (New York: Routledge, 2009), p. 41.
38. Paulina Palmer, *Contemporary Women's Fiction: Narrative Practice and Feminist Theory* (Jackson: University of Mississippi, 1989).
39. Zimmerman, *Safe Sea of Women*, p. 2.
40. Adam Mars-Jones, ed., *Mae West is Dead* (London: Faber & Faber, 1983), p. 42.
41. Adam Mars-Jones, *Monopolies of Loss* (London: Faber & Faber, 1992), p. 3.
42. Lilian Mohin and Anna Livia, eds., *The Pied Piper* (London: Onlywomen Press, 1989), p. ix.
43. Helen Sandler, ed., *The Diva Book of Short Stories* (London: Diva Books, 2000), p. ix.
44. Margaret Reynolds, ed., *The Penguin Book of Lesbian Short Stories* (London: Viking, 1993), p. 394.
45. Sara Ahmed, *The Promise of Happiness* (Durham, NC: Duke University Press, 2010).
46. Joanne Winning, ed., *The Crazy Jig* (Edinburgh: Polygon, 1992), p. 4.
47. Toni Davidson, 'Introduction', *Borderline* (Edinburgh: Mainstream Publishing, 2001), pp. 9–10, p. 10.
48. Sandler, ed., *The Diva Book of Short Stories*, p. viii.

49. Justin Gowers, 'Britain Does Not Publish Enough Gay Fiction', Books Blog. *The Guardian.* Web. 25 June 2007, n.p. www.theguardian.com/books/booksblog/2007/jun/25/britaindoesnotpublishenoug (accessed 22 September 2014).
50. Zoë Strachan, ed., *Out There* (Glasgow: Freight Books, 2014), p. 9.

19
Stories of Jewish Identity: Survivors, Exiles and Cosmopolitans

AXEL STÄHLER

'The first short stories ever written were of course Jewish short stories.'[1] The confident, if controversial, claim of the British Jewish writer Gerda Charles (born Edna Lipson) posits the historical Jewish affinity with the short story. What she has in mind are the biblical stories of Joseph and Potiphar's wife (Genesis 39) and the books of Ruth and Esther. In a similar vein, Joseph Leftwich charts the Jewish narrative tradition as a tradition of the short story through legends, fables and parables from the Bible to the Talmud and Rabbinic literature to more recent folk tales and, eventually, the Jewish contribution to the cultural production of the modern nations in languages other than Hebrew or Yiddish.[2]

The focus of this chapter is on the British Jewish short story in English, which in the past has suffered a surprising lack of recognition. There is, to date, no comprehensive anthology, though there have been various attempts in the Anglophone world at anthologizing Jewish short stories. In order to gain a sense of the development of the British Jewish short story and its place in the larger context of English (or perhaps better Anglophone) and Jewish literature it is therefore useful to explore its manifestation in some such collections which are, after all, dedicated to categorization and, at least implicitly, to the negotiation of a canon.

Anthologies, by their very nature, need to define criteria of inclusion and exclusion which extend beyond the question of literary quality. Seen in a comparative historical perspective, such collections accordingly chart shifts in the approach to Jewish secular writing pre- and post-Holocaust, from its emergence in the middle of the nineteenth century to (almost) the present day. Significantly, as such they suggest a trajectory of the global evolution of the Jewish short story while simultaneously indicating, more specifically, patterns of the perception of British Jewish short stories in changing contexts. Indeed, it is possible to discern two putative phases of anthologizing British Jewish short stories in the Anglophone world, which negotiate between these two parameters.

The first phase was initiated in 1933 when the poet, translator and critic Joseph Leftwich published *Yisröel: The First Jewish Omnibus* with James Heritage in London. In 1963 a collection of *Modern Jewish Stories* was published by Faber and Faber and less than two decades on, in 1979, *The Penguin Book of Jewish Short Stories*, edited by the British Jewish writers Gerda Charles and Emanuel Litvinoff, respectively. The second phase arguably becomes manifest with the publication in 1998 of *The Oxford Book of Jewish Stories*, edited by the Mexican-American Jewish writer Ilan Stavans, and of Bryan Cheyette's *Contemporary Jewish Writing in Britain and Ireland*.

The tension between these two approaches – of understanding Jewish short stories either in individual national contexts or as part of much wider, transnational and transcultural Jewish creativity – usefully illustrates the perennial problem of how to position and contextualize the work of Jewish writers. As Leftwich observed in 1933, 'It is the old question again, whether the Jews are a nation or a religious community.'[3] The issue is further confused by the movement of individual writers, which blurs arbitrarily imposed national, if not linguistic, boundaries. Post-war Jewish culture in Britain was dominated by émigré writers, which to some extent reflects the pattern of Britain's emerging multicultural society in general. Another, perhaps even more significant factor was Jewish displacement as a result of the Holocaust. Yet even before the Second World War Jewish writing in Britain reflected the impact of exile and migration.

While these two approaches are not necessarily mutually exclusive, in most of the anthologies which include a British Jewish element the predominant trajectory nevertheless appears to have been one of subsuming short stories by Jewish writers from different cultural and national backgrounds under a Jewish label. In what follows I will explore some of the tensions between the 'national' and 'transnational' trajectories.

Anthologizing British Jewish Short Stories

In the 'English Section' of *Yisröel*, Leftwich included nineteen writers from the first half of the nineteenth century to the time of publication. His choice comprises Benjamin Disraeli, Grace Aguilar, Mathilde Blind, Amy Levy, Alfred Sutro, Israel and Louis Zangwill, Samuel Gordon, S[amuel] L[evy] Bensusan, M[yer] J[ack] and Gertrude Landa ('Aunt Naomi'), W[alter]

L[ionel] George, Gilbert Frankau, Paul Selver, Hannah Berman, G. B. [Bertha Gladys] Stern, Sarah Gertrude Millin, Louis Golding and Cecil Roth. Most of these names, if not entirely forgotten, are today shrouded in obscurity. Some, such as the historian Cecil Roth, are not known primarily for their literary output; others, such as the dramatist Alfred Sutro, achieved recognition mainly in other genres; some, such as Hannah Berman and Sarah Gertrude Millin, were not British in the more narrow sense. Both were born in Lithuania and at a young age migrated with their families to Ireland and South Africa, respectively, though Berman later settled in England. Their inclusion suggests that Leftwich understood 'English' to mean Anglophone rather than British. His choice is moreover indicative of the increasing significance of Anglophone Jewish writers in South Africa and of the tentative beginnings of Jewish writing in English in the Anglophone diaspora outside the imperial centre and America, the latter meriting a section of its own in his anthology.

Leftwich's editorial decisions clearly reflect the pre-war period and as such are in striking contrast to both Charles's and Litvinoff's post-war choices. A revised edition of *Yisröel* was issued in May 1945, twelve years after its first publication. Between them, the editions span a period that coincides precisely with the rise of Nazi rule in Germany and the end of the Second World War. As early as 1933, the proliferating antisemitism in Nazi Germany must have suggested an ominous portent to Leftwich, the implications of which for his own project he could not ignore, even though he could not have foreseen its eventual cataclysmic impact. Extrapolating from the situation in Germany but reversing the perspective, he asks:

> Is there really such a thing as a specifically Jewish culture that spreads all over the world through all cultures and traditions, and that works through in spite of environment and education and language and common fate and common interest with your fellow-countrymen who are not Jews? (p. xxix)

His answer is of ingenuous simplicity, if tantalizingly vague: 'Writers are descended one from the other. There is a cultural lineage as well as a physical' (p. xxix). Leftwich consequently rejects, or at the very least casts doubt on, the 'blood' model of Jewishness and insists instead on multidirectional processes of hybridization in different linguistic contexts.

Yet even within a more unified linguistic sphere, there appears to be little uniformity. Indeed, the stories gathered by Leftwich in the English section of his anthology – arranged chronologically according to the writers' date of birth and spanning the whole of the nineteenth century from 1804 (Disraeli) to 1899 (Roth) – are as diverse as their authors' backgrounds. Some of them have no obvious Jewish content, such as Disraeli's 'Ixion in Heaven' (1832–3), Sutro's 'The Bread on the Waters' (1891), Bensusan's 'Death' (1933?), George's 'Ave, Amor, Morituri Te Salutant' (1927) and Selver's 'Well, I'm Blowed' (1929). Others are set in a vaguely Jewish milieu or have characters with Jewish names, yet do not address specifically 'Jewish' themes, such as Blind's 'Leopold Sontheim's Confession' (1885), Louis Zangwill's 'Prelude to a Pint of Bitter' (1933?), Landa's 'My Venetian Singer' (1933?) and Stern's 'Cinderella's Sister' (1921). Golding's 'The Doomington Wanderer' (1933?) is set mainly within the Jewish community of the author's eponymous fictional rendering of Manchester, in which he also set his best-selling novel Magnolia Street (1932). Others, such as Israel Zangwill in 'The Sabbath Breaker' (1893) and Berman in 'The Horse Thief' (1933?), write of Jewish life and traditions in Eastern Europe. In contrast, Gordon's 'The Miraculous Kaddish' (1933?) is set in all likelihood in London's East End, though this is never made explicit. Curiously, Leftwich excluded the much more influential ghetto tales of Israel Zangwill – such as those collected in his *Ghetto Tragedies* (1903) and *Ghetto Comedies* (1907) – which elaborated a thematic link of the Jewish experience in the East End with a literary tradition that had evolved since the second half of the nineteenth century among Jewish writers from central and eastern Europe.

Compared with the literature of post-war multiculturalism, very few of these texts negotiate identities. Rather, where they are concerned with Jewish identities at all, they project Jewishness most frequently in an apologetic mode in response to established stereotypes. In the process new stereotypes of the quaint humanity of the Jew were created. Identity conflicts, hybridity, mimicry and similar issues proliferating in post-war Jewish literature, are not yet a concern of these earlier writers. However, antisemitism and racial stereotyping are already recurrent themes. Stories such as Levy's 'Cohen of Trinity' (1889), M. J. Landa's 'Two Legacies' (1933?), Frankau's 'An Outlier from His Tribe' (1933?) and Cecil Roth's 'The Martyr' (1932) engage with manifestations of both on different levels.[4]

In a purely literary sense, Levy's story is certainly the most accomplished of these four. Yet it is, in its engagement with antisemitic stereotypes, perhaps also the most ambivalent. It is about a Jewish writer expelled from Cambridge because he 'had entirely failed to follow up on his preliminary distinction' and who eventually kills himself at the peak of his unexpected literary success.[5] As in her earlier novel *Reuben Sachs* (1888), if more subtly, Levy castigates in her story the materialism of Anglo-Jewish society as well as its internal divisions and Jewish ('tribal') characteristics. While Cohen's fierce individuality is emphasized, he is nevertheless perceived in relation to the imagined sleazy chaos of his family home and his characterization conforms so closely to prevalent antisemitic stereotypes as to challenge them. The story's impact is reinforced by the implicit non-Jewishness of Levy's narrator, whose ambivalent response to Cohen is as an object of distantly amused scrutiny. However, what appear to be manifestations of the author's Jewish self-hate should rather be seen as the desire for a frank and unbiased characterization, untainted by the 'allosemitism' decried much later by Zygmunt Bauman, which posits the Jew as the perpetual other.[6]

Sarah Gertrude Millin's 'Why Adonis Laughed' (1929) demonstrates no overt affinity with Jewish themes. The writer, praised by Leftwich as 'perhaps the most important woman writing to-day in English literature, and one of the greatest writers of our time' (p. 169), is viewed less enthusiastically today for what has been called her 'obsession' with 'the supposed dire consequences of miscegenation'.[7] It is nevertheless the perceived potential of interracial conflict and ambiguity which makes her story stand out from the others in Leftwich's collection, although it needs to be understood within the specific context of her own South African background.

This particular story has been described as 'a "white peril" narrative',[8] which places the focus on the (alleged) rape of the young black woman Dinah by her white master. While never made explicit, the connotations carried by the young woman's name support this reading. In Genesis 34, Dinah, Jacob's daughter with Leah, is raped by Shechem and her violation subsequently brings destruction on the offending Canaanites at the hands of the Israelites. As such, the name answers not only to the rape narrative suggested by Graham but also to anxieties of racial retribution. But the true point of the story is, I would suggest, another one, and it may also have been Leftwich's reason for including it in his anthology: not only does David's harsh service for Dinah recall Jacob's wooing of Rachel (see Genesis 29:15–30), but Dinah and David – the black 'boy' who marries her without being aware of her violation, which is suggested only by the birth of a light-skinned baby – are the only characters in the story with biblical Jewish names. Both of these implicit associations of the poor River Kaffirs with the Jews are significant because they relate to negotiations of Jewish racial positioning in pre-war South Africa. Ultimately, the story appears to reflect, through the vicarious example of Dinah and David, on the racial insecurity experienced by Jews in South Africa, and it is this which not only distinguishes it from all the other stories in the English section of Leftwich's anthology but which makes 'Why

Adonis Laughed' and its racialized context anticipate the post-war preoccupation with ethnic identity.

Poignantly laying claim with its Hebrew/Yiddish main title to a specific national and cultural identity, Leftwich's *Yisröel* is a significant early attempt at establishing a canon. As such it is all the more striking when compared with its revised editions of 1945 and 1963. The Yiddish section remained the longest in the anthology and was evidently considered by Leftwich to be paradigmatic of the transnational nature of Jewish fiction, more than the increasingly diminished English or the surprisingly slim American sections. In contrast, the British Jewish writer Gerda Charles identified in the introduction to her own anthology, *Modern Jewish Stories* (1963), a significant shift in contemporary Jewish writing: 'In general, outside Israel ... the great, splendid achievement is with the English-speaking countries: England, the Commonwealth and, above all, America'. Indeed, Charles noted how difficult it was to balance the American Jewish preponderance, although she concluded with restrained optimism that 'the last few years have seen an unprecedented rise in the number and quality of Anglo-Jewish creative writers'.[9]

Indeed, the publication of Charles's anthology coincided with the rise of what later in the very same year, 1963, would be styled the 'Jewish New Wave'.[10] This, in turn, needs to be seen in context with the rapid and sweeping cultural change which affected all of Britain after the war and which saw in the wake of the *Windrush* generation the emergence and gradual ascendancy of a plurality of ethnic voices, most conspicuously of those conveniently but controversially gathered under the label of Black British literature. The anthology's blurb recognized the emergence of a 'contemporary Jewish scene' and associated the 'Jewish renaissance' with these developments. Yet the qualities which give 'the best Jewish writing its distinctive flavour' are confidently identified as 'respect for suffering, regard for moral good, underlying optimism, unfailing humour'.[11] Conspicuously, the image of Jewishness sketched here is fully compatible with constructions of Englishness and corresponds to stereotypical notions of the British support of the underdog and the stiff upper lip. And while reference to the 'Jewish renaissance' may, if perhaps subliminally, suggest the rebirth of Jewish writing after the cataclysm of the Holocaust, the blurb eschews direct mention of Jewish victimization or of the Holocaust. Even the criterion of 'respect for suffering' suggests a bystander's perspective rather than that of the sufferer. As such, the blurb engages in a simplification of the editor's much more diffident reflections, arguably in order to emphasize Jewish whiteness or even Englishness and, subtly, to demarcate Jewish writing in Britain and the Commonwealth from the multicultural proliferation of 'coloured' writing.

In her introduction, Charles matter-of-factly conceded that there was not much to be gleaned from Eastern Europe and Germany in the wake of the Holocaust. Less than two decades on, the editor of *The Penguin Book of Jewish Short Stories* (1979), the British Jewish writer Emanuel Litvinoff, nevertheless once again emphasized the significance of Jewish cultural production in Yiddish and its transformative impact on a transnational scale.[12] Alongside Anglophone Jewish writers, Litvinoff therefore privileges Yiddish writers – from pre-Holocaust Eastern Europe and from America – as well as Israeli authors, the one exception being Isaac Babel, whose language was Russian. The only British Jewish short story writers Litvinoff included in his collection, in addition to one of his own texts, were Dan Jacobson and Muriel Spark. 'Fanya', from Litvinoff's *Journey through a Small Planet* (1972), is set in London's East End like most of the fictionalized memoir and relates the disappointment of an orphan girl in her romance with a Yiddish actor from America, even while it suggests the decline of Yiddish culture in Britain.

Jacobson's 'The Zulu and the Zeide' (1959) is perhaps the writer's most frequently anthologized story. It had already been included by Charles, as well as the 1963 edition of *Yisröel*, and – having been adapted, in 1965, for a Broadway musical – continues to be reprinted. As in Millin's 'Why Adonis Laughed' three decades earlier, racial positioning is the main theme of the story. Yet in Jacobson's narrative, as indicated by its title, a direct connection is drawn between blacks and Jews in South Africa. Jewish whiteness is no longer an issue in this story. The parameters have subtly shifted. The concern is now rather with Jewish complicity in the apartheid system and the obfuscation of the affinities between both ethnic groups by the arriviste Jewish whites.

More intriguing is Litvinoff's choice of Spark. In a Jewish context the mainstream writer was clearly marginal. Indeed, 'The Gentile Jewesses' (1963), reprinted by Litvinoff, is one of the very few open engagements of the prolific writer with her part-Jewish heritage. Through its exploration of ostensibly irreconcilable paradoxes, the story challenges the validity of established notions of essentialism and enacts a quest for belonging that nevertheless embraces multiple identifications of equal validity as articulated in the oxymoron of the title, a description the narrator accepts, in emulation of her grandmother and mother, also for herself.[13]

Spark was certainly not part of the 'new wave' of British Jewish writing, though as Cheyette observes, her hybrid background 'enabled her to become an essentially diasporic writer with a fluent sense of self'.[14] Yet the marginality of Spark in the Jewish context and the way in which it is elided in Litvinoff's collection is worthy of note. Thus, in the short biography prefaced to the story itself, it is mentioned that Spark 'was born in Edinburgh of part-Jewish origin on both sides of her family'.[15] No mention, however, is made of her conversion to Catholicism in 1954, nor of her reluctance to engage with 'Jewish' themes.

Read synoptically, these earlier anthologies – edited by Leftwich, Charles and Litvinoff – seem to chronicle the decline of the Jewish short story in Britain: from the wide-ranging panorama offered in Leftwich's *Yisröel* to Charles's carefully optimistic appraisal, which coincided with the 'new wave' of Jewish writing in Britain of which she herself was a proponent, to Litvinoff's almost complete elision of the British segment in his anthology. This trajectory was confirmed two decades later in *The Oxford Book of Jewish Stories* (1998), edited by Ilan Stavans. This anthology eschews the 'national/linguistic' principle of categorization and follows a chronological trajectory that emphasizes the editor's transnational approach. Simultaneously, however, Stavans deliberately chose to represent a specific secular Jewish tradition originating in the Yiddish writing of Sholem Jacob Abramovitsh (better known by his pen-name Mendele Mocher Seforim) in the middle of the nineteenth century, which forced the editor 'to eliminate predecessors in non-Jewish languages, such as Benjamin Disraeli and Heinrich Heine, as well as early practitioners in Yiddish and Hebrew, such as Abraham Mapu and Isaac Meir Dick' – a decision which seems counterproductive and potentially misleading.[16]

More explicitly than any of the preceding anthologies, Stavans's collection promotes the comprehensive construction of a transnational 'Jewish' canon, which is developed in the editor's introduction and supported with various reading aids – such as a chronology of modern Jewish literature, 1767–1997 (pp. 471–81), and a thematic index detailing, as central concerns of modern Jewish stories allegories, antisemitism and the Holocaust, biblical themes, domestic affairs, interreligious and ethnic relations, Israel and the diaspora, modernity, mysticism and the kabbalah (pp. 483–5). Israel Zangwill, Dan Jacobson and Elias Canetti are the only British Jewish authors to be included in the anthology. Canetti's 'The Sacrifice of the Prisoner', an excerpt from his monumental novel *Die Blendung* (1935; *Auto-da-Fé*), rather than a short story proper, is identified in Stavans's thematic index as an allegory, while both

Zangwill's 'Tug of Love' (1907) and Jacobson's 'The Zulu and the Zeide' are listed under domestic affairs and modernity, with the latter also being recorded under interreligious and ethnic relations, a particular concern which Jacobson, as discussed above, shares with Millin and which arguably originates in the authors' South African background. Thus reduced to the historical example of Zangwill and two émigré authors (one of whom, the Nobel laureate Canetti, continued to write in German and later chose to live in Switzerland), the British Jewish short story has almost completely been written out of Stavans's narrative of the Jewish short story.

However, in the same year, 1998, a dedicated attempt was made by the scholar Bryan Cheyette in his anthology of *Contemporary Jewish Writing in Britain and Ireland* to reverse this trajectory. While not exclusively focused on the short story, this anthology nevertheless gathers significant samples of the genre. Cheyette's book was the first in the *Jewish Writing in the Contemporary World* series and needs to be seen in this context. 'Each volume', as general editor Sander L. Gilman explains, 'will focus on one culture and the writing of Jews in that culture today. The complexity of this project is that in moving from time to time, from language to language, from culture to culture, all of these terms take on fine differentiations.' The purpose of the series is 'to make writing by young and notable Jewish writers available to an American reading public that recognizes only a few categories of "Jewish" writing'.[17]

Cheyette's particular objective is 'to focus on one specific narrative by tracing a history of extraterritorial or diasporic British-Jewish literature from the early twentieth century to the present day' (p. xiii). Significantly, the editor's emphasis throughout 'is as much on the Englishness of Jewish writing as on a supposedly authentic Jewishness', because one cannot, as he suggests, understand the writers in his anthology 'without taking note of the national context in which they produce their works' (p. xiii). For Jewish writers in Britain this meant, as Cheyette argues, that 'most have had to write against the dominance of an oppressive Englishness' (p. xiii).[18]

One arena in which this struggle was enacted was the literary engagement with the central Jewish experience of the Holocaust, which pitches narratives of Jewish victimization against British defiance and victory – competing narratives that ultimately are incompatible and, potentially, irreconcilable. Accordingly, in Cheyette's anthology of British and Irish Jewish writing, the Holocaust has been given much prominence – in contrast to the earlier collections, in which the literary response to the Holocaust has been excluded from their British Jewish segments.

From Un-thology to Anthology: The Holocaust in British Jewish Short Stories

When Leftwich revised his 1933 volume in 1945, the experience of the Holocaust was perhaps still too immediate to expect an anthology like *Yisröel* to be informed by it. Yet even so one may wonder at the editor's decision to omit Grace Aguilar's 'The Fugitive'. Aguilar is not only significant as one of the earliest Jewish writers in Britain to achieve national, and indeed international, recognition. Frequently responding in her fiction, like the Moss sisters after her, to stereotypes of Jewish femininity as they were elaborated in historical romances such as Walter Scott's *Ivanhoe* (1820), she also keenly addressed the persecution of the Jews in both her fiction and her non-fiction.[19]

First published posthumously in 1852 in the collection *Home Scenes and Heart Studies*, 'The Fugitive', like Aguilar's successful novel *The Vale of Cedars; or, The Martyr* (1850), details Jewish suffering under the Inquisition in Spain. However, as historical fiction, it most importantly offered its author 'a way of writing modern Anglo-Jewish history'.[20] Aguilar's persecution narrative, written about a century before the Holocaust and focusing on a period another century before that, might easily have served Leftwich as a reflection on the contemporary conflagration during which England, yet again, had been the only stalwart in Europe to oppose the oppressor. Yet even at this early juncture he might have felt that to compare the earlier persecution in any way with that of his own day could demean the latter.

While in 1945 Leftwich was faced not only with the ineffability of the Holocaust but also with a distinct lack of literary engagement with the so recent catastrophe, in the English section of the 1963 edition of *Yisröel* he included Alexander Baron's 'The Anniversary' (1954). Published by Yoseloff in New York, this edition of the anthology addresses a specifically American Jewish readership with different sensibilities, which may account for the new acknowledgment of the Holocaust. Baron (born Joseph Alexander Bernstein) recounts in his text a ceremony commemorating the tenth anniversary of the beginning of the mass deportations of Jews from Paris in 1942. It exposes how 'the protecting shell of present time' is broken among the audience when the testimony of an unknown speaker – '"Who is she?" Another voice: "No one. A survivor"' – evokes the anguish of the so-called *rafle du Velodrome d'Hiver*.[21]

The emotional impact of Baron's short text is such that one wonders at the assurance with which Gerda Charles dismissed contemporary short stories of the Holocaust as lacking in power.[22] But not only 'The Anniversary' challenges such an assumption. Brian Glanville was at the crest of the new wave of Jewish writing in Britain and Charles included his 'A Betting Man' in her *Modern Jewish Stories*. While it is perhaps more indicative of Glanville's work, which increasingly focused on sport, and on football in particular, it is not this story that I want to discuss here but the one that Charles chose to ignore. Like 'A Betting Man', 'The Survivor' was first published in Glanville's 1961 collection, *A Bad Streak and Other Stories*.

'The Survivor' is about an Eastern European Jewish refugee boy taken in by an Anglo-Jewish family after the war and subsequently turned Israeli sailor. From time to time he still visits. Marion, the Levinson's daughter, feels him to be a 'vague, latent menace', a sentiment that is only intensified over the years and reflected also in his increasingly alarming behaviour to which the young girl's mother turns a blind eye.[23] When he eventually rapes Marion, it is implied that the experience of the Holocaust cannot be domesticated, that the damage done to the individual is transmitted to and wreaks havoc also in the supposedly safe haven inhabited by the Levinsons.

By the time Stavans's and Cheyette's collections were published (1998), the Holocaust had of course made it into the anthology and both include various texts that engage directly or indirectly with the Holocaust. Though born in America, Ruth Fainlight has long been considered to write in the British Jewish tradition and 'Another Survivor' (1978), reprinted by Cheyette, addresses a topic in relation to the Holocaust that also resonates with a specifically British context. Fainlight's protagonist was on the *Kindertransport*, a British rescue effort that allowed 10,000 children of Jewish descent to leave Germany and Nazi-occupied territories between 1938 and 1940. The story chronicles how Rudi, having repressed all memories of his parents for a long time, in middle age gradually begins to transform the bland house he shares with his new family with antiques in an attempt to recreate his childhood home in Berlin. Eventually, he (ab)uses his adolescent daughter by fashioning her into a likeness of his mother. Yet his overarching sense of guilt finally erupts in violence when, disturbed by the likeness he has created, he tears his mother's dress off his daughter to shatter the illusion, to single her out as his victim as someone else must have singled out his mother. To her distraught cry of 'Fascist!' he leaves the house to wander the streets 'until he reaches the end of his endurance and drops in his tracks'.[24]

Fainlight's story addresses the phenomenon of survivor's guilt and the trauma of the Holocaust, suggesting also its impact on subsequent generations. It is predicated on its distance from the historical event of the Holocaust: the ineffable is investigated through its effect on the lives of survivors and bystanders. As in 'The Anniversary' and 'The Survivor', the safe insulation 'within the present', in Baron's words, 'a blessed, a necessary protection', is breached and the devastating mental damage exposed as a menace barely hidden by the protective shell of life after the Holocaust.[25] The un-thologizing of Holocaust stories arguably is another layer of this shell, while the gradual incursion of Holocaust stories into the anthology signals an increasing willingness, or even the compulsion, to acknowledge and to confront the historical event and its continuous impact.

Beyond the Anthology

As the proximity of the original publication dates of Baron's and Glanville's stories suggests, interest in the Holocaust increased after the middle of the 1950s among British Jewish writers, though it never achieved the prominence it has in American Jewish writing. One British Jewish writer for whom 'the Holocaust is a literary obsession that haunts his pseudoautobiographical persona', is Clive Sinclair.[26] Efraim Sicher illustrates this contention with 'The Creature on My Back' (1979), which in Sinclair's macabre and darkly humorous style shows the narrator struggling with an evil-minded (imaginary) creature on his back, which attempts to claim him and his posterity to Holocaust victimhood. Yet when he confides in a psychologist, he is told that he is lucky: 'You have a creature on your back. Such things are not common in Canada. It may yet go away. As for myself, I have a number on my arm. A souvenir of Europe.'[27]

The Holocaust informs many of Sinclair's stories if frequently more subtly. 'The Luftmensh' (1979) is of particular interest because it articulates another of its author's obsessions: the critical engagement with Israel. A connection is drawn between the Holocaust, survivor's guilt, the demise of Yiddish culture, slavery, the American Civil Rights Movement and Israel – and all that in the guise of a detective story with a nod, moreover, towards Philip Roth and his novel *The Ghost Writer* (1979) as well as the American Jewish writer's preoccupation with the confusion of identities. The writer Smolensky hires his namesake Joshua Smolensky, private eye and narrator of the story, to find another author whom he met at a colony of writers – in Philip Roth's former room, 'no less'.[28] Almost like a *dybbuk* (in Jewish folklore an evil spirit which possesses a living person), the Yiddish writer Victor Stenzil has taken possession of Smolensky the author by commissioning him to tell the story of his life – like a ghost writer – because he can no longer write in the language of the victims of the Holocaust. Initially reluctant, Smolensky finally agrees: 'The fact is that Victor grew, in the space of a single day, from an object of irritation into a living obsession. He became my subject, and I his' (p. 53). There is a clear echo here of the creature on the back. Victor's obsession, which condemns him to silence, is the Holocaust he did not experience.

One motif recurrent in many British Jewish short stories – as in Jewish stories more universally – is that of the wanderer. Sinclair's 'Luftmensh' and his other 'road' story of 'The Creature on My Back' are cases in point. Though one should be wary of attributing this thematic preoccupation merely to age-old stereotypes of the 'wandering Jew', the historical precariousness informing much of the Jewish experience may well be held to account for it. For this reason the attempt to produce narrative coherence beyond the single short story form, while nevertheless focusing in individual sketches on the wanderer, as it surfaces for instance in Gabriel Josipovici's collection *Goldberg: Variations* (2002) and Tamar Yellin's *Tales of the Ten Lost Tribes* (2008), is of particular interest.[29]

As suggested by the title of his collection, Josipovici follows with his thirty interconnected short stories the musical pattern set by Johann Sebastian Bach's *Goldberg Variations* (1741; BWV 988). The collection adapts the story of the harpsichord virtuoso Johann Gottlieb Goldberg, who supposedly played the variations to his patron to help him find the elusive sleep he craved. Josipovici's main narrator, the German Jewish writer Samuel Goldberg, is similarly employed by the country gentleman Tobias Westfield Esq. as a kind of reverse Sheherazade to battle his insomnia with nightly new stories. In addition to this formal model, and certainly no less significantly, Josipovici also engages in his stories with Paul Klee's 1940 painting *Wander-Artist (Ein Plakat)*.

The fragmentary, mosaic-like nature of Josipovici's short pieces, which range a-chronologically and non-sequentially from the eighteenth century to the present and occasionally confuse Goldberg with a persona more like that of the author, confronts the reader with ever-shifting perspectives on apparently disparate occurrences, which eventually, however, weave together past and present and return the reader matter-of-factly to the cycle's beginning – as does the repetition of Bach's theme in the conclusion of his variations.

The writer's representation of the Wander-Artist as a unifying device in particular suggests an interpretative key. A closer look at his twenty-seventh 'variation', entitled eponymously with Klee's picture, is especially illuminating in this context: 'Here I am, one hand raised in mock salute, on my way to the other side', it begins from the perspective of the stick figure-like image. 'To the other side of what? It does not matter. The other side.' Klee created the figure in the last year of his life, after he had been suffering from (undiagnosed and fatal) scleroderma for several years. Josipovici's reading of the Wander-Artist emphasizes its existential dimension. 'It does not matter', he continues the figure's imagined soliloquy, 'where I have come from. You could say that I am only alive when I come into view and where I am going is anyone's guess' (p. 179).

It seems more than likely that Josipovici's personal life as an émigré writer may have informed his *Goldberg: Variations*. Yet wandering is also at the heart of Tamar Yellin's *Tales of the Ten Lost Tribes* (2008), which is another collection of interlinked short stories. Yellin too, though born in the north of England, has a cosmopolitan family background. Her father was 'a third generation Jerusalemite and her mother the daughter of a Polish immigrant', and the writer describes 'the creative tension between her Jewish heritage and her Yorkshire roots' as a defining feature of her work (p. 157).

While this certainly is true of her first collection of short stories, *Kafka in Brontëland* (2006), it may be less so of *Tales of the Ten Lost Tribes*, in which the motif of wandering, a significant element also in her earlier collection, emerges as a structural principle. The circular structure of the collection sees the narrator in the concluding story in her own heart of darkness, travelling up-river in an exotic land 'deeper and deeper into the heart of the forest' (p. 151). Racked with fever, left by her guide, and unable to communicate with the locals, she clutches a charm she exchanged as a child with her wayward and disillusioned explorer-wanderer uncle for a diamond ring purloined from her mother.

As with Josipovici's *Variations*, each of Yellin's stories is 'valid' in itself but they nevertheless add up to more than the sum of the parts. 'Menasseh', the last of the ten stories, each named after one of the ten lost tribes of Israel, culminates in the inconclusive search for a mythical Jew called Isidore, like another Kurtz, from Conrad's 'Heart of Darkness', of whom conflicting stories are told. Isidore is the epitome of the wanderer and the 'perpetual foreigner' (p. 118). The sense of unfulfillment, of the agonisingly and perpetually disappointed search for belonging, pervades Yellin's whole collection.

While there are many stories by British Jewish writers published independently, the relatively recent proliferation of interweaving story cycles, such as Josipovici's and Yellin's, suggests not only the increasing prominence of these writers in a larger British context but also an emerging pattern of the pursuit of the transcendence of the meaning of individual stories, of the amplification of the sum of the parts. Jenny Diski's *The Vanishing Princess* (1995) and Elena Lappin's *Foreign Brides* (1999) are relevant here. The former is contained by two interrelated frame stories. The latter has a similar framing device in that the protagonist of the first story returns in the last, two decades on, and it too addresses forms of displacement in its twelve stories of those 'who have chosen to follow their partners to countries that are not their own'.[30] While Diski's stories have no obvious Jewish content but are strongly informed by the writer's feminist attitude, Lappin combines a frequently Jewish focus with a similar feminist approach.

Michelene Wandor's *False Relations* (2004) is another collection that blends the author's avowed feminism with a specifically Jewish perspective.[31] Moreover, as in Josipovici's *Goldberg: Variations*, Wandor explores musical resonances in her own stories of wandering. Like the Jewish composer Salamone Rossi, who appears in the title story and who worked in seventeenth-century Mantua under the patronage of the Gonzaga, some of these stories are set in or revolve around the Italian city. Yet the more pervasive connecting device in this case is, beyond musical allusions, the figure of 'the Jewish Princess' whose trajectory the reader follows in different stories from her expulsion from Spain in 1492 in 'Song of the Jewish Princess' to Mantua in 'Corridors of Light and Shadow', to the present in England in 'Toccata and Fugue', and finally to the biblical past in 'The Story of Esther and Vashti'.

Most of Wandor's stories embody a form of polyphony in that they interweave the dialogue of two typographically and stylistically distinct threads of narrative that illuminate one another. The promise of co-existence and of mutual understanding elaborated in 'False Relations' is transposed in the last story to the context of modern-day Israel. In 'Yom Tov', a middle-aged woman returns from abroad to visit the kibbutz where, as a child, she was saved by an Israeli Arab during a terrorist raid. By chance the man, shot in the act and 'despised by both sides' (p. 188), drives her taxi. On the way they realize that they both 'know the same piece of music' – one of Bach's French suites (p. 187). It connects them across the divides of Arab–Jewish and of time. Once again the story is also split into two narrative strands – the present and the woman's retrospective on the hazily remembered events of the terrorist attack. Yet like the false relations they are, there is no final convergence between both narratives, nor is there an open acknowledgment between the woman and her driver, the girl and her rescuer.

With wandering as a focus, the stories discussed in this concluding section confirm the paradigm of extraterritoriality observed by Bryan Cheyette. This is a paradigm that certainly did not yet apply in the pre-war period, in which the thematic concerns of British Jewish short story writers were as varied as their backgrounds. Nor was the narrative of the decline of the Jewish short story after the Second World War, written strong in the English segments of anthologies of Jewish short stories since 1933, particularly convincing. In fact, Cheyette's own collection of 1998 suggests the continuous presence of Jewish short stories in British writing. The fact that in more recent years Jewish writers have increasingly also worked on collections of short stories that seek to impart the narrative amplification of their cyclical structure demonstrates the increasing visibility of the Jewish short story in English and indicates its trajectory beyond marginality. In addition, contemporary stories by younger writers, such as Naomi Alderman, progressively appear to focus on the specificities and localities of Jewish life in Britain, although whether or not a new paradigm is developing must, for the time being, remain open to conjecture.

Notes

1. Gerda Charles, ed., *Modern Jewish Stories* (London: Faber & Faber, 1963), p. 9.
2. Joseph Leftwich, ed., *Yisröel: The First Jewish Omnibus* (London: James Heritage, 1933), pp. xix–xxii. The first revised edition was published in 1945 by James Clarke in London with a slightly modified subtitle as *Yisröel: The Jewish Omnibus*. In 1963 another revised edition was published by T. Yoseloff in New York, in which the content was updated and significantly changed.
3. Leftwich, ed., *Yisröel* (1933), p. 29.
4. It proved impossible to establish first publication dates for several of the short stories collected by Leftwich. All those stories for which the date 1933 is given here, and to which a question mark has been put, are listed in bibliographical reference works for the first time in relation to Leftwich's *Yisröel*; they may, nevertheless, have been published previously.
5. Leftwich, ed., *Yisröel* (1933), p. 51.
6. Zygmunt Bauman, 'Allosemitism: Premodern, Modern, Postmodern', in *Modernity, Culture and 'the Jew'*, ed. Bryan Cheyette and Laura Marcus (Cambridge: Polity, 1998), pp. 143–56.
7. *The Oxford Companion to Twentieth Century Literature in English*, ed. Jenny Stringer (Oxford University Press, 1996), s.v. 'Millin, Sarah Gertrude', p. 451.
8. Lucy Valerie Graham, *State of Peril: Race and Rape in South African Literature* (Oxford University Press, 2012), p. 79.
9. Charles, ed., *Modern Jewish Stories*; both quotations on p. 12.

10. See Tosco R. Fyvel, 'The Jewish New Wave', *Jewish Chronicle* (13 September 1963), New Year Section, pp. 37, 44.
11. Charles, ed., *Modern Jewish Stories*, dustjacket.
12. Emanuel Litvinoff, ed., *The Penguin Book of Jewish Short Stories* (Harmondsworth: Penguin, 1979).
13. Litvinoff, ed., *The Penguin Book of Jewish Short Stories*, p. 347.
14. Bryan Cheyette, 'Imagined Communities: Contemporary Jewish Writing in Great Britain', in *Contemporary Jewish Writing in Europe: A Guide*, ed. Vivian Liska and Thomas Nolden (Bloomington: Indiana University Press, 2007), pp. 90–116 (p. 94).
15. Litvinoff, ed., *The Penguin Book of Jewish Short Stories*, p. 344.
16. Ilan Stavans, ed., *The Oxford Book of Jewish Stories* (Oxford University Press, 1998), p. xi.
17. Bryan Cheyette, ed., *Contemporary Jewish Writing in Britain and Ireland* (London: Halban, 1998), pp. ix and x.
18. Ruth Gilbert's 2013 study of *Writing Jewish*, focusing on contemporary Jewish writing in Britain since the 1990s, seamlessly connected with Cheyette's introduction, which extended to the time of its publication (1998) and it became clear that the boundary between both coincides also with an important shift in British Jewish writing. This shift, as Gilbert contends, manifests itself in British Jewish writers 'confronting the interface between Jewishness and "Englishness"' and in 'shaking off a culture of reticence and self-censorship which arguably inhibited previous generations of Anglo-Jewry'. See Ruth Gilbert, *Writing Jewish: Contemporary British-Jewish Literature* (Basingstoke: Palgrave Macmillan, 2013), p. 9.
19. See, for example, Michael Galchinsky, *The Origin of the Modern Jewish Woman Writer: Romance and Reform in Victorian England* (Detroit, MI: Wayne State University Press, 1996).
20. Michael Ragussis, *Figures of Conversion: 'The Jewish Question' and English National Identity* (Durham, NC: Duke University Press, 1995), p. 149.
21. Leftwich, ed., *Yisröel* (1963), pp. 111, 110.
22. Charles, ed., *Modern Jewish Stories*, p. 12.
23. Brian Glanville, 'The Survivor', in *A Bad Streak and Other Stories* (London: Secker & Warburg, 1961), pp. 107–18 (p. 111).
24. Ruth Fainlight, 'Another Survivor', in Cheyette, ed., *Contemporary Jewish Writing*, pp. 73–80 (pp. 79, 80).
25. Leftwich, ed., *Yisröel* (1963), p. 110.
26. Efraim Sicher, *Beyond Marginality: Anglo-Jewish Literature after the Holocaust* (Albany: State University of New York Press, 1985), p. 161.
27. Clive Sinclair, 'The Creature on My Back', in *Hearts of Gold* (Harmondsworth: Penguin, 1982), pp. 85–97 (p. 97).
28. Clive Sinclair, 'The Luftmensh', in *Hearts of Gold*, pp. 51–63 (p. 51).

29. Gabriel Josipovici, *Goldberg: Variations* (Manchester: Carcanet, 2002) and Tamar Yellin, *Tales of the Ten Lost Tribes* (New Milford and London: Toby Press, 2008).
30. Elena Lappin, *Foreign Brides* (London: Picador, 1999), dustjacket.
31. Michelene Wandor, *False Relations* (Nottingham: Five Leaves, 2004).

20

New Voices: Multicultural Short Stories

ABIGAIL WARD

In thinking about ideas of newness and multiculturalism, it seems wise to begin with some historical contexts. Although the mid-twentieth century Caribbean migration that has come to be symbolized by the arrival of the SS *Empire Windrush* in June 1948 is often understood to be the 'beginning' of non-white arrival in Britain, there was in fact a black and Asian presence in Britain long before the late 1940s. As Peter Fryer writes in his memorable opening to *Staying Power* (1984), 'There were Africans in Britain before the English came here. Some were soldiers in the Roman imperial army that occupied the southern part of our island for three and a half centuries. Others were slaves.'[1] If we look at the post-war period, however, there is little sense of this longer history of black residence in Britain. The apparent 'forgetting' of this pre-1948 black history in Britain has been crucial in refuting the legitimacy of black habitation in Britain in the post-war years. Admitting that black people have lived in Britain longer than (in Fryer's words) 'the English' makes it difficult to cast them as recent intruders, or even visitors, to the country. The rhetoric of invasion was used by figures like Enoch Powell, who gave voice to a discontent earlier expressed in the series of post-war 'anti-black' riots, such as those of 1958 in Nottingham and Notting Hill, and the associated increase in racist violence and police brutality.[2]

It is also important to remember that migrants were writing long before they arrived in Britain. In the Caribbean, the short story was already a popular genre in the first half of the twentieth century, as shorter pieces of writing were more easily printed and disseminated in local news and magazine publications.[3] As Bill Schwartz has argued, 'West Indian emigrants came from societies well advanced in the prerequisites of breaking from colonialism ... The typewritten novels and poems in their suitcases, their mimeographed manifestos, their music: all were testament to the depth of emergent anti-colonial sensibilities.'[4] As this quotation suggests, much of this literature was political, expressing discontent at Empire. This period of writing in Britain has been typified by Sam Selvon's novel *The Lonely Londoners* (1956), which contrasts migrants' optimism and hope for a new life in Britain with the difficulties these men and women were little prepared for. As we see in this chapter, though, later twentieth- and twenty-first-century writing by migrants and their children is not necessarily any less political.

In writing about the multicultural short story, care is needed. The meaning and usefulness of the term 'multicultural' is often contested and challenged. A. Sivanadan, for example, has been careful to distinguish between 'multiculturalism as an outcome of the struggle for equality emanating from below, and multiculturalism as government policy imposed from above'.[5] The focus in this chapter from 1948 to the present also means we have seen a significant change in the positioning of non-white and postcolonial writers in Britain. These concerns notwithstanding, this chapter traces some developments in post-war short story writing by writers who are commonly known as 'postcolonial', 'migrant', 'black British', or 'British Asian'. Of course, there are many writers who might also be included in this chapter but are not for reasons of space, including Peter Ho Davies, Patricia Duncker, George Lamming and Ben Okri, to name just a few. The writers under focus in this chapter – Sam Selvon, Pauline Melville, E. A. Markham, Salman Rushdie, Hanif Kureishi, Jackie Kay and Zadie Smith – have been chosen to reflect a spectrum of diasporan perspectives on Britain, and to explore a trajectory in what may be termed 'multicultural' writing in Britain.

Sam Selvon was born in Trinidad in 1923 and worked as a journalist for *The Trinidad Guardian*, as fiction editor of *The Guardian Weekly*, and for the BBC. He was a prolific short story writer and often used the term 'ballad' to describe his stories, suggesting their link with musical and oral forms of transmission. Correspondingly, much has been written on Selvon's innovative use of Creole in his stories and novels. As Maria Grazia Sindoni argues, 'he experiments with a language that is neither English nor Trinidad Creole, but an artificial fusion where two languages merge and blend to yield an innovative and precocious response to the difficulties brought about by decolonisation'.[6] We can see this language at play in the story 'Finding Piccadilly Circus' (1950), which – like many of his early short stories – was later incorporated into *The Lonely Londoners*. In addition to Selvon's use of Creole, the Trinidadian qualities of this story are evoked by the use of a Caribbean frame of reference to describe London and its weather, for example: 'the wind pass through [his clothing] like if it is a mosquito net, and right there you should know yuh pardner start to shiver like he had malaria fever'.[7] Cultural differences are many; upon arrival, the narrator is amazed that there are white porters at the train station, and various aspects of British life are thus jokingly explored and defamiliarized, including unemployment benefit: 'wite people who ain't working looking at me cut-eye, like if they too vex that Ah come in they country and getting money for nothing' (p. 124). We see here an early indication of resentment at the migrants' presence, but also how the narrator shrugs it off as a joke, pointing to his resilience and good humour. The ultimate comedy, and reason for the story's title, is his confusion that Piccadilly Circus has no circus, and Lyons has no lions. In this way, Selvon explores with humour potentially distressing issues of communication and cultural dislocation.

As this defamiliarization suggests, Selvon's stories illustrate not only the impact of migration on the migrant, but also on the host city. This 'creolization' of Britain can, of course, be seen in his use of calypso. The calypso had long been used in the Caribbean as a form of storytelling and, often, protest. Early *Windrush* pioneers like Lord Kitchener brought the calypso to a British audience, and many of the writers from this period drew on this form in their stories. As John McLeod argues, Selvon 'turn[s] frequently to calypso for the resources which influence a vision of London as something other than the terrifying experience of objectification, economic hardship, racism and loneliness'.[8] McLeod points out that for many people calypso was not only a humorous form of complaint against the social order, but also a source of strength enabling them to overcome hardships and their sense of displacement. Like the calypso, the short story provides Selvon with a concise form in which to critique conditions for migrants and also – through the notion of a shared experience – to provide a comforting sense of familiarity and belonging.

Selvon's story 'Calypso in London' opens with such a critique of London, which is bleak, cold and inhospitable. Yet, this sombre backdrop is vital in inspiring creativity, and leads the character Mangohead to start composing 'a calypso that would tell everybody how life treating him':

> It had a time in this country
> When everybody happy excepting me
> I can't get a work no matter how I try
> It look as if hard times riding me high. (p. 127)

While this cry of hardship might seem to be very specific to the position of migrants in British cities at this time, on hearing this verse, his Calypsonian expert Hotboy tells him: 'You think we still in Trinidad? This is London, man, this is London. The people want calypso on topical subject' (p. 128). Hotboy's words collapse the distinction between London and Trinidad, minimizing the differences in living conditions between the metropolitan centre and island home: London is not all it was supposed to be.

Mangohead is a good example of how Selvon's male protagonists often live off their wits, and creatively reinvent the London around them, whether by song, story or dance. In 'Working the Transport', the character Small Change creates a new dance trend, the hip and hit (made up to impress a girl), which is soon the fashionable dance in the clubs.[9] This migration, therefore, sees the creolization, or 'Caribbeanization' of London. We learn in the story 'Come Back to Grenada' that, though migrants are assimilating, they are also changing Britain, too:

> Long time George used to feel lonely little bit, but all that finish with since so much West Indian come London. All kind of steel band fête all about in the city, in St Pancras Hall, pan in Piccadilly Circus and even jumping up in the road when the Lord Major did riding in he coach.[10]

This is an important moment suggesting that migrants are creolizing the city, which now 'have so many spades that you bouncing up with one every corner you turn' (p. 174).[11] Initially, while home is very much the Caribbean, and a continued source of comfort for Selvon's characters, for George, the increased numbers of Caribbean migrants to London means that his sense of home gradually shifts: 'When he think 'bout home it does look so far away that he feel as if he don't belong there no more' (p. 177). Mike Phillips and Trevor Phillips have also explained, as 'the prospect of return faded', so too did 'the sense of "home" as the place where we would feel most secure and comfortable. Instead "home" became the distant spot on the map where we had our origins.'[12]

Also part of the *Windrush* generation of writers, E. A. Markham was born in 1939 in Monserrat, and travelled to Britain in 1956. Like Selvon, Markham often draws on humour to illustrate the determination and resilience of Caribbean migrants in Britain. In his story 'Mammie's Form at the Post Office', for example, the protagonist Mammie is attempting to send money back to the West Indies, so that her relatives' graves can be properly maintained, but struggles with the young post office clerk, who appears to antagonize her at each step. To begin with, Mammie's use of 'home' to describe the Caribbean causes substantial communication problems:

The boy pretended he didn't understand what she was saying, and then asked if she wanted to send money ABROAD. She had to correct him and tell him she was sending her money HOME: that was where she is from. She was indignant that first, they treated you like a foreigner, and then they denied you your home.[13]

This is a telling exchange: the clerk presumably assumes Britain is her home, suggesting a vision of Britain that is less culturally exclusive than other stories by this generation of writers might suggest. Yet Mammie reads his incomprehension as an insult; other challenges include being given the wrong form to complete, because 'West Indies was the same as Bangladesh' (p. 337) and, ultimately, she leaves without completing the transaction. This story, then, explores the problems of communication for migrants to Britain yet, like Selvon's narrator, Mammie maintains her humour and is not beaten by this encounter, resolving to go to another post office the following day. For both writers, the short story form is important in enabling them to create distinct snapshots of some of the diverse experiences of migrants from the colonies to London at this point in the middle of the twentieth century.

The impact of this generation of migrants on later authors can be seen by looking at the stories of Pauline Melville. Melville was born in 1948 in Guyana, before moving to Britain and becoming a successful actor and then writer. She has been awarded a series of prizes for her debut collection of stories, *Shape-Shifter* (1990) and first novel, *The Ventriloquist's Tale* (1997). Many of her short stories explore multicultural perspectives on life in Britain with a humour and use of language that evokes Selvon's tone, such as 'Mrs da Silva's Carnival' from *The Migration of Ghosts* (1998). As the title suggests, Mrs da Silva is not just a participant in the Notting Hill Carnival, but a driving force and formidable character: 'The sight of Mrs da Silva's enormous behind, swinging rhythmically from side to side like a huge demolition ball capable of knocking down the houses on either side of the street, has inspired a multitude of revellers.'[14] This story shares the jovial resistance of Selvon's calypsonian prose and, although the police are trying to keep people away from the carnival, we are informed by the narrator that the centre of the street is Mrs da Silva's 'rightful place' (p. 38). Despite the heavy-handed police presence, therefore, the spirit of carnival cannot be broken: '"Let the police hit themselves up they own backside," she chortles defiantly as the band plays' (p. 41).

Also like many of Selvon's characters, Salman Rushdie had what he has called a 'dream-England' before his arrival in Britain, which he soon came to realize was, 'no more than a dream'.[15] Rushdie was born in 1947 in Mumbai (then Bombay) and, from 1961, he was educated at Rugby School in Warwickshire, before attending the University of Cambridge. He is the most well-known writer to feature in this chapter and, though his novels have attracted much more critical attention than his short stories, the collection *East, West* (1994) offers some interesting responses to migrant life in Britain in the latter half of the twentieth century. The title of this collection emphasizes a consistent interest of Rushdie's, which is the interplay and connections between East and West. In his essay 'Imaginary Homelands' (1982) he writes about the Indian writer's exile from India: 'Sometimes we feel that we straddle two cultures; at other times, that we fall between two stools. But however ambiguous and shifting this ground may be, it is not an infertile territory for a writer to occupy.'[16] As Rushdie suggests here, while diaspora can lead to overwhelming experiences of dislocation and unbelonging, it has – it would seem – also encouraged migrant writers to explore creatively their liminal positions, in the spirit of Mangohead's calypsos.

'The Courter', published in *East, West*, is narrated, for the majority of the story, by a young Indian boy living in London in the early 1960s. The narrator and his siblings enjoy a hybrid identity; his younger sister's 'lullabies were our cover versions of recent hits by Chubby Checker, Neil Sedaka, Elvis and Pat Boone'.[17] While Damian Grant has argued that this London is 'at one remove from social reality', in part 'because of the mediatized world he constructs for himself', this collection of childhood Western singers, fashions and television programmes, alongside the narrator's love for India, and ayah (or nanny), suggests that this story amply reflects Rushdie's interest in 'East, West' connections.[18] As he has explained in interview, 'the most important part of the [collection's] title was the comma. Because it seems to me that I am that comma – or at least that I live in the comma.'[19] Naturally, the story feels very autobiographical.

His ayah, Mary, is known as Certainly-Mary, for her habit of always saying 'Certainly-yes' or 'certainly-no', and her mispronunciation of English consonants also leads to Mecir's occupational change from 'porter' to 'courter'. This humour through mispronunciation and translation continues when the narrator's father is slapped by a female chemist for asking if she had nipples (for the baby's bottle), rather than teats, recalling Selvon's character's bafflement and confusion over words in London. Ultimately, Mary feels unwell, and decides to return to India; the narrator wonders, 'was it that her heart, roped by two different loves, was being pulled both East and West?' (p. 209) Though the narrator acknowledges that he, too, has 'ropes around [his] neck [...] pulling [him] this way and that, East and West, the nooses tightening, commanding *choose, choose'*, he refuses to make this decision, choosing 'neither', 'and both' (p. 211). This defiant stance solidifies his intentions to live – like Rushdie – with contradictions.[20]

Like Rushdie's narrator, the protagonist of Melville's story 'Eat Labba and Drink Creek Water', from *Shape-Shifter*, is also torn between East and West – this time, Guyana and Britain. She dreams she 'returned [to Guyana] by walking in the manner of a high-wire artist, arms outstretched, across a frail spider's thread suspended sixty feet above the Atlantic attached to Big Ben at one end and St George's Cathedral, Demerara, at the other'. Yet, it is not as simple as returning to the country of birth (which may, as her imagery suggests, be anything but easy), as her narrator acknowledges, 'whichever side of the Atlantic we are on, the dream is always on the other side'.[21] These dreams suggest that even if – in contrast to Rushdie's narrator – the diasporan subject *did* choose between East and West, there will not necessarily be a straightforward resolution of identity or of the conception of 'home'.

Hanif Kureishi's stories also explore British Asian identities but, unlike Rushdie, Kureishi was born in England (in 1954 in Bromley, Kent). His father, who was originally from India, had come to Britain in 1947; Kureishi's mother was white English. For Hari Kunzru, Kureishi 'has become a symbol of British multiculturalism', so it is perhaps particularly apposite that he appears in this chapter, though – ironically – and like Rushdie, Kureishi has voiced concerns over the term.[22] Kureishi has claimed little difficulty in harmonizing his identity; as he explained in his essay 'The Rainbow Sign' (1986), 'I wasn't a misfit; I could join the elements of myself together.'[23] This doubleness, or dual heritage, has also led him to be wary of racial binaries; just as racist white Britain is alienating, so too is the other extreme: 'I had to live in England, in the suburbs of London, with whites. My mother was white.'[24] His Britishness means that, unlike 'first-generation' migrants like Selvon or Rushdie, his writing lacks the distinctive use of Creole or dialect explored in stories thus far.

Though critics like Bettina Schötz have seen Kureishi's short stories as 'postethnic', and 'a crucial turning point in his *oeuvre*, making a shift in focus from inherently political themes such as British Asian ethnicity to the private difficulties, worries and fears of predominantly white, middle-aged male individuals', many of the stories in his collection *Love in a Blue Time* (1997) feature mixed-race (white English and Indian) children in Britain, which suggests an ongoing interest in ideas of belonging and race.[25]

In 'The Rainbow Sign', Kureishi explained that, through his writing, he wanted to explore 'a new way of being British': 'The two countries, Britain and Pakistan, have been part of each other for years, usually to the advantage of Britain. They cannot now be wrenched apart, even if that were desirable. Their futures will be intermixed' (p. 102). We might be tempted to read these comments alongside Kureishi's own 'intermixed' identity, and this theme of racial mixing, as mentioned, may be found in several of his stories, including 'We're Not Jews'. This story is set in the 1960s and focuses on a mixed-race child, Azhar, who is experiencing racist bullying from white children at school. Initially, Azhar's white mother Yvonne can't understand why he's so hurt by their taunts, but soon encounters racism first hand, from Little Billy and his father, Big Billy. The perpetuation of racism, passed through generations, is suggested not just by the shared name of the Billys, but also in the child's emulation of his father's racist gestures: 'Big Billy was hooting like an orang-utan, jumping up and down and scratching himself under the arms – one of the things Little Billy had been castigated for [by the headmistress].'[26]

Yvonne becomes a victim of their bullying, when they refer to her as 'a slut who marrie[d] a darkie' (p. 43), though she carries her own prejudices: 'She refused to allow the word "immigrant" to be used about Father, since in her eyes it applied only to illiterate tiny men with downcast eyes and mismatched clothes' (p. 44). Similarly, her comment 'we're not Jews' (p. 45) reveals her own tendency to single out other minority groups as potential targets for victimization. The story ends with Azhar's incomprehension at home – not understanding what his uncles are saying in Urdu or Punjabi, though at school he is called 'Paki'. Azhar, it would seem, is caught unhappily between two worlds and, unlike Kureishi, is unable to 'join the elements of [him]self together'.

In the story 'With Your Tongue Down My Throat', we find another mixed-race narrator, Nina (who, again, has a white English mother and an Indian father). Nina learns that she has a half-sister in India, where her father now lives, and tries to imagine her: 'A girl materialises under a palm tree, reading a Brontë novel and drinking yogurt. I see a girl being cuddled by my father. He tells stories of tigers and elephants and ricksaw wallahs.'[27] This humorous, exoticized version of her sister illuminates one of the ways in which ethnic identities are 'read'. Nina's disappointment on meeting Nadia, who is dressed in Western clothing, is evident: 'you look as if you live in Enfield' (p. 65). The similarity of the names, Nadia and Nina also suggests a kind of twinning: 'My sister! My mirror' (p. 65). Yet, like Homi Bhabha's 'mimic men', who are *almost the same, but not quite*', the sisters are *not* the same.²⁸ For Bhabha, colonial mimicry was the desire for a 'reformed, recognizable Other', but the slippage of mimicry, or its 'ambivalence', is crucial in casting the colonial as a '"partial" presence'.²⁹ Nadia might be Nina's "Indian" self, should she too have grown up in India, but she is different from Nina: 'made from my substance, and yet so other' (p. 66). Nadia symbolizes different things throughout the story; whilst she is an exotic other/self to Nina, for Nina's mother she symbolizes 'betrayal by [Nina's] father', to which Nina ironically responds: 'Symbolises? [...] But she's a person' (p. 64).

As the story progresses, Howard, the mother's television script-writer boyfriend, reveals that he, in fact, is the narrator. The reader is forced to confront the fact that Howard has been projecting Nina's thoughts all along. This switching of frames reminds us of the way in which white people have historically 'spoken for' – and projected onto – non-white people. With Howard's voice revealed, we see that it has been his fabrications of 'the exotic' and cultural misrepresentations all along, not Nina's.

While 'My Son the Fanatic' also features a young mixed-race character, like Kureishi's novels *The Buddha of Suburbia* (1990) and *The Black Album* (1995), it explores generational splits. Parvez is a Punjabi taxi driver who migrated to England; his son, Ali, was born in this country, but gradually becomes scathing of his father's corrupt Western ways. Parvez, for example, counts among his closest friends a prostitute named Bettina, and he drinks alcohol: 'Each time Parvez took a drink, the boy winced, or made a fastidious face as an accompaniment [...] Ali had a horrible look on his face, full of disgust and censure. It was as if he hated his father.'³⁰ While Parvez's view of success is assimilationist, in that he hopes for the successful integration into Britain of both himself and Ali, for his son the country's freedoms have led to it becoming 'a sink of hypocrites, adulterers, homosexuals, drug takers and prostitutes' (p. 122).

They are unable to resolve their differences, and the story ends with Parvez's violent assault of Ali, and Ali's question: 'who's the fanatic now?' (p. 127). Parvez's enthusiasm for Britain appears to have motivated his violent, drunken behaviour, and Helga Ramsey-Kurz argues that, in revealing his bias towards Islam, along with Parvez's 'naivety, short temper, patriarchal airs, his unreasonable dismay at Ali's sudden show of prudence, and his paranoid suspicion that Ali is on drugs ... Kureishi effectively erodes both the validity of the father's judgement and his reading of Ali as a fanatic.'³¹ I would suggest instead that Kureishi merely presents the scene without judgement or comment. Parvez had previously rescued Bettina from a violent client, so we may be encouraged to consider whether or not his actions here are a similar response to what he sees as an attack on not just Bettina (whom Ali has verbally abused), but also the West. Alternatively, Parvez could be seen as attempting to 'rescue' Ali from himself, or from 'fanatical' Muslim beliefs.

London, perhaps inevitably, looms large in post-war stories concerning ethnicity and identity. Despite this metropolitan dominance, however, there are noteworthy stories with more regional or provincial settings. The short stories of Jackie Kay, which are often set in smaller cities around Britain, are representative of this more regional focus. Born in Edinburgh to a white Scottish mother and a black Nigerian father in 1961, Kay was adopted by a white couple and brought up in Glasgow. Kay is best known for her several poetry collections and the novel *Trumpet* (1998), which follows the fortunes of Joss Moody, a transvestite jazz musician living in Glasgow. Her story collection *Why Don't You Stop Talking* (2002), which contains a wealth of pieces about life in Britain, is also notable, however. As Kay has commented, a short story is 'like a wee picture that reveals a big picture. Like a quick but very penetrating glance at somebody's life that often reveals something you're not expecting.'[32] Such unexpected moments might include the story 'Shell', in which a character slowly turns into a tortoise, or 'Shark! Shark!', where the character Brian's irrational fear of sharks (even though he lives inland) ultimately leads to a violent nightmare, and heart attack and thus – ironically – his death is caused by a shark.

Kay's story 'Out of Hand' speaks back to Selvon and Markham's generation, relating the story of a female migrant on the *Windrush*. The story images the moment of the arrival of the *Windrush* in terms of its ultimate impact and memorialization in Britain: 'Rose McGuire Roberts came down those *Windrush* steps. She already felt memorable as she was doing so.'[33] We can see in this quotation the way in which this arrival was immediately historicized and, fittingly, Rose soon goes to the cinema, where the Pathé news item at the start is about the *Windrush*. As the narrator describes: 'Rose sees herself for a brief moment in black-and-white coming down the ship's steps with her red hat on' (p. 163). The looks Rose receives from fellow cinema-goers suggest not jealousy, as she imagines, but an early hostility to her presence in the country: 'A lot of them stare at her as they leave [. . .] Only the stare is not friendly like you would expect. Well, maybe they are jealous!' (p. 164). These stares foretell her future treatment in Britain where, though a skilled nurse, she is placed on night shift, with 'all the rubbish jobs, all the jobs she shouldn't be doing' (p. 165). The racism exceeds the tasks she is assigned, as overtly racist comments are addressed to her from the patients for whom she is caring: 'You there! It's all your fault. You've brought your diseases with you. None of us would be in here if it weren't for you' (p. 166). Though this outburst is upsetting enough to Rose, the hurt is compounded by the fact that 'nobody intervenes' (p. 167). This lack of action in speaking out against racism is also evident in Markham's story 'A Place for Simon', where Simon is the name given by the narrator to racist white Britons. As the narrator recounts, 'I first met him on a train. I was aware of his voice before I met him.' Simon, in this instance, is a schoolboy who loudly exclaims that the train's lateness is 'because it was a holiday train, filled with foreigners: they didn't really expect *us*, did they, to put on our best trains, just to make the foreigners comfortable and take them up to London?' As the narrator notices, 'There was no argument; there was a silence, which I interpreted as assent.'[34] In both Kay's and Markham's stories, then, we see inaction and silence from white observers as a validation of racism.

In 'Out of Hand', though, we also see racism figured as a physical threat when, in 1958, 'the year of the Nottingham riots', Rose and her husband are confronted by a group of white people who shout: 'Go back to your own country!' (p. 168). As she reflects, 'How come she thought England was her country? How did that happen? How was it that she thought when she got on that *Windrush* that she was coming home?' (p. 168). Here, Kay raises another significant issue regarding 'home' for the first generation of post-war Caribbean migrants, which was the colonial relationship to Britain that encouraged migrants to view it as the 'motherland'. This issue is not raised in stories by Selvon and Markham, for whom the Caribbean is (at least initially) 'home', even though the passenger list from the *Windrush* stated quite clearly that these were *British* subjects. Some of the men had visited during their service in the Second World War and accordingly, for many, their journey to Britain was indeed a journey home.

The *Empire Windrush* is later referred to in 'Out of Hand' as a 'huge fiction of a ship' (p. 169); Phillips and Phillips have argued that 'the moment of arrival captured by the *Windrush* has become a symbol for all those occasions when we, or any of the other black people who have become part of the British nation, stepped off our separate gangplanks'.[35] The mythologizing of this moment of arrival has also been seen not only in the way in which the *Windrush* became a shorthand way of referencing the period of post-war migration to Britain by Caribbean migrants, but also – arguably – how it eclipsed earlier 'arrivals' by black people outlined at the start of this chapter.[36]

Kay's stories 'Why Don't You Stop Talking' and 'Trout Friday' also explore ideas of racism and alienation, though from points later in the twentieth century. In 'Trout Friday' Melanie, whose father is Trinidadian and mother is white Irish, is concerned with racial labels and identity politics in Britain: 'She'd read somewhere that people with her colour of skin were now being called *beige*. Somehow she didn't like *beige*; it made her think of fashion and clothes [. . .] *Beige Britain*' (p. 69). She rejects other pejorative labels:

> *half-caste* [. . .] sounded insulting and she didn't like *mixed-race* because it made her feel muddled. Certainly not *mulatto*, it made her think of mules [. . .] Most upsetting of all, she didn't like it when other black people described her as being *red* or *high yellow* because that made her feel like a primary colour. (pp. 69–70)

This concern over labelling intersects with Kay's comments about the persistent coalition between race and nationality in Britain, where to be British or, in Kay's case, Scottish – it is assumed – is to be white: 'I still have Scottish people asking me where I'm from. They won't actually hear my voice, because they're too busy seeing my face.'[37] In *The Black Atlantic* (1992) Paul Gilroy has written about attempts 'to construct the nation as an ethnically homogeneous object';[38] writers like Kay arguably disrupt such categorization and homogeneous ideas of nation. Unlike Markham's Mammie, who was born in the Caribbean, and certain that was still her home, then, Kay's protagonists tend to be born in Britain, and are very much British, if not always 'at home' with a British nationality.

Another writer interested in the coalition of race and nationality is Zadie Smith, whose first novel *White Teeth* was published to much acclaim in 2000. Smith was born in London in 1975, of black Jamaican and white English parents, and has affinities with both Kureishi and Kay, describing herself as being 'about as post-post-postcolonial as it's possible to be'.[39] Although she has not yet published a collection of short stories, several of her stories have been published in newspapers and story compilations. In *The Embassy of Cambodia* (2013), Fatou, from the Ivory Coast, is working – without wages – as a nanny and maid for an Asian family in Willesden, North West London. This story gestures towards the phenomenon of 'new slaves' in Britain, and particularly the case of Mende Nazer, whose autobiography, *Slave* was co-written with journalist Damien Lewis. Smith's narrator reveals that 'in a discarded *Metro* [. . .] Fatou read with interest a story about a Sudanese "slave" living in a rich man's house in London. It was not the first time that

Fatou had wondered if she was a slave.'[40] As it happens, Mende was kept as a slave in Willesden by the Sudanese diplomat, Abdel al-Koronky. Fatou notices the differences between herself and Mende: 'Fatou could read English – and speak a little Italian – and this girl in the paper could not read or speak anything except the language of her tribe' (p. 7). However, it is clear to the reader that there are similarities between their predicaments, for example: 'nobody beat Fatou, although Mrs Derawal had twice slapped her in the face' and, 'just like the girl in the newspaper, she had not seen her passport with her own eyes since she arrived at the Derawals' (p. 7). She also reveals that her wages are kept by the Derawals in exchange for her food and lodging. While she concludes, 'no, on balance she did not think she was a slave' (p. 7), she is perhaps trying to convince herself: the reader may reach another conclusion.

After Fatou saves the youngest child from choking on a marble, the parents' uneasiness and embarrassment at having to be thankful to her leads them to dismiss her. The story ends with Fatou waiting by the bus stop: 'Many of us walked past her that afternoon, or spotted her as we rode the bus, or through the windscreens of our cars, or from our balconies. Naturally, we wondered what this girl was doing [...] We worried for her' (p. 21). This suggests a typical response to such a sight; a pang of concern, but also a reluctance to reach out or speak to people like Fatou. Pietro Deandrea argues that, all too often, 'new slaves' are spectralized; they barely register in people's minds and are, in many ways, unknowable: 'the main obstacle here resides in *finding* the *human material*, and in finding basic data about their spectralised lives. Who are they? Where do they live, where are they imprisoned and exploited? How many of them?'[41] Smith's story imagines the life of just one of these many ghosts in Britain today. Like Markham's train passengers who were reluctant to challenge the voice of Simon, or Kay's silent hospital workers, Smith perhaps warns of the dangers of silence. If not condoning racism, nevertheless in this story, silence does nothing to help Fatou's situation, or answer the questions posed by Deandrea above; rather, silence denotes a passive complicity in her fate.

While Britain's population has always comprised a mix of origins, ethnicities and cultures, the influence of the post-war generation of migrants to Britain shaped not only the literature Britain was producing, but also the country itself. While an earlier generation of migrants explored the pull of conflicting ideas of 'home' in their work, for later writers their identity as British is perhaps less complicated, though the persistence of racism and the coalition of race and nationality mean questions of identity for non-white writers are still being posed and worked through. What is clear, though, is that these migrants and their children have had an enormous impact on Britain. As Kwesi Owusu puts it,

> From the early days of post-war immigration and settlement, when Black people in Britain saw themselves predominantly as 'guests' of British society, to current trends stressing citizenship ... it often seems that we have come full circle – a fast-moving circle, with its complex patterns of junctions, crossroads and critical thresholds, all intricately bound to stories waiting to be told.[42]

From Selvon's creative post-war Caribbean migrants to Smith's silenced and oppressed twenty-first-century Nigerian worker, short story writers in Britain have used the form as a succinct way of highlighting issues of inequality and oppression, but also resistance and survival. As Owusu indicates, representation – the telling of tales – is at the heart of multicultural life in Britain, in which the short story plays an important, if often overlooked, role.

Notes

1. Peter Fryer, *Staying Power: The History of Black People in Britain* (London and Sterling: Pluto Press, 1984), p. 1.
2. For accounts of the violence against black people in the post-war period, see Mike Phillips and Trevor Phillips, *Windrush: The Irresistible Rise of Multi-Racial Britain* (London: HarperCollins, 1998).
3. See Louis James, 'Writing the Ballad: The Short Fiction of Samuel Selvon and Earl Lovelace', in *Telling Stories: Postcolonial Short Fiction in English*, ed. Jacqueline Bardolph (Amsterdam and Atlanta, GA: Rodopi, 2001), pp. 103–8 (p. 104).
4. Bill Schwartz, 'Introduction: Crossing the Seas', in *West Indian Intellectuals in Britain*, ed. Bill Schwartz (Manchester University Press, 2003), pp. 1–30 (p. 3).
5. A. Sivanadan, 'Britain's Shame: From Multiculturalism to Nativism', 22 May 2006, www.irr.org.uk (accessed 8 March 2015), para. 6 of 15.
6. Maria Grazia Sindoni, *Creolizing Culture: A Study on Sam Selvon's Work* (New Delhi: Atlantic, 2006), p. xii.
7. Sam Selvon, 'Finding Piccadilly Circus', in *Foreday Morning: Selected Prose 1946–1986* (Harlow: Longman, 1989), pp. 123–6 (p. 123). Subsequent page references are given in parentheses in the text.
8. John McLeod, *Postcolonial London: Rewriting the Metropolis* (London and New York: Routledge, 2004), p. 27. Susheila Nasta also explores the influence

of calypso on Selvon's writing about London in *Home Truths: Fictions of the South Asian Diaspora in Britain* (Houndmills and New York: Palgrave, 2002), pp. 78–9.
9. Samuel Selvon, 'Working the Transport', in *Ways of Sunlight* (1957; London: Longman, 1979), pp. 132–8.
10. Sam Selvon, 'Come Back to Grenada', in *Foreday Morning*, pp. 166–77 (p. 175).
11. This phenomenon is humorously explored in Louise Bennett's poem 'Colonisation in Reverse' (1966), in *Writing Black Britain 1948–1998: An Interdisciplinary Anthology*, ed. James Procter (Manchester University Press, 2000), pp. 16–17 (p. 16).
12. Phillips and Phillips, *Windrush*, p. 4.
13. E. A. Markham, 'Mammie's Form at the Post Office', in *Taking the Drawing Room through Customs: Selected Stories 1972–2002* (Leeds: Peepal Tree, 2002), pp. 336–47 (pp. 336–7). Subsequent page references are given in parentheses in the text.
14. Pauline Melville, 'Mrs da Silva's Carnival', in *The Migration of Ghosts* (London: Bloomsbury, 1999), pp. 25–44 (p. 25). Subsequent page references are given in parentheses in the text. This playful and defiant articulation of black female power echoes Grace Nichols's poetry collection *The Fat Black Woman's Poems* (London: Virago, 1984).
15. Salman Rushdie, 'Imaginary Homelands', in *Imaginary Homelands: Essays and Criticism 1981–1991* (London: Penguin and Granta Books, 1991), pp. 9–21 (p. 18). In his many essays, he has written candidly about racism in Britain – which, he asserted in 1982, was 'not a side-issue' ('The New Empire Within Britain', *Imaginary Homelands*, pp. 129–38 (p. 129)).
16. Rushdie, 'Imaginary Homelands', p. 15.
17. Salman Rushdie, 'The Courter', in *East, West* (London: Jonathan Cape, 1994), pp. 175–211 (p. 180). Subsequent page references are given in parentheses in the text.
18. Damian Grant, *Salman Rushdie* (Plymouth: Northcote House, 1999), p. 105.
19. Cited in D. C. R. A. Goonetilleke, *Salman Rushdie* (Houndmills and London: Macmillan, 1998), p. 131.
20. Rushdie has admitted that the protagonist is 'determined not to choose [between Britain or India, or East or West]. In that sense, he is quite like me' (cited in Nasta, *Home Truths*, p. 133).
21. Pauline Melville, 'Eat Labba and Drink Creek Water', in *Shape-Shifter* (London: Picador, 1991), pp. 148–64 (pp. 148–9).
22. Hari Kunzru, 'Erotically Unmoored: Hanif Kureishi's Collected Short Stories', in *The Financial Times*, 13 March 2010, www.ft.com/cms/s/2/a133d f7a-2d4f-11df-9c5b-00144feabdco.html (accessed 8 March 2015). See Catherine Fildes, 'An Interview with Hanif Kureishi', 26 April 2010, http://literateur .com/an-interview-with-hanif-kureishi/ (accessed 7 January 2015) and Rushdie, 'New Empire', p. 137.

23. Hanif Kureishi, 'The Rainbow Sign', in *My Beautiful Laundrette and Other Writings* (London: Faber & Faber, 1996), pp. 73–102 (p. 75).
24. Kurieshi, 'Rainbow Sign', p. 78. In *The Buddha of Suburbia*, Karim also described himself as 'a new breed as it were, having emerged from two old histories' ((London: Faber & Faber, 1990), p. 3).
25. Bettina Schötz, 'The Exploration of Community in Hanif Kureishi's Short Fiction', in *The Literary London Journal*, 10 (2013), 2, www.literarylondon.org/london-journal/autumn2013/schotz.html (accessed 28 February 2015), para. 2 of 26; 1 of 26.
26. Hanif Kureishi, 'We're Not Jews', in *Collected Stories* (London: Faber & Faber, 2010), pp. 41–50 (p. 42). There is, of course, the similarity between 'bully' and 'Billy'.
27. Hanif Kureishi, 'With Your Tongue Down My Throat', in *Collected Stories*, pp. 60–103 (p. 63). Subsequent page references are given in parentheses in the text.
28. Homi K. Bhabha, *The Location of Culture* (London and New York: Routledge, 1994), p. 86.
29. Ibid.
30. Hanif Kureishi, 'My Son the Fanatic', in *Collected Stories*, pp. 116–27 (p. 121). Subsequent page references are given in parentheses in the text.
31. Helga Ramsey-Kurz, 'Humouring the Terrorists or the Terrorised? Militant Muslims in Salman Rushdie, Zadie Smith, and Hanif Kureishi', in *Cheeky Fictions: Laughter and the Postcolonial*, ed. Susanne Reichl and Mark Stein (Amsterdam and New York: Rodopi, 2005), pp. 73–86 (p. 79).
32. Jackie Kay, 'Don't Tell Me Who I Am', interview with Libby Brooks, *The Guardian*, 12 January 2002, www.theguardian.com/books/2002/jan/12/fiction.features (accessed 26 January 2015), para. 12 of 24.
33. Jackie Kay, 'Out of Hand', in *Why Don't You Stop Talking* (London: Picador, 2003), pp. 159–69 (p. 162). Subsequent page references are given in parentheses in the text.
34. E. A. Markham, 'A Place for Simon', in *Drawing Room*, pp. 348–54 (pp. 348, 349).
35. Phillips and Phillips, *Windrush*, p. 6.
36. As Procter points out in his General Introduction to *Writing Black Britain*, 'If 1948 has come to signal the "beginnings" of a postwar black British history, it has also come to conceal a number of other, contradictory, pasts' (pp. 1–12 (p. 3)).
37. Kay, 'Don't Tell Me', para. 1 of 24. See also Kay's poem, 'So You Think I'm a Mule?', in Procter, ed., *Writing Black Britain*, pp. 202–4.
38. Paul Gilroy, *The Black Atlantic: Modernity and Double Consciousness* (London and New York: Verso, 1993), p. 3.

39. Zadie Smith, 'In Conversation with Kurt Andersen', www.nypl.org/sites/default/files/events/smith043006.pdf (accessed 28 February 2015), para. 69 of 137.
40. Zadie Smith, *The Embassy of Cambodia* (London: Penguin, 2013), p. 16. Subsequent page references are given in parentheses in the text. The significance of this story in relation to London fiction is considered briefly in Chapter 16.
41. Pietro Deandrea, 'Contemporary Slavery in the UK and its Categories', in *Black Arts in Britain: Literary, Visual, Performative*, ed. Annalisa Obie and Francesca Giommi (Rome: Aracne, 2011), pp. 167–85 (p. 179).
42. Kwesi Owusu, 'Introduction: Charting the Genealogy of Black British Cultural Studies', in *Black British Culture and Society: A Text Reader*, ed. Kwesi Owusu (London and New York: Routledge, 2000), pp. 1–18 (p. 13).

21

Settler Stories: Postcolonial Short Fiction

VICTORIA KUTTAINEN

People, not Plots

> Miss Mansfield does not write what one usually thinks of as a 'short story'. She is interested in people, not plots.[1]

To open with Robert Littell's observation about the modernist short story writer Katherine Mansfield is to undertake the kind of re-reading, re-positioning and re-framing that the postcolonial perspective often suggests. Each of the writers discussed in this chapter has typically been understood in terms of their contribution to national literature or to a literary school or style more broadly. As a case in point, Katherine Mansfield has traditionally been classed as a modernist whose stylistics were informed by her distance from New Zealand and her exposure to metropolitan literary experiments, allowing her to exceed the conditions of her colonial upbringing to create universal art.[2] More recently, however, scholars have re-evaluated the effects of her colonial upbringing and subsequent exile on her writing to demonstrate ways in which she might instead be understood as a paradigmatic settler postcolonial writer.[3] To understand these writers and their work in these terms is a gesture towards claiming for them a common set of stylistics informed by their shared postcolonial condition in settler domains.

Here the term 'postcolonialism' is used in its widest sense, not as a marker of contemporary periodicity or of time *after* political independence, but rather as a signal of the enduring aftermath of colonialism, in which the problematics of settlement are discernible in the first wave of colonization through to the present day.[4] This scope extends from the work of short story writers typically understood as 'colonial', in whose writing the motifs of place and displacement and the themes of longing and belonging take root, to the work of contemporary writers whose stories are more often read in terms of postmodernism.

Reading through these optics draws attention to the common thread of exile and alienation that is present in nineteenth- and twentieth-century fiction. This frame also focalizes through a postcolonial lens what Lyotard has identified as postmodernism's central feature, 'incredulity toward meta-narratives', as writers such as Peter Carey or Janet Frame grapple with colonial legacies that have persisted in ideological forms long after independence.[5] While the conditions of settler colonialism, and the artistic reaction to it, are distinct in each domain and epoch as well as particular to each writer, productive interpretations of their work can be gleaned by reading them alongside one another, across large geographical distances and time spans, in terms of the artistic and existential response to settlement. Relationships to heritage, to forbears and to place are, after all, thematized and problematized in much of the work discussed in this chapter.

Short Fiction and the Postcolonial

The experience of postcolonialism informs not only the themes but also the structure of the short story as a favoured genre in former settler colonies. Frank O'Connor famously claimed that the short story held a special attraction to 'submerged population groups',[6] including colonized and otherwise marginalized people, and critics have repeatedly observed synergy between the short story form and the postcolonial condition.[7] However, theorists of settler postcolonialism such as Alan Lawson and Stephen Slemon have noted that the conditions of postcoloniality in settler domains translate to a kind of 'in-between' status for settlers, whose position of marginality in relation to the imperial centre is also marked by privilege in relation to indigenous peoples colonized by their settlement.[8] The form of the short story can also be seen to straddle this hybrid position in relation to marginality and centrality. The emergence of short stories and sketches in the settler colonies, at the time when the long novel was popular in England, has been linked by critics to a perception of the unsuitability of inherited literary forms in colonial domains. As a mode of the short story often favoured by settler writers, the brief sketch form, for instance, has been observed to logically emanate from settings where observations of people and place, rather than history or plot, are narrative preoccupations.[9] The form has proved eminently suitable to adaption in local contexts because of its capacity to capture the rhythms, cadences and silences of oral expression (as discussed by John Thieme in this volume). The oral and slice-of-life impressions of colonial life register strongly, for instance, in the work of Henry Lawson, Olga

Masters, Frank Sargeson or Alice Munro, all of whom are masters of the genre. Yet, paradoxically, although the short story form allowed colonial writers to capture fresh impressions in colonies where forms and metaphors inherited from the Old World ill suited foreign experiences and settings, it also allowed colonial writers to engage with and extend the literary tradition of Europe, from the short tales of Boccaccio and Chaucer to the *comptes* of Chekhov and Maupassant. As a genre, the short story form is thus highly adaptable to the hybrid status and conditions of settler postcolonialism.

Certainly there are also pragmatic explanations for the affinity between colonial writers and the short story form. Writers such as Henry Lawson found publication for short stories in the 'land of newspapers' and magazines that constituted colonial print culture.[10] Outlets overseas also gave short story writers the chance to return colonial writing 'Home' to London or Europe and have remained important avenues to disseminate their work through cosmopolitan circuits long after national publishing networks have been well developed.[11] Practically and philosophically, then, the medium of the short story has been an important conduit between metropole and colony that has registered the tensions between home and exile.

New Zealand

As perhaps the most peripheral of all Britain's settler colonies, an Antipodean island nation shadowed by its dominant colonial neighbour, Australia, New Zealand has produced a rich yield of short story writers, from Katherine Mansfield to the present day, whose work can be interpreted as postcolonial. In her recent postcolonial re-reading of Mansfield's work, Janet Wilson, for instance, has demonstrated that her corpus is haunted by a 'problematics of location' characteristic of the settler postcolonial condition. In her interpretation of Katherine Mansfield's depictions of an idyllic yet often lonely or alienated New Zealand childhood in stories such as *Prelude* (1918) or 'At the Bay' (1922) or the oblique coming-of-age story 'The Garden Party' (1922), Wilson identifies an 'obsession with "home"' as well as a perpetual sense of displacement.[12] This dynamic of unsettlement oscillates between a desire to escape and to belong, both in the colony and in Europe. Similarly, Mansfield's centre of interest in these stories frequently shifts subjective positions. A naïve outsider's observations of Europeans, as in 'The Little Governess' (1915), mark an exilic point of view; a colonial who is brought up in the finest image of émigré English society in 'The Garden Party' (1922), but is nonetheless beset by a sense of detachedness and provincialism, marks a settler point of view; and the participant-observer filled with longing for the perceived sense of indigenous belonging, especially in Mansfield's 'Maata' stories, marks the alienated perspective of the postcolonial writer in relation to indigenousness. In these three alternating points of view, Mansfield's obsession with people and place emerges; her writing is striated by what critics have identified as the settler postcolonial 'problematic'.[13]

Mansfield's refined, impressionistic style has been praised for its striking, almost unintelligible originality, while at the same time attracting accusations of stylistic mimicry, attaching to Mansfield the label of the 'English Chekhov'. In this respect her work also embodies the ambivalence of the settler postcolonial position, as described by Alan Lawson: haunted by anxieties and accusations of imposture (a dynamic in postcolonial writing described further by Dawson and Nolan) while at turns so strikingly original that the settler postcolonial subject and her writing lack, as Lawson suggests, 'the key to full intelligibility'.[14] Whatever can be said of it, Mansfield's fiction is subtended by themes of exile and alienation.

In stark contrast to the alienated perspective of Mansfield – who was in perpetual exile and wrote from a position of distant, cool observation of her characters, risking exotic romanticization of settler colonial Pakeha and Maori characters – New Zealand's Frank Sargeson represents such characters from an insider's point of view. Also a keen observer of human behaviour, committed to narratives centred on people not plots, Sargeson's position as writer is not of detachedness but of intense intimacy with his characters. His perspective is not unlike that of a barstool confessional, capturing the lexicon and deeply textured lives of the New Zealand working class in his monologue-style sketches. The worlds of his characters are small and cramped; family life is oppressively intimate and family members' perceptions of each other are often tragi-comic, filled with laconic affection and sometimes derision: 'Oh Lord! It's a good job everybody isn't like my uncle' the narrator exclaims in 'Conversations with My Uncle' (1935).[15] And: 'Oh Lord, I don't know what to do about Frances. I've asked her why she doesn't get married, and she's asked me who'd marry her? Who would, indeed!' the narrator confides about his middle-aged cousin who keeps house for his father in 'In the Midst of Life' (1935) (p. 18). Small-town life is equally claustrophobic; a milkman says of a working-class woman in 'A Piece of Yellow Soap' (1935): 'Sometimes I used to pass her along the street, out of working hours. She acknowledged me only by staring at me, her eyes like pieces of rock' (p. 13). And although Maori characters are often observed from Pakeha perspectives,

Sargeson uses this technique to reveal more about Pakeha stereotypes of the indigenous other than Maoris themselves, as in 'White Man's Burden' (1936).

Sargeson's ability to capture the rhythms and patterns of New Zealand life confidently conveys the distinctiveness of life in New Zealand settings, and indeed his work has been of deep significance to New Zealand's cultural nationalism. Yet for all Sargeson's intimate acquaintance with his people and their recognizably Kiwi idiosyncratic characteristics, the characters he portrays are still marked by the spectre of postcolonial unsettlement. His characters remain outsiders and fringe-dwellers, drifting, alienated and only semi-articulate, as in the case of the beach hermit Fred Holmes in 'The Last Adventure' (1937), the juvenile delinquent in 'A Good Boy' (1971) or the borderline sexual deviant George in 'I've Lost My Pal' (1938). It is no coincidence that this story of the clashes and desires of normalized, dysfunctional mateship should first appear in the Australian magazine *Man*; Sargeson's characters are principally boys and men, who typically hold positions of superiority over women, exert dismissive attitudes and are strongly inflected by the puritanism of their Scots–Irish heritage even as they live in reaction and rebellion against the culture that sustains them.

Carrying on the tradition of chronicling the distinctive voices and milieu of New Zealand, Janet Frame marked out literary ground from a female perspective. Even as Frame was nurtured and mentored by Sargeson, famously living in his garden shed while she wrote her first novel, *Owls Do Cry* (1957), Frame's work found its ideal readers with the proliferation of feminist psychoanalytic theory in the work of Hélène Cixous and Luce Irigaray. These opened up broad-scale questioning of how patriarchal social structures and normative modes of expression may have limited the rich and complex forms of female subjectivity that writers such as Frame explored. The subsequent development of feminist literary theory provided ways of reading that challenged classifications of mental illness as a form of labelling and defining women who did not conform to patriarchal expectations, and stimulated appreciation of the complexity of Frame's narrative project. Frame's writing takes up the perspective of the alienated outsider, as well as the challenging task of recording subversive, incomprehensible female experience, and joins to these the deep textures and everyday experiences of life in peripheral, often rural, New Zealand. Her experimental forms of expression explore the gaps and silences in what can be considered worth writing about. Yet the hope of liberation offered by Frame is markedly ambivalent; for her, language is dubious, as it fails not only to render comprehensible the complexity of authentic, lived female experience, but also to capture the experience of place in New Zealand through sets of metaphors and linguistic conventions imported from elsewhere. As Gina Mercer perceptively writes, 'Janet Frame has always written from the position of the other. Her perspective is that of the outsider, the marginalized, the oppressed and repressed' and she is particularly concerned with those 'denied the power of a voice and place'.[16] Institutionalized characters frequently recur in her stories for more generalized kinds of incarceration by society.

Nature, however, is not an escape but a place colonized by the colonial gaze in ways that anticipate ecocritical perspectives. In the eponymous story of Frame's first short story collection, *The Lagoon* (1951), for instance, the tidal lagoon promises to reveal rich sea treasure such as 'a baby octopus if you are lucky', but equally as likely 'the drowned wreckage of a child's toy-boat', signifying the anti-pastoral register that seductively promises 'an under-water moon, dim and secret' but more often returns one's own reflection: 'your image tangled up with sea-water and rushes and bits of cloud'.[17] In 'Swans', a story book-ended by hope and then despair for the family pussycat, Gypsy, who is discovered dying, Mother, Fay and Totty take a train-ride to the seaside, eagerly anticipating the fixtures of colonial leisure ('merry-go-rounds and swings and slides, among people, other girls and boys and mothers') and 'the place to get ice-creams', only to arrive, unaccompanied by their father's guidance, at 'the wrong sea' where there was 'no place, only a shed with forms that have bird-dirt on them and old pieces of news-papers stuffed in the corner and writing on the walls, rude writing' (pp. 47–8). Often in Frame's writing, as in this story, the settler ideals of family and permanence are dashed, exposed as flimsy, and even subject to tragic yet almost inevitable betrayal; mother's childlike assurance that 'things would be all right' and Totty's firm trust that 'mother knew always' are both ruined by the discovery of the dead cat at the end of the story. A sense of dislocation pervades both of these stories, and it is transferred to the landscape: the lagoon of the narrator's childhood is transformed with the development of the tourist town of Picton, the location of the idyllic seaside spot is elusive, and innocence is shattered by experience. Language in 'Swans' is subject to concealment, misunderstanding and misdirection; in 'The Lagoon' the narrator strives to understand the stories of her grandmother, whom she recalls as the exotic daughter of a Maori princess, only to learn later from her aunt that instead her grandmother was 'a murderess' and the scandalous details had been printed in the tabloid *Truth*. This story, like many of Frame's, reflects upon the nature of story, fact, fiction, exposure and concealment. 'It's an interesting story', her aunt reflects, 'I prefer Dostoevksy to *Truth'* (p. 10). Such is a characteristically loaded and ambivalent statement for a Frame story: does the aunt prefer the reality of European high literature to the stuff of everyday family life in New Zealand? Or does she prefer literary truths to tabloid truths? These sets of questions resonate across a settler postcolonial landscape that is peopled with characters as alienated and eccentric as Sargeson's, who are repeatedly trying to find ground to stand on, whether to transform their colonial experiences into something more palatable by standards set somewhat randomly elsewhere, or to translate their experiences out of a non-native language ill-fitting the landscape and experience of life in New Zealand into something that resonates as true, honest and real.

Australia

While New Zealand has historically relied on a trans-Tasman print culture and a steady stream of imported Australian magazines, Australia can hardly be understood as a dominant nation in global terms of comparison to Europe or America. Parallels rather than differences between New Zealand and Australia are more usefully drawn, as writers in both countries struggled to articulate and find publication for stories that expressed their native experience. Yet, cultural nationalism found a voice in Australia much earlier than in New Zealand. Henry Lawson's *Bulletin* stories of the 1890s might be seen as equivalents to Frank Sargeson's 1940s sketches in *Truth* in terms of their relative importance to each nation's cultural nationalism. Both authors captured the cadences and rhythms of local speech and the atmosphere of local place in striking ways, and both portrayed lonely, wandering characters clinging to ideals of working-class mateship while often beset by feelings of alienation and exile. But rather than finding a settled sense of tradition in the settler colony, literature which began by writing back to English standards and expectations has become caught in cycles of self-referentiality in Australian literature. Henry Lawson's once radically innovative Australian bush tale 'The Drover's Wife', for instance, has become a site of seemingly endless postcolonial rewriting. While it captures the loneliness and exile of a mother and her son in the harsh Australian bush, and chronicles their forced self-sufficiency, writers and critics have taken it up for its romanticizing of femininity, its overwrought symbolization of the bush as female and of the mother as nation, and for its structure that centres the action of the story around the importance of the absent father figure, the ever-mythologized male drover.

In this, settler postcolonial short fiction responds not only to the conventions of Europe but also to the nationalistic conventions that often risk becoming a new form of domination. Perhaps the first short story to 'write back' to Lawson's 'Drover's Wife' was Barbara Baynton's 'Squeaker's Mate' (1902), whom the narrator describes as 'the best long-haired mate that ever stepped in petticoats'. Here the wife is portrayed not as stranded or bereft but as an equal co-labourer of her husband, a lazy bludger who exploits her loyalty and hard work. Where Lawson's 'The Drover's Wife' is a romantic and even heroic ballad of nationalism, 'Squeaker's Mate' is written in the gothic register, exposing the sexism at the heart of settler Australia. Just as 'The Drover's Wife' is known only by her title as wife, the woman in this story remains nameless until the last few paragraphs, when we learn her name is Mary. Her subjectivity and worth are deemed only in terms of her labour value to Squeaker, whose self-centred and cruel treatment of her is starkly revealed after a tree falls on her, and his reaction is to resent the extra workload her injury has brought him as he leaves her to die while he cruelly brings another woman into the house to replace her.

Both Baynton and Lawson thematized the land in ways that more contemporary writers would continue to take up, or send up, well into the twentieth century. In a series of later stories that have continued to 'write back' to 'The Drover's Wife', the settler tradition comes under intense scrutiny and even parody in postmodern stories. As discussed at length by Ken Gelder and Paul Salzman in *The New Diversity: Australian Fiction 1970–88*, Murray Bail and Frank Moorhouse assumed an 'anti-realist position, denoting fiction as artefact, a fabulation';[18] each explicitly re-wrote 'The Drover's Wife', drawing it into patterns of playful intertextuality and even transmedia, as Bail also references Russell Drysdale's 1945 painting 'The Drover's Wife'. Bail's narrator is a suburban dentist who cries imposture or inaccuracy over the original painting, which we know is itself non-original: 'The woman depicted is not "The Drover's Wife". She is my wife', he avers in his 1975 story of the same name. In Moorhouse's 1987 'The Drover's Wife' an Italian student of Australian culture, Franco Casamaggiore, delivers a paper at an academic conference in which he explains that the 'Drover's Wife' is a 'national joke, an "insider-joke" for those who live in that country', over-interpreting the figure of the wife as an extended metaphor for sheep, signalling the Australian male's uncomfortably close relationship to the national animal.[19] In these playfully metafictional responses to the classic

Henry Lawson story, even the idea of an interpretable national culture becomes an insider's joke, and each of these writers extends the short story form by veering into inventive tales that work to free writing in Australia from carrying the burden of representing the nation.

Arriving on the literary scene as a maverick in the 1970s, Peter Carey actively took on the task of debunking a number of Australian nationalist myths, particularly in the short story collection *The Fat Man in History* (1974), now considered a contemporary classic. In one of Peter Carey's classic fables 'American Dreams', the nature of Australian character and heritage, which the nation's literature is so often expected to perform, is called into question as Mr Gleason builds a miniature replica of his home town, complete with all its inhabitants, which becomes a magnet for busloads of paying American tourists; the model of the small town is at first a point of civic pride, marvelled upon for its accuracy, but it becomes an ersatz tourist trap that imprisons even its own inhabitants when civic pride and identity are drawn into patterns of commodity culture and neo-liberal global tourism. Frank Moorhouse's *The Coca-Cola Kid* (1985) would continue to push the boundaries of the short story collection in Australia, moving it beyond ossified tradition and bush tales into the landscape of late capitalism and Americanized consumer culture set adrift on the allure of sex, drugs and rock and roll. Yet, for all their innovation, these writers continued to draw on themes of alienation and rootlessness that are remarkably consistent with those themes in Lawson and Baynton. Further, their work has been scrutinized, like Lawson's, for its masculine preoccupations. While strongly more realist than the inventive fables of the so-called 'beautiful liars' of the 1970s, Jessica Anderson's stories could be said to treat the settler tradition somewhat more radically; her stories, which amount to a feminization of the Australian city, are written against a male-centred outback tradition in Australian fiction.

Despite these modern and postmodern responses to an overemphasis on the bush in Australian literature, and a turn to city landscapes, the thematization of the land is a broad Australian preoccupation, which Elizabeth Jolley's fiction takes up from her own migrant settler position. English-born, Jolley emigrated to Western Australia in her late thirties and released her first book of short fiction, *Five-Acre Virgin and Other Stories* at the age of fifty-three. Like Frame, Jolley's work explored issues of identity and invoked self-reflexivity and forms that would later be recognized as feminist and postmodern but which were profoundly experimental for their time, often hampering their publication. Over the next twenty-five years, Jolley was prolific in her output, publishing fifteen novels, three works of non-fiction and six collections of short stories. Jolley shares with Frame an interest in the effects of large institutions: schools, boarding houses and hospitals, for instance. Her work takes society's misfits as its central characters, and both a sadness and a dark sense of humour underpin her portrayal of the subjective experience of marginalized and alienated people. Yet where Frame's work tends towards weird melancholy, Jolley's fiction veers into absurdist sharp-witted irony. These oppositional poles of absurdist humour and profound melancholy are also present in Canadian short fiction, as manifestations of the ways that writers have worked through the ongoing aftermath of colonization there.

Canada

As Catherine Nash has argued, 'the idea of place' very often concerns both the 'sensual, lived experience of the local environment' as well as 'the abstract level of the nation'.[20] This is a nation always-already riven by what novelist Hugh MacLennan first called, in the title of his 1945 novel, Canada's 'Two Solitudes', a phrase that has subsequently been adopted as shorthand for the gulf in communication between Anglo- and French-Canada. This is the context in which Canadian short story writers have problematized the idea of the nation as a unified and coherent place. Regionalism has a long tradition in the history of Canadian short fiction, from Duncan Campbell Scott's *In the Village of Viger* (1896), a collection of stories that chronicle provincial French Canadian life, to Stephen Leacock's humorous portraits of small-town Ontario in *Sunshine Sketches of a Little Town* (1912), Emily Carr's sketches of Northwest Coast indigenous life in *Klee Wyck* (1941) and Ethel Wilson's portraits of Vancouver in *The Innocent Traveller* (1949). Through these and more, Canada's masterful short story writers have critically challenged the idea of 'nation as empire' with perhaps even more regularity than their Australian parallels.[21] As intensely regional as these stories are, they are also underscored to greater and lesser degrees by the notion of travelling, a trope that stresses the tension between the rural idyll and the regional backwater, intimate attachments to place and feelings of claustrophobia brought on by small-town family life, and the threats and allures of metropolitan life elsewhere in Canada, south of the border, or overseas.

Mavis Gallant embodies this tension. Like Mansfield, Gallant lived most of her life outside her home country but was also an outsider within it; just as Mansfield felt as estranged in Pakeha, New Zealand, as in London or Europe, so Mavis Gallant's life was marked by exile at home and abroad.

From her childhood, her experience of being born into an English-speaking Protestant family in Montreal and sent to a French-Catholic boarding school in Quebec crystallized her experience of living across the 'two solitudes' that characterize Canadian experience. Whether she is writing about French or English Canada or Europe – where she moved in 1950 to become a writer, remaining in Paris until her death in early 2014 – Mavis Gallant's hallmark as a writer is her evocation of the unsettled nature of twentieth-century experience, and especially the feeling of exile. As Martha Dvorak described in her obituary of Gallant, she is 'best known for her stories of cultural dislocation, of borderlines' of characters out of place.[22] In 'The Moslem Wife' (1976) Gallant writes powerfully of the charms of interwar travel and expatriate life, only to reveal deftly how characters cannot escape their families even when they want to, and the ways in which bohemian lives abroad, apparently free, are in fact intensely fragile as they quickly snap back into established, conservative patterns of gender and nation with the onset of the Second World War. Similarly, she writes of characters set adrift from family as in 'Baum, Gabriel, 1935–()' (1979), the story of a German-Jewish refugee in Paris who is the only surviving member of a family destroyed by the Holocaust. Gallant's output was prolific: over a hundred of her short stories were published in *The New Yorker* and her *Collected Stories* (1996) amounted to over a thousand pages but contained only half of her work. The epic sweep of Gallant's writing takes in the sociological complexity of whole lives but crystallizes these to poignant details in polished form. Likewise, the global span of her work takes in strangers who meet while travelling or living abroad, but also deeply engages with the lineaments of local life in Montreal, particularly in her autobiographical Linnet Muir stories.

In contrast to the global scope of Gallant's *oeuvre*, Alice Munro's stories are mostly centred on home, but also represent a tension between belonging and alienation as well as near and far. Another prolific contributor to *The New Yorker*, Nobel Laureate Alice Munro is a beloved national icon in her native country and is widely regarded as one of the most significant short story writers in the world. Her early years in south-western Ontario and her early marriage spent on the West Coast of British Columbia established a pattern of oscillation between those two regions that is sustained across the body of her work. These settings inform her masterful portrayal of regional Canada and its vernacular community identity.

Munro's portraits of people are psychological masterpieces that bear witness to the complexity of human experience from a place of intimate knowing. While Gallant writes from an outsider's perspective, pursuing the stories of wandering and diasporic characters, Munro writes from an insider's perspective, giving voice to the often un-voiced rural Canadian experience and chronicling the loneliness and isolation of those who are exiles at home. In this, Munro could be said to represent a Canadian corollary of Frank Sargeson, while Mavis Gallant's exilic status and outsider's point of view invite comparisons with Katherine Mansfield. Yet, unlike Sargeson, Munro represents a deeply feminine point of view and sensibility. In an early story, 'Boys and Girls' (1964), later included in her first short story collection *Dance of the Happy Shades* (1968), Munro establishes her interest in the way women's lives are circumscribed by social pressures, driving intuition and self-knowledge underground: these concerns signal a shared interest with Janet Frame and other feminist writers of the 1970s and 1980s. *Lives of Girls and Women* (1971) centres on Del Jordan growing up on the fringe of the fictionalized rural Ontario town Jubilee, while in *Something I've Been Meaning to Tell You* (1974) the way other women police each other's lives by gossip also crystallizes as an early theme in Munro's work, a theme that emerges strongly in the relationship between Rose and her step-mother Flo in the short story collection *Who Do You Think You Are?* (1978), which can also be read as a rural female *Bildungsroman* and story of identity.

Munro's vividly realized, profoundly personalized regions find parallels in Margaret Atwood's personalization of the Toronto region of her childhood and young adult years. Yet, Atwood's stories, which are in some ways a Canadian parallel of Jessica Anderson's, showcase an urban Canada and an emerging feminist consciousness in various stages of coming into awareness of the sometimes subtle, and at other times agonizingly obvious, injustices of being a woman in a patriarchal society. In her anti-realist mode, Atwood's stories rival Peter Carey's fabulist, allegorical, blackly comic and intensely metafictional style; her collection *The Stone Mattress* (2014) playfully conjoins both styles. In the opening triptych, connected short stories treat the Toronto of the 1960s, ironizing the self-consciousness of the city's writers, while the other stories are almost in rebellion against this realism, releasing Canadian writing from the burden of seriousness (a mantle that the author seems to suggest this postmodern nation was never *really* of the constitution to carry), into the realm of ghost stories, vampire tales, folk tales, pulp horror and metafictional phantasmagoria.

Atwood's contemporaries Margaret Laurence and Sandra Birdsell have felt less released from the burden of working through issues of individual, group and national identity through their fiction, however. Ultimately, their work, like Janet Frame's fiction in relation to Elizabeth Jolley's writing, is unable to take comfort in absurdist play. Both writers interrogate the notion of lineage and heritage, and both writers probe the silences, complicities and myths of the settler family in attempts to come to terms with indigenous people who have been and continue to be deeply affected by settlement. Laurence's *A Bird in the House* (1970) and Birdsell's *Agassiz Stories* (2002) take up the theme of land but also the micro-politics of place and relations in general, to uncover beneath the intensity of personal experience an understanding of the privileges of white settler Canada and the racial inequities that underpinned the myth of unified white, British settler Canadian descent and identity.

South Africa

The issue of racial inequality has of course been inescapable in the literature of South Africa, a nation even more divided than Canada's 'two solitudes' across linguistic, race and ethnic lines. Amidst this diversity it is impossible to task a single writer with the burden of speaking the nation with a unified voice, or expressing in a representative way *the* postcolonial milieu, but one voice does emerge most clearly from the South African context, and it is that of Nobel Laureate Nadine Gordimer. During the formalization of racial segregation under the official policy of apartheid enforced by the National Party regime, a flourishing of urban black short fiction was stimulated by the platform of *Drum* magazine, but it would be a first generation South African, daughter of an Eastern European Jewish father and an English mother, Nadine Gordimer, whose writing about alienation and racial conflict from a deeply humanistic perspective would ultimately achieve international literary recognition. As critics have noted, there is an obvious tension in Gordimer's position as South Africa's most famous literary voice as a privileged white attacking the apartheid regime, whose work is informed by a deep love of South Africa and a commitment to its land and peoples. Through these paradoxes and tensions, Gordimer works out her own postcolonial identity. It is perhaps unsurprising, then, that Gordimer's writing increasingly explored coming to terms with her own complicity as a white writer.

Early in her *oeuvre*, her ambivalent and highly charged prose showed a propensity for literary experimentation or exploration, but as Barbara Eckstein has observed, Gordimer's novels gradually moved towards a more explicit political vision as the writer's own political activism developed. Her short stories, however, retained the deep engagements with personal relationships present from her earliest collection, *Face to Face* (1949), in which the public and the private are interwoven and in which state policy affects attitudes and experience at the same time as personal preconceptions erect barriers.[23] Much of Gordimer's work interrogates the way a heavily repressive and restrictive society prevents different groups from knowing each other, and shows these in terms of constrained narrative possibilities that engage with race and space in daily life at the phenomenological level of experience, grappling with what Dominic Head observes are the fundamental principles of apartheid, the 'geopolitics of apartheid and its policies of space control'.[24] Her fiction both embodies and attempts to overcome these restrictions — as in Munro's work — through limited points of view, atomized characters, ironic distancing and ambiguity.

In 'The Catch' (1957) white characters relax the social rules of the apartheid regime that prevent them from interacting with the sorts of people they meet on holiday and which preclude the kind of friendship that develops between them. Yet, when some white friends turn up, they fall back into their own racial enclave and Gordimer masterfully narrates the tacit petty allegiances and betrayals that ensue. The 'catch' of the title alludes both to the fish caught by their Indian friend at the fishing resort and the bind they find themselves in when they attempt to overcome the racial prejudices of their class. In 'What Were You Dreaming?' (1991) Gordimer uses dialogic presentation to give readers insight into how white anti-apartheid supporters remain oblivious to the way their self-congratulatory liberal ideologies serve their own sense of smug self-righteousness. The story begins with a black man's monologue, revealing his pragmatic tactics of dealing with whites who give him lifts in their cars: he tells them what they want to hear to get to where he wants to go. On this particular occasion he is offered a lift by a white South African woman who is also chauffeuring an Englishman. The black passenger soon realizes he has become a showpiece in a pantomime meant to illustrate to the Englishman the terrible suffering of blacks under the oppressive apartheid regime. He performs his oppression to service the prurience of the white spectators. The reader sees into the black character's logical reasoning, and also into the limits of the white characters' self-serving attempts at demonstrating their empathy.

As Head has observed, 'Gordimer's importance as a short story writer stems from her ability to utilize certain formal properties of the genre', especially ambiguity, which allows Gordimer to extend what Head calls the 'single effect' of the kind of revelation or exposure we might associate with a Mansfield story to a kind of double exposure, in which a kind of productive ambiguity reveals the entrenched positions of two characters, unable to see beyond their own limited perspective, while the reader is able to see into the position of each.[25] In Gordimer's story 'Once Upon a Time' (1989), this double exposure is laid bare in a tragic way, as the reader sees both inside the structures that white South Africans have created to protect themselves, and outside their walls, to the complex and seemingly unresolvable social and racial problems of emergent post-apartheid South Africa. As the narrator tries to find rest in her 'haunted' house at night, it is revealed that the cause of the apparent haunting is that the foundations of the narrator's home are insecure, literally under-mined by years of extracting wealth from the land. Similarly, the frame story reveals that settlers have become prisoners of their own precariously conceived middle-class lifestyles: a young boy is tragically caught in the barbed fence of the family's secure compound in an increasingly militarized, gated white community, and the tragic ending to the story displays that the only kind of 'children's stories' conceivable in this milieu are ones that end tragically.

As with Canadian, Australian and New Zealand writers of the short story, the unsettled perspective that manifests in Gordimer's later, clearly postcolonial stories, in which security is eroded from within and without, has a long history that can be traced to the earliest short stories in the colony. The profound tensions between native and settler, as well as Afrikaner and English, are present, for instance, in Olive Schreiner's pioneering writing. In Schreiner's well-known Boer War story 'Eighteen-Ninety-Nine' (first published in 1906 and collected in *Stories, Dreams and Allegories* 1923), exile, displacement and orphanhood are underscored even in the earliest passages of the narrative, as the Boers flee the English to the Transvaal, in pursuit of dreams of self-sufficiency that are only ever fleetingly attained. The story in general emphasizes the vulnerability of women and children in a landscape that offers beauty and promise but is marked by a seemingly endless cycle of planting and harvesting that yields only further dispossession and death.

Numerous settler stories in South Africa take up the trope of dislocation that underpins colonial settlement. Whether in terms of the endless drifting in the heavy, melancholic story of poor whites in Pauline Smith's 'Desolation' (1925) or in stories set against the background of the trip 'Home' to London, for instance in Sarah Gertrude Millin's 'Up from Gilgal' (1924) or Arthur Shearly Cripps's 'The Black Death' (1918). In these stories, geographical dislocation often translates to psychological and even physical unsettlement, an obsession with racial purity connected to the insecure social status of the colonial subject and shifting, as well as relative standards of wealth, propriety, class and sufficiency. These themes persist in different forms even in the recent, multiracial and global, transnational stories of Zoë Wicomb. In 'Ash on my Sleeve' (1987), for instance, the character Frieda returns to South Africa after many years living in exile in London, to be confronted with the domestic claustrophobia, persistent paternalism and outright sexism that continues to mark South African life in the new multiracial post-apartheid era. Wicomb focuses on questions of identity, and specifically middle-class 'coloured' identity in the new South Africa, where the cultural dominance of 'English' influence has to be negotiated. For the character Frieda, this also involves a level of self-interrogation about her own sense of superiority. In Wicomb's 'Another Story' (1990) routes and roots are further thematized, along with intercultural encounters. The question of who is the fool and who is the sophisticate – the metropolitan ex-colonial who longs wistfully for the simplicity and belonging of colonial family life, or the cunning colonial, whose remaining life in South Africa has been characterized by the base needs of survival – plays upon the mind of the reader as an unanswerable question. The identity of the exploited and the exploiter has become so mixed up in this postcolonial scene that even the genre of this short story is unclear, appearing as a hybrid of the nineteenth century colonial family romance and the modern hardboiled detective tale.

As a whole the short story form has been an adaptable genre in these milieux, lending itself to the compelling treatment of a variety of postcolonial themes and topics: grappling with the displacement and alienation often felt in a relatively new colony, as in the bush tales of Henry Lawson; exploring tensions between longing and belonging, as in the work of Katherine Mansfield; capturing the local vernacular, as in the sketches of Frank Sargeson; rebelling against nationalism as local form of imperialism, as in the short fiction of the so-called 'beautiful liars' of Australian postmodern fiction like Peter Carey or Frank Moorhouse; trying to find a female voice and sense of agency and subjectivity, as in the work of Janet Frame or Elizabeth Jolley; or exploring how the forms of the short story can be used to probe racial myths of unified British descent, as in the work of Margaret Laurence or Sandra Birdsell, and to understand white privilege and complicity, as in the work of Nadine Gordimer, or the persistence of unsettlement, in the transnational stories of Zoë Wicomb. Themes of alienation and displacement as well as community and individual identity pervade the work of all these writers. Yet this is perhaps the most heavy burden placed on the short story: to work out how literature can mean anything, or make a difference, in the face of atrocities and atrocious inequities caused by settlement, from the ongoing aftermath of apartheid in South Africa to the continued marginalization of Aboriginal people in settler colonies in the postcolonial present. Whatever its response, the short story has proved to be an eminently human form, committed as ever to multiple perspectives, to persistence and to adaptability. In the postcolonial domain, the form also bears witness to the persistence of unsettlement, and demonstrates its enduring capacity to accommodate and capture, from multiple perspectives, the endurance of tragedies, misunderstandings, inequities and injustices that persist in colonialism's long wake.

Notes

1. Robert Littell, 'Katherine Mansfield's *The Garden Party and Other Stories*', *New Republic* (5 July 1922), p. 166.
2. See C. K. Stead, 'Katherine Mansfield as Colonial Realist', *Commonwealth*, 4 (1997), Spring, pp. 13–17; or Lydia Wevers, '"The Sod Under My Feet": Katherine Mansfield', in *Opening the Book: New Essays on New Zealand Writing*, ed. Mark Williams and Michele Leggott (Auckland University Press, 1995), pp. 33–48.
3. See for instance Salkat Majumadar, 'Katherine Mansfield and the Fragility of Pakeha Boredom', *Modern Fiction Studies*, 55 (2009), 1, pp. 119–40. See also Janet Wilson, '"Where is Katherine?" Longing and (Un)belonging in the Works of Katherine Mansfield', in *Celebrating Katherine Mansfield: A Centenary Volume of Essays*, ed. Gerri Kimber and Janet Wilson (London: Palgrave, 2011), pp. 251–71 and Janet Wilson, Gerri Kimber and Delia da Sousa Correa, eds., *Katherine Mansfield and the (Post)colonial* (Edinburgh University Press, 2013).
4. This is the definition of the 'postcolonial' invoked by Bill Ashcroft, Gareth Griffiths and Helen Tiffin in *The Empire Writes Back: Theory and Practice in Post-Colonial Literatures* (New York: Routledge, 1989).
5. Jean-Francois Lyotard, *The Postmodern Condition: A Report on Knowledge*, trans. Geoff Bennington and Brian Massumi (Minneapolis: University of Minnesota Press, 1984), p. xxiv.
6. Frank O'Connor, *The Lonely Voice: A Study of the Short Story* (Cleveland: World, 1963), p.18.
7. See for instance the following: Jacqueline Bardolph, ed., *Telling Stories: Postcolonial Short Fiction in English*, Proceedings of the Nice Conference of the European Association for Commonwealth Literature and Language Studies, March 1988 (Nice: EACLALS, 1989); Lucy Evans, *Communities in Contemporary Anglophone Caribbean Short Stories* (Liverpool University Press,

2014); Victoria Kuttainen, *Unsettling Stories: Settler Postcolonialism and the Short Story Composite* (Newcastle Upon Tyne: Cambridge Scholars Press, 2010); W. H. New, *Among Worlds: An Introduction to Modern Commonwealth and South African Fiction* (Erin, Ontario: Porcepic, 1975); and Lydia Wevers, 'The Short New Zealand Story', *Southerly*, 53 (1993), 3, pp. 118–36.

8. Alan Lawson, 'A Cultural Paradigm for the Second World', *Australian-Canadian Studies*, 9 (1991), 1–2, pp. 67–78; Stephen Slemon, 'Unsettling the Empire: Resistance Theory for the Second World', *World Literature Writing in English*, 30 (1990), 2, pp. 30–41.
9. See for instance W. H. New, *Dreams of Speech and Violence: The Art of the Short Story in Canada and New Zealand* (University of Toronto Press, 1987); Ian Reid, 'Generic Variations on a Colonial Topos', in *The Tales We Tell*, ed. Barbara Lounsberry, Susan Lohafer, Mary Rohrberger, Stephen Pett and R. C. Feddersen (London: Greenwood Press, 1998), pp. 83–90; Gillian Whitlock, 'The Bush, the Barrack Yard and the Clearing: "Colonial Realism" in the Sketches and Stories of Susanna Moodie, C.L.R. James and Henry Lawson', *The Journal of Commonwealth Literature*, 20 (1985), 1, pp. 36–48; and Lydia Wevers, 'The Short Story', in *The Oxford History of New Zealand Literature in English*, ed. Terry Sturm (Auckland: Oxford University Press, 1991), pp. 201–68.
10. Toni Johnson-Woods, 'Beyond Ephemera: Serialisation of Fiction in Nineteenth Century Popular Australian, US and UK Periodicals', unpublished dissertation, University of Queensland, 2000, p. 64.
11. Stephen Torre, 'The Short Story Since 1950', in *The Cambridge History of Australian Literature*, ed. Peter Pierce (Cambridge University Press), pp. 419–51 (pp. 419–20).
12. Wilson, 'Where is Katherine?', pp. 252, 251.
13. Kuttainen, *Unsettling Stories*, p. 10.
14. Carrie Dawson and Maggie Nolan, eds., *Who's Who? Hoaxes, Imposture and Identity Crises in Australian Literature* (Brisbane: University of Queensland Press, 2004); Alan Lawson, 'Difficult Relations: Narrative Instability in Settler Cultures', in *The Paths of Multiculturalism: Travel Writing and Postcolonialism*, ed. Maria-Alzira Seixo, John Noyes, Graca Abreu and Isabel Mouthinho (Lisbon: Edicoes Cosmos, 2000), pp. 49–60 (p. 57).
15. Frank Sargeson, 'Conversations With My Uncle', in *The Collected Stories of Frank Sargeson* (Auckland: Longman Paul, 1964), p. 10. Subsequent page references to this edition are given in parentheses in the text.
16. Gina Mercer, *Janet Frame: Subversive Fictions* (St Lucia, Queensland: University of Queensland Press, 1994), p. 1.
17. Janet Frame, 'The Lagoon', in *The Lagoon and Other Stories* (Christchurch: Paxton Press, 1961), p. 7. Subsequent page references to this edition are given in parentheses in the text.

18. Ken Gelder and Paul Salzman, *The New Diversity: Australian Fiction 1970–88* (Melbourne: McPhee Gribble, 1989), p. 14.
19. Murray Bail, 'The Drover's Wife', in *Contemporary Portraits and Other Stories* (St Lucia, Queensland: University of Queensland Press, 1975), p. 55; Frank Moorhouse, 'The Drover's Wife', in *Room Service* (1985; rpt Harmondsworth: Penguin, 1987), p. 100.
20. Catherine Nash, 'Remapping the Body/Land: New Cartographies of Identity, Gender, and Landscape', in *Writing Women and Space: Colonial and Post-Colonial Geographies*, ed. Alison Blunt and Gillian Rose (New York: Guildford, 1994), p. 228.
21. W. H. New, 'Beyond Nationalism, On Regionalism', *World Literature Written in English*, 23 (1984), pp. 1, 12–30, p. 15.
22. Martha Dvorak, 'Obituary: Mavis Gallant (1922–2014)', *Journal of Commonwealth Literature*, 49 (2014), 2, pp. 147–56 (p. 147).
23. Barbara Eckstein, 'Pleasure and Joy: Political Activism in Nadine Gordimer's Short Stories', *World Literature Today*, 59 (1985), 3, pp. 343–6 (p. 343).
24. Dominic Head, *Nadine Gordimer* (Cambridge University Press, 1994), p. xii.
25. Head, *Nadine Gordimer*, p. 165.

22

After Empire: Postcolonial Short Fiction and the Oral Tradition

JOHN THIEME

The spread of the English language as a consequence of imperialism and English's popularity as a lingua franca in the age of globalization have significantly broadened the range and timbre of short stories written in English. This chapter examines ways in which the short story has been refashioned by Anglophone postcolonial writers, with a particular focus on how the incorporation of oral elements has reinvigorated the genre. In African and Asian societies that were subjected to British colonization, the transformations that the short story has undergone have been particularly influenced by traditional tale-telling modes. In the Anglophone Caribbean, where the majority populations are Afro-Caribbean descendants of slaves and Indo-Caribbean descendants of indentured labourers, the lines of cultural continuity have been more fractured, but there has also been an uneasy, yet highly productive dialogue between the conventions of the English short story and the oral traditions of local communities. The genocide of the pre-Columbian indigenous peoples of the region left few survivors to bring their narrative traditions into print, but the fiction of Guyanese-born writers Wilson Harris and Pauline Melville has brought aspects of their legends into the short story. Elsewhere in the Americas and in Australasia, despite suffering violence and dispossession at the hands of settler populations, indigenous voices have survived to articulate the experiences of their communities in short fiction.

The vast range of themes and forms to be found in African short stories makes it difficult to generalize about ways in which writers across the continent have employed the genre, but some commonalities exist. In pre-colonial sub-Saharan African societies, tale-telling was a lynch-pin of cultural continuity, serving as a vehicle for imparting ethical instruction as well as a medium of entertainment, and the griot, or storyteller, occupied a revered role in communities, acting as the oral repository of their collective wisdom. Postcolonial African writers have sometimes seen themselves as the linear descendants of griots, charged with a similar responsibility to educate the recipients of their work, while also entertaining them through the power of story.[1] However, as Helon Habila points out, 'It's a sad but apparently undeniable fact that the short story has always taken second place to the novel in Africa.'[2]

Around the time that various African states attained independence, the availability of African writing in English was particularly facilitated by the English publishers Heinemann, whose influential African Writers Series was founded in 1962 and initially edited by Nigeria's foremost storyteller, Chinua Achebe. It brought the continent's newly emergent literatures to an international audience and, printed in low-cost paperback, it was also an invaluable source of texts for West African readers until the 1980s, when a decline in African, particularly Nigerian, book sales, brought about by economic factors, led the publishers to turn to a format that made its volumes less affordable in Africa itself. The Heinemann series had not published many short story collections by individual African writers, but it had made a significant contribution to the dissemination of work in the genre by bringing out a dozen anthologies. The short story remained a poor relative of the novel, but by this time a number of influential post-Independence magazines had also fostered work in the genre. These included *Black Orpheus* and *Okike* (Nigeria), *Transition* (Uganda) and *Drum* and *Staffrider* (South Africa). Since the millennium various initiatives have helped to stimulate interest in the short story. Founded in 2000, the Caine Prize, an annual award for the best new story by an African writer, has helped to remedy the comparative neglect of the genre, and in 2013 the journal *African Literature Today* addressed the lack of critical attention by publishing a special issue on the short story.[3]

The relationship between the oral tale and the contemporary short story has been an ambivalent one. While postcolonial short story writers have often assumed a stance akin to that of the griot, their heightened concern with social commentary has led them towards more realistic modes of representation than those employed in traditional storytelling, where animal fables and tales in which humans interact with supernatural beings have loomed large. The animal fables are often aetiological: tales such as 'Why the Tortoise Shell is Cracked' offer causal explanations of how particular animals acquired their distinctive characteristics. Tales in which humans encounter supernatural beings are similarly set in a mythical past and, while they can often be read allegorically as offering commentary on the present, they lack the immediacy of response to social conditions that characterizes many African short stories.

The relationship between the vernacular tale and the short story has been further complicated when the primary medium for the latter has been English. African writers have debated the appropriateness of using European languages as a medium of expression. Chinua Achebe's response to this was to develop a spare form of English prose in order to capture the distinctive idioms of Igbo speech. This is particularly evident in his historical novels about village life, *Things Fall Apart* (1958) and *Arrow of God* (1964), where the scribal narrative mode incorporates an extensive range of oral elements, including proverbs, similes and fables, and such elements also figure in the short stories of Achebe's *Girls at War* (1972). This collection brings together stories written between Achebe's student days in the early 1950s and the early 1970s, and taken as a whole the volume chronicles changes in Nigerian society across decades that saw the advent of colonial rule, the coming of Nigerian Independence and the teething troubles of post-Independence society. Stories such as 'The Madman' and 'Akueke' read like episodes in Achebe's village novels, while the early 'Polar Undergraduate' shows his playful irony being lavished on the habits of some of his Ibadan student contemporaries. The two longest and most significant stories in the collection, 'Vengeful Creditor' and 'Girls at War', expose the corruption Achebe sees as widespread in post-Independence Nigeria. The former offers a moving picture of the personal consequences of a failed socialist policy to bring about universal primary education and, more generally, illustrates the disparity between the socially privileged and ordinary people. The title story shows the idealism associated with the first phase of the Nigerian Civil War being supplanted by venal opportunism and betrayal.

Flora Nwapa stands out among Nigerian women writers of Achebe's generation, both as a fiction writer and as a pioneering publisher of local writing. Her short story collections *This is Lagos* (1971) and *Wives at War* (1980) complement Achebe's complex exploration of codes of manhood in Igbo society by placing particular emphasis on the socialization of women. An incipient feminist, though she resisted the label herself, Nwapa took the view that the traditional status of women in West African society had been eroded during the colonial era and saw the restitution of a more balanced model of gender relations as a crucial component of the project to revive the values of pre-colonial African society.

The short stories of Ghana's Ama Ata Aidoo also explore the perceived failings of post-Independence West African society, particularly focusing on the mistreatment of women. In *No Sweetness Here* (1970), characters move from country innocence to city experience, with Aidoo evincing a clear preference for Ghana's rural north over the Westernized southern world of the capital, Accra. A number of the stories dramatize the bewilderment felt by ordinary people in the face of exploitation by the privileged new elite of Ghanaian society. The appropriately titled 'For Whom Things Did Not Change' ends with an ingenuous character asking a question that voices the volume's central subject: 'My young Master, what does "Independence" mean?'[4] Unanswered though it is, the question provides a fitting conclusion to a polyphonic story, which offers a particularly fine example of Aidoo's accomplished handling of point of view. In *The Girl Who Can* (1997), Aidoo addresses the struggles that African women continue to face decades after Independence with the same blend of wry irony and social protest that informs all her work. Now, though, there is a greater emphasis on women's capacity for self-empowerment. The geographical sweep of Aidoo's later short stories is broader and *Diplomatic Pounds* (2012) includes several in which migration, a perennial subject of her writing, is as much concerned with the displacement caused by travel between Africa and the 'developed' West as by internal movements within Ghana.

At the same time as the Anglophone short story was making an impact in West Africa, there were parallel developments in popular fiction. Midway between the oral tale and the literary short story, various forms of local pulp writing that catered to the tastes of an urban-orientated newly literate class grew rapidly in popularity from the 1950s onwards. Among the best-known writing of this kind was Onitsha market literature, a genre of chapbooks that took its name from the Igbo-speaking commercial town in south-eastern Nigeria where the writing originated. Onitsha pamphlets include didactic parables, instruction manuals and plays, as well as short fiction that represents a distinctive departure from both traditional tale-telling and the 'literary' fiction of writers like Achebe and Nwapa. Onitsha was, however, only one instance of such writing. Similar work, circulating outside traditional publishing channels, has appeared in various parts of Nigeria and Ghana, where, as Stephanie Newell points out, 'Local publications ... are complex hybrid discourses', in which proverbial lore often provides the basis for generically mixed fiction that confounds the conventions of the Western novel and short story.[5]

Several post-Millennium West African novelists have also made significant contributions to the short story. Helon Habila's *Waiting for an Angel* (2002), a novel that reflects on the difficulties facing the Nigerian writer, lends itself to being read as a short story sequence. It was developed from Habila's earlier Nigerian-published *Prison Stories* (2001), a collection which includes 'Love Poems', winner of the 2002 Caine Prize. Chimamanda Ngozi Adichie acknowledges having been inspired by her Igbo precursors Achebe and Nwapa, and incidental references to Achebe in her stories 'Jumping Monkey Hill' and 'The Headstrong Historian' (in *The Thing Around Your Neck*, 2009) signal the extent to which she is self-consciously responding to an established tradition of Nigerian short story writing. Unlike the first generation of Anglophone West African short story writers, she is able to mediate between carefully observed social experience and the precedents established by her literary predecessors. Her short fiction is at its best in stories such as 'Imitation' and 'Arranged Marriage' (also included in *The Thing Around Your Neck*) that depict the dilemmas faced by diasporic African women in America.

In East Africa there has been a similar convergence between the short story and the oral tale, and folk discourse's fascination with mystery, foreboding and guilt has found its way into the print story. Such motifs inform some of the stories in Kenya's most acclaimed novelist Ngugi wa Thiong'o's early collection *Secret Lives* (1975) and they are also prominent in the short fiction of his compatriot Grace Ogot, whose *Land without Thunder* (1968) and *The Other Woman* (1976) combine elements from precolonial Luo folklore with more realistic social commentary, often highlighting the tension between traditional codes and modern mores. Uganda's Taban lo Liyong'o's *Fixions* (1969) also draws on Luo myths, while pursuing a distinctive experimental approach, in which there is scant regard for Western notions of the well-made story. M. G. Vassanji's *Uhuru Street* (1992) depicts the lives of an Asian community in Dar es Salaam seen through the nostalgic eyes of an author who has migrated to North America. Its focus on a street full of eccentrics suggests affinities with another diasporic Asian short story cycle, V. S. Naipaul's *Miguel Street* (1959), but Vassanji's Tanzania is more affectionately rendered than Naipaul's Trinidad. More recent short story writing in Kenya and Uganda has been stimulated by organizations and publications such as the Kwani Trust in Kenya and Fountain Publishers and FEMRITE in Uganda. These have fostered local talent and developed writing communities outside the constraints of metropolitan publication and the award of the Caine Prize to Binyavanga Wainaina (Kenya) and Monica Arac de Nyeko

(Uganda) has further strengthened the feeling that the short story is an ideal means for representing the rapidly changing post-Millennium realities of East African society.

Pride of place among Zimbabwean short story writers must go to Dambudzo Marechera and Petina Gappah. The title-novella of the anarchic Marechera's *House of Hunger* (1978) is accompanied by nine challenging short stories, notable for their surrealist juxtapositions and a focus on 'madness' which, whether the stories are set in what was then Rhodesia or England, suggests it is societally induced. There is a similar view of 'madness' in 'The Annexe Shuffle', one of the stories in Gappah's *An Elegy for Easterly* (2009). However, the prose style of this highly accomplished collection, which depicts the human consequences of living in a country where rampant inflation and corruption permeate every aspect of daily life, is altogether more controlled and stories such as 'The Mupandawana Dancing Champion' observe life with a mordant irony.

Botswana's best-known novelist, South African-born Bessie Head's *The Collector of Treasures* (1977) is a collection of tales that draws on folkloric motifs. Set in Head's adopted homeland, the stories particularly focus on the impact of modernity on traditional village life and women's struggles against male abandonment and neglect. Within South Africa itself the beginnings of a black short story tradition have been traced back to the newspaper writing of the dramatist and journalist R. R. R. Dhlomo in the 1920s and 1930s. Many of Dhlomo's successors in the genre have testified to the resilience of black South Africans during the apartheid era. Es'kia Mphahlele's stories in *The Living and the Dead* (1961) and *In Corner B* (1967) dramatize his belief in the distinctiveness of 'Afrikan Humanism'. Mbulelo Mzamane's *My Cousin Comes to Jo'burg* (1980) takes a more light-hearted view of black African endurance, deploying the familiar trope of the country cousin who proves extremely able to thrive in an urban situation. Miriam Tlali's *Soweto Stories* (1989) employs a style which brings the urban vernacular into dialogue with Standard English to attest to the hardships of black South African township life. It devotes particular attention to the predicament of women who are oppressed by the patriarchal values of traditional society as well as the doctrines of white supremacy.

The short stories of Alex La Guma, several of which are collected in *A Walk in the Night* (1967), reflect on the ironies and ambiguities surrounding the interstitial situation of 'coloured' South Africans during the apartheid years. Zoë Wicomb's *You Can't Get Lost in Cape Town* (1987) sketches the movement of its protagonist, Frieda Shenton, from a rural upbringing in South Africa's

Namaqualand to a university education in Cape Town and a return to her roots after a period away in England. Rich in personal details, the stories dramatize Frieda's sense of alienation, using poetic imagery and disorientating time-shifts that reflect her psychic unease as a coloured South African, though many aspects of the vignettes that make up her fragmentary autobiography, such as her adolescent worries about her body image and an account of her Cape Town abortion in the title story, also speak across cultures.

Ahdaf Soueif's *Aisha* (1983) is a similar linked short story sequence by a writer from the opposite end of the African continent. As in *You Can't Get Lost in Cape Town*, several of the individual stories are cameos that reflect the protagonist's movement between cultures and, again like Wicomb, Soueif is intensely personal in her handling of detail. *Aisha*'s stories foreground cultural differences between the Egypt of the title-character's early years and her expatriate life in London, where her liberal attitude to her husband's serial marital infidelities distances her from the social mores of her Egyptian upbringing. Both *Aisha* and Soueif's later collection, *Sandpiper* (1996), employ an understated lyrical English which opens up multiple angles of vision on its cross-cultural themes. Like the stories of the inaugural Caine Prize winner, Leila Aboulela (Sudan), and Nuruddin Farah (Somalia), her work is an instance of the increasing use of English by writers who have grown up in countries outside the Commonwealth.

In the twentieth-century Caribbean, the short story was a more widely used genre than in Africa, but although West Indian writing received considerable acclaim in Britain in the 1950s and 1960s, the short story found little favour with metropolitan publishers during this period. V. S. Naipaul's first written book, the short story collection *Miguel Street*, was not published until his reputation had been established by the success of his first two novels and comparatively few Caribbean writers had collections of their stories published abroad until the 1980s. Nevertheless, the Caribbean short story had a long pedigree prior to the 1980s and had thrived in other contexts. Little magazines such as *Trinidad* and *The Beacon* (Trinidad), *Kyk-over-al* (Guyana) and the long-running Barbadian magazine, *Bim*, which had a region-wide appeal, were all important forums for the Caribbean short story. In the 1930s, the Trinidadian 'Beacon Group' published notable social realist fiction by the distinguished black radical C. L. R. James and two significant writers of Portuguese descent, Alfred Mendes and Albert Gomes. These writers' stories particularly focus on the middle-class encounter with 'yard' life, a subject that bridged the gap between an English-derived literary culture and those living in the lower echelons of the island's society. *Bim*'s long-serving editor Frank Collymore was instrumental in publishing a wide range of stories by many of the leading Caribbean writers of the 'independence generation', including Sam Selvon, Roger Mais and Austin Clarke, while *Kyk-over-al*, edited by the poet A. J. Seymour, played an important part in furthering the development of Guyanese fiction. In the 1940s and 1950s, the BBC's 'Caribbean Voices' radio programme, broadcast to the Caribbean from London and edited at various points by Una Marson, Henry Swanzy and, more briefly, Naipaul, provided an important outlet for short story writers such as Selvon, Michael Anthony and Andrew Salkey, as well as Naipaul himself. English-published anthologies were another publication venue for Caribbean short stories in this period and collections such as Salkey's *West Indian Stories* (1960) and *Stories from the Caribbean* (1965), and Kenneth Ramchand's *West Indian Narrative* (1966; revised 1980) played a significant role in bringing Caribbean stories to both a Caribbean and an international readership. Subsequent anthologies have included *The Penguin Book of Caribbean Short Stories* (1996), edited by E. A. Markham, and the impressively wide-ranging *Oxford Book of Caribbean Short Stories* (1999), edited by Stewart Brown and John Wickham.

The short story has been a particularly appropriate medium for bringing the Caribbean gift for oral narrative into print. Many stories from the region draw on the speech patterns of everyday Caribbean life; others take their inspiration from specific forms of Afro-Caribbean tale-telling. The latter group includes stories about Anancy, the wily spiderman trickster figure of Akan folklore, and a range of fictions that draw on Trinidadian calypso and related Carnival forms. Anancy was brought to the Caribbean by slaves transported from Africa and stories about him were passed from mouth to mouth across the generations, undergoing significant changes in the process of oral transmission in their new environment. Anancy stories have been particularly popular in Jamaica, where he has been seen as an embodiment of the slaves' descent to subterfuge to combat the harshness of their situation on Caribbean plantations and, after Emancipation, their continuing struggle against discrimination and impoverishment. Print collections of Anancy stories were published from the early twentieth century onwards, but in the 1960s and 1970s, at a time when African retentions were being rediscovered in Caribbean society, they achieved a new degree of popularity and were adapted into literary stories by writers who reinvented them to comment on contemporary social situations. In Andrew Salkey's *Anancy's Score* (1973), the spiderman is depicted as a spellbinding storyteller, whose gift for vernacular narrative has helped to ensure the survival of West African culture in the Caribbean. The stories in Salkey's collection are also interesting for embodying a philosophy that moves beyond the dog-eat-dog survival ethic of earlier Caribbean Anancy tales and in this respect they are closer to their Akan precursors, where, although Anancy's exploits are celebrated, he is not exempt from censure when his trickery transgresses the society's moral codes. Written in a style that moves between Creole and Standard English, *Anancy's Score* also reflects on the linguistic situation of Caribbean people, using Anancy as a knowing manipulator of language, whose strategies combat oppression. Salkey returned to the figure in *Anancy, Traveller* (1992), a volume which displays less of the playful humour that characterizes the traditional tales.

Like the Anancy story, the narrative form of many Trinidadian calypsoes makes them akin to short stories, even if their primary mode of communication has been through performance, with vinyl and more recently digital media providing popular compositions with a continuing after-life. Calypso, Trinidad's most vibrant narrative medium, had its origins in the nineteenth century, but came of age in the post-Second World War period. Among its most acclaimed exponents, The Mighty Sparrow (Slinger Francisco) and The Mighty Chalkdust (Hollis Liverpool) have been particular masters of the narrative calypso. Calypso compositions have commented on virtually every aspect of Trinidadian social and political life, in Sparrow's case with a particular emphasis on the man–woman relationship and in Chalkdust's with a longstanding concern to highlight social and political injustices. Calypsonians traditionally compete for the title of Calypso Monarch at Trinidad's annual Carnival and, along with calypso, Carnival themes and forms have been major influences on numerous Trinidadian stories. The short stories of Naipaul's *Miguel Street* and Selvon's *Ways of Sunlight* (1957) both demonstrate affinities with calypso. However, while Naipaul uses calypso intertexts to deflate the aspirations of the inhabitants of his fictional Port of Spain street, the vernacular London-set stories of the second half of Selvon's collection relate to the folk form in an altogether more sympathetic manner. Carnival themes and forms also have an integral role in Earl Lovelace's collection *A Brief Conversion* (1988) and Willi Chen's *King of the Carnival* (1988), the first collection of short stories by an Anglophone Caribbean writer of Chinese descent. Lovelace's fictions employ a sympathetic form of irony that is markedly different from Naipaul's use of the mode, along with a style in which long, sprawling sentences convey the free-flowing rhythms of carnivalesque experience. They provide a panoramic portrait of the performance aspects of the island's culture, focusing on artists such as the Carnival figure of the Midnight Robber, fire-eaters and bottle dancers, as well as the drama played out in everyday activities like playing draughts, Baptist hymn-singing, stickfighting and gambling.

In Barbados, Timothy Callender, many of whose stories were first broadcast on radio, developed a particular kind of orally inflected short story that captures the speech rhythms of the tale-teller. Appealing to implied listeners and readers with interjections such as 'Hey', Callender's primarily comic stories include the Faustian 'A Deal with the Devil' and pieces such as 'Peace and Love' and 'The Boyfriends', which deal with sexual rivalries. The best of his stories are included in *It So Happen* (1975). Frank Collymore's stories are collected in the posthumously published *The Man Who Loved Attending Funerals* (1993), a volume which demonstrates his eye for the eccentric and macabre aspects of Caribbean life and sometimes veers into a Poe-like gothicism.

Guyana's Rooplall Monar's *Backdam People* (1985) gives a vivid picture of the hardships of Indo-Guyanese estate life in the middle years or the twentieth century, doing so in a style that draws on the distinctive rural Creole spoken by his subjects. Pauline Melville's prize-winning first collection, *Shape-Shifter* (1990), includes stories set in Guyana and London, several of which have affinities with Latin American magic realism. Shape-shifting metamorphoses are a central trope in the stories, but Melville usually leaves open the question of whether those purporting to have magical powers really possess a shamanistic capacity to transform experience. Her second collection, *The Migration of Ghosts* (1998), which includes several stories set in mainland Europe, displays the same talent for mixing narrative modes and moving between different levels of reality. It includes her finest story to date, 'The Parrot and Descartes', a complex fable which suggests that the 'unity of magic and science' has been sundered in post-Cartesian Western thought.[6] Guyana's most acclaimed novelist, Wilson Harris, has produced a small group of short stories, among which 'Kanaima' (1964), a fable set in the Guyanese interior which draws on Amerindian mythology, is particularly outstanding.

Jamaica's Olive Senior is arguably the finest Caribbean short story writer to have emerged to date and her being awarded the inaugural Commonwealth Writers Prize for her first collection, *Summer Lightning* (1986), was a watershed moment in the history of the Caribbean story. Earlier notable collections by writers from Jamaica include *Gingertown* (1932) by Claude McKay, who migrated to America and became an important figure in the Harlem Renaissance of the 1920s and 1930, and two undated 1940s volumes, *Face and Other Stories* and *And Most of All Man*, by Roger Mais. Mais played a significant role in the Jamaican nationalist movement of the late colonial period and wrote numerous stories for publications associated with the independence struggle. The posthumously published *Listen, the Wind* (1986) brings together many of his best stories and shows his skill in depicting the everyday realities of both rural and urban Jamaican life.

Yet nothing prior to *Summer Lightning* quite rivals its subtle complexities of tone and its capacity to reflect the discursive splits in Jamaican society. This is particularly evident in the long final story, 'Ballad', a linguistic *tour de force* that dramatizes the conflict between the colonial educational curriculum and rural folk culture. The ingenuous girl narrator, Lenora, is asked by her teacher to write about the most unforgettable character she has ever met and starts to tell the story of an ebullient local woman, Miss Rilla, who has infringed middle-class sexual taboos by having a series of love affairs, some of them with younger men. Her teacher tells her that Miss Rilla is not an appropriate subject for a composition, but Senior's story subverts this by instating Miss Rilla as its subject and having Lenora write about her in a form of Jamaican Creole. The story presents Miss Rilla as an embodiment of the vibrancy of the folk culture and a joy in life which flouts the codes of respectable colonial society and, as a vernacular ballad, it employs a form and register that distances it from the language of the schoolroom. Reflecting on her own practice in the story, Senior has spoken of it as a breakthrough for her, since her immersion in the persona of the narrator released her to write from her own experience and enabled her to capture the particular cadences of other characters' voices. Elsewhere in *Summer Lightning*, Senior moves between the oral and the scribal and in so doing spans a broad range of the Jamaican linguistic continuum. Several stories in the volume, including the title story and 'Bright Thursdays', are left open-ended, requiring readers to participate in bringing them to completion, and Senior has spoken of this as a conscious strategy to bring about a partnership between writer and reader, akin to the 'call and response' aspects of African-derived music.[7]

Like *Summer Lightning*, Senior's second collection, *Arrival of the Snake-Woman* (1989), which mainly employs Standard English, makes recurrent use of a child's perspective to cast light on the social divisions in Jamaican society. In *Discerner of Hearts* (1995), Senior once again leaves several of her endings open, inviting readers to complete the meaning. Several stories in this volume raise issues relating to 'madness', which in various guises appears to be a socially induced consequence of colonialism and its legacy. In 'The Case Against the Queen', the narrator's uncle returns to Jamaica after a period living in England and, dressed in a three-piece suit, parades his madness by taking the same walk every day in the afternoon sun, without ever speaking to anyone. In 'You Think I Mad, Miss?', the first-person Creole narrator, who is begging on the streets, accosts a series of passers-by and through the fragments of her life story that she tells them gradually reveals how she came to be in her present situation.

Prior to the 1980s, female voices were underrepresented in the Caribbean short story, despite the important role that women have played in ensuring the continuity of the societies' tale-telling traditions. This situation has changed dramatically since then and Senior's contemporaries Velma Pollard and Lorna Goodison have also made significant contributions to the development of the distinctive sociolect of the Jamaican short story. Pollard's characteristic narrative method in *Karl and Other Stories* (1994) and *Considering Woman I and II* (1989 and 2011) is to expand outwards from a puzzling initial episode to provide insights into the situation from which this has arisen. Her concise stories deal with the situations of women in various stations in life, usually moving towards conclusions which, as with Senior, invite reader participation in the completion of meaning. Best known as a poet, Goodison is also an accomplished teller of stories that offer vignettes of Jamaican life. Her collections *Baby Mother and the King of Swords* (1990) and *Fool-Fool Rose Is Leaving Labour-in-Vain Savannah* (2005) particularly focus on the predicaments of the socially disadvantaged and women whose illusions about love lead to disappointments, a theme that is also at the heart of the title story of her collection *By Love Possessed* (2011).

Senior and Goodison settled in Canada, but have remained distinctively Jamaican writers in their choice of subject matter and idiom. Noteworthy collections by several other Caribbean women who now live outside the region move between the Caribbean and European and North American settings, reflecting the internationalization of the Caribbean short story. These include Alicia McKenzie's *Satellite City* (1992), Dionne Brand's *Sans Souci* (1988), Michelle Cliff's *Bodies of Water* (1990) and *The Store of a Million Items* (1998), and Merle Collins's *Rain Darling* (1990). Migrations, in their many and variant forms, have made the definition of exactly what constitutes a Caribbean story a disputed issue, and internationally acclaimed writers such as Jean Rhys and Jamaica Kincaid have frequently been appropriated into metropolitan canons. However, Rhys's stories that draw on her

Dominican girlhood, such as 'The Day They Burned the Books' and 'Pioneers, Oh, Pioneers', which appear in *Tigers Are Better-Looking* (1968), and Kincaid's Antiguan-set stories, such as 'Girl' and 'In the Night', which are included in *At the Bottom of the River* (1983), bear the indelible imprint of these two very different writers' intense response to the Caribbean worlds of their childhood as well as enriching the broader compass of the short story in English.

The relationship between the oral and the scribal has been rather different on the Indian subcontinent, where there is a time-honoured tradition of short narrative and the spoken and the written have coalesced across the centuries. Episodes from revered ancient texts such as the Sanskrit epics *The Ramayana* and *The Mahabharata* have routinely been retold or performed for audiences unable to access them in written form. In such retellings the episodes have often taken on the status of individual fables, akin to the stories of the *Panchatantra*, a compendium of tales that Salman Rushdie has referred to as India's equivalent of Aesop.[8] This kind of tale-telling has influenced a certain type of modern Anglophone Indian short story, in which, as in the fiction of R. K. Narayan, mythic levels underpin an apparently realistic surface. Narayan has retold stories from the epics and *puranas* (Sanskrit sacred legends) in his *Gods, Demons and Others* (1964) and his shortened prose versions of *The Ramayana* (1972) and *The Mahabharata* (1978), and intertexts from classical Hindu discourse also inform several of his novels and short stories.

The first significant body of Indian short stories in English appeared in the late nineteenth century at a time when the presence of the British Raj was influencing the local intelligentsia, particularly in Bengal, but it was in the 1930s that Anglophone Indian fiction came of age. During this decade the so-called 'Big Three' of Indian fiction in English, Mulk Raj Anand, Raja Rao and Narayan, raised the profile of Anglophone Indian writing both at home and abroad, particularly in Britain, where all three were published.

Anand's prolific short story output spans a broad range of narrative modes and themes, but he is at his most powerful in realist pieces such as 'Old Bapu', 'The Thief' and 'Lajwanti', which protest against the plight of India's oppressed and disadvantaged groups. Anand's *Selected Short Stories* (2006), edited by Saros Cowasjee, provides an excellent introduction to his work in the genre. Like his novels, Narayan's short stories are centred on his imagined South Indian town of Malgudi, a location that has been compared with Hardy's Wessex and Faulkner's Yoknapatawpha County. Written over a period of sixty years, his stories reveal ambiguities and transformations that undermine the commonly held view that Malgudi is a microcosm of a settled timeless India. They employ a wry ironic tone, which never descends into broad satire, to expose the follies and foibles of everyday South Indian life. Many of his best short stories are included in *A Horse and Two Goats* (1970), *Malgudi Days* (1982) and *Under the Banyan Tree* (1985). Like Narayan, Raja Rao came from a South Indian Brahmin background. The stories in his collection *The Cow of the Barricades* (1947) centre on the rural world of the Indian south and, as Stefano Mercanti points out, they draw on the conventions of the *shtala purana* (village folk-tale).[9] However, although on one level the use of this form involves an act of homage to a traditional South Indian narrative mode, Rao's attitude towards the social world he portrays is detached and several of the stories depict the abuses and injustices of village life. In Rao's later collections, *The Policeman and the Rose* (1978) and *On the Ganga Ghat* (1989), the Anglophone short story is taken in a strikingly new direction, as the representation of social experience gives way to allegories that explore his belief in Vedantic Hinduism.

The three writers' use of English reflects a consciousness of the problematics of employing the colonizer's tongue. In the Foreword to his novel *Kanthapura* (1938), Rao famously spoke of the problem of having to 'convey in a language that is not one's own the spirit that is one's own', going on to say that 'Our method of expression therefore has to be a dialect which will some day prove to be as distinctive and colourful as the Irish or the American. Time alone will justify it.'[10] Time has indeed done so, though now numerous regionally inflected varieties of English are used in contemporary Indian fiction and the word 'dialect' seems inappropriate. After India attained Independence, Hindi and English were enshrined in the Constitution as national languages. It was intended that English would be phased out after a period of fifteen years, but at the end of this period opposition from the nation's non-Hindi-speaking states led to its retention as an 'associate language' and this, together with the growth of English as a medium for global communication, have insured its continuation as a pan-Indian language that has lost most of its associations with colonialism. English is now spoken by an ever-increasing number of Indians, with the corollary that there has been a boom in English-language publishing and Anglophone fiction.

Several other notable short story writers followed in the wake of the 'Big Three'. Beginning with *The Mark of Vishnu* (1950), Khushwant Singh's numerous collections display a journalist's panoramic eye for observing and commenting on the particularities of Indian social life as well as a range of international experiences. *The Portrait of a Lady* (2009) brings together many of his best stories from different periods in his career, including 'Karma', 'Black Jasmine' and the title story. The delicately realized stories of Attia Hosain's *Phoenix Fled* (1953) evince nostalgia for a pre-Partition India in which traditional ethical codes unite communities and classes. Written from a cosmopolitan Muslim viewpoint, they are not overtly elegiac, but nevertheless lend themselves to being read as a lament for a vanished way of life.

In the closing decades of the twentieth century, encyclopaedic novels such as Rushdie's *Midnight's Children* (1981), Shashi Tharoor's *The Great Indian Novel* (1989) and Vikram Seth's *A Suitable Boy* (1994) established a vogue for representations of India writ large, but the short story continued to flourish, particularly in the hands of women, who in India have as yet been less prone to write at epic length. The filigree-like surface of the stories in Anita Desai's collections *Games at Twilight* (1978) and *Diamond Dust* (2000) conceals a steely resolution; their subtly understated mode captures a gamut of poignant human emotions without ever descending into sentimentality. Stories such as 'Surface Texture' and 'The Man Who Saw himself Drown' embrace levels of psychological complexity that can appear disconcertingly at odds with the quietly observant style in which they are written. Githa Hariharan's stories 'The Remains of the Feast' and 'Gajar Halwa' (in *The Art of Dying*, 1993) are brilliant dramatizations of the importance attached to food and eating habits in Indian culture. In the former, a dying nonagenarian Brahmin woman asserts her independence and infringes caste taboos by eating forbidden food and drinking aerated drinks.

Another significant development in Anglophone Indian fiction since the 1990s has been the emergence of a group of works that defy classification by blurring the boundaries between the novel and short story and in so doing resist conventional Western generic labels. Hariharan's novel *When Dreams Travel* (1999) displays a self-conscious interest in traditional storytelling in a subversive continuation of *The Thousand and One Nights*, in which, as in the American John Barth's *Chimera* (1972), Scheherazade's sister Dunyazade becomes a leading protagonist. Vikram Chandra's novel *Red Earth and Pouring Rain* (1995) is similarly metafictive in its interweaving of tales that employ a mythic narrative mode and a realist story of a contemporary road journey undertaken by a young Indian and his friends. Chandra followed this with *Love and Longing in Bombay* (1997), in which five loosely linked short stories achieve a cumulative force through their relationship with one another.

Subtitled *A Novel in Parts*, Anita Nair's *Ladies Coupé* (2001), another fiction in the tradition of collections such as *The Canterbury Tales* and *The Thousand and One Nights*, uses a frame-narrative as a vehicle for the telling of multiple stories. During the course of a single night, five very different Indian women narrate their life histories to the middle-aged protagonist, Akhila. They tell their tales in a women's train carriage that is an emancipating space for both female narrative and for Akhila herself, and her exchanges with her fellow-passengers release her from the routine of her unfulfilled life and a belief that women's destinies are dependent on their relationship to men.

Sri Lanka's most acclaimed fiction writer who has 'stayed home', Punyakante Wijenaike is less overtly feminist, though she is often concerned with women's predicaments. In *The Third Woman* (1963) and *The Rebel* (1979) she writes about characters whose life histories reflect the changing face of the island's society over several decades, usually without directly addressing the traumas caused by the island's civil war. Diasporic Sri Lankan-born writers such as Romesh Gunesekera and Chandani Lokugé have been less reticent about illustrating the impact that the country's troubled recent history has had on ordinary people. Both Gunesekera's *Monkfish Moon* (1992) and Lokugé's *Moth* (1992) convey a sense of the violent forces that lurk just below the surfaces of everyday life in stories that evoke a sense of threat through restrained, yet powerful prose.

Pakistan's Daniyal Mueenuddin's linked short story sequence *In Other Rooms, Other Wonders* (2009) is set in a very different terrain from those of Gunesekera and Lokugé, but it, too, depicts human tragedies being played out in a landscape of love and loss. The dexterous handling of the contrast between the beauty of the natural world in which the stories are set and the savagery of their conclusions marks Mueenuddin out as the finest Pakistani short story writer of his generation. Other notable Pakistani short story collections include Aamer Hussein's *Mirror to the Sun* (1993) and *Insomnia* (2007), and Tahira Naqvi's *Attar of Roses* (1997).

In addition to the writers discussed above, numerous diasporic writers of South Asian origin demonstrate an umbilical, if sometimes tenuous, relationship with their ancestral homeland. Like much of his fiction, Salman Rushdie's short story collection *East, West* (1994) travels between India and the West and several of the stories revolve around cultural intertexts. Bollywood rubs shoulders with Hollywood in a manner that suggests the extent to which hitherto discrete cultures have become linked in the global village. Diasporic issues are also central to the short stories of American-based Bharati Mukherjee and Jhumpa Lahiri. Mukherjee's collections

Darkness (1985) and *The Middleman* (1988) put their main emphasis on assimilation; Lahiri's *The Interpreter of Maladies* (1999) takes a more considered look at the displacements and translations that occur in recently established and evolving migrant communities. The Canadian-based Rohinton Mistry's *Tales from Firozsha Baag* (1987) is altogether more Indian-rooted. It focuses on the residents of a Parsi apartment building, combining comedy with a despairing humanism and displaying an ambivalent emotional attachment to the Bombay of Mistry's youth.

The intersection of the oral and the written that characterizes many of the short stories discussed above is also a notable feature of stories written by indigenous peoples in 'settler' societies; their stories frequently rework precolonial tale-telling traditions to comment on contemporary situations. Thomas King's 'The One About Coyote Going West' and Jeanette Armstrong's 'This Is a Story' (both included in King's anthology *All My Relations*, 1990) challenge majoritarian Canadian discourses, albeit in very different ways. In New Zealand/Aotearoa, Witi Ihimaera has re-envisioned the society from a Maori point of view. In *Pounamu, Pounamu* (1972), the first short story collection by a Maori writer, he does so through a series of simply told narratives, most of which employ the voice of a boy or young man, whose innocent vision provides a highly appropriate vehicle for seeing the geopolitical world in which he is coming of age through fresh eyes. In *The New Net Goes Fishing* (1977) Ihimaera's perspective is less restrained and several of the stories protest against the marginalization of Maori in Pakeha-dominated society. Both these collections draw on Maori storytelling traditions, but Ihimaera is a writer who moves between the oral and the scribal and he has also published the more 'literary' *Dear Miss Mansfield* (1989), which he calls a 'small *homage*' to New Zealand's most famous short story writer and in which, using techniques such as the epiphany, he demonstrates an indebtedness to her Modernist short story technique.[11] However, although his stories sometimes respond to Katherine Mansfield's work in a straightforwardly derivative way, more often there is a gentle, never fully developed irony, which suggests that her liberalism and capacity to see beyond surface realities remain blinkered by her upper middle-class upbringing. Ihimaera's stories offer a more inclusive approach by closing the distance between the well-to-do and the poor and by breaking down barriers between Maori and Pakeha, women and men, gay and straight and Aotearoan and European-oriented cultural perspectives. In short, his stories move between an approach that inserts Maori oral traditions into the print story and work that engages in a dialogue with a classic modern short story writer and as such it can be seen as a metonym for the manner in which the postcolonial short story has related to the English conventions associated with the genre. Sometimes it extends the range by insisting on the importance of oral demotic voices; at other times it is content to work closer to more 'literary' conventions, while invariably evoking a suggestion of difference that disturbs many of the assumptions that have historically been associated with the short story form.

Notes

1. As Wole Soyinka puts it, 'the artist has always functioned in African society as the record of *mores* and experience of his society *and* as the voice of vision in his own time', 'The Writer in the African State', *Transition*, 31 (1967), p. 13.
2. Helon Habila, Introduction, in *The Granta Book of African Short Stories* (London: Granta, 2011), p. ix. See also Ernest Emenyonu, 'Editorial: Once Upon A Time Begins A Story', *African Literature Today*, 31 (2013), p. 1.
3. 'Writing Africa in the Short Story', *African Literature Today*, 31 (2013).
4. Ama Ata Aidoo, *No Sweetness Here* (London: Longman, 1979), p. 29.
5. Stephanie Newell, *Ghanaian Popular Fiction: 'Thrilling Discoveries in Conjugal Life' & Other Tales* (Oxford: James Currey, and Athens, Ohio: Ohio University Press, 2000), p. 9.
6. Pauline Melville, *The Migration of Ghosts* (London: Bloomsbury, 1998), p. 109.
7. Olive Senior, '"Whirlwinds Coiled at My Heart": Voice and Vision in a Writer's Practice', in *Crosstalk: Canadian and Global Imaginaries in Dialogue*, ed. Diana Brydon and Marta Dvořák (Waterloo, Ontario: Wilfrid Laurier University Press, 2012), p. 28.
8. 'A Tall Story: How Salman Rushdie Pickled All India', *Arena*, BBC2, 1982.
9. Stefano Mercanti, *The Rose and the Lotus: Partnership Studies in the Works of Raja Rao* (Amsterdam and New York: Rodopi, 2009), p. 2. Rao mentions the *shtala purana* in his Foreword to *Kanthapura* (1938; Delhi: Orient Paperbacks, 1992), p. [5].
10. Rao, Foreword to *Kanthapura*, p. [5].
11. Witi Ihimaera, *Dear Miss Mansfield: A Tribute to Kathleen Mansfield Beauchamp* (Auckland: Viking, 1989), p. 9; italics in original.

23
Ghost Stories and Supernatural Tales

RUTH ROBBINS

In 1887, Oscar Wilde published 'The Canterville Ghost', a parody which satirically rehearses some features of the Victorian ghost story. A mansion is leased to an American family named Otis. The family is warned that the owners 'have not cared to live in the place' themselves, since a great aunt 'was frightened into a fit ... by two skeleton hands being placed on her shoulders'.[1] The Americans take up residence nonetheless, and with the sturdy rationalism of the New World, turn the tables on the ghost. Clanking chains, suits of armour that move of their own accord and a recurrent blood stain have no effect on the new tenants. The blood stain is cleaned up with Pinkerton's Champion Stain Remover; the younger Otis boys play pranks on the ghost, mimicking his own behaviour back at him; and the family refuses to believe that there is anything frightening about him at all. Exhausted by his impotence, the ghost agrees to his own exorcism, and the story ends with the Americans in possession of a stately home now without its supernatural tenant.

Wilde's story pokes affectionate fun at the well-worn conventions of the ghost story. Like many parodies it works as both a joke against, and a homage to, the genre. Without the presumption that any reader can immediately pick up the references to the form, there would be no tale to tell and no comedy from the incongruity of a ghost who turns out to be more afraid of the people he is meant to be haunting than they are of him. As the editors of one ghost-story anthology put it, 'The successful ghost story ... depends on using the conventions creatively.' When we read a ghost story, 'we know that we are to be shown a climactic interaction between the living and the dead, and usually expect to be unsettled by the experience'.[2] Wilde's atypical example shows that the ghost story's effects depend on our recognition of, and agreement to accept, the rules of the genre – ironic perhaps, in a genre that is also supposed to surprise and to shock. The elements I foregrounded – local knowledge of a haunting, the empty untenanted house and a repertoire of ghostly behaviours – were clichés, by 1887. In fact, they were clichés well before that, but where earlier writers focused on their potential to provoke an enjoyable shiver, Wilde declares for the Otises' worldview, and demands that the ghost oils his chains, because ghosts are rather inconvenient to modern life.

That assertion of modernity's power is at odds with the ghost story's normal values, which depend on the potent incursion of the past into the present, and on the presumption that the past continues to exert its influence. Discussing the genre, Julia Briggs argues that 'If ... the form depends upon the existence of a tension between an outmoded, but not entirely abandoned belief and a[n] enlightened scepticism, such tension was notably present during the last [nineteenth] century, when the material and spiritual conceptions of life were locked in a continual conflict which no intellectual could entirely avoid'.[3] For other commentators, Briggs's Freudian explanation of the seepage of the past into the present has been superseded by more materialist reasoning. Simon Hay goes so far as to suggest that the psychoanalytic framework is so deeply indebted to the ghost story that psychoanalysis can never explain a ghost story's effects.[4] To use Freud alone to explain how ghost stories work is, in Hay's view, to employ a circular argument. He locates the form's potency in the social rather than the psychic: 'the key concern of the [ghost] story is class mobility' (p. 6), he says, evidencing his claim with readings of ghost stories where a quasi-feudal past is overturned and then re-established (for instance by the rightful heir inheriting property). Andrew Smith makes the case that the circulation of wealth (paper money is a phantasm representing so much real gold) is the motivating force in the ghost story's construction. The objects that money can buy, which become possessions (and which are often behind the 'possession' of a haunted subject) are spectral too: the labour that went into their manufacture is hidden by the polished surface of the finished object, but the object is 'haunted' by that labour, he suggests.[5] Kate Krueger has also recently suggested that the domestic labour on which Victorian domestic comfort depended was ghostly too – hidden from view in Victorian, or even 1950s England, where servants were meant to be neither seen nor heard and a woman's housework was meant to be done before her husband returned from his work.[6] Unlike Hay, however, both Smith's and Krueger's readings of ghost stories remain partially indebted to psychoanalysis, and both make the case that it is a matrix of material, social and psychological factors that are the reasons for the psychic disturbances that ghosts cause.

Most of the social structures whose disturbance accounts for the ghost story's popularity in the Victorian period no longer hold true by the 1920s. 'The Canterville Ghost' signals how a rigid social structure, in which it paid to know one's place, was already under threat. If the very people who were meant to be most terrified by spectres were unmoved because they were not bound by the class conventions of their locale, and if the writer did not play by those social rules, the audience has no obligation to them either. Ironically too, the Freudian explanation for domestic terrors also undoes the need for ghosts. The trauma of the family romance with its repressed violence is explanation enough for the alienation of terrorized subjects. The ghost-story genre demanded the acceptance of the social order and a residual belief in the supernatural. As those elements departed, the ghost story changed and faded, like a spectre in sunlight. The rest of this chapter considers psychic, social and material reasons for its popularity and its relative demise by focusing on the conditions for its popularity, and on the psychological and social narratives it illuminates.

The Victorian Material World and its 'Spiritual' Consequences

The Victorian period was an age of progress, transformed by new ideas in science and technology. So there is some irony in the fact that the vindictive past returned so frequently to disturb the present. It was a period of unprecedented technological change. At the beginning of the century, an educated person would have been able to understand the key scientific knowledge of the day; by its end, that grasp of the material world had slipped away from ordinary people and science looked increasingly like magic. The beliefs of the past also came under assault from new scientific discourses: the ancientness of the past and the evolutionary story of the species both led to a loss of faith in some of the old forms of belief in Christianity; and the harnessing of electricity and the invention of photography, for instance, were both signs of progress which also supported, paradoxically, a belief in the supernatural. Photography was quickly set to work by sincere believers and by charlatans, to 'prove' the existence of ghosts. Double exposures showing 'spirits' made the spiritual seem real.[7] Similarly, electricity, which cannot be seen, but which can be felt, is also ghostly, if one cannot understand how it works.

The Victorians defined themselves as modern, but ordinary domestic arrangements remained 'ancient', situated by the necessity for fires for warmth and light. For most of the century the home was only dimly lit; towards the latter part of the century gas was piped into homes for lighting, and only by its very end did the extremely wealthy benefit from electric light. Middle-class homes – even relatively poor ones – employed domestic servants because the management of a house (carrying water and coal, cleaning up after coal and water) was hefty work. The shape of a family amongst the reading classes was almost always inclusive of people who were employees not relations. The home – and its proxies, the hotel, the inn – was the most likely setting for both the telling of the ghost story and its plot. Many Victorian stories begin with the telling of tall tales round a fire, which testifies to what seems to have been a real social situation, and which was a social setting which was familiar culturally if not experientially. The Victorian ghost story very often refers back to an oral tradition as in the case of Sheridan Le Fanu's 'An Account of Some Strange Disturbances in Aungier Street' (1853):

> It is not worth telling, this story of mine – at least, not worth writing. Told, indeed, as I have sometimes been called upon to tell it, to a circle of intelligent and eager faces, lighted up by a good after-dinner fire on a winter's evening, with a cold wind rising and wailing outside, and all snug and cosy within, it has gone off ... well ... Pen, ink, and paper are cold vehicles for the marvellous, and a 'reader' decidedly a more critical animal than a listener.[8]

Some of the key markers of the genre are here: a domestic setting for the telling of a tale, a winter's night outside and the suspension of disbelief that comes from a 'good after-dinner' feeling; it is cosy, but there is also threat. The narrator's comment on the 'critical' frame of mind of the reader, contrasted with the credulity of the listener, is also part of the set-up. Oral narrators draw strength from eye-witness authority. Other examples are even cosier in their framing. In Elizabeth Gaskell's 'The Old Nurse's Story' (1852), a safe domestic setting for narrative is constructed in the narrator's mode of address: 'You know, my dears, that your mother was an orphan ... and I dare say you have heard that your grandfather was a clergyman.'[9] This is storytelling as gossip by someone whose affection for her audience ('my dears') is not in doubt.

The material setting of many examples of the genre points to the relationship between past and present that is also the genre's key plot point. The modern Victorian home is permeated by the past. The hearth represents ancient as well as contemporary comfort, but it also provides very poor light to see by. What you can only half-see is hard to interpret. Everyday objects can take on an uncanny life of their own, as in Algernon Blackwood's 'The Kit-Bag' (1908), where a young man staying in a hotel en route to a climbing holiday, borrows a rucksack from a friend, only to find that this commonplace object has taken on a life of its own, and is following him around the room. In the half-light of a poorly illuminated hotel bedroom, he cannot be sure of his senses: 'It is difficult to say at what point fear begins, when the causes of that fear are not plainly before the eyes.'[10] Turning the light on doesn't help because it shows that the ghost is real. Throwing light on the subject, however, often does destroy its power to frighten. In a world where light is not easily obtained, it is not surprising that there were powerful effects to be had from shadowy vision. Fear is most easily constructed when the situation is not clearly legible. As Srdjan Smajić has argued, understanding how we 'see' (and how we do not see clearly at all times) is central to understanding the Victorian obsession with the ghost story.[11]

The domestic comfort of having servants to do the hard labour of household management may be another explanation for the ghostliness of the Victorian home, which was, after all, often inhabited by extra people who were meant to remain unseen. (Children, like servants, were meant to be unseen and unheard, and are often uncanny figures in the ghost story as a consequence of their not-quite human status.) In grander Victorian houses, there were separate stairways and passages for the servants, so that no one would see them. It is no surprise, therefore, that in Henry James's 'The Turn of the Screw' (1897), it is rogue servants who haunt the House at Bly, particularly given that the haunted governess is a young and impoverished gentlewoman who has not been used to a grand household. And it is notable that this most sophisticated and literary example of the ghost story is, like the Wilde story with which this chapter began, saturated with features derived from the genre's popular form. It opens with ghost stories being told round a fire at Christmas, nodding to the oral tradition of which is it not otherwise a part. The governess's story is then told to a more select audience. She herself is a new tenant in an unhomely home, and veers between rationalist and romantic explanations of the events that haunt her just like the credulous servant witnesses of other earlier tales.

Houses that are not quite 'home' are a key setting for the ghost story. A family moving to London for the Season, or to the Hills in India to avoid the hot weather, seeks a house to rent, and finds one, ridiculously or suspiciously cheaply. Mrs De Wynt, one of the correspondents in Rhoda Broughton's epistolary tale 'The Truth, the Whole Truth, and Nothing but the Truth' (1868) locates such a house for her best friend, and describes her stupefaction at finding such a wonderful house at so small a rent as three hundred pounds a year (actually an enormous sum in 1868; this is the world of the extremely wealthy): 'With that suspiciousness that is no characteristic of you, you will immediately begin to hint that there must be some terrible unaccountable smell, or some odious inexplicable noise haunting the reception rooms. Nothing of the kind, the woman [who showed me the house] assured me.'[12] The question of smell is one thing; in an era before drains and sewers were fully the responsibility of the authorities, and when indoor lavatories were a new invention, the assumption that cheap housing would have poor sanitation was understandable.[13] The question of an unexpected noise in the reception rooms – because floorboards and door frames do creak – is equally unexceptional. The ghost story, however, uses the situation of the unfamiliar house to unsettle readers and characters alike.

Creepy feelings can extend outside the home, especially when a familiar landscape is rendered strange by atmospheric conditions or even the forces of history. In Elizabeth Bowen's late example 'The Demon Lover' (1945), Mrs Drover, returns to her family home in London during the Blitz to pick up some unconsidered trifles. The familiar landscape of London is rendered queer by the aftermath of the bombings and the illegibility of street patterns caused by the blackout. In this landscape, Mrs Drover gets into a taxi, apparently driven by the ghost of a former lover, and is driven off into who-knows-what fate, despite the evidence of modernity that surrounds her. The place where home is has become distinctly unsettling at this juncture of history.

The Freudian Uncanny

Despite Hay's doubts, there is still something to be said for Freud's account of how we are frightened by narratives. Material conditions have their effects on the mind; the mind interprets the material in relation to the effects of the material – it *is* a circular argument, as Hay suggests, but there are connections between what a place is like and how it feels to inhabit it. The comments above on domestic settings are part of this explanatory frame. Freud's connection of the social to the psychological is still a usable tool.

In his account of the Uncanny (1919), Freud focuses on the home as the locus for shivering, momentary uncertainties. He traces the etymology of the German word *unheimlich* (literally 'unhomely'), showing that it always contains its opposite – *heimlich*, homely. The homely, domestic and familiar are at the root of feelings related to the uncanny, weird and strange. Freud also argues that 'doubts whether an apparently animate being is really alive; or conversely whether a lifeless object might not in fact be animate' is a good starting point for the investigation into the uncanny. [14] Dolls, waxworks and corpses are likely to provoke a shudder of misrecognition in which the perceiver cannot at first distinguish between life-likeness and life itself. To these elements, Freud's account adds the uncanny effect of the double (the literal twin, or the spectral sense that an individual is in fact divided into several constituent parts) and the uncanny effects of repetition, where the same act is compulsively re-enacted. (Genre is, of course, also a form of repetition, and ghosts in stories often return compulsively and repeat the same actions as the sign of the trauma they both inhabit and inflict.) Freud concludes that the home is the most likely site of uncanny experience or of haunting, explaining this in part by the repressed traumas of individual lives, and, since everyone suffers from repression, there is a broader implication: generally people have homes and families, and generally they repress their desires and traumas – so generally they may be expected to be haunted. It is a shift from the individual psyche to a much wider – social and cultural – potential to be affected by the strange within the walls of the family home.

In ghost stories, where many of the reasons for a ghost to appear come from family tensions, overbearing parental authority, rivalries between siblings, disputed inheritances or love affairs where sisters or brothers are rivals, the haunted house bears the traces of the violent emotions and the violent actions that emotions have provoked. Emotional propriety (loving the correct suitor, honouring one's ancestors) and property (which one inherits from those ancestors if everyone's behaviour has been 'proper') become inextricably intertwined. But proper behaviour in the Freudian account is a corollary of repression, particularly the repression of affective and desiring relationships. As Freud's work became better known, it found its way into the ghost story. D. H. Lawrence's 'The Rocking-Horse Winner' (1926) shows a small boy, desperate for his mother's love, intuiting that the way to her heart is money. He is possessed by the haunting refrain 'There *must* be more money', which appears to be his home speaking his mother's desire out loud. He rides his rocking-horse to discover the names of winners of horse races, so that his uncle can bet on them and his mother can have the money she craves. But his mother remains unsatisfied by material wealth, and doesn't notice the boy's decline into death at the end of the tale. The money satisfies neither her material desires nor his emotional needs. May Sinclair's *Uncanny Stories* (1923) are also about the psychic pain caused by love that is either unrequited or unexpressed within families. In 'The Token' a young wife longs for her husband to express his love for her; his stiff upper lip never wavers, however; and she dies of a broken heart (or, more prosaically, of heart disease) after a blazing row about a paperweight given to her husband by George Meredith, which she believes he cares for more than he cares for her. Her ghost haunts his rooms, desperate for his love to be expressed. This happens only after the intercession of the husband's sister, who makes him speak his love: 'I was mad with caring for her!' he shouts; and now the ghost knows it, she vanishes forever.[15] In 'The Intercessor' a dead child haunts its parents, distraught because her mother did not love her when she was alive; and in 'If the Dead Knew' a mother haunts her son, who feels guilt for having wished her dead so he could marry the girl he loves. These are writers making knowing use of the Freudian account of family relations.

These are not the only uncanny elements the ghost story can trace. There is also a great deal of psychological terror to be derived from other instances where what one expects to be known and knowable – the evidence of your eyes – turns out to be deceptive. Many of the words attached to ghosts, such as 'spectre' or 'apparition', are words that are to do with 'seeing', of knowing the world around you through visual perception. Freud's uncanny originally focuses on the home; but there are other forms of interpretation in which one expects certainty, and where uncertainty is profoundly disturbing. In his essay on 'Femininity' (1933) Freud comments on the 'unhesitating certainty' with which we expect to be able to identify a person's sex.[16] And although he concludes that such certainty is illusory, the uncertainty that derives from not being able to trust the senses to tell someone's gender is uncanny. This is not a widely exploited source of fear, but in the ghost stories of Vernon Lee it is central. The counter-tenor or castrato singer whose feminine voice belies his masculine body ('A Wicked Voice' (1890)), or the young woman in travesty who haunts in the shape of a boy ('The Phantom Lover' (1886)) are two examples of gender incongruity deployed to uncanny effects, which come from the strange desirability of spectres who do not conform to gender norms, and who unsettle the heteronormative certainties of those who perceive them.[17]

There are also ghost stories which are wish-fulfilments. When Arthur Machen published a short story called 'The Bowmen' in 1915, the public was quick to presume its authenticity. 'The Bowmen' narrates how the ghosts of the Agincourt long-bowmen come to the rescue of contemporary soldiers at the first Battle of Mons in 1914. They have apparently been summoned into being by the accidental invocation of St George by one of the British soldiers. The story is wish-fulfilment in its writing and in its reception. The tale is propaganda, which reassures an English audience that God is on their side. But its aftermath, in which its truth was asserted by the reading public and by multiple alleged eye-witness accounts of the angels of Mons, despite Machen's protestations of the story's fictionality, suggests that the wishes of its readers were amply fulfilled by a story which is not haunting at all, unless one happens to be a German infantryman.[18]

The Marxist Spectre

Marx's *Communist Manifesto* (1848) opens with the spectre of communism haunting Europe. For Marx fear is generated both by the overthrow of old social systems and by feudalism's refusal to die. This 'vision' of a potentially monstrous future and an undead (already monstrous) past has proved fruitful for ghost-story critics, who have seen it as exemplifying the imaginary enactment of class struggle. Simon Hay's reading of Charlotte Riddell's 'The Open Door' (1882) draws out themes that were common to the nineteenth-century ghost story. The protagonist reinstates his family fortunes by demonstrating his bravery in a spot of ghost-hunting. An old house has been let on a long lease to a new tenant. The tenant cannot live in the house because it is haunted by 'a door that won't keep shut'.[19] Phil is commissioned by both owner and tenant to find out why. There is a murderer at large – the widow of the previous owner has murdered her husband and continues to frequent the place to uncover a will in her favour; but the door is not kept ajar by her means: the recalcitrance of this inanimate object is, we are meant to infer, the result of a ghost. When Phil finds the murderess (who nearly gets him too) he is instrumental in restoring the social order, clearing the name of the murdered man's son and restoring the house to peace. His fortune is made on the back of this action and he gets to marry the girl he loves.

Hay's reading of this story emphasizes its class dimension: the restoration of a family to its proper place in society, and the resolution of an affair that had threatened relations between an old money (the house's owner) and new (the tenant). What had risked becoming a class war (even one politely fought in the courts) is avoided. The last words of the story, however, belie the 'happily-ever-after' scenario: 'there are times when a great horror of darkness seems to fall upon me, and at such periods I cannot endure to be left alone' (p. 282). Even the apparently satisfactory restoration of the social order leaves its psychic traces at the end of the story; Phil is still haunted by the spectre not of communism but of a feudal past he has helped to restore.[20]

Class is a particular concern of the English and it never quite leaves the English ghost story. The Victorian ghost story makes the emphasis on social relations extremely clear. Commonly, the first witness of any ghost in a domestic setting is a credulous, generally working-class, often female, servant. The horror only truly arises at the point when a credible eye-witness, upper class, leisured, educated, professional, sceptical and usually male, is also convinced of the reality of the haunting.

Small groups of middle-class men, professional, academic, rational and intelligent, are those most usually haunted in the stories of M. R. James (1862–1936). These are men who are not strictly 'at home' in the tales, since they inhabit college rooms and hotels. They share antiquarian interests and a prosaic fascination with golf. They are almost always homosocial beings, living without the company of women. Part of James's effectiveness comes from this context: such men are (generically, anyway) the least likely of all groups to be haunted. But they are, repeatedly, caught up by a vindictive past, often accessed through the accidental acquiring of some ancient object which then proceeds to terrify them. In James's own words: 'Many common objects may be made the vehicles of retribution and ... malice. Be careful how you handle the packet you pick up in the carriage-drive.'[21] His focus is on the damage that is done in mundane situations. In 'Whistle and I'll Come to You, My Lad' (1904), an ancient whistle, a seemingly harmless archaeological relic, whistles up a terrifying apparition which haunts an elderly professor on a golfing holiday on the East Coast of England. In 'The Mezzotint' (1904), a museum curator comes across an old engraving, which inexorably tells the story of a judicial murder and the revenge that followed. He and his colleagues are powerless to intervene in the playing out of the story over several hours on the day they receive the mysterious picture. The impression is that the story will repeat for all eternity, and no one can stop it.

In the stories of Robert Aickman (1914–81), which owe much to James, class is also a central element. His protagonists do not understand the social world because they are socially awkward and intellectually commonplace, so that the terrors that haunt them might be supernatural, or might just be the psychic disturbances caused by social unease. It is not property as such that is at stake, but the means to negotiate the social terrain in which they are never quite at home. In 'The Trains' (1951) two young female hikers get lost in a valley they cannot navigate.[22] Their (possibly lesbian) pleasure in each other's company is soured because they are so lost. They are 'rescued' from their predicament into a house in the valley, a house from which they have seen a ghostly woman waving at trains, only to find themselves embroiled in a murder and an imprisonment from which there appears to be no escape. As is typical with Aickman, the story is unresolved. The stories, written from the 1950s to the 1970s, are throwbacks to an earlier age and depend on there being social rules with which the stories' actors are unfamiliar. In many of Aickman's stories there is also an unresolved sexual tension that combines in uneasy ways with the class story.

In Elizabeth Walter's 'Come and Get Me' (1973) a soldier on exercises in remotest Wales is haunted by a figure at the window of an abandoned house. The ghost is that of a young man who had apparently deserted from his regiment in the Second World War. Local rumour has it that he had killed himself by drowning. In fact, his father, disgusted by his son's alleged cowardice, had imprisoned him in the house to avoid the stigma of a court martial. When the young lieutenant returns a year later in company with an old officer who had known the original family, it turns out that the story is more macabre. The imprisoned ghost had not deserted but had been betrayed by the very officer who is now investigating the apparition. The ghost kills his betrayer by luring him onto a rotten staircase from which they both fall. The ghostly figure is found to be just a skeleton, the old officer a fresh body. This is a story about class because it is focused on codes of appropriate behaviour, in this case in the closed world of the army's officer class. Breaking faith with those codes leads to consequences as stark as any that arise from the misappropriation of property by theft, murder or inappropriate affection.

Like genre itself, the ghost story depends to a very large extent on rules that are bent or broken. As societies become less convinced by those rules, the conditions that facilitate the ghost story are harder to rely on, and the motivations for ghostly behaviours are increasingly incredible. The ghost story is usually a conservative genre. Either it returns the reader to a safe status quo, or, when it refuses to do so, readers and eyewitnesses are left wishing that it had.

Unmotivated Ghosts

Some of the best ghost stories come from a slightly different tradition that overlaps with the weird tale. These are stories where ghostly activity appears utterly unmotivated, and the narrative does not dissolve the obscurity or explain anything at all. In the works of J. Sheridan Le Fanu, for instance, weird things sometimes happen to people who appear to have done nothing to deserve them, and the extremes of psychological torture that they suffer cannot be explained. A very famous example is 'Green Tea', in which an utterly harmless clergyman, Mr Jennings, is haunted by the hallucination of a small devilish monkey. He seeks treatment for his condition, which may be explained by heredity (his father saw a ghost); or by over-consumption of the stimulant, green tea; or by nervous exhaustion brought on by overwork. But frankly, none of the explanations is proportionate to the torments he suffers. The monkey seems to come from nowhere, and is not susceptible to treatment by Jennings's doctor/theologian consultant, Martin Hesselius, who in fact, blames the clergyman himself for his own affliction: 'the complaint under which he really succumbed, was hereditary suicidal mania', Hesselius tells us.[23] Hesselius's certainty is not, however, backed up by the feel of the tale. He is an ineffective doctor whose patient dies, and no one knows why.

This tradition is picked up in the works of Algernon Blackwood (1859–1961), where the 'ghosts', if they are ghosts, are often rooted in nature. Trees are malevolent ('Willows' (1907)); a whole French village turns into a herd of cats at night, and glories in the predatory instincts of feline kind ('Ancient Sorceries'(1908)).[24] No explanation is offered. Observers of these phenomena act as eyewitnesses, watch with horror, and then run away. The situations are never resolved or explained. These are tales that relate much more strongly to the weird tale than to the ghost story. But they are related generically because of their intent to provoke the reader's shudder.

A more obviously ghostly version of this narrative trajectory away from social and psychological frames comes from the *oeuvre* of Charles Dickens. Dickens was fascinated by ghosts. In his Christmas stories, most famously *A Christmas Carol* (1843), he brings the ghostly to bear on the present for moralistic purposes. However, his most interesting ghost tale, 'No.1 Branch Line: The Signal-Man' (1866), operates on an entirely different level.

The railway was a resolutely modern setting in 1866. But that confident modernity is overlaid with foreboding. The branch line of the title is located in an ancient landscape that has many of the features of the sublime. 'The cutting was extremely deep, and unusually precipitate. It was made through a clammy stone, that became oozier and wetter as I went down', the narrator tells us.[25] The signalman is cut off from the civilization for which he provides technical support. He seldom rises from the cutting; but he has made attempts to use his time to educate himself in foreign languages and in algebra. These two forms of study are related, for they are both 'puzzles' to the signalman, the rest of whose existence is made up of interpreting and acting on very simple signals from further up the line.

The signalman is unsettled because he is haunted by a figure who shouts a warning that cannot be acted upon because it is also a puzzle. The evidence is that his warnings should be heeded (the spectre has already predicted two serious incidents), but there is no evasive action that the signalman can take to prevent the railway accident that the spectre foretells and he is paralyzed by his impotence. On the narrator's third visit to his new friend at the signal box, he discovers that the man has been killed by a train despite the shouted warnings of the driver. The driver, to the narrator's horror, repeats both the reported words and the gestures of the ghost as he describes how the accident happened.

Unlike the more traditional ghost tales, this ghost is not out to right wrongs or to punish a malefactor. The signalman is blameless. There is no explanation of his haunting. This is a nihilistic tale about the inevitability of human tragedy and hopelessness of human agency. Cause and effect are disrupted. Evidence does not lead to action; interpretation is merely contingent and understanding fleeting. The signalman does not deserve his fate, just as in later stories by Blackwood, M. R. James and Sheridan Le Fanu, the protagonists do not deserve theirs.

A Genre in Decline

The conditions that made the ghost story popular did not survive beyond the First World War. Ghost stories continue to be written, but the genre has been overtaken by other genres. The hauntings of the earlier form have been overtaken by the psycho-social discomforts charted by the high culture forms of short fiction.

Two notable examples by contemporary women writers, Jane Gardam's 'Dead Children' (1994) and A. S. Byatt's 'The July Ghost' (1982) stand as elegies for the genre. In Gardam's story the children, despite the title, are not dead, but grown up, lost to their mother through the natural process of maturing. The story centres on two scenes in a London park, separated by thirty years, and told in the first instance from the point of view of the protagonist's two children, who encounter a very elderly lady in a clearing and are a bit frightened of her, and then retold from the elderly lady's point of view in the present. The haunting is really about the fact that life goes on and nothing can stop its inexorable processes. The children in the earlier narrative of the encounter have met up with the ghostly figure of their mother, now an old woman whom they do not recognize. The second telling has the older woman meeting her children as they were when they were still invested with all her hopes for the future. It is an unsettling but not a horrifying tale, in which the supernatural is made to speak about the psychology of ageing and change.[26]

Byatt's story is more distressing. A narcissistic man seeks new digs to escape from an abandoned lover. The house he moves into belongs to a woman with whom he starts a new affair, though one with a macabre twist, for his access to the woman comes from the fact that, unlike her, he can see the ghost of her dead son. Though the man's is the point of view from which the narrative is constructed, the woman's story is much more interesting and much sadder. Her son has been killed in a car accident. His ghost – a happy child ghost who is not a problem to anyone – appears to everyone in her vicinity except for her and she is desperate to see him:

> 'I'm too rational to see ghosts [. . .] I thought ghosts were what people *wanted* to see, or were afraid to see . . . [. . .], and the best hope I had [. . .] was that I would go mad enough [that . . .] I might actually have the illusion of seeing or hearing him come in. Because I can't stop my body and mind, waiting, every day, every day. I can't let go'.[27]

Being 'too rational to see ghosts' sums up the problems for the genre today. In a neat reversal, class discomfort – from which the education to be 'too rational' comes – and psychic pain are caused not by the disruption of an apparition, but by its lack. The mother could be comforted if she could believe in an afterlife, but she knows that life comes only to a 'sliced-off stop' (p. 505). In the story's final lines, the young man leaves the bereaved mother, telling the ghost child he has to go because: 'What are we in this house? A man, a woman and a child, and none of us can get through' (p. 512). It is a story of family breakdown. But we no longer really need the ghost to act as a motive for the emotional pain that is just as easily understood as the contemporary human condition.

Notes

1. Oscar Wilde, 'The Canterville Ghost' (1887), *The Complete Works of Oscar Wilde*, ed. Merlin Holland (Glasgow: HarperColllins, 1994), pp. 184–204 (p. 184).
2. Michael Cox and R. A. Gilbert, Introduction to *The Oxford Book of Victorian Ghost Stories* (Oxford University Press, 1993), p. xi.
3. Julia Briggs, *Night Visitors: The Rise and Fall of the English Ghost Story* (London: Faber & Faber, 1977), p. 16.
4. Simon Hay, *A History of the Modern British Ghost Story* (Basingstoke: Palgrave 2011), p. 5. Hay writes: 'for Freud . . . the psyche was modelled on the classic haunted house, both its attic and its cellar populated with ghosts . . . in the shape of repressed traumas and desires, just waiting for the right moment to pop . . . out of the closet in the form of neurotic symptoms or slips of the tongue'.
5. Andrew Smith, *The Ghost Story, 1840–1920: A Cultural History* (Manchester University Press, 2010), pp. 11–17. See also, Mary Poovey, *The Financial System in Nineteenth-Century Britain* (Oxford University Press, 2003); and Fredric Jameson, 'Cognitive Mapping', in *Marxism and the Interpretation of Culture*, ed. I. Grosberg and C. Nelson (Urbana: University of Illinois Press, 1988), pp. 347–57.
6. Kate Krueger, *British Women Writers and the Short Story, 1850–1930: Reclaiming Social Space* (Basingstoke: Palgrave, 2014), especially chapter 2.
7. See for example, John Harvey, *Photography and Spirit* (London: Reaktion Books, 2007); and Clement Cherous, Andreas Fischer, Denis Canguilhem and Sophie Schmit, *The Perfect Medium: Photography and the Occult* (Yale University Press, 2005). Both of these two books show how the fakers faked ghost photography, but also discuss why the public was so prepared to be fooled. Marina Warner's *Phantasmagoria: Spirit Visions, Metaphors, and Media into the Twenty-First Century* (Oxford University Press, 2006) discusses some of the material conditions that led to belief in the spirit world.
8. J. Sheridan Le Fanu, 'An Account of Some Strange Disturbances in Aungier Street', in Cox and Gilbert, *Victorian Ghost Stories*, pp. 19–36 (p. 19).
9. Elizabeth Gaskell, 'The Old Nurse's Story' (1852), in Cox and Gilbert, *Victorian Ghost Stories*, pp. 1–18 (p. 1).
10. Algernon Blackwood, 'The Kit-Bag' (1908), in Cox and Gilbert, *Victorian Ghost Stories*, pp. 480–9 (p. 483).
11. Srdjan Smajić, 'The Trouble with Ghost-Seeing: Vision, Ideology and Genre in the Victorian Ghost Story', *English Literary History*, 70 (2003), 4, pp. 1107–35.
12. Rhoda Broughton, 'The Truth, the Whole Truth, and Nothing but the Truth' (1868), in Cox and Gilbert, *Victorian Ghost Stories*, pp. 74–82 (p. 75).
13. The 'letting' situation is very common indeed. In Cox and Gilbert, alongside Broughton's story there are at least four others in which this basic situation is

repeated, included Le Fanu's 'Account', the anonymous 'The Story of Clifford House' (1878), B. M. Croker's 'To Let' (1890), and Charlotte Riddell's 'The Open Door' (1882). The middle two, save for their settings, are virtually the same story as Broughton's 'The Truth'.

14. Sigmund Freud, 'The Uncanny' (1919), in *The Penguin Freud Library, Volume XIV: Art and Literature*, trans. James Strachey, ed. Albert Dickson (Harmondsworth: Penguin, 1983), p. 341, 347.
15. May Sinclair, *Uncanny Stories*, ed. Paul March-Russell (1923; London: Wordsworth, 2006), p. 56.
16. Sigmund Freud, 'Femininity' (1933), in *The Essentials of Psycho-analysis*, ed. Anna Freud (Harmondsworth: Penguin, 1991), p. 413.
17. For a fuller discussion of this tendency in Lee's work, see Ruth Robbins, 'Apparitions can be Deceptive: Vernon Lee's Androgynous Spectres', in *Victorian Gothic: Literary and Cultural Manifestations in the Nineteenth Century*, ed. Julian Wolfreys and Ruth Robbins (Basingstoke: Macmillan, 2000), pp. 182–200. A good range of Vernon Lee's stories is collected as *Supernatural Tales* (London: Peter Owen, 1987).
18. Arthur Machen, 'The Bowmen' (1915), in *The White People and Other Weird Stories* (Harmondsworth: Penguin, 2011), pp. 223–6. Daphne du Maurier reprises this theme in her Second World War Story, 'Escort', where the ghost of a ship from Nelson's navy protects a North Sea frigate from attack by a German submarine. Daphne du Maurier, 'Escort', in *The Rendezvous and Other Stories* (London: Virago, 2007), pp. 156–74.
19. Charlotte Riddell, 'The Open Door' (1882), in Cox and Gilbert, *Victorian Ghost Stories*, pp. 256–82 (p. 257).
20. Hay, *A History of the Modern British Ghost Story*, pp. 2–17.
21. M. R. James, 'Stories I Have Tried to Write', in *Collected Ghost Stories* (Ware: Wordsworth's Classics, 1992), pp. 643–7 (p. 646).
22. Robert Aickman, 'The Trains' (1951), in *The Wine-Dark Sea* (London: Faber & Faber, 2014), Kindle Edition.
23. J. Sheridan Le Fanu, 'Green Tea', in *In a Glass Darkly* (1872) (Ware: Wordsworth, 2008), pp. 3–32 (p. 32).
24. Both of these stories are collected in Algernon Blackwood, *Ancient Sorceries and Other Weird Stories*, ed. S. T Joshi (Harmondsworth: Penguin, 2002).
25. Charles Dickens, 'No. 1 Branch Line: The Signalman' (1866), reprinted in John Grafton, ed., *Classic Ghost Stories* (New York: Dover Thrift Editions, 1998), pp. 19–29 (p. 20).
26. Jane Gardam, 'Dead Children' (1994), in *The Stories* (London: Abacus, 2014), pp. 309–18.
27. A. S. Byatt, 'The July Ghost' (1982), reprinted in J. A. Cuddon, ed., *The Penguin Book of Ghost Stories* (Harmondsworth: Penguin, 1984), pp. 499–512 (p. 505).

24

The Detective Story: Order from Chaos

ANDREW MAUNDER

Agatha Christie's 'Tape Measure Murder', published in 1950 at the tail-end of the so-called 'Golden Age' of the British detective story, betrays typical features: a closed community, in this case a respectable English village, but where violence lies repressed beneath gentility.[1] A middle-aged housewife dressed in a kimono lies strangled, her neck bearing the marks of what appears to be a narrow belt. There are suspects, and there are official investigators – but it is left to an amateur detective, in this case a sedentary old spinster, Jane Marple, to puzzle her way through the series of scattered facts before revealing the truth on the final page. The crime is described as 'old fashioned' and the story certainly seems so. But, sixty years on, its appeal remains. If such texts have sometimes been neglected in surveys of literary history, it is not because of a shortage of materials, nor of heavyweight supporters – which have included T. S. Eliot, W. H. Auden and Gertrude Stein – but because detective stories have often been perceived as superficial and one-dimensional: the focus on the puzzle has been seen to diminish the 'literary'.

Indeed, for a long time, the literary establishment maintained a condescending stance to this popular and commercial genre. In 1944, Edmund Wilson described the detective genre as 'sub-literary', 'degrading to the intelligence' and existing 'somewhere between smoking and crossword puzzles'. 'I hope never to read another of her books' was his verdict on Christie. He judged Arthur Conan Doyle's Sherlock Holmes stories 'stagy' and melodramatic, although he had enjoyed them as a child.[2] Doyle, Christie and their kind are accused of enacting a form of confidence trick on the public, giving them the same thing over and over again; yet these unpretentious writers never made great claims for their stories, beyond their timeless appeal.

The recognition received by detective stories and their writers has never, therefore, been straightforward. The form is seen as not quite literature but has been held up as the epitome of pure storytelling. The 1920s are a case in point: the moment when the familiar structures of the detective short story seemed to stand in opposition to modernist short story writers' apparent disdain for plot. The modernist aesthetic preferred 'obliquity', which Virginia Woolf described as 'the things one doesn't say'.[3] The years after the First World War were also famous in cultural terms for providing an environment where 'human character changed', as Woolf put it, into something 'modern' and less certain.[4] In contrast, fictional detectives are invariably characterized by their certitude: as a form, the detective story tends to be extremely certain in its answers; it deals in mystery but is not generally enigmatic. As a form of storytelling with a strong narrative drive, it is characterized by its working towards a quick, tidy ending, making things explicit, and concluding on the satisfying restoration of the status quo. 'The universal desire to see the hidden things brought to light, to know exactly what took place on a given occasion, by whose agency and how', was how one 1894 commentator described its appeal. This has remained a powerful driver.[5]

Although the short detective story as we now recognize it tends to be associated most strongly with the 1890s and then the 1920s and 1930s, myths of origin abound, some stretching back to the story of Oedipus. Others have located the beginnings in collections of semi-fictional case studies such as *Richmond: Scenes from the Life of a Bow Street Runner* (1827). This dating fits with the establishment of a force of 'bobbies' in 1829 and the subsequent Police Acts, including in 1877 the establishment of the Criminal Investigations Department; all these focused attention on law enforcement and the criminal. The periodical press also played a role in feeding demand for crime stories, supplying readers with 'shilling shockers' and with reports of real-life detective exploits, including Charles Dickens's influential 'Inspector Field' articles in *Household Words* (1850–1).

There is another school of thought which points to the American Edgar Allan Poe as the father of the detective story, beginning suddenly with 'The Murders in the Rue Morgue' (1841). Some ingredients are very recognizable. A locked room creates a sense of entrapment and mystery. The detective, C. Auguste Dupin, is a quirky, analytical person observed from the point of view of a dim assistant. It is through such admiring eyes that the sleuth's methods and final demystification of the crime are shared with readers, thus creating one of the form's distinctive features; we get two stories: one in the present, which describes the investigation, and then the explanation, which originates in the past but also explains the present.[6]

Because Poe's influence on the detective genre was not immediate, other formative examples have been offered, including Wilkie Collins's 'The Diary of Anne Rodway' (1856) and Ellen (Mrs Henry) Wood's 'Johnny Ludlow' tales featuring a boy detective (1868–87). Most histories, however, suggest it was not until the 1880s that the developed version appeared: Arthur Conan Doyle's Sherlock Holmes novella *A Study in Scarlet* (1887), followed by the first series of short stories beginning with 'A Scandal in Bohemia', in *The Strand* (1891). It was Doyle, so this suspiciously tidy narrative goes, who, influenced by Poe, realized that the detective could be the central attraction.

Strangely, another thing that Doyle helped do was to encourage the idea that detective stories belonged to a lower rank of creativity; they were a side-line allowing him financial freedom to pursue more 'literary' projects. When interviewed, he explained: 'there is no great originality required in devising ... such a man [Holmes], and the only possible originality which one can get into a story about a detective is in giving him original plots and problems to solve'.[7] This idea that detective stories required little creativity became popular. In 'Our Short Story Writers' (1895), the *Pall Mall Gazette* explained how it was 'easy to construct detective stories. Having imagined some crime or other event, the narrator goes back and makes signs on the wall ... then brings along his detective, who sees these signs and displays his marvellous sagacity.'[8] All that the writer had to remember was that he or she needed to work backwards; the ending and the explanation shaped the rest of the story. Later the *Pall Mall* returned to the subject, suggesting that romance should always be excluded, and there should be no diatribes on social issues: 'the duty of the author is to attend strictly to business, and to introduce into his pages nothing that does not directly bear upon the central mystery and its solution'.[9] The story would proceed from a suppressed or partial idea of the truth to an explanation of it, with the reader able to devour it in a satisfying single sitting. Then the story would finish; no love interest, no proselytizing.

By the end of the nineteenth century, the appetite for detective stories appeared unstoppable: 'magazines being bought up with the utmost avidity', as the *Westminster Review* noted in 1897, purely to read 'literature which revels in the machinations of evil-doers, and in the checkmating movements of those whose perilous business it is to keep such wretches in constant fear and trembling'.[10] By this time the landscape had expanded to include pioneers Catherine Louisa Pirkis (1841–1910), 'Dick Donovan' [Joyce Emerson

Muddock] (1843–1934), L. T. Meade [Elizabeth Meade Smith] (1844–1914), Grant Allen (1848–99) and Arthur Morrison (1863–1945) – reliable money-spinners who developed detective short stories into a sub-speciality, with narratives which mimicked the procedures of real-life detectives (as they were understood) and enabled more than one magazine to keep afloat. They had to compete with what Wilkie Collins had termed 'the rank and file of hack writers', who made anonymous livings selling stories to 'penny dreadfuls' and boy's magazines.[11] These included Harry Blyth (1852–98), the creator of Sexton Blake, billed as the 'great detective' but invariably regarded as a poor man's Sherlock Holmes.

By this time other recognizable ingredients had begun to appear. Arnold Bennett in his work as a reviewer for London's *Evening Standard* was willing to be seduced by elegance of style, but noted that this was an unusual feature of detective stories. He was accordingly captivated by M. P. Shiel's Poe-inspired Prince Zaleski tales, in which the cannabis-smoking aesthete solves cases ensconced on a chaise longue.[12] But Bennett was exasperated by the detective story's artificiality, its treating crime as a game. This was especially true of the short story, where lack of space (combined with laziness) meant that detectives were mere 'calculating machines, impossible seers, and outrageous fools, drawn ... on a background of plain cardboard'. Rounded characters and convincing environmental details were always lacking. Nor were such stories worth reading for their insights into actual police procedure. 'I should like to know', Bennett wrote, 'how many [writers] ... have ever talked familiarly with a detective ... or even seen a detective' (pp. 278–9). Overall, Bennett's attitudes to detective stories remained ambiguous and fluctuated between occasional appreciation of the imaginative processes involved and ridicule for the simplistic version of the world offered.

But why did detective stories become popular? One explanation is the reformulation of attitudes to law enforcement, a shift from the eighteenth-century sense of the criminal as folk hero – Jack Sheppard or Dick Turpin – to seeing him as deviant and needing policing. The nineteenth century also saw an increasing interest in criminology. Charles Darwin, Francis Galton and Henry Maudsley in the 1860s and 1870s helped biologize crime. Later works by Cesare Lombroso and Max Nordau suggested that crime could be attributed to genetics. Criminal anthropology maintained that criminals could be recognized as physically different from 'normal' people and were programmed differently. Writers exploited this by inventing fiendish masterminds who vied with their detectives for dominance. Conan Doyle's

'Napoleon of crime', Professor Moriarty, is presented – half jokingly – in 'The Final Problem' (1893) in this way as having 'hereditary tendencies of the most diabolical kind'.[13] Conan Doyle famously created Moriarty as a means of killing off Holmes, but he is also an example of the tendency to make the criminal a focus for public concerns, a scapegoat for unresolvable crimes. L. T. Meade and Robert Eustace's Madame Sara, 'Sorceress of the Strand' (1902), was another example, as was Sax Rohmer's Dr Fu Manchu (1912), this portrayal notable for its cultural stereotyping and tapping into fears about the 'yellow peril' invading Britain. Literary detectives became heroes capable of fixing these villains. Indeed this casting of the detective short story series as a form of fiction that is really about the elemental struggle between good and evil, which works by continually bringing relief to middle-class anxieties by creating supra-human figures who re-install order and expel undesirables, has been reiterated many times. In 'The Resident Patient' (1894), Dr Watson tells readers of *The Strand* that Sherlock Holmes is precisely this kind of city-watcher, who 'loved to lie in the very centre of five millions of people, with his filaments stretching out and running through them, responsive to every little rumour or suspicion of unsolved crime' (p. 423).

This sense of amateur detectives as vigilantes was appealing but so, too, were the details – accrued through successive stories – about the methods used to neutralize criminals. As well as all his other gimmicks, part of Holmes's strength comes from cod-scientific ratiocination or 'reasoned hypothesizing' as Umberto Eco terms it.[14] Nowhere does Holmes demonstrate this more than in the meeting with a new client in 'The Adventures of the Norwood Builder' (1903). 'I assure you', Holmes tells him, 'that, beyond the obvious facts that you are a bachelor, a solicitor, a Freemason and an asthmatic, I know nothing whatever about you' (p. 497). Arthur Morrison's Martin Hewitt, who appeared in twenty-five stories, between 1894 and 1903, initially as a replacement for Holmes in *The Strand*, is less of an exhibitionist than his hawkish predecessor, and more affable, but uses similar methods and also hypnotism to solve puzzles. Hewitt, like Holmes, is able to 'read' crime scenes. He is quick to deduce that it is a trained parrot who has committed the jewel theft in 'The Lenton Mysteries' (1894) or that in 'The Case of Laker Absconded' (1895) the missing clerk, far from being an embezzler, has actually been kidnapped, his hard-won respectable identity stolen by a criminal gang.

All this could seem ludicrous, as could the oddball amateurs solving crimes. They prompted complaints from real detectives, who recognized neither themselves nor their painstaking methods in the tidy ten-page narratives that littered popular magazines. For readers, this did not seem to matter. An idiosyncratic investigator, a thrilling pursuit topped by the meting out of poetic justice gave colour to drab lives. This was the pitch given in 1893 by Arthur Humphreys of Hatchard's bookshop, who attributed the 'great demand' to weary commuters and their wives. 'Women never seem to tire of . . . detective stories; they like mystery, a substantial splash of sensation.'[15] For women readers detective stories, especially those featuring such self-confident women as Doyle's Irene Adler, Catherine Pirkis's 'lady detective', Loveday Brooke (1894) and George Sims's Dorcas Dene (1897), offered visions of what might be.

Eagerness to glimpse into another (darker) world was also catered for in G. K. Chesterton's stories featuring Father Brown. These go beyond concerns with the solving of crimes to encourage interest in rehabilitation. Chesterton introduced the priest-detective in 'The Blue Cross' (1910), eventually publishing fifty-three stories over twenty-five years. Brown's clerical hat and scruffy umbrella mark him as eccentric in the familiar mould. But he is spiritual and theological whereas rivals like Sherlock Holmes and Martin Hewitt are secular and scientific. Whilst Holmes generally remains distant from the criminal, Brown gets up close 'inside a murderer [. . .] into the posture of his hunched and peering hatred'.[16] Nor does Brown have any interest in forensics or the fashionable anthropological approach whereby the criminal is read 'as if he were a distant prehistoric monster' (p. 465). Instead, the priest uses his knowledge of people and of himself, together with an awareness of evil. The convergence of good and evil recurs frequently, epitomized in the Jekyll and Hyde-influenced 'The Man in the Passage' (1913). Hints of the Roman Catholic confessional also feature. 'The Invisible Man' (1911) ends with Father Brown in deep conversation with a murderer 'and what they said to each other will never be known' (p. 77). Taken together, the stories embody Chesterton's claim that the Catholic Church was to all intents and purposes 'an enormous private detective', except that it pursued crimes 'not in order to avenge, but in order to forgive them'.[17]

If the works of Doyle and Chesterton represent two traditions of the detective story, those of E. W. Hornung are another. Although the epitome of middle-class respectability (Hornung was Doyle's brother-in-law) Hornung's Raffles series – *The Amateur Cracksman* (1899), *The Black Mask* (1901) and *The Thief in the Night* (1905) – are examples of how detective stories could seem to walk a critical tightrope, safe but containing scandal, as well as escapism. Arthur J. Raffles is a charismatic sportsman but also an outsider, aesthete and sometimes a thug, who thumbs his nose at the law by running a parallel career as a burglar.[18] Playing cricket not only opens doors into well-stocked houses but is part of Raffles's philosophy that everyone needs a good cover story. Robbery is just another kind of sport with its own rules: Raffles is willing to steal in a house where he is invited but deems it bad manners to take anything from the host. Instead he robs the illicit Jewish diamond buyer Rueben Rosenthal in 'A Costume Piece' (1898) and the arrogant aristocrats in 'Gentleman and Players' (1898). While it is difficult to miss the stories' ingrained snobberies, also striking are their coded suggestions of homosexuality. Raffles's sole relationship is with his chum, Harold 'Bunny' Manders, who narrates. There have been suggestions that Hornung took Oscar Wilde and Lord Alfred Douglas as his models. Certainly Bunny finds Raffles 'irresistible' (p. 6) and is often jealous of women, notably in 'The Gift of the Emperor' (1898). Within the confines of this kind of reading, Hornung's writings can just as easily be read 'straight'– that is they can produce a different (heterosexual) interpretation; equally it is possible that there may be hints in the text which point to ways in which another interpretative community – a male homosexual audience – could be specifically targeted. When the stories appeared the public lapped them up, but others were cautious about this thief-hero, Conan Doyle warning that they were 'dangerous in their suggestion'.[19]

Doyle's comments are a reminder that there has always been a tendency to see the craving for detective stories as a kind of illness: addictive, weakening and corrupting. In the post-Darwinian 1890s, anxieties regarding cultural descent ran high. For some, the craving for detective stories was symptomatic of degeneration not only of literature but of moral values, evidence, claimed the *Westminster Review* in 1897, of how a 'collective mattoidism' had taken hold. While on the one hand it is a reference to Lombroso's popular theories about the mentally-stunted criminal 'type', on the other the comment implies dumbing down (p. 437). Moreover, there was a fear that readers would take their 'cue' from what they read. In 1895, Britain was electrified by revelations from the Robert Coombes trial. Coombes, thirteen, had murdered his mother, concealing her death. At the trial considerable weight was placed on his reading, which comprised mainly crime-related stories. Such evidence was highly troubling, and fears about the trafficking between real-life and fiction, as well as the effect of American models, were topics of conversation for years. In 1899 the debate over the mischievous ideas which crime-ridden stories were deemed to encourage flared up again. A Sherlock Holmes tale 'The Jew's Breastplate' (1899), dealing with the theft of a jewel from the British Museum, was deemed to be the inspiration behind thefts from the Natural History Museum in April 1900. Predictably, the *Daily News* suggested that any popular crime writer 'wields an influence which he himself perhaps scarcely appreciates', though it did concede that 'it would be unfair to make him responsible for the imitative tendencies of weak-minded persons'.[20]

Before 1914, Conan Doyle remained the biggest draw and continued producing Holmes stories until 1927, baulking at suggestions for updating – putting Holmes and Watson on a motor-cycle, for example. Martin Hewitt stories also remained popular. So, too, were those featuring Baroness Emma Orczy's the 'old Man in the Corner' (1901), who solves crimes sitting in a teashop. However, by 1905, the *Academy* was recording another development: the appearance of 'modern scientific methods', or forensics.[21] Although it is rare nowadays to hear Richard Austin Freeman spoken of with affection, he won plaudits for his invention of the inverted detective story, in which the culprit is revealed early on and the story shows the means by which he or she is tracked down. This narrative method is often at work in the short stories starring Dr John Thorndyke. The title of his collection, *The Singing Bone* (1912), is symptomatic of Freeman's central idea that in a detective story a corpse always 'talks', if only about how it was robbed of life. Thorndyke painstakingly pieces together forensic clues: white footprints on the linoleum by the bedside of the poisoned woman, or the dental plate found some distance from a skull in a haystack. Ernest Bramah's Max Carrados stories (1911), featuring a blind man who uses other senses to solve cases, and Hesketh Prichard's Canadian backwoodsman, 'November Joe' (1912), who tracks down criminals using the skills of native North Americans, likewise became 'must-haves' for magazine editors. Partly they suited the vogue for tales of derring-do; with their emphasis on direct male action they became a kind of celebration of imperial manliness. This is only the top of a very long list, which also includes hundreds of stories published by the *Windsor Magazine, Pearson's, Nash's* and others.

If the period 1880–1914 represents one phase of the modern detective story, the next, 1914–45, is often described as its 'Golden Age'. During and after the First World War, magazines continued to publish detective stories, at times without discrimination. Some writers continued to shake their heads at the prurient philistinism of the resulting works – H. G. Wells being a notable example. They continued to be fearful, too, about the messages given to young people. However, it was the writers actually producing detective stories who now made the loudest claims for respectability. They included

Richard Freeman, who stressed the need to distinguish between 'serious' formal, detective stories and the 'crude and pungent sensationalism' of the vulgar thriller, whose sole object was 'to make the reader's flesh creep'.[22] Freeman was not immune from this latter failing and in 1913 had written the 'Hunter of Criminals' stories for *Pearson's* (1913). Professor Humphrey Challoner, whose wife has been killed by an unknown burglar, devotes his life to luring criminals into his house and killing them in the hope that one of them is his wife's murderer, forming an extensive collection of body parts along the way.

It was Dorothy L. Sayers, however, who in numerous articles and interviews, and as editor of the anthologies *Great Short Stories of Detection, Mystery and Horror* (1928, 1931, 1934), made the most passionate response to the form and, convinced of its relevance to contemporary society, took up the project of championing it. For Sayers, writing in the aftermath of the First World War, searching for literary works that could help audiences resist the debilitating influence of modern life, the detective story was a potentially fortifying and provocative form, which provided the possibility of a moral art, putting the reader in touch 'with the greater realities'.[23] Although it has been fashionable to disparage Sayers, a would-be intellectual whose outlook, like that of her contemporary Agatha Christie, can seem based on a narrow and snobbish analysis of society, her views were extremely influential in the rehabilitation of the detective story in the 1920s and 1930s. The form could also be used, Sayers argued, as a social commentary. Her story 'The Unsolved Puzzle of the Man with No Face' (1924) is part of this idea. A mutilated corpse turns up on the beach, prompting a group of train passengers to discuss it. The violence makes them think of Mussolini's Fascisti but they are forced to acknowledge that the answer is closer to home, that it might be an ex-soldier sent over the edge by his experiences of the trenches.[24] Having encouraged men's violent instincts on behalf of the state it was no surprise, Sayers's argument goes, that they found their training difficult to shake off.

The most popular of the post-war writers, Agatha Christie, offered a more comforting prospect. *The Mysterious Affair at Styles* (1920) introduced Hercule Poirot, the fussy Belgian with a passion for order. Eighty novels followed but also 130 short stories. Christie disliked the short story form, feeling that novels gave her more scope for complex crimes. Nonetheless, in the 1920s and 1930s she published the collections *Poirot Investigates* (1924) and *Murder in the Mews* (1937), as well as twenty Miss Marple stories beginning with *The Thirteen*

Problems (1932). Another Poirot collection, *The Labours of Hercules*, appeared in 1947 after serialization in *The Strand Magazine*. Having ambitions as a playwright, Christie also adapted stories into plays, notably 'A Witness for the Prosecution' (1933), an exposé of the weakness of the British judicial system. 'Three Blind Mice', about a psychopath killing guests in an isolated hotel, was successively a radio drama and a short story (1950) before premiering as *The Mousetrap* (1952) and becoming the world's longest running play. One of Christie's final published works, her *Autobiography*, sums up her career, and records her bleak vision of the modern world, her dislike of violence and her belief in the detective story as a moral fable in which good must always triumph.

Christie's work gained her legions of fans but her dizzying success, which seemed to come with little obvious talent for writing stylish prose, prompted resentment. In 'The Simple Art of Murder' (1944), Raymond Chandler accused exponents of the 'classic' detective story, of whom Christie was the leading light, of being 'too little aware of what goes on in the world'.[25] But to criticize Christie on her inability to provide a gritty portrayal of 1930s Britain was to miss the point. Robert Graves noted that such stories are not mimetic and 'no more intended to be judged by realistic standards than one would judge Watteau's shepherds and shepherdesses in terms of contemporary sheep farming'.[26] Christie's are works hymning the joys of an older England which never really existed.

The ambiguous response to Christie's stories owes much to the confusion that her roles as middle-brow entertainer and moralist provoke. It also has to do with their apparent simplicity. They are small-scale, told largely through dialogue and populated by 'flat' characters – Chandler used the term *'papier maché* (p. 232) – whose very flatness ensures no distraction from the central puzzle. Christie claimed to believe in 'fair play', thus clues are always offered but so unobtrusively that they tend to be overlooked. The village-set story 'Tape Measure Murder' (cited earlier), in which the clue to the killer is in the title, is a case in point. Moreover, finding a corpse in the well-kept surroundings in which Christie's characters live is always seen as incongruous, an extra-ordinary event which sends shockwaves around the community, the effect being, claimed W. H. Auden in 'The Guilty Vicarage' (1948), like those engulfing a proud homeowner who discovers a dog making 'a mess on a drawing-room carpet'.[27]

Other inter-war attractions – and these could be duplicated at length – included H. C. Bailey's Reggie Fortune (1919; a doctor who assists Scotland Yard), Freeman Willis Crofts's Inspector Joseph French (1924; a suave

Scotland Yard detective with a knack for cracking unbreakable alibis or 'futzing around with [train] timetables', as Chandler put it (p. 225)), Margery Allingham's Albert Campion (1929; a bespectacled young fogey) and Dorothy L. Sayers's Lord Peter Wimsey (1923; an amateur criminologist in spats). The latter was a curious success and has, since his first appearance, been a figure liable to provoke mixed emotions. It has become commonplace to suggest that Sayers created Wimsey as a means to escape her frustrations as a spinster in post-1918 London, lacking romantic and professional fulfilment. Whether such writing was therapeutic or not, Sayers attempts a sophisticated jazz-age world in which Lord Peter, asking silly, seemingly innocuous questions discovers more than the police. In 'The Entertaining Episode of the Article in Question' (1922) Wimsey unmasks a jewel thief by recognizing 'a slim shingled creature' with thick ankles as a famous female impersonator, Jacques Sans-cullotte (p. 28). The revelation depends on Wimsey – and the reader – noticing that the impersonator uses the wrong gender for a French word and thus gives himself away as a man pretending to be a woman.

A contemporary reader approaching the Wimsey stories can find their central figure grating. His 'what Ho!' catchphrase appears a caricature of an upper-class man, whilst Sayers's sprinkling the dialogue with foreign phrases and obscure learning can seem pretentious. Nonetheless, Wimsey became an iconic figure – *The Strand*'s cover for March 1938 shows him in colour, stylishly attired in top hat and white tie. His popularity impelled Sayers to keep going until 1939. For Sayers, like Christie, short stories were profitable side-lines and despite confessing herself bad at writing them she produced three collections: *Lord Peter Views the Body* (1928), *Hangman's Holiday* (1933) and *In the Teeth of the Evidence* (1939). Then she decided that Wimsey no longer suited the times, that exhibiting relish in elaborate 'private murders' seemed in bad taste in the light of bigger world events and that she wanted to devote her energies to more serious intellectual pursuits.[28]

In the 1930s the idea of the literary detective as front cover star did not seem outlandish. C. Day Lewis described the reading public's adulation of their favourites as a kind of cult; Wimsey, Reggie Fortune, Miss Marple, each in their own way seemed 'the Fairy Godmother of the twentieth century folk myth', a 'Divine' being.[29] Yet with the outbreak of War, attitudes changed. Christie and her contemporaries would still enjoy the financial satisfactions of well-crafted work but the contempt they came in for from detractors like Chandler was added to by new writers less ready to deal in genteel conjuring tricks and a tidy finish, and more inclined to capture the disturbances of the modern world.

All this was flagged up by George Orwell in two essays: 'Raffles and Miss Blandish' (1944), in which he celebrated the late-Victorian and Edwardian detective story as an intellectual exercise – unlike the modern gangster 'thriller' epitomized in the nasty work of James Hadley Chase – and 'The Decline of the English Murder' (1946), where he mourned the demise of 'our great ... Elizabethan period' of murder. This, Orwell suggested, spanned 1850–1925 and included such notable cases as Thomas Neill Cream, Florence Maybrick, Dr Crippen and Edith Thompson; all involved domestic crimes against a backdrop of bourgeois respectability, prompted by sex, jealousy or money. The contrast between these famous cases, products of 'a stable society', and the so-called 'Cleft Chin Murder' of 1944 in which a G.I., Karl Hulten, and his British girlfriend, Elizabeth Jones, went on a spree of robbery and murder, was striking. Orwell discerned a new kind of 'meaningless' murder set against 'the anonymous life of dance-halls and the false values of the American film'. The fact that such viciousness was what newspaper readers seemed to want was proof of how British culture had been changed by 'the brutalizing effects of war'.[30] A series of repulsive murders in the decade following 1945 committed by men with twisted personalities – Neville Heath, John Haigh, John Christie – helped reinforce this sense of a loss of innocence. By the mid-fifties, teenage 'delinquents' were well into their stride, whilst the 'Teddy Boys', with their coloured suits and worship of rock'n'roll, embodied a new culture of selfishness and violence.

Read in this light, it is not difficult to see how post-1945 detective stories seemed to drift away from the neat puzzle formula towards new American-influenced dystopias of drive-by shootings and police corruption. Following Dashiell Hammett and Chandler, critics have discerned a British version of their 'hard-boiled' school, a place of 'urban chaos, devoid of spiritual and moral values', in which organized criminals wield more power than the law enforcers, where justice is never served and no one talks.[31] It was a school filled in Britain by writers like Frank Dubrez Fawcett, Harold Kelly and Stephen Francis (writing under the pseudonyms of Ben Sarto, Darcy Glinto and Hank Janson), who churned out cut-price paperbacks aimed at the mass market and who took prosecutions for obscenity as occupational hazards. In contrast, veterans like Christie and Allingham and Gladys Mitchell had not lost their readerships but refused to get caught up in unfamiliar subjects, believing that detectives did not have to be on first-name terms with gangsters and prostitutes. Mitchell's 'A Light on Murder' (1950), featuring psychologist Adela Bradley, retains the familiar ingredients of the locked-room mystery: there are four men in a lighthouse; one is stabbed.[32] For her part, Christie declared herself shocked at the subject matter of the new generation: 'One would have thought that the community would rise up in horror against such things; but now cruelty seems almost everyday bread and butter.'[33] Similar difficulties in coming to terms with change are expressed in Phyllis Bentley's 'Miss Phipps and the Invisible Murderer' (1966), in which the spinster detective's distaste towards the bee-hived victim does not stop her uncovering the unsavoury truth, but is mixed up with a sense that the promiscuous young woman got what was coming to her, sexual revolution or not.[34]

What hampered the post-war detective short story was not simply its lack of direction. The shrinking of the magazine market, coupled with the sense that the detective short story was 'for the most part middle-aged and graying around the temples', its main practitioners having been born before 1914, also led to suggestions that its best days were over.[35] One such 'graying' story writer was P. G. Wodehouse who, in 1950, lamented the collapse of *The Strand*, sometime home of Holmes, Hewitt, Wimsey and Poirot, asking 'Where can [a writer] sell his stories?' Wodehouse's inability to sell stories may well have had something to do with disapproval of his undistinguished war, in which he controversially made pro-German broadcasts before departing for the United States, but his own view was that magazines died because of the demand that stories be written to a formula and relying on 'names' (printing anything by anyone famous even if it was sub-standard).

With reduced magazines putting paid to the short detective story – or forcing writers to look to American outlets such as *Ellery Queen's Mystery Magazine* (1941–) – the outlook for the classic detective story as opposed to the cold-war thrillers of Eric Ambler and Ian Fleming, was poor. The form seemed to splinter into different types, a point made by Sally Munt, who suggests that the resulting post-war stories should be seen in terms of Harold Bloom's framework of influence 'where each writer is fully aware of writing within the shadow of his predecessor, but revises his text to push out the form and relate it to his particular milieu'.[36] The debt owed by Edmund Crispin's Gervase Fen stories (1953; 1979) to John Dickson Carr's 1920s stories, which had featured the fat, cape-wearing Dr Gideon Fell (a character inspired in turn by G. K. Chesterton) has long been acknowledged. More recently Colin Dexter has explained of his Inspector Morse stories that he modelled their structure on the whodunnit schema inspired by Christie, but used Oxford landmarks as an attempt to recreate the kind of memorable cityscape perfected by Chandler in his 1940s depictions of Los Angeles.[37] The few short stories by former jockey Dick Francis collected in *Field of Thirteen* (1998) take the archetype of the hard-boiled detective but put him in the class-based world of English horseracing.

Alongside this there emerged another group of writers who, influenced partly by the American Patricia Highsmith, wrote stories which were less about whodunit but 'why?' Questions of psychology and environment became more important than the hunt for clues. 'I murdered Brenda Goring for what I suppose is the most unusual of motives' is how Ruth Rendell's 'The Irony of Hate' (1977) begins, and the emphasis on the twisted or arresting human personality has remained a feature of post-war detective fiction, evident in Rendell's work.[38] The short stories making up *The Fallen Curtain* (1976), *The Fever Tree* (1982) and *Blood Lines* (1995) are uneven, but Rendell's habit of encouraging sympathy and identification with her criminals, encouraging readers to see the world through their eyes, is clearly in evidence. 'Murder itself is not interesting' she writes, but 'the impetus to murder, the passions and terrors which bring it to pass ... exert compulsive fascination.'[39]

What Rendell shared with several younger contemporaries who have emerged since the 1990s is the idea that the crime that has been committed can be just one of several problems which need solving, but is probably the only one which can be. The label 'state of the nation' has been used, not a tag likely to be given to Christie's works, but bestowed here because of a new tendency to go beyond puzzle-solving. Thus Val McDermid has written of crime writing's 'unique ability' to point to 'how we live now' and her stories collected in *The Writing on the Wall* (1997), whilst undeveloped, suggest how detective stories really can seem bound up with wider societal issues. 'The Ministry of Whisky' (2011), about an unhappy wife who plots the murder of her husband after seeing how an acquaintance trapped in an abusive marriage gained acquittal for the same crime, presents a glimpse into the disillusionment lurking beneath everyday lives. As the story concludes, no crime has been committed but it seems as if it is about to be.

From the first, McDermid, and her fellow Scot Ian Rankin, have also been praised for standing separately from 'English' detective traditions, instead using stories as vehicles which comment on Scotland's identity and self-definition. In interview, both writers extoll Scotland's long tradition of crime writing stretching back to James Hogg's *Private Memoirs and Confessions of a Justified Sinner* (1824) as proof that 'Scots prefer the dark night of the soul to tea with the vicar'.[40] Theirs is a move to stake out a kind of *Scots noir* far from the fake Scotland sold to tourists. More familiar is the choice of detective figure. Like many of his predecessors, Rankin's John Rebus is characterized by his unsuccessful relationships and his solitariness. Unlike them, he seems to find little compensation in a professional career, carried out in a corrupt world where powerful people pull the strings and justice is invariably tainted. Certainly short stories like 'Playback', 'The Dean Curse', 'The Gentlemen's Club' – the latter centring on the apparent suicide of a teenage girl at an exclusive school – suggest a distaste for the over-privileged. In a nod to an English forebear – Sergeant Cuff in Wilkie Collins's *The Moonstone* (1868) – 'The Gentlemen's Club' shows the detective as outsider forced to penetrate the upper echelons of society, whose members do not believe that the usual rules apply to them. Yet when the culprit, having been confronted by Rebus, is left alone to face his conscience, the bleakness of the vision seems Chandleresque. This literary hybridity is made explicit in another story, 'A Good Hanging' (1992). Faced with the death of a drama student, the detective's thought processes appear as inscrutable as those of Conan Doyle's detective, something his careerist assistant Brian Holmes rues: 'Why did Rebus always have to work from instinct, and always alone, never letting anyone in on whatever he knew or thought he knew? Was it because he was afraid of failure? Holmes suspected it was.'[41] Brian Holmes himself occupies an uncertain position; he is not a Watson, and neither is he a Sherlock; but like nearly every literary detective he ends up rubbing shoulders with both.

The desire to 'be' a Sherlock Holmes has remained an important impetus behind the detective story even as the cultural landscape has changed. Holmes seems omnipresent – on television, as well as in print – but what modern detectives cannot hope for is the kind of civilizing function for which Holmes's gifts and peculiar intelligence seemed to equip him: the kind of function that Chesterton and Christie had in mind, or said they had, but which writers since have struggled to make convincing. Yet there is still a sense that being a detective matters and, for authors, a sense that upholding the traditions matters as well. This is a feeling captured in many of the stories in David Stuart Davies's more recent anthology *Crime Scenes* (2008). Fashions are transient – as the forgotten reputations of people like Sax Rohmer or R. A. Freeman attest – but the appeal of the detective story remains constant, its complicated mixture of lofty idealism and commercial gain retaining a very basic appeal.

Notes

1. Agatha Christie, 'Tape Measure Murder', in *Ms Murder: The Best Mysteries Featuring Women Detectives, by the Top Women Writers*, ed. Marie Smith (London: Zanadu, 1989), pp. 26–37 (p. 26).
2. Edmund Wilson, 'Who Cares who Killed Roger Ackroyd?', in *Literary Essays and Reviews of the 1930s and 40s* (New York: Library of America, 2007), pp. 677–83 (pp. 679, 681, 659 and 687).
3. Letter to Janet Case, 19 November 1919, in *The Letters of Virginia Woolf*, ed. Nigel Nicholson and Joanne Trautmann, 6 vols. (New York: Harcourt, 1975–80), II, p. 400.
4. Virginia Woolf, 'Mr Bennett and Mrs Brown' (London: The Hogarth Press, 1924), in Michael J. Hoffman and Patrick D. Murphy, eds., *Essentials of the Theory of Fiction*, 2nd edn (Durham, NC: Duke University Press, 1996), pp. 24–39 (p. 26).
5. Unsigned Article, 'How We got the Suez Canal Shares', *The Friend of India and Statesman*, 19 December 1894, p. 6.
6. See Marty Roth, *Foul and Fair Play: Reading Genre in Classic Detective Fiction* (Athens: University of Georgia Press, 1995), pp. 1–22.
7. Anon., 'Sherlock Holmes: History of a Great Idea', *Northern Echo*, 17 December 1900, p. 4.
8. Anon., 'Our Short Story Writers', *Pall Mall Gazette*, 28 August 1895, p. 4.
9. Anon., 'Murder and Mystery', *Pall Mall Gazette* 24 July 1900, p. 4.
10. 'A. C.', 'Crime in Current Literature', *Westminster Review*, 147 (April 1897), pp. 429–40 (p. 437).
11. Wilkie Collins, 'Dramatic Grub Street', *Household Words*, 17 (1858), pp. 265–70 (p. 269).
12. Arnold Bennett, 'Some Good Detective Stories', *Evening Standard*, 3 May 1928, in *Arnold Bennett: The Evening Standard Years*, ed. Andrew Mylett (London: Chatto and Windus, 1974), pp. 151–3.
13. Arthur Conan Doyle, *The Complete Sherlock Holmes* (London: Penguin, 1983), p. 471. All quotations from the Sherlock Holmes stories are from this edition, with subsequent page references given in parentheses in the text.
14. Umberto Eco, *A Theory of Semiotics* (Bloomington: Indiana University Press, 1976), pp. 131–3.
15. Unsigned Article, 'What We Read', *Woman's Herald* (16 March 1893), p. 58.
16. G. K. Chesterton, 'The Secret of Father Brown', in *The Complete Father Brown* (Harmondsworth: Penguin, 1981), pp. 461–7 (p. 465). All quotations from the Father Brown stories are from this edition, with subsequent page references given in parentheses in the text.

17. G. K. Chesterton, 'The Divine Detective', in *A Miscellany of Men* (1912) (Beaconsfield: Darwen Finlayson, 1969), pp. 155–8; p. 155; p. 156.
18. E. W. Hornung, 'Gentlemen and Players', in *The Collected Raffles* (Oxford University Press, 1996), pp. 35–51 (p. 35). All quotations from the Raffles stories are from this edition, with subsequent page references given in parentheses in the text.
19. Arthur Conan Doyle, *Memories and Adventures*, quoted in Peter Rowland, *Raffles and His Creator: The Life and Works of E. W. Hornung* (Windsor: Nekta, 1999), p. 138.
20. Unsigned Article, 'Copy Cat Crimes', *Daily News*, 1 May 1900, p. 5.
21. Unsigned Article, 'The Passing of the Detective', *Academy* (30 December 1905), pp. 1356–7 (p. 1356).
22. R. A. Freeman, 'The Art of the Detective Story' (1924), in *The Art of the Mystery Story*, ed. Howard Haycraft (New York: Grosset & Dunlop, 1946), pp. 7–19 (p. 9).
23. Letter to Mrs G. K. Chesterton, 15 June 1936, in *The Letters of Dorothy L Sayers 1899–1936*, ed. Barbara Reynolds (London: Hodder 1995), p. 394.
24. Dorothy L. Sayers, 'The Unsolved Puzzle of the Man with No Face', in *Lord Peter Views the Body* (London: Victor Gollancz, 1928), pp. 249–82 (p. 250). All quotations from the Wimsey stories are from this edition, with subsequent page references given in parentheses in the text.
25. Raymond Chandler, 'The Simple Art of Murder', in *The Art of the Mystery Story*, ed. Haycraft, pp. 222–37 (p. 231).
26. Robert Graves and Alan Hodge, *The Long Weekend: A Social History of Great Britain* (1940; rpt Manchester: Carcanet, 2006), p. 236.
27. W. H. Auden, 'The Guilty Vicarage', in *Harper's Magazine* (May 1948), pp. 606–12 (p. 608).
28. Letter to James Sandoe, 6 Jan. 1944, in *The Letters of Dorothy L. Sayers*, ed. Reynolds, pp. 2–3.
29. 'Nicholas Blake' [C. Day Lewis], 'The Detective Story – Why?', in *The Art of the Mystery Story*, ed. Haycraft, pp. 398–405 (p. 400).
30. George Orwell, 'Decline of the English Murder', in *Decline of the English Murder and other Essays* (Harmondsworth: Penguin, 1986), pp. 9–13 (pp. 9, 12, 13).
31. George Grella, 'The Hard-Boiled Detective Novel', in *Detective Fiction*, ed. Winks, pp. 103–20 (p. 105).
32. Gladys Mitchell, 'A Light on Murder', in *Ms Murder*, ed. Smith, pp. 132–9.
33. Agatha Christie, *An Autobiography* (London: Fontana, 1977), p. 452.
34. Phyllis Bentley, 'Miss Phipps and the Invisible Murderer', in *Ms Murder*, ed. Smith, pp. 155–69.
35. Dennis Vanetta, *The English Short Story 1880–1945* (New York: Twayne, 1985), p. 35.

36. Sally Munt, *Murder by the Book* (London: Routledge, 1994), pp. 3–4.
37. Colin Dexter, 'Inspector Morse', in *The Lineup: The World's Greatest Crime Writers Tell the Inside Story of Their Greatest Detectives*, ed. Otto Penzler (London: Quercus, 2011), pp. 117–38.
38. Ruth Rendell, 'The Irony of Hate' [original title, 'Born Victim'], in *A Moment on the Edge: 100 Years of Crime Stories by Women*, ed. Elizabeth George (London: Harper, 2002), pp. 189–206 (p. 189).
39. Ruth Rendell, 'Introduction', *An Anthology of the Murderous Mind* (London: Vintage, 1996), pp. vii–xi (p. vii).
40. Val McDermid, 'Living the Tartan Noir, How Scottish Crime Fiction Mirrors Society', *New Statesman*, 143 (28 February 2014), p. 44.
41. Ian Rankin, 'A Good Hanging', in *The Complete Short Stories* (London: Orion, 2005), pp. 83–103 (pp. 98).

25
Frontiers: Science Fiction and the British Marketplace

PAUL MARCH-RUSSELL

In his pioneering survey, *New Maps of Hell* (1960), Kingsley Amis observed that science fiction (sf) is preoccupied with 'the idea as hero' rather than subtle uses of language, narrative or characterization.[1] Martin Scofield subsequently adapted Amis's definition of sf to his analysis of the American short story 'in which the overall idea, rather than character, plot or "themes" in the usual sense, dominates the conception of the work and gives it its unity or deliberate disunity'.[2] Unlike Amis, who tended to prefer his sf to be either escapist adventures or satirical exercises, Scofield's adaptation allows him to define the short story in self-reflexive terms: 'a work that is dominated by a single guiding idea or mood and achieves a perceptible overall artistic coherence' (p. 5). Symptomatic of the taxonomic problems that underwrite both sf- and short story criticism, 'the idea as hero' can paradoxically refer to a story that is thematic and plot-driven, atmospheric and impressionistic. Not only does the short story lie at the intersection between high and low culture, between the little magazine and the mass-market periodical, as Tim Armstrong has observed, but so too does science fiction.[3] As Farah Mendlesohn has argued, 'whatever else it is, sf literature is not *popular*'; it exists 'at variance from the standards and demands of both the literary establishment and the mass market'.[4] Sf and the short story complement each other not only formally but also culturally: their liminal position questions the assumptions by which critics have often discriminated between what is or is not literary. Yet, as Nicola Humble has noted, 'there is something wrong with the way in which we have mapped the literary field of the first half of the twentieth century'.[5] This 'something wrong' is accentuated when we attempt to re-map not only the short story but also sf as part of literary production since the 1890s.

The Scientific Romance

The genealogy of science fiction is a notoriously tangled family tree. Critics have variously traced its origins to ancient and classical texts, such as *The Epic of Gilgamesh* and Lucian's 'A True History'; to the intellectual and religious convulsions between Protestantism and Catholicism in the seventeenth century; and to the impact of the Industrial Revolution upon Mary Shelley's *Frankenstein* (1818).[6] However, reading the development of British sf in conjunction with the short story helps to disentangle at least part of this narrative, since its emergence was greatly impeded by the same market conditions that hampered the short story. Despite Darko Suvin's attempt to create a taxonomy of British sf that traces its origins to the 1840s, he concedes that a critical threshold was reached only at the start of the 1870s – supposedly, even, a single day (1 May 1871), when Edward Bulwer-Lytton's short novel, *The Coming Race*, was published anonymously, George Chesney's *The Battle of Dorking* began serialization in *Blackwood's Edinburgh Magazine* and Samuel Butler submitted his episodic novel, *Erewhon*, to his publishers Chapman and Hall.[7]

Although to some extent these novels were written as satires, what is more significant is the degree to which they were taken seriously by their readers. Chesney, writing in the wake of the Franco-Prussian War (1870–1), warned of a future conflict with Germany in which an unprepared Britain would be defeated. Chesney's tale not only inspired the sub-genre of the invasion novel but also codified much of the political rhetoric surrounding the balance of power and the late nineteenth-century arms race.[8] Bulwer-Lytton, too, prophesied a future war but from below, from a subterranean variant of the human species known as the Vril-ya with super-evolved powers and a mysterious, destructive energy source. Although the scenario of the hollow earth was hardly new, it nevertheless played upon the anxieties and expectations stirred in readers' imaginations by the impact of geology and evolutionary theory. A Darwinian rhetoric also underscores Butler's utopian fantasy of machines that supersede human authority and in which humans are no more than 'a machinate mammal'.[9] Within a decade of Butler's satire, though, 'urban life was *itself* a machine ensemble, with everyday communication, public spaces and popular culture increasingly routed through machines'.[10]

These pioneering novels established many of the preoccupations of late Victorian sf. The title of Charles Howard Hinton's book of mathematical lectures, *Scientific Romances* (1886), seems to have conferred the name by which this new genre was most widely known. Significantly, Hinton also included a short story, 'The Persian King', whose tone hovers somewhere between Edward Abbott's *Flatland* (1884), Lewis Carroll's *Alice* books, and the satirical art-tales of Oscar Wilde. Ostensibly a dramatization of Hinton's belief in a fourth-dimensional hyperspace, the story also contains a moral warning against the abuse of power to be found in later sf. Its strength, however, comes from such striking imagery as 'The roads became choked with grass, the earth encroached on the buildings, till in the slow consuming course of time all was buried – houses, fields, and cities vanished, till at length no trace was left of aught that had been there.'[11]

As Brian Stableford has argued, the social, economic and publishing conditions that enabled the rapid emergence of the short story in the 1890s also accelerated the development of scientific romance.[12] The thirst for wonder, evident in the conclusion to Hinton's story, became a key ingredient of the late Victorian literary marketplace. As H. G. Wells famously wrote, 'Short stories broke out everywhere', and with that came a licence unhindered by the previous constraints of serialization, the three-volume novel and the circulating libraries: 'I would discover I was peering into remote and mysterious worlds ruled by an order logical indeed but other than our common sanity.'[13] Later, Wells reflected on his methodology: 'the fantastic element, the strange property or the strange world, is used only to throw up and intensify our natural reactions of wonder, fear or perplexity . . . The thing that makes such imaginations interesting is their translation into commonplace terms and a rigid exclusion of other marvels from the story. Then it becomes human.'[14] Although short story critics have tended to value Wells for his commercial acumen, Wells's comments indicate that he was also motivated by aesthetic aims, and that the lessons of Poe had been well learnt.[15]

As is commonly known, *The Time Machine* (1895) originated as an early short story ('The Chronic Argonauts' (1888)) whilst *The War of the Worlds* (1898) should ideally be read alongside two other stories, 'The Crystal Egg' and 'The Star' (both 1897). Wells's early reputation was established with tales such as 'The Flowering of the Strange Orchid' and 'The Stolen Bacillus' (both 1894), which translated the biological and evolutionary concerns of his scientific journalism into a form that was not only readily available for a mass audience but also fitted the demands of the new periodicals, such as the *Pall Mall Gazette, Pearson's Magazine* and *The Strand*, with which Wells became identified. In pre-revolutionary Russia, where Wells's political and scientific ideas exerted profound influence, his short stories were almost as inspirational as his novels. Yevgeny Zamyatin's observation that Wells's utopias are 'always dynamic, built on collisions, on conflict' can be applied as much to 'A Story of the Days to Come' (1897) as to the novel, *When the Sleeper Wakes* (1899), which followed it.[16] It is tempting also to read Wells in terms of Boris Èjxenbaum's account of O. Henry as a parodist: 'he thought in schemes, in formulas, like an expert theoretician'.[17] 'The New Accelerator' (1901), for example, concludes with the narrator's impartial statement, 'like all potent preparations it will be liable to abuse . . . we have decided this is purely a matter of medical jurisprudence and altogether outside our province',[18] a sly parody of the formulaic disclaimers used by commercial entrepreneurs.

At the same time, Wells was also working within popular and short fiction, forms that were often likened to the increasingly mechanical rhythms of everyday life.[19] Intelligent imitators, such as Rudyard Kipling in 'With the Night Mail' (1905), foregrounded this association by calling attention to the printed text: Kipling's travelogue of international flight turns into an aerial log, correspondence, a book review, advertisements; 'extracts from the magazine in which it appeared'.[20] Conversely, E. M. Forster's dystopia, 'The Machine Stops' (1909), satirizes attempts 'to "keep pace with the sun", or even to outstrip it': 'The globe went eastward quicker still, horrible accidents occurred, and the Committee of the Machine ... declared the pursuit illegal, unmechanical, and punishable by Homelessness.'[21] Forster's story embodies a modernist strain that became dominant during post-war Bloomsbury: the separation of a vital Art from a robotic Culture. This tension, though, was also articulated in the contemporaneous debate between Wells and Henry James, in which Wells's equally modern vision of literature would be excluded from the emerging orthodoxy of Modernism.[22]

Even within sf, Wells's legacy is mixed. For New Wave writers such as Brian Aldiss and Christopher Priest, reacting against the conventions of American pulp sf, Shelley and Wells offer mythical starting-points not only for the genre itself but also for a uniquely British tradition within that history.[23] Such a reading, however, not only selectively reinterprets genre history but also presents a less complex picture of Wells than the one that emerges from the backdrop of the late Victorian literary marketplace. In contrast, another New Wave writer, raised within the American auspices of colonial Shanghai, J. G. Ballard, regarded Wells as having 'had a disastrous influence on the subsequent course of science fiction'.[24] For pioneering academic critics of sf such as Suvin, Wells's notion of the single variant gave him the basis for his influential model of cognitive estrangement. Yet as Istvan Csicsery-Ronay has observed, Wells's method, which served the structure of his short stories so well, breaks down within the shifting and multiple realities not only of Philip K. Dick but also of contemporary British writers such as Paul McAuley, China Miéville and Jeff Noon.[25] The Wellsian scientific romance suggests neither an inclusive definition for British sf nor the sf genre nor, even, the sf short story. It does, however, mediate a series of unresolved tensions.

The Inter-War Period

After the First World War, the periodical market that had established writers such as Wells went into decline, and with it the scientific romance. This is not to suggest that literary sf disappeared altogether, but what did almost vanish was the short fiction;[26] the writers of the inter-war period worked mainly within the novel. Where the short scientific romance did survive, though, was in the form of the essay, most notably in the *To-day and To-morrow* pamphlet series launched in 1923 by Kegan Paul.

The first of the contributions, *Dedalus, or Science and the Future*, was by the evolutionary biologist J. B. S. Haldane. His essay depicts a bio-engineered utopia, in which disease has been eradicated, famine has been defeated by the creation of new foodstuffs, and population growth has been regulated by the use of eugenics and artificial reproduction. The whimsical touches that Haldane added to his vision formed the basis for his later piece, 'The Last Judgment' (1927). Taking the form of a 'broadcast to infants on the planet Venus some forty million years hence', Haldane's story imagines a series of far-future scenarios including the collapse of industrial civilization, global destruction, genetic re-engineering of the human body and the terraforming of other worlds.[27] In his best-selling novel, *Last and First Men* (1930), Olaf Stapledon took a number of these scenarios and extended them into whole chapters within a vast future history. As many readers who were entranced by Stapledon's vision were also frustrated by his text's resistance to classification:[28] its chronicle-like structure fragments into so many interrelated episodes which, like the best short stories, demand to be scrutinized rather than skimmed.

Stapledon was admired not only by his contemporaries – from Haldane's sister, Naomi Mitchison, to J. B. Priestley and Virginia Woolf – but also by the first generation of British sf fans turned writers, amongst them Aldiss and Arthur C. Clarke. In 1948, Clarke invited Stapledon to speak to the British

Interplanetary Society (BIS). Although Stapledon was famously unaware of the existence of science fiction, his novels were consumed by fans such as Aldiss, Clarke and Walter Gillings along with the American pulps that were transported to Britain as ballast in the holds of transatlantic vessels, and then sold in bargain bins at stores such as Woolworth's. A few British writers, such as John Beynon Harris (better known as John Wyndham) and most notably Eric Frank Russell, published in the pulps whilst fans such as Clarke, Gillings and Sam Youd (the real name of the sf writer John Christopher) occasionally featured in the correspondence pages of American magazines such as *Astounding Science Fiction*. What emerges from a review of the origins of British fandom is its hybrid nature. Instead of either an unbroken lineage from Wells to Stapledon to Clarke (Stapledon admitted to Wells in 1931 that he had read only 'The Star' and *The War of the Worlds*), or the interruption of that lineage by the importation of American science fiction (the term popularized by Hugo Gernsback, editor of *Amazing Stories*, in 1927 but not commonly used in Britain until the 1950s), British fandom is characterized by its magpie attitude in pursuit of the wondrous. To take Clarke as an instance: he praised not only Stapledon but also Wyndham Lewis's high modernist fantasy, *The Childermass* (1928); he admired Wells and his antithesis, C. S. Lewis; he was drawn to the social science fiction of *Astounding*'s editor, John W. Campbell, but was also inspired by the pseudo-science of Charles Fort's *Lo!* (serialized in 1934 by Campbell's predecessor). Just as there is no pure sf, so there is no pure British lineage.[29]

Even the first British sf magazines have their starting-point in an American initiative: the Science Fiction Leagues (SFL) that Gernsback encouraged his readers to form so as to create a coherent network of clubs and associations. Maurice Hanson was the branch secretary of the SFL in Nuneaton and it was he who launched the fanzine, *Novae Terrae*, in 1936. By the following February, it had become the official organ of the Science Fiction Association founded in Leeds by, amongst others, Clarke, Gillings and John Carnell. In September 1937, Hanson moved to London, where his flat-mates were Clarke and William F. Temple, both members of the BIS. Their scientific optimism complemented the fanzine's pedagogic elements; dual qualities that extended the missionary zeal of the SFL.

That June, though, Gillings launched Britain's first adult sf magazine, *Tales of Wonder* (1937–42), published by The World's Work, a branch of William Heinemann. Consciously modelled upon *Amazing Stories* rather than its more sophisticated successor, *Astounding*, the magazine was successful not only in attracting work by the few established British writers within the American pulps but also in publishing stories and articles by, amongst others, Clarke and Temple. Like Gernsback, Gillings included a letters page that featured correspondence from future writers such as Kenneth Bulmer and Charles Eric Maine. The outbreak of the Second World War increasingly affected the production of *Tales of Wonder*, especially once Gillings had been enlisted. Similarly, Carnell's attempt to re-launch *Novae Terrae*, retitled as the magazine *New Worlds* in 1939, proved futile. As Mike Ashley puts it, whilst British sf languished in the 1940s, 'American science fiction was enjoying a Golden Age' with consequences for how sf would be perceived in Britain after 1945.[30]

The White Horse Circle

In the late 1940s, a number of short-lived British magazines (amongst them Gillings's *Fantasy* and Leslie J. Johnson's *Outlands*) appeared, prompted by a desire to emulate their American counterparts and to address the new Atomic Age. The only title to survive, though, was Carnell's *New Worlds*, finally launched in 1946 but seemingly doomed when its publisher, Pendulum, collapsed in 1948. Instead, the coterie of writers who met with Carnell at the White Horse pub in New Fetter Lane (fictionalized in Clarke's *Tales from the White Hart* (1957)) formed their own company: Nova Publications. In 1949, the fourth issue of *New Worlds* was published and gradually the magazine ceased to be an imitator of *Astounding* and achieved its own identity. Both the look and the content of the magazine were more subdued than its illustrious American counterpart, less space-operatic in orientation. Although Carnell's most important writers were Clarke and Wyndham, during the early 1950s he created a stable of regular contributors, which included Bulmer, Christopher, E. C. Tubb and James White. The success of *New Worlds* meant that Nova could launch a sister-title, *Science Fantasy*, in 1950 edited by Gillings, until he was replaced by Carnell at the end of 1951. Rivals also appeared, most notably *Authentic* (1951–6) and *Nebula* (1952–9). Although established writers, such as Tubb, would appear across the main titles, the introduction of competition into what had been a non-existent marketplace encouraged editors to look for new talent (discoveries included Aldiss, Ballard, Barrington J. Bayley and Michael Moorcock), to diversify their content and to publish innovative stories by American writers that could not find an outlet within their home market. From 1954 to 1963, Nova Publications became part of the technical trade publisher,

Maclaren and Sons, which gave *New Worlds* and *Science Fantasy* a financial stability that their competitors lacked.

Despite this florescence in magazine publication, however, genre science fiction was regarded as an American phenomenon and was subject to the anti-Americanism of the period.[31] The BBC avoided the label when promoting two of its pioneering sf series, *Journey into Space* (1953–6) and *The Quatermass Experiment* (1953), whilst *The Eagle*'s flagship serial, 'Dan Dare, Pilot of the Future', was self-consciously pitched against American pulp comics.[32] Even the best-selling novel that had in many respects precipitated the popular acceptance of sf, Wyndham's *The Day of the Triffids* (1951), was written and marketed as a Wellsian satire rather than the pulp sf of Wyndham's American output.

This neutrality towards sf was also evident in the magazines with their subdued appearance, tendency towards more socially oriented fictions, and greater openness to fantastical elements. Although *New Worlds* tended towards the more hard-science story, with Carnell editing both it and *Science Fantasy*, it was not uncommon for writers such as Aldiss and Ballard to cross between the titles. Female authors were conspicuous by their absence but, with their greater sense of social appeal and comparatively greater licence than the American pulps, male authors did tend to feature women more (most notably in the female utopia of Wyndham's 'Consider Her Ways' (1956)) or sexual themes (such as Temple's 'The Lonely' (1955)). Even the 'beautiful but insane' women that occur in Ballard's early surrealistic fantasies can be read as symptomatic of the magazines' relatively greater social freedom.[33] Religious themes, frequently taboo in the American market, were also tackled, most famously in 'The Nine Billion Names of God' (1953) and 'The Star' (1955) by the otherwise secular Clarke. Christopher who, unlike Clarke, was sceptical about the possibilities of human progress, poignantly captured in his tale of space exploration, 'Christmas Roses' (1949), developed a rare skill for alien points of view: the Loch Ness Monster in 'Monster' (1950) and sentient plants in 'The Tree' (1954). The White Horse circle was not exclusively a ghetto, as Doris Lessing recalls: 'My disappointment with what I thought of as a dull group of people, suburban, provincial, was my fault. In that prosaic room, in that very ordinary pub, was going on the most advanced thinking in this country.'[34] Clarke's increasingly high media profile also meant that the serious scientific speculations associated with the White Horse circle gained a gradual mainstream recognition. This process was aided and abetted by the publication of anthology series, most notably Edmund Crispin's *Best SF* (1955–70),

Aldiss's *Penguin Science Fiction* (1961–4) and Amis and Robert Conquest's *Spectrum* (1961–6). These anthologies were notable not only in being edited primarily by mainstream literary figures but also in being published by mainstream presses such as Faber and Penguin. They helped to popularize and cement an early canon of sf but they also reprinted British and American writers together, thereby pushing the public recognition of authors especially associated with the White Horse circle.[35]

The New Wave

The World Science Fiction Convention was held in London in 1957, a sign of the growing significance of British sf. Aldiss and Ballard met there for the first time, but neither of them was impressed by the proceedings. Ballard recalled: 'the Americans were hard to take, and most of the British fans were worse. In Paris science fiction was popular among leading writers and filmmakers like Robbe-Grillet and Resnais, and I assumed that I would find their counterparts in London, a huge error.'[36] Although Aldiss was more a fan of sf than Ballard was, both looked to modernist and European innovations as part of their inspiration. The structure of Aldiss's first collection, *Space, Time and Nathaniel* (1957), outlined an emergent preoccupation of the New Wave – the perception of identity in relation to space and time – whilst the story 'Psyclops' (1956) introduced the stream-of-consciousness techniques that Aldiss would develop as the Acid Head War stories of the late 1960s (republished as *Barefoot in the Head* (1969)). In his roles as an editor at Penguin and joint-editor with Harry Harrison on the short-lived journal, *SF Horizons* (1964–5), Aldiss was ideally placed to promote greater literary standards within sf.

Yet, despite Ballard's prolific output and Moorcock's introduction of his fantasy anti-hero Elric, the decisive factor in the emergence of the New Wave (as Judith Merril would popularize it in the United States) was economics. As Ashley notes, 'The rising popularity of pocketbooks in Britain ... was starting to have an effect on magazine distribution and sales.'[37] Commenting upon his third readers' survey in *New Worlds* (April 1964), Carnell concluded that 'the day of the specialized s-f magazine, published for the devout band of followers, is almost over'.[38] Having already contracted with Corgi Books a paperback anthology series, *New Writings in SF*, Carnell relinquished control of both *New Worlds* and *Science Fantasy*. The magazines were picked up by the soft-porn publisher, Roberts & Vinter, with Moorcock installed as editor of the former and the Oxford art dealer, Kyril Bonfiglioli, editing the latter. The financial instability of *New Worlds* for the rest of the 1960s would underscore Moorcock's increasingly avant-garde stance.

For the first three years, however, Moorcock's instincts were constrained by his publisher. With the collapse of Roberts & Vinter in 1967, and the last-minute award of an Arts Council grant thanks to Aldiss's intervention, Moorcock was able to achieve what he had sketched-out in 1964: a large-size format with 'good quality illustrations', specializing 'in experimental work by writers like [William] Burroughs and artists like [Eduardo] Paolozzi', which 'would attempt a cross-fertilization of popular sf, science and the work of the literary and artistic avant-garde'.[39] Moorcock's fictional model was the first of Ballard's condensed novels 'The Terminal Beach' (1964), reluctantly published by Carnell, whose apocalyptic response to the Atomic Age was registered not only in terms of the psychological breakdown of its protagonist but also in the textual fragmentation: the non-linear use of sub-sections, interpolated documents and hallucinations that form impenetrable blocks of data in concert with the labyrinthine architecture of the abandoned nuclear test-site. Until 1967, however, such experimental fiction as well as the work of the coterie that surrounded Moorcock jostled with more conventional fare by established writers. Not only did this arrangement make better commercial sense, it also meant that continuities could be drawn between the pre- and post-Carnell eras. In particular, the theme of entropy – often taken as a defining characteristic of New Wave sf – extended a leitmotif evident in Wells and Stapledon but also in the conceptual framework to Aldiss's interlinked collection, *The Canopy of Time* (1959) (*Galaxies Like Grains of Sand* in the United States (1960)).[40] Similarly, despite Aldiss's caricature of Wyndham's apocalyptic fiction as cosy catastrophes, the justification of cannibalism on Darwinian lines in Wyndham's 'Survival' (1952) prefigures Ballard's visceral horror.

In July 1967, *New Worlds* moved to its larger-size format. With the end of Roberts & Vinter, *Science Fantasy* (retitled *Impulse* in 1966 and then, briefly, *SF Impulse*) was absorbed into its sister-title. In his tenure as editor, though, Bonfiglioli had made significant discoveries in Daphne Castell, Christopher Priest, Keith Roberts, Josephine Saxton and Brian Stableford. Roberts, especially, would make an important contribution to the style and content of *New Worlds* but, taken together, this grouping should be regarded as formulating an alternative New Wave. Parts of Roberts's *Pavane* (1968), an episodic alternate history set in a Catholic England, had been published in *Impulse*; the text's episodic nature seems to articulate the impossibility of either fully expressing or comprehending a radically different historical past. Part of another, even more violently equivocal text, Ballard's *The Atrocity Exhibition* (1970), had also appeared in *Impulse*. The disparate publishing history of Ballard's text, scattered across such sf and non-sf magazines as *Ambit*, *Encounter*, *New Worlds* and *International Times*, seems to embody the New Wave's propensity for fragmentation and dissemination.

These propensities were articulated in *New Worlds* through the twin procedures of cybernetics and assemblage. Stories by such writers as Ballard, Michael Butterworth, Langdon Jones, John Sladek and Pamela Zoline were imbued both with the organizational principles of cybernetics and the contextual practice of assemblage that seeks to uncover 'new energies and images through juxtaposing found materials or by directing aesthetic attention to an existing but previously ignored context'.[41] The erotic charge of assemblage effectively unseated the computer logic of cybernetics by randomizing the text (adding to the entropy or informational overload). This randomization of the text meant also the obliteration of the page and of conventional reading strategies: photographs, illustrations, collages, unusual fonts and layouts all contributed to the disintegrating boundaries between text, image and page.[42] In this sense, the short story became a module within a mobile network of shifting signs and processes. This motility is most clearly seen in the stories involving Moorcock's protean anti-hero, Jerry Cornelius, not only in their seemingly arbitrary construction but also in Moorcock's farming-out of the character to other writers so that authorial intention is further displaced within an anarchic, communal ethos.

Such artistic strategies can also be read as a symptomatic response to *New Worlds'* ever-worsening financial position after its temporary ban by the retailer W. H. Smith over the serialization of Norman Spinrad's novel, *Bug Jack Barron* (1969), and the eventual suspension of its Arts Council grant. In 1971, *New Worlds* was reborn as a paperback quarterly following in the footsteps of Carnell's *New Writings*. Although the New Wave undoubtedly introduced new styles and content into the production of sf, it failed to create Moorcock's ideal of a 'literature for the space age'.[43] It also failed to increase significantly the number of women writers and, although *New Worlds* featured a number of new British authors, most notably M. John Harrison and Ian Watson, perhaps its greatest boon was to expatriate Americans such as Sladek, Zoline and Thomas M. Disch. Although experimental short fiction would have to look beyond the sf genre – and, in this respect, Malcolm Bradbury's *Penguin Book of Modern British Short Stories* (1988) is an effective illustration of the mainstreaming of techniques pioneered in *New*

Worlds – Moorcock's periodical has remained a touchstone for all successive UK sf magazines.

Interzone to the Present Day

Interzone was launched in 1982 by a collective consisting of fans and freelance critics, which included John Clute, Malcolm Edwards, Colin Greenland, Roz Kaveney and David Pringle. Gradually, this group diminished until by 1988 Pringle was sole editor and publisher although some members of the former collective, most notably Clute, remained as contributors. The magazine was launched with the declared aim of recapturing *New Worlds'* former grandeur, and several of its earliest writers were either ex-New Wavers or significant non-genre authors such as Angela Carter. This mix was itself a reflection of how the British sf story had survived during the 1970s in non-genre magazines, for example, Emma Tennant's *Bananas*.

By the middle of the 1980s, however, *Interzone* had begun to establish its own identity, beginning with an editorial in Number 8 (summer 1984) by Greenland and Pringle that called for a 'radical hard sf': 'It may be fantastic, surrealistic, "illogical", but in order to be radical *hard* SF it should explore in some fashion the perspectives opened up by contemporary science and technology'.[44] For a time, radical hard sf was used as a synonym in the United States for the emerging cyberpunk movement such that *Interzone* became a gateway for these writers. But, the magazine also provided a venue for British authors who were seeking to get beyond the New Wave's blanket dismissal of genre sf.[45] Iain M. Banks's 'A Gift from the Culture' (1987) was an early sampler of the space operatic utopia that he had conceived as far back as the early 1970s. During the 1980s and 1990s, *Interzone* fostered an entire generation of British authors – amongst them, Stephen Baxter, Nicola Griffith, Peter F. Hamilton, Simon Ings, Gwyneth Jones, Paul McAuley, Ian McDonald, Kim Newman, Alastair Reynolds, Charles Stross and Liz Williams. Some, such as Baxter, Hamilton and Reynolds, responded to the call of Greenland and Pringle as an updating of genre sf to create what has been dubbed 'the New Space Opera'.[46] Others, reacting to the advances in genetic engineering, nanotechnology and virtual reality, responded in stories of mounting complexity (McAuley, Stross) sometimes on a global economic scale (McDonald). Still others addressed the call in terms of its formal disparity, mixing, bending and commenting upon the porousness of generic boundaries (Ings, Newman). Despite the overall masculine tone and content of the magazine, the presence of women writers was relatively higher than its predecessors: women writers appearing in *Interzone* have included Griffith, Jones and Williams, but also authors such as Storm Constantine, Mary Gentle, Tanith Lee and Lisa Tuttle, each perhaps responding to the lack of a doctrinaire statement upon what is or is not sf.[47] Non-genre writers, such as Toby Litt and Nicholas Royle, have also appeared, further blurring the boundaries, whilst the presence of several non-English and non-Anglophone writers, including Geoff Ryman (Canadian but a long-term UK resident), has queried *Interzone*'s identification as an exclusively *British* sf magazine. As if marking *Interzone*'s legacy in both the sf and short story fields, one of its protégés, Chris Beckett, won the Edge Hill Short Fiction Prize in 2009 with his collection *The Turing Test* (2008).

By this point, however, Pringle had relinquished the role of editor to Andy Cox, formerly editor of *The Third Alternative* (1994–2005; retitled *Black Static*, 2005–), and Cox's TTA Press. However, the number of writers who appeared in both *Interzone* and *The Third Alternative* – amongst them, Neal Asher, Tony Ballantyne, Eric Brown, Peter Crowther, Graham Joyce, Chris Kenworthy and James Lovegrove as well as the former New Wavers Harrison, Priest and Watson – suggests less an absorption and more an assimilation. With its promotion of both slipstream and weird fiction, *The Third Alternative* was a key document in the so-called 'British SF Boom' of the early twenty-first century, but equally the generation of writers that Pringle established at *Interzone* can be seen as creating the necessary platform.[48] These developments, though, can also be read as part of a historical pattern in which, from the Victorian scientific romance to the beginnings of British genre sf and the New Wave, science fiction in the United Kingdom has always been a hybrid form and generic classifications have never been rigorously applied. In this respect, the acknowledged influence upon Ballard and Moorcock of Maurice Richardson's surreal comic tales, *The Exploits of Engelbrecht* (1950; originally published in the little magazine, *Lilliput*, with illustrations by Gerard Hoffnung and Ronald Searle, republished by Butterworth's Savoy Books in 2010), should also be noted.

In the absence of overly rigid definitions, the British sf short story may have the capacity to thrive within the publishing conditions of the twenty-first century. Yet, as the novelist and short story writer Nina Allan has observed, 'British writers have not thus far made any great inroads into the predominantly US-based online publishing scene'.[49] A possible exception is *Strange Horizons* (2000–), edited since 2010 by the UK-based Niall Harrison, but otherwise the only consistent online outlet for British short fiction is *Arc* (2012–), a subsidiary of *New Scientist* edited by Simon Ings. Although it is subscription only, *Arc*'s clearly stated editorial policy to publish fiction that explores the applications and social effect of future technologies, and its ability to pay professional rates, has meant that the magazine has been able to attract established authors such as Harrison, McAuley, Reynolds, Jeff Noon, Adam Roberts and Tricia Sullivan (US-born but a long-term resident of the United Kingdom).

To some extent, *Arc*'s direction has complemented the 'mundane sf' tendency spearheaded by Ryman, first in *Interzone* Number 216 (2008), and then in the anthology, *When It Changed* (2009), published by the mainstream short story press, Comma. Both *Arc* and Ryman's anthology are also notable in featuring writers from across the genre divide, in Ryman's case, well-known sf authors such as Ings, Jones, Roberts, Williams, Paul Cornell, Ken MacLeod and Justina Robson, non-genre writers such as Patricia Duncker and authors who occupy a liminal space between genres such as Frank Cottrell Boyce, Sara Maitland and Adam Marek. Following the success of both *When It Changed* and Maitland's contribution, 'Moss Witch', as runner-up at the 2010 BBC National Short Story Prize, Comma has published three further volumes edited on similar lines: *Litmus* (2011), *Bio-Punk* (2012) and *Beta-Life* (2014). Meanwhile Roberts's contribution, 'Hair', became the basis for his British Science Fiction Association (BSFA)-shortlisted novel, *By Light Alone* (2011).

Adam Roberts's career is indicative of current trends. Most of the stories that comprise his collection *Adam Robots* (2013), long-listed for the 2014 Edge Hill Prize, were not originally published in magazine form, but appeared in anthologies with small presses such as Solaris (owned since 2009 by Rebellion) or NewCon, the brainchild of the sf writer Ian Whates. Like many other contemporary sf and fantasy writers, Roberts made his reputation via the novel – although works such as the award-winning *Jack Glass* (2012) often feature episodic structures. In this respect, Roberts also contributed to the series of novellas that initiated Pringle's current venture, PS Publishing, in 1999. Although continuing to publish sf collections, most notably selected works of Jones, McAuley and Watson, PS has tended towards the dark fantasy and weird fiction associated with Jurassic London, Anne Perry and Jared Shurin's not-for-profit imprint that works in partnership with museums and galleries. Their anthology *The Lowest Heaven* (2013), showcasing emerging writers such as Sophia MacDougall, James Smythe and E. J. Swift, is an indication of the valuable work to be done by small presses.

Yet, as Allan comments, 'the sheer profusion of small press titles' which 'have taken the place of magazines' for novice writers has also created 'a ghetto in recent years'. Allan's conclusion is that a solution 'must lie with the writers', and she cites Ian Sales, Tim Maughan and Robert Shearman as authors who have circumvented the conventional routes for, respectively, 'the self-published chapbook', 'the small independent imprint' and 'the single-author collection'.[50] To these names, though, can also be added Noon who, having experimented with flash fictions in *Pixel Juice* (1998) and compositional techniques derived from the cutting and mixing of electronic dance music in *Cobralingus* (2001), is currently exploring the imaginative possibilities of the 140-character twitter post. As a now largely self-published author, Noon is not only promoting his work to a dedicated readership but also using that medium as the basis of his post-human message. Although this interface between artistic expression and technological media might appear to be the height of postmodernism, in many respects it is an extension of the metatextuality of the short story to be both a passive and a critical reflection of an increasingly mechanized mass culture. If Wells were to board his time machine to the present, the current condition of the sf short story might not appear to be so alien to him after all.

Notes

1. Kingsley Amis, *New Maps of Hell* (London: Victor Gollancz, 1960), p. 137.
2. Martin Scofield, *The Cambridge Introduction to the American Short Story* (Cambridge University Press, 2006), p. 5.
3. Tim Armstrong, *Modernism: A Cultural History* (Cambridge: Polity Press, 2005), pp. 51–3.
4. Farah Mendlesohn, 'Introduction: Reading Science Fiction', in *The Cambridge Companion to Science Fiction*, ed. Edward James and Farah Mendlesohn (Cambridge University Press, 2003), p. 1.
5. Nicola Humble, 'Sitting Forward or Sitting Back: Highbrow v. Middlebrow Reading', *Modernist Cultures*, 6 (2011), 1, pp. 41–59 (p. 42).
6. See respectively James Gunn, *The Road to Science Fiction*, vol. 1 (New York: New American Library, 1977); Adam Roberts, *The History of Science Fiction* (Basingstoke: Palgrave, 2005); and Andrew Milner, *Locating Science Fiction* (Liverpool University Press, 2012).
7. Darko Suvin, *Victorian Science Fiction in the UK: The Discourses of Knowledge and Power* (Boston: G. K. Hall, 1983); and Suvin, 'Victorian Science Fiction, 1871–85: The Rise of the Alternative History Sub-Genre', *Science Fiction Studies*, 10 (1983), 2, pp. 148–69 (p. 148).

8. See not only I. F. Clarke's critical study, *Voices Prophesying War, 1763–1984* (Oxford University Press, 1966), but also his anthologies, *The Great War with Germany, 1890–1914* (Liverpool University Press, 1997) and *The Tale of the Next Great War, 1871–1914* (Liverpool University Press, 1995).
9. Samuel Butler, *Erewhon* (New York: Dover, 2002), p. 136.
10. Roger Luckhurst, *Science Fiction* (Cambridge: Polity Press, 2005), p. 29.
11. Charles Howard Hinton, *Scientific Romances* (London: Swan Sonnenschein, 1886), p. 101.
12. Brian Stableford, *Scientific Romance in Britain 1890–1950* (London: Fourth Estate, 1985), pp. 11–17.
13. H. G. Wells, 'Introduction to *The Country of the Blind*' (1914), in *Complete Short Story Omnibus* (London: Gollancz, 2011), p. 952.
14. Wells, preface to *Seven Famous Novels* (New York: Knopf, 1934), pp. vii–viii.
15. See, for example, Harold Orel, *The Victorian Short Story: The Development and Triumph of a Literary Genre* (Cambridge University Press, 1986).
16. Yevgeny Zamyatin, *A Soviet Heretic*, trans. Mirra Ginsberg (London: Quartet, 1991), p. 288.
17. B. M. Èjxenbaum, 'O. Henry and the Theory of the Short Story', in *Readings in Russian Poetics*, ed. Ladislav Matejka and Krystyna Pomorska (Cambridge, MA: MIT Press, 1971), p. 262.
18. Wells, *Omnibus*, p. 545.
19. See, for example, Angelique Richardson, introduction to *Women Who Did: Stories by Men and Women, 1890–1914* (London: Penguin, 2005), pp. xlv–xlviii.
20. Rudyard Kipling, *Actions and Reactions* (London: Macmillan, 1909), p. 109.
21. E. M. Forster, *Collected Short Stories* (London: Penguin, 1954), p. 119.
22. See, especially, J. R. Hammond, *H. G. Wells and the Modern Novel* (New York: St Martin's Press, 1988), pp. 24–41; and Simon J. James, *Maps of Utopia: H. G. Wells, Modernity, and the End of Culture* (Oxford University Press, 2012), pp. 1–35.
23. See, respectively: Brian W. Aldiss, *Billion Year Spree* (London: Weidenfeld and Nicolson, 1973); and Christopher Priest, 'British Science Fiction', in *Science Fiction: A Critical Guide*, ed. Patrick Parrinder (London: Longman, 1979), pp. 187–202.
24. J. G. Ballard, *A User's Guide to the Millennium* (London: Flamingo, 1997), p. 197.
25. Istvan Csicsery-Ronay, Jr., *The Seven Beauties of Science Fiction* (Middletown, CT: Wesleyan University Press, 2008), pp. 70–2.
26. See Stableford, *Scientific Romance in Britain 1890–1950*; and also Andy Croft, *Red Letter Days: British Fiction in the 1930s* (London: Lawrence & Wishart, 1990).
27. J. B. S. Haldane, *Possible Worlds* (London: Chatto & Windus, 1927), p. 292.
28. On Stapledon's reception, see Robert Crossley, *Olaf Stapledon: Speaking for the Future* (Syracuse University Press, 1994), pp. 191–3.

29. For a contrary view, see Nicholas Ruddick, *Ultimate Island: On the Nature of British Science Fiction* (Westport, CT: Greenwood Press, 1993).
30. Mike Ashley, *The Time Machines: The Story of the Science-Fiction Pulp Magazines from the Beginning to 1950* (Liverpool University Press, 2000), p. 134.
31. See for example Arthur Koestler, 'The Boredom of Fantasy', *The Listener*, 48 (1953), pp. 891–3.
32. For further details, see Derek Johnston, 'The BBC Versus "Science Fiction": The Collision of Transnational Genre and National Identity in Television of the Early 1950s', in *British Science Fiction Film and Television*, ed. Tobias Hochscherf and James Leggott (Jefferson, NC: McFarland, 2011), pp. 40–9.
33. J. G. Ballard, *Vermilion Sands* (London: Vintage, 2001), p. 11.
34. Doris Lessing, *Walking in the Shade: My Autobiography, 1949–1962* (London: HarperCollins, 1997), p. 34.
35. For example, as the production notes to *Doctor Who* acknowledge, the anthologies were extensively used to gauge an idea of science fiction. See 'The Genesis of *Doctor Who*', BBC Archive, www.bbc.co.uk/archive/doctor who/6400.shtml (accessed 1 December 2014).
36. J. G. Ballard, *Miracles of Life* (London: Harper Perennial, 2008), p. 194.
37. Mike Ashley, *Transformations: The Story of the Science Fiction Magazines from 1950 to 1970* (Liverpool University Press, 2005), p. 231.
38. John Carnell, 'Survey Report 1963', *New Worlds*, 141 (1964), pp. 2–3; 121–2 (p. 122).
39. Michael Moorcock, introduction to *New Worlds: An Anthology* (London: Flamingo, 1983), p. 11.
40. On entropy see especially Colin Greenland, *The Entropy Exhibition: Michael Moorcock and the British 'New Wave' in Science Fiction* (London: Routledge and Kegan Paul, 1983).
41. Stephen Fredman, *Contextual Practice: Assemblage and the Erotic in Postwar Poetry and Art* (Stanford University Press, 2010), p. 3.
42. On the role of text and image in *New Worlds*, see David Brittain, *Eduardo Paolozzi at New Worlds: Science Fiction and Art in the Sixties* (Manchester: Savoy, 2013).
43. See Michael Moorcock, *Into the Media Web: Selected Short Non-Fiction, 1956–2006*, ed. John Davey (Manchester: Savoy, 2010), pp. 363–4.
44. Quoted in Kathryn Cramer, 'Hard Science Fiction', in *Cambridge Companion to Science Fiction*, ed. James and Mendlesohn, p. 194.
45. In addition to the essay collections above by Ballard and Moorcock, see M. John Harrison, 'A Literature of Comfort' (1971), in *Parietal Games: Critical Writings by and on M. John Harrison*, ed. Mark Bould and Michelle Reid (London: SF Foundation, 2005), pp. 84–8.
46. For further details, see Luckhurst, *Science Fiction*, pp. 222–30.

47. Gentle, Jones, Lee and Tuttle also appeared, alongside Saxton, Zoline, Zoe Fairbairns and Naomi Mitchison, in Jen Green and Sarah Lefanu's historically nuanced anthology, *Despatches from the Frontiers of the Female Mind* (London: The Women's Press, 1985).
48. On the British SF Boom, see the special issue of *Science Fiction Studies* 30 (2003), p. 3.
49. Nina Allan, 'The Art and Business of Short Fiction', in 'The State of British SF and Fantasy: A Symposium', *Strange Horizons* (28 July 2014), www.strangehorizons.com/2014/20140728/1britsf-a.shtml#allan (accessed 4 December 2014).
50. *Ibid.*

26

Weird Stories: The Potency of Horror and Fantasy

ROGER LUCKHURST

The weird story is most commonly associated with American pulp magazine fiction. In March 1923, Clark Henneberger published the first issue of *Weird Tales: A Magazine of the Bizarre and Unusual* in the standard pulp format of 128 untrimmed 7 x 10-inch cheap acidic pages with bright, lurid covers. It became closely associated with the work of H. P. Lovecraft, maestro of slimy ooze, tentacular horror and degenerate back-sliders in prose marked by a breathless pile-up of adjectival modifiers and exclamation marks. 'The Thing cannot be described – there is no language for such abysms of shrieking and immemorial lunacy, such eldritch contradictions of all matter, force, and cosmic order. A mountain walked or stumbled. God!' reads one of Lovecraft's most celebrated tales.[1]

Lovecraft wrote long tales, rarely dynamic in narrative but instead thick with accumulated descriptions of eerie landscapes and extreme psychological states of lone male figures. The shorter length was dictated mainly by pulp concerns (his editors often cut down and streamlined his sentences better to fit the rhythm of pulp style), but Lovecraft was also very committed to Edgar Allan Poe's insistence on a heightened 'unity of impression' that the short story could deliver.[2] 'Atmosphere, not action, is the great desideratum of weird fiction', Lovecraft declared.[3] Lovecraft and his circle, which included prolific short story writers Clark Ashton Smith, Henry Whitehead and Robert E. Howard, perfected the 'weird menace' story in the early 1930s, in tandem with the emergence of the 'horror' film. The film-board classification 'H for Horrific' appeared in 1932 alongside the Universal studio adaptations of *Frankenstein* and *Dracula*, but these films were often called 'weird' by their first reviewers. The weird story is an elaboration of the eighteenth-century gothic romance, not quite the same as gothic but a strange and interstitial form on the way to somewhere else: modern horror.

'Weird menace' was a capacious pulp category that stretched from supernatural tales of the vengeful dead back from the grave via grim urban noir stories of sexual threat or actual torture to exotic jungle terrors of kidnap and cannibalism. These were the mass sensation fictions of the American culture industry, the so-called 'shudder pulps' seeking to register thrills in the physiology of the bodies of those suffering economic hardship.[4] Hundreds of titles had tens of millions of readers, although the star writers of the day who poured out millions of words to order – writers like Seabury Quinn or Theodore Roscoe – have been largely forgotten. When Lovecraft died in 1937, he had only one small book publication outside his pulp and amateur magazine stories and so also seemed destined for obscurity. When his dedicated followers founded Arkham House to publish collections of his short stories in the 1940s, the eminent literary critic Edmund Wilson deigned to notice them, only to dismiss the developing cult of Lovecraft with the view that 'the only real horror of most of these fictions is the horror of bad taste and bad art'.[5]

After the Second World War, the epithet 'weird' was most often found in the titles of horror comics (*Weird Chills, Weird Horrors, Weird Fantasy, Weird Science, Weird Tales of the Future*, etc.). This was a boom which began in 1949, stuffing the pages of comics with graphic depictions of rotting corpses, axe murderers and dismemberment, armies of the undead and busty damsels in distress, squeezed in the giant pincers or obscene tentacles of alien creatures. Death came swiftly and repeatedly and always with a mordant laugh. The graphic horror and violence of the weird comics produced a moral panic, fanned by Fredric Wertham's alarmist account, *The Seduction of the Innocents*, which blamed early comic reading on later delinquency, drug-use and criminality in adolescents. After Werthem's appearance before the Senate Subcommittee in Juvenile Delinquency in April 1954, this brand of comics was regulated out of existence within six months.[6]

The association of the weird with American pulp forms has resulted, I think, in a profound aversion to taking the term seriously or in understanding how it might categorize certain modes of English short story writing since the 1880s. In *The Uses of Literacy* in 1957, Richard Hoggart lamented that Americanization was fast erasing authentic working-class culture in England with an imported glut of 'crime, science fiction and sex novelettes'.[7] It has been established that the organized British Left were fully in support of the censorship of horror comics.[8] For a long time, the weird was the pulp menace from America. The guttering flame of its memory was preserved by small presses and passionate amateur experts, bibliographers and editors far beyond the academy: S. T. Joshi, E. F. Bleiler, Richard Dalby. Only since 2003, when the British writer M. John Harrison coined the term 'The New Weird' for a group of specifically English authors seeking to defy the relatively identifiable generic markers of science fiction, gothic or fantasy to create something hybrid and slippery and new, has the term come to be reassessed. Harrison was tentative about the New Weird, posing it as a series of questions rather than an identifiable kind of writing: 'Who does it? What is it? Is it even anything?'[9] Even so, it travelled back across the Atlantic and the anthology *The New Weird* appeared in America in 2008. In an exercise of retrofitting a literary tradition for this contemporary genre, a vast anthology, *The Weird: A Compendium of Strange and Dark Stories*, appeared in 2011, claiming roots in the early twentieth century and incorporating figures as diverse as Franz Kafka, Gustav Meyrink, Jorge Luis Borges, Rabindranath Tagore and Stefan Grabinksi into the weird mode.

This active invention of a tradition as a tactic of legitimation is typical of weird fiction writing. Lovecraft's long essay, *Supernatural Horror in Literature*, composed in 1925, shaped his own literary influences into a distinct lineage, arguing that the weird descended from the German Romantics and French decadents but culminated in four modern British masters: Arthur Machen, Algernon Blackwood, Lord Dunsany and M. R. James. The concentration of writers from the British Isles in Lovecraft's list (the first three decidedly from the fringes, though), suggests that 'weird fiction' might have a certain explanatory power, provided we grasp its provisional nature and resist the idea that the weird is an established but somehow 'lost' tradition. What follows is a consideration of the weird as an inflection or tone, a *mode* of writing rather than a *genre*, 'not a kind but a method, a way of getting something done' that exists in the interstices of other forms of the fantastic.[10]

Lovecraft defines weird fiction as 'a literature of cosmic fear', as distinct from 'the literature of mere physical fear and the mundanely gruesome'. He continues:

> Such writing, to be sure, has its place, as has the conventional or even whimsical or humorous ghost story ... The true weird tale has something more than secret murder, bloody bones, or a sheeted form clanking chains according to rule. A certain atmosphere of breathless and unexplainable dread of outer, unknown forces must be present; and there must be a hint, expressed with a seriousness and portentousness becoming its subject, of that most terrible conception of the human brain – a malign and particular suspension or defeat of those fixed laws of Nature which are our only

safeguard against the assaults of chaos and the daemons of unplumbed space.[11]

This description establishes several crucial elements. The weird is distinguished from both the trappings of the gothic romance – the apparatus of clanking chains, oneiric labyrinths and conventionalized spectres – and also from its metaphysics. The gothic romance was a Protestant nightmare of feverish Catholicism, stuffing a fantasy Europe with mad monks, ravished or ravishing nuns, arbitrary feudal tyranny and debilitating superstition. This was established by Horace Walpole's founding gothic text, *The Castle of Otranto* in 1764, but continued as a fictional apparatus at least until Bram Stoker's *Dracula*. In contrast, the weird for Lovecraft is rooted in the North, is 'Nordic' (a term Lovecraft used as a racial and explicitly racist term) and thoroughly materialist. The disturbance in Lovecraft comes not from the transgression of spiritual or secular moral orders, but from an opening out to a vast, indifferent and inhuman universe. 'All my tales are based on the fundamental premise that common human laws and interests and emotions have no validity or significance in the vast cosmos-at-large', he wrote to the *Weird Tales* editor, Farnsworth Wright, about 'The Call of Cthulhu'. This is materialist horror, in which 'a negligible and temporary race called mankind' is confronted with a 'boundless and hideous unknown – the shadow-haunted *Outside*' that terrifies in its dethronement of all anthropocentric thought.[12] Weird writer and theorist China Miéville suggests that this eerie affect is a fractured sublime, which no longer leads to spiritual or cognitive heights, but rather 'allows swillage of that awe and horror from "beyond" back into the everyday – into angles, bushes, the touch of strange limbs, noises, etc. The weird is a radicalized sublime backwash.'[13]

Lovecraft's quartet of English masters of the weird have to be somewhat shoehorned into this materialist framework, though. Arthur Machen, who began to publish in the 1880s, was a conservative Anglican who claimed to follow the original English Catholic church before schism, whose oddly fractured fictions lambasted materialism and mocked the scientific naturalism of his day with sometimes ecstatic religious visions but mostly horrifying glimpses of supernatural or atavistic forces obtruding into the dreary streets of *fin-de-siècle* London. For the central device of his intrusion fantasies, Machen used the Catholic doctrinal term *perichoresis*, 'an interpenetration' of spiritual orders, an in-mixing of the sacred and the profane.[14] Algernon Blackwood was similarly something of a spiritual seeker, a member of the Theosophical Society in the 1890s and briefly (like Machen) a member of the ritual magical group, The Hermetic Order of the Golden Dawn. He was also a serious student of Eastern religions. Blackwood's stories conjure the sense of other realities pressing themselves forcefully on the limited human range of the spectrum, whether from unimagined exteriors or unknown interior psychical strata. The invisible threat is never manifested in formal religious frameworks, however – nothing as vulgar as angels or demons. M. R. James was an entirely more conventional figure – English, Protestant and of the establishment. He generated dark antiquarian fantasies from rootling around in medieval incunabula, catching the last whisps of Catholic demonology and witch-hunts within relatively conventional ghost story club tale structures. Lord Dunsany's fragments from an invented cycle of myths and fables of ancient deities in *The Gods of Pegana* (1905) are considerably weirder, however – an odd, private cosmogony that seemed to pastiche the forms of Irish nationalist myth-making typical of W. B. Yeats and his circle at the same time. This quartet suggests that the weird before Lovecraft was less materialist than a body of fiction that registered the growing instability of orthodox Christian natural and supernatural paradigms. The disordered visions of the weird are compromise formations, a mark of disturbance to traditional orders, religious longing distended into very strange shapes. One might see them as of a piece with other symptoms of crisis, such as the diverse kinds of 'occulture' in the late nineteenth century – psychical research, the magical and pagan revivals and mystical esotericism.[15] The generic slipperiness and unexpected trajectories of weird fiction offer their own formal rendering of that crisis in their irresolution.

'Weird' fiction began to creep into the titles of collections of ghost stories and supernatural tales in England in the 1880s. There was little particularly to distinguish, say, Charlotte Riddell's collection *Weird Stories* (1882) from the traditional gothic tale or Victorian ghost story, although Grant Allen's eclectic *Strange Stories* (1884) is more symptomatically conflicted, being composed of ghost stories and supernatural tales written by a man with ambitions to be a serious scientific naturalist and was thus contemptuous of the very form employed. It is really Machen's early work, however, that establishes the paradigm of English weird fiction. Machen's early fame rests on the scandal of the book of two long stories he contributed to the quintessential Decadent 'Keynotes' series in 1894, *The Great God Pan and The Inmost Light*. *Pan* is a collection of fragments by different narrators artfully arranged in the manner of Stevenson's *Strange Case of Dr Jekyll and Mr Hyde* (1885), which together begin to hint at an unspeakable neurological experiment on a young girl's brain that produces access to other realities and (we infer) a coupling that results in a demonic child, Helen. Helen's career in lascivious sexual vampirism leaves a trail across London of men committing suicide from either panic or pleasure or an intolerable combination of both. The fragments crest towards revelations they cannot articulate, breaking off in terror, or sidestepping into arcane invocations of obscure Latin sources to conceal truths from the uninitiated. Machen is one of many Decadents to pervert the myth that the announcement of the death of Pan in Plutarch's 'On the Decline of Oracles' is the mark of the end of Paganism and the birth of the Christian era. The story subverts Elizabeth Barrett Browning's pious poem, 'The Dead Pan' (1844) by suggesting that atavistic pagan gods still lurk in the ancient woods of the Welsh borderlands or the atavistic convolutions of the brain and whose influence can seep insidiously into the streets of the imperial metropolis. Machen thus establishes the weird's insistent collision of urban modernity with ancient survivals.

'The Inmost Light' is built from another set of fragments that piece together a monstrous experiment in the occult sciences, this time on the suburban edges of London, a borderland Machen encountered with dread. The story is of Horror in Harlesden, a contribution, the narrator says, towards 'the science of the great city; the physiology of London, literally and metaphorically the greatest subject that the mind of man can conceive'.[16] A doctor extracts the soul of his submissive wife in an ugly new terraced house, capturing it as the dancing, inmost light of a jewel, leaving her an unnerving husk and the doctor a haunted, ruined man. The crab-like advance of plot, with sudden breaks and apparently random shifts, the lurch in tone from jaunty cynicism to holy terror, is striking, awkward, and entirely Machen's signature. *The Great God Pan and the Inmost Light* was loudly condemned by outraged reviewers, the *Westminster Gazette* famously terming it 'a nightmare incoherence of sex'.[17] It was soon caught up, purely by association, with Oscar Wilde's arrest and downfall in early 1895, which suppressed the more overt provocations of the Decadent Movement overnight. Yet Machen actually amplified the sense of transgression with *The Three Imposters* (1895), an even more convoluted set of overlapping short stories, featuring recurrent characters and a spurious quest, which ratcheted up the physical horrors of biological degeneration, abject fear and murderous violence. It contains the famous interpolated narrative, the 'Novel of the White Powder', which ends with the physiological dissolution of a student of the occult, his liquefied remains dripping through the ceiling of his boarding house. The book comes to an end with the discovery of a body 'torn and mutilated in the most hideous fashion, scarred with the marks of red-hot irons, a shameful ruin of the human shape. But upon the middle of the body a fire of coals was smouldering; the flesh had been burnt through.'[18] These are very early graphic visions of 'body horror', yet at the same time Machen consistently foregrounds the artifice of these interpolated tales, undercutting any terror by making the reader aware that these are tall stories told within the frame of the narrative to credulous idiots.

After these provocations, Machen seemingly embraced a life of obscurity, inhabiting those margins where the minor writer ekes out an existence in jobbing journalism or hack writing, surfacing occasionally with a modest masterpiece all the more valued by adepts for its sheer obscurity and unavailability. Machen repeatedly mythologized his poverty and obscurity in later fictions, writing the long novel *The Hill of Dreams* for years (one of the best books about writer's block ever painfully committed to paper), and in his several autobiographies written after a revival of interest in his work in the 1920s. *Far Off Things* recounted his disastrous failed apprenticeship in writing and in London living in the 1880s; he even collected and published a selection of his worst reviews as a celebration of his aesthetic 'failure'. Machen is one of London's 'shadowy immanences' for Iain Sinclair, the poet and writer who has most sought to recover the forgotten denizens of London's 'ghetto of the weird'.[19] Sinclair revels in the para-literary world of London's vanished second-hand book dealers, where the pulp fiction promised something magical and rare beyond 'orthodox bibliography' but with all that hermetic wisdom slowly rotting back into the wood-mulch from which it came.

There is a certain paradox, though, in Machen's success as a legendary failure, his major presence as a 'minor' writer, no longer sustained just by adepts and small presses but now appearing in Penguin Classics and included in Cambridge University Press literary histories. The English weird, with its strong associations with the Decadent movement, can be seen as part of a reaction to the commerce of literature as an industry, resistant to the easily consumable 'light' reading of the new mass circulation magazines that helped invent the form of the short story in the 1880s. Instead, the weird actively seeks crabbed, difficult prose, transgressive or oddly evasive content, genre slippage and elusive authors as emblems of aesthetic resistance to market logics. This investment has if anything intensified in the later stages of the conglomeration of multinational publishing houses. Lavish small press reprints of the weird and wonderful clearly emerge in dialectical relation to the behemoths of Random House and Amazon. Sinclair denounces London's

'CGI dystopia' by praising Machen and his fellows: 'They honour obscurity.'[20]

If the rarefied palette of Machen's weird stories risks being coarsened by mass production and wider interest, there is always something rarer to bring to the table: Count Stenbock's vanishingly obscure *Studies of Death* (1894), for example, or Robert Murray Gilchrist's Decadent gothic tales in *The Stone Dragon* (1894). Stenbock, who died at thirty-five with only a handful of delicate and perverse publications, was a far greater success at failure than Machen. The weird must constantly reinscribe just where the margin lies, since what is valued as obscure is an inevitably moveable feast.

Machen opens another key avenue of weird fiction. Whilst the meaning of 'weird' is rooted in notions of doom or the dread power of Fate in Old English and other northern dialects, the *Oxford English Dictionary* notes that there is also a cluster of meanings that associates 'weïrd' (with a diaeresis) with 'weyard' or 'wayward'. This association was developed entirely from Shakespeare's punning around the 'Weird Sisters' in *Macbeth*, a text whose staging of supernatural forces was a key influence on the eighteenth-century gothic revival. Thus, the weird might mean 'suggestive of the supernatural; of a mysterious or unearthly character', but it also means 'out of the ordinary course, strange, unusual; hence, odd, fantastic'. It resonates with *wayward*, defined as 'disposed to go counter to the wishes or advice of others, or to what is reasonable; wrong-headed, intractable, self-willed' or 'perverse' (*OED*). One of Machen's many autobiographical writings from the 1920s was called *The London Adventure; or, The Art of Wandering*, the subtitle anticipating the argument that books on the city must act like perambulations around the metropolis, subject to chance and accident, wrong-turns and disorientation, a willingness to seek to get lost, and thus become open to fugitive moments of deliverance and joy – 'the magic touch which redeems and exalts the dullness of things' surprised from 'unknown, unvisited squares' or 'railway arches'.[21] The possibility of levering open other realities by stumbling across them drives a number of Machen's short fictions, such as 'A Fragment of Life' (1904) or, much later, 'N' (1936). This tactic, elevated to the *dérive* or 'drift' by the Parisian avant-gardists The Situationist International a generation later, makes the wayward traversal of the city an act of resistance to totalitarian urban planning.[22] Machen's tactic for weirding London has been adopted by Iain Sinclair for his whole career, as he happily confesses.

We can take the waywardness of the weird to be also a matter of the slipperiness of form, the refusal to fit into sequential narrative or generic expectation. In his fascinating theory of literature, Nicholas Royle places *veering* as central to it, 'responding to what is on the move and uncertain in the very moment of reading, to what is slippery, unpredictable and chancy in the experience of literature'. Although Royle associates 'turning, sliding and shifting' in the text as the mark of the literary 'masterpiece', an entirely unexamined category, and has nothing to say about genre fiction even in his chapter on ghosts, the waywardness of the veer is another useful entry into the tangents of the weird tale.[23]

This effect of veering explains how weird fiction can be conceived to expand beyond the expected orbit of gothic or horror writers. Thus, I think Rudyard Kipling deserves to be considered as one of the most influential weird writers, precisely for the way he veers in and out of genres in his early collections.

Kipling's early Indian tales were constantly described by their first readers as 'weird' for their exotic oddity, their uncertain tone and their confounding of expectations.[24] They were often published first as gossip tales in the pages of the *Civil and Military Gazette* in India, perhaps sometimes hard to distinguish from factual reportage from the very frontline of empire, which was already full of strange anecdotes and odd rumours. Since they came from 'beyond the pale', beyond 'the Borderline where the last drop of White blood ends and full tide of Black sets in', they proved hard for readers in England to categorize: they came literally out of nowhere.[25] Kipling's early short fiction used the currency of the supernatural to explore the misfiring cultural exchanges at the colonial frontier, where native superstition might be mocked but also subtly incorporated by the colonial administrators who must improvise in the contact zone.[26]

A good example is 'At the End of the Passage' (1890), first published in the *Boston Herald* and *Lippincott's Magazine* before being pirated in an American collection of stories, *Mine Own People*. It concerns four young Englishmen working entirely alone at their professions at the edge of Empire – one on the Indian survey, one in the Civil Service as advisor to a client ruler, one a Doctor and one Assistant Engineer. They travel hundreds of miles each Sunday merely to see a fellow white face and bicker gently over whist and stave off despair. Suicide haunts them as a way out of the intolerable heat and pressure, and Hummil, the engineer, is close to crack-up. He lies sleepless at night in the 104-degree heat, rigid with terror at his dreams of 'a place down there' and 'a blind face that cries and can't wipe its eyes'.[27] These enigmatic images are left dangling in the story, unmotivated and naggingly under-explained. Hummil confesses something we are not allowed to hear.

Then soon enough, Hummil is haunted by the 'figure of himself', that deathly double or fetch, standing on the verandah and evading capture: 'It slid through the house' (p. 206). Attempts by the doctor to treat his friend inevitably fail and the double conforms to convention in heralding death and Hummil is found lifeless, a look of abject terror on his face. In the last section of the tale, the doctor tries an experiment in optography – that is, taking a Kodak photograph of the retina of the dead man, just to see if it has recorded anything. There is another strange occlusion in the tale as the reader gets not the developed image, but 'the sound of something being hammered to pieces' as the doctor destroys the camera in the bathroom. 'There was nothing there', he says when he emerges, then immediately contradicts himself: 'It was impossible' (p. 211). The story ends inconclusively, with self-cancelling statements.

This is a weird story in its strange slippages, occlusions and absences. It has tinges of the supernatural, but oddly the oppressive atmosphere of menace derives much more from the evocation of Indian summer heat and the tedium of bureaucratic administration than the belated slide towards ghost story. In John Bayley's study, *The Short Story*, where Kipling features as a pivotal figure of the new phase of the form, 'At the End of the Passage' keeps recurring as a puzzling enigma in his argument because the story starts out in the territory of Chekhov but ends up in full-blown Edgar Allan Poe: 'the true horror', Bayley worries, gets 'overlaid by the false nightmare', all that 'mumbo-jumbo out of Poe', terrors that are 'incongruously added on'.[28] Bayley seems anxious to police generic boundaries, to drag Kipling from the slavering jaws of the gothic – 'the comfortable department of the macabre', he calls it – and back into proper literature (p. 66). Yet this strange veering from one genre to another, achieved in such a surprising and casual set of clausal turns, is the signal that Kipling was employing modes that might now be called 'weird'. Of course Kipling could be conservative and didactic, but he also authored numerous tales that were oneiric, hazy and haunting in their irresoluteness. They are full of weird transmissions, mocking native superstition at one moment ('In the House of Suddhoo'), then fully imbibing the possibilities of fragmentary telepathic communication the next ('Wireless'). Their ghosts – if that is what they are – are fugitive and flicker beyond grasp ('Mary Postgate'). Something in these stories defeats the very Chekhovian realism that they initially appear to deploy.

The weird does not always need the apparatus of horror, then: it can manifest in a subtle veering or waywardness that leaves the reader confounded at the slow mutation of the story out of one horizon of expectation and into a wholly different space. Kipling's most bemusing tales twist gently beyond grasp, requiring multiple readings before the reader understands that the pieces remain deliberately incomplete, the kernel of the story closed and enigmatic. This tactic of evasion is something consistently used by Walter de la Mare in his short fiction, which from the start (in the 1890s) was sometimes explicitly supernatural, but more often than not was marked by 'a consistent texture of the unusual' and 'a constant threat of unreality'.[29]

This veering is also evident in the early short stories from the 1940s of the writer William Sansom. Sansom certainly fits the bill for obscurity, having been a successful advertising man and fiction and travel writer, whose evident facility in slick commercial prose resulted in his rapidly vanishing from the post-war literary canon. His early stories, published by the Hogarth Press in the collections *Fireman Flower* (1944) and *Something Terrible, Something Lovely* (1948), are compellingly odd, a mix of influences ranging from Kafka's abstract and opaque allegorical mode, via Surrealism (the London International Surrealist Exhibition in 1936 was an important influence on Sansom) and the New Apocalyptics, the group of poets around Dylan Thomas who embraced more symbolic and expressionistic styles in reaction to the political realism of the thirties. Sansom was on the edges of Thomas's literary and drinking circles in London. A selection of Sansom's stories was published as an act of recovery by Tartarus Press in 2002, who also publish Arthur Machen, giving Sansom the imprimatur of the 'weird'.

'Fireman Flower' emerged from his experience in the London Fire Service during the Second World War. As a fireman, he worked alongside that other oddity of a writer, Henry Green. The story typifies Sansom's mix of realistic detail with an extraordinary ability to slip sideways into more symbolic and oneiric modes. The intensely subjective narration restricts the fighting of a gigantic warehouse blaze to the dissociated subjective state of Fireman Flower, who roves through the building on an increasingly allegorical quest to find the true 'kernel' of the flames. From intensely observed heightened reality, Flower moves through corridors and rooms that seem to hold slightly different ontological statuses, as bubbles of memory, dream or symbolic desire. The tone moves waywardly from particularized depiction to abstract philosophical discussion and ecstatic exalted states tinged with sublime terror in a way that is difficult to convey in short quotations. A similar sense of busted allegory, of symbolic registers that defy easy 'translation', hovers around brief tales like 'The Little Fears', which establishes the setting of a dreary coffee bar with careful description but then elevates it into a stage for an intensely paranoid gothic psychic storm in the severely damaged focalizing narrator. Extreme psychic states allow stubs of detective fiction, thriller, pulp weird menace and gothic romance to appear suggestively in these tales, but always with a sense that expected trajectories of generic forms are being unnervingly undermined and left irresolute.

Some of Sansom's stories suggest that the distending traumas of the War are finding a way of being registered in formal distortion, in the waywardness of the weird. This is particularly true of the work of Robert Aickman, whose stories convey a profound sense of traumatic aftermath in dusty and diminished byways of post-war Britain. Aickman's work is increasingly being understood as a crucial development in the trajectory of the English ghost story after the 'Golden Age' between 1880 and 1920, but it never sits straightforwardly in gothic conventions, being defiantly wayward. Aickman is therefore weird *and* weïrd. Aickman was a diffident, conservative elitist, who disdained popular horror fiction, and Lovecraft in particular. When he began his famous anthologies of ghost stories in 1964, he declared 'there are only about thirty or forty first-class ghost stories in the whole of western literature', an act of canon formation in which he shamelessly included himself.[30] He was the grandson of the Victorian and Edwardian gothic and detective writer Richard Marsh and named the literary agency he ran in Gower Street after his colourful ancestor. Aickman published forty-eight long stories between 1951 and his death in 1981, usually of about ten thousand words, the necessary length to accumulate detail but also to allow for the glacial slide from realism into something more fantastical. For these stories, he eschewed the term 'ghost story' and preferred the epithet 'strange' over 'weird'. The stories are certainly marked by an aversion to the explicit, and a sense of having missed the main significance of the tale is a common readerly reaction. Glen Cavaliero calls them 'weird jigsaw puzzles from which the central piece is missing'.[31] S. T. Joshi professes continual bemusement and his own assessment is perhaps appropriately inconclusive: 'There is no question that Aickman belongs somewhere within the realm of weird fiction; but where exactly his place is in that realm is a singularly vexing question.'[32] Again, Aickman's value has long been tied to his relative obscurity – cherished by the weird cognoscenti and the literary end of horror fiction, but almost entirely ignored by the academy – although on the centenary of his birth Faber reissued four of his collections in 2014, another indication of the revived interest in the mode.

Aickman writes of poisonous haunting in environments of extraordinary decay and collapse, redolent of post-war decline and austerity. Elizabeth Jane Howard, with whom he co-published his first short stories in 1951, recalled that his conversation harped entirely on the view that 'everything had declined ... We were approaching the end of a civilization'.[33] In 'The Hospice', somewhere on the outskirts of Wolverhampton, the narrator, having run out of petrol, is forced to stay overnight in a hotel whose regime unfolds in surreal, Kafkaesque detail, guests force-fed vast heavy meals of comfort food whilst chained to long tables (Aickman's vision, perhaps, of the stultifying post-war 'nanny' welfare state). In 'The Unsettled Dust', a grand aristocratic house is in severe decline and taken over by the state, the place choked with clumps of dust which are stirred – perhaps – by a vengeful haunting that emerges out of the twisted hatred of the family's surviving sisters, mere tenants of their own legacy now, two women waiting upon the extinction of their name. In 'The Trains', two women fall between the squares of a map on a walking tour in an unspecified 'North', finding shelter in an odd house in Quiet Valley. There, they become entrapped in an awful temporal loop, doomed to be the very spectres they have seen waving at the shrieking trains on the track that thunders past the house.

Aickman's principal theme was sexual anxiety, as he professed in his disarmingly honest memoir *The Attempted Rescue*, about his warring parents and dismal childhood. His mother confessed to her son that her wedding night 'was worse than I could ever have believed possible', and that he was the disappointing product of their sole union. He feared and loathed his errant father, yet also entirely imbibed his father's nostalgia for a Golden Age before the Great War: 'Everything that happened to my father, and his whole generation, after 1914, was a weary, skeletal epilogue', Aickman said, thus effectively doubling the weight of the post-war trauma that imbues his work.[34]

In 'The Swords', one of Aickman's weirdest and most poisonous works, a young travelling salesman is staying in revolting digs in Wolverhampton. There, he stumbles into a fairground to see a show that invites the sparse audience to plunge blunt, rusty swords into the body of a listless, passive showgirl. The narrator, having run away from this sadistic scene, is invited to spend £10 (a vast sum) on a private show only for this initiation into the adult sexual world to end in an utterly disturbing detail: 'I caught hold of her left arm by putting both my hands around her wrist, and tried to drag her up towards me ... I was still holding on to her hand and wrist with my two hands, and it took me quite some time to realize what had happened. What had happened was that I had pulled her left hand and wrist right off.'[35] The girl rushes away, clutching her severed arm and leaving a trail of curdled sexual shame. Sex is always difficult and phantasmatically violent in Aickman.

If 'The Swords' is eloquent about men's violence, many stories concern hapless male travellers ensnared by alluring succubi who might drag them out of their dreary constraint for a while but their moment of bliss carries a deathly price. It happens in Greece with two sirens in 'The Wine-Dark Sea', in Venice in 'Never Visit Venice', and on an unspecified island between England and Ireland in 'The View'. A man's serial marriages are routinely destroyed by a vicious sexual haunting in 'The Fetch', amongst the most explicit of his stories in reading the disturbances of the weird mode as an emanation of sexual dysfunction. Aickman shares absolutely Philip Larkin's diminished, disappointed post-war world, but adds to it *vagina dentata*.

Is the weird, then, ultimately a male mode of anxiety about the weird and wayward sisters who determine their fate? Lovecraft's sexual terror – most overt in 'The Dunwich Horror' – is part and parcel of his panic and disgust at the idea of racial inter-mixing. Some of this panic seeps into Aickman, too. Even in the recent revival, it has been noted that the author who coined the 'New Weird', M. John Harrison, often features female characters who suffer unnerving illnesses or are literally collapsing in decay at the touch of entropic male self-pity.[36] This is strongest in his extraordinary story, 'Running Down', another excoriating vision of England's post-war decline.[37] Harrison, deeply read in weird fiction, evokes these Aickmanesque sexual hauntings in stories that carry names like 'The Great God Pan', overtly tipping its hat to the tradition, a story in which magic rituals from the psychotic end of the 1960s leaves a toxic trail of illness, depression, hallucination and bizarre obtrusions from other realities. Magical possibilities curdle in cruel aftermaths amidst precisely detailed English landscapes in Harrison's short fiction: fantasy where fantasy is disallowed or cancelled.[38]

The weird mode may look like a symptomatic club of masculine anxiety, but in fact it is entirely possible to take another trajectory through from the *fin-de-siècle* to the present day to make women writers occupy the centre of weird fiction. Instead of Arthur Machen, we could start with Vernon Lee's *Hauntings* (1890), a Decadent collection that also explicitly eschews gothic tropes for psychology and strange, wayward turns of plot. The pioneer modernist of stream-of-consciousness techniques, May Sinclair, published *Uncanny Stories* in 1923, shimmering and enigmatic tales that emerge from the overlapping terrains of psychoanalysis (she was among the first in England to train in Freud), mysticism and psychical research.[39] At mid-century, as Sansom and Aickman scratched about in obscurity, the most wildly successful writers in this mode were Shirley Jackson in America and Daphne du Maurier in England. Both are routinely eclipsed because the weird connoisseur despises middle-brow success most of all, and yet du Maurier's exploration of twisted desire is entirely in keeping with the analysis of the weird story elaborated here. There is, Nina Auerbach suggests, a 'defining weirdness' about du Maurier that the domestication of her as 'author of *Rebecca*' tends to eclipse.[40] Cruel twists of desire abound from du Maurier's earliest short stories, which have been interpreted within a gothic frame.[41] Eventually, though, we return to the strangeness of Venice in du Maurier's 'Don't Look Now', of the art of wandering waywardly and getting lost in a city of ghosts, where weird sisters can spy the dead child and foresee the husband's death even as he tries to fend off their mannish oddity and psychical powers. Du Maurier's code-word for her same-sex desires was her 'Venetian' mood ('I glory in my Venice, when I am in a Venice mood' she wrote to one lover).[42] It allows one to reflect that this whole female lineage sketched out through the weird is also a 'lesbian' one, although many of the writers would have refused the identification. This reconfirms the weird as a twisting, labyrinthine mode, not an easily definable genre, and one that uses the bizarre and oneiric shifts of plot and tone to find ways of saying the unsayable. This is the reason it exists in fugitive, interstitial forms, and why it has been hidden for so long in histories of English literature. The revival, briefly called the New Weird and driven by M. John Harrison's and China Miéville's conviction that it can have potentially revolutionary possibilities, has made this sliver of interstitial writing visible anew for a time. It feels timely because it is a form highly responsive to the shifting ontology of what it means to be human in the twenty-first century.

Notes

1. H. P. Lovecraft, 'The Call of Cthulhu', in *Classic Horror Tales*, ed. R. Luckhurst (Oxford University Press, 2013), p. 49.
2. Edgar Allan Poe, 'The Philosophy of Composition', in *The Selected Writings of Edgar Allan Poe*, ed. G. R. Thompson (New York: Norton, 2004), pp. 675–84 (p. 677).
3. H. P. Lovecraft, 'Notes on Writing Weird Fiction', in *Miscellaneous Writings*, ed. S. T. Joshi (Sauk City: Arkham House, 1995), pp. 113–16 (p. 116).
4. See Robert Kenneth Jones, *The Shudder Pulps: A History of the Weird Menace Magazines of the 1930s* (West Linn, OR: Fax Collectors Editions, 1975).

5. Edmund Wilson, 'Tales of the Marvellous and Ridiculous', in *Classics and Commercials: A Literary Chronicle of the Forties* (London: Allen, 1951), p. 288.
6. See Bart Beaty, *Fredric Werthem and the Critique of Mass Culture* (Jackson: University of Mississippi Press, 2005).
7. Richard Hoggart, *The Uses of Literacy: Aspects of Working Class Life, with Special Reference to Publications and Entertainments* (London: Chatto & Windus, 1957), p. 205.
8. Martin Barker, *A Haunt of Fears: The Strange History of the British Horror Comics Campaign* (London: Pluto, 1984).
9. M. John Harrison, 'New Weird Discussions: The Creation of a Term', in *The New Weird*, ed. Jeff and Ann VanderMeer (San Francisco: Tachyon, 2008), p. 317.
10. Veronica Hollinger, 'Genre vs. Mode', in *The Oxford Handbook of Science Fiction*, ed. R. Latham (Oxford University Press, 2014), pp. 139–51 (p. 140).
11. H. P. Lovecraft, *Supernatural Horror in Literature* (New York: Dover, 1973), p. 15.
12. Lovecraft, letter to Farnsworth Wright, 5 July 1927, in H. P. Lovecraft, *Selected Letters, Volume II: 1925–29*, ed. A. Derleth and D. Wandrei (Sauk City: Arkham House, 1968), p. 150.
13. China Miéville, 'Weird Fiction', in *The Routledge Companion to Science Fiction*, ed. Mark Bould, Andrew Butler, Adam Roberts and Sherryl Vint (Abingdon: Routledge, 2009), pp. 510–15 (p. 511).
14. Arthur Machen, 'N', in *Tales of Horror and the Supernatural* (Horam, Sussex: Tartarus Press, 1998), p. 280. 'Intrusion fantasy' is discussed as a distinct sub-genre in Farah Mendlesohn, *Rhetorics of Fantasy* (Middletown: Wesleyan University Press, 2008).
15. See Christopher Partridge, *The Re-Enchantment of the West: Alternative Spiritualities, Sacralization, Popular Culture and Occulture* (London: T. & T. Clark, 2006).
16. Machen, 'The Inmost Light', *Tales of Horror and the Supernatural*, p. 154.
17. Quoted from the lengthy selection of citations of negative reviews in Machen's own 1916 preface to *The Great God Pan*, reprinted in Creation Books edition (London, 1996), p. 26.
18. Machen, *The Three Impostors*, ed. D. Trotter (London: Dent, 1995), p. 154.
19. Iain Sinclair, *Our Unknown Everywhere: Arthur Machen as Presence* (Newport: Three Impostors, 2013), pp. 9, 12, 20.
20. Sinclair, *Our Unknown Everywhere*, p. 28.
21. Arthur Machen, *The London Adventure; or, The Art of Wandering* (London: Martin Secker, 1924), pp. 48, 11.
22. See Simon Sadler, *The Situationist City* (Cambridge, MA: MIT Press, 1999).
23. Nicholas Royle, *Veering: A Theory of Literature* (Edinburgh University Press, 2011), pp. viii, 28.

24. For early reception, see Stephen Arata, 'A Universal Foreignness: Kipling in the Fin de Siècle', *English Literature in Transition*, 36.1 (1993), pp. 7–38.
25. Quotations from the opening paragraph of Rudyard Kipling, 'His Chance in Life', in *Plain Tales from the Hills*, ed. D. Trotter (London: Penguin, 1990), p. 91.
26. See Roger Luckhurst, *The Invention of Telepathy 1870–1900* (Oxford University Press, 2002), pp. 173–80.
27. Kipling, 'At the End of the Passage', in *Life's Handicap: Being Stories of Mine Own People* (London: Macmillan Pocket Edition, 1923), pp. 203, 204. Subsequent page references are given in parentheses in the text.
28. John Bayley, *The Short Story: Henry James to Elizabeth Bowen* (Hemel Hempstead: Harvester, 1988), pp. 66, 35.
29. Lana Hartman Landon, 'Walter de la Mare', in *British Short Fiction Writers, Dictionary of Literary Biography*, 162 (Detroit: Gale, 1996), p. 76.
30. Robert Aickman, 'Introduction', in *Fontana Book of Great Ghost Stories* (1964; London: Fontana, 1979), p. 7.
31. Cited in R. B. Russell, 'Introduction' to Robert Aickman and Elizabeth Jane Howard, *We Are For the Dark* (Leyburn: Tartarus Press, 2011), p. ix.
32. S. T. Joshi, *The Modern Weird Tale: A Critique of Horror Fiction* (Jefferson: McFarland, 2001), p. 222.
33. See Elizabeth Jane Howard, *Slipstream: A Memoir* (London: Macmillan, 2002), p. 179.
34. Robert Aickman, *The Attempted Rescue* (London: Gollancz, 1966), pp. 20 and 26.
35. Robert Aickman, 'The Swords', in *Cold Hand in Mine* (London: Faber & Faber, 2008), p. 23.
36. See Mark Bould, 'Old, Mean and Misanthropic: An Interview with M. John Harrison', in *Parietal Games: Critical Writings By and On M. John Harrison*, ed. M. Bould and M. Reid (London: Foundation Studies in Science Fiction, 2005), pp. 326–41.
37. For more detail on Harrison and this story in particular, see my essay 'Post-Imperial Melancholy and the New Wave in the 1970s', *Foundation*, 93 (2005), pp. 76–88.
38. His short stories are collected in M. John Harrison, *Things That Never Happen* (London: Gollancz, 2004).
39. For more detailed commentary on Lee and Sinclair, see my *The Invention of Telepathy* (Oxford University Press, 2002).
40. Nina Auerbach, *Daphne du Maurier: Haunted Heiress* (Philadelphia: University of Pennsylvania Press, 2000), p. 127.
41. See Avril Horner and Sue Zlosnik, *Daphne du Maurier: Writing, Identity and the Gothic Imagination* (London: Macmillan, 1998).
42. Cited in Auerbach, *Daphne du Maurier*, p. 157.

27

Experimentalism: Self-Reflexive and Postmodernist Stories

DAVID JAMES

'The short story is a young art', wrote Elizabeth Bowen in 1937: 'as we know it', she contends, 'it is the child of this century'. It sounds curious to think of short fiction as still in its infancy or at least early adolescence by mid-century, when we recall the form's earlier trailblazers such as Thomas Hardy, Henry James and, of course, Edgar Allan Poe. Bowen must therefore have had some other context of generic transformation in mind, one that affects the story 'as we know it' now, rather than as it has come to be known and traditionally valued. Modernism, in her account, changed the short story's conditions of possibility: it now 'may be said to stand at the edge of prose', not only because 'poetic tautness and clarity are so essential to it' but also because 'it is nearer drama than the novel' and nearer still to cinema, whose medium is 'itself busy with a technique'. Being 'of the same generation', both film and short stories 'have been accelerating together', such that for Bowen they continue to hold certain 'affinities' which are critically instructive: 'neither is sponsored by a tradition; both are, accordingly, free; both, still, are self-conscious, show a self-imposed discipline and regard for form'.[1]

Bowen draws the literary-historical net quite tight here. And one might question her characterization of short stories as modernism's progeny alone, their progression tied to parallel developments in other idiomatically twentieth-century artistic media. But her emphasis on the formally self-conscious and self-disciplining nature of such narratives would remain prescient in the decades to come. Beginning its map of transitions in the short story some twenty years after Bowen's Faber anthology, this chapter traces the aesthetic consequences of the genre's creative self-reflexivity across an era in which its increasing experimentalism contended at times with its increasing marginalization. However much the short story's popularity fluctuated, stylistic advances in the genre flourished after the Second World War. Writers from Britain and Ireland can't exactly be paralleled with the explicit modes of postmodern self-referentiality that shaped both the topics and the techniques of iconic North American experimentalists like John Barth and Donald Barthelme. Nonetheless, as they responded to earlier twentieth-century modernist innovations in perception, duration and interiority, writers finding a home with English presses in the 1950s, 1960s and beyond initiated radical renovations that weren't simply about 'continually blur[ring] the lines', as Charles May puts it, between short 'fiction and an analytical discourse about fiction'.[2] Though less ostentatious or self-analysing than their American contemporaries, perhaps, British and Irish writers offered varieties of compositional reflexivity that still tested the referential limits of fictional language, the very purpose of character and the world-making functions or fabrications of narrative itself.

National differences aside for a moment, though, to what extent might the short story be peculiarly suited to the central tenets of postmodernist thought and artistic practice? If postmodern culture paradigmatically 'values the fragment over the whole', in Richard Lee's words, 'the surface over the "depths," derivation over "originality"', this could well be 'one reason to value short fiction as the genre that speaks most directly to the parochial and local rather than the totalizing narratives of the novel'.[3] Certainly, post-war and contemporary short stories often capitalize on the fragmentary and protean nature of perceptual experiences. But simply to align this feature with postmodernism's hallmark opposition to conceptual, social and ideological forms of totality would be to miss what has remained so vital to short stories, even when they're being most adventurously experimental: the provision of miniature wholes of their own, irrespective of inconclusive or suspenseful endings. As Bowen herself proposed, the 'mark' to which the best short stories aspire is 'the completeness, or spherical perfection, latent in any story that is projected rightly'. She goes on to add that the 'story should have the valid central emotion and inner spontaneity of the lyric' and remain 'as composed, in the plastic sense, and as visual as a picture' (p. 14). Bowen's comparisons here anticipate not only H. E. Bates – who in his 1972 preface to the second edition of *The Modern Short Story* (1941) argued that 'the short story is to fiction what the lyric is to poetry', for in 'its finest mould the short story is, in fact, a prose poem' – but also the Argentine novelist, essayist and short story writer Julio Cortázar.[4] For Cortázar, the short story is akin to 'the idea of the sphere, the most perfect geometric form in the sense that it is entirely closed in on itself and each one of the infinite points of its surface are equidistant from the invisible central point'. This 'marvel of perfection that is the sphere as a geometrical shape' is Cortázar's exemplary analogy for a 'perfectly executed short story'. Unlike the novel – which in this model can only 'evoke the image of a polyhedron, of an enormous structure' – the short story 'tends, by definition, toward sphericity, to close in on itself'.[5]

In the end, these blueprints are intentionally suggestive rather than set in stone. Indeed, between such contrasting ways of imagining what the story can do – between spherical self-enclosure and disintegrative self-exposure, between the modernist will-to-integrity and the postmodern pursuit of fragmentariness – a whole spectrum of priorities abound for late twentieth-century writers who neither repudiate modernism's commitments entirely nor fully embrace postmodernism's mischievous involutions. What unites them, if anything, is the sense in which the 'short story', in Claire Larriere's terms, 'has always been, and will always be, a voice of rebellion'.[6] Parts do indeed tend to rebel against wholes in postmodern times. Stories appear not only 'rhizomatic, intertextual and anti-mimetic', in Luisa Rodriguez's phrase, 'but also seem to be under construction', insofar as 'their different components can be assembled and reassembled *ad infinitum*'.[7] Such are the obstacles to advancing a purely 'organic' conception of short fiction as a genre that integrates through its formal and figurative coherence alone the events upon which it so briefly – often inconclusively – concentrates the reader's attention.

Still, even that most hermeneutically daunting of writers, Samuel Beckett, has prompted some critics to see infrastructures where others see only indeterminacy. It might seem counterintuitive to trace something like Cortázar's 'architectural obligation' towards integrity in Beckett's short fiction, given the resolutely anti-representational impulse of his recursive, grammatically heterodox prose.[8] Nonetheless, certain designs do shadow the dissolution. Indeed, Hugh Kenner described Beckett's *Texts for Nothing* as a 'short work with no real subject but its own queer cohesion'.[9] And likewise, more recently, Mark Nixon pans back to view continuities across the idiosyncratic stages of Beckett's narrative *oeuvre*, suggesting that maybe we're not meant 'to view these prose pieces as separate, individual entities, but as an on-going corpus of writing circling around what *From an Abandoned Work* calls "all the variants of the one"'.[10]

Beckett is a key figure in the short story's post-war transition from modernism's formidable command of structure, image and epiphany to postmodernism's linguistic disintegration, thematic enigmas and self-ironizing exhibitionism. At the fulcrum of this phase lies *Texts for Nothing*, written originally in French between 1950 and 1951, before appearing in English in 1967. Devoid of depth of character and progression in any recognizable or consistent sense, these short prose pieces pre-empt the interpretive challenges that their own rhetorical density and digressions provoke. 'I never went looking for extravagant meanings', remarks the voice of Text I, laying down the gauntlet for readers early on by hinting at a stance they themselves might be better off assuming when entering the semantic maze to come.[11] In the ensuing pages, not only do signifiers become dysfunctional – 'words too, slow, slow, the subject dies before it comes to the verb, words are stopping too' – but the narratorial reflections on subsiding and diminishing vocabularies cut loose from any stable provenance (p. 8). In the end, 'what matter who's speaking' (p. 11), remarks the narrative voice of Text III, epigrammatically capturing Beckett's impulse to unyoke the self from the very medium through which selfhood normally achieves articulacy.

It's that 'self-reflexive concern' in Beckett's short prose 'with writing about writing', as Shira Wolosky puts it, which 'extends beyond the question of the status of fiction and the faculty of fiction-making, to implicate language as such', addressing in effect 'language as a question'.[12] This is perhaps Beckett's most tangible legacy for subsequent generations of short story writers, who may not aim to be so formally self-disintegrative, philosophically elusive or theologically allusive but who, as we shall later see, call attention to both the vexations and virtuosities of fiction-making itself. These writers would also inherit Beckett's tendency to undermine the short story's capacity for epiphanic resolution, shedding critical light, as *Texts* does, on the reprieve that epiphanies fleetingly offer speakers who are reaching for remnants of agency: 'Yes, there are moments, like this moment, when I seem almost restored to the feasible. Then it goes, all goes, and I'm far again, with a far story again, I wait for me afar for my story to begin, to end, and again this voice cannot be mine. That's where I'd go, if I could go, that's who I'd be, if I could be' (p. 19). A gossamer epiphany here seems aborted or held tantalizingly beyond the narrator's grasp, leaving the subject second-guessing his/her ability to consider self-determination, even self-expression, in 'feasible' terms. Agency turns out to be a 'far story', one in which the narrating self appears forever 'afar' – detached from both intention and effectuation.

Telling a story thus becomes more than a mere playful act of writerly self-dramatization for the Beckett of *Texts*. Potentially comic, at times existentially farcical, the quest for self-narratability also reveals a darker underside:

No, grave, I'll be grave, I'll close my ears, close my mouth and be grave. And when they open again it may be to hear a story, tell a story, in the true sense of the words, the word hear, the word tell, the word story, I have high hopes, a little story, with living creatures coming and going on a habitable earth crammed with the dead, a brief story, with night and day coming and going above, if they stretch that far, the words that remain, and I've high hopes, I give you my word. (p. 28)

Narrative conceived as a clarifying, affirming way of relating the self to the world, connecting 'living creatures' to 'a habitable earth', is reserved here as a wishful prospect, the object of speculation. But 'words' can and do 'remain' in Beckett's universe, even as 'high hopes' are dashed. Language's materiality – if only in the guise of 'a brief story' – endures, emblematizing how these short prose works, 'in denying self-denial and negating negativity', can actually give way 'to reproductive and inventive energy'.[13]

Samuel Beckett 'of all living is the man I believe most worth reading and listening to'.[14] Such was the opinion of the working-class avant-gardist, B. S. Johnson, who despaired of the reluctance of post-war intellectual culture to foster and reward adventurously innovative fiction. Johnson indeed quotes Beckett directly to reinforce his insistence that in the late twentieth century – with the lessons of modernism overtaken by more prevalent and popular forms of social realism – 'to find a form that accommodates the mess . . . is the task of the artist now' (p. 17). But Johnson was vocal about the way that searching for alternative modes comprised only half the battle: experimenters in the 1960s and 1970s needed a reading public prepared to recognize their advances. On this point – and speaking somewhat on behalf of other determined avant-gardists of the time such as Christine Brooke-Rose, Eve Figes and Ann Quin – Johnson was adamant that they 'have a right to expect that most readers should be open to new work, that there should be an audience in this country willing to try to understand and be sympathetic to what those few writers not shackled by tradition are trying to do and are doing' (p. 29). Affirming her own commitment to 'constant literary innovation', Figes concurred that 'old modes seem hopelessly inadequate'. She encapsulated something of the militant hostility that figures like Johnson, Alan Burns and Gabriel Josipovici shared towards the seeming complacency and inertia of mainstream British culture by declaring that what 'matters is that the writer should shock into awareness, startle, engage the attention' and 'above all . . . not engage in the trade of reassurance'.[15] In a more confessional and occasionally self-deprecating tenor, Burns admitted to 'writing short prose pieces in a rather pressured, affected style', formulating a 'snapshot method' that 'flirt[ed] with the notion of disconnection'. Disjuncture and imagistic brevity in this case sprung 'partly from an immature wish to shock', as Burns puts it, from an impulse to 'go to an extreme, make a break, an iconoclastic need to disrupt or cock a snook at the body of traditional literature'.[16] Opposing both a British public whose tastes appeared to be easily satiated by realism and reactionary writers easily dissuaded from taking risks, such experimenters – however much, like Johnson, they 'object[ed] to the word *experimental* being applied' to their work – represented a spirited revival, initiating a phase of narrative renovation in which short forms could play leading roles.[17]

Surveying the climate for such transformations, though, Johnson himself was far from upbeat. Unlike Elizabeth Bowen, who three decades earlier had deemed the 'present state of the short story' to be 'on the whole, healthy', reckoning that nowhere was the 'attack on convention ... being better directed' and that ultimately 'its prospects are good' (p. 18), Johnson observed with Zulfikar Ghose in the early 1960s that 'the form is in decline'. This was 'due to no fault inherent in the form'; again, audiences were to blame. 'The short story deserves', they urged, 'but seldom receives, the same precise attention to language as that given normally only to a poem'.[18] Johnson's own efforts, in collaboration with Ghose, to warrant that kind of attention are brisk and variable. His stories certainly do exhibit incredible verve at the level of the sentence, exploiting the present tense ('Perhaps It's These Hormones') and the rhetorically idiosyncratic personas or digressions that characterize first-person narration ('Clean Living is the Real Safeguard'). 'Broad Thoughts from a Home' is theatrically experimental: set out in typographically interruptive fashion, the dialogue in the main narrative is interspersed with explanatory annotations detailing who is being addressed and sketching reactions before they are vocalized. With these programme notes to its own creation, the story offers a meta-compositional anatomy lesson in the use of allusion, tone, sentiment, literary influence and scenic movement or selection. In a climactic yet self-mockingly '*Magnanimous gesture*', Johnson presents the reader 'with a choice of endings to the piece': four options, including one (the so-called '*Variable*') where 'the reader is invited to write his [sic] own ending in the space provided below. If this space is insufficient, the fly-leaf may be found a suitable place for any continuation.'[19] Such are the kind of metafictional antics for which Johnson, for all his seriousness about the future of a British avant-garde, became renowned. Breaking the fourth wall here – as he famously did the same year in the novel *Albert Angelo* – Johnson summons us to participate in the text's own terminal reformation, as though experimentation of a diegetic, structural or stylistic kind was simply not enough.

Yet a good deal of the pathos in Johnson's fiction is generated when his priorities shift from textual shock-tactics for the sake of artistic non-conformism towards frank observations of daily life. This social dimension to innovation in short fiction brings late twentieth-century avant-gardists into conjunction with writers with whom they might otherwise appear incompatible. Ian McEwan, for instance, was surely having a jibe at the textual autopsies of Brooke-Rose, J. G. Ballard and Johnson himself when insisting in 1978 that 'experimentation in its broadest and most viable sense should have less to do with formal factors like busting up your syntax or scrambling your page order, and more to do with content'. However, McEwan's proposed alternative – the 'representation of states of mind and the society that forms them' – actually complements what those writers whom he considers 'inaccessible and too often unrewarding' were pursuing all along.[20] Although less conspicuously responsive, at least superficially, to topical matters of immediate social concern, Leonora Carrington's mythopoeic stories reverberate with the wider implications and formations of mental states. Sometime partner of Max Ernst, and one of the longest surviving artists to have participated in the Surrealist movement, Carrington wrote 'small and concentrated potions', as Marina Warner describes them, 'in which the oddest elements from metaphysics and fantasy, daily routine and material life are simmered together'.[21] This encounter between the fantastic and the quotidian shapes 'The Seventh Horse' (written in New York in 1941, published in 1943). A husband (Philip) reproaches his wife (Mildred) for her imperious treatment of an ensnared horse in their garden, a creature called Havelino. Havelino's point of view then occupies the narrative before she instructs a fat, apparently flightless bird to spy on the couple as their relationship disintegrates, leaving Philip to take off in 'a great ecstasy of love' with a 'beautiful black mare' as though 'they were one creature'.[22] The successive shifts in narrative perspective and implied centres of sympathy are radically unpredictable, such that Carrington disorients the reader not only by fantastically blending different species and stylized events but also by perpetually displacing the stance of observation and articulation. As a writer who, when growing up, 'understood clearly and correctly that her parents meant to control every aspect of her life', Carrington challenges normative gender relations and familial hierarchies with suitably unruly manipulations of form.[23]

Entrapment also figures as the opening conceit of 'A Mexican Fairy Tale' (written in Mexico City in the early 1970s and published in 1975). Juan, a boy from San Juan, notices the pigs under his watch are scared by a plangent voice crying from inside a ruin. He goes off to implore a local patriarch, Don Pedro, for a ladder that will allow Juan to scale the ruin. The narrative swerves via the ensuing episode to Pedro's perspective: we're told that his 'family were afraid of him', while he in turn 'was terrified of his boss', a gangster figure 'who wore neck ties and dark glasses and lived in the town and owned a black motorcar'.[24] Meanwhile, the voice appealing to Juan turns out to be a hummingbird of sorts that morphs into 'a girl, a wind', causing Juan's pigs to faint 'with utmost fright' (p. 153). After instructing a cactus, doubling as a servant (Piu), to roast the pigs, 'the bird whirled so fast she turned into a rainbow and Juan saw her pour herself into the Pyramid of the Moon in a curve of all colours' (p. 154). Another servant, Black Mole, coerces Juan to devour all the pigs before then unsheathing a sword and slicing him up 'into small pieces just like Piu had sliced himself up to feed the pigs' (p. 154). We then switch scenes to Don Pedro in full masculinist swing, bellowing at his wife to bring dinner while his daughter María flinches 'behind a large maguey ... She thought: He's beating my mother. A thin yellow cat dashed past in terror. The cat is also afraid, if I go back he will beat me, perhaps he will kill me like a chicken' (p. 155). Led to the dismembered Juan by a dog she considers 'is an ancient', María proceeds to sew him back 'together with neat stitches' (p. 156). After Juan loses his heart, as 'a black vulture swooped out of the air, snatched the heart in its claws, and flew off toward the Pyramid of the Moon', María and Juan descend her father's ladder 'into the dark Earth' which then closes around them in the shape of a 'smile [that] is still there, a long crack in the hard clay' (pp. 156, 157). In a climactically accelerating sequence, Mole returns to set up a subterranean pyre upon which Juan and María jump to be burned as 'one whole being' who 'will return again to Earth' (p. 158). We're told in the final line: 'So this story has no end' (p. 158). Struck by the blur of telescoping events, Carrington's reader too might wonder whether a denouement is possible or even desirable. Her fantasy is structurally accumulative, for the sheer pace of merging scenes exceeds logical spatio-temporal parameters, often moving in a different tempo to characters' apparent desires and motivations.

Such are the exegetic challenges posed by Carrington's short fiction of which, like her paintings, she forever refused to offer her own interpretations. With compressed duration, segmented focus, and capriciously non-teleological development, her stories retool the very phenomenology of reading. They test our capacity to form mental pictures of rapidly captured oneiric realms, prioritizing fantastical thought-experiments over empathic engagement. By entering this 'inner world' of Carrington's '"hypnagogic vision" where consciousness and the unconscious merge', we're compelled to rethink what it means to visualize narrative through connected scenes and to entertain instead the short story as a rather impish mode that collects without necessarily synthesizing an ever-expanding array of entities and events.[25]

Derailing the reader's quest for correlations between parts and whole, points and sphere, is itself an effect of Carrington's Surrealist adventures, just as undoing the reader's assumptions about gender embodiment typified Angela Carter's own spectacular reanimation of fairy tale in the interests of critique. Subjected by Carter to transgressive and darkly satiric treatment in collections such as *Fireworks* (1974), *The Bloody Chamber* (1979) and *Black Venus* (1985), the ontological complexities, personal compromises and contradictions of sexual identity would occupy an increasingly central place for late twentieth-century writers responding to the legacies and diversifications of feminist politics. Carter was daring in her process of generic parody and adaptation, unflinching in her framing of eroticism and violation. Meanwhile, the young Ian McEwan would prove to be more tendentious still in his early psychopathologies of desire. It's not 'enough to talk about men and women in social terms', he reflected in 1983, not 'enough to be rational' about the relation of sexual self-identity to pleasure. This conviction plays out across two psychologically probing and unsettling volumes, *First Love, Last Rites* (1975) and *In Between the Sheets* (1978), in which McEwan dramatizes the sense that 'there is something intractable about the sexual imagination, and what you desire is not, very amenable to programmes of social change'.[26]

In the title story of his second collection, McEwan's protagonist, Stephen, is an audacious writer whose inventive artistic life is counterpointed with his stilted private life. He is 'terrified' by his wife's orgasms, and his sexual self-expression has become all but privatized.[27] Internalized desires are repressed but involuntarily resurface, initially when Stephen wakes in the opening sequence in the aftermath of a wet dream, and later when he feels compelled to acknowledge 'the experimentation in his writing, the lack of it in his life' (p. 100). This pursuit of polarities, whether emotional or intellectual, is a recognizable trope in McEwan's fiction. Across mid-career novels like *Black Dogs* (1992) and *Enduring Love* (1997), inward conflicts broaden out into antithetical worldviews: masculine rationality versus feminine intuitiveness; ontic versus phenomenal existence; the advancements of hard science versus the solace of spirituality. Some critics have regarded these positions, when grafted onto characters, as overly formulaic. But perhaps the short story is more suited to McEwan antinomies, since his condensed treatment of irreconcilable affects and incompatible behaviours amplifies rather than schematizes the psychological drama.

In the case of 'In Between the Sheets', McEwan admitted that he 'was uneasy about' Stephen 'pursuing his writing in a way that takes him away from any real relationship to a point when he is deeply fearful of women and their pleasure'. While this 'connection' may feel 'too simple', McEwan argued that 'short stories demand simple and incisive sets of oppositions'.[28] What's also incisive about this particular story is the disturbing force with which its perspective aligns us with Stephen's increasingly erotic if confused notions about his own daughter. On a night when his daughter has invited another girl – with whom she already appears to have a preciously intimate, semi-erotic friendship – for a sleepover, he hears his daughter make a sound that was 'so utterly familiar that only now as he advanced very cautiously along the hallway did he know it to be the background for all other sounds, the frame of all anxieties'.[29] We are led to the very brink of an appalling scenario in which a man's own sexual uncertainties are enacted upon or resolved by his daughter, but it emerges that her murmurs were nothing more than restlessness and he quickly reverts back to the role of a comforting father. This superficial closure is by no means corrective, still less reassuring: the afterglow of discomfiture lingers beyond the final lines. With an unbalanced protagonist focalizing the narrative, his 'frame of all anxieties' serves also as our principal frame of comprehension, consolidating the way that 'complicity as a condition of writing' in McEwan's world is also a tangible 'consequence of reading'.[30]

This may have been one of McEwan's most controversial stories, contributing to his being 'labelled as the chronicler of comically exaggerated states of mind', a connoisseur of the macabre.[31] But it wasn't his favourite. For that we need to consider 'To and Fro', which McEwan described as 'a fifty-five-page story condensed into about eight pages', making it 'more like a poem'.[32] Among his most stylistically adventurous, 'To and Fro' is once again premised on a simple opposition. A man lies in bed admiring the subtle contours and motion of his sleeping partner's physique, while being haunted by a prolonged nightmare in which his predatory colleague, Leech, stalks nocturnal thoughts of his workplace:

> If I can lie in the dark I can see in the dark pale skin on the fragile ridge of cheekbone, it carves a dog-leg shape in the dark. The deep-set eyes are open

and invisible. Through almost parted lips a point of light glints on saliva and tooth, the thick belt of hair blacker than the surrounding night. Sometimes I look at her and wonder who will die first, who will die first, you or me? The colossal weight of stillness, how many more hours? (pp. 107–8)

Reflections accumulate across paratactic clauses, sometimes connecting but sometimes diverging from each other in image and subject. This phrasing enables McEwan to simulate at the level of the sentence an alternation between observation and speculation, capturing mental modulations from fact to fear: 'First here comes Leech, no first here am I towards the end on one morning, reclining, sipping, private, and Leech comes by, salutes me, claps me on the back a cordial, vicious blow between the shoulder blades below the neck' (p. 108). Again the percussive syntax embodies and accentuates the visceral nature of the encounter: part of an ordinary routine, the macho greeting is predictable but no less predacious for being so expected. Towards the close, Leech appears to be insinuating himself into the narrator's psychic as well as physical life: 'Are we the same? Leech, are we? Leech stretches, answers, bats, pushes, pretends, consults, flatters, stoops, checks, poses, approaches, salutes, touches, examines, indicates, grips, murmurs, gazes, trembles, shakes, occurs, smiles, faintly, so very faintly, says, Open your . . . the warmth? . . . open your eyes, open your eyes' (p. 115). The list of counterpointing verbs condenses a day of workplace antics, postures and gestures into a single catalogue. External snapshots are all we have to build up a portrait of Leech's interiority, as mannerisms stand in for, or else only hint at, clear motives. McEwan thereby restricts characterization to a taxonomy of traits, while fulfilling that objective he would describe later in his career 'to represent, obviously in a very stylized way, what it's like to be thinking' and thereby to show 'how much our recollections can play into what we accept as reality – how much perception is distorted by will'.[33]

If such distortions are morally disarming for the reader, they often seem all the more so when arising from everyday circumstances. One specialist navigator of this quotidian terrain is Graham Swift, who returned to the short form with *England and Other Stories* (2014) after several decades of novel writing. It was Swift's first collection, though, *Learning to Swim* (1982), that singled him out as an experimenter who could take the short story into new existential and ethical domains precisely by bringing ordinary lives into disturbing close-up. In 'Seraglio', we follow a husband and wife on holiday in Istanbul, a vacation that's less of an escape or restorative break than a routine, one of their many habits – including excursions to theatres and upmarket restaurants – that distract from the brute reality of their childlessness. Their eight-year relationship is itself a 'story': his affair, early in their marriage, has never been disclosed. At the same time, he holds his wife accountable for the miscarriage that left her unable to conceive again, because he assumes that 'having suffered herself without reason, she wanted to be blamed for it'.[34] Against the toxic backdrop of this indictment, the man admits that 'this became our story: our loss and its recompense', the 'result' of which being that they 'lived on quite neutral terms with each other' (p. 8). At first glance, then, this narrative would appear to be a showcase of formal self-reflexivity: staging a couple who feel that they are 'not like real people' but rather 'like characters in a detective novel', waiting for the 'mystery to be solved' as to 'who killed our baby' (p. 9). But Swift is a metafictionist of more subtle intent, rarely infected by any postmodern eagerness to unpack technique for its own sake. Consequently, the self-referential aspect of storytelling isn't advertised but threaded instead into the ensuing drama – one part of the narrative's emotive whole, so to speak, rather than imposed and emblazoned from without – as the man reflects on how their contrived routine, 'like all stories, kept us from pain as well as boredom' (p. 9). The very poignancy of 'Seraglio' coincides with yet another level of self-consciousness: the man's awareness of their own tendency as a couple to indulge in the consolation of a selective and protective story about themselves. 'All stories are told', he admits, 'like this one, looking back at painful places which have become silhouettes, or looking forward, before you arrive, at scintillating facades' (p. 13).

In the title story of the collection, Swift shifts into a more detached third-person mode. With another semi-estranged couple as its focus, each imagining the directions their lives might have otherwise taken, 'Learning to Swim' retains the formality of 'Mr Singleton' and 'Mrs Singleton' to deal forensically with the inner lives of the pair it tracks. Swift counterpoints style and subject matter: choosing a kind of documentary impartiality to give us an insider's account of the destructive consequences of gendered expectations, mutual misunderstandings and undisclosed desires. We learn that 'Mrs Singleton had thought she was the shy, inexperienced, timid girl', and yet 'overnight she discovered that she wasn't this at all' when she realized she 'had to educate him into moments of passion, of self-forgetfulness which made her glow in her own achievement' (p. 196). Mr Singleton, meanwhile, is physically assured, a confident swimmer; but in other ways, he remains afflicted by his own sense of inadequacy. After a baffling and belittling experience of sitting through a symphony concert, 'as they filed out, he had almost wept because he felt like an insect', going as far as to suspect that Mrs Singleton 'had arranged the whole business so as to humiliate him' (p. 197). Conflicts between them erupt, but their expertise in domestic contestation appears to be matched by their agility in conceding ground, 'for though Mr Singleton inflicted the first blow he would always make himself more guilty than he made her suffer, and Mrs Singleton, though in pain herself, could not resist wanting to wrap him up safe when his own weakness and submissiveness showed and his body became liquid and soft against her' (p. 204). The symmetry in the sentence's construction here, moving between their respective perspectives, emulates the curious equilibrium the couple achieve through quarrels. Indeed, the story alternates in an even-handed manner between these viewpoints to trace a recurrent 'pattern' of accusation and supplication, finally pursuing them together like 'miners racing each other for deeper and deeper seams of guilt and recrimination' (p. 213). The story's very composition thereby reflects syntactically and performs structurally the geometric dance of combat and collusion it conveys.

This evocatively performative dimension to the short story has attracted writers like McEwan, Clive Sinclair and A. L. Kennedy, who have extended the genre's scope for exploring desire and sexual identity in idioms that range from the comic to the thoroughly disquieting. But for others, such as Jon McGregor, it's not so much erotic but visibly everyday realms that yield the most enlivening material, drawn as he is to 'the idea of lives pivoting on single moments and lives being changed by passing remarks and stray comments and accidents and coincidences'.[35] McGregor's 'In Winter the Sky' from his 2012 collection *This Isn't the Sort of Thing that Happens to Someone Like You*, works from the perspective of a man resolved to tell his partner of an incident in which he killed a drunk pedestrian straying onto the road. After the hit-and-run, he tries to bury the guilt. Reminiscent of the dissident typographic provocations of B. S. Johnson's work, McGregor's story uses a split layout which includes free indirect discourse focalized alternately by the man and woman set on the verso, and a typographically varied poem eulogizing the landscape's seasonal changes on the recto. With its oblique meditation on the story's regional setting –

> the beauty of this place is not in the names but the shapes
> the flatness / hugeness / completeness of the landscape.
> Only what is beneath the surface of the earth is hidden
> ~~(and sometimes not even that)~~
> and everything else is made visible beneath the sky[36]

– the unfolding, intermittently revised poem offers a prologue to the rest of McGregor's collection, whose stories are all attached to specific place-names even though their precise relation to these sites doesn't always seem prominent initially. Elsewhere in the volume, McGregor moves to the other end of the innovation spectrum, pulling back from the textual ruptures of 'In Winter the Sky' and 'The Last Ditch'. In the touching 'Airshow', we follow a commemorative visit to an airfield where the story's 'grandfather' served during the Second World War, a base 'from which squadrons had flown out to destroy whole towns; burying households beneath rubble, igniting crematorial fires, busting dams and drowning entire valleys. Some civilians were killed. The war was won' (p. 50). Throughout, McGregor's style matches in its laconic restraint the reserved and reflective presence of this elderly man: 'He lifted a finger, as though to point something out, and withdrew it. They walked along the verge for a short distance. The grandfather wasn't much inclined to talk about the place, it seemed' (pp. 49–50). The frequent commas create delicate pauses, slowing the momentum of the narration in tempo with the grandfather's poised state of contemplation. There is a quietness about McGregor's sparseness: his strategic minimalism isn't so much about leaving description out as leaving more silence in, working 'carefully', in Toni Morrison's phrase, 'with what is *in between* the words', with 'what is not said'.[37] Indeed, the whole impact of McGregor's story hinges on what the veteran doesn't mention:

> As they drove past, the grandfather turned to look at the people in the car-park. He didn't say anything. He watched them through the back window. He didn't say anything as they drove through Coningsby, past the church and over the river and out along the main road to the motorway. He waited until they got back to the house, and as they helped him out of the car he asked just what it was those people with the binoculars had thought they might be waiting to see. (p. 51)

Simple, denotative sentences beginning with the pronoun here together build a sense of suspense, delaying the point at which this seemingly preoccupied man might give us an insight into what he's been thinking up until now. Inviting us to project bereavement or trauma onto silence and inscrutability, the story inventively refuses our access to the emotional interiority of its focal character. Intensity thus coexists with, or is born out of, incomprehension, even though events themselves are easy to follow as the story plays out against the backdrop of an unexceptional visit. Tracking the grandfather closely yet entirely from the outside, the narrative's form encourages us to feel aligned and almost in touch with his perspective on events when in fact we're witnessing an enigma – at the end leaving us to wonder what it is, as readers, we 'might be waiting to see'.

Form itself has a plot of its own to relay in cases like this, as in many of those stories surveyed above. Which reminds us of Cortázar's praise of the short story's *sphericity*: its enclosing, economical form is not so much the container as the catalyst for what makes its narrative so impactful. Although the appeal of overtly self-conscious experimentation may have gradually waned in recent years, writers like McGregor epitomize how an emerging generation is no less stylistically innovative than its late-modernist and postmodern predecessors. The genre's longer trajectory after mid-century reveals that it has moved from being a metafictional testimony to its own perpetual reconstruction towards a form that ingeniously enfolds and enacts what it shows – without compromising the dramatic immediacy that makes short stories so deliciously or disturbingly suspenseful in the first place.

Notes

1. Elizabeth Bowen, 'Introduction: The Short Story', in *The Faber Book of Modern Stories*, ed. Bowen (London: Faber & Faber, 1937), p. 7. Subsequent page references to this edition are given in parentheses in the text.
2. Charles E. May, *The Short Story: The Reality of Artifice* (New York: Twayne, 1995), p. 89.
3. Richard E. Lee, 'Crippled by the Truth: Oracular Pronouncements, Titillating Titles, and the Postmodern Ethic', in *The Postmodern Short Story: Forms and Issues*, ed. Farhat Iftekharrudin, Joseph Boyden, Mary Rohrberger and Jaie Claudet (Westport, CT: Praeger, 2003), p. 109.
4. H. E. Bates, 'Preface to the New Edition', *The Modern Short Story: A Critical Survey* (1941; London: Michael Joseph, 1972), p. 12.
5. Julio Cortázar, 'Los caminos de un escritor' ['The paths of a writer'], translated by María del Pilar Blanco, from *Clases de Literatura, Berkeley, 1980* (Mexico City: Alfaguara, 2013), p. 30.
6. Claire Larriere, 'The Future of the Short Story: A Tentative Approach', in *The Tales We Tell: Perspectives on the Short Story*, ed. Barbara Lounsberry, Susan Lohafer, Mary Rohrberger, Stephen Pett and R. C. Feddersen (Westport, CT: Greenwood Press, 1998), pp. 195–200 (p. 196).
7. Luisa María González Rodriguez, 'Intertextuality and Collage in Barthelme's Short Fiction', in *Short Story Theories: A Twenty-First Century Perspective*, ed. Viorica Pâtea (Amsterdam: Rodopi, 2012), pp. 249–50.
8. Cortázar, 'Los caminos de un escritor', p. 31.

9. Hugh Kenner, *A Reader's Guide to Samuel Beckett* (London: Thames & Hudson, 1973), p. 119.
10. Mark Nixon, 'Preface', in *Texts for Nothing and Other Shorter Prose, 1950–1976*, ed. Nixon (London: Faber & Faber, 2010), p. viii.
11. Samuel Beckett, *Texts for Nothing*, in *Texts for Nothing and Other Shorter Prose*, ed. Nixon, p. 4. Subsequent page references are given in parentheses in the text.
12. Shira Wolosky, 'The Negative Way: Samuel Beckett's *Texts for Nothing*', *New Literary History*, 22.1 (Winter 1991), pp. 213–30 (p. 215).
13. Wolosky, 'The Negative Way', p. 227.
14. B. S. Johnson, *Aren't You Rather Young to be Writing Your Memoirs?* (London: Hutchinson, 1973), p. 17. Subsequent page references are given in parentheses in the text.
15. Eva Figes, 'Note', in *Beyond the Words: Eleven Writers in Search of a New Fiction*, ed. Giles Gordon (London: Hutchinson, 1975), p. 113.
16. Alan Burns, 'Essay', in *Beyond the Words*, pp. 63, 64.
17. Johnson, *Aren't You Rather Young*, p. 19.
18. B. S. Johnson and Zulfikar Ghose, *Statement Against Corpses* (London: Constable, 1964), p. 7.
19. B. S. Johnson, 'Broad Thoughts from a Home', in *Statement Against Corpses*, p. 75.
20. Ian McEwan, 'The State of Fiction: A Symposium', *The New Review*, 5.1 (1978), p. 51.
21. Marina Warner, 'Introduction', in Leonora Carrington, *The Seventh Horse and Other Tales*, translated by Katherine Talbot and Anthony Kerrigan (London: Virago, 1989), pp. i–xiii (p. xii).
22. Leonora Carrington, 'The Seventh Horse', in *The Seventh Horse*, p. 71.
23. Susan L. Aberth, *Leonora Carrington: Surrealism, Alchemy, and Art* (Farnham: Lund Humphries, 2010), p. 28.
24. Carrington, 'A Mexican Fairy Tale', in *The Seventh Horse*, p. 152. Subsequent page references are given in parentheses in the text.
25. Warner, 'Introduction', p. ii.
26. John Haffenden, 'Ian McEwan' (1983), in *Conversations with Ian McEwan*, ed. Ryan Roberts (Jackson: University of Mississippi Press, 2010), pp. 26–46 (pp. 35, 36).
27. Ian McEwan, 'In Between the Sheets', in *In Between the Sheets and Other Stories* (London: Jonathan Cape, 1978), p. 98. All quotations from McEwan's stories are from this work, with subsequent page references given in parentheses in the text.
28. Haffenden, 'Ian McEwan', p. 29.
29. McEwan, 'In Between the Sheets', p. 104.
30. Kiernan Ryan, *Ian McEwan* (Tavistock: Northcote House, 1994), p. 18.

31. Haffenden, 'Ian McEwan', p. 30.
32. Christopher Ricks, 'Adolescence and After' (1979), in *Conversations with Ian McEwan*, p. 24.
33. McEwan, interview with Zadie Smith, *The Believer*, 3.6 (August 2005), p. 50.
34. Graham Swift, 'Seraglio', in *Learning to Swim and Other Stories* (1982; London: Picador, 2010), p. 7. Subsequent page references to this edition are given in parentheses in the text.
35. Jon McGregor, interview by Caroline Edwards, *Contemporary Literature*, 51.2 (Summer 2010), pp. 220–1.
36. Jon McGregor, *This Isn't the Sort of Thing that Happens to Someone Like You* (London: Bloomsbury, 2012), p. 21. Subsequent page references to this edition are given in parentheses in the text.
37. Elissa Schappell, 'Toni Morrison: The Art of Fiction' (1992), reprinted in Carolyn C. Denard, ed., *Toni Morrison: Conversations* (Jackson: University Press of Mississippi, 2008), p. 66.

28

Satirical Stories: Estrangement and Social Critique

SANDIE BYRNE

The widely held view that the short story is a better vehicle than the novel for the expression of alienation from or tension with dominant or normative social values deserves particular scrutiny in connection with satire. Indeed, it might be expected that the satirical short story would be especially suited to an oppositional or political stance. Satirical short stories of the nineteenth century, however, are rarely strongly or stridently adversarial.

Helmut Gerber asserts that writers of the nineteenth and early twentieth centuries observed, represented and commented on political and cultural events and movements, in ways 'just as sensitive to the world they lived in as writers are now and just as concerned with discovering the appropriate artistic form for the raw material the times offered the artist'.[1] He finds that writers of nineteenth-century short stories had 'perhaps a more specific rebellious spirit', since they had 'satisfactory labels with which to identify an enemy: villa-ism, the President of the Immortals, Mrs Grundy, Fleet Street, Circulating, and all the other symbols of life-denying, nay-saying forces'.[2]

These enemies are the targets of novels, a play, and non-fiction polemic rather than short stories (Thomas Hardy, *Tess of the d'Urbervilles* (1891/2); Thomas Morton, *Speed the Plough* (1798); George Moore, 'Literature at Nurse, or Circulating Morals' (1885)), and it is significant that they are 'satisfactory labels': abstractions, fictions and metonyms rather than named individuals or groups. Whilst satire flourished in the nineteenth century, in journalism, pamphlets and poetry, particularly in periodicals such as *Punch, or the London Charivari* (launched 1841), *Fun* (1861) and *Judy, or the London Serio-comic Journal* (1867), short stories of the period (with some notable exceptions) more often used parody, burlesque or pastiche. Characteristic of pastiche and travesty in periodicals is the two-part version of the stories in George Egerton's

(Mary Chavelita Dunne Bright) *Keynotes* (1893), particularly 'A Cross-Line' in a series titled 'She-notes', by 'Borgia Smudgiton' with 'Japanese fan [sic] de siècle illustrations by Mortarthurio Whiskersly'.[3]

Victorian and early twentieth-century periodicals and albums also ran a lively commerce in author-to-author pastiche skits. Anthony Trollope, for example, mimics Bret Harte in 'Never, never – Never, never' (1875) and Max Beerbohm's *Christmas Garland* (1912) imitates the style of Henry James, Rudyard Kipling, A. C. Benson, H. G. Wells, G. K. Chesterton, Thomas Hardy, Frank Harris, Arnold Bennett, John Galsworthy, G. S. Street, Joseph Conrad, Edmund Gosse, Hillaire Belloc, George Bernard Shaw, Maurice Hewlitt, George Moore and George Meredith.[4] The popularity of Conan Doyle's Holmes stories soon engendered its own pastiche industry, for example Allan Ramsay's 'The Adventure of the Table Foot' (1894) starring Thinlock Bones.[5] The personal appearance, habits and prejudices of authors also become targets of satire, for example the representation in Vernon Lee's (Violet Paget) 'Lady Tal' (1911) of Henry James as Jervase Marion, an etiolated middle-aged author who cannot believe a woman capable of writing a serious novel. Whereas Beerbohm's pastiches provide the pleasure of amused recognition, 'Lady Tal' is more than a humorous portrait of the artist, but satirizes the construction of identity, particularly female identity, through kaleidoscopic speculation, gossip, misunderstanding and misinterpretation, the fragments of which are never resolved by authorial revelation of the 'true' self of Lady Tal.

Caricature of authors was endemic in the twentieth century, for example, Oscar Wilde in Ella Hepworth Dixon's 'The World's Slow Stain', from *One Doubtful Hour* (1904); George Bernard Shaw as Sherard Blaw in H. H. Munro's (Saki) 'The Infernal Parliament', from *The Square Egg and Other Sketches* (1929) and elsewhere in his work; and Ezra Pound as Archibald Cox in Richard Aldington's 'Nobody's Baby', from *Soft Answers* (1932). Even more enduringly popular has been pastiche of generic rather than individual authors' tropes and styles, as a vehicle for social critique. Trollope's 'Not if I Know it' (1882) mimics and inverts the conventions of Christmas stories of redemption and forgiveness by making the conventional change-of-heart tale seem to be based entirely on the profit motive, a trope anticipated by *Punch* several decades before, in its brief pastiche of the denouements of commercial Christmas stories, 'Christmas Books for Men of Business' (1847). Trollope's 'John Bull on the Guadalquivir' (1860) is a cringe-inducing satire of English materialism, vulgarity and xenophobia in a mistaken-identity tale, while 'Christmas at Thompson Hall' (1876) uses the conventions of farce to satirize sexual anxieties and to expose social forces that exaggerate the import of a harmless mistake (a respectable woman going into the wrong bedroom) to that of a shameful sexual misdemeanour. Trollope burlesques pseudo-medievalism in 'The Gentle Euphemia' (1866); Dickens pokes fun at sentimental accounts of courting couples in *Sketches of Young Couples* (1840), and of young men in *Sketches of Young Gentlemen* (1838).

In addition to producing satirical portraits of real writers and their styles, nineteenth-century humorous short fiction continued the tradition of employing stereotypes and stock characters. Oscar Wilde borrows off-the-shelf Americans for 'The Canterville Ghost' (1887) to represent national characteristics, both negative and positive: materialism, pragmatism, lack of imagination and bad taste, in opposition to English sensitivity to the products, people, traditions and ideals of the past; and practicality, kindness and energy, in opposition to the hidebound and class-riddled English.

George Gissing's characters are neither stereotypes nor stock, but his target is also British society. His stories anticipate satirical short fiction of the later twentieth century, holding up to censure and ridicule the dogged imposition of outworn social mores in 'The Scrupulous Father' (1900) and hypocrisy in 'The Pessimist of Plato Road' (1894). Satire of editorial and publishing practice in Gissing's 'The Lady of the Dedication' (1882) anticipates one of the specific targets of twentieth-century short fiction: the media. The critical reception of his turn to short stories was mixed: *The Times* thanked him for the three out of thirty stories that ended happily, and noted his new system of aggravating the reader by instead of giving a gloomy ending giving none at all;[6] *The Bookman* congratulated him on making rapid strides towards a high place as a writer of short stories, and observed that there were no wasted words or preambles in his straightforward and forcible narratives.[7]

At the turn of the century, Saki critiques 'civilized' urban Edwardian adult society with characters estranged from or outside that society. Children reveal the hypocrisies and cruelties of cold-hearted adults in 'The Lumber Room' (1914), mercilessly torment the weak in 'The Open Window' (1914), get the upper-hand on the patronizing or duplicitous in 'The Boar-Pig' (1914) or are coolly indifferent to the gruesome end of their tormentors, as in 'Sredni Vashtar' (1911). Animals reveal nasty little secrets in 'Tobermory' (1911) or are agents of revenge for the unloved child ('Sredni Vashtar') or on the dull in 'The Lull' (1914). Most characteristically, charming, languorous youths effortlessly change into murderous werewolves in 'Gabriel-Ernest' (1909) or glide between the lazily bored and the needle-sharp (Reginald in

Reginald (1904) and *Reginald in Russia* (1910) and Clovis in *The Chronicles of Clovis* (1911)). Vain and effete, these characters turn two activities into artforms, dressing and living off the less deserving (that is, the less young, attractive, witty or greedy). Callousness seems to link the savage wit of one to the blood-thirstiness of the other, but the verbal satire of the former occasionally has a social function, as when Reginald asks a duchess in mid-platitude whether she has ever walked the Embankment on a winter night in 'Reginald at the Theatre' (1904). More sustained satire is provided in 'Cousin Teresa' (1914), whose joint target is the fatuity of music-hall numbers, and the honours system.

The media, war, gender relations and the British class system each become a target of twentieth- and twenty-first-century short fiction, but as in the nineteenth century the objects are more often general and social than specific: the life-denying forces of moral, mental, emotional and aesthetic inertia. Dennis Vannatta asserts that the short story, like lyric poetry, has always seemed 'more suited to the dramatization of individual emotional and psychological concerns' than to wider issues, adding that perhaps few of us would 'want to read serious dramatizing of the problems of, say, socialized medicine'.[8] Twentieth-century short fiction does represent precisely that, but just as often with broad-brush facetious and farcical comedy than with direct statement or sharp satire.

Nineteenth- and early twentieth-century satire of publishing becomes, in late twentieth-century short stories, satire of the television and film industry. Evelyn Waugh satirizes the form of film scripts in his early story 'The Balance' (1926) and the insanity of the all-powerful producer and film-scripting-by-committee in 'Excursion in Reality' (1932); Malcolm Bradbury's 'Who Do You Think You Are?' (1976) satirizes TV panel and reality shows through a cast of shallow, vain and meretricious 'experts' whose immersion in theories makes action barren and identity and authenticity impossible. Martin Amis's 'Career Move' (1992) satirizes by inversion, making poets the recipients of large advances, media attention, and courtship by agents and film companies, while script-writing doesn't pay. A sonnet opens in 437 theatres and takes £17 million in the first weekend, whereas action film-scripts are taken by laptop-produced broadsheets and obscure pamphlets. The author of *Offensive from Quasar 13* eventually receives a cheque for £12.50, which bounces. Poets don't have it all their own way, however. Their work is subject to the familiar process of intervention, interference and disassembling. Though the medium changes, the same forces of greed, philistinism, vanity and envy are shown to outweigh artistic considerations.

The satirical representation of war and violent conflict in short fiction does not necessarily satirize armed combat. Alun Lewis's 'The Last Inspection' (1942) takes place in a military railway depot where men are preparing for the inspection of a new line. Because the officers linger too long over speeches and toasts to victory at a retirement lunch for a brigadier who has done very little for the war effort, the inspection is cancelled. The hard-worked men are cynical but jovial. When they return the primped engine to the shed, one of them learns that there is a telegram for him. He turns grey at the thought of his wife and children in Shoreditch. '"Oh Christ," said Fred. "Oh Christ. Oh Christ"'.[9] There is no elaboration about the disparity between the lives of the officers and the men, and no authorial intervention to emphasize the message that civilians as well as combatants suffer in wartime; the story speaks for itself.

The 'Troubles' in Ireland have supplied material for short fiction as well as for better-known drama and novels. Frank O'Connor's 'Guests of the Nation', published under the name Michael O'Donovan in 1931, satirizes unthinking bloodshed by showing the difficulty of executing long-term British hostages who have become humanized to their captors. Flann O'Brien's 'The Martyr's Crown' (1950) reduces the fight for nationhood to a farcical pub story, and martyrs who die for Ireland's freedom to a woman who (allegedly) has sex for the cause, or at least to prevent a house search. Satire merges with black humour in John Morrow's 'Place: Belfast/Time: 1984/ Scene: The Only Pub' (1979). Whilst watching the inauguration ceremony of Ireland's new leader on TV, the narrator admiringly reminisces about the stages of 'The Bishop's Game' (following the idea of a sequence of moves in chess), which got the new leader into place. In retaliation for the mistaken bombing of a school bus, there was an attack that killed the leader's wife. Knowing that her death has little propaganda value, the leader shot her dogs, knowing also that in Crufts week this will gain English sympathy. Dog lovers, led by Peter Hain under the tricolour, marched on Downing Street. Car workers held a mourning strike and a special capital punishment bill was rushed through so that two Protestants could be hanged and, in 1984, a declaration of intent withdrawn. During the monologue, the narrator warns his auditor to watch what he says, since you never know who's listening.

Future imagined wars have also been the object of satire, as, for example, those brought about by unregulated technology in H. G. Wells's dystopic scientific romances, and the stories of Martin Amis. The introduction to *Einstein's Monsters* (1987), 'Thinkability', is a powerful, thoughtful polemic, which offers no more solution to the threat of nuclear war than the imperative to *think*. The five stories dramatize the stages from nuclear anxieties to nuclear aftermath. Echoing Wyndham Lewis's *The Wild Body*, Amis's author's note suggests that humankind is less than our idealized illusion of the human and humane: we are as much Einstein's monsters as are nuclear weapons. Amis acknowledges a debt to J. G. Ballard for 'The Time Disease', about a post-apocalyptic world in which tedium is courted and excitement avoided. To catch time is to de-age.

Like Amis and Ian McEwan, who were once bracketed as 'neo-nasties' for their representations of horrors and perversities, Fay Weldon and Angela Carter have included the violent, the shocking and the supernatural. The two represent opposed modes of fictionalizing gender relations and inequalities. Weldon's astringent short fictions depict women and men in permutations of the roles of victim, martyr, enemy, ally, exploiter and oppressor. Characterization is broad brush-stroke and plot-driven; more important are the power relations, uneasy alliances and conflicts between characters, and the working-out of the situations that grow out of those relations. The style of the narratives is often stripped, staccato and detached, comprising short, often declarative, sentences, many aphoristic or gnomic, interspersed with longer exposition.

Siân Mile characterizes Weldon's fiction as feminist punk, an interventionist endeavour perpetrated in 'transitory revolting gestures'.[10] These gestures dramatize what Finuala Dowling calls the discontent of women not as neurotic lamentations of maladjusted individuals, but as 'a response to a social structure in which women are systematically dominated, exploited and oppressed'.[11] 'Alopecia' (1976) in *Watching Me, Watching You* (1981) is one of many stories which whilst representing men as oppressors and abusers does not as a corollary represent women as faultless or innocent. Had the women who noticed Erica's hair-loss had a sense of sisterhood, and not dismissed it as alopecia, the cycle of abuse would not have continued. Ironically, the woman most in denial about Erica's abuse, her friend Maureen, marries Erica's abusive husband. Meg, the newly wed young woman in the title story of *Polaris and Other Stories* (1985), has a strong sense of herself as wife and her responsibilities to her husband, Timmy, their home and his dog. While Timmy is away on a tour of duty in a nuclear submarine, Meg, like the other wives, envisages him in danger, in cramped, difficult conditions, and feels that it is her part to be self-sufficient and austere whilst working on their unfinished and uncomfortable isolated house. In fact the crew have made a comfortable domestic environment and spend much of their time preparing and eating gourmet meals. A more experienced naval wife, Zelda, who could and should be a supportive friend to Meg, is at best an ambivalent ally, counselling Meg to think only of Timmy and put his needs first, yet introducing her to the rakish Tony. In 'Down the Clinical Disco' (1991), Weldon echoes Waugh's distrust of state-institution psychiatry, through two people deemed insane, who have learned how to perform 'normality', particularly in terms of gender-appropriate behaviour, and do so obsessively, always aware that they are observed, determined not to be returned to Broadmoor.

Angela Carter's narrative blocks are folk- and fairy-tale-like, but the simple bases of the stories of *The Bloody Chamber* (1979) conceal sophisticated structures. Carnival elements of violence, cruelty and transgression often involve inversions of power so that the young, seemingly powerless girls growing into their sexual power can tame or destroy the powerful males, in for example, 'The Erl King' (1977) and 'The Company of Wolves' (1977), or are saved by an older woman, as in 'The Bloody Chamber' (1979), or reveal themselves to be akin to the wolf/tiger, as in 'The Tiger's Bride' (1979). Each represents a transformation of the conventional victim. Whereas some of Weldon's men may be called beasts in the loosest sense, Carter represents the alien and otherness of the male as animal or fantastical. This paradoxically inverts the usual association of the female with Nature and requires the women to employ against the males qualities of intelligence and reason not conventionally associated with fairy-tale heroines. Carter's successful heroines refuse the female persona established by Sade's prototype masochist-martyr Justine, which she deplores in *The Sadeian Woman* (1979).

In the nineteenth century, Trollope and Gissing used realist frameworks with plausible characterizations to make conventions, hypocrisies and habits of mind targets of satire. The ills are social, but succumbing to them is (at least to an extent) a matter of individual choice. In Wyndham Lewis's fictions, the humanity of the individual is eroded by the animal-instinctual, rendering futile any representation of the individual in conventional modes of characterization, aiming at psychological depth. In this deployment of puppets and grotesques, Lewis's shorter fictions may be the ancestors of stories by Martin Amis and Will Self, though in other ways the stories could hardly be more different.

It can be difficult to discuss the short stories of authors who also wrote in other genres without discussing the authors' styles, themes and subjects as a whole. This is particularly true of Wyndham Lewis, a point that extends to his visual as well as his verbal art, since he offered painting and writing as part of the same satiric enterprise. Lewis's *BLAST 1* manifesto (1914) gave, within its bullet-point fusillade of things to be blasted, humour: 'Quack English drug for stupidity and sleepiness'. It 'blessed', however, specifically English satirical humour: 'great barbarous weapon of the genius among races', especially Jonathan Swift, for his 'solemn bleak wisdom of laughter'.[12] 'Constantinople our Star' in *BLAST* 2 (July 1915) asserts that 'The English "Sense of Humour" is the greatest enemy of England', far worse than that of 'poor' Germany. It is a 'perpetual, soft, self-indulgent (often maudlin) hysteria.'[13]

In his pamphlet 'Satire and Fiction' (1930), Lewis insists that satire is degraded if it becomes moral, because moral judgements are constantly changing, and ethics are tied to religion. Whilst deploring the substitution in the post-First World War world of moral with political and economic values, Lewis argues that these should not be the specific targets of satire. Satire need not have specific targets; it need not be in opposition to, or for, anything. He asked,

> how can satire stand without the moral sanction? you may ask. For satire can only exist in contrast to something else [. . . .] 'satire' for *its own sake* [. . .] is possible [. . . .] Satire and laughter are ugly, but essential: *'laughter'* [. . .] has a function [. . .] similar to art. It is the preserver much more than the destroyer. And, in a sense, *everyone* should be laughed at or else *no one* should be laughed at. It seems that ultimately that is the alternative.[14]

In 'Studies in the Art of Laughter', Lewis insists that satire works on the surface, without 'the hot innards of Freud-infected art'; it is 'metallic' and 'external'; it is 'very *cold'*.[15]

In his capacity as 'The Enemy', Lewis identifies and highlights moral problems, but his short stories, collected in *The Wild Body: A Soldier of Humour and Other Stories* (1927), *Rotting Hill* (1957) and the posthumously published *Unlucky for Pringle: Unpublished and Other Stories* (1973), provide no character dialogue, interior monologue, or narrative voice to point out the moral or offer solutions: they are essays in a new human mathematic.[16]

'Cantleman's Spring-Mate' (1917) was deemed offensive by the American authorities, who invoked Section 211 of the US Criminal Code (preventing the distribution of obscene material). The offending section was a scene in which Cantleman, an officer soon to go to the Front, rapes/seduces a woman, Stella. The episode takes place in a section infused with the images of awakening sexuality and sensuality of spring, which compels plant- and animal-life to copulation and fecundity. Cantleman cannot escape the overmastering force, the 'sex-hunger' that he has seen impel a sow to a hog. The story suggests that, equally bestial, humankind is similarly compelled to acts of both sex and power, but is enervated because it clothes the sex-drive and will-to-power in romantic illusions. Cantleman has been reading Hardy's *The Trumpet-Major*, set, like the story, during wartime, but his perception of nature is far from that of Hardy's characters, and Lewis's association of Stella with nature is far from that of Hardy's of women and nature in *Tess of the D'Urbervilles* and other fiction. The woman is associated with the compulsive force of Nature: her child-bearing hips have 'animal fullness',[17] and she has the 'amplitude and flatness of a mare'; 'With a treachery worthy of a Hun, Nature tempted him towards her' (p. 42). Cantleman decides that women are contaminated with Nature's hostile power and so may be treated as spies or enemies, and feels that in Stella's body he is 'raiding the bowels of Nature'. As Stella puts her arms around his neck when he gives her a ring, he feels that 'consent' flows up into Stella's body from 'all the veins of the landscape' (pp. 42–3). This act is made parallel to a later violent act of war: 'When he beat a German's brain out it was with the same impartial malignity that he had displayed in the English night with his Spring-mate' (p. 43).

The Wild Body includes rewritten versions as well as new stories, loosely tied together as a series of Rabelaisian adventures in Brittany and in the Basque region. The narrator is Ker-Orr, whose function is to encounter and be the 'showman' of the antics of the plebiscite 'puppets' represented as base, without aesthetic sense or intellect; and the more animalistic, the more mechanistic. In 'Inferior Religions', one of the essays accompanying the stories, Lewis explains that their daily round, in hotel or restaurant, is no less circumscribed than that of a donkey powering a wheel. The first story in the collection, 'A Soldier of Humour' (1917), completed at the front, during the Battle of Messines Ridge, is set in Bayonne, a Breton city made representative of modernity's commercialism and consumption. Faced with a choice of hotels – the Fonda del Universo and the Fonda del Mondo – Ker-Orr finds that they are identically strange: constructed of glass and glaring surfaces, saturated in harsh revealing light. In this glare, everything in the hotel presents itself as 'the goods' yet is gratuitous and cheap, including an inhabitant, Valmore, a Frenchman who has adopted Americanism. Valmore insolently assumes an air of superiority that Ker-Orr resents, casting himself as the indigenous 'Redskin' and Valmore as the colonizing force about to overcome his tribe. Their relationship perhaps represents British resentment of post-war indebtedness to America and fear of cultural imperialism manifest in American commodities and fashions that were flooding Britain when the story was redrafted. Having left Bayonne, Ker-Orr books into a hotel in Galicia, where he is allotted an airless, windowless cupboard, and finds that Valmore is the owner. He recruits three 'authentic' Americans as his 'army' for an 'operation' to triumph over Valmore by forcing him to defer to the Englishman, but in order to keep them to the plan, Ker-Orr has to try to detach them from their fascination with a set of pornographic pictures. As Ker-Orr watches, he registers that the language of battle has been infiltrated by the register of performance in his mind: 'the stage analogy affected me [. . .] I must await my cue [. . .] I was the great star' and he too fans out the pornographic cards.[18] The American commodification and reification has affected him and he is as much a role-player as Valmore. The 'triumph' is merely a bottle of champagne at Valmore's expense and three numbers played by the orchestra of English light comedy music.

In 'The Rot', in *Rotting Hill* (1951), whose title is attributed to Ezra Pound, dry rot afflicting a Notting Hill flat, caused by bombs and six years of standing empty, and the inefficiency of the electricians and painters brought in to repair it, stands for the rot in post-war British society, but so also does the client, 'Mr Lewis'. In the mind of the one conscientious worker, the carpenter who half-demolishes the flat (enthusiastically beginning the work of destruction long before the work of construction can start), Lewis stands for the lazy petit-bourgeois imperialist: 'worse, as he saw it, than the rotten [. . .] I belonged to the rot – to a rotten social class'.[19] For Lewis, the builders stand for workers over-empowered by Socialism, yet finally he does not complain about the feckless, noisy young builders, nor about the rot left in his flat, but lets them boisterously celebrate the end of their 'bondage' to the job.

Critical opinion of Lewis's stories has been as divided as that about his novels and non-fiction. A contemporary review referred to Lewis's 'inordinate vocabulary of scorn' and his creation of 'bestial or preposterous figures', finding the 'noise and fury' of his writing too much.[20] T. S. Eliot referred to 'Cantleman's Spring-Mate' as 'one of the finest pieces of prose in the language', and to Lewis as the 'most fascinating personality of our time'.[21] Though Lewis's stories include grotesque representations of women, some critics have argued that his writing is not misogynistic. Juliet Mitchell asserts that he disliked the forcing of women into either the feminist or the feminine class, both of which are of the 'unthinking puppet-groups' that Lewis hated.[22] More recent critical work sees Lewis's satire in a line of descent from Juvenal,

Rabelais, Donne, Jonson and Swift, and, in particular Menippean satire, for its use of exaggeration and rhetorical play and its attack of engrained attitudes. The stories of *The Wild Body* and *Rotting Hill* observe from the outside; they set their puppet grotesques moving on a fantastical stage but no interior monologue or authorial intervention draws a moral lesson, any more than accompanying notes elucidate morality from Lewis's paintings.

Waugh's more Horatian 'An Englishman's Home' (1939) uses the politics of a small fictional village to satirize English society between the wars, in particular the territorial impulse, vanity and the not-in-my-backyard preoccupation.[23] Beverley Metcalfe has retired to the countryside and bought a house with surrounding grounds that give him a pleasant view and desirable privacy, but has not chosen to purchase an adjoining field that once belonged to his property. When he learns that a newcomer has bought the field and plans to use it as an industrial site, all his territorial instincts are aroused. He tries to awaken a community spirit so that his neighbours, three types of lower gentry, will join with him to out-bid the newcomer, but no one wants to spend money on a field that will mostly benefit Metcalfe. They suggest that he should public-spiritedly shoulder the financial responsibility himself. Things seem to be at an impasse when one of the villagers cunningly suggests that the local boy scouts need a camping place, and that it should be named for any benefactor who would provide it. Metcalfe buys the field at a hugely inflated cost. The irony of the story is that the proposed plans were completely bogus, a scam run by a country landowner to pay the tax on his own estate.

In later stories Waugh's characters are living in the ruins of civilization, a wasteland of inept and corrupt yet all-powerful leaders, insane systems and sheep-like, moronic citizens. The targets of 'Mr Loveday's Little Outing' (originally 'Mr Cruttwell's Little Outing', 1935) are both the state health system and ignorant do-gooders. A much-loved and trusted inmate of a mental asylum has been acting as an informal assistant in the decades since he murdered a woman. Following the efforts of a bored daughter of a minor aristocrat who has been incarcerated in the same place, he is released. Amid the regretful farewells and good wishes of the staff and patients, Mr Loveday leaves, but soon returns, having had a lovely day out, and murdered again.

In 'Scott-King's Modern Europe' (1947) a schoolteacher is accidentally invited as a guest of honour at a festival to celebrate the leading poet of 'Neutralia', a country that has suffered 'every conceivable ill the body politic is heir to'. Scott-King, urged to laud Neutralia as a Utopia that has kept out of the world war, realizes that it is a totalitarian dictatorship. He is tricked and manipulated and suffers numerous misfortunes, but in condemning the catalogue of modernity constituted by Neutralia, Waugh's narrator seems to express opprobrium to incompetence and oppression, mediocrity and corruption, in equal measure.

In Waugh's short stories, as in *Brideshead Revisited* (1945) the Second World War has lost any chivalrous or heroic impetus and become an irrational series of pointless, disorganized events ordered by incompetents and louts, and in the aftermath the lunatics and the swindlers are running things. 'Love Among the Ruins' (1953) satirizes the justice and prison system ['the new penology'], education, psychoanalysis and social welfare/workers. In the New Britain there are no criminals, only victims. Mountjoy Prison, a large country house, once the home of a soldier maimed in the Second World War and awarded the Victoria Cross who has been sent to a home for the handicapped, is made a luxurious rehabilitation centre, from which Miles Plastic, to his annoyance, is released. Miles is set to work at the Euthanasia Service, where hundreds of the 'welfare-weary' made miserable by modern life queue for state-provided poisoning by cyanide. His boss, Dr Beamish, is disgusted by the dependency of modern people: surrounded by free natural resources for suicide, they come to the state to be killed, unlike his own parents, who hanged themselves with their own washing-line. Miles falls in love with Clara, a ballerina whose mandatory sterilization has given her a beard, which has debarred her from dancing. After becoming pregnant, she has an abortion and another operation that removes the beard but replaces her face with a taut salmon-pink rubbery mask. Miles returns to Mountjoy and burns it to the ground, killing its occupants. As the only rehabilitated criminal available, he is promoted to Propaganda, pushed into an arranged marriage and made ready to tour the country as the prime example of Modern Man. He acquiesces, but during the wedding ceremony is ill at ease; we see him fidgeting and igniting his cigarette lighter, presumably ready once again to set the place on fire. Unusually, 'Love Among the Ruins' names real people of the 1930s and 1940s, including Aneurin Bevan and Anthony Eden. W. H. Auden and Stephen Spender are ridiculed as Parsnip and Pimpernel, two 1930s poets published by the Left Book Club; Pimpernel one of the first 'patients' of euthanasia, Parsnip always pushed to the back of the queue.

Like Waugh, Angus Wilson draws a picture of England as a nation of snobs, hypocrites, the moribund and the criminal. His collections *The Wrong*

Set (1949) and *A Bit Off the Map* (1957) continue Waugh's preoccupation with markers of class and class aspiration and pretension. The stories chronicle the changing social and moral climate of the country as its political climate moved from Clement Attlee's to Churchill's to Eden's governments. D. J. Taylor asserts that they dramatize England's 'new people jockeying for position, and its old people fighting a desperate rearguard action against the colonising tide'.[24] The title story of *The Wrong Set* mocks ingrained racism, ignorance and prejudice. Jockeying for position in 'Realpolitik' takes the form of politicking in a gallery by one of the 'new people', a nasty ambitious new manager, who bullies a group representative of old values: an idealist, an older woman, an older ex-army man and a loyal secretary. In 'Crazy Crowd' a lower middle-class boy, Peter, visits the upper middle-class family of his fiancée, Jennie. The family is strongly united and its members immediately fall into clearly familiar long-held roles; the females fuss, serve and bully the males; the siblings tussle and squabble and bond. Conversation consists of in-jokes and showing off. Everyone has Theories forcibly aired. They pride themselves on their 'craziness', their cheerful eccentricity, which is in fact overbearing egotism. Peter is confused and offended, and aims to leave, but is stopped by sex, stage-managed by Jennie. 'Significant Experience' is another monologue about an experience with an older woman (in Marseilles), in which a middle-class Oxford boy's arrogant assumption of superiority and lack of self-knowledge reveals his egotism, selfishness and inhumanity.

British society of the 1950s as represented in Wilson's *A Bit Off the Map* is made up of fakes, bores, inadequates and the despairing. The title story begins as the monologue of a young man, Kennie, patronized by a would-be intellectual, vaguely revolutionary, nihilistic group, 'The Crowd', but turns from first- to third-person narrative with multiple perspectives and ends in violence as Kennie, looking for truth, having mistaken cant and puff for solidity, kills a geriatric colonel. In 'A Flat Country Christmas', set in 1949, two pairs of friends are clinging together, estranged from familial and social roots by geographical and class mobility, and, isolated on a large, featureless, uniform modern housing estate, they congratulate themselves on having broken class barriers through shared military experience. Pretence and superficiality get them through political differences, but one of the group, stuck in a uniform housing estate in bleak, muddy fields, ends depressed and despairing.

'Rex Imperator' from *Such Darling Dodos* (1950), like some of the stories of Fay Weldon, focuses on the relationship between an elderly couple and their house, making attachment and threat to ownership representative of the rearguard's clinging to (self-) possession, autonomy and stability. A shower of ungrateful and self-seeking parasites surrounds Rex, a wealthy, once-strong, elderly man. Rex's physical decay seems to presage the loss of control of his dependants, but a flash of spirit reasserts his – albeit temporary – dominance. The title story of the collection exposes both the ageing dandy, nostalgic for the frivolity of the 1920s (and his academic relatives, nostalgic for the more serious Socialism of the 1930s), and the swings of fashion that have restored his superficial values.

In some ways, Malcolm Bradbury is the inheritor of both Evelyn Waugh, about whom he published a critical work, and Angus Wilson, whose work he admired and who was his colleague at the University of East Anglia. Like the earlier writers, Bradbury is a sharp observer of verbal nuance and the markers of class, hypocrisy, manipulation and pretension, in speech and action. His short stories, collected in *Who Do You Think You Are?* (1976), have some of the same targets as his longer fiction and non-fiction – psycho-babble, media-speak and theory-jargon – and cover some of the same ground geographically and thematically. That collection also equals Max Beerbohm's feat of pastiche, in a set of mini-stories in the styles of Angus Wilson, C. P. Snow and Kingsley Amis (Jim Dixon is brought together with Lewis Eliot in the story 'An Extravagant Fondness for the Love of Women'), Iris Murdoch, John Braine, Muriel Spark, Lawrence Durrell, John Osborne (in a verse-play), Alan Sillitoe, J. D. Salinger and James Joyce.

'Composition', one of Bradbury's many campus fictions, represents post-humanist theory as rendering a life confused, sterile, amoral and inauthentic. 'Nobody Here in England', also set on an American university campus, targets the greed and inhumanity in academic acquisition as an old woman is pandered to for the important archive material she claims to have in her gift; which turns out to be a bottle of (allegedly) George Bernard Shaw's sperm. The woman is destructive, disruptive and grotesque, yet more sympathetic than the plastic people who surround her.

Whereas urban working-class characters appear in Waugh's stories at most as walk-on parts speaking Mockney – as, for example, in 'The Balance' (1926) – they are at centre stage in the work of later authors, including that of Amis and Self. Amis's 'State of England' (1986) in *Heavy Water and Other Stories* (1998) is presented through the eyes of Big Mal, a divorced bouncer. Mal is alienated from family, because he has left his wife, Sheilagh, and son, Jet (he speaks to his wife incoherently, by mobile phone, though they are feet apart); from place, specifically Jet's private school; from people, such as other fathers, because he feels that they are judging him; and from English society, because a new confusion of classes and ethnicities leaves him unconfident, unsettled and uncertain.

Often bracketed with Amis, Will Self is described by Jules Smith as 'undoubtedly Britain's leading satirical writer, whose dystopian visions, outrageous scenarios and pungent uses of language combine to hold up a distorting mirror to the self and society'.[25] His narrators share with some of those of Fay Weldon and Martin Amis a deadpan and detached voice, and with Martin Amis the sense of estrangement and alienation. His characters, like some of Amis's, are often emotionally stunted, their reading of the world and others without affect, though driven by the will to power. The reappearance of characters such as Zack Busner, in separate stories, for example, adds to the distancing effect, and Busner himself contributes to a recurring theme in Self's fiction: the failure of psychiatrists and other mental health workers either to heal or to produce viable, rigorous, disinterested research. In 'The North London Book of the Dead' (1991), life after death is shown to be more or less the same as life before death, and just as mundane. The dead of London just move to another part of the city, a place so segmented and imperceptive that they are rarely discovered. The narrator has lost his mother but is far from prostrate with grief: like most of Self's characters, he has little emotional empathy or drive, other than for drugs, and even the desire for a hit is about the craving, not its fulfilment. In 'The Nonce Prize' in *Tough, Tough Toys for Tough, Tough Boys* (1998) two prisoners enter a short story competition. Each convict's 'story' has been constructed by narrative, words that lead to one false verdict in court, and another in the competition: the judge in court convicts a drug-dealer who has been framed for a terrible child-murder, and the literary judge awards the prize to a psychopathic murderer, believing that the story 'Little Pussy' clearly demonstrates compelling moral irony in a brilliant representation of an affectless psychopathic mind. 'A Rock of Crack as Big as the Ritz', a prelude to 'The Nonce Prize', remodels Scott Fitzgerald's satire of wealth as status with the device of a seam of crack cocaine in a run-down house; enough to flood the market or, if carefully harvested and rationed, to make its finder rich, as long as he doesn't touch the product, which, eventually, he does.

Sharing some of Self's affectless minimalism, Toby Litt began his enterprise of publishing a succession of books with titles starting with every letter of the alphabet, each in a different genre, with *Adventures in Capitalism*. 'It Could Have Been Me and it Was' targets the mindless credulousness engendered by the blizzard of advertising promises and claims. The narrator believes that such a promise has been fulfilled when he wins the lottery, so undertakes to believe everything he sees or hears. It sends him insane, and, institutionalized, he is forbidden all access to media, apart from the works of Charles Dickens, perhaps a nod to the fate of Tony Last in Waugh's *A Handful of Dust* (1934). 'After Wagamama but Mostly Before' opens with a scene that ruthlessly mimics the mannerisms and obsessions of slaves to fashion and pretension. The dehumanized factory atmosphere of the Japanese fast food restaurant removes all the usual pleasures of dining out, which is immaterial to the diners, who aren't there for those pleasures. Minor characters in one scene appear in or are focalizers of other scenes, and among the fictional characters are fictional versions of 'real' celebrities: Yoko Ono, Quentin Tarantino, Keanu Reeves, Mrs Bobbit, Paul Getty Jnr. Reality and representation are permeable. In a scene set in a Japanese bedroom, a character says that the craftsman on a TV documentary was her father, and produces the lacquered egg that he is shown creating. The egg, thrown at the screen passes through it. A film treatment suggested by a minor character is picked up and a pre-production party announced in which characters become further interchangeable as they are ordered to attend the party disguised as one another.

Frank O'Connor asserts that the short story is by its very nature 'remote from the community – romantic, individualistic, and intransigent'.[26] The skits, pastiches and satirical mimicry of the nineteenth and early twentieth centuries are mostly good-hearted and far distanced from, or at odds with, that which they depict. Many twentieth-century satirical short stories are angrier, their narrators positioned as more alone, isolated and estranged from their worlds. Such stories hold up mirrors to society as though to invite change. Yet in the twenty-first century, the mirror reflects reflections, sliding surfaces. The perception of a society of endless reification and valueless materialism, particularly represented by advertising, marketing and the media, generates a style without much character development, depth, affect or apparent narratorial engagement.

Notes

1. Helmut Gerber, *The English Short Story in Transition, 1880–1920* (New York: Pegasus, 1967), p. xv.
2. *Ibid.*
3. *Punch, or the London Charivari* (19 March 1894), p. 109.
4. Max Beerbohm, *A Christmas Garland* (London: Heinemann, 1912).

5. Zero, pseudonym of Allan Ramsay, 'The Adventure of the Table Foot', *The Bohemian*, 2:1 (January 1894).
6. Unsigned review, *Times* (14 February 1898), p. 10.
7. Unsigned review, *Bookman* (December 1897), p. 106.
8. Dennis Vannatta, 'Introduction', in *The English Short Story 1945–1980*, ed. Vannatta (Boston: Twayne, 1985), pp. ix–xx (p. xviii).
9. Alun Lewis, 'The Last Inspection', in *The Last Inspection* (London: George Allen & Unwin, 1942), pp. 9–14 (p. 14).
10. Siân Mile, 'Slam Dancing with Fay Weldon', in *Fay Weldon's Wicked Fictions*, ed. Regina Barreca (Hanover, NH and London: University Press of New England, 1994), pp. 21–36 (p. 30).
11. Finuala Dowling, *Fay Weldon's Fiction* (Madison, NF: Fairleigh Dickinson University Press; London: Associated University Press, 1998), p. 43.
12. *BLAST* 1 (July 1914) dated 20 June 1914, pp. 8, 17.
13. *BLAST* 2, 'War Number' (July 1915), p. 11.
14. Percy Wyndham Lewis, *Men Without Art* (London: Cassell, 1934), pp. 88–9.
15. Percy Wyndham Lewis, 'Studies in the Art of Laughter' (1934); reprinted in *Wyndham Lewis, Enemy Salvoes: Selected Literary Criticism*, ed. C. J. Fox (London: Vision Press, 1975), pp. 41–9 (p. 44).
16. Lewis edited and largely wrote the three issues of *The Enemy: A Review of Art and Literature* published in 1927–9.
17. Percy Wyndham Lewis, 'Cantelman's Spring-Mate', in *The Ideal Giant, The Code of a Herdsman, Cantelman's Spring-Mate* (London: The Little Review, 1917), p. 38. Subsequent page references to this story are given in parentheses in the text.
18. Percy Wyndham Lewis, 'A Soldier of Humour', in *The Wild Body: A Soldier of Humour and Other Stories* (London: Chatto & Windus), pp. 57–9.
19. Percy Wyndham Lewis, *Rotting Hill* (London: Methuen, 1951), p. 95.
20. Rachel Annand Taylor, 'Some Modern Pessimists', *Spectator*, 139. 5 (17 December 1927), p. 863.
21. T. S. Eliot, 'Literature and the American Courts', *The Egoist*, 5.3 (March 1918), p. 39; Eliot, Review of *Tarr*, *The Egoist*, 5: 8 (September 1918), pp. 105–6.
22. Juliet Mitchell, 'Women and Wyndham Lewis', *Modern Fiction Studies*, 24.2 (1978), pp. 223–31.
23. The story includes the first of many of Waugh's characters to be named 'Cruttwell' after his tutor and Dean (later Principal) of Hertford College, C. R. M. F. Cruttwell, against whom Waugh sustained a vendetta.
24. D. J. Taylor, 'From Darling to Dodo', *The Guardian*, 24 August 2013, p. 16.
25. Jules Smith, essay on Will Self for the British Council, http://literature.britishcouncil.org/will-self
26. Frank O'Connor, *The Lonely Voice* (London: Macmillan, 1963), p. 21.

29
Comedic Short Fiction

RICHARD BRADFORD

The comic short story might too easily be dismissed as an appendix to a subgenre: a lightweight variation on the novel's junior partner. In some instances this classification is well deserved, with authors making use of brevity as the opportunity to dress in respectable literary garb an extended joke or an exercise in parody. At the same time, it is possible to locate those who regard as a challenge the combining of humour that is more than trivial with the demands of a compact, pressurized narrative.

At the close of the nineteenth century short fiction was becoming established as a popular alternative to the full-length novel, and one of the first, and certainly one of the most popular, practitioners of the comic form was Barry Pain. Pain was a journalist who found that the rise of the weekly magazine, aimed mostly at the lower middle-class suburban reader, created the opportunity for literary writing that guaranteed payment by submission. This in itself was partly responsible for the consolidation of short fiction in late Victorian and Edwardian Britain. Such pieces could be read in a single journey by individuals commuting in and out of the city on the ever-expanding rail network, and magazines such as *Cornhill*, *Punch* and the *Daily Chronicle* regularly made room for stories of one to two thousand words alongside their mixture of current affairs, gossip and reviews.

Pain's most famous stories (1900–13) involve the eponymous 'Eliza'. Their popularity has endured to the extent that in 1992 BBC 2 adapted them as ten-minute screen performances and in 2006 BBC Radio 4 followed suit with a week-long serialization. The narrator is Eliza's husband but we never learn of his first name, nor indeed of the married name he shares with Eliza, because she never uses his name in the conversations between them that make up most of the dialogue. This might seem a curious gesture on Pain's part, but we gradually discern a connection between the partial anonymity of the first-person narrator, through no fault of his own, and the general temper of the pieces. For readers with a taste for magazine fiction Eliza's husband would have been faintly familiar. In 1888–9, in *Punch*, George and Weedon Grossmith magnetized a considerable readership with the dull pomposity of Charles and Caroline ('Carrie') Pooter. There are degrees of continuity from issue to issue – given that the Pooter household, their friends, his work and their son, endure as features of Pooter's account – yet each separate entry established for itself a degree of thematic autonomy. Pain's stories maintain this balance between an ongoing fictional scenario and a self-contained narrative, emphasizing the latter in the title of each entry. The Weedons and Pain make use of unwitting self-caricature as their principal comic device, with both Pooter and the unnamed husband of Eliza as victims of their own fidgety solipsism and self-deluding social ambitions. But Pain, to his credit, puts a twist on the precedent set by the Weedons by causing us to wonder about who exactly is laughing at whom. We begin to suspect that Eliza never uses her husband's name because she no longer takes him seriously.

The story entitled 'Miss Sakers' opens in typical fashion, with Eliza's husband making an observation that reflects his combination of self-importance and absurdity:

> On Saturdays I always get back from the office early. This particular Saturday afternoon I looked at our chimneys as I came down the street. I thought it very queer, but, to make certain, as soon as I got into the house I opened the drawing room door. It was just as I thought. I called up-stairs to Eliza, rather sharply.
> She came down and said, 'Well, what's the matter?'[1]

To his consternation, the maid Jane has lit the fire in the drawing room. 'It is our rule', he informs the reader, 'to have the drawing room fire lit on Sundays only' (p. 33). The disclosure of the cause of this threat to his sense of order and authority – the arrival of the vicar's daughter, Miss Sakers – is painfully slow because he appears unable to address straightforward questions or accept replies without providing himself and the reader with egregious explanations and digressions. We begin to see him as an unbearably solipsistic figure, an impression confirmed when we look more closely at the contrast between his orations and Eliza's barbed replies.

> 'At this very moment,' I added, 'the drawing room fire is flaming halfway up the chimney. It seems we can afford to burn half a ton of coals for nothing. I cannot say that I was aware of it.'
> 'You *are* satirical!' said Eliza. 'I always know when you are being satirical, because you move your eyebrow, and say, "I am aware", instead of "I know". I told Jane to light the fire myself'. (p. 34)

We never learn of Eliza's true feelings for her husband, but it is evident from their exchanges that she is wearily aware of being attached to a man who is by parts ludicrous and irritating. That he is oblivious to his dearest Eliza's view of him adds a particularly dark level of comedy to this revival of Pooter. Eliza's unnamed husband's account is, quite literally, The Diary of a Nobody.[2]

Some might regard Pain's creation as an improvement on the Weedons', at least in terms of the implied class-based partisanism of social satire. Pooter – along with his successors such as H. G. Wells's Mr Polly – involved a potential conflict between the victim of the comedy and those who take amusement from the spectacle. He was based on a stereotypical notion of the person who, just like him, travelled to the city each day by train and assuaged their boredom by reading stories in magazines such as *Punch*. Perhaps, then, the kind of reader who took greatest satisfaction from Pooter's displays of earnest social ambition were those who were, by birth or otherwise, part of the cultivated middle-class world of the West End to which Pooter hopelessly aspired. They were watching him from the outside, with smug amusement. The one person who shares this perspective is Eliza herself, trapped as she is in the bleak farce that he has brought upon both of them. We cannot but admire the manner in which Pain marshals his genre to his purpose. Because his stories are very short indeed – some being little more than two pages in length – we take away from them painfully economic snapshots of a relationship in which one individual exists in a state of self-delusion which is quietly, economically, undermined by his wife. Pain was part of the golden age of experimentation in the comic short story in Britain, and experimentation in this context does not refer to avant-garde innovations in form and style – modernism, humour and short fiction were by their nature uncomfortable bedfellows – but rather to a less dramatic line of development: Pain and a few others began to look at what could be done by making classic realism funny.

H. G. Wells was equally adventurous, but with radically different outcomes. 'The Truth About Pyecraft' appeared in *The Strand* magazine in 1903 and while it is now treated as a typically Wellsian hybrid of realism and science fiction it was, at the time, ground breaking. The story begins with an unremarkable, if sardonic, account of the uneven friendship between Mr Pyecraft and Mr Formalyn, co-members of a prestigious London club. Pyecraft is repulsively obese, even by the indulgent hedonistic standards of the Edwardian era. Too greedy to consider 'weight-loss' by diet, Pyecraft harasses Formalyn into disclosing a formula devised by his Hindustani great-grandmother, which achieves all it promises, except that its Hindu originators had addressed the notion of 'weight loss' as a rather different existential issue. Pyecraft, still very fat, finds himself floating close to the ceiling in the spacious sitting room of his Bloomsbury residence. He is no smaller but he can now defy gravity, and, only on Formalyn's advice, returns to ground level assisted by several volumes of the *Encyclopaedia Britannica*. The story is grotesquely amusing and it is difficult to imagine it stirring outright laughter in even the most soulless reader. Pyecraft is not endearing; but his fate is grim, and as the story closes it remains unresolved.

Wells's piece makes us aware of the uneasy distinction between comedy and outright cruelty. We are forced to take a step back, contemplate the very notion of mockery and caricature as abstractions rather than something that we partake of involuntarily; and we wonder about whether compassion, even guilt, should accompany our appetite for the humorous depiction of fellow human beings. It is unlikely that Wells could have achieved this in a full-length novel, even a novella, because our sense of surprise and uncertainty at how we should react is a concomitant feature of the work's compression of the credible with the fantastic.

The aesthetic of surrealism was born in the 1920s, but this and other short stories by Wells anticipate it in their capacity to juxtapose the familiar with the improbable and outrageous. G. K. Chesterton was comparably unnerving. Known best for his rather eccentric detective novels, Chesterton disclosed a taste for the bizarre and fantastic in short story collections such as *The Club of Queer Trades* (1905). The 'club' involves those who seem to be involved in an unexceptional pursuit or form of employment – vicar, house agent and so on – while able to exchange their apparent profession for exceedingly strange activities, sometimes for financial gain, often arbitrarily. In 'The Awful Reason For The Vicar's Visit', the Rev. Ellis Shorter, of Chuntsey, in Essex, detains the narrator with a tale of his current and enduring state of distress, involving his having been obliged to dress as an old lady. His story is curious, complex yet oddly believable, at least until he discloses his, and his friend's, actual trade. They are 'Professional Detainers', employed to transfix individuals with stories of their curious dilemmas, stories that are by parts improbable, convincing and compelling. Their purpose is to postpone an arranged sequence of events, in this case to cause the narrator to be late for a meeting with Captain Fraser. Fraser will then use the spare two hours to convince his lover to leave with him on a voyage to South Africa.

It is impossible to ascertain the purpose of these pieces fully. They are short stories certainly, and they involve a peculiar blend of farce, satire and formal anarchy; but beyond that we remain confused and indeed fascinated. They are rather like prose versions of Brecht before his time but with beautifully incoherent dialogue, yet they are informed also by a mood of middle-class Edwardian insouciance. No one has made sense of them or explained their import convincingly. The early twentieth-century reader might detect an echo of Conan Doyle, except that Holmes's deductive acumen is exchanged for a perverse brand of illogic. We even begin to wonder if the anonymous narrator's accounts in Chesterton's pieces seem so authentic because he is an obsessive fantasist – or, in truth, mad. Walter Allen, in his classic study *The Short Story in English* (1981), seems at once transfixed and perplexed by the Edwardians. He offers a spellbound account of Saki's 'Sredni Vashkar' (1911) but refuses to commit himself to a classification of what kind of writing it is. His description of it as 'a masterpiece of the psychology of a lonely, emotionally neglected and imaginative childhood' serves it well enough, but it also pays no account to the utter sense of the grotesque and bizarre in which the tale of Conradin and Mrs de Ropp is enshrouded.[3] The story sits uneasily between the horrific and the darkly preposterous.

Saki's 'Tobermory' takes us to the comfortably louche setting of Lady Blemley's house party, and in some respects it seems intent on caricaturing the superficialities and hypocrisies of the genteel classes, except that it also involves a string of merciless insults directed at the guests by the eponymous talking cat. Comedy can force us to look again at behaviour, people and ideas, to feel embarrassed about what we and our peers once took for granted, or it can just cause a jolt, perhaps make us laugh, at something incongruous or absurdly improbable. In 'Tobermory' Saki challenges us to deal with both simultaneously for the duration of the story.

Perhaps the most fascinating and obdurately inscrutable comic story of this period is Max Beerbohm's 'Enoch Soames' (1916). Soames, of the title, is an invention, an aspiring poet disappointed that the literary establishment seems indifferent to his talents. The two other principal characters are very real: the narrator, and Soames's friend, is Beerbohm, and the artist William Rothenstein also appears in the piece. Rothenstein was an esteemed painter, a friend of Beerbohm, and in the story we hear that he had done a portrait of Soames, a version of which, by Rothenstein himself, appeared in later editions. It is as if the authentic living figures are set upon bringing to life a man who is otherwise a verbal confection. Soames, despairing of his lack of esteem, does a deal with the Devil to have himself transported a hundred years hence to see if his legacy, if any, has endured. He will spend an afternoon and early evening (2.10pm to 7.00pm) in the Reading Room of the British Library scouring journals, newspapers and more substantial critical works for some record of how the twentieth century cultural establishment has evaluated his writing.

There is an intriguing after-life to Beerbohm's tale. In 1997, 'Teller', a performing artist with no forename, published an article in *The Atlantic* reporting how he, together with a group of people connected with literature and the theatre, had assembled in the Reading Room exactly a hundred years from the day that Soames set off on his time-travelling adventure. They report that they did indeed witness an incongruously dressed, somewhat emaciated figure – whom they describe as the living embodiment of Rothenstein's portrait – but, before they could approach him, he slipped away among groups of other browsers. Teller does not even hint that he has staged some kind of self-parodic 'event' and thus, intentionally or otherwise, he raises a question about similar pieces from the period. Clearly, neither Beerbohm nor, one assumes, Teller expect that their readers will treat what they have written as remotely credible. Teller is an entertainer, a performance artist, but one might credit Beerbohm with a more serious objective. Specifically, satire tinged with elements of pathos and tragedy, is used to offer a portrait of the effects of aesthetic over-ambition and self-delusion in *fin-de-siècle* London. But if he expects the reader to take this seriously, why does he frame the story within a late nineteenth-century version of Dr Faustus? Equally, we first assume that Wells's portrait of the ghastly Pyecraft involves an exploration of hubris combined with lazy hedonism, and we then have to ask ourselves if the spectacle of Pyecraft floating around the room reduces this to a level of arbitrary absurdity. By its nature, the short story has a propensity for overemphasis. In novels, moments of savagery, improbability, excess, tragedy or outrageous humour can be absorbed into the broader textual fabric, even deflected – given the space available – by antithetical actions or moods. Short fiction rarely allows for such balance and redistribution, which is why, in many of the cases already considered, the comedic and fantastic often overwhelm everything else.

Between the 1920s and the 1940s few British writers attempted to tackle the conflict between earnest 'literary' purpose and unfocused, sometimes bizarre humour that was evident in the work of Wells and Beerbohm. Instead, comedic short fiction became little more than a compact variation upon the comic novel, and the best-known practitioner of this compromise was P. G. Wodehouse. Wodehouse is without doubt one of the finest comic writers in English. His dialogue has the ironic dynamism of Wilde and his prose administers laughter as an anaesthetic for the less desirable features of existence. Yet even his most devoted admirers have not proposed that his achievements are contributions to the pantheon of literary classics, or that he breaks new intellectual ground. He is, as he has himself often declared, a gifted stylist and entertainer. It would, therefore, be preposterous to regard his stories of the inter-war English gentry as properly satirical. All his characters are faintly ludicrous, sometimes mildly poignant, but we are never invited to dislike them as individuals or to treat the social system that indulges them as anything other than amiably silly. His short stories are portraits, brief performances by figures we often find fairly absurd – but never quite come to dislike – who operate in circumstances that most of his readers would treat as, by parts, enviable and idyllic, irrespective of their own class and status.

Most of Wodehouse's stories, and indeed his novels, feature the double act of Bertie Wooster and his butler/private secretary, Jeeves. Wooster is the archetypical upper-class fool, often saved from humiliation and potential prosecution by the steadying presence of Jeeves. The latter's background is mysterious, but he routinely outranks his employer in terms of attendance to the chivalric 'code' of the English gentleman. Largely, they conduct their clownish business within the world of country-house weekends and the apartments and grand terraces of Mayfair and Kensington, but even when Wodehouse ventures beyond the closed circle to engage with more contentious matters, buffoonery seems to endure as the all-consuming factor. In 'Comrade Bingo' (1922), for example, Wooster is strolling through Hyde Park and finds himself berated at Speakers' Corner by a heavily bearded representative of the Heralds of the Red Dawn, whose political mantra is the 'massacre of the bourgeoisie, [the] sack[ing] of Park Lane and disembowel[ment] of hereditary aristocracy'. The revolutionary is recognized by Bertie's companion, Lord Bittlesham. He is, Bittlesham points out, his own nephew and Bertie's old friend Richard 'Bingo' Little. Bingo's true motive is to court the Herald member Charlotte Corday Rowbotham, daughter of a wealthy, rabidly communist activist. One might, charitably, regard the piece as a satirical portrait of upper middle-class political hypocrisy, the ongoing attraction of revolutionary socialism for those made guilty by their privileged status, though not quite enough to fully renounce it. One might; but it is impossible to treat the social and political registers of the story as significantly different from any other of the settings and contexts that Wodehouse marshals for his comic enterprises. Satire is simultaneously humorous and judgemental, but Wodehouse takes a more uniformly liberal stance by refusing to take anything seriously.

Compositionally, there is an interesting – and unexpected – point of comparison between Wodehouse and Richmal Crompton, who began her *Just William* stories in 1922. While these stories are generally seen as children's fiction, she originally conceived William as a young adult.[4] The lower middle classes enjoyed Wodehouse's fiction, but Crompton's original conception lacked some of the appeal of the Wodehouse model: she had planned a series of tales based on a young man, and his gang of friends, who spent their lives in the suburbs. Her problem was that suburbanites, after leaving school, were generally expected to work for a living, unlike Bertie and his pals, for whom money was a constantly available resource. Hence she was obliged to turn her hero and his friends into eleven- and twelve-year-olds. There is an intriguing, though entirely unintended, message in her adjustment of class and age. For those who envy Bertie's world of game-playing and irresponsibility, overlaid partially in an atmosphere of harmless humour: don't grow up.

Before the middle of the twentieth century the personnel and settings of short comic fiction were almost exclusively middle to upper class. The lower orders had featured in novels from Dickens onwards and Leslie Halward published his first collection of stories on working-class life in Birmingham, *To Tea on Sunday*, in 1936, but it seemed by consensus inappropriate to present the lives of the poverty-stricken and dispossessed in a manner that would provide amusement for others. Either that or the bourgeoisie and gentry offered a richer gallery of comedic raw material for writers who, in most cases, shared this background. After the Second World War, fiction and poetry began to reflect, albeit in erratically varied ways, the legacy of the post-war Labour settlement, the most significant turning point in British politics and society since the beginning of the Industrial Revolution. Most of the new generation of writers were anti-modernist, more concerned with absorbing and refracting the environment of the 1950s than toying with the nature of representation.

Kingsley Amis was probably the most important member of the group of writers who dominated fiction from the early 1950s to the mid-1970s, at least if we judge significance in terms of Dickens's success in eroding the distinction between 'literary' writing and mass appeal. It should also be noted that Amis altered the status of 'comedy' as a literary sub-genre, in the sense that, since

Romanticism and the advent of the nineteenth-century classic realist novel, it had been systematically relegated to a league of literary endeavour lower than that occupied by the likes of John Dryden, Jonathan Swift, Alexander Pope, Henry Fielding and Tobias Smollett. There has, of course, been a permissible brand of abstract humour, characterized by Samuel Beckett, Harold Pinter, Dylan Thomas and others, but this is rather different from the type that Amis regards as a precondition for good writing and good living, a mantra offered by Nash the common-sense psycho-therapist of *Stanley and the Women* (1984): 'The rewards for being sane may not be very many but knowing what's funny is one of them. And that's an end of the matter.'[5]

When reading Amis's novels we are continuously aware of a presence which hovers behind and around the narrator, always ready to pounce and never willing to allow a piece of dialogue or a solemn proclamation to get past without puncturing whatever pretension to absolute validity it might carry with it. He was an ever-smiling counterbalance to inflexibility and grim profundity. Some of his short stories are economic adaptations of this technique. 'Dear Illusion', a savage attack on the hypocrisies of the literary world, is a typical example. More frequently, however, he makes use of the narrative brevity to explore the opportunities and challenges of comedy. In 'Who or What Was It?' (1972) Amis and his then wife, the writer Jane Howard, are staying at the hotel, The Green Man, after which he named his 1969 novel. They reflect on 'who' exactly the narrator was, 'what' happened during his story and decide to seek some assistance:

> 'I'm not going to be like a bloody fool in a ghost story who insists on seeing things through alone, not if I can help it – I'm going to give Bob Conquest a ring. Bob's an old chum of mine, and about the only one I felt I could ask to come belting up all this way (he lives in Battersea) for such a ridiculous reason.'[6]

Robert Conquest is not at home, but the collaboration would not have been the first, since the two of them co-wrote a novel called *The Egyptologists* (1965) in which a group of middle-class male acquaintances set up a pseudo-academic society that is an ingenious sham. It might have been a coincidence, but in the spring of the same year Conquest published an article in *Critical Quarterly* on 'Christian Symbolism in *Lucky Jim*'. The article was an elaborate spoof, with references to Mrs Joyce Hackensmith's *The Phallus Theme in Early Amis* (Concord, 1957) and a reading of Jim's drunken lecture as a symbolic re-enactment of the crucifixion, but such straight-faced absurdities were not entirely incongruous in the sophisticated critical world of 1965, since many of the journal's readers seem to have taken it seriously. The darker side of the joke emerges in the fact that for someone more interested in the 'conscious exertion of critical reading' than in the enjoyment of a comic novel, the article would read as an ingenious and illuminating piece of work.[7] The farce continued with the publication of a poem by Amis called 'The Huge Artifice: an interim assessment' (1967). As its title suggests, the poem is a series of solemn reflections on the work of a contemporary writer.

> We can be certain, even at this stage,
> That seriousness adequate to engage
> Our deepest critical concern is not
> To be found here.[8]

The 'assessment' continues with references to 'questionable taste', 'coarse/Jokes' and 'a grave strategic lapse'. The story 'Who or What Was It?', along with the interconnected fabric of spoof articles and verse, posed the question of whether conventional comic writing could ever be taken seriously in an era when heavyweight criticism had time only for literature that tackles fundamental issues of existence and representation, and was especially drawn to modernist writing. In 'To See The Sun' Amis adapts himself to the Smollettian epistolary technique, updated to the setting of 1925. The readers' perspectives are granted principally via the letters of Stephen Hillier to his wife, Connie, and to his Oxford colleague, A. C. Winterborne, and through the journal of Countess Valvazour, an attractive Balkan noblewoman whom Hillier hopes will assist him with this tedious enterprise in historical scholarship. To cut a very complicated story short, Countess Valvazour and Hillier have a brief affair, which is drawn to a tragic and peculiarly moving conclusion because of the Countess's socially and emotionally limiting condition as a vampire.

The most striking juxtaposition of the narrative is between the horribly familiar euphemisms and formalities of middle-class Englishness and the substance of the actual story. It is an intriguingly effective experiment in how far the polarities of surface and substance can remain distinct. The average reader might find it difficult to fully suspend disbelief with the story of a 150-year-old woman who looks twenty-nine, drinks blood, and who finally departs as 'a thin wisp of hair, no more than four or five stands (which) has disintegrated before I could reach it'.[9] The point is that the fantastic improbability of Hillier's experience is matched by the coy restraint with which he relates these experiences to his wife and his colleague. He could just as easily be lying to his wife about a very ordinary affair or confiding in his friend about an ethereally romantic experience in foreign parts. The story is an accessible and disturbing engagement with the nature and existence of absolute truth. We cannot 'believe' the story, but in a related sense Hillier enacts and practises a strategy of evasion and subterfuge which we have come to accept as a social convention, a convention given more credibility by its use by the 'Englishman abroad' of the 1920s.

'Mason's Life' is Amis's shortest work of fiction. In about a thousand words he creates the peculiarly familiar circumstances of one man, Mason, having his quiet drink disturbed by the presence of an apparent lunatic, called Pettigrew, who insists that Mason is a figment of his imagination. Amis very skilfully edges the reader towards a sense of empathy with Mason, the reasonable and tolerant individual who has to accommodate the deranged idiocies of the sort of person who has been known to lurk in the bar rooms of life and fiction. The surprise comes in the closing paragraph.

> Mason grabbed the other by the arm, but that arm has lost the greater part of its outline, had become a vague patch of light already fading, and when Mason looked at the hand that has done the grabbing, his own hand, he saw with difficulty that it likewise no longer had fingers, or front or back, or skin, or anything at all.[10]

It would be wrong to treat these pieces as mere curiosities. They raise questions about the nature of fiction just as challenging as any one might encounter in James Joyce. But they do so by continually examining the relationship between serious literary endeavour and what many would treat as the inconsequential, the improbable and the amusing. Such stories oblige us to look again at how we routinely classify comedic writing, and how we evaluate the effects it can create.

Amis's near contemporary J. G. Ballard attempted something similar in his collection *The Atrocity Exhibition* (1970), a series of short stories involving very real events and individuals interwoven with frameworks and mannerisms that disrupt any claim they might have to documentary realism. We perceive them as literature for want of any other suitable classification and they deserve the title of comic at least in terms of their being, by parts, outrageous and grotesque. The most notorious (given that it caused one bookseller to be prosecuted for displaying obscene material) was called 'Why I Want to Fuck Ronald Reagan'. It is written in the style of a scientific paper and documents a number of experiments conducted to measure the psychosexual appeal of the then Governor of California.

By comparison with Amis and Ballard's experiments with comedic short fiction, Malcolm Bradbury's *Who Do You Think You Are?* appears conventional, verging on the reactionary. The first half is made up of caricatures of the kind of figures who had already become easy victims in drama, fiction and the media of the 1970s – notably, academics, social workers and psychologists – and the second is a sequence of parodies of authors such as Muriel Spark, John Osborne, John Braine and Lawrence Durrell. Bradbury exhibits a good deal of skill throughout, yet one feels that his stylistic displays do little to advertise the potential of the humorous short story as anything more than a vehicle for exhibitionism. It is as though an actor is advertising his versatility via a combination of mimicry and stand-up comedy.

Few would associate Kingsley Amis with the postmodern but there are extraordinary parallels between his and Ballard's short fiction and Will Self's two volumes *The Quantity Theory of Insanity* (1991), a collection of conventionally brief stories, and *Cock and Bull* (1992), two novellas. Doris Lessing wrote of the first that 'absurdity unfurls logically from absurdity, but always as a mirror of what we are living in – and wish we didn't'.[11] In 'Cock', Carol, an otherwise submissive wife, grows a penis and rapes her husband Dan; and in 'Bull', John Bull, a quintessentially male rugby player, acquires a vagina at the back of his knee and is seduced by his (male) doctor by whom he – or, to be more anatomically specific, his leg – becomes pregnant. These characters are outstandingly credible and they, like their reader, are confounded by the intrusion of the unimaginable into their routine existences. Self's brand of postmodernism, which he shares with the likes of Ali Smith, Toby Litt and David Mitchell, involves a compromise between features that most would treat as conventional and quasi-realistic with the shock effect of a sudden alteration in time scale, perspective or credibility. Self, however, gives special emphasis to shifts between the familiar and the utterly absurd, such that we are not certain if we are expected to laugh at the spectacle or be faintly repulsed by it. Once again the comedic is the testing ground for experiments with the nature of fiction and, curious as it might seem, Self belongs within a lineage that includes Wells, Chesterton, Beerbohm, Amis and Ballard.

James Burr's *Ugly Stories for Beautiful People* (2007) is a collection that builds on this legacy. 'It' tells of people who disappear up their own behinds, which might sound like a variation upon the well-known, mildly absurd vernacular phrase, but Burr very cleverly suspends the preposterous, unimaginable moment of anal self-consumption so that when it occurs we suddenly realize that we have missed the clues leading towards it that he has sewn into the preliminary account. It is effectively a reworking of Amis's 'Mason's Life' with an especially generous dose of grotesquery. 'Life's What You Make It' shows how a woman's largely contented life, or at least her perception of it as such, is gradually threatened by another far less agreeable version. Events and circumstances are the same in these almost parallel universes, but in one they compel happiness, and in the other unsettling discontent. Is this merely a conventional account of how an individual drifts towards mild depression? It might initially seem so, but we do begin to suspect that she is experiencing something close to a supernatural notion of parallel existences. Once again a notion of the absurdly inconceivable, often with a lightness of touch, is allowed to intrude upon skilfully wrought depictions of the mundane and believable.

One of the most popular practitioners of the comic short story in the early twenty-first century is Neil Gaiman. In a BBC interview in 2010 ('Short Stories Are Like Vampires', 11 June 2010) he stated that the genre's endurance was guaranteed because it 'seems at this point in time to be a wonderful length for our generation ... [a] perfect length for your ipad, your Kindle or your phone'.[12] As a fifty-year old, his notion of 'our generation' probably includes those who don't regard social media as concomitant with literacy, and in this regard he is making the challenging claim that the short story appears to have found a host in the early twenty-first century just as welcoming as was the magazine at the close of the nineteenth. For sceptics, however, his statement also implies that short fiction is ideally suited to those who regard a diminished attention span and intellectual impatience as entitlements. Gaiman's fiction belongs to the market-orientated brand of postmodernism initiated by Will Self: self-consciously strange and often implausible, yet built on the foundations of the readable and the familiar.

One of his best-known comic short stories is 'The Case of Four and Twenty Blackbirds' (first published in 1984 and released as a sixteen-page ebook by HarperCollins in 2008). Stylistically it is a well-executed imitation of detective-noir writing; the wry presence of Philip Marlowe has returned. His new manifestation has to deal with clients who have experienced macabre versions of nursery rhymes, beginning with a visit to his office by the sexy, blonde, Jill Dumpty, who informs him that her brother, Humpty, did not fall but was murdered. Gaiman's PI breezes through these weird, morbid refashionings of childhood fantasy and diversion without unease and the rest of the world surrounding him and his peculiar clients is outstandingly normal. One might treat this as earnest satire, an invitation to consider the parallels between the 'adult' sub-genre of crime fiction and the world of fantasy and illusion that attracts children to nursery rhymes and fairy tales; but in doing so, one would also have to wonder about the extent to which we should indulge a somewhat adolescent version of lampoon as satire. Gaiman could be seen as belonging to the tradition that predates the postmodern, taking us back to Wells and Saki and including Kingsley Amis; but that raises the questions of where he ranks in this company. In the end, the answer to this question depends on the reader's tastes and preferences; but it cannot be denied that he obliges us to consider the difference between short comedy as a diversion that does not greatly exhaust our attention, and the genre as a platform for the exploration of the complex potentialities of comedy.

Comedy, in its most elementary form, involves moments of sudden inconvenience, embarrassment or farce. As readers, spectators or viewers we partake of something that ought to involve a nuance of guilt, given that we are enjoying, from the outside, events we would generally prefer to avoid in our own lives. Full-length comic novels are prone to an excess of these, and often reinforce the status of the genre as a minor, secondary literary form. An abundance of comedic incidents or an over-sustained mood of ironic, deadpan narration can lead to tedium (and here Amis is notable in overcoming this challenge). It is for this same reason that short fiction has proved itself to be both a hospitable and a taxing vehicle for explorations of the still unresolved question of how serious writing can be reconciled with a mood that is bizarre, improbable, grotesque and – by virtue of the combination of these elements – comedic. The short story allows just enough space for authors to seduce the reader into an acceptance of the ordinary and routine, and, for the same reason of economy, to challenge their sense of complacency.

Notes

1. Barry Pain, 'Miss Sakers', in *Eliza* (Boston: Dana Estes Company, 1904), p. 33. Subsequent page references to this edition are given in parentheses in the text.
2. George and Weedon Grossmith's *The Diary of a Nobody* (featuring Pooter) was first published in book form in 1892, by J. W. Arrowsmith, Bristol.
3. Walter Allen, *The Short Story in English* (Oxford: Clarendon Press, 1981), p. 87.
4. See Mary Cadogan, *The Woman Behind William: The Life of Richmal Crompton* (London: Macmillan, 1993).
5. Kingsley Amis, *Stanley and the Women* (London: Hutchinson, 1984), p. 285.
6. Kingsley Amis, *The Complete Short Stories* (London: Penguin Classics, 2013), p. 247.

7. Robert Conquest, 'Christian Symbolism in *Lucky Jim*', *Critical Quarterly*, 7:1 (March 1965), pp. 87–92.
8. Kingsley Amis, *Collected Poems 1944–79* (London: Hutchinson, 1979).
9. Amis, *The Complete Short Stories*, p. 234.
10. Amis, *The Complete Short Stories*, p. 350.
11. Will Self, *The Quantity Theory of Insanity* (1991; London: Bloomsbury, 2007), back cover blurb.
12. 'Short Stories Are Like Vampires', BBC Radio 4, broadcast 11 June 2010.

30

Short Story Cycles: Between the Novel and the Story Collection

GERALD LYNCH

Readers know when they are reading a book of short stories that is more than a miscellaneous collection yet clearly not a novel: James Joyce's *Dubliners* (1914) is not only different from a collection of stories such as Ian McEwan's *First Love, Last Rites* (1975) but also obviously different from *A Portrait of the Artist as a Young Man* (1916). The stories in books such as *Dubliners* both stand on their own and gather accretively to form more meaningful communities of fictions that, in turn, enlarge the meanings of each individual story. As such, the short story cycle is a middle-way genre, and its growing popularity may be accounted for in its suitability for the increasingly distracted reader's preference for brevity and the human need for continuity in aid of greater understanding. Coherence in such books of related independent stories can be achieved weakly by means of a frame narrative, a similar theme, a distinctive style, or a compositional device (such as structuring the whole on a musical or painterly subject), or achieved strongly by means of shared setting (*Dubliners*), focus on one character (Alice Munro's 1978 *Who Do You Think You Are?*), or recurrent characters and narrators (Kate Atkinson's 2002 *Not the End of the World*). These kinds of books the present chapter calls short story cycles, while recognizing that a number of other descriptors – series, sequence, novel in stories, composite, etc. – continue to compete for acceptance in critical-theoretical discussions of this comparatively new fictional form.

The determination of inclusion in the genre category of short story cycle depends on precision or looseness of definition. Complicating matters, many books published as novels – by publishers wary of the paying public's resistance to any title that includes 'short story' – are actually short story cycles (or sequences, composites, etc.). (Exceptionally, Faber and Faber advertised Kazuo Ishiguro's sombre *Nocturnes: Five Stories of Music and Nightfall* (2009) as a 'short story cycle'.) In addressing the question of definitional precision/imprecision, this chapter maintains a more precise understanding of what constitutes a short story cycle; nevertheless, as wide a reference as possible will be made throughout to various books of short fictions that, if not precisely story cycles, are also clearly not miscellaneous collections or novels. And if, on the one hand, there are collections of short stories that display features of the story cycle without achieving through setting and character the coherence and cyclical structure of *Dubliners* or *Who Do You Think You Are?*, there are at the other end of the narrative spectrum many modern and contemporary novels that, in experimenting with the elements of the traditional novel, fragment and arrange their narratives in ways that suggest short story cycles. For example, and to suggest an extreme instance, it is not unreasonable to view modernism's nonpareil novel *Ulysses* (1922), with its eighteen highly distinctive episodes, as Joyce's second great short story cycle, while in the long modern period 'anti-novels' persist and proliferate in story-cycle-like works such as Julian Barnes's *The History of the World in 10½ Chapters* (1989), Jane Rogers's *Mr Wroe's Virgins* (1991) and Rachel Cusk's 'novels', *The Lucky Ones* (2003), *Arlington Park* (2006) and *The Bradshaw Variations* (2008).

The short story cycle in English is a modern genre, emerging in its developed form only at the turn of the twentieth century. More accurately, it is a sub-genre of the short story, which began only some hundred years earlier in the practice and theorizing of Edgar Allan Poe. The recent arrival of the short story cycle may help to explain why it continues to excite contentious discussions of nomenclature and definition. And even though the present chapter is titled 'short story cycles' and begins in the first paragraph above with fairly declarative definition, neither what we call this new fictional form nor, for that matter, precisely what kind of book we are talking about when we talk about short story cycles is a settled critical question.

Of course stories were being told and recorded long before Poe subjected the short fictional narrative to analysis in terms of a Romantic aesthetic and thus began the formal systemization of a new genre. Although the Old Testament contains some well-crafted short stories ('Job', for example), short story cycles can be said to have begun with Western civilization's first epic, with the excursus-recursus tales of the *Odyssey*, which coalesced from popular stories that Homer made memorable with the 'incidentals' of mnemonic versification. A sounder literary-historical footing for the English story cycle can be established in frame narratives such as the folk tales that were gathered and shaped into *The Decameron* by the fourteenth-century's

Boccaccio. (This attenuated line of influence is somewhat affirmed by modern Australian author Christina Stead's short story cycle *The Salzburg Tales* (1934), which takes *The Decameron* for its model.) Similarly influential, the lasting influence of *The 1001 Arabian Nights*, the death-defying serial that first appeared in English translation in 1706, must be acknowledged. Yet more formally influential than either of these for the English short story cycle is Geoffrey Chaucer's *The Canterbury Tales* (1475), which is reminiscent of the *Odyssey* in being versified stories told in a frame format, but with multiple participant narrators (so owing something also to *The Decameron*). Story cycles such as Stead's *Salzburg Tales* probably owe much to *The Canterbury Tales*. In the eighteenth century, episodic/picaresque novels such as those of Henry Fielding and Tobias Smollett, and of course Jonathan Swift's *Gulliver's Travels* (1726), can be seen as nearer prose predecessors of the story cycle not only for their intermittent narratives but also for the intra-textual relevance of their seemingly wayward interpolated tales.

Nearer still, the modern origins of English short story cycles can be located in the late eighteenth and early-to-mid nineteenth centuries, in the various collections of character and comic and nature sketches that were moving (if mainly in this retrospectively recognized teleology) towards the genre that readers recognize today as the short story cycle. From about the middle of the nineteenth century onwards, such short fictional and quasi-fictional collections and 'Victorian miscellanies' must have been influenced by Charles Dickens's popular first book, *Sketches by Boz* (1836), whose title alone points to both its miscellaneous and coherent characteristics; and ditto for Dickens's second book of fiction, *The Pickwick Papers* (1836). A like claim, if not as immediate for the English short story cycle, can be made for the importance of Russian Ivan Turgenev's serial *A Sportsman's Sketches* (1852), the book that Sherwood Anderson, author of the first modern American story cycle, *Winesburg, Ohio* (1919), considered 'one of the great books of the world', and which Irish short story writer and theorist Frank O'Connor described as perhaps 'the greatest book of short stories ever written'. O'Connor goes pertinently further, anticipating the subject of the present chapter (as there had long been short stories per se): 'Nobody, at the time it was written, knew quite how great it was, or what influence it was to have in the creation of a new art form.'[1] Also in an anticipatory role was Anthony Trollope's mostly forgotten two-series *Tales from All Countries* (1861, 1863), which take the English character abroad to various countries, as the title suggests, and achieve coherence through that touring character-type in dissimilar fictional situations. (Interestingly, David Mitchell's story cycle,

Ghostwritten (1999), utilizes the same device of international travel and settings, if with greater cyclical design; and Toby Litt's *Life-Like* (2014) puts recurrent characters Paddy and Agatha through their fictional paces in various countries in its cyclical exploration of the deleterious effects of increasing globalization.) Even Robert Browning's book-length narrative poem, *The Ring and the Book* (1868), in its dramatic monologues of many narrators representing various perspectives testifying to the conflicting circumstances of an old Italian murder mystery, can now be recognized as contributing to the form that would emerge as the modern short story cycle.

But the short story cycle in English comes to mature form not in England but in North America, in American Sara Orne Jewett's *The Country of the Pointed Firs* and Canadian Duncan Campbell Scott's story cycle of a community in Western Quebec, *In the Village of Viger*, both published, remarkably, in the same year, 1896. (Thomas Hardy's frame narrative, the literary portrait gallery *A Group of Noble Dames* (1891), is also an important contributor to the new genre but has weak claim to being a contrived short story cycle as the present chapter understands the emergent genre.) *In the Village of Viger*, the more accomplished fiction of the two originals, was the first to weave for literary artistic purpose *as* a composed short story cycle the various nineteenth-century narrative strands – nature sketch, character sketch, comic anecdote, tall tale, gothic tale, local-colour writing, fable and romantic tale – that preceded the arrival of the modern short story cycle in *Dubliners*. (Testifying to the integrity of *Viger* as an intact short story cycle, as an aesthetic whole, Scott in his lifetime refused permission for any of its obviously independent stories to be separately published.)

Throughout the twentieth century and beyond, the story cycle continues to be well suited to writers intent on portraying a particular region or community, its history, its characters and its communal concerns. These regions and communities can be as different from one another as the world of Canadian Norman Duncan's *The Soul of the Street: Correlated Stories of the New York Syrian Quarter* (1900), the Fenland village of E. B. Swain's *The Stoneground Ghost Tales* (1912), the small-town ironic idyll of Stephen Leacock's *Sunshine Sketches of a Little Town* (1912), or the darker American version of Anderson's *Winesburg, Ohio*, the dismal moral landscape of Joyce's Dublin or the Port of Spain, Trinidad, of V. S. Naipaul's *Miguel Street* (1959), the North Queensland of Australian writer Thea Astley's *Hunting the Wild Pineapple* (1979), and the Greece of Cusk's *Outline* (2014), to distinguish but a few in the panoply. Other story cycles, such as Dylan Thomas's *Portrait of* the Artist as a Young Dog (1940), Munro's *Who Do You Think You Are?*, Margaret Atwood's *Moral Disorder* (2006) and Tessa Hadley's *Clever Girl* (2013), focus on the growth of a single character, thereby illustrating in the story cycle the interest in individual psychology since the rise of modernism, though such characters are also necessarily determined by conditions within the particular communities of their beginnings (for example, rural South Wales and the recurrent town of 'Tawe' in Thomas's cycle). The adaptability of the story cycle as an alternative form of the *Bildungsroman/Künstlerroman* can be seen in, for example, Toby Litt's *I Play the Drums in a Band Called Okay* (2008), which in twenty-six vignettes of varying styles, convincingly represents the life cycle of a rock band. Moreover, this bio-fictional use of the story cycle apparently appeals to female writers especially (for example, Munro, Atwood, Hadley and, to a lesser degree, Rogers and Cusk), who have used its lacunal narrative structure as an alternative to the purportedly patriarchal presumption inherent in the *Bildungsroman/Künstlerroman* novel as established by Joyce's *A Portrait of the Artist as a Young Man*.

The past half-century or so has seen an acceleration in the publication of short story cycles in all English-speaking countries, with examples from British, Irish, Canadian, Indian, Australian, New Zealand and American literatures being far too numerous to include even in a catalogue survey.[2] As climactic evidence of its international popularity, in 2014 the Nobel committee awarded the prize in literature to the English-speaking world's preeminent writer not only of short stories but of story cycles, Alice Munro.

To return to what was anticipated above, there are a number of reasons for preferring the phrase short story cycle for this deceptively diffuse genre. *Cycle* carries enriching historical associations not only with the classical works already mentioned (as well as with those by Dickens, Trollope and Hardy) but also with such other contributory cyclical and seasonal literary forms as calendars, liturgies, miracle plays and sonnet cycles. 'Cycle' aptly describes the dynamic spiralling movement of 'recurrent development' identified by the genre's first theorist, Forrest Ingram.[3] And cycle best captures the return function of the ideal story cycle's concluding story. Compelling contending terms will persist. Duncan's *The Soul of the Street: Correlated Stories of the New York Syrian Quarter* introduced a first competing descriptor for this evolving genre in 1900, and much later in the century Thea Astley forwarded the simplest description in the subtitle of her 1979 story cycle *Hunting the Wild Pineapple and Other Related Stories*.

Writers and critics can also be proprietary and culturally nationalistic when describing the development of the short story cycle. Gerald Kennedy, for example, argues that what he calls 'story sequences' are a distinctively American genre: 'Although recent collections by such writers as Alice Munro, Angela Carter, Gabriel García Márquez and Italo Calvino remind us that the proliferation of short story sequences is truly a global phenomenon, still the pragmatic affinity for short stories that shaped the literature of the United States decisively in the nineteenth century seems to persist in our national avidity for organized story collections.'[4] Regardless, a poised balance between the part and the whole is definitive of short story cycle form, and American culture has always stressed the melting-pot *unum* over the multicultural *pluribus*, whereas in, say, Canadian history the inverse has obtained.[5] Such cultural nationalism aside, Kennedy confirms the impression of an increasing international popularity of short story cycles in many countries and languages along with England and English-speaking cultures. And the differences in views of the story cycle's national aptness point up an intriguing feature of the genre's development: the short story and subsequently the story cycle appear to thrive in countries and cultures as they strive to establish or recuperate national identity and character: nineteenth-century America, twentieth-century Ireland and Canada, and perhaps even England of the past few decades. Frank O'Connor's early theoretical study of the short story posited it as the vehicle of 'the lonely voice', and W. H. New compellingly showed that the short story has been the genre of choice in neighbouring countries on the margins of dominating cultures (Canada and New Zealand are New's focus, but Ireland offers another obvious example).[6]

Ingram elaborated his identification of the short story cycle's distinguishing dynamic – 'recurrent development' – in this way: it is 'a book of short stories so linked to each other by their author that the reader's successive experience on various levels of the pattern of the whole significantly modifies his experience of each of its component parts'. Here, Ingram established the fundamental feature of the outer form of the short story cycle: its unique relation of the integrity of each individual story and the whole collection, or what he somewhat mystically called 'the tension between the one and the many'. With more precision, Ingram usefully described a tripartite system for categorizing story cycles according to the ways in which they were conceived and compiled. He categorized them as (1) 'composed', that is, cycles which 'the author had conceived as a whole from the time he wrote its first story', designed cycles such as Kazuo Ishiguro's *Nocturnes: Five Stories of Music and Nightfall*; as (2) 'arranged', that is, ones that 'an author or editor-author has brought together to illuminate or comment upon one another by juxtaposition or association', a cycle such as Kate Atkinson's *Not the End of the World* (2002); and as (3) 'completed', that is, 'sets of linked stories which are neither strictly composed nor merely arranged', but ones that were completed when their author recognized the links within a group of stories, a series such as Hardy's *A Group of Noble Dames*.[7] But Ingram's helpful, if speculative and biographical, categorizing goes only so far in assisting readers' apprehension of this form that occupies the generic space between the miscellany of short stories and the novel, between the discontinuous and the more obviously coherent narrative forms.

A sounder way to begin describing and categorizing story cycles is first to recognize what lends the cycle its strongest coherence, the centripetal force, so to speak, that holds discrete stories in a unified cyclical structure – that which actually makes a story sequence a story cycle. As observed in the first paragraph of this chapter, from their beginnings story cycles have been unified primarily for being set in one place: a rural territory, a town, a city, a suburb, as is evidenced in such classics as Turgenev's *A Sportsman's Sketches*, Leacock's *Sunshine Sketches of a Little Town*, Anderson's *Winesburg, Ohio*, Joyce's *Dubliners*, or the rural Ireland of Eric Cross's *The Tailor and Ansty* (1942) – cycles whose very titles most often highlight the different stories' focus on the one place. In the later twentieth century, Adam Thorpe's episodic story cycle *Ulverton* (1992) represents the persistent British interest in rural settings. Similarly, the constitutive importance of place is foregrounded in the Caribbean neighbourhood of Naipaul's *Miguel Street*, in the Montreal Jewish-emigré enclave/ghetto of Mordecai Richler's *The Street* (1969), in Pat Barker's north-east England and feminist working-class *Union Street* (1982) and in the suburban Parkside of British author Simon Mason's *Lives of the Dog-Stranglers* (1998). (Apparently, the urban geography of the street offers a useful organizing principle for story cycles.) In the alternate categorizing system being proposed here, the other major class comprises cycles that are unified by focus on one character, such as Munro's *Lives of Girls and Women* (1971) and Hadley's *Clever Girl*, which spotlight the growth of Del and Stella respectively, and which best represent the story cycle's aforementioned adaptability as *Bildungsroman/Künstlerroman*; or such cycles are unified by the same group of characters or character-narrators, as in Naipaul's *Miguel Street*, Richler's *The Street* and Cusk's *The Lucky Ones* and *Arlington Park*.

There are of course additional techniques and devices that deserve attention for strengthening the coherence of short story cycles: such strong features as framing stories, as in the book-ending 'The First Adam' and 'The Last Adam' of Jane Gardam's *The Pangs of Love* (1983); or a single recurring narrator-character, as with Leverson in Australian Thea Astley's *Hunting the Wild Pineapple*; or even a suggestive ordering of the stories (although this is the weakest claim to story cycle status among miscellaneous collections). But only three lesser unifying elements merit recognition after the two major ones of place/setting and character. There are many miscellanies of short stories that acquire unity by means of consistent thematic focus. D. H. Lawrence's *The Woman Who Rode Away* (1928), for example, qualifies as one such, with its different stories intently invested in recurrent gender power-struggles and sexual exoticism against a background of presumed civilized degeneration. Similarly, Angela Carter's collections *The Bloody Chamber* (1979) and *Black Venus* (1985) qualify, with their contemporary versions of fairy tales and re-creations of the lives of historical figures, respectively. Gardam's *Going into a Dark House* (1994) features stories that focus preponderantly on death; and Helen Simpson's *Hey Yeah Right Get a Life* (2000) fairly exhausts the exhausting lives of isolated young mothers. (Hadley's *The Lucky Ones* could well be a story cycle counter to, and perhaps even a critique of, Simpson's favourable attention to such lives of suburban desperation.) And there are numerous story collections that impress readers as more than usually unified by a strong, distinctive style, as in any of Ali Smith's collections of stories in her characteristic experimental style.

There are also story collections that cohere, if somewhat artificially, around a structural device, such as Stead's *The Salzburg Tales*, modelled, as observed above, on one of the genre's classic influential works, *The Decameron* (and also, perhaps, on *The Canterbury Tales*); A. S. Byatt's *The Matisse Stories* (1993), each of which is conditioned by one of the great artist's paintings; Ishiguro's *Nocturnes*, with each story tuned to a musical image; and New Zealand writer Witi Ihimaera's *Dear Miss Mansfield* (1989), which presents a series of responses to the country's greatest short story writer. But such seeming story cycles are more accurately described as series or sequences that exploit a device to lend aesthetic wholeness to collections that, however accomplished for containing great short stories, never quite achieve the unity and intra-textuality of a true short story cycle. So, for definitional purposes, it is best to remain wary of including collections from any of these minor categories of thematic focus, distinctive style and enabling device, simply because on such bases – and especially regarding theme and style – claims for status as a short story cycle could be made for almost any miscellaneous collection. As genre theorist Alastair Fowler cautioned regarding such capaciousness of definition, 'over-extending a critical type, as perhaps William Empson did in *Some Versions of Pastoral*, makes it in the end vacuous'.[8]

With that cautionary note sounded, it would be a mistake not to credit the roles played by theme and style and device in strengthening the coherence of short story cycles unified primarily by place and/or character. Further, what is true of any elementary categorizing system is true of the one being proposed here; namely, that the two major categories of place and character overlap, sometimes indistinguishably as primary unifying elements, and that the lesser elements of coherence are also variously interwoven in contributing to a story cycle's unity. For instance, the Fenland village of Swain's *The Stoneground Ghost Tales* is unified also by the recurrence of ghost-hunter Rev. Batchel. Hanratty, Rose's hometown, serves also to unify Munro's *Who Do You Think You Are?* North Queensland's 'Mango', the place, is as much a contributor to the continuity of Astley's *Hunting the Wild Pineapple* as is recurrent narrator Leverson, and the various settings of Hadley's *Clever Girl*, if Bristol most affectingly, contribute as significantly to that story cycle's sameness as does protagonist Stella. Somewhat contrarily, story cycles unified primarily by place, such as Thorpe's *Ulverton*, are not dependent on a single recurring character, though one may be present. When character is structurally contributory in cycles unified primarily by setting, it is usually a group of characters that provides the coherence. Cycles unified primarily by one recurrent character *are* invested also in place because, of course, the place of origin or extended residence plays an essential role in the formation, revelation and understanding of character. All of this supports the contention here that the short story cycle primarily accommodates writers intent on anatomizing a territory or place – rural, urban or suburban – and only secondarily those writers interested in presenting a *Bildungsroman* narrative as the *discontinuous* story of a life.

But even if this alternate system of categorizing story cycles according to what contributes most to their coherence – setting and character – takes us further than does a system that must often speculate on the conditions that governed the cycle's composition (Ingram's categorizing), definition by setting and character still risks compromising the uniqueness of the story cycle fundamentally. In this respect, even basic categorizing should be viewed as a good way to begin understanding a theoretically complex and diverse genre, but not as an end in itself. Something troubling persists in the useful recourse to recurrent setting and character (let alone a constituent theme, a consistent style or tone, or a clever device). Such an approach still risks assessing story cycles finally as failed novels, which would be to judge their success according to inappropriate generic features and reader assumptions – the very thing to be avoided with a new genre. As Fowler cautions, 'when rules of the wrong genre are applied, they naturally seem arbitrary and oppressive' (p. 28).

For it is the traditional novel, from Samuel Richardson's *Pamela* (1740) to Martin Amis's *Money* (1984), that presents a continuous narrative of character, place, theme and style, however scrambled the elements and chronology may sometimes have been, from Laurence Sterne's *The Life and Opinions of Tristram Shandy* (1759) to Amis's *Time's Arrow* (1991). The novel coheres most obviously in narrating a continuous event unfolding over a comparatively extensive period of time (even if, as with *Time's Arrow*, the temporal trajectory is reversed), and despite flashbacks. Short stories, including those of a story cycle, because they come rapidly to focus on climactic events, continue to be distinguished for their concision. Even the most tightly unified story cycles will lack the traditional novel's chief advantage as a completed action, as temporally continuous, and as a comprehensive narrative design. There is something essential to short stories that is decidedly un-novelistic, an aesthetic effect (as Poe realized at the genre's inception) that is indeed closer to that of lyric poetry – the illuminating flash of a revelatory event rather than the steadily growing light of causal relations.[9] The sequence that is a story cycle signals a different code: recognizing a place and understanding a character's life as seen stroboscopically, as held still momentarily, in bursts of epiphanic insight, strangely fragmented into kaleidoscopic arrangements, unfolding unfamiliarly for readers accustomed to the space and pace of novels.

Consequently, the success of a story cycle should not be judged in terms of its approximation to the achievements of a good novel. Its success should not finally depend on the extent to which it is unified even by place or character, nor, for that matter, should it ultimately be judged according to an aesthetic grounded in the desirability for continuous unfolding and closure. Although saying so may appear to contradict much that has been written to this point, it is important to hold this paradoxical essence of short story cycles in mind, and not only because such an anti-novelistic aspect of the short story cycle may account also for its emergence and rise in the modern period. The story cycle is also unique for the paradoxical way it often represents the *failure* of place and character to unify a vision that remains tantalizingly whole yet fundamentally suspicious of coherence and completeness. Consider: place as setting, Dublin, not only gives coherence to the disparate stories of Joyce's great story cycle but also insinuates a form of disunity, for place in that cycle fails to provide what may be called coherence-as-meaning. *Dubliners* is about the ways in which traditional Irish-Catholic culture is falling apart in the onslaught of an increasingly meaningless metropolitan modernity viewed – suggestively in Cubist fashion – from multiple perspectives and in the various pitiable contexts of its stories.

This paradox can be understood in terms of the outer and inner dynamic of the short story cycle, a concept borrowed here from genre theorists René Wellek and Austin Warren.[10] Dublin, the setting of the stories, the fictional place, represents the outer dynamic that gives most coherence and unity to the stories of the cycle, while 'Dublin', as Joyce's figure of a gasping old Ireland at the turn of the twentieth century, represents the inner principle that destabilizes. Here is another example, this time from the second major category of story cycle types, that of character: in similar manner the character Rose finally does not satisfyingly unify Munro's *Who Do You Think You Are?* That story cycle is also about the possibility/impossibility of essential identity and selfhood – how they are formed and represented, how such identity may only ever be provisionally achieved. Rose is both the recurrent character who knits the stories together, as the outer dynamic that confirms readers' expectations of consistent character development in a *Bildungsroman*, and the fictional figure of a destabilized self, as a form of inner principle threatening ideas of coherent character, identity and selfhood. Often each story of a cycle explores such problems of (dis)continuity and (in)coherence, only to defer their desired solutions to the next story in the cycle (suggesting Ingram's 'recurrence' principle), whose conflict both repeats and advances those of its predecessors, until readers reach the final story of the cycle, which, as one result of its cumulative function, returns them to the preceding stories in the context of the whole cycle. Story cycles viewed with regard to their outer and inner forms, whether cycles of place or character, seldom close on a grounding essence or reassuring presence. For such reasons the short story cycle can also be considered a modern anti-novel, fragmenting the continuous narrative's treatment of place, time, character and plot, in multiple perspectives that indeed suggest a literary approximation of the cubist aesthetic.

Story cycles develop in what Ingram called 'the dynamic patterns of recurrence and development', which make the first and last stories of key significance.[11] This chapter concludes, then, with a few examples of the functioning of first and last stories, showing some of the ways in which they establish and confirm a cycle's meanings. In doing so, I take as focal texts two short story cycles that informed consensus would agree exemplify cycles of place and character respectively, *Dubliners* and *Who Do You Think You Are?*

Opening stories in cycles of place introduce the setting of the ensuing stories as the essential condition of the cycle's meanings. In *Dubliners* 'The Sisters' does so by presenting a dark and deathly place as thematic and metaphoric condition of the stories that follow. Even the story's title, signalling both familial relation and Catholic vocation, anticipates the fussy matriarchy and religiosity that rules Joyce's dismal Dublin. The first paragraph proceeds to foreground what will be the recurrent atmosphere of a turn-of-the-century crepuscular city: 'night after night . . . lighted in the same way, faintly and evenly'. Confinement and suffocation are typical of the stories that follow. A dying religious figure seems always hovering, as here the first story begins, 'There was no hope for him [a priest] this time.' The lexical register of the subsequent stories is tuned by the opening paragraph's 'dead' and 'deadly', 'corpse' and 'paralysis'. A typical boy initiate (sometimes as boy-man in subsequent stories) struggles to comprehend the puzzling pervasive lifelessness. The opening paragraph ends adumbrating the cycle's recurrent trope of a fatal confusion of romantic adventure, sexuality and religion.[12] In such ways the opening stories in cycles of place introduce into the contained, the framed, community its most disturbing element: in 'The Sisters' this is death, a dying religion and a moribund atmosphere (if one that produced, contrarily, James Joyce and the brilliant *Dubliners*).

Cycles whose primary unity is provided by a character begin, in *Bildungsroman* fashion, with a story of the protagonist's childhood, detailing the event that establishes a pattern repeated with variation (recurrent development) in the ensuing twistings and turnings of individual stories. 'Royal Beatings', the first story of Munro's *Who Do You Think You Are?*, presents the perverse shaping conditions of the protagonist Rose's life in small-town Hanratty. There, she must make her way in a place where violent males rule and dramatizing females such as stepmother Flo and the deformed Becky Tyde create their own rituals for managing the unmanageable experiences of life in a man's world where, fictionally speaking, females effectively hold the only interest. This opening story recounts two beatings, one orchestrated by the town's males and fatal, the other a shady matriarchal *pas-de-trois* of sorts (the royal beating of Rose by her father), which is arranged by drama-queen Flo and brings about catharsis in the tense mother–daughter relationship. Because in Munro's fictions romantic-sexual love is the primary means of seeking identity, 'Royal Beatings' dramatizes this first remembered confusion of pain and shame and parental love in Rose's life. In the subsequent stories, Rose must try to make an identity for herself looking for love under the power of patriarchy and eventually as a professional actress. The character is no slouch in that endeavour, though the cycle's first story prepares readers not to expect a comforting answer to the titular identity question.

The concluding stories of cycles present the most serious challenges to readers and critics, as they bring to fulfilment the preceding recurrent patterns, sometimes re-introducing many of the earlier stories' major characters and images, and restating the cycle's main thematic interests. In doing so, concluding stories most clearly distinguish the story *cycle* from its cousins, the series or sequence of related stories and such miscellanies as are unified by style, tone and device. For example, in the contemporary story cycle, the final 'chapter' of Cusk's *Arlington Park* functions in exemplary manner as a story cycle's capping, or *return*, story: a dinner party brings together the five females of the preceding five stories and revisits their crises and boredoms. 'Underground' in David Mitchell's *Ghostwritten* is equally worthy of distinction in functioning as the final story of a contemporary cycle, providing recapitulation and synthesis for its much-travelled characters (and readers) in a capping crescendo of reiterations. But regardless of such contemporary examples of mastery, the ideal instance of a return story remains Joyce's 'The Dead'.

Its title alone functions as closing gloss on the denizens of Dublin, while figuratively thumping the lid on those morbid themes introduced in 'The Sisters'. The story cycle's preoccupation with stultifying Dublin and its stifled characters is likewise remembered and epitomized in 'The Dead': the claustrophobic atmosphere of a pretty seasonal party, 'the Misses Morkan's annual dance' (p. 175), shut in on itself on a winter's night; the circumscribed ambitions of the focalizing consciousness, fastidious Gabriel Conroy, one of Joyce's boyish men possessed of little soul and no sparking smithy; his dutiful, affected service to his beleaguering relations; his self-conning conjugal love that mounts only in anticlimactic frustration; his wife's maudlin longings for impassioned devotion. No other return story ends so fittingly, either in itself or for the cycle it finishes, with such thudding finality, as when demigod Joyce brings lyrically home to Gabriel the blunt epiphany of his delusory, desultory, dead-end life: 'His soul swooned slowly as he heard the snow falling faintly through the universe and faintly falling, like the descent of their last end, upon all the living and the dead' (p. 223).

Only the closing and titular story of Munro's *Who Do You Think You Are?* can bear comparison with 'The Dead' as a short story cycle's perfect return story. 'Who Do You Think You Are?' returns readers to the cycle's title and, as the stories have shown, more meaningfully to its implied challenge respecting the constructedness of female selfhood. This last story also returns protagonist Rose most fully and finally to her place of origin, the small town of Hanratty, the first home which remains, changed and in the absence of romantic-sexual love, as the one entity capable of providing an acceptable answer to that key titular question. The answer would seem to be as follows: 'You' are indelibly who you were and where you came from; you are and are not limited by those foundational components, but you ignore or deny them at peril of losing your soul. So you had better return, reconnoitre, revitalize.

As said, the return stories of cycles also reprises characters from earlier stories. In Munro's, for example, Rose's stepmother Flo, the key shaper of Rose's personality, who was left for dead in the preceding story, 'Spelling', is resurrected to act a key role in reconnecting Rose to her home-town origins. In the end, at home, Rose confesses her faults and experiences a mysterious sense of forgiveness for her felt sin of shallowly acting her life, and that absolution seems to entail a kind of confirmation of the identity she has fled and sought throughout the cycle. Thus what gets confirmed at the end of *Who Do You Think You Are?* is a middle-aged woman's acceptance of self-identity as connected intimately to an unattractive place of origin. The enigmatic closing sentence of this story cycle is appropriately interrogative, and therefore open-ended: 'What could she say about herself and Ralph Gillespie, except that she felt his life, close, closer than the lives of men she'd loved, one slot over from her own?'[13] 'One slot over from her own' is both a spatial and an implicitly temporal figure that places Rose alongside Ralph, who is her only remaining connection to the formational influences of her hometown of Hanratty, the place that is granted something of a metaphysically signifying power respecting identity and selfhood.

The main function of a short story cycle's return story is to remind readers of earlier preoccupations in light of the determinant events of the concluding story. Comfortable closure mostly remains provisional in return stories, for although they may tempt with hints of resolution, they also destabilize. This is not to say that the meanings of story cycles always remain indeterminate, only that open-ended return stories would appear to be another of the family features of the genre. When such conventions are worked by writers of Joyce's and Munro's genius, the result is cycles that return to their beginnings, or their elusive centres, without ever quite closing the circle or resting in a believable essence, as 'The Dead' turns readers back into the now heavily ironized events of the story and imaginatively forward to predict Gabriel Conroy's future in terms of the spiritually dead-end lives of his spiralling downwards fictional predecessors. Similarly, *Who's* Rose can be projected into a continuing middle- and eventual old-age of growing self-knowledge, probably lived alone, and never in a resting condition of knowing comfortably who she is. Respecting their subjects and themes, their places and characters, and even the genre's preferred name, story cycles are invested in processes.

In terms of Alastair Fowler's hereditary metaphor for defining genre, there is now a recognized family of short story cycles in English, whose members constitute a gallery of shared features and display an abiding interest in the centrality of setting and place.[14] Readers may understandably resist the quasi-mystical implications of Fowler's proposition that literary influence can work along generic lines much as genetic traits pass along the spiralling helixes of a family's DNA. Such wary readers might wonder: did Joyce, in choosing to compose the innovative *Dubliners* as a short story cycle, really write under the influence of the cultural ethos and traditions that contributed to the form of fellow Irishman George Moore's cycle *The Untilled Field* (1903) – regardless of whether Joyce had read the earlier book or not (he had)? I believe that the answer is yes. Although evidence in such questions, especially when asked of works separated by centuries and great distances, remains elusive, suppositional, the purported presence and operation of such a family tree/literary-cultural subconscious has at least been variously attested by such trustworthy eminences as T. S. Eliot, M. M. Bakhtin, Jorge Luis Borges and Northrop Frye.[15]

The roots of the short story cycle family can be found in Classical epic and European Renaissance narratives that were woven from stories that had been going around since people first told tales to make mysterious life tolerable and themselves collectively a coherent community in time. Practically, for England and the English-speaking world, the short story cycle has its historical beginnings in the eighteenth century, in epistolary and picaresque novels.

The rise of magazine culture over the ensuing decades encouraged the development of personal essays, character and nature sketches, and the short story itself. Such works were first organized and published as occasional miscellanies, and then in composed books by single authors such as Charles Dickens, Anthony Trollope and Thomas Hardy. In North America, the first fully formed modern short story cycles coalesced also from the various strands of sketches and tales (encouraged by the local-colour vogue in fiction, which would have heightened the abiding interest in place) and came to first fruition in story cycles by Sara Orne Jewett and, especially, Duncan Campbell Scott. Then the modern deluge, first most sublimely in Joyce's *Dubliners*. From that point, 1914 onward, the short story cycle has become – for reasons of cultural and geo-political nationalisms, aesthetic aptness and even reader attentiveness – a favoured form of both fiction writers and readers who are increasingly engaged in the space between the novel and the short story miscellany.

Notes

1. Sherwood Anderson quoted in Forrest L. Ingram, *Representative Short Story Cycles of the Twentieth Century: Studies in a Literary Genre* (Paris: Mouton, 1971), p. 148; Frank O'Connor, *The Lonely Voice: A Study in the Short Story* (London: Macmillan, 1963), p. 46; Ingram makes O'Connor's observation the epigraph to his own pioneering study.
2. Already in 1989 Susan Garland Mann, *The Short Story Cycle: A Genre Companion and Reference Guide* (New York: Greenwood, 1989), could end her book (pp. 187–208) with an annotated listing of some 120 short story cycle titles – with most being from the contemporary period – and still claim that 'many other works could have been included' (p. xiii); as might be expected, her definition of the story cycle is generously inclusive.
3. Ingram, *Representative Short Story Cycles of the Twentieth Century*, p. 20.
4. Gerald J. Kennedy, ed., *Modern American Short Story Sequences: Composite Fictions and Fictive Communities* (New York: Cambridge University Press, 1995), p. viii.
5. See Gerald Lynch, *The One and the Many: English-Canadian Short Story Cycles* (University of Toronto Press, 2001), pp. 20, 190.
6. Frank O'Connor, *The Lonely Voice: A Study in the Short Story* (London: Macmillan, 1963); W. H. New, *Dreams of Speech and Violence: The Art of the Short Story in Canada and New Zealand* (University of Toronto Press, 1987).
7. Ingram, *Representative Short Story Cycles of the Twentieth Century*, pp. 19 and 15–18.
8. Alastair Fowler, *Kinds of Literature: An Introduction to the Theory of Genres and Modes* (Cambridge, MA: Harvard University Press, 1982), p. 33.

9. Edgar Allan Poe, *Selected Writings of Edgar Allan Poe: Poems, Tales, Essays and Reviews*, ed. David Galloway (Harmondsworth: Penguin, 1982), pp. 443–6, 480–92.
10. René Wellek, and Austin Warren, *Theory of Literature*, 3rd edn (New York: Harcourt, Brace, Jovanovich, and World, 1962), p. 231.
11. Ingram, *Representative Short Story Cycles of the Twentieth Century*, p. 20.
12. James Joyce, *Dubliners* (1914; Markham: Penguin, 1977), p. 9. Subsequent page references to this edition are given in parentheses in the text.
13. Alice Munro, *Who Do You Think You Are?* (Toronto: Macmillan, 1978), p. 206.
14. Fowler, *Kinds of Literature*, p. 41.
15. T. S. Eliot, 'Tradition and the Individual Talent', in *The Sacred Wood* (London: Methuen, 1920), pp. 47–59; M. M. Bakhtin, *Problems of Dostoevsky's Poetics*, trans. and ed. Caryl Emerson (1963; rpt Minneapolis: University Minnesota Press, 1984), p. 89; Jorge Luis Borges, 'Nathaniel Hawthorne', in *Other Inquisitions 1937–1952*, trans. Ruth L. C. Simms (Austin: University Texas Press, 1964), pp. 47–65; Northrop Frye, 'Conclusion to *Literary History of Canada*' (1965); reprinted in *The Bush Garden: Essays on the Canadian Imagination* (Toronto: Anansi, 1971), pp. 213–51.

31

The Novella: Between the Novel and the Story

GERRI KIMBER

The novella – often considered to be the most sophisticated mode of short fiction – has attracted some of the most renowned authors writing in English from the middle of the nineteenth century onwards. It is, however, a complex mode, so complex, in fact, that no one seems quite able to define it. The question of length is often taken as a starting point to identify a prose form mid-way between a novel and a short story, but this tells us nothing about the specifics of its formal features, or aesthetic effects. This problem is compounded, because – as Malgorzata Trebisz observes – there are no particular literary techniques used exclusively by any one of the fictional prose forms: similar techniques can be found in the short story, the novella and the novel.[1] According to Robert Scholes, the difference lies in the *purpose* for which certain techniques have been used within all three genres.[2] Trebisz extends this argument further, noting that 'there do exist certain techniques which statistically occur more frequently in the novellas than elsewhere' (p. 2). This chapter will examine such techniques, using a variety of authors associated with the novella genre: Joseph Conrad, Henry James, James Joyce, Katherine Mansfield, D. H. Lawrence, H. E. Bates, Alan Sillitoe and Ian McEwan. Mansfield in particular, in revising her novella 'The Aloe' into the more condensed 'Prelude', offers an unrivalled opportunity to witness the creation of one of modernism's most celebrated short fictions.

Ian McEwan, a contemporary author whose use of the novella is a vital component of his literary endeavours, has an almost messianic zeal for the genre, affirming – controversially – that 'the novella is the perfect form of prose fiction'. Examining its long tradition, he reveals how the genre demands very different qualities in a writer from the novel, citing the demands of economy which 'push writers to polish their sentences to precision and clarity, to bring off their effects with unusual intensity, to remain focused on the point of their creation and drive it forward with functional single-mindedness, and to end it with a mind to its unity'. He goes on to discuss 'Heart of Darkness', noting how

> Conrad's famous contribution to the tradition is typical. It begins with exquisite artifice, in 'luminous space' – Marlowe [sic] gearing himself up to tell his story while he and his friends sit in a yacht at anchor in the Thames estuary at dusk. As the light drops, the notion of darkness is set before us, and will be relentlessly pursued through a hundred pages or so.[3]

Indeed, Conrad's novellas use the capacity shorter fiction has for implication and suggestion to create brooding tales about the murky psychological effects of imperialism on its agents, with 'Heart of Darkness' (1899; first book publication 1902) considered one of the finest exemplars of the genre. Henry James's sophisticated (and elusive) engagement with morals and social mores are very well illustrated in his novellas, and especially in 'Daisy Miller' (1878). James frequently uses the contradictory aspect of the novella – the open-endedness it shares with the short story, complicated by its greater density – to draw his readers in to the problems at the heart of his stories. These can be ironic or knowing, as in his account of the elusiveness of literary meaning in 'The Figure in the Carpet' (1896), or, in a more profound vein, they can examine larger questions of life and death, as in 'The Beast in the Jungle' (1903).

James Joyce's novella 'The Dead' (1914) is considered by McEwan to be *the* 'great novella': 'it was the particular demands of the novella, the way it lays on the writer a duty of unity and the pursuit of perfection, that brought him to shape in this fashion one of the loveliest fictions in the English language'.[4] Amongst modernist short fiction writers, Katherine Mansfield's longer stories *Prelude* (1917; first published 1918) and 'At the Bay' (1921; first published 1922) are considered particularly fine examples; episodically structured, they too can be classified within the novella spectrum. D. H. Lawrence's sometimes verbose and loosely plotted novels have not always worn well in a modern world; conversely his tightly constructed stories and novellas such as 'The Fox' (1922) and 'The Woman Who Rode Away' (1925) still have a powerful afterlife in their ability to convey suppressed emotion.

The argument that the novella is the most sophisticated manifestation of short fiction writing is reinforced by the careers of H. E. Bates and Alan Sillitoe. Bates's prominence in the English short story is established earlier in this volume; here the focus is on his interest in the novella towards the end of his career, when some of his finest work was produced. 'The Triple Echo' (1970) is Bates's most noteworthy novella, in which delicate nature imagery is interwoven effectively with social and psychological themes. Sillitoe's novellas, 'The Loneliness of the Long Distance Runner' (1959) and 'Out of the Whirlpool' (1987), reflect a different world of northern working-class youth in conflict with society and the law. Sillitoe's bleak, existential view of life, confined by the British class system and where escape comes at terrible personal cost, is reflected in the characters of his anti-heroes, Colin Smith and Peter Grant. The continuing relevance of the novella today – and also, conversely, the continuing critical uncertainty about the genre's place in prose fiction – is demonstrated in the work of Ian McEwan, notably in *The Comfort of Strangers* (1981) and *Amsterdam* (1998). Although his novellas have been criticized (most notably the Booker-winning *Amsterdam*), McEwan has proved himself a consummately skilful novella writer and defender of the genre.

It is commonly believed that the word 'novella' is a diminutive of the word 'novel', and of course, as novellas are smaller in size, this would make sense. Historically, however, the English word for 'novel' comes from the Italian word 'novella' (meaning 'little new thing') and is not in fact a diminutive at all. William Giraldi's historical analysis explains how 'the seventeenth-century novella was the forerunner of both the novel and the modern short story, a fact that gets neglected in our foregrounding of the novel and the short story while brushing aside the novella like a refugee who has arrived unannounced from a distant land'. He notes that English writers were not initially in favour of the novella form, 'and indeed, with some possible few exceptions – J. A. Cuddon cites Aphra Behn's *Oroonoko* (1688) and William Congreve's *Incognita* (1713) – they seem to have skipped over it and gone straight to the novel'.[5] Thus, the genre's origins can be seen to have firmer historical roots than might at first be imagined. Indeed, as 'romans', in their even earlier incarnation, they were, as might be expected, romances, manifesting as travel or quest stories in Boccaccio's *Decameron*, Chaucer's *Canterbury Tales* and Marguerite de Navarre's *Heptameron*. However, it was with the Romantic German form of the *Novelle* in the late eighteenth and early nineteenth centuries that the genre really came into its own, with exponents such as Goethe and Kleist. Reworked and modernized, the Novelle would culminate in Thomas Mann's much-lauded novella, *Der Tod in Venedig* (*Death in Venice*, 1912).

Mary Doyle Springer in *Forms of the Modern Novella* (1975), presents a list of formal functions that she considers only this genre can realize, including immediacy of range, condensation of action and restrictions on time and number of characters, thereby allying it inevitably closer to the short story than the novel. Length, of course, is a determining (but vague) feature. The basic understanding is that it has to be shorter than a novel: for Springer, 'a common length [is] between 15,000 and 50,000 words'.[6] Judith Leibowitz believes the novella's purpose is 'so to shape its narrative that the effect will be of intensity and expansion ... an intensive analysis of a limited area with wide, undeveloped implications'.[7] Tony Whedon considers another factor, the notion of time, noting that 'novellas work through refracting and splicing time'.[8] There can be frequent tense changes, together with flashbacks or flash-forwards and a compression of time when compared to a novel. For Whedon, novellas 'are often concentric, onion-like, and one reads them by peeling away layers of scenes and exposition and time (and meaning) until one has a revelation of character' (p. 566).

Joseph Conrad's 'Heart of Darkness' is one of the most celebrated and discussed novellas – alongside Thomas Mann's 'Death in Venice' perhaps – but many other Conrad novellas are also worthy of attention, notably, 'An Outpost of Progress' (1898), 'The End of the Tether' (1902), 'Youth: A Narrative' (1902) and 'Typhoon' (1903). In its form and content, 'Heart of Darkness' is strikingly different from most other books written at the time, and anticipates more overtly modernist texts to appear in the next three decades or so of the twentieth century. Conrad himself was aware that his achievement was innovative: 'I am *modern*, and I would rather recall Wagner the musician and Rodin the sculptor who both had to starve a little in their day ... They had to suffer for being "new".'[9] Of course, 'make it new', that famous modernist dictum coined by Ezra Pound, is foreshadowed by Conrad's statement here, and using the form of the novella also intimates a breaking free from the more established verbosity to be found in the standard Victorian novel. Its content challenges the Victorian belief in progress and moral improvement as a certainty. The overtly pessimistic portrayal of bewilderment and alienation foreshadows the uncertain era in which it was written, with the work of Freud, Darwin and Marx contributing to a fragmentation of the old, ordered view of the world, with seemingly nothing to replace the empty void of discarded values. Indeed, the inscrutable utterance of 'The horror! The horror!' in the closing pages might be said to signal this historic predicament.[10]

The narrative structure of Conrad's novella is predicated on uncertainty; the absence of an omniscient narrator, the unreliability of Marlow the protagonist's second-hand tale, the self-reflexive comments, the absence of standard characterization and even names all contribute to this self-consciously anxious text as it journeys both literally and metaphorically, one journey taking us to the depths of the Congo, the other taking us into the self and a descent into the unconscious. Anticipating Prufrock's exclamation from 1917, 'It is impossible to say just what I mean!', this text offers a profoundly disturbing and nuanced meditation on a collapsing imperial society and era.[11] In its novella form, as Trebisz confirms, 'Marlow's report on Kurtz in *Heart of Darkness* becomes the tale about the difficulty of telling a tale. The "double" convention, so frequent in the novella, exemplifies best the reconciliation of the metaphoric and the realistic.'[12]

The iconic status of 'Heart of Darkness' is such that Conrad's other fine novellas tend to remain resolutely in its shadow. 'The End of the Tether' was collected in the same volume as 'Heart of Darkness': *Youth: A Narrative and Two Other Stories* (1902). Unlike its more famously enigmatic stablemate, this story contains well-developed characterization in Massy, Sterne and Van Wyk, and particularly in the tragic hero-protagonist Captain Whalley. Psychological motivation, as always in the novella, substantiates and enhances the tightly structured plot, which tells the story of an elderly sea captain, Whalley, who falls on hard times, starts to go blind and in a moment of existential crisis chooses to end his own life by drowning with the ship he commands, whilst the rest of the crew escape. Money is a central theme here: Massy, the owner of the *Sofala*, the ship that Whalley captains, is addicted to gambling and has ruined himself. Desperation and greed force Massy to take extreme measures, to the extent that he deliberately arranges the wreck of his own ship in order to collect the insurance. Whalley, having discovered the plot, and knowing that his incipient blindness will terminate both his career as well as his hopes of restoring his own financial fortunes in order to provide for his daughter, takes advantage of the situation for one final act. Not wishing his body to be recovered – and in a bitter and ironic twist to the story – he places in his own jacket pockets the scrap-iron Massy had secreted in order to deflect the compass and scupper the ship: 'Again he had a flash of insight. He was indeed at the end of his tether ... [It] was unseemly that a Whalley who had gone so far to carry a point should continue to live. He must pay the price' (p. 246). And presaging the deliberate choice made by Colin Smith in Sillitoe's 'The Loneliness of the Long Distance Runner' *not* to win the race and secure his path to an easier life (and also foreshadowing the theme of blindness in 'Out of the Whirlpool', which is the fate of the protagonist there), Whalley's choice affirms the notion of a personal moral code that will allow no deviation: the deliberate finality of his action is unambiguous in its meaning.

If the two previous novellas in Conrad's collection are concerned with the themes of maturity ('Heart of Darkness') and old age ('The End of the Tether'), the title novella in this collection of 1902, 'Youth: A Narrative', concerns itself with just that, namely, a young man's first journey (to the East). As in 'Heart of Darkness', using the construct of a 'framed' narrative, an unnamed outer-narrator introduces the characters – including the inner-narrator Marlow, whom we have met before, and who subsequently takes over the story. Here, we have not an old sea-captain driven to despair at the end of his life, or a mature man about to realize some profound truths about the world he inhabits, but a young second mate aged twenty, on the steamship *Judea*, recounting the numerous adventures that befall the vessel and her crew as she makes her way with her cargo of coal from the Tyne to Bangkok. Marlow survives the many perilous adventures of the voyage and believes, twenty years on, as he narrates his tale, that the journey was the making of him, though seemingly not without cost – clearly, the illusion of youth does not match up to reality: 'our weary eyes looking still, looking always, looking anxiously for something out of life, that while it is expected is already gone – has passed unseen, in a sigh, in a flash – together with the youth, with the strength, with the romance of illusions' (p. 39). The strength of the narrative here is predicated to a far greater extent on all the disasters – and they are numerous – which befall the *Judea*, underpinning, more overtly than in the other novellas, Conrad's views on masculinity, colonialism and heroism.

Conrad wrote his best work using the length of the novella, as, arguably, did Henry James, in stories such as 'Daisy Miller: A Study', 'The Aspern Papers' (1888), 'The Pupil' (1891), 'The Figure in the Carpet', 'In the Cage' (1898) and 'The Beast in the Jungle' (1903). James's gothic ghost story 'The Turn of the Screw' (1898), also utilizes the technique of a framed narration seen in 'Heart of Darkness' and 'Youth: A Narrative'. Trebisz (quoting Roger Ramsay) notes how in these novellas 'Conrad was finding his genius, James was playing with his'. As she makes clear, 'the exploitation of the point of view had been recognized by both authors as the very method of making the most of their relatively brief works' (p. 66). The problem of how reality is perceived, and how it is articulated, is foregrounded in many novellas. The novella has a self-reflexive quality, which is due in no small part to its length constrictions, insisting on an intimacy arising out of relative brevity. Henry James's focus of attention, for example, is not so much on action and events, but on the revelation of a situation or a state of mind.

'Daisy Miller: A Study' is a case in point. The novella's heroine, Daisy, trying to live the life of a 'New Woman' in a Victorian world, has a naïve view of the world, represented by the simple summer flower she is named after, unfettered by the conventions which restrict the man who tries to pursue her and subsequently condemns her, Frederick Winterbourne. His name directly confirms his character's antithesis to Daisy – he is winter-born, with all that implies; as 'winter' takes hold, so the 'daisy' withers and dies: 'Daisy's pathetically bare April grave in the fabled Protestant cemetery at Rome is the kind of heartless empty space whose silence reverberates throughout James's early tales of failed courtships and narrowly averted marriages'.[13] Springer believes that the form of the novella is especially appropriate for fictions whose principle of coherence is 'serious or restrainedly tragic, seldom or never ... comic'. The degenerative or pathetic tragedy is another narrative type to which the novella appears particularly suited, and 'Daisy Miller' is a clear paradigm of such a mode, since, as with 'Death in Venice' (and also 'The End of the Tether'), 'its relentlessness and the depth of the misery expand it beyond the single episode which often characterizes the short story'. Here, the central character is driven relentlessly, as Springer observes, towards 'unrelieved misery or death'.[14]

In James's 'The Figure in the Carpet', an unnamed narrator – a literary critic – searches for the elusive, secret meaning in the works of an author called Hugh Verreker, who hints that this secret figures in his work 'like a complex figure in a Persian carpet'.[15] A young woman, Gwendolyn, to whom the secret is eventually told, dies in childbirth, and the secret dies with her. Ultimately, the narrator arrives at no resolution to this mystery, and by extension, no insight into his own limited awareness. Viewed by some critics as an attack on literary critics in general, the story provides a focus on hermeneutics that foregrounds a dialogue on the process as well as the purpose of reading, confronting simplistic notions of interpretation. Similarly, in 'The Beast in the Jungle', the themes of loneliness, love, fate and death are considered in a story that confronts – and ridicules – the idea of a search for the 'ultimate' experience, finally challenging the meaning of life itself. The protagonist, John Marcher, believes that at some point in his life a catastrophic or spectacular life-altering event will occur, lying in wait for him like a 'beast in the jungle'. As a result, his life is in stasis and he will not allow himself to fall in love, marry or have children because of his certainty – burnt into his soul as strongly as any religious creed – that this event will happen. When he meets May Bartram, a woman he used to know, she remembers this hidden secret of his, but despite her best attempts Marcher will not commit to her, so stubborn is his belief that marriage is not for a man such as he, with his exceptional fate. He waits and waits – and so does May – until he finally comes to the catastrophic realization that nothing will ever happen, that he has wasted his whole life for nothing, and that he has also determined May's fate of wasting away her own life in an ultimately futile love for him. Standing by her tomb, the horror of his past life now confronts him:

> This horror of waking – *this* was knowledge, knowledge under the breath of which the very tears in his eyes seemed to freeze [...] But the bitterness suddenly sickened him, and it was as if, horribly, he saw, in the truth, in the cruelty of his image, what had been appointed and done. He saw the Jungle of his life and saw the lurking Beast.[16]

Here, Springer's notion of the 'degenerative' situation is realized in the character of Marcher, where both irony and pathos play out in the tragedy of his life: 'an essentially static character is combined with a learning situation, whereby the pathos emerges at the end and the "education" is seen to be fruitless – Marcher learns "too late"'.[17]

Undoubtedly influenced by James's psychological, structurally complex narratives, modernist writers shaped the novella for their own purposes. James Joyce's 'The Dead' is an early modernist text, written in 1907, but not published until 1914 in the collection *Dubliners*. In the manner of later modernist texts such as *Mrs Dalloway* (1925) and Joyce's own *Ulysses* (1922), with the action nominally taking place in one day – in this case one particular evening – the representation of the political fragility of decaying colonial Ireland is mirrored in the personal history of the protagonist, Gabriel Conroy, as the narrative explores his shifting reflections on his entire life, during the Morkan sisters' annual dinner dance. In recognizing its early modernist features, Daniel R. Schwarz comments: '[i]ts multiple perspectives, dense linguistic texture, and complex unity remind us that "The Dead" was written as Picasso was [painting] *Les Demoiselles d'Avignon*'.[18] The emotionally powerful language of the epiphany which ends the story: 'His soul swooned slowly as he heard the snow falling faintly through the universe and faintly falling, like the descent of their last end, upon all the living and the dead', prompts

Ian McEwan to note that in this novella, 'the young Joyce surpassed himself'.[19]

A contemporary of Joyce's, Katherine Mansfield had met Joyce in Paris in the summer of 1922, after the publication of *Ulysses*. Joyce had noted at the time that she seemed to have far more of an understanding of the book than did her critic husband, John Middleton Murry.[20] Her most celebrated (and longest) stories can be classed as novellas: *Prelude* (1917) and 'At the Bay'. These pieces present us with the minutiae of the daily life of one solidly middle-class family – the Burnells – in colonial Wellington. The capacity of the novella to discover significance in the diurnal is pinpointed in Leibowitz's remark that 'the novella tends to crystallize a large segment of experience, often a whole lifetime, by selecting important moments of that life or by selecting an event which alters its total pattern'.[21] Here, in both stories, the action takes place in a single day, and almost nothing happens of any consequence.

One technique which acts as a marker for these particular stories is the way they begin – *in medias res*, cutting straight through to the action from the very first line, as if a stage direction is being given, occasionally with the use of temporal constructions implying a prior knowledge of the event being described: 'There was not an inch of room for Lottie and Kezia in the buggy';[22] 'Very early morning' (p. 342). In addition, the theatrical/cinematic tone is enhanced in these two novella-length stories by their division into sections or 'scenes'; both are divided into twelve scenes (with 'At the Bay' having an additional four-line scene at the end).

Both stories have an identical narrative style, reflecting their modernist origins: an omniscient point of view, combined with multiple limited points of view represented as free indirect discourse; together with a plotless form, the result is an intimate method of storytelling, where, for certain moments, we become intimate with the character on the page. This use of free indirect discourse would become a hallmark of Mansfield's narrative technique, together with the episodic nature of certain stories and their theatrical quality; as Mansfield remarked in a letter, discussing *Prelude*, 'What form is it you ask? . . . As far as I know, it's more or less my own invention.'[23] Some years later she referred to 'the *Prelude* method – it just unfolds and opens'.[24] Andrew Gurr takes these ideas one stage further, claiming a link with Eliot: '"Prelude" was in all sorts of ways an innovation. Its form, twelve episodes or scenes . . . was original in fiction, its closest kin perhaps being the associative form Eliot developed at the same time for *The Waste Land*.'[25] Mansfield, ever the innovator and seeker after new experiences, was fascinated with the new medium of the cinema. Her narrative art reflects this interest in the deliberate cinematic impression of so many of the stories; it is as if the narrator has a moving camera, panning across, then focusing in, which provides both novellas discussed here with their unique 'pictorial' characteristics. (McEwan, as we shall see, also recognizes the importance of a cinematic quality in the novella.)

'The Aloe' would become the draft for the more polished *Prelude*. As Vincent O'Sullivan notes, 'If critics can now say that "a good case could be made for the short story being the most flexible of all forms and, as such, the key to 'modernism'", and refer to its range as "analytical or lyrical, dramatic or rhapsodic", that is partly because of what Mansfield did, and did for the first time in [these] two versions.'[26] A comparison of the equivalent passages from 'The Aloe' and *Prelude*, reveals how the former was condensed, its verbosity tightened, the images made more direct, fashioned into polished, lyrical, *modernist* prose. Such a comparison also offers a perfect exemplar of how the novella differs from a novel. At sixty-nine pages, 'The Aloe' easily fits into the definition of a novella. Its condensed counterpart, *Prelude* at half the length does too, but 'The Aloe' has far more items introduced – people, animals, images – and much more lengthy descriptions. Here is the same passage in both texts: ('The Aloe') 'Dawn came sharp and chill. The sleeping people turned over and hunched the blankets higher – They sighed and stirred, but the brooding house all hung about with shadows held the quiet in its lap a little longer'; (*Prelude*) 'Dawn came sharp and chill with red clouds on a faint green sky and drops of water on every leaf and blade'. Almost three lines in the first instance are condensed to just over one line in the second. In *Prelude* a scene is presented, and the reader must visualize the image, subjectively, for him- or herself.

D. H. Lawrence, Mansfield's contemporary and erstwhile friend, wrote novels, novellas and short stories, but it is his shorter fiction, some would argue, that has stood the test of time. His novellas include 'The Fox' (first published in 1922), 'The Captain's Doll' (1923), 'The Ladybird' (1923), 'The Woman Who Rode Away' (1925), 'The Princess' (1925), 'St Mawr' (1925), *The Escaped Cock* (1929) and *The Virgin and the Gypsy* (1930). 'The Fox' tells the story of two women, Nellie March and Jill Banford, who struggle to make a living on a small farm, and who are at the mercy of a rogue fox that is killing their chickens – and their livelihood. In this story, the 'fox' is not merely a wily animal but also represented as a predatory male called Henry

Grenfield. Grenfield attempts to woo March and ostracize Banford, whom he eventually kills. Banford, physically weaker than her friend, is no match for the predatory Grenfield – indeed as he becomes closer to March, so in turn March's feelings towards the real fox become more ambivalent, and Banford's warnings as to his true intentions fall on deaf ears. As Keith Sagar notes, 'the imagery throughout has established Henry as the hunter, indeed the fox, with Banford and March both in their different ways his victims. It is all along March's submission which he seeks ... he simply replaces the fox in March's consciousness.'[27] Lawrence uses the novella form to good effect in both 'The Fox' and 'The Woman Who Rode Away' to convey suppressed emotion.

Trebisz notes that with the passage of time, Lawrence's work evinces a 'gradual movement from realism towards symbolism', a development illustrated by these two novellas.[28] 'The Woman Who Rode Away', one of Lawrence's most shocking stories, recounts a woman's solitary religious quest to Mexico, which brings both danger and self-discovery: kidnapped by Chilchui Indians, she becomes their sacrificial victim as they attempt to make some kind of cosmic reconnection. The protagonist's esoteric discourse with one of the Indians enables her finally to acquiesce in her own sacrifice and understand her role in the universe. As Marianna Torgovnick notes: 'the "Indian" speaks in a way very similar to Lawrence's Gypsies, miners, and other "dark men". He is the spokesman for Lawrence's theories about women, theories laced with a fear of female power.'[29] The novella, according to Springer, is particularly suited to the '"apologue" [which] makes use of the characters and what happens to them to maximize "the truth of a statement or statements," a principle which other critics variously call "allegory," "parable," or sometimes "fable"'.[30] Apologues are not to be confused with action plots. In the former, character is subordinate to the message being conveyed; in the latter, we are expected to care what happens to the characters. Springer uses both of these novellas by Lawrence as examples to illustrate this difference. 'The Woman Who Rode Away' may therefore be considered an apologue, since 'character and plot, diction, scene, and all other aesthetic details have been systematically subordinated to the making of the reader's apprehension of the story's final statement' (p. 27), that is, that the phallic principle will always overcome the female. Thus, Lawrence directs the reader to feel no emotion for the woman in the story, so that her impending death is not viewed as distressing. However, in 'The Fox', any message 'is formally subordinate to the making of a serious action' (p. 30).

There is no resolution in this story, only ambiguity: March's redemption, in her unsatisfactory marriage to Grenfield, is incomplete.

H. E. Bates (1905–74) became prolific as a novella-writer in the latter stage of his career. *The Cruise of the Breadwinner* was published in 1946, and he went on to publish twenty-two novellas between 1953 and 1970.[31] These appeared in five collections: *The Nature of Love* (1953); *Death of a Huntsman* (1957); *An Aspidistra in Babylon* (1960); *The Golden Oriole* (1962); and *The Four Beauties* (1968). Arguably his best novella was his last, *The Triple Echo*, published separately in 1970. In this novella, delicate nature imagery is interwoven very effectively with his social and psychological themes and their tragic dénouement. There are certain resonances here with 'The Fox'. The story centres on Alice Charlesworth, the wife of a soldier in the Second World War, left to run the family farm while her husband is a prisoner of the Japanese. Isolated and lonely, she befriends a young soldier, Barton, in a nearby barracks who, detesting army life, eventually deserts and moves into the farmhouse. As a disguise, he assumes the persona of her sister and grows his hair. So good is his disguise that one particular officer looking for him (since he is now classed as a deserter), ends up inviting him to a local dance, an invitation he foolishly accepts. By the end of the night, Barton is unmasked and goes on the run. After his eventual capture, Alice, in her despair, shoots Barton dead with her husband's gun, alongside his captor. As with 'The Fox', it is as a result of external intrusion that safety and love are destroyed. The story is, partly, a bitter response to the way war destroys the lives of non-combatants.

Alan Sillitoe's novellas, 'The Loneliness of the Long Distance Runner' and 'Out of the Whirlpool' reflect a rather different, post-war world of northern working-class youth, at odds with the law and with society. Sillitoe's bleak, existential view of life, confined by the British class system and where any attempt at escape comes at terrible personal cost, is reflected in the characters of his anti-heroes, Colin Smith and Peter Grant. 'The Loneliness of the Long Distance Runner' is written with the memories of the deprivations of the war, fifteen years earlier, still felt in the British population. The class system is also still in place and, for the working class, poverty and hunger are not uncommon. There is an overall sense of disillusionment with post-war Britain, coupled with anger at the perceived lack of opportunities for the working class. Smith's father has died of throat cancer, and during his illness the family has lived on next to nothing. Smith ends up in borstal for petty theft, yet is determined to defy the rules and remain true to himself and his class, reflecting the post-war Labour government's working-class policies of social security, better housing and free medical treatment. This sense of new-found power and rights, together with resentment towards upper-class authority, infects the novella's narrator, since for him, there are only two classes: 'In-law' and 'Out-law', and the working class are 'Out-laws'. Heroism is ultimately a game that only the 'In-laws' believe in. Reflecting on the governor of the prison and the class he represents, Smith's opinions are clear: 'He's dead as a doornail. If he ran ten yards he'd drop dead [...] At the moment it's dead blokes like him as have the whip-hand over blokes like me.' The class divide for Smith, is clear-cut: 'I'd rather be like I am – always on the run and breaking into shops for a packet of fags and a jar of jam – than have the whip-hand over somebody else and be dead from the toe-nails up.'[32] In his refusal to toe the line, when offered the chance of an early release if he comes first in a long-distance running race, he stops before the finish line and refuses to continue, because he wants to show the governor what 'honesty' is: 'I'll stick this out like my dad stuck out his pain' (p. 51). Forced to do menial tasks for a further six months, he claims 'the work didn't break me; if anything it made me stronger' (p. 53). Finally out of borstal, he is left defiant and still stealing, deliberately *unchanged*.

'Out of the Whirlpool', written almost thirty years later, reflects similar themes. In this case, 'honesty' or self-truth for the young protagonist, Peter Grant, results in a similarly bleak, self-destructive outcome. At eighteen, Grant is an orphan living with his grandmother and working in a furniture factory, having dropped out of school at fourteen. He becomes involved with a middle-aged widow, Eileen Farnfield, living with her for a time before returning to his grandmother, a more experienced, but no less isolated young man. Two women let Grant down: first his mother, dying when he was only fourteen. His anger at the beginning of the novella is palpable, symbolized by watching a row of houses being demolished: 'He craved to witness a spectacular annihilation [...] a house pulled out by the roots so that not even rubble remained'. The wealthy, property-owning Eileen Fairfield takes pity on him and offers him a handyman's job, and they soon become lovers. She lets him down by taking another lover behind his back. He uses a gun he has found and cleaned up to attempt to kill the man who has usurped him, but the gun backfires in his face and leaves him blinded. Paradoxically, although now sightless, he 'sees' the world more clearly. Back living with his grandmother, he finds himself in the garden: 'his boots went into the hard and crusty snow. That was real. He could smell the cold, and taste the snow. Therefore, he could see it'.[33] This novella, with its strong echoes of Lawrence's novel *Lady Chatterley's Lover* (1928), confirms once again the class

The Novella: Between the Novel and the Story

divide which typifies Sillitoe's fiction; not even love can bridge the perceived social incompatibility.

Ian McEwan, as noted above, has reinvigorated the use of the novella, another (and perhaps little recognized) sign of his pre-eminence in late twentieth-century and early twenty-first century literature. *The Comfort of Strangers* (1981), one of his earliest works, is a macabre, gothic story of murder and double-crossing, set in Venice (the novella has been compared to Mann's 'Death in Venice'), where a couple on holiday are deceived by a local couple purporting to be their friends, resulting in the murder of the man and the hospitalization of the woman. The enigmatic and haunting beauty of the city is contrasted with the sordid, sadomasochistic life of the 'strangers', who envelop and eventually control the lives of the visiting couple. On publication, the book was criticized, not only for its lurid subject matter, but also because, as with McEwan's first longer fiction, *The Cement Garden* (1978) it was considered to be 'only' a long short story – in other words, a novella. With *Amsterdam* (1998), McEwan proved himself once more a consummately skilful novella writer, using the technique of flashbacks and the division of the book into five sections. The book has been called 'an exquisite social satire or moral fable' – even a burlesque.[34] Also part psychological thriller, the plot centres on three former lovers of the same woman: a foreign secretary, a composer and a newspaper editor. As the narrative unfolds, the discovery of sleazy photographs of the foreign secretary cross-dressing embroils the other two former lovers into a bitter plot as they become mortal enemies, determined to exact revenge on each other, finally leading them both to Amsterdam, and, ultimately, to their own deaths.

The book's overt political influence marked the end of a long period of Conservative rule – mired in the 'politics of sleaze' at its demise. Indeed, the plot is enmeshed in this sleaze, as McEwan satirizes and ultimately ridicules those who, as Dominic Head notes, 'had flourished under a government they had despised for almost seventeen years'; nevertheless, 'the narrative tone is detached, befitting the clinical dissection of amorality in the two principals'.[35] In an interview after the book's publication, McEwan makes important points on its novella form: 'For a long time I wanted to get back to the kind of form, the short novel that could be read in three or four hours, that would be one intact, complete, absorbing literary experience.' Numerous drafts 'involved a process of making it leaner and leaner until I really couldn't lose any more of it'.[36] Here we see how condensed narrative, reworked over several drafts (as with Mansfield), produces novellas of startling brilliance.

This chapter has considered examples from over a hundred years of English novella writing, a tradition which, thanks to McEwan and other contemporary writers such as Will Self, is still alive today, despite a degree of prejudice against the form. The journalist Toby Clements believes that McEwan is 'lucky to be allowed to publish novellas', claiming an unknown writer of the genre would find it very difficult to obtain a publisher: 'Because they don't sell well, publishers don't like them, and so they remain the reserve of the well-established writer with a guaranteed readership.'[37] Indeed, the novelist Stephen King claims the genre can inspire fear in authors: 'At some point, the writer wakes up with alarm and realizes that he's come or is coming to a really terrible place ... an anarchy-ridden literary banana republic called the "novella".'[38] Yet this also signals the technical skill required to master the form. Clements also quotes Philip Rahv's list of what constitutes the novella: 'compositional economy, homogeneity of conception, concentration in the analysis of character, and strict aesthetic control'. The novellas discussed in this chapter can all be said to conform to at least one if not all of these characteristics, representing a genre with an enduring tradition in English literary history.

Notes

1. Malgorzata Trebisz, *The Novella in England at the Turn of the XIX and XX Centuries: H. James, J. Conrad, D. H. Lawrence* (University of Wroclaw, 1992), p. 2.
2. Robert Scholes, 'Towards a Poetics of Fiction: An Approach Through Genre', *NOVEL: A Forum on Fiction*, 2.2 (Winter, 1969), pp. 101–11.
3. Ian McEwan, 'Some Notes on the Novella', *New Yorker*, 29 October 2012, www .newyorker.com/books/page-turner/some-notes-on-the-novella (accessed 9 November 2014).
4. McEwan, 'Some Notes on the Novella'.
5. William Giraldi, 'The Novella's Long life', *Southern Review* (Autumn 2008), pp. 793–81 (p. 794).
6. Mary Doyle Springer, *Forms of the Modern Novella* (Chicago University Press, 1975), p. 8.
7. Judith Leibowitz, *Narrative Purpose in the Novella* (The Hague: Mouton, 1974), pp. 17–18.
8. Tony Whedon, 'Notes on the Novella', *Southwest Review*, 96.4 (2011), pp. 565–71 (p. 566).
9. Frederick R. Karl and Laurence Davies, eds., *The Collected Letters of Joseph Conrad, Volume II: 1898–1902* (Cambridge University Press, 1986), p. 418. (Letter to William Blackwood, 31 May 1902.)

10. Joseph Conrad, *Youth, Heart of Darkness, The End of the Tether*, ed. Owen Knowles (Cambridge University Press, 2010), p. 117. All quotations from Conrad's novellas are from this edition, with subsequent page references given in parentheses in the text.
11. T. S. Eliot, 'The Love Song of J. Alfred Prufrock', in *Collected Poems 1909–1962* (London: Faber & Faber, 2002), p. 6.
12. Trebisz, *The Novella in England*, p. 23.
13. Vivian R. Pollak, ed., *New Essays on 'Daisy Miller' and 'The Turn of the Screw'* (Cambridge University Press, 1993), p. 2.
14. Springer, *Forms of the Modern Novella*, pp. 13, 12.
15. Henry James, 'The Figure in the Carpet', in *The Aspern Papers and Other Stories* (Oxford World Classics, 2013), p. 136.
16. James, 'The Beast in the Jungle', in *Tales of Henry James*, ed. Christof Wegelin and Henry B. Wonham (New York: Norton, 2003), pp. 339–40.
17. J. H. E. Paine, *Theory and Criticism of the Novella* (Bonn: Bouvier, 1979), p. 84.
18. James Joyce, *The Dead*, ed. Daniel R. Schwarz (Boston: Bedford/St Martin's, 1994), p. 81.
19. McEwan, 'Some Notes on the Novella'.
20. See Claire Tomalin, *Katherine Mansfield: A Secret Life* (London: Viking, 1987), p. 224.
21. Leibowitz, *Narrative Purpose in the Novella*, p. 52.
22. Gerri Kimber and Vincent O'Sullivan, eds., *The Collected Fiction of Katherine Mansfield*, 2 vols. (Edinburgh University Press, 2012), II, p. 56.
23. Vincent O'Sullivan and Margaret Scott, eds., *The Collected Letters of Katherine Mansfield*, 5 vols. (Oxford: Clarendon Press, 1984–2008), I, p. 331 (11 October 1917).
24. Mansfield, *Letters*, IV, p. 156 (1 January 1921).
25. Andrew Gurr, 'Katherine Mansfield: The Question of Perspectives in Commonwealth Literature', in *The Critical Response to Katherine Mansfield*, ed. Jan Pilditch (Westport, CT: Greenwood Press, 1996), pp. 197–206 (p. 201).
26. Katherine Mansfield, *'The Aloe' with 'Prelude'*, ed. Vincent O'Sullivan (Manchester: Carcanet, 1983), p. 8.
27. Keith Sagar, *The Art of D. H. Lawrence* (Cambridge University Press, 1976), pp. 116–17.
28. Trebisz, *The Novella in England*, p. 53.
29. Marianna Torgovnick, *Primitive Passions: Men, Women, and the Quest for Ecstasy* (University of Chicago Press, 1998), p. 50.
30. Springer, *Forms of the Modern Novella*, p. 12.
31. See Dennis Vannatta, *H. E. Bates* (Boston: Twayne, 1983), p. 108.
32. Alan Sillitoe, *The Loneliness of the Long-Distance Runner* (London: W. H. Allen, 1959), p. 14. Subsequent page references given in parentheses in the text.
33. Alan Sillitoe, *Out of the Whirlpool* (London: Hutchinson, 1987), pp. 14, 122.

34. Peter Childs, ed., *The Fiction of Ian McEwan* (Basingstoke: Palgrave Macmillan, 2006), p. 118.
35. Dominic Head, *The Cambridge Introduction to Modern British Fiction, 1950–2000* (Cambridge University Press, 2002), pp. 12, 46.
36. 'An interview with Ian McEwan', *Bold Type*, Random House, December 1998, www.randomhouse.com/boldtype/1298/mcewan/interview.html (accessed 9 November 2014).
37. Toby Clements, 'Ian McEwan is lucky to be allowed to publish novellas', *Daily Telegraph*, 15 October 1912, www.telegraph.co.uk/culture/books/9609841/Ian-McEwan-is-lucky-to-be-allowed-to-publish-novellas.html (accessed 9 November 2014).
38. Quoted in Joe Fassler, 'The Return of the Novella: The Original Longread', www.theatlantic.com/entertainment/archive/2012/04/the-return-of-the-novella-the-original-longread/256290/ (accessed 9 November 2014).

32
The Short Story Visualized: Adaptations and Screenplays

LINDA COSTANZO CAHIR

The job and joy of readers of short stories are, in part, to visualize what is on the pages. Inevitably, each reader sees the text differently, as the words connote – imply and suggest meaning – in ways that instigate connections with a reader's knowledge and past experiences. When filmmakers adapt short stories to large and small screens they take these highly connotative print texts and translate their readings of them into moving images that come with or without attending spoken words. Their way of visualizing – of reading – the literary text invariably differs from viewers' readings, which should deepen each viewer's own discernment of the literary work, while simultaneously asking that a perspective other than one's own be considered.

In translating a short story into a cinematic text, the complex question of fidelity to the literature arises. Readers often assume that a page-to-screen filmmaker should be faithful to the literature by recreating the story, setting and characters in exacting compliance to what was written. Many filmmakers do see this as their key goal and strive for visual duplication of the literal world as described in the short story. This literal mode of adaptation, at its best, can create the sensation of film conjuring reality, of making readers feel that, as they watch the story-based movie, they are experiencing – entering and getting lost in – the very world that the writer has created.

However, the majority of short story-based films are not literal adaptations: they are traditional ones. A traditional adaptation allows filmmakers to alter particular details of the short story as they deem appropriate and necessary, while staying close to the narrative contours of the literature. These alterations may be in service of the filmmaker's inventive, stylistic or interpretive values, or for more practical concerns such as contemporary tastes, mores, political climate, censorship, equipment limitations, pressures in casting and budget restrictions. Short stories are particularly prone to traditional film adaptations as their brevity may require expansion of their source material to fit a feature-length movie.

A third approach to film adaptation of short stories regards faithfulness to the literal details of the narrative as less important than faithfulness to exploring the literature's integral meaning. Instead of replicating narrative information, these filmmakers recreate what they see as the essential importance – individuation – of the literary work. The adaptations, consequently, are free to reshape the literal details of the short story in extreme and innovative ways that sculpt what the filmmaker deems most essential to the parent literary text. Simultaneously, this approach asserts that the short story-based film is an independent, self-standing work, with its own aesthetic principles. It values the individuation of the film itself, and, in more experimental cases, draws attention to the idea that the movie is not a facsimile of the short story it is adapting, as literal film translations are deemed to be; instead, it is a fully independent form commenting on, interpreting and re-envisioning the short story, while also detaching from it. Such radical translations may explore theoretical issues raised by the very act of adaptation or may simply explore modes of creating cinematic equivalents of literature, as they see it.

In considering the strength of a short story-based film, an awareness of the three adaptation modes – literal, traditional and radical – is of consequence, since an exploration and evaluation of the merits of the film adaptation should take into account the adaptation mode and the values it was attempting to achieve.[1] A radical film adaptation should not be held to the standards of a literal film, and *vice versa*. In the short story-based films and screenplays discussed throughout this chapter, this paradigm always lingers in the fore or background.

Because it is so story-driven, with even small narrative details important, detective fiction adapted to film usually employs either a literal or a traditional approach. One notable exception is the work of Arthur Conan Doyle, as film translations of his Sherlock Holmes short stories exist in each of the three adaptation modes. During the silent era, strict replication of the literal details of a story was not attempted and, perhaps was not even possible given the brief duration of early silent movies. Instead, radical film adaptations emerged. Conspicuous examples of this can be seen in the prevalence of Sherlock Holmes films that emerged in the silent era, with *Sherlock Holmes Baffled* (1900) providing an early model. Produced for a Mutoscope machine that allows viewing by one person only, the film (less than a minute in duration) visually narrates the tale of a man in the process of robbing a well-appointed home when Sherlock Holmes enters. The robber inexplicably disappears before Holmes's eyes, then reappears, only to disappear again, leaving a very baffled, cigar-smoking, pistol-shooting Sherlock Holmes. Beyond the title of the movie, there seems to be little reference to the physical or psychological details of character or to any one, specific Conan Doyle story. Instead, the movie appears to have appropriated the title in response to the cultural popularity of Sherlock Holmes at the time. Rather than exploring the substance of the literature, the movie, instead, showcases the visual magic (corporeal disappearance before our very eyes) that film of the time was capable of. Mutoscope audiences in 1900, unaware of the nuances of stop/start camera work, would have been as astounded as Holmes was to see the robber inexplicably vanish.[2]

Silent film era movies based on Sherlock Holmes stories were made in abundance. Of the surviving information, films worth noting include: *Held for Ransom* (United Kingdom, 1905), the story of a kidnapped millionaire's child, rescued by Holmes; *Un rivale di Sherlock Holmes* (Italy, 1907), a movie lauded for being 584 feet in length; *A Fool for Luck* (United States, 1908), where an ambitious young man who wants to be like Holmes enrols in a detective correspondence course; and *Sherlock Hochmes: The King of Detectives* (Hungary, 1908), a comic characterization of Holmes being all-knowing. While modern viewers may be tempted to judge these early films as having so little in common with Conan Doyle's short stories as to disqualify them as adaptations, they are, arguably, radical adaptations in that they are faithful to two fundamental radical translation values: that the movie should not be a facsimile of the story, and that alterations to the parent text may be done in service to the filmmaker's values. However, these alterations may be judged as so excessive and so self-involved as to discredit them as legitimate variations on Arthur Conan Doyle's short stories.

The first interesting film adaptation of Conan Doyle's work is arguably the silent film, *Sherlock Holmes* (1922). Also the first Conan Doyle-based film that has a page to stage to screen arc, the movie was adapted from a play by William Gillette that was 'based on the stories of Sir Arthur Conan Doyle'. The film begins with an inter-title taken from Conan Doyle's 'Adventure III: A Case of Identity': 'Life is infinitely stranger than anything which the mind of man could invent. We would not dare to conceive the things which are really mere commonplaces of existence.' While the plot of *Sherlock Holmes* has nothing in common with 'A Case of Identity', the theme of the quote fits the story of this film. When arch-villain Professor Moriarty frames Prince

Alexis for a crime he did not commit, Sherlock Holmes (John Barrymore) is called to intervene, which he does with acute, other-worldly intellect and dramatic panache. *Sherlock Holmes* suggests that integral to Conan Doyle's short stories is the complex characterization of both Holmes and Dr Moriarty. At heart, the film, while lacking in literal details of particular stories, does explore the nature of *both* characters as 'stranger than anything the mind of man could invent'. As film, *Sherlock Holmes* asserts importance for being one of Barrymore's more impressive early roles and for bringing a sophistication of film approaches that earlier cinematic treatments of Conan Doyle's stories lacked. Shot in a studio and on location (Switzerland and Cambridge, England), defined by an early *noir* sense of lighting, framed with a classical approach to composition, edited with an elegance of continuity and memorable for its engaging, character-defining acting, *Sherlock Holmes* has much to recommend close study. However, the excellence of the movie is, arguably and ultimately, overtaken by a trivial script that loses any sense of the deeply engaging plots that Conan Doyle famously constructed.

What each of these silent-era film adaptations of the Conan Doyle Holmes stories share, in addition to the radical approach, is the expanding ambition to find cinematic equivalents of a fully word-based art form. How each movie negotiates this quandary provides a map for the evolution of cinema, itself; and, as the silent-era technology grew increasingly sophisticated, so did the filmic approaches to exploring cinematic equivalents of the word-based art of literature.

The short stories of Sir Arthur Conan Doyle rank as the most frequently filmed stories of the silent era, with these movies invariably being radical adaptations of Sherlock Holmes stories. This era, with its aggressively evolving and increasingly sophisticated film techniques, allowed for traditional film adaptations, a convention which persists even today in large- and small-screen adaptations of the Sherlock Holmes short stories. The Golden Age of Arthur Conan Doyle adaptations emerged in the 1939–46 series of fourteen Sherlock Holmes movies, which have now reached almost legendary status because of their capacity to be reasonably and traditionally faithful to the narrative details of the literature, while imprinting a distinct cinematic impression of what Sherlock Holmes (Basil Rathbone), Dr Watson (Nigel Bruce) and the nineteenth-century England of their lives and adventures looked like.

While many readers of the Sherlock Holmes stories expect literal adaptations of the tales, strict literal renderings of the stories are rather uncommon.

However, in 1984, Granada Television embarked on the ambitious task of adapting each of the Sherlock Holmes short stories in a series entitled *The Adventures of Sherlock Holmes*. Granada was unable to complete the full filming that it had planned (the series came to an abrupt end in 1994 when Jeremy Brett, who played Sherlock Holmes, died), but the episodes they did complete stand as conspicuous examples of a literal translation of Conan Doyle's stories. Filmed in self-standing episodes adapted closely from individual Holmes stories (slightly renamed), the series attempted to reproduce explicitly the visual and narrative information of the stories. The series's commitment to visual replication was so sincere that there are scenes in episodes that attempt to recreate the very *Strand* magazine illustrations which had accompanied a story's original publication. However, while these adaptations respect actualities of character and narrative details and demonstrate skill in replicating them, they fall flat in exploring the subtleties of meaning inherent in Conan Doyle's literary texts.

Since 1946 barely a year has gone by that has not seen a feature-length or short film, an animated short or feature, or a television show based on or referencing Arthur Conan Doyle's detective. Sherlock Holmes is the most frequently portrayed character in cinema and television, and extremely varied approaches have emerged since the early twentieth century: celebrated adaptations (*Sherlock Jr.*, 1924; *The Hound of the Baskervilles*, 1939); deeply flawed ones (*Sherlock Holmes in New York*, 1976; *The Hound of the Baskervilles*, 1978); big budget, period spectacles (*The Adventures of Sherlock Holmes*, 1939; *Sherlock Holmes: A Game of Shadows*, 2011); humorous films (*Without a Clue*, 1988; *The Adventure of Sherlock Holmes' Smarter Brother*, 1975); animated movies (*Sherlock Holmes and the Baskerville Curse*, 1983; *Sherlock Holmes in the 22nd Century*, 1999); and provocative adaptations (*The Private Life of Sherlock Holmes*, 1970; *Sherlock*, BBC series 2010, 2012, 2014).

Detective fiction, with its story-driven narratives, lends itself well to adaptation in film, and while Sherlock Holmes adventures are the stories most frequently translated to small and large screen, there have also been a multitude of television adaptations of short stories by Agatha Christie, G. K. Chesterton and Ruth Rendell, which are, overall, satisfying as traditional adaptations and charming in their depictions of Miss Marple, Hercule Poirot, Father Brown and Inspector Wexford, even when they cartoonize these principal detectives. Writers Julian Symons and Dorothy Sayers, whose short detective stories adapted for television share the writerly value of exploring the psychology of violence behind respectable, ordinary faces, also share a talent for screenwriting as their filmography writing credits attest. While Symons and Sayers write provocative stories that rely less on narrative details of detection and more on psychological inquiry to create suspense, the screen adaptations of their short stories remain consistently unremarkable.

In contrast to Symons and Sayers, Daphne du Maurier, whose writing has been viewed as melodramatic and lacking intellectual complexity, has written works that result in remarkably interesting films. While film adaptations of two of her novels have attained canonical status (*Rebecca*, 1940 and *My Cousin Rachel*, 1952), the adaptation of two of her short stories, 'The Birds' and 'Don't Look Now,' rank among the more interesting studies in the aesthetic correspondence that can resonate between a short story and the film adaptation of it. In fact, the films based on these two du Maurier stories manage to deepen our insights into and appreciation of the parent literature.

In 1960, when Alfred Hitchcock decided to adapt du Maurier's short story, 'The Birds', he had the experience of having filmed, back to back, two other works of hers: the less successful costume drama, *Jamaica Inn* (1939), and the archetypal Hitchcock film, *Rebecca* (1940). In the twenty years since then, Hitchcock's approach to adapting du Maurier's work changed appreciably. *The Birds* emerged as a radical adaptation of du Maurier's short story. Set in a 1950s fictional coastal town in Cornwall, the original story centres on an everyman, Nat Hocken. Injured during the Second World War, but working part-time on the Trigg farm, Nat, alone, notices increasingly odd and aggressive behaviour from birds, which, in ever-escalating suspense, grows into a series of apparently unprovoked and increasingly fatal attacks by the birds on humans. The story ends in ambiguity, as Nat and his family, surrounded by the death of everyone in their neighbourhood and listening to worldwide accounts of similar bird attacks, anxiously await their personal and global fate.

Hitchcock changed the setting of du Maurier's story to 1960s Bodega Bay, California, and transformed the main character, Nat Hocken, into Melanie Daniels (Tippi Hedren), a beautiful and wealthy San Francisco socialite. Melanie impulsively decides to spend the weekend in the coastal town of a young attorney, Mitch Brenner (Rod Taylor), whom she had just met in a pet shop. Arriving in Bodega Bay, she brings Mitch a present she has bought him from the store – Hitchcock's darkly comic touch: two lovebirds. Melanie's injury by a swooping seagull, similar to Nat's initial gull attack, is a portent of the intensifying bird attacks that Hitchcock constructs in visual variation on du Maurier's descriptions. The filming of the bird attacks presented a huge, well-documented, technical challenge for Hitchcock, who succeeded in rendering the escalating eerie, suspenseful and ultimately horrifying tone of the short story, and, like the story, the film creates the terror, contrary to most works of suspense, largely in open spaces and in bright, broad daylight.

In *The Birds* Hitchcock succeeds in mounting psychological insights so suggestive and intriguing as to give birth to an entirely new way of reading Daphne du Maurier's work. Hitchcock's film, with its ambiguous ending similar to du Maurier's ending in spirit if not in letter, raises the question, what do the birds mean or signify? Early critics saw the birds as ecological warnings of the need to change polluting behaviour, as cosmological agents of a god-force dissatisfied with human behaviour, as the annunciators of the perils and arbitrariness of life and as existential manifestations of irrationality and chaos. Lacanian theorists (Robert Samuels and Slavoj Žižek) and feminist scholars (Raymond Bellour and Camille Paglia) began to explore complexities of linguistic and filmic language as signifiers in Hitchcock's adaptations, the effects of psychic injury, the deconstruction of existing relations of power and the roles of passivity and dominance. The vast and varied interpretive approaches to the film ushered in a revisiting of parallel considerations of du Maurier's short story. As the story enriched the film, the film, in turn, enriched the story.

The best literature-to-film translations will do this; they will cross-fertilize. This happened yet again with a second film adaptation of a du Maurier short story, Nicholas Roeg's traditional film translation of her 'Don't Look Now'. The film largely reconstructs the story elements of du Maurier's work, but makes minor alterations to heighten visual import and to expand the forty-five-page story into a feature-length, 110-minute film. In *Don't Look Now* (1973), Roeg retains the setting – Venice – and the four principal characters, as written, and the film narration closely follows the plot structure of the original. In du Maurier's story, John and Laura Baxter, grieving over the recent accidental death by drowning of their young daughter, Christine, are accosted in Venice by an old woman who tells them, 'You see, she isn't dead, she is still with us ... Don't be unhappy any more. My sister has seen your little girl.' This eerie declaration is made more curious when John and Laura seem to catch glimpses of Christine as they walk the watery streets of Venice. As the story progresses, Laura speaks to the two old sisters and wants to believe in their compassion and in the veracity of their alleged spiritual visions. John, however, asserts that they are 'fraudulent' and is angered that they are attempting to 'practice their mediumistic tricks on him'.[3] Uncertainty surrounds the paranormal, an issue further complicated by the fact that, throughout the story, there are distinct situations which suggest that John is clairvoyant, even as he tries to deny it to himself.

The opening sequence of *Don't Look Now* departs from the literature by cross-cutting two scenes that do not appear in the story: the circumstances of Christine's drowning and contemporaneous actions involving her father, who, while working, has the sudden and uncanny experience of sensing that his daughter is in peril. John Baxter (Donald Sutherland) is an art historian and an expert in church restoration, a minor, but particularly interesting, film amendment to the short story. In this initial sequence, John is reviewing slides of photographs he took of a church and seems surprised to see something that he evidently hadn't noticed before: the back view of a young girl who appears to be his daughter. The image somehow telegraphs danger, and John rushes out to find Christine, who has drowned wearing the same red coat that the young girl in the photo had on. In the opening sequence and throughout the film, John Baxter studies, closely and intensely, photographic images. He is expertly trained at scrutinizing what he sees and at determining its authenticity. This action becomes a trope suggestive of themes at the heart of both the film and the short story: can we trust the authenticity of what is before our very eyes? Is it safe and reliable to believe in the actuality of what we see? The human eye, much like the camera's eye, is limited to the material world. Is there a domain – a domain that a church signifies – beyond the material? Roeg's use of disjunctive montages and his blurring of the lines of the supernatural and psychological conspire to deepen the themes raised by du Maurier's story.

At heart, though, both the film and the short story seem to be asking if these questions, *in this context*, are themselves inauthentic, since the asking may merely be the understandable effect of the parents' grief, their deep psychological longing and need to believe that their daughter may still exist somewhere and that they may be able to see her just one last time. In asking these same questions, the film audience and the readership are made complicit in the metaphysical fiction because, like the Baxters, they want to believe that it is possible for John and Laura to make contact with their dead daughter. *Don't Look Now*, with its cinematic beauty and complexity, with its filming of the watery byways of Venice which evoke, in ways that the story may not, the heartrending memory of the death by water of Christine, caused people to read and reread 'Don't Look Now' and to see it as much a tale of neo-gothic suspense as a meditation on metaphysical possibilities, on the psychology of grief and the divergent modes through which a mother and a father may attempt to deal with it, and on reader-response theory. It is a page-to-screen adaptation where each of the two texts benefits from illumination by the other.

While their story-driven narratives contribute to the popularity of film versions of detective and suspense literature, film versions of science fiction are also popular, but for a different reason. Science fiction is constructed around what film does best: visual detail and the magic of making what does not really exist. Film adaptations of the early science fiction novels of H. G. Wells (*The War of the Worlds*, 1897; *The Time Machine*, 1895; *The Invisible Man*, 1897; and *The Island of Dr Moreau*, 1896) are as abundant as they are varied in quality. However, there is also a significant roster of films based on the short stories of Wells. In 1902 Georges Méliès filmed *A Trip to the Moon* (*Le voyage dans la lune*), a black-and-white silent, sixteen-minute film now of canonical stature. Often included on lists of the one hundred greatest movies, *A Trip to the Moon* is an amalgam of Jules Verne's novel, *From the Earth to the Moon* (1865), and H. G. Wells's long short story, 'The First Men in the Moon' (1901). Important as the first science fiction movie, *A Trip to the Moon* dazzled 1902 audiences with its special effects showing Professor Barbenfouillis and his crew (a loose rendering of Wells's lunar crew, Dr Cavor and Mr Bedford) landing on the moon, with impressions of Earth from that vantage point. Film historians marvel at the technique and composition of Méliès' silent film, with the picture of the space capsule landing precisely on the moon's right eye now an iconic image.[4] The silent era also saw film versions of lighter Wells short stories. *The Tonic*, *Daydreams* and *Blue Bottle* were made as three separate, two-reel silent films that formed the compendium, *H. G. Wells Comedies* (1928), co-directed by Wells's son, Frank Wells, along with Ivor Montagu.

A versatile author, H. G. Wells also wrote screenplays and film scenarios, and his stories were adapted (posthumously) for *BBC's Sunday-Night Theatre* in the 1950s. However, it is his science fiction novels and short stories, and the film adaptations of them, for which he is still best known. The 1936 film adaptation of Wells's 'The Man Who Could Work Miracles' (1898) has continued as something of a charming favourite. With the narrative arc and much of the dialogue taken directly from the story, but with the addition of minor scenes and characters that did not appear in the literature, the movie is a traditional adaptation of the Wells story about George McWhirter Fotheringay, 'a little man' inexplicably given the power to perform miracles. Part science fiction, part fantasy and part allegory, the story is a light meditation on the uses and misuses of power. The movie also adds a frame structure that features three minor deities, underlings of 'The Master', who fully disdain humankind and state: 'If they had power, they would be no better.' They decide to test this premise by giving one human, George Fotheringay, the ability to perform miracles. He does, and the 1936 movie's special effects show George flipping an oil lamp without touching it, raising a bed, commanding the disappearance and reappearance of Constable Winch into the flames of Hades and performing the mildly risqué act of re-attiring Maggie Hooper (Sophie Stewart) in 'splendid robes like those of Cleopatra in the movies'. The film is flawed by inflated music, choppy editing, distracting key lighting and stage-delivered dialogue. These flaws are made incidental, however, by the performance of Roland Young who, even without Wells's 'erect red hair, a moustache with ends that he twisted up, and freckles' creates a George Fotheringay so charming as to be memorable.[5]

One of the most memorably prodigious science fiction films ever made, *2001: A Space Odyssey* (1968), resulted from the collaboration of two British greats: the writer Arthur C. Clarke and the filmmaker Stanley Kubrick. Using Clarke's short story 'The Sentinel' as a starting point, Clarke and Kubrick co-wrote the screenplay, which Clarke eventually expanded into a novella, *2001: A Space Odyssey*. Structured in four separate but related vignettes, *2001* speculates intelligently on the evolution of humankind. Cinematically stunning, philosophically evocative, hauntingly ambiguous and eerily memorable for its approach to characterization, the film often makes the roster of critics' ten greatest films.

Because of the highly visual nature of science fiction and the story-driven nature of detective and suspense fiction, these genres are generally suited to film adaptation, as is a related genre, espionage. Although most of the better-known espionage adaptations are based on novels (those of British writers Ian Fleming, Graham Greene, Frederick Forsyth, Len Deighton and John le Carré, for example), there are also notable film adaptations of shorter works. Alfred Hitchcock based two of his espionage thrillers, *Secret Agent* (1936) and *The Man Who Knew Too Much* (1934, 1956), on short stories.[6] The two separate versions of *The Man Who Knew Too Much* were each moderately flawed, story-driven adaptations of the 1922 G. K. Chesterton story of the same title. *Secret Agent*, Alfred Hitchcock's critically successful

1936 suspense film, is an adaptation of W. Somerset Maugham's espionage stories, 'The Traitor' and 'The Hairless Mexican', both from the short story collection, *Ashenden: Or the British Agent* (1928). Maugham's compendium of stories was also the basis of the 1991 four-part BBC1 series *Ashenden*. The BBC series and the espionage films are, understandably, plot-driven adaptations of the literature.

While the genres discussed above (detective, suspense, espionage and science fiction) make for hospitable transitions to film, other literary genres can be more difficult for film to negotiate. Great dramatic fiction, for example, often leads the reader into the interiority of characters, into an introspection of character thoughts, feelings and motivations. Film can reconstitute plot and can produce, in a split second, an abundance of visual detail that literature cannot possibly replicate even in pages and pages of description, but it is less naturally suited to representing the interiority that literature explores so naturally. A second example taken from Maugham's writing illustrates this very point.

W. Somerset Maugham's short story 'The Letter' narrates the ever-shifting details surrounding the point-blank shooting of Geoff Hammond by Leslie Crosbie. Maugham's omniscient narrator recounts in vivid and protracted detail Mrs Crosbie's description of what happened that night: Hammond began with unwanted declarations of love, which she rebuffed, kindling his ensuing physical assault of her. Later she succinctly summarizes the ordeal: 'He tried to rape me, and I shot him.' Leslie Crosbie has the full support of her husband, Robert, who believes the killing is justified, even laudable, stressing this by rhetorically asking the attorney they have hired, 'is it murder to exterminate noxious vermin?'[7] The attorney, Howard Joyce, inevitably starts to piece together strands of evidence: circumstantial evidence (the firing of six shots seems excessive for self-defence); and material evidence (a desperate letter Leslie has written to Hammond). As further proof emerges, it becomes clear that Leslie Crosbie had been having a long-term affair with Hammond, who, unbeknown to her, had been simultaneously supporting an Asian mistress. When Leslie discovers the truth, she kills him in jealous anger. The story's magic is not in its plot details, which are generally foreseeable, but in defending attorney Howard Joyce's internal reactions to the quiet waves of emerging truths that he would prefer not to see, in his inner weighing of legal versus moral obligation and in his moments of insight and disgust. The delicacy of the writing comes through in the subtle shifts of internal response that Leslie Crosbie must navigate in reaction to the shifts in evidence mounting against her. In 'The Letter' the most significant responses are interior – Robert Crosbie's later reaction to his wife's infidelity – and Maugham is quietly powerful in cataloguing them all.

The challenge before filmmakers who attempted adaptations of 'The Letter' was how to make the deeply private and interior, exterior. There are three unremarkable attempts: a 1929 early sound film; a 1947 version (*The Unfaithful*); and a 1982 adaptation for American television. Although the 1929 film is praised for its acting, each of these movies is little more than melodrama. However, the 1940 adaptation is an entirely different case. Directed by William Wyler, produced by Hal B. Wallis, and starring Bette Davis (Leslie Crosbie), Herbert Marshall (Robert Crosbie) and James Stephenson (Howard Joyce), *The Letter* is a remarkable example of dramatic film exploring character interiority. Through savvy camera placement, movement and lighting (cinematographer, Tony Gaudio), precise editing (George Amy and Warren Low), emotionally heightening music (composer, Max Steiner) and effectively nuanced film acting, *The Letter* stands as a testament to film as a collaborative art form.

The Letter was a traditional adaptation of Maugham's short story, with the most significant alterations of the literature done in compliance with the American censorship demands of The Production Code, then under the direction of William Hays. Since neither unpunished murder nor adultery was allowed to be depicted on screen, the screenplay, perforce, modified Maugham's plot details, making Geoff Hammond's mistress into his wife, who, contrary to the story's ending, kills Leslie Crosbie to avenge her husband's murder. A Production Code insistence that Maugham's language be softened resulted in the movie's now-famous tag line: 'He tried to make love to me and I shot him.' The film's opening sequence is legendary, with a leisurely tracking shot that moves down the rubber trees of the Crosbies' Singapore plantation, through thatched huts where native workers doze in moonlight heat, past a perching white cockatoo, and onto a veranda where the quietude is harshly interrupted by a series of two pistol shots; a well-dressed man stumbles out, and a woman follows holding a smoking pistol, which she deliberately fires into him four more times. The woman's face is remarkably expressionless, signalling an interior state where her act is possible only because she emotionally disengages from her conduct. Steeped in the hypocrisy of colonial justice, *The Letter* – with its remarkably subtle performances enhanced by deep-focus long shots juxtaposed against tight framing – moves beyond melodrama to a domain affecting in its portrayal of characters' interior motivations, passions and fears.

Character interiority unfolds in stirring ways in *Odour of Chrysanthemums* (2002), a short film (just twenty-eight minutes long) based on D. H. Lawrence's story of the same title. The film respectfully follows Lawrence's account of Elizabeth Bates, a young wife and mother in a Nottinghamshire mining village. Elizabeth bitterly assumes that Walter Bates, her abusive husband, is late in returning home from work because of his chronic detours to the local pub. On this day, however, Walter has been killed in a mining accident. His coal-painted body is brought home, and as Elizabeth attempts to make a resting place for it, she moves a small vase of chrysanthemums, the flower she associates with the first bloom of their love and of other small, tender moments she has shared with Walter. The symbol of the chrysanthemums is evocative, implicit and compassionate, and as deep and complex as Elizabeth's feelings are in looking at her dead husband and the chrysanthemum vase beside him.

The film *Odour of Chrysanthemums* narrates Lawrence's story with extraordinary insight. Produced, directed and photographed by Mark Partridge, who also co-wrote the screenplay, the film, while apparently a traditional adaptation of Lawrence's story, assumes the avant-garde values of pure cinema. In the *camera stylo* convention, Partridge uses his camera as a writer uses a pen. The result is a highly visual creation, and while not a silent movie, the film's verbal and aural modes are of minimal consequence. As a film 'Odour of Chrysanthemums' communicates most deeply through its construction of moving images, with the camera doing so much more than merely narrating the story. The interacting values of composition, stasis and movement come together in memorable sequences that recreate the momentously sad realizations that Elizabeth Bates (Geraldine O'Rawe) undergoes. The stylistic arrangement of everything in the frame – the *mise-on-scène* – is suggestive of the paintings of Johan Vermeer: the composition of domestic interior scenes, the use of Vermeer colours (earth tones of ochre and umber and natural blues of lapis lazuli), and extraordinary chiaroscuro lighting. In *Odour of Chrysanthemums* Partridge's camera writes for Lawrence and it writes beautifully, expressively, and implicitly.[8]

In stark contrast to the film *Odour of Chrysanthemums*, the film *The Dead* (1987), relies heavily on dialogue and music and falls short at delineating the character interiority so central to James Joyce's short story of the same title. A reverent obeisance to Joyce's words nullifies the inventiveness necessary to create filmic equivalencies of them. Like Lawrence's 'Odour of Chrysanthemums', Joyce's story is constructed around an alienated married couple (Gabriel and Gretta Conroy), a wife's complex reaction to the death of a man she once loved and the epiphany that comes in realizing the deathly isolation that the couple share. Joyce's stream-of-consciousness technique presents the free flow of Gabriel's thoughts and sensations, creating the wonderful illusion that the reader is inside Gabriel's mind.

Film has a long history of exploring techniques for creating stream of consciousness in its medium; however, *The Dead* explores none of these methods.[9] Instead, voiceover narrations reading Joyce's literature present the interiority that the camera would achieve in more inventive filmmaking. However, the visual and aural recreations of Joyce's Dublin are intriguing: the Morkan sisters' home and annual dance; the plates of goose and ham and spiced beef; Bartell D'Arcy singing 'The Lass of Aughrim'; the backlighting of Gretta Conroy standing remotely on the stair landing listening to D'Arcy; the Gresham Hotel of the early twentieth century; and the snow blanketing Dublin. James Joyce once remarked that his novel *Ulysses* depicted Dublin so accurately that were it destroyed, Dublin could be reconstructed brick by brick from his descriptions. The film *The Dead*, a slavishly reverent film adaptation, studied to the point of stultification, could claim Dublin's reconstruction by its frame-by-frame depictions. The movie works effectively as a companion piece to Joyce's story, recreating the literal sights and sounds of Gabriel Conroy's stultified world. Ironically, however, given Joyce's theme of paralysis, there is also something stagnant about it.

Angels and Insects (1995) does an equally skilled job of depicting the sights and sounds of its world, aristocratic Bredely Hall of Victorian England and the parallel insect studies of its central character, entomologist and explorer William Adamson (Mark Rylance), who has fallen in love with Eugenia Alabaster (Patsy Kensit), the daughter of Sir Harald Alabaster (Jeremy Kemp). The unbridled passion that William Adamson (a word play on Adam's son) experienced among the Amazon natives contrasts with the sophisticated propriety of Bredely Hall (a play on well-bred and breeding), but when William marries Eugenia he becomes entangled in a family degeneracy, kept secret, but which he comes to discern with the help of Lady Alabaster's companion, Matty Crompton (Kristin Scott-Thomas). From a screenplay based on A. S. Byatt's allegorical story 'Morpho Eugenia', *Angels and Insects* is as painstaking a recreation of its literary world as is *The Dead*. To that, however, it adds a visual audacity that captures the weirdness, the startling chill, the intensity of perversion and the formidable beauty that weaves throughout Byatt's story. Under the direction of Philip Haas, the cinematography (Bernard Zitzermann), the editing (Belinda Haas), the screenplay (Philip and Belinda Haas), the art direction (Alison Riva) and the costumes (Paul Brown) conspire with the actors in this visual study of propriety and free-ranging passion. Working and re-working the author's device of insect behaviour as a trope for the complicated society of Bredely Hall, the movie searches for filmic equivalents of what Byatt put on the page. While uneven in its degree of success in negotiating this ambition, *Angels and Insects* is as uninhibited in its ventures as its main character, William Adamson, was in his Amazonian affairs.

Rather than painstakingly recreating the world of the short story or ambitiously exploring the integral meaning of the literature, some screen adaptations have simply celebrated the story's entertainment value. This has given rise to an entire short story-based television industry that, in rare instances, produces shows so enjoyable and noteworthy as to be memorable. The most legendary of these is *Alfred Hitchcock Presents* (1955–62). A mixture of irony and camp and horror and suspense, the American television series opened weekly with the now-iconic black silhouette of Hitchcock accompanied by Gounod's 'Funeral March of a Marionette'. Hitchcock's amusingly droll introductions to the episodes often lampooned the products of the very sponsors of that evening's telecast, adding to the iconoclastic tone of the show. Preferring to work from published short stories rather than original teleplays, Hitchcock based episodes on works by British writers Dorothy L. Sayers, Eric Ambler, Louis Pollock, Roald Dahl, John Collier, Stacy Aumonier, Thomas Burke, Ann Bridge, Rupert Croft-Cook, Saki (Hector Hugh Munro) and A. A. Milne.

In the tradition of *Alfred Hitchcock Presents*, Roald Dahl's *Tales of the Unexpected* emerged as a popular British television series (1979–88). Originally based on Dahl's collection of sixteen stories of the same title, the show was characterized by Dahl's signature writing device: twisting, unforeseen endings. Over the show's ten-year span, various Dahl stories were used, with additional writers contributing original teleplays, also. The combination of the unexpected story twists and Dahl's own introduction to many of the episodes resulted in an uncommonly entertaining, long-running series. Both *Alfred Hitchcock Presents* and *Tales of the Unexpected* were spun-off into publications of short story collections with their sales enhanced by the pioneering marketing tool of television tie-ins.

One of the longer running British television series (1963–present), the esoteric *Doctor Who*, is based on original source material, not on previously published short stories. Like Hitchcock's and Dahl's shows, *Doctor Who* has generated series tie-in short story collections. More interestingly, though, *Doctor Who* has ushered in a significant moment in the history of the short story. Fans of the show write their own stories based on series characters and events, and they share these writings on various Internet sites. From this, a significant Internet sub-culture of writers has emerged; and, while not inspired by a short story itself, *Doctor Who* has the distinction of inspiring active global, colonies of short story writers.

In rare instances the imprint left by particular film adaptations of short stories are so affecting as to elicit a collective response. The Granada TV series, *Country Matters* (1972–3), based on short stories by A. E. Coppard and H. E. Bates, galvanized audiences in their appreciation of the series' unsentimental observations of early twentieth-century British country life. In its relentless detail of place, circumstances and character, *Country Matters* provoked insights into the often-harsh realities of countryside existence, while doing so with praiseworthy cinematic crafting.

Short stories chosen for film adaptation are, invariably, high-concept works. They are, in some way, unique and inordinately visual. They have a clear emotional focus and a plot that can be pitched in a pithy line or two. Some have great literary value, while others do not. What they all share is a quality that attracts filmmakers to the infinity of approaches they can employ in adapting the story to the screen. In each case, the film's inception did not surge, *sui generis*, from the creative imagination of a filmmaker, but rather from the conceptual values of a concise and evocative short story.

Notes

1. Linda Cahir, *Literature into Film: Theory and Practical Approaches* (Jefferson, NC: McFarland & Company, Inc., 2006), pp. 13–18.
2. The silent film, 'Sherlock Holmes Baffled' can be seen in entirety on YouTube; most films cited in this chapter are available in total or part there. However, since YouTube sustains a fluid archive of holdings, availability of titles is ever changing.
3. Daphne du Maurier, 'Don't Look Now', in *No, But I Saw the Movie*, ed. David Wheeler (New York: Penguin, 1989), pp. 65–110 (pp. 70–1 and 73).
4. Four subsequent films were made of H. G. Wells's 'The Men in the Moon': 1919 (Gaumont), silent; 1964 (Columbia); 2010 (Can Do Productions); and 2010 (Praxinoscope LLC), a 3-D version.
5. H. G. Wells, 'The Man Who Could Work Miracles', in *The Complete Short Stories of H. G. Wells*, ed. John Hammond (London: Phoenix, 1999), pp. 399–412 (p. 399).

6. Hitchcock filmed Chesterton's short story twice, in 1934 and 1956. When François Truffaut asked why, Hitchcock described the 1934 version as the work of an amateur and the 1956 version as the product of a professional.
7. W. Somerset Maugham, 'The Letter', in *Collected Stories* (London: Alfred A. Knopf, 2004), pp. 565–98 (pp. 575 and 568).
8. Mark Partridge was the director of photography for the successful Inspector Lynley Mysteries (series IV and V) for BBC Television.
9. Stream-of-consciousness technique poses a conundrum for filmmakers, since, by definition, it is a non-visible state. Alain Resnais's movies are interesting given this issue and Hain Callev's book, *The Stream of Consciousness in the Films of Alain Resnais* (New York: McGruer Publishing, 1997), is particularly instructive.

33
The Short Story Anthology: Shaping the Canon

LYNDA PRESCOTT

One of the ways in which short stories are like poems (rather than like novels) is that they lend themselves to being collected for publication in anthologies. According to the *Oxford English Dictionary* the original meaning of 'anthology', in ancient Greek, was 'a collection of the flowers of verse, i.e. small choice poems, *esp.* epigrams, by various authors'. In fact, 'flowers' and 'choice' are appropriate terms for the first literary anthologies in Britain that appeared during the publishing boom of the second quarter of the nineteenth century: these were gift-books, containing a mix of poetry and prose that would be suitable for young women readers. Annuals such as *The Keepsake* were designed as elegant, illustrated gift-books, published each autumn in time for Christmas and New Year present-giving. *The Keepsake*, which ran from 1828 to 1857, enjoyed enormous sales figures and included in its roster of contributors some of the best-known writers of the day, including Walter Scott, Harrison Ainsworth and Mary Shelley (most of Shelley's short fiction was first published in this way). The concept of annual short story anthologies has remained an important one in the development of the genre: sifting and circulating stories in yearly compilations helps to maintain the genre's visibility in the literary marketplace as a form of writing which is 'of the moment'. But there are numerous cross-currents in the tide of anthologies that regularly wash the shorelines of bookshops, classrooms or the virtual fringes of the Internet, and more specialized collections range across named periods, places, themes or sub-genres. Although the majority of short story anthologies are commercially oriented, often featuring specific genres such as fantasy or ghost stories, literary anthologies can occupy influential spaces in terms of helping to shape tradition. They can not only build and perpetuate the reputations of particular writers and particular short stories, but they can also influence the formation of canons.

The Short Story Anthology: Shaping the Canon

The routes by which individual stories find their way into anthologies are various. The 'standard' route would probably begin with the short story being published in a magazine, then, if the writer is sufficiently successful, it might be gathered with other stories in a single-authored collection; from here an anthologist might single it out for reprinting amongst a number of stories by other writers. For example, V. S. Pritchett's 'A Family Man' first appeared in the *New Yorker* in 1977, then two years later was published with eight more of Pritchett's recent stories in *On the Edge of the Cliff*, then in 1987 Malcolm Bradbury selected it for *The Penguin Book of Modern British Short Stories*. The first stage, magazine publication, is easier to achieve than the second, a single-authored collection: unless a writer has already built a reputation, usually as a novelist (though Pritchett would be an exception here), the market for single-authored short story collections is uncertain. So adventurous anthologists might go back to magazines, or perhaps short story compilations associated with a specific prize or project, to find less well-known writers and stories. Such 'prize or project' volumes could themselves be viewed as anthologies, sometimes bringing contemporary stories into print for the first time. However, the canon-forming function of anthologies is most clearly evident when there is a longer historical perspective on the selection.

There are two ways in which short story anthologies can employ such historical perspectives: general anthologies are often organized chronologically, whilst more specialized collections carve up the history of the genre into periods. At the 'origins' end of the historical sweep, anthologists of English short stories are arguably dealing with a less clearly delineated field than compilers of American short stories. This is not simply because studies of American literature have traditionally paid considerable attention to the evolution of nineteenth-century tales and short stories but also because in the United States the nature of the genre was debated in formal terms from an early date, beginning with Edgar Allan Poe's 1842 review of Nathaniel Hawthorne's *Twice-Told Tales*. In contrast, the English short story in the nineteenth-century was less well defined and, although commercially successful, was paid less attention than the realist novel. Dickens's work is a case in point. Although a story such as 'The Signal-Man' can often be found in short story anthologies, the editor of his *Selected Short Fiction* noted in 1976 that 'many of the assorted stories and sketches which Dickens produced throughout his career defy conventional categorization and now lie buried in remote corners of his collected works'.[1] 'The Signal-Man' was a comparatively late story, which Dickens produced for the Christmas number of his weekly magazine *All the Year Round* in 1866. *All the Year Round* and its predecessor, *Household Words*, were amongst the few English middle-range magazines catering to the kind of readership equivalent to the popular American *Harper's Monthly* (another key difference in the way the short story developed on opposite sides of the Atlantic). For the most part, the British short story market was divided along serious versus popular lines, and it is the stories published in upmarket periodicals such as *Blackwood's Edinburgh Magazine*, *The Monthly Magazine* and, later, titles such as *Belgravia* and *The Strand Magazine* that have found their way into anthologies of nineteenth-century short stories.

Retrieving short fictional texts from the earlier part of the nineteenth century is more problematic than selecting from the abundance of stories published in the century's later decades. One compilation that manages century-long coverage is the Routledge anthology, *Nineteenth-Century Short Stories by Women* (1998), with original publication dates ranging from 1804 to 1898. Women's writing has been a productive field for anthologists. As Susan Hill, the editor of the *Penguin Book of Modern Women's Short Stories* (1991) pointed out, over half the short stories written during the twentieth century were written by women, but this was not a new development. Writing stories for magazines and annuals was a steady source of income for significant numbers of nineteenth-century women writers. The Routledge anthology includes twenty-eight stories, some by writers well known as novelists, such as Maria Edgeworth (with 'The Limerick Gloves' from her *Popular Tales* of 1804), Elizabeth Gaskell (represented by one of her *Household Words* stories, 'A Manchester Marriage', 1858) and Margaret Oliphant (whose 'A Story of a Wedding Tour' appeared in *Blackwood's* in 1898). Over half of the stories in this anthology are from the 1890s, reflecting the rise of 'little magazines' such as *The Yellow Book*, which, though short-lived (1894–7), proved an influential outlet for women's fiction.

Several of the writers represented in the Routledge anthology also appear in *The Broadview Anthology of Victorian Short Stories* (2004), though for the most part different stories are selected. An exception is Mary Shelley's *Keepsake* story of 1833, 'The Mortal Immortal', which not only appears in both these modern anthologies but was already a favourite in nineteenth-century collections. The novelist Charles Gibbon reprinted it in his two-volume anthology, *The Casquet of Literature, being a Selection of Prose and Poetry from the Works of the Most Admired Authors* (1873–4), and during the 1890s it appeared in further English and American collections. As a story of 'the supernatural' with thematic links to Shelley's earlier novel, *Frankenstein*, it has featured in several genre-based anthologies, including Sam Moskowitz's *Masterpieces of Science Fiction* (1966). Another story that appears in both the Routledge anthology of women's short stories and the Broadview *Victorian Short Stories* is Mary Elizabeth Braddon's 'Eveline's Visitant' (1862). This, too, has been appropriated for genre-based anthologies, including the 2005 *Wordsworth Book of Horror Stories*.

Routledge's *Nineteenth-Century Short Stories by Women* can be seen as part of the later twentieth-century's recovery of women's literature that was stimulated by works of feminist criticism such as Ellen Moers's *Literary Women* (1976) and Elaine Showalter's *A Literature of their Own* (1977). At the same time, new feminist publishers, notably Virago (founded 1973) and the Women's Press (founded 1978), promoted both fictional and nonfictional writing, including some anthologies. Again, sub-genres can be seen to flourish, as in the Women's Press wittily titled collections of crime stories, *Reader, I Murdered Him* (edited by Jen Green, 1989) and *Reader, I Murdered Him, Too* (edited by Helen Widrath, 1995). Although many of the authors in these collections are American, United Kingdom-based contributors include the prominent Scottish crime writer Val McDermid. Back in the mainstream of literary short stories, Virago published in 1986 one of the best-known anthologies of twentieth-century women's short stories, *Wayward Girls and Wicked Women*, subtitled *An Anthology of Subversive Stories*, edited by Angela Carter. Again, only a minority of the eighteen authors represented are English, but Carter sets the tone with her own story of a dominatrix marionette, 'The Loves of Lady Purple'. *Wayward Girls and Wicked Women* was republished by Penguin Books in 1989 with a back-cover blurb declaring that 'They are discontented, bad mannered and won't play by the rules', a more sensationalist claim than Carter's comment in her introduction that the women in the anthology's stories 'at least contrive to evade the victim's role by the judicious use of their wits'.[2] The thematic nature of the collection aside, *Wayward Girls and Wicked Women* indicates how an anthology can be shaped by its editor's affiliations or individual traits, in this case, Carter's adventurous and politicized approach to fiction-writing.

Thematic or period-based anthologies are clearly a boon to college or university teachers compiling booklists, since they enable breadth of reading without making undue demands in terms of length. Like other titles from this publisher of academic texts and editions, *The Broadview Anthology of Victorian Short Stories* is designed with the student in mind, and it comes with an introduction by the editor, Dennis Denisoff, outlining the literary and social historical context for the collection, short introductions to each of the authors represented, footnotes to the stories themselves and five substantial appendices. At secondary school level, too, short story anthologies have provided breadth and variety within a single set of covers for English teachers seeking to extend their pupils' reading range. The English Association, which was founded in 1906 primarily to develop English Studies in schools, published its own short story anthologies under the title *English Short Stories of Today*, the first of which appeared in 1939. The selection of stories was designed to showcase the work of eminent authors, including two best known as short story writers, M. R. James and Saki (Hector Hugh Munro), alongside major figures such as H. G. Wells and the 1932 Nobel Laureate, John Galsworthy. Although the stories were selected as being suitable for schoolchildren, this did not preclude some adventurous choices, notably Evelyn Waugh's 'Mr Loveday's Little Outing', Mr Loveday being a psychopath and his 'little outing' being for the purpose of committing another murder. A second series of *English Short Stories of Today* appeared in 1958 and Oxford University Press took over the publication with further volumes in 1965 and 1976. By the time of the fourth series in 1976 the list of authors included what would then have been called 'Commonwealth writers', such as Chinua Achebe, V. S. Naipaul and R. K. Narayan: here we can see the inclusive potential of short story anthologies aiding new developments in canon-formation as postcolonial writers came to the fore.

The fact that Oxford University Press reprinted collections originally published by the English Association indicates that the grey area between 'academic' and 'trade' books can be quite wide where short story anthologies are concerned. But some anthologies compiled for educational use declare their intended readership very clearly in their titles. The poet, novelist and educationist David Holbrook edited three volumes for Cambridge University Press under the title *People and Diamonds: An Anthology of Modern Short Stories for Use in Secondary Schools*, a two-volume publication in 1962 followed by a third (confusingly numbered 'volume 2') in 1965. Holbrook does not restrict himself purely to English writers – for example, the 1965 volume opens with F. Scott Fitzgerald's 'The Diamond as Big as the Ritz' – but the other four stories in this anthology include what might be considered 'classic' English stories. 'Odour of Chrysanthemums', probably the most famous of D. H. Lawrence's short stories, is here, along with 'The Machine Stops', which is equally prominent amongst E. M. Forster's short story output.

Like so many anthologists, Holbrook also turns to Joyce's *Dubliners*, in this case selecting 'The Boarding House', to follow 'Odour of Chrysanthemums' – the stylistic contrasts all the more striking across the stories' largely domestic settings. The only story in this volume not still widely read is T. F. Powys's 'Lie Thee Down, Oddity!' Powys's idiosyncratic stories were reprinted fairly regularly in anthologies from the middle of the twentieth century, such as Faber's 1964 *Modern Short Stories*, edited by Jim Hunter, where again 'Lie Thee Down Oddity!' appears in the company of stories by Lawrence and Fitzgerald. During the later part of the twentieth century Powys's work tended to fade from view, but the 2011 re-issue by Faber of his short story collection *God's Eyes A-Twinkle* (along with several of his novels) suggests that his stories have not slipped out of the canon entirely; it may be that his frequent inclusion in anthologies has helped to shore up his reputation.

The middle decades of the twentieth century were gala years for anthologies of 'modern' and/or English short stories. John Hadfield's collection of 20 *Modern Short Stories*, which included American as well as English writers, was first published by Dent in 1939 and was still in print, under the title *Modern Short Stories to 1940*, in 1984. Also in 1939 Oxford University Press brought out, in their World's Classics series, *Modern English Short Stories*, edited by Phyllis M. Jones, spanning the years 1888–1937. This was followed up in 1956 by a second series, *Modern English Short Stories 1930–1955*, edited by Derek Hudson, who concluded his introduction with: 'This much is certain – that these stories do not derive from a dying art. Among them perhaps one or two will live to speak, fifty years hence, for English literature.'[3] The idea of one or two short stories speaking 'for English literature' was always going to be a rather suspect proposition, and from a twenty-first-century vantage-point it looks as though a good proportion of Hudson's authors, let alone the stories through which they are represented, are either neglected or forgotten. Who now reads the stories of Frances Towers (1885–1948), John Moore (1907–67), Christopher Sykes (1907–86) or Nigel Kneale (1922–2006), even if the latter's BBC Quatermass serials are remembered enthusiastically? Amongst the still firmly canonical writers in the anthology, the stories selected have not proved to be the most enduring: Virginia Woolf's late story 'The Duchess and the Jeweller' and Elizabeth Bowen's 'Maria' are not now considered as high points of their authors' art, although Hudson does better with Rosamond Lehmann, whose 'A Dream of Winter' continues to appear in more recent anthologies.

In fact, despite the great number of English/modern short story anthologies that appeared in the middle of the twentieth century, a sense of uncertainty seemed to hover around the short story's status and achievements. Part of this uncertainty centred on the challenges of narrative experimentation and modernist innovation. As Derek Hudson rather quaintly describes it in the introduction to his 1956 anthology,

> The modern short-story writer has had to steer between the Scylla of popular journalism and the Charybdis of preciosity. It has seemed, at times during the past twenty-five years, that some of our distinguished writers were bent on establishing an era of plotlessness which might drive the intellectual short story out of the reach even of a 'general reader' sympathetically disposed to experiment. (p. xiii)

Hudson was not the first anthologist to draw attention to such problems. In 1937, Elizabeth Bowen discussed some of the formal features of new short stories in her introduction to the *Faber Book of Modern Stories*, which T. S. Eliot asked her to edit. Here she coined the term 'free story' to describe an approach to narrative and characterization that deployed cinematic techniques, 'oblique narration, cutting, the unlikely placing of emphasis'.[4] But behind the scenes Bowen was expressing a different kind of uncertainty about the contemporary short story: the following extract from a letter written in 1936 from her home in Ireland to her friend William Plomer (whose work was included in the Faber anthology) may simply reflect the trials and tribulations of anthologists at any time, but it may also point to a gulf between, on the one hand, the kind of early twentieth-century short stories that have achieved longevity through the later accretion of literary analysis and criticism, and, on the other hand, the mass of stories being published at the time:

> Yes indeed I am doing those abominable short stories (the collection I mean). As far as I ever do read here, I read nothing else. 4/5 of what I try out shows a level of absolute mediocrity; arty, they are, and mawkishly tender-hearted. Quite a large number of short stories are told, do you notice, by hikers. 'As I crossed the horizon' they so often begin, and the heroine is generally just called 'the woman'.[5]

However, in her introduction to the anthology Bowen expresses her judgements on the contemporary short story largely through a distinction between 'commercial' short stories that are suitable for popular magazines and 'the free story' that, whilst it may be non-commercial, is often dissatisfying. Her eventual choices for the anthology included stories by

A. E. Coppard, Stephen Spender, the Irish writers Frank O'Connor and Seán O'Faoláin (whose 1932 collection *Midsummer Night Madness* she particularly admired) along with her own story 'The Disinherited'. Like Virginia Woolf in her 1924 essay 'Mr Bennett and Mrs Brown', Bowen opted for the year of the first Post-Impressionist exhibition as a cultural and artistic turning point, and invited readers of the anthology to 'study the development of the short story in English since, roughly, 1910, to notice its variations and watch its trends'.[6]

Bowen's stated aims of tracing changes and demonstrating variety are shared by the editor of two of the most reprinted English short story anthologies of the twentieth century, Christopher Dolley. Whilst some anthologies explicitly foreground the evaluative nature of their selection – Christopher Isherwood's *Great English Short Stories*, which he edited in 1957 from New York, is refreshingly direct on this score – Dolley announces several different motivations for assembling his collections. His editorial foreword to the *Penguin Book of English Short Stories*, first published in 1967, begins with a word about the publisher's list. This is no surprise, since Dolley, unlike most of the anthologists mentioned so far, was neither a writer nor a teacher but the manager of Penguin's Education division. In 1969 he became chairman and managing director of Penguin Books, following Allen Lane's retirement, but found time to edit a *Second Penguin Book of English Short Stories* in 1972. His foreword to the first collection begins: 'This volume of English short stories is the first in the series to be published by Penguins [sic]. Other volumes will include Modern Short Stories and American Short Stories.' The plan to focus on modern short stories perhaps reflects the recognition, increasingly clear by the 1960s, that modernism as a literary movement had elevated the generic status of short stories; the planned publication of a volume devoted to American short stories is equally telling, as it registers, again, the achievements of American writers but at the same time establishes a separate space for the English short story. Dolley's foreword continues:

> The aim of this collection is to appeal to the reader at large. No attempt has been made to conduct a historical survey of the English short story, and the collection starts in the mid nineteenth century, from which date the short story developed as a recognizable genre. . . . The short story still flourishes, and the aim of this collection is to give some idea of the variety and individuality which the genre has developed over the last hundred years.[7]

As with Hudson's defensive 'these stories do not derive from a dying art' a decade earlier, Dolley's assertion that 'the short story still flourishes' hints at some continuing anxiety about the genre's health. The very fact that this anthology was reprinted so frequently, sometimes twice a year, most recently in 2011, and is still available as an e-book, indicates that such anxieties were unnecessary. No doubt the anthology's educational uses contributed to its popularity: during the later 1960s and 1970s, as adult education expanded, the *Penguin Book of English Short Stories* could be found in many a Workers' Educational Association book-box and on the shelves of university extramural department libraries, providing a compact introductory text for part-time students of literature courses.

Dolley's editorial foreword to the *Second Penguin Book of English Short Stories* in 1972 began with a note about Penguin's advances in the short story field, now that anthologies of French, Italian and American short stories were available as companion volumes to the first *Penguin Book of English Short Stories*, but again the anxious note creeps in: 'Their publication has demonstrated that, far from continuing its supposed decline, the short story is enjoying a revival all the more encouraging when viewed against the gloom surrounding the future of the literary novel.' Although Dolley had disclaimed, in his foreword to the first volume, any intention of conducting a historical survey of the English short story, his retrospective view in the second foreword takes a different line:

> The first *Penguin Book of English Short Stories* set out to survey the history of the genre in its present form and inevitably the need for compression made the choice difficult. I am grateful therefore that this volume allows me to widen the range of authors representative of the best English short story writing and at the same time to bring the selection forward in time so that it includes writers who are still at the height of their powers.[8]

In fact, two-thirds of the writers included in the second volume were there in the first. Although Dickens has been dropped, some later nineteenth-century stories from Hardy and Kipling are again included. Joyce Cary, whose stock was higher in the third quarter of the twentieth century than it is now, appears in both volumes, but Conrad, Wells, Maugham, Huxley and Waugh make way for T. F. Powys, E. M. Forster and a new trio of writers 'still at the height of their powers': Robert Graves (who actually by 1972 was nearing the end of his working life), Muriel Spark and Kingsley Amis. The three living writers represented in the 1967 volume, V. S. Pritchett, Graham Greene and Angus Wilson, have further stories in the 1972 volume; in fact, it seems that no anthology of English short stories would be complete without V. S. Pritchett, 'widely regarded as the finest English short story writer of the twentieth century' according to the Royal Society of Literature, which now funds a prize in his name for the best unpublished story of the year. Graham Greene and Angus Wilson are better remembered as novelists, but their short stories continue to be read, perhaps partly because of their visibility in anthologies. In some cases, a writer's second story in the 1972 volume is from the same original collection. This is inevitable with Joyce, and as Dolley had chosen the final, acclaimed *Dubliners* story 'The Dead', for the first anthology, he falls back on 'Ivy Day in the Committee Room' for the second. The two stories by D. H. Lawrence, 'Fanny and Annie' in 1967 and 'The Horse Dealer's Daughter' in 1972, are both from Lawrence's 1922 collection, *England, my England*. All in all, the *Second Penguin Book of English Short Stories* capitalized on a good marketing opportunity but did not break much new literary ground.

Meanwhile, Penguin Books were building their list of short story anthologies by identifying separate traditions within as well as outside the British Isles. *The Penguin Book of Scottish Short Stories* appeared in 1970, compiled by J. F. Hendry, whose introduction speaks of bringing together writers who will provide 'a composite picture of the various facets of Scottish writing today'. So this is a twentieth-century collection including stories by George Mackay Brown, Lewis Grassic Gibbon, two stories by Ian Hamilton Finlay and several by women writers: Elspeth Davie, Margaret Hamilton, Dorothy K. Haynes, Naomi Mitchison and Muriel Spark. A number of these authors reappear in the *New Penguin Book of Scottish Short Stories* (1983) edited by Ian Murray, and, despite the 'New' claim in the anthology's title, they are sometimes represented by the same story, in Spark's case 'The House of the Famous Poet', and in Edward Gaitens's 'A Wee Nip'. But where the 1983 volume does differ significantly from the earlier anthology is in its appeal to a Scottish tradition of short story writing by including nineteenth- as well as twentieth-century writers, notably Walter Scott, James Hogg, Margaret Oliphant and Robert Louis Stevenson. Stevenson is represented by 'The Beach of Falesá', one of his stories of the South Pacific which had been for many years out of print until it was included in the Penguin version of *Dr Jekyll and Mr Hyde* edited by Jenni Calder in 1979. Since its appearance in Murray's anthology, and subsequent collections of Stevenson's *South Sea Tales*, 'The Beach of Falesá' has become an increasingly prominent item in Stevenson's output during the canon-shift associated with the rise of postcolonial studies.

Welsh short stories also featured on Penguin's lists. A collection edited by Gwyn Jones and titled simply *Welsh Short Stories*, had been published by Allen Lane in 1941, and it reappeared in expanded form as a World Classic from Oxford University Press in 1956. A new Oxford edition was published in 1971, then Penguin took up the baton again in 1976 when Alun Richards edited the *Penguin Book of Welsh Short Stories*, to be followed in 1993 by the *New Penguin Book of Welsh Short Stories*, also edited by Richards. These five anthologies shaped by Gwyn Jones and Alun Richards effectively established a canon of Welsh twentieth-century short story writers, including E. Tegla Davies, Caradoc Evans, Rhys Davies, Kate Roberts, Dylan Thomas and D. J. Williams. The 1976 anthology was especially influential, being adopted as a school and college textbook. A third of its twenty-four stories are translated, reflecting the parallel development of Welsh-language and Anglo-Welsh literature, with the short story a prominent genre for both. Welsh publishing houses have also promoted short story anthologies, for example, *A View across the Valley: Short Stories by Women from Wales, c.1850–1950*, edited by Jane Aaron, was published by Honno, an independent co-operative press dedicated to Welsh women's writing, in 2005. More recently, Parthian Books published two volumes of the Library of Wales's *Story* anthologies (2014), edited by Dai Smith, with eighty stories spanning the twentieth century.

During the Second World War Penguin also brought out their first Irish short story anthology: *Modern Irish Short Stories*, a slim volume edited by Alan Steele and Joan Hancock, appeared in 1943, the first of several collections with the same title from different publishers. There were also numerous anthologies published under the briefer title *Irish Short Stories*, beginning with a Faber collection in 1932, edited by George A. Birmingham. However, the best known of these compilations is the *Modern Irish Short Stories* edited by Frank O'Connor for Oxford University Press in 1957 and reprinted ten times before being re-issued as *Classic Irish Short Stories* in 1985. O'Connor announces in his introduction:

> I believe that the Irish short story is a distinct art form: that is, by shedding the limitations of its popular origin it has become susceptible to development in the same way as German song, and in its attitudes it can be distinguished from Russian and American stories which have developed in the same way. The English novel, for instance, is very obviously an art form while the English short story is not.[9]

O'Connor goes on to develop his point with reference to several of the stories in the anthology, notably George Moore's 'Home Sickness' from his 1903 collection, *The Untilled Field*, which he judges to be 'a masterpiece'. Joyce's 'The Dead' also appears in this anthology, along with Elizabeth Bowen's 'Summer Night' – Bowen, he concedes, 'has her place in English literature, but she also has her corner in Irish'.

Another eminent short story writer claimed by both English and Irish literary traditions is William Trevor. In 1989 Trevor edited the monumental *Oxford Book of Irish Short Stories*, which was re-issued in 2010 and looks set to remain an influential collection. The anthology begins with seven folk tales translated from Irish before moving on to Oliver Goldsmith ('Adventures of a Strolling Player') and Maria Edgeworth ('The Limerick Gloves' again). Trevor's choice from Joyce's *Dubliners* is, unsurprisingly, 'The Dead', and he includes two stories each from Sean O'Faoláin and Frank O'Connor. The anthology moves forward to the present day with stories by John McGahern, Bernard MacLaverty and Desmond Hogan. Trevor's own story, 'Death in Jerusalem' features Irish characters, as does Elizabeth Bowen's 'Her Table Spread', the two Anglo-Irish writers claiming their Irish corners.

Sitting alongside the multiple anthologies exploring and establishing national traditions within the British Isles, there are further collections devoted to specific locales, especially cities. For example, the Edinburgh-based Mainstream Publishing produced two short story anthologies in the 1980s consisting wholly of stories set in Glasgow or written by Glasgow writers, *Streets of Stone* (1985) and *Streets of Gold* (1989), both edited by Moira Burgess and Hamish Whyte. London has, of course, had its share of dedicated anthologies, some arising from short story competitions, for example, the 1993 *Smoke Signals* sponsored by the London Arts Board, and some building on earlier magazine publication, such as the *London Magazine* collections, again with the evocative title *Signals*. It is not only literary magazines that have contributed to this kind of anthologizing: in 1993 Julie Burchill was commissioned to compile an anthology of stories set in or about London and published by Penguin to celebrate *Time Out*'s twenty-fifth anniversary. For volume two of the 'Time Out' *Book of London Short Stories* (2000) the editor was a writer, Nicholas Royle, who had already edited *Time Out* books of New York and Paris short stories, and has gone on to be a prolific anthologist. In Birmingham, while the locally based Tindal Street Press was enjoying funding from Arts Council England between 1998 and 2012, it published several short story anthologies focused on the city and its people. *Birmingham Noir*, edited by Joel Lane and Steve Bishop in 2002, was a collection of twenty-three crime stories, and its sister anthology,

Birmingham Nouveau, edited by Alan Mahar the same year, brought together short stories from a *Birmingham Post* competition interspersed with photographic sketches from the newspaper's staff. Another Tindal Street publication from this period arose out of writing workshops that were held at community venues across the city as part of a millennium project: *Whispers in the Walls*, edited by Leone Ross and Yvonne Brissett is subtitled *New Black and Asian Voices from Birmingham* and for most of the authors this was the first time any of their work had been published.

Another twenty-first-century anthology that grounds itself in specific places is *England Calling: 24 Stories for the 21st Century* (2001), edited by Julia Bell and Jackie Gay. Each story is identified by author, title and place-name. Most of the place-names refer to English cities – Newcastle, Coventry, Bath, London (twice) – but some denote counties or less specific areas – Cheshire, Cornwall, Black Country, off the M4. The stories are previously unpublished, but the authors include some well-known literary names such as David Almond and Peter Ho Davies, alongside the comedian Alexei Sayle and journalist Julie Burchill. The editors' introduction launches straight into the issue of what Englishness means at the start of the twenty-first century in a country that is 'restless, uneasy, questioning and devolving'. English fiction has often been firmly grounded in a sense of place, but the story writers represented in this anthology, the editors say, 'are not only telling stories of the landscapes of England, but peeling back the layers of Englishness in the process – Englishness as it is now: multicultural, messy, survivalist'.[10] Bell and Gay are quite explicit in their call for fiction to articulate, or at least explore, national identity and culture at a time when Scottish and Welsh devolution are raising new questions about that identity. *England Calling*, like the city-based collections mentioned above (amongst numerous other examples), operates with a dual rationale: to showcase new short stories and to foster a sense of community. Whether or not such anthologies turn out to be influential in shaping literary canons will depend not only on the quality of the short stories themselves but also on the way that literary studies evolve, and, where educational curricula are concerned, the extent to which devolutionary currents impinge on the map of English writing.

Meanwhile, the showcasing of new writing gathers pace elsewhere in various kinds of anthologies. Some are directly linked to international literary prizes, for example, the Bristol Short Story Prize, which has generated anthologies of the winning and short-listed stories since 2008. The Manchester Writing Competition, linked to the Creative Writing school at Manchester Metropolitan University, includes a short story section, and the finalists' work appears in an archive that functions as a virtual anthology. Although competitions like those based in Bristol and Manchester attract large numbers of submissions, their rules admit only previously unpublished work, so unlike traditional anthologies the finalists' collections have been through a single 'sifting' process rather than several. For many years there has been no British equivalent of the annual *Best American Short Stories* series, which selects around twenty stories published in US and Canadian magazines each calendar year. The American series, established in 1915, has a distinguished history, and for numerous now-famous short story writers having their work appear in *Best American Short Stories* has been an important step in confirming their literary reputations. The annual anthology, which regularly makes the best-seller lists for fiction, includes a mix of established writers and relative newcomers: the 2013 volume, for example, features a fair number of university teachers of Creative Writing alongside writers with long-established reputations, including Lorrie Moore and Alice Munro, whose featured story, 'Train', was published in *Harper's Magazine* around the time that she received the Nobel Prize for Literature. During the 1920s there was a short-lived American enterprise to publish an annual anthology of *Best British Short Stories*, organized by the now-defunct Boston publishing house of Small, Maynard & Company. The idea of an annual anthology was revived in the United Kingdom by Penguin Books with their *Firebird* anthologies in the early 1980s, though this series, too, proved to be short-lived. However, a twenty-first-century version of the annual anthology was launched in 2011 by the Norfolk firm, Salt Publishing, with Nicholas Royle as editor, and the *Best British Short Stories* series, with six issues to date, is establishing itself as a significant outlet for good new writing. Only a small minority of the stories have previously appeared in single-authored collections, and in some cases the anthology brings stories into print for the first time, their initial publication having been online. Although the *Best British* anthologies have not yet featured any Nobel Laureates, they do include some well-known names, such as, in the 2014 volume, the award-winning poet and fiction writer David Constantine. His story 'Ashton and Elaine' is reprinted from a collection titled *Red Room: New Short Stories Inspired by the Brontës* – another reminder of the sheer variety of sources trawled by twenty-first-century short story anthologists.

Whilst annual anthologies of new writing reassert the short story's contemporary relevance and vitality, it is the longer sweep of anthologies connecting older writing with more recent work that makes them, in the end, the more influential shapers of tradition. This chapter concludes by looking at two major late twentieth-century anthologies from publishers who have dominated this field, *The Penguin Book of Modern British Short Stories* (1987) edited by Malcolm Bradbury, and *The Oxford Book of English Short Stories* (1998) edited by A. S. Byatt.

Bradbury's anthology is restricted chronologically from 1945 to the mid-1980s, but is not confined to English writers. He includes a significant number of Irish authors (Samuel Beckett and Edna O'Brien as well as Elizabeth Bowen and William Trevor), Dylan Thomas from Wales and Muriel Spark from Scotland. The category 'British writer' had begun, by the 1980s, to include a larger proportion of authors born outside Britain, so Jean Rhys and Doris Lessing are joined by younger writers, Salman Rushdie and Kazuo Ishiguro. Ishiguro is just one of the successful graduates of the University of East Anglia's (UEA) Creative Writing programme, founded in 1970 by Malcolm Bradbury and Angus Wilson, to be included in this anthology: others are Clive Sinclair, Rose Tremain and Ian McEwan. These four, along with another clutch of Bradbury's contributors, Martin Amis, Julian Barnes, Adam Mars-Jones, Salman Rushdie and Graham Swift, had also featured in *Granta* magazine's 'Best of Young British Novelists' list in 1983. So, as far as the younger generation of writers is concerned, there are strong connections in Bradbury's anthology with *Granta*, one of the most prestigious literary magazines in the United Kingdom, and the pioneering UEA Creative Writing programme. Bradbury contributes one of his own short stories along with 'More Friend Than Lodger' by his UEA colleague, Angus Wilson, and a very recent magazine story from his former University of Birmingham colleague, David Lodge. An academic flavour pervades the collection in other ways, too, with stories that include Samuel Beckett's 'Ping', through to the experimentalist B. S. Johnson's 'A Few Selected Sentences' and the anthology's final story, Adam Mars-Jones's 'Structural Anthropology'. Another marked feature of this anthology is that its list of contributors, featuring many of the major names in post-war fiction writing, includes so many writers who are known primarily as novelists. Bradbury acknowledges this much in his introduction, arguing that in the period covered by the anthology novels and short stories have shared 'new kinds of self-questioning and a fresh enquiry into the nature and the proper conditions of a fiction'.[11] However, he also includes several writers whose reputations have been built on their achievements as short story writers, principally V. S. Pritchett and William Trevor, but perhaps Alan Sillitoe, whose stories are as highly regarded as his novels and poems, belongs in this category, too.

The Short Story Anthology: Shaping the Canon

Bradbury's anthology, like Dolley's *Penguin Book of English Short Stories*, lends itself well to academic use, but the final collection to be considered here is clearly addressed to the 'general reader' as well as students and scholars. Like Trevor's *Oxford Book of Irish Short Stories*, A. S. Byatt's *Oxford Book of English Short Stories* has a monumental feel. Whereas Bradbury's anthology was constrained by period though not nationality, Byatt's collection ranges from the middle of the nineteenth century to the present, but she confines herself to English writers. However, she says in her introduction that in making her selection 'I was very carefully *not* looking for stories that would give images of England, or of the Empire; I very carefully tried to have no preconceptions of any "English" styles or subject-matter.'[12] The stories are arranged chronologically, and from the outset it is clear that Byatt is not merely perpetuating existing canons. Her nineteenth-century stories include 'The Sacristan of St Botolph' by William Gilbert, father of the more famous dramatist, and 'Little Brother' by Mary Mann, Thomas Hardy's contemporary, whose subject matter was drawn from rural communities in East Anglia. Hardy is there, too, along with Dickens and Trollope, but Byatt's table of contents continues to surprise, her twentieth-century stories including 'Landlord of the Crystal Fountain' by Malachi Whitaker (actually Marjorie Olive Whitaker), known in her day as the 'Bradford Chekhov', and 'My Flannel Knickers' by Leonora Carrington. The stories she selects by better-known short story writers also reveal some original choices. A. E. Coppard's 'Some Talk of Alexander' is much less well known than, say, 'A Field of Mustard' or 'Dusky Ruth', and similarly with Saki she opts for the less-anthologized 'The Toys of Peace'. Byatt's comments on Saki suggest another perspective on the value of anthologies: 'Saki's tales should not be read in bulk, for their idiosyncratic shockingness is diminished by proximity to other idiosyncratic shocks of rather the same kind, and his talent begins to look like a limited series of tricks' (p. xxi). There is no dominant mode in the collection of thirty-seven stories, and Byatt's introduction refers to social realism, fantasy, ghost stories, 'stories of sensibility' (Hardy, Elizabeth Taylor, H. E. Bates and D. H. Lawrence) and 'rollicking stories of insensibility, Saki and Waugh, Wodehouse and Firbank' (p. xvii). Several of Bradbury's younger generation of short story writers appear in Byatt's anthology, too, but her final story is the (then) very recent 'Dead Languages' by Philip Hensher.

The impact of *The Oxford Book of English Short Stories* on the reputation of the short story as a genre remains to be seen. At the level of the individual writers featured in the anthology, Byatt's selection adds yet more status to some already well-known stories, such as Graham Greene's 'The Destructors' and J. G. Ballard's 'Dream Cargoes', but it also brings semi-forgotten texts back into the limelight and speculates on the potential of some contemporary stories to endure. First published in 1998, it has already been reprinted several times in the United States as well as the United Kingdom, but, unlike Dolley's best-selling Penguin anthologies of English short stories a generation earlier, Byatt's collection breaks some new ground. However, whilst women writers are fairly well represented, the selection of authors from later decades does not include any Asian or Black British writers: Byatt's canon, unlike Bradbury's, remains firmly white.

Notes

1. Charles Dickens, *Selected Short Fiction*, ed. Deborah A. Thomas (Harmondsworth: Penguin, 1985), p. 11.
2. Angela Carter, ed., *Wayward Girls and Wicked Women* (London: Virago, 1986), p. xii.
3. Derek Hudson, ed., *Modern English Short Stories 1930–1955* (London: Oxford University Press, 1956), p. xiv.
4. Elizabeth Bowen, ed., *The Faber Book of Modern Short Stories* (London: Faber & Faber, 1937), p. 12.
5. Victoria Glendinning, *Elizabeth Bowen: Portrait of a Writer* (London: Weidenfeld & Nicolson, 1977), p. 118.
6. Bowen, ed., *The Faber Book of Modern Short Stories*, p. 7.
7. Christopher Dolley, ed., *The Penguin Book of English Short Stories* (Harmondsworth: Penguin, 1967), p. 5.
8. Christopher Dolley, ed., *The Second Penguin Book of English Short Stories* (Harmondsworth: Penguin, 1972), p. 7.
9. Frank O'Connor, ed., *Classic Irish Short Stories* (1957; Oxford University Press, 1985), p. ix.
10. Julia Bell and Jackie Gay, eds., *England Calling* (London: Weidenfeld & Nicolson, 2001), pp. ix–xi.
11. Malcolm Bradbury, ed., *The Penguin Book of Modern British Short Stories* (London: Viking, 1987), p. 13.
12. A. S. Byatt, ed., *The Oxford Book of English Short Stories* (Oxford University Press, 1998), p. xv. Subsequent page references to this edition are given in parentheses in the text.

34
The Institution of Creative Writing

AILSA COX

The discipline of creative writing began to emerge strongly in US institutions in the middle of the twentieth century, although it had already begun to establish itself before the Second World War: the pioneering Iowa Writers' Workshop was founded as early as 1936 (and creative writing had been taught at Iowa for many years before that). In the United States, the relationship between the teaching of creative writing in Higher Education and literary production has been notable in the period since 1945.[1] There was a significant expansion of Master of Fine Arts (MFA) programmes in the 1980s and 1990s, with far-reaching consequences for literary culture. In Britain, the first MA programmes were founded by mavericks in the 1970s: Malcolm Bradbury and Angus Wilson at the University of East Anglia, and the poet David Craig at Lancaster. It took a generation for creative writing to establish itself in British universities: initially, such courses were considered eccentric, a flashy American import. Yet, since then, the growth has been dramatic: by 2015 the National Association of Writers in Education (NAWE) calculated that there were over two hundred MA courses available, with at least fifty universities also offering PhD supervision.[2] Current undergraduate provision varies from option modules within an English degree to full-blown joint- and single-honours courses. While some individuals remain sceptical about the discipline's academic credentials, most universities have embraced creative writing, if only because of its attractiveness to students.

Those short story writers who do not have some kind of university affiliation, as graduates, teachers or honorary professors, would seem to be in a minority. Even fewer are without some experience of the creative writing workshop, either in Higher Education or some other context, for instance the residential courses run by the Arvon Foundation. Mark McGurl, in his influential study of 2009, argues that the involvement of so many American writers in creative writing programmes has produced a marked self-consciousness and reflexivity in their work. This chapter is necessarily more speculative and inconclusive than McGurl's, but it will follow his lead in suggesting that the partnership between short story writers and the academy has left its traces on the genre. I shall be considering writers who have studied or taught creative writing (in several cases both), and others who position themselves outside the discipline yet are in some senses implicated in its practices. The focus is mostly on the texts themselves, but I shall discuss the role played by creative writing in the short story's increasing popularity, and ways in which short story writers have formulated their individual poetics and concepts of authorship through the fiction itself. Before turning to the texts and their writers I shall briefly outline the nature of creative writing as pedagogy, and the challenges this brings both for its supporters and for universities when it is incorporated into the curriculum of Higher Education.

The writers' workshop is central to creative writing teaching, combining the close reading of the students' own drafts with a non-hierarchical approach to learning. Mark McGurl, Michelene Wandor, Rebecca O'Rourke and others associate creative writing pedagogy with the progressive ideals of 1960s educationalists. The origins of creative writing in the United Kingdom lie not only within the academy, but also in community and adult education, and the self-running groups affiliated to the Federation of Worker Writers and Community Publishers in the 1970s and 1980s. In this context, the workshop was a means of empowering the individual and providing an outlet for voices marginalized by mainstream literature. A. L. Kennedy's prize-winning first collection, *Night Geometry and the Garscadden Trains* (1990) was published while she was Writer-in-Residence for Hamilton and East Kilbride Social Work Department; her series of autobiographical essays, *On Writing*, reflects on the many workshops she has run both in the community and within higher education. Kennedy is scathing about nameless institutions that, as she sees it, exploit would-be writers with a substandard product, churning out individuals who will never fulfil their initial promise, fit only to teach more aspiring writers in their turn. At the same time, she speaks idealistically of her own contact with students at Warwick University, and the potential of the right kind of workshop to transform lives. The wrong kind of workshop infantilizes students with writing exercises and imposes a group dynamic on an individual process. The right kind of workshop concentrates on personal growth, inspiration and professional advice through a whole range of activities inside and outside the classroom.

Michelene Wandor has also pointed out some of the drawbacks in the workshop method, notably the 'irreconcilable conflict at the heart of the

Romantic/therapy axis'.[3] By this, she means an inherent contradiction within the dual focus on the text and its author. How can the workshop simultaneously operate as a space for individual confidence-building and self-expression, and as a critical device? A pedagogy based on student participation, self-reflection and political empowerment also conflicts with the consumerist rhetoric unleashed by recent changes in university funding and the raising of tuition fees. Creative writing MAs have long been viewed as a type of apprenticeship, often visited by publishers and agents; this vocational aspect is increasingly emphasized in the undergraduate curriculum. But not all graduates will become professional writers, and those who do are likely to supplement their income through teaching.

In *Exploding English*, his 1990 study of warring tendencies in English studies, Bernard Bergonzi looks forward to a 'different relationship' between the practising writer and the academy, 'a more direct and sustaining one, even a form of patronage'.[4] To a large extent, his vision has been fulfilled, but there remains some ambivalence on both sides of the relationship. As Marina Warner puts it, 'teachers of creative writing need to live in at least two worlds – at the university and in a room of their own'.[5] A few, mostly high-profile writers in permanent positions fulfil a role that is essentially that of writer-in-residence, with minimal teaching commitments. It is this type of writer in particular that McGurl compares to the varsity athlete, conferring prestige on the university and enhancing the value of its degrees: 'but whereas varsity athletics typically symbolizes the excellence of competitive teamwork, creative writing and the other arts testify to the institution's systematic hospitality to the excellence of individual self-expression'.[6] However, many of the salaried workforce struggle to reconcile Warner's 'two worlds', especially since their credentials as teachers derive from their ongoing practice and their publishing record. Most university teachers feel divided between their duties to their students and their own research; but writers are also expected to embody what they preach, or else to risk accusations of inauthenticity or bad faith. The benefits of a university post, both financial and otherwise, generally outweigh the disadvantages. Many writers enjoy the stimulus of teaching and belonging to a community of writers, but traces of self-doubt and the fear of compromise can sometimes become manifest in their publications.

The introduction of creative writing programmes in the United Kingdom coincided with the increasing influence of critical theory in literature departments. Paul Dawson takes into account the views of those who see these twin currents as polar opposites in an ongoing struggle between critic and practitioner. As he suggests, this is, in many respects, a false division, since the discipline of creative writing has developed its own research and pedagogical strategies, not entirely incompatible with poststructuralist thinking.[7] Will Self's designation as Professor of Contemporary Thought at Brunel University disguises his involvement in creative writing, a discipline he frequently derides. Yet this appointment might also be regarded as indicative of creative writing's evolution beyond purely practical considerations of craft and technique. It also highlights its cross-disciplinary potential as a variety of intellectual enquiry. Nonetheless, the public disavowal of creative writing expressed not only by Self, but also by Hanif Kureishi and, on occasion, A. L. Kennedy, is related to a deeper ambivalence, shared by many other practitioners, towards the hand that feeds them. Later in this chapter I shall discuss Ali Smith, as an example of a writer who resists creativity's incorporation into the academy by positioning herself as an outsider.

If, as many believe, the short story's popularity has increased in recent years, this is largely due to the growth of creative writing courses.[8] Short stories offer the new writer a route into publication through small press magazines such as *ShortFiction*, published at the University of Plymouth; or the student cohort's own anthologies, such as the one produced annually at the University of East Anglia. The increasingly popular category of 'flash fiction' (generally defined at a maximum 750 words) is easily adapted for live readings and student showcases.[9] Most importantly, short fiction is ideally suited to the workshop process, as a self-contained piece of prose can be completed, critiqued and revised within a few weeks. As Graham Mort explains, its other attraction is the potential for experimentation:

> Like a poem, a story can be shaped as a kind of architectural form of language. It's also possible to experiment with narrative technique – voice, point of view, the exploration of consciousness – and not get locked into one kind of narrative style. So stories are malleable enough to work on and short enough to sacrifice if they go wrong.[10]

Mort is a prize-winning poet who has also published two short story collections (*Touch*, 2010; *Terroir*, 2015) whilst serving as Professor of Creative Writing and Transcultural Literature at Lancaster University. Like Alison MacLeod at Chichester, he exemplifies the teacher-practitioner, integrating his own practice with the development of creative writing as a distinctive academic discipline. Both have been members of the Higher Education committee of NAWE, which produced a Research Benchmark Statement in 2008, clarifying, in precise detail, the principles and methodologies underpinning research in creative writing. These principles include its speculative, exploratory and interdisciplinary nature, and the validity of the writing process itself as a form of research activity, alongside more traditional aspects such as researching the form or using source-based material.

MacLeod and her colleagues at Chichester also instigated *Thresholds*, an online forum originally aimed at postgraduates, but now a more general resource for short story writers, including short essays, interviews and reflections on the form from current practitioners and predecessors, such as Flannery O'Connor, Eudora Welty and Raymond Carver.[11] The existence of the forum illustrates the many ways in which new media have helped sustain an interest in short story writing. While there is some experimentation with hypertext and interactive storytelling, notably from Kate Pullinger (while working at the Universities of De Montfort and Bath Spa), the effects have been on the dissemination of short fiction rather than its form. Literary journals are easier to distribute online than as print copies; short stories can also be transmitted as podcasts or apps. Most significantly for the health of the short story, writers are able to promote publications and communicate with one another through informal networks that often owe their origins to university courses.

Short story theory has evolved mostly through the attempts of its practitioners to validate the form by defining its generic specificity. In the broader sense, as Malcolm Bradbury observes, 'one of the virtues of the story is that it shows us that in every serious work of fiction the writer is saying something crucial about the form he or she is using'.[12] Bradbury's *Penguin Book of Modern British Short Stories*, published in 1987 and still widely used today, announced an earlier revival of interest, exemplified by the younger writers in the anthology. Amongst these younger writers, Angela Carter, Graham Swift, Clive Sinclair, Ian McEwan, Kazuo Ishiguro, Rose Tremain and Adam Mars-Jones were all associated with the University of East Anglia, as students, teachers or writing fellows. Clare Hanson's monograph, *Short Stories and Short Fictions, 1880–1980* (1985) shared Bradbury's faith in 'a resurgence of interest and confidence', claiming an increase in magazine outlets and the number of single author collections. Like Bradbury, she believes that 'the short form is the form for innovation, and many of the best young writers are turning first to short fiction'.[13] The young writers she cites are Ian McEwan, Clive Sinclair and Adam Mars-Jones.

As is well known, Ian McEwan was the first to graduate from the MA in creative writing set up by Bradbury and Wilson in the 1970s. Like the work of Sinclair and Mars-Jones, his two collections challenge their readers with a combination of transgressive subject matter and postmodern pastiche, incorporating forms of discourse taken from the media and from academic disciplines including history, psychoanalysis and the material sciences. 'Solid Geometry' (*First Love, Last Rites*, 1975) is a Borgesian display of mock erudition, incorporating passages from a Victorian diary compiled by the narrator's great grandfather. The fogeyish narrator becomes so absorbed in the diary, including its second-hand account of a startling geometrical experiment, that he neglects his wife's emotional and sexual needs. His attempt to reproduce the experiment with his wife's body succeeds in making her vanish from material reality. A preserved human penis, also inherited from the narrator's great-grandfather, represents abstract, phallocentric knowledge which is placed in opposition to lived experience; in her rage, the narrator's wife smashes the bottle. In that sense, the story is an attack on conventional learning. Yet the wife's disappearance also enacts a wish-fulfilment for its author, or indeed for any writer frustrated by external distractions. McEwan's humour is in some respects an in-joke, dependent on a shared familiarity with the types of discourse that are being parodied in the story.

The short story resurgence identified by Bradbury and Hanson was not so much in evidence during the 1990s; by 2002, the English and Scottish Arts Councils were launching a 'Save Our Short Story' campaign, defending what was now perceived as an endangered species. Richard Todd's 1996 study, *Consuming Fiction: The Booker Prize and Fiction in Britain Today*, identifies a synergy between the major prizes, the media and the bookshops that raised the public profile of the literary novel at the expense of the short story. McEwan's career exemplifies the financial and critical success available to writers who have been able to reconcile postmodern self-reflexivity with the pleasures afforded by a strong narrative drive within the format of the literary novel. While McEwan continues to produce novellas alongside longer works of fiction, these early publications are his only short story collections to date.

The postmodern strand in British short story writing continued in the work of Will Self and Toby Litt, another UEA graduate, whose *Adventures in Capitalism* (1996) and *Exhibitionism* (2002) embrace consumerism and popular culture with satirical relish. 'Please Use a Basket' (*Adventures in Capitalism*) is narrated by the cardboard figure of a shop assistant, who stands behind the stack of wire baskets at a chain of chemist shops. 'You know me', the story begins, 'I'm the Boots *Please Use a Basket* girl', assuming a familiarity with British popular culture in the 1990s that may no longer be taken entirely for granted.[14] As she speaks, the narrator gradually transforms from mass-produced image to a real life checkout assistant who, angered by capitalist hegemony, has become a Marxist agitator. Litt contrasts the obtrusive cardboard figure inside the store and her unrecognizable original standing on the street, hectoring pedestrians with copies of *Socialist Worker*. One is obeyed, the other ignored. 'The Audioguide' (*Exhibitionism*) also makes startling use of narrative voice, in order to animate the manipulative strategies of consumer culture. This story is narrated through an imaginary earpiece with direct access to 'the Gallery of the Museum of Your Head'.[15] Addressing the reader directly, the audio guide imposes the implicit and explicit rules of the gallery visit to explore the fragmented subjective states housed in its various rooms, finally subverting the narrative's restrictive frame by challenging the predictability of this 'crude and conceited' device (p. 54).

As may be suggested by Litt's handling of the modern psyche as a rickety assemblage of external signs and internal drives, he willingly engages with poststructuralist thinking, breaching the division that still exists, in some English departments, between creative writing and critical theory. 'When I met Michel Foucault' (*Adventures in Capitalism*) begins with a quotation from the eponymous Foucault that could serve as an epigram for his entire career: 'I am no doubt the only one who writes in order to have no face' (p. 189). With each novel, he has switched genres, moving between crime fiction to chick lit or science fiction, in an effort to disrupt aesthetic continuity, and thus evading, theoretically at least, Michel Foucault's 'author function'.[16] Because of its fragmentation, short fiction is arguably the form best suited to Litt's mercurial tendencies. The later collections, *I Play the Drums in a Band Called Okay* (2008) and *Life-Like* (2014) are both story cycles; the stories may be read as self-contained narratives, and indeed some of them have been published individually, but they also accumulate meaning in relation to one another. Taking as its subject overlapping circles of kinship and acquaintance, through a loosely connected network of disparate characters, *Life-Like* juxtaposes realist accounts of family life with pastiche twitter feeds and medical bills that recall the formal inventiveness of the first two collections.

The best-known writer in this postmodern strand is Ali Smith who, like Helen Simpson and Kate Atkinson, abandoned a conventional academic career in English Literature for life as a freelance writer. In *The Creative Writing Coursebook* (2001), Smith claims that she suffers irritable bowel syndrome at the very thought of teaching a creative writing workshop.[17] Despite this aversion, the self-reflexivity of her short fiction could be tailor-made for the creative writing classroom. Her fourth collection *The First Person and Other Stories* (2008) is a systematic investigation of narrative technique, with those 'other stories' including 'Present', 'The Third Person' and 'The Second Person'. 'The Third Person' reflects on the nature of storytelling, ending with a sequence of comments on the effects of third person narration.

The merging of autobiography, essay and fiction is even more overt in 'True Short Story', at the start of the collection. The story is a response to some remarks made by *Prospect* magazine's deputy editor, Alex Linklater, at the launch of the National Short Story Prize in 2005, comparing the 'capacious old whore' of the novel with that 'nimble goddess', the short story.[18] In Smith's fictionalized rendition, the first person narrator interrogates the sexist metaphor, which in this telling transforms 'goddess' to 'nymph', allowing the author's wordplay to encompass fly fishing and nymphomania. It also enables her to relate her personal poetics to the myth of Echo. In Greek mythology, Echo is punished for her loquacity by losing the powers of speech; she has no voice of her own, but can only repeat the end of other people's sentences. When the self-obsessed Narcissus ignores her, she fades away into nothing but the traces of other speakers' final words. Smith juxtaposes that voicelessness with an account of female disempowerment during the narrator's postgraduate studies at Cambridge. This reminiscence introduces the figure of Kasia, who may be identified with Kasia Boddy, herself an authority on the short story, to whom the collection is partly dedicated. Her supposedly real life story is the 'true short story' of the title. Of course most readers will not be in a position to judge its factual accuracy, but we are clearly invited to identify the biographical author with the autodiegetic narrator whom Kasia calls Ali. Kasia is in hospital, after treatment for cancer. The urgency of lived experience is implicitly contrasted with the dilettante conversation between two male characters discussing literature in terms of whores and nymphs, an interchange that dramatizes and extends Linklater's original remarks. The National Short Story Prize was an initiative from the 'Save Our Short Story' campaign; in Kasia's one-woman campaign for effective drug treatment there is rather more at stake than pedantic generic distinctions.

'True Short Story' includes a textbook summary of comments on the characteristics of the short story, paraphrasing a number of sources, including Walter Benjamin, Franz Kafka and Grace Paley, but both the story's anecdotal structure and its blurring of generic boundaries suggest that this is a form that defeats the very notion of a 'true' definition. As Smith puts it in *Artful* (2012), a later collection of story/essays based on a lecture series, the short story is 'an elastic form'.[19] Both Smith's short stories and her longer fiction are polyphonic, constructed as a dialogue between competing voices. Smith's declaration that 'this story was written in discussion with my friend Kasia' draws attention to the dialogic aspects of her work, subverting patriarchal concepts of authorship as a unified, controlling presence. The interplay of voices is further celebrated by a final reference to Echo in the closing lines: 'so when is a short story like a nymph? When the echo of it answers back'.[20] Smith re-appropriates the Greek myth, referred to earlier in the story, so that Echo's ability to capture the speech of others becomes an act of self-assertion. Echo does not have one voice, but many, and when she speaks each voice is re-articulated in answer to itself. Smith's closing sentences affirms a generic affinity between the short story and the production of meaning through the dialogic process.

If the figure of Echo symbolizes text as boundless dialogue, that of Narcissus might suggest the writer's imperative to conceptualize a division between the story's implied author and the living self; or, in Margaret Atwood's words, 'the Author, capital A, and the person whose double he or she is'.[21] Like Toby Litt's work, Smith's stories often resemble the technical exercises recommended in creative writing handbooks; but they transcend the mechanical 'craft' of fiction, offering instead a philosophy of writing from a practice-based perspective. Her affirmation of a multiplicious and fluid subjectivity is often interpreted as a challenge to rigid notions of gender and sexuality, but it can also be related to the temporary dissolution of the self within the writing process.

Artful is based on a lecture series at St Anne's College, Oxford, an instance of creative writing infiltrating the heart of British academia, and epitomizing Smith's ambivalent relationship to institutional life. Smith deliberately trivializes high cultural values in this volume, turning the literary text into a game or a puzzle based on random correspondences, wordplay or coincidence. Like McEwan, she positions herself outside the institution, rejecting traditional academic discourse, and offering a different way of knowing the world, grounded, despite its postmodern credentials, in first hand experience and in serendipity. Unlike a conventional academic essay, fiction grants its author permission to roam freely between high art and popular culture, paraphrasing Walter Benjamin or Alice Munro without any obligation to cite her references. Writers such as McEwan, Smith and Litt rely on the reader's ability to read the signs, whether they point to literary theory or to the ephemera of marketing campaigns: 'Mr Kipling, as you no doubt already know, makes *exceedingly* good cakes'.[22]

Smith's writing is just one example of the importance of voice in contemporary fiction, especially short fiction. As Mark McGurl demonstrates, the concept of 'voice' has become indispensable in the teaching of creative writing, whether as the self-expressive need to 'find your voice'; or as a 'pedagogical reflection of literary modernism's fascination with the artifice and mobility of personae [. . .] easily assimilable to later postmodern accounts of fractured and multitudinous subjectivity'.[23] The short story genre is strongly rooted in orality, and tends to foreground the act of narration.[24] The defining role of 'voice' in the aesthetics of short fiction is inescapable in the title of *The Lonely Voice* (1962), Frank O'Connor's influential study, which defines the distinction between the short story and the novel as 'a difference between pure and applied storytelling'. O'Connor regards the short story as an outlet for a fundamental sense of isolation, whether spiritual or social in its origins.[25] In her most personal essay in *On Writing*, 'Proof of Life', A. L. Kennedy also attributes an existential primacy to 'voice', as a means to gain personal authenticity and generate collective transformation: 'All over the world, we may be able to read the start of a story where people with nothing to lose start writing and speaking and screaming so unstoppably that they become different people and make a different world.'[26]

The workshop method often includes reading out loud; stories with a strong and distinctive narrative voice, especially those narrated in the first person, have an immediate appeal for the listener. Jackie Kay's 'Wish I Was Here' (*Wish I Was Here*, 2006) exemplifies the confessional monologue, using present tense to convey the narrator's thoughts and experiences directly to the reader. In Anne Enright's 'What You Want' (*Yesterday's Weather*, 2009), the first-person narrator voices her thoughts (which have obvious demotic appeal), about luck, the lottery, religion and what to do if offered three wishes. An additional factor in favour of the dramatic monologue is the commissioning of stories by writers such as Kay and Enright by BBC Radio, one of the major outlets for contemporary short fiction in the United Kingdom. Some of these stories exploit an ironic distance between the narrator, the implied author and the reader. For instance, Hanif Kureishi's 'Weddings and Beheadings' (*Collected Stories*, 2010) is ventriloquized through a character who films the gruesome executions broadcast from some remote and violent region: 'You don't know me personally. My existence has never crossed your mind. But I would bet you've seen my work.'[27]

An anxiety often expressed about creative writing is that it might produce a stagnant orthodoxy amongst a generation of disciples following their teacher's style. This is a concern addressed indirectly by Philip Hensher in his defence of the subject.[28] In fact, the variety of styles and approaches amongst MA alumni such as Lucy Wood, Zoe Lambert, Carys Bray, Jane Feaver, Anne Donovan, Mark Illis and Tom Vowler, reflects the diversity of the form in general. But if there are pronounced tendencies that characterize the short story in the British 'programme era', the exploration of voice and viewpoint is the most prominent. This interest is not confined to first-person narration. It also extends to the use of free indirect discourse in stories such as Jon McGregor's 'Which Reminded Her, Later' (*This Isn't the Sort of Thing That Happens to Someone Like You*, 2012), where the character's voice is so tightly integrated into the narration that the reader inhabits her consciousness.

Other tendencies include the enduring influence of Angela Carter and the fairy tale, as in Lucy Wood's Cornish-themed *Diving Belles* (2012); another is the increasing popularity of themed collections and the short story cycle. Mark Illis's *Tender* (2009) consists of key moments from the lives of a single family across a period of thirty years; Kazuo Ishiguro's *Nocturnes* (2009) is subtitled 'five stories of music and nightfall'. Rachel Cusk's *The Lucky Ones* (2003) and *Arlington Park* (2006) can both be read as short story cycles; most of the chapters in her *Outline* (2014) can also be read independently of one another. Themed collections are easier to market than miscellaneous volumes, but also add an extra level of meaning, in the resonance between one story and another; Kirsty Gunn's *Infidelities* (2014), for instance, uses its mildly provocative title to compare notions of faithfulness in both life and art. More tightly integrated short story cycles, such as those by Illis and Cusk, and the earlier examples from Litt, use a fragmented narrative form to convey discontinuity in their characters' lives and to explore the fractured connections between them. It is sometimes argued that this hybrid genre has an advantage over the conventional novel in its resistance to linearity and narrative closure. However, as Paul March-Russell points out, 'increasingly, the boundaries between the novel and the short story cycle are dissolved, so that the question becomes not what defines the short story cycle, but what defines the novel?'[29] The rise of creative writing within the institution has encouraged experimentation through a heightened awareness of form and technique.

Outline's shadowy protagonist is a writer, teaching at a summer school in Athens; incorporating the many unwritten stories she encounters, the book becomes a meditation on the relationship between storytelling and writing. Interviewed for the journal *Short Fiction in Theory and Practice*, Cusk draws a distinction between the act of writing and the instinctual need to frame lived experience within tidy narrative patterns, expressed as oral storytelling within everyday conversations: 'And in my experience of teaching creative writing at Kingston University, I often see a confusion or merging together of these two things – telling a story and writing.'[30] Writing, she insists, demands a heightened self-consciousness and a separation from reality. These are radical comments, challenging the conventional view, in creative writing pedagogy, of fiction writing as an extension of oral storytelling, and of the pre-eminence of voice in contemporary short fiction.

The summer school in *Outline* is taught by two writers. The other tutor, the Irishman Ryan, has a position at a university, like Cusk herself. But his writing career, based on the book of short stories he wrote on an American scholarship, has ground to a halt:

> I don't know about you, Ryan said, but I actually don't have time to write, what with the family and the teaching job. Especially the teaching – it's the teaching that sucks the life out of you. And when I do have a week to myself, I spend it teaching extra courses like this one, for the money. If it's a choice between paying the mortgage and writing a story that'll only see the light of day in some tiny literary magazine—.[31]

Self-seeking and adulterous, Ryan is at least frank in his admission that he has sacrificed artistic integrity for the sake of a bourgeois lifestyle. John, in Toby Litt's short story cycle *Life-Like*, is equally solipsistic, his lechery almost destroying the would-be writer, Agatha, and her family, after a routine seduction on a residential course.

The authors of these stories seem to project their own moral and professional anxieties onto their unattractive doubles. A writing exercise used by Litt himself at his own workshops plays an important role in Agatha's relationship with John. Unlike Litt and Cusk, A. S. Byatt has not taught on a creative writing programme; nonetheless, her fiction shares similar concerns. In Byatt's story 'Raw Material' (*Little Black Book of Stories*, 2004) Jack Smollett is another character who turns to teaching after his writing career fails to live up to its promise, running a long-established group at a leisure centre. When, for the first time, he recognizes genuine talent in a new member, Cicely Fox, the others react by attacking her work. Cicely Fox's deafness stands for her isolation and detachment from social interaction; it also signals her absorption in the interior process of language, the quality that re-awakens Smollett's own love of writing: 'He was fired up, not only on Cicely Fox's behalf, but more darkly on his own. For the class's rancour, and the banal words in which it expressed that rancour, blew life into his anxiety over his own words, his own work.'[32]

Byatt's story is an excursion into the Grub Street of the twenty-first century, a territory that extends beyond Jack Smollett's leisure centre to include the university campus. It also recalls Cusk's distinction between storytelling and writing. The injunction to 'write what you really know about' is revisited after Miss Fox's horrific and inexplicable murder (p. 187). Smollett cannot describe the experience of finding her body; but his students instinctively transform the material into the melodramatic fictional patterns that mediate their own experience. This is, in fact, the reality they know. The class's writing is, as Smollett has always acknowledged to himself, a form of therapy, not only in a cathartic sense, but also because it boosts their self-esteem to consider themselves professional writers. In an interview with the *Scottish Review of Books*, Janice Galloway speaks scathingly of students she taught at Glasgow University who were expecting 'tricks that will turn you into J. K. Rowling'.[33] The suggestion, repeated in Byatt's story, is that creative writing feeds false aspirations when it reduces writing to a set of mechanical rules; the standard formulae, made familiar by the handbooks and repeated *ad nauseam* in writers' workshops everywhere, do not apply to genuine artistry.

The concerns of short story writers about artistry demonstrate the truism that every form of patronage comes with a price. Despite its many tensions and internal contradictions, the pact between the institution, the students and the public, has sustained a growth in short story writing and, more importantly, reading in the United Kingdom. Small independent presses, such as Salt and Comma, so essential to short story publishing, depend to an increasing extent on creative writing students, alumni and tutors. Freight Books was founded by former creative writing postgraduates from Glasgow University, and one of its first publications was an anthology of their work. Nicholas Royle is one of many writers, especially those with fractional contracts, who differentiate between their academic role and their 'outside' life. In that 'outside' life, he has edited numerous anthologies, including a *Best British Short Stories* series for Salt; he has also founded his own press, Nightjar, issuing individual short stories as signed limited editions. While in principle these activities are separate from each other, in practice his roles as advocate, practitioner and mentor for the form and its writers blur the boundaries between the institution and the larger creative economy.

The increased availability of creative writing courses may be regarded as an aspect of widening access to higher education in the late twentieth and early twenty-first centuries. The discipline has egalitarian origins, and is especially attractive to mature students; indeed, in exceptional circumstances MAs may be taken by students without a first degree. Tessa Hadley was a former teacher, but her writing career began in her forties, with an MA at Bath Spa University, where she is now Professor of Creative Writing. She is also a literary critic, and, for those familiar with her work, there is a discernible connection between her own practice and her reflections on other women short story writers, such as Alice Munro, Elizabeth Bowen and Katherine Mansfield. Like Munro, in particular, she exploits the short story's elliptical properties to suggest the inexpressible and inexplicable within domestic experience. Her advice to her own students – 'what you're writing should hurt and make you feel slightly anxious, and almost ashamed' – calls for a risky emotional investment that can scarcely be measured by the sort of learning outcomes associated with more traditional subjects.[34]

Hadley's stories often expose the nuances of class identity. 'A Mouthful of Cut Glass' (*Married Love*, 2012) is set in the 1970s and concerns a second-year undergraduate, Sheila, visiting her boyfriend's family in Birmingham. Born in a slum with an outside toilet, Neil is an exotic at Bristol University, and Sheila admires him for underplaying his working-class credentials. All seems to go well, the parents treating her politely, until she overhears Neil's mother speaking in 'her real voice, the one she used with people she was comfortable with'.[35] Her description of Sheila's accent as a 'mouthful of cut glass' is mortifying to the vicar's daughter (p. 47). Neil's stay with her own rickety and slightly eccentric family in rural Suffolk is punctuated by small embarrassments; yet Sheila observes, with some unease, it is characterized by ready absorption into this environment.

As a fragmented form, the short story is especially able to engage with discontinuity, fleeting encounters and fractured identities such as those presented in 'A Mouthful of Cut Glass'. Once again recalling Munro, Hadley often shows characters self-consciously reading experience or unpacking everyday expressions. The story ends almost with a psychic hall of mirrors, as Sheila strives to read Neil's state of consciousness from the other side of the rectory's French windows: 'she would have liked to see her life as he saw it, stripped of its ordinariness; she wished that she could possess him as he only was when he was alone' (p. 57). Earlier, her dissection of his mother's odd expression, 'a mouthful of cut glass', with its violent collision between two separate clichés, is juxtaposed with a university essay on Medea. This focus on perception and linguistic analysis suggests that, for Hadley's protagonists, lived experience is analogous to literature; reality is interpreted, or even authored, like a text. In a world where hierarchies of class and gender are breaking down, or even inverted, and codes of behaviour are far from transparent, textuality offers a means through which to negotiate confusion. The lonely voice in her stories is often that of the bookish young woman who serves as a proxy for the author, and who invites identification from readers who may potentially be writers themselves.

Paradoxically, despite the growth of a short story culture stimulated by creative writing MAs, the novel still remains the ultimate goal for alumni of these courses. Despite the deep affection felt towards the short story, it functions in many respects as a shop window for agents and publishers in the market for novels. Lucy Wood, Tom Vowler and Carys Bray have all followed up acclaimed collections with debut novels. Indeed, Bray's story 'Scaling Never' (*Sweet Home*, 2012) became the nucleus of *A Song for Issy Bradley* (2014), which switches viewpoints between family members dealing with a child's sudden death. Slightly edited, Bray's story appears as chapter 9 in the novel. Nonetheless, the institution of creative writing has subsidized the least lucrative form of literary endeavour, apart from poetry, and promoted its readership. In partnership with the Small Wonder festival, Chichester University sponsors an annual Award for Lifetime's Excellence in Short Fiction; the recipients at the time of writing have been William Trevor and Edna O'Brien. The Edge Hill Prize, inaugurated by the university in 2007, remains unique as the only British prize rewarding the author of a published short story collection. Both initiatives are intended to be active interventions, raising the status of the form alongside the range of prestigious prizes launched in recent years, such as the National Short Story Prize, the Sunday Times EFG Short Story Award and, in Ireland, the Frank O'Connor International Short Story Award (2005–15).

What is clear from this survey, despite the selectivity necessary in a synoptic overview, is that short story writing is not only deeply embedded within creative writing MAs, but that the work of its practitioners responds to the questions asked by creative writing about form and technique, and about the nature of authorship itself. No matter how far the discipline is integrated into the curriculum, or how rewarding the academy's patronage may be, writers will always prefer to conceive of themselves as outsiders, which suggests that O'Connor's 'lonely voice' is finding a new and apt relevance.

Notes

1. See Mark McGurl, *The Program Era: Postwar Fiction and the Rise of Creative Writing* (Cambridge, MA: Harvard University Press, 2009).
2. National Association of Writers in Education, 'Writing Courses', www.nawe.co.uk/writing-in-education/writing-at-university/writing-courses.html (accessed 28 February 2015).
3. Michelene Wandor, *The Author is Not Dead, Merely Somewhere Else: Creative Writing Reconceived* (Basingstoke: Palgrave Macmillan, 2008), p. 131.
4. Bernard Bergonzi, *Exploding English: Criticism, Theory, Culture* (Oxford: Clarendon Press, 1990), p. 9.
5. Marina Warner, 'Diary', *London Review of Books*, 36:17 (11 September 2014), pp. 42–3. Available on www.lrb.co.uk/v36/n17/marina-warner/diary (accessed 28 February 2015).
6. McGurl, *The Program Era*, p. 408.
7. Paul Dawson, *Creative Writing and the New Humanities* (Abingdon: Routledge, 2005).
8. See Sam Baker, 'The Irresistible Rise of the Short Story', *Daily Telegraph*, 18 May 2014. Available on www.telegraph.co.uk/culture/books/10831961/The-irresistible-rise-of-the-short-story.html (accessed 28 February 2015).
9. For flash fiction definitions see Paola Trimarco, 'Short Shorts: Exploring Relevance and Filling in Narratives', in *Teaching the Short Story*, ed. Ailsa Cox (Basingstoke: Palgrave Macmillan, 2011), pp. 13–27.
10. Tom Vowler interview with Graham Mort, *ShortFiction*, www.shortfictionjournal.co.uk/?page_id=515 (accessed 28 February 2015).
11. *Thresholds: Home of the International Short Story Forum*, http://blogs.chi.ac.uk/shortstoryforum/ (accessed 28 February 2015).
12. Malcolm Bradbury, 'Introduction', in *The Penguin Book of Modern British Short Stories* (London: Viking, 1987), p. 14.
13. Clare Hanson, *Short Stories and Short Fictions, 1880–1980* (Basingstoke: Macmillan, 1985), p. 159.
14. Toby Litt, *Adventures in Capitalism* (London: Penguin, 2003), p. 63.
15. Toby Litt, *Exhibitionism* (London: Penguin 2003), p. 43. Subsequent page references to this edition are given in parentheses in the text.
16. Michel Foucault, 'What is an Author?', in *Textual Strategies: Perspectives in Post-Structuralist Criticism*, ed. Josué V. Harari (London: Methuen, 1979), pp. 141–60.
17. Ali Smith, 'Creative Writing Workshy', in *The Creative Writing Coursebook*, ed. Julia Bell and Paul Magrs (Basingstoke: Macmillan, 2001), pp. 24–8 (p. 24).
18. Quoted in Michelle Pauli, 'Short Story Scores with New Prize and Amazon Project', *The Guardian*, 23 August 2005. Available on www.theguardian.com/books/2005/aug/23/news.michellepauli (accessed 28 February 2015).

19. Ali Smith, *Artful* (London: Penguin, 2013), p. 29.
20. Ali Smith, *The First Person and Other Stories* (London: Penguin, 2009), p. 17.
21. Margaret Atwood, *Negotiating with the Dead* (Cambridge University Press, 2002), p. 54.
22. Litt, *Adventures in Capitalism*, p. 27.
23. McGurl, *The Program Era*, p. 234.
24. See Mary Louise Pratt, 'The Short Story: The Long and the Short of It', in *The New Short Story Theories*, ed. Charles E. May (Athens, OH: Ohio University Press, 1994), pp. 91–113.
25. Frank O' Connor, *The Lonely Voice: A Study of the Short Story* (London: Macmillan, 1963; repr. 1965), p. 27, 18.
26. A. L. Kennedy, *On Writing* (London: Vintage, 2014), pp. 336–7.
27. Hanif Kureishi, *Collected Stories* (London: Faber & Faber, 2010), p. 611.
28. Philip Hensher, 'So You Want to Be a Writer', *The Guardian*, 14 March 2014. Available on www.theguardian.com/books/2014/mar/14/creative-writing-courses-advice-students (accessed 29 July 2016).
29. Paul March-Russell, *The Short Story: An Introduction* (Edinburgh University Press, 2009), p. 105.
30. Elke D'hoker, 'Painterly Stories: An Interview with Rachel Cusk', *Short Fiction in Theory and Practice*, 3.2 (2013), pp. 253–9 (p. 255).
31. Rachel Cusk, *Outline* (London: Faber & Faber, 2014), pp. 46–7.
32. A. S. Byatt, *Little Black Book of Stories* (London: Vintage, 2004), p. 210. Subsequent page references are given in parentheses in the text.
33. Janice Galloway, 'The SRB Interview', *Scottish Review of Books*, 5.2, 2 September 2009, www.scottishreviewofbooks.org/index.php/back-issues/volume-five/volume-five-issue-two/10-janice-galloway-the-srb-interview (accessed 28 February 2015).
34. Alex Clark, 'Tessa Hadley: A Life In Writing', *The Guardian*, 28 February 2011. Available on www.theguardian.com/books/2011/feb/28/tessa-hadley-life-writing-fiction (accessed 28 February 2015).
35. Tessa Hadley, *Married Love* (London: Jonathan Cape, 2012), p. 47. Subsequent page references are given in parentheses in the text.

35
Short Story Futures

JULIAN MURPHET

Post-book?

The happy fortunes of the modern short story form since the late nineteenth century were underwritten by very specific material and technical circumstances. What Benedict Anderson has aptly called print capitalism underwent significant recalibrations as the larger industrial economies entered into their imperial-monopoly phases, not least the introduction of photomechanical reproduction technology and, with it, the launch of magazine and periodical culture and the penny press. Nowhere was this more the case than in the 'Gilded Age' United States, where an unrestricted literary market in bowdlerized British novels meant that local periodicals offered the best available venue for local writers (such as Nathaniel Hawthorne, Edgar Allan Poe and Herman Melville) to prosper in; but the metropolitan oases of Russia, France and Germany also fostered lively subscription magazine cultures, triggering momentous formal innovations from the likes of Anton Chekhov, Guy de Maupassant and E. T. A. Hoffmann. In Britain, meanwhile, this state of affairs fomented the propitious conditions – which Henry James in c.1910 called 'a world of periodicals and editors, of roaring "successes" in fine' – in which Robert Louis Stevenson, H. G. Wells, Arnold Bennett and Rudyard Kipling were to leave their distinctive marks on a form whose centre of gravity arguably lay elsewhere.[1]

There is an argument to be made that, at the very historical apex of the age of the book – the Gutenberg galaxy's apotheosis in the 'world republic of letters' with its meridian in Paris at the end of the nineteenth century – this notable shift to shorter forms in cheap and disposable periodical formats had already augured a momentous recalibration of literary energies, whose long-term results we can perhaps see around us today.[2] That is to say, the situation of which James complains in his preface to *The Wings of the Dove* – namely, 'the fact that the work had ignominiously failed, in advance, of all power to see itself "serialised"' – is one in which books, the very physical bulk of the codex as such, already seemed doomed to a saurian extinction in the face of the lither and more adaptable species of shorter fiction.[3] It is a hypothesis introduced by that inaugural moment in Honoré de Balzac's *Lost Illusions* when Lucien pens the revolutionary two-page *feuilleton* that seals his fate on the far, and contemptible, side of the novel itself: the shorter, journalistic form betokens the demise of the longer. Of course, during the modernist period the uneven technical and material development of long- and short-form prose fiction under monopoly capitalism created a space in which both the short story and the novel might distinctively prosper as aesthetically rigorous forms. But the irreversible gravitation of financial rewards towards the shorter forms had arguably already signed the death certificate of the aesthetically serious novel as a commercially viable entity at the time that James was writing.

The ambient, more anthropological reasons behind this historical tipping point are likewise endemic to the history of capitalism: the oft-noted erosion of 'attention' thanks to a plethora of cultural and social distractions; the ever-tightening noose of the synchronized clock around everyday pursuits, including leisure; the paucity of available times and spaces for sustained acts of reading; the accelerating cycles of fashion and cool; the increasing competition from other mechanical and electronic media; and so on. None of this offered succour to a form whose expansive origins lay in the voluminous cultural space allotted for reading in a pre-industrial economy. But all of it augured well for a form implicitly free from the restrictive economy of the codex as the gold standard of a literate culture: the short story was, in both inception and evolution, a 'post-book' form, and so sheds light on the present literary conjuncture. For if we are not yet even remotely 'post-book' in terms of the diversity of available published titles today, the story is different when we assume the perspective of what John Thompson calls the 'diversity of the *marketplace*' as such – that is, the ever-narrowing range of what is noticed, bought and consumed.[4] When this constricted market is compared to the immense versatility and range of online and digital textual formats, whose signal advantages – of being easily accessed and updated, affordable, searchable, portable, easily stored, and of having inter- and hyper-textual capabilities, and the capacity for multimedia – seem to mire the codex in some antediluvian estuary of drying sands, the writing on the wall for the book seems stark indeed. Even if academics are inclined to agree that books, as André Schiffrin laments, 'have traditionally been the one medium in which two people, an author and an editor, could agree that something needed to be said, and for a relatively small amount of money, share it with the public', the widespread migration of reading habits from the printed page to the continuously refreshed, pixelated screen has tended to confirm the short story's initial declaration of independence from the codex by privileging brief and memorable bursts of cultural information.[5] Rather than the extended narrative reach and aesthetic complexity of the novel, it is the short story that today's predominant textual forms – the blog entry, the tweet, the status update, the email, the SMS – have come to resemble. And this affinity, in which the first and the ultimate 'post-book' forms of writing meet and coalesce, is propitious for new aesthetic experimentation in the short narrative format.

Promising Signs

We can take the measure of such promising hybridity in a few, select efforts by writers and publishing houses over recent years. It is important to note at the outset that none of these forms is particularly distinguished aesthetically, especially as regards the estimable history of the short story form: there is nothing here to trouble the reputations of Heinrich von Kleist, James Joyce or Jorge Luis Borges. What matters, rather, is to observe the resilience and adaptability of the short narrative format within a rapidly changing media ecology that looks certain, in the long term, to lay the printed codex to dignified rest. For it is in such experimental attempts that we begin to see how much better adapted the short narrative form is to medial migration and transmission than the bulkier and less convertible novel.

Scots writer Ewan Morrison, who disheartened many at the Edinburgh Writers' Festival in 2011 with his timely speculations about the precarious futures of the printed book and the very category of professional writers as such, has attempted to encode in his stories the apocalyptic paradox that defines our moment in cultural history. His 2005 collection, aptly entitled *The Last Book You Read* (and sold predominantly as an e-book), explores the chronic dysfunctions affecting human intimacy in the age of the Internet.[6] At its core is a story written in the form of a one-sided series of email responses to a public posting on a fictional noticeboard. That posting had called for confidential information about the habits of male adulterers, and the long and increasingly desperate trail of one man's email responses runs the full scale of confessional attitudes, from swaggering misogynist braggadocio to wallowing guilt and depression. Presented entirely from within the 'voice' of this series of electronic missives, the story exploits all the usual idiomatic resources available to the literary remediation of digital communication – SMS abbreviations like '4 U' and '@ work'; the random typos of hasty composition; the peculiarly immediate and hectoring tone of much email correspondence; and the use of 'attachments' of more extended prose, broken up into inevitable bullet points. But the narrative's larger point has to do with the automated alienations and systemic technological disconnections that define our late-postmodern sociality: the fact that the most intimate and private psychological data are routinely circulated between 'persons' who most likely do not exist, by servers and databases run by algorithms and robots. Our chronically unreliable narrator, who moves between two or three names and as many email addresses, and at key metafictional moments wants us to believe that he is a struggling writer (signing off once as Jack Nicholson from *The Shining*), sends his simulated confessions into an electronic void with all the existential despair of a Dostoevsky protagonist.

In 2008, Penguin publishers in conjunction with Six to Start games development company launched an experimental 'alternate reality game' called 'We Tell Stories'. In this online initiative, six established authors used a variety of Internet platforms – including Google Maps, blogs, Twitter and a number of other innovative delivery systems – to publish their short narrative tributes to well-known works of fiction published under the Penguin Classics imprint, such as John Buchan's *The Thirty-Nine Steps*, Charles Dickens's *Hard Times* and Lewis Carroll's *Alice's Adventures in Wonderland*. Husband and wife team Nicci French (Nicci Gerrard and Sean French) took as their source text Emile Zola's *Thérèse Raquin*, and typed out onto a basic blog-like interface, in real time, the alternating perspectives of a jaded older man and a fiercely romantic younger woman on their short-term and low-rent relationship, in their contribution *Your Place and Mine*.[7] Though it is now simply archived like any other text on the 'We Tell Stories' website, for those who engaged with the experiment as a real-time literary event, there was the sense of the short story form being opened up by the dynamism of a 'live feed' from two irreconcilable sources in the real. That is, the form for a brief moment lost its inevitable sense of temporal foreclosure in the preterite tense – which Fredric Jameson calls the *récit*'s 'mark of irrevocable time, of the event that has happened once and for all' – and entered, even if virtually, the existential flow of information in the present.[8] That the text lacked much in the way of literary distinction thus, at least for the brief duration of its performance, raised the stakes of its fictionality and added to its plausibility as a document of the real. In his *Slice*, meanwhile,

Toby Litt unleashed a still more ambitious project, predicated in content on M. R. James's ghost story 'The Haunted Dolls' House', over multiple platforms including Livejournal, WordPress, gmail, flickr and Twitter.[9] Also dispatched live, and similarly alternating between the perspective of a teenage girl and her parents, Litt's efforts on these various websites between 24 and 28 March 2008, strained at the very formal limits of the well-wrought tale by demonstrating how radically distributed and partitioned the once single stream of narrative information has become in the age of social networking. The written word having lost the hegemony it had unquestionably enjoyed when James wrote his tale, today, Litt effectively shows, we consume story more as a web of discrete and complexly interwoven streams of data: visual, textual, symbolic (emoticons play a vital part) and auditory. So too, Naomi Alderman's contribution, *Alice in Storyland*, distributed its narrative information across a dizzying number of emails, text messages, live online events and specially created websites, even going so far as to permit a certain degree of interactivity and the influence of 'readers' on the outcome of the plot.

Yet such remarkable freedom was effectively paid for by the corporate patronage of a major publisher looking to enhance sales of actual books. In the result, what seems to have mattered most about 'We Tell Stories' is how impossible it would have been to 'monetize' its products, strung up as they were on a number of free-to-air online platforms and tailor-made, non-firewalled websites. These were, conspicuously, not commodities, and as Ewan Morrison had argued, it was precisely this non-profitability of online story materials that portended the worst for 'the author' as a professional identity – just as the digitization of music and of motion pictures is having disastrous consequences on the profitability of those creative industries. So it was with a kind of inevitable corporate logic that Amazon then launched a new category of literary commodity, the Kindle Single in 2011, and thereby sought to bridge the yawning chasm between the traditional categories of fiction and the actual life of words today in digital formats. The Singles are modelled on the one-track popular music 45-rpm records of the vinyl days of yore, or more obviously on the single mp3 files through which most people consume music today. Just as the long-playing record or album is a relic of the past, so too the novel, it is once again suggested, may be bypassed in favour of its discrete narrative elements or units – cheap e-book 'Singles', downloadable onto your tablet or other device at the click of a button. Although the format, generally novella-length and still adhering to Poe's standard definition of readability in a single sitting, caters to readers of both fiction and non-fiction alike, it might persuasively be argued that in fact the non-fiction Singles fare better as free-standing textual artefacts. The fiction is as a rule heavily generic short story material, written by established (and on the whole American) authors whose print runs had perhaps been on the decline on the open marketplace. This emphatic conservatism at the level of form, contradicting so flagrantly the exuberant experimentalism of the 'We Tell Stories' venture, is the aesthetic price paid for what has turned out to be a relatively remunerative alternative to standard forms of publication. Within a year of the launch, over two million Singles had sold, and some authors were earning between $9,000 and $65,000 per unit, thanks in large part to the quality control ensured by literary heavyweight David Blum, protecting the initiative from vanity press accusations. But the survival of some vestigial or nostalgic 'literary' prestige in such a context is a mixed blessing at best; the language used in a glowing *Atlantic* magazine report modulates schizophrenically, but aptly, between an aesthetic and a financial idiom of praise: 'the fact is a new genre is emerging as a result of e-reading technologies, one that is proving successful both editorially and financially. All of this stands in evidence that in its Kindle Singles brand, Amazon is investing in a serious business model behind a quality editorial product'.[10]

Inevitably, then, the publishing majors (all of them run, as André Schiffrin gloomily points out, by international conglomerate media empires capitalized in the vicinity of tens of billions of dollars) would seek to test the viability of a wholesale conversion from printed to digitized text by exploiting the literary cachet of their most illustrious authors.[11] This means not only ensuring that the literary heavyweights on their lists sign off on the marketing rights to digital editions of their back catalogues, but, even more, convincing some of them to participate in trials and exhibitions that demonstrate the viability of online and networked textual forms within the still legitimate literary 'rules of art' in Bourdieu's sense: that is, to leverage the still active 'author function' in order to open up new forms of corporate profitability with or without the material commodity of a printed text – or at least to use the former to push sales of the latter one last time. And no form is better suited to such exhibitions than the short story. Roddy Doyle's work for Jonathan Cape (owned by Random House) in *Two Pints* (2011) and *Two More Pints* (2014) consists of a long series of relatively brief Facebook status updates on Doyle's page, posted in 'real time' by the author on mostly trivial issues of the day (celebrity deaths, local politics, public events), and then collected and curated for publication in book form. Why they qualify as fiction rather than essays or what Coetzee called 'strong opinions' is because

Doyle has taken the liberty of projecting his topical reflections through an imagined stichomythic exchange between two grizzled Dublin pub regulars. Written entirely in dialogue without any authorial intrusions or descriptions at all, these condensed passages of inebriated banter perform the kind of generational parallax that the transition from book to digital text betokens for an ageing reading public. Time and again, the interlocutors reflect on the sheer oddity of, and their exteriority to, the digital hegemon: 'Would you ever let yourself be digitally enhanced', one asks; 'See your man in America who twittered his dick', queries the other; after reflecting that everything looks better on an HD TV set, his companion parries 'Does it make the fuckin' economy look better as well?'[12] Slight in its ambitions, but canny in its method, *Two Pints* and its sequel harness the compulsive chattiness of their host medium (Facebook) for a wistful disquisition upon felt existential cleavages between embodiment and sociability in a post-book world. The micro-stories of which they are compiled manage the awkward task of transforming topical ephemera into wrought comic gems by way of the acute self-consciousness of their mediatic 'betweenness' (which is what, finally, 'medium' means).

If this winking effort from a publishing major to smooth the logic of transition marks out one predictable end of a complex spectrum, we should similarly expect a counter-effort from the other direction. The giants of industrial technology and particularly companies heavily invested in mobile electronic devices have made the same kind of move with well-known author 'brands', albeit without a physical book as the envisaged end-product. BlackBerry's ambitious involvement in Neil Gaiman's Keep Moving Project in 2013, resulted in a year-long collaboration between the writer and his extensive fan base on a large multimedia 'text' entitled *A Calendar of Tales*, and authored, as the website has it, 'by Neil Gaiman and You'.[13] That text, consisting of twelve vaguely interrelated stories based on the months of the year (as classical and old-fashioned a fairy-tale conceit as the form could tolerably stand today), has a simple but promising genesis: 'On February 4th 2013 Neil Gaiman [. . .] tweeted twelve questions to the world, one for each month of the year. From the tens of thousands of responses he received, Neil picked his favourite answers and wrote twelve short stories inspired by them. Releasing these back to the world, Neil asked people to contribute art to illustrate the stories.' So, the official emphasis here lies squarely upon interactivity and an open 'Web 2.0' approach: less the idea of an author releasing his prefabricated materials on new-fangled platforms than one of the inextricable sociality of text. Which is to say, the concept of textuality implicit in this project is one dependent upon BlackBerry's technical specializations as a social networking tool, and not on the codex as a point-to-point medium. However, that corporate sponsorship vitiates the very 'Web 2.0' promise it cynically proffers. The privileging of Twitter as the primary instrument of authorial inspiration not only builds a partner company into the conceptual infrastructure, but, given the intense competition and selectivity involved, tends of necessity towards the bare minimum of actual user interaction. For instance, 'February' is framed thus: '@neilhimself asked: "What's the strangest thing that ever happened to you in February?" @TheAstralGypsy replied: "Met a girl on a beach, searching for her grandma's pendant, lost 50 years ago. I had it, found previous Feb".' These last 107 characters, selected from hundreds of thousands submitted, thereby serve as an alibi for a networked interactivity that never properly gets off the ground. Similarly the graphic artworks chosen to accompany each tale are rigorously selected from a pre-determined aesthetic palette in conformity with Gaiman's well-established 'graphic novel' track record; their function is, pedestrianly enough, merely to illustrate what has already been written. The project is an intriguing, but ultimately disappointing attempt to capitalize upon the extensive base of online fan fictions by absorbing them under the sanctioned umbrella of corporate PR. In effect, *A Calendar of Tales* served as one immense, year-long advertisement for BlackBerry with a captive audience of Gaiman's committed followers. The tales are weak, the prose flaccid, and the 'artwork' ghastly; but aesthetics was never the point of the project.

No recent experiment has been odder, perhaps, than David Mitchell's 2014 live-Tweeted short fiction, 'The Right Sort'.[14] In a context of ever-greater interest in the 140-character medium for extremely condensed narration – think only of Mashable's 'Margaret Atwood Twitter Contest' which selected ten users' single-tweet short stories, or Twitter-users' Short Horror Stories – Mitchell's effort is puzzling on a number of counts.[15] First, given the various contractual arrangements that Mitchell has with his publishers, the Twitter story appears under the 'imprint' of Sceptre Books, which therefore claims proprietary copyright over the 280-entry narrative, along with Mitchell and Twitter itself: it is therefore not a Twitter story like yours or mine. Second, this is clearly a short story whose larger form is conceived on a very traditional model: there are conventional characters, in a more or less plausible (albeit warped) fictional world; there is copious dialogue in quotation marks; there is a pivotal turning-point and an epiphany; and above all, rather like Gaiman's work, there is a hidebound preconception that the short story is where romance (the fantastic, the grotesque, the uncanny) goes to hide in a novel-ridden universe of literary realism. Third, at a more local level, the individual tweets are paradoxically treated as autonomous units – the prose, conforming to the 140-character procrustean bed, contracts into periods characterized by brevity and parataxis; ostensible 'literariness' is at a merciful minimum, which agrees aesthetically with the first-person voice of a humble schoolboy; and there is very little of what we might describe as Twitter enjambement, or syntactical carry-over between tweets. Fourth, however, and most damningly, there is absolutely no effort to mediate between form and content at the level of mediatic self-consciousness; for all the tale's ultimately unfathomable ontology, we are essentially cast into a world in which Rhodesia is still a state, many decades before Twitter could have existed, and which therefore forecloses the possibility of a story told in real time through live tweets, and asks the impossible of the medium: namely, to imagine it as a neutral container for fiction, rather than a communicational node of interactivity. As an indication of the missed opportunity, consider the fatuity, in a tweet, of accounting for its stylistic brevity with the explanation: 'Valium breaks down the world into bite-sized sentences. Like this one. All lined up. Munch-munch.' Mitchell, it would appear, has signally failed to grasp the formal opportunity of his experiment, though he has written by far the most aesthetically rewarding of all the stories here considered. That paradox would seem to indicate the uneven development between form and medium that most acutely characterizes our present.

Conditions and Futures

How might we more accurately characterize the lines of technical and existential force governing the present and near-future conditions for short narrative production? How might 'convergence culture' oblige a serious rethink of what it is to tell a story in the first place?[16] How does the prevailing 'regime of computation' affect the underlying assumptions about what story is, what its rules are, and where it might be heading?[17] Of course, in the brief space available one can only scratch at the surface of a vast agglomeration of factors.

The principal point to make is that literature has historically been a one-way 'representational' medium, while the media that define our epoch and the world of the near future are above all 'connective'.[18] That is, during the 500-year long age of the book, the function of the written word was principally to give rise to images that offered a picture of the world or of some other, imaginary, one. The emergence of connective media in the twentieth century (telephony, radio and television) constituted a first, decisive push against the regime of representation – these media thrived above all not by giving pictures (though they did that too), but by integrating scattered subjects within a network of broadcast simultaneity and light-speed transmissions. The second, and conclusive moment came with the launch of the personal computer, and (with its unstoppable spread) the Internet, mobile devices and our full paraphernalia of connective digital technology. With the inevitability of an achieved revolution, digital code has subsumed all representational media: the great films of the past, the great music, and of course the full literary archive, all have been transcoded into digitally readable files for instant playback on the humblest smartphone. In other words, 'representationality' has been swallowed up by connectivity, without our critical vocabularies or existential framework altering sufficiently to make sense of the transformation.

While we continue to think in terms of distinct and somehow irreconcilable cultural forms – music, cinema, literature, performance – in fact the technology (and the capital behind it) has done the reconciling for us. The key to grasping our present conjuncture lies in the concept of 'convergence', which simply means the technical obsolescence of any concept of media purity or discrete channels of information.[19] The future of the short story form, indeed the future of narrative itself, depends upon a radical understanding of the hollowing out of the old humanist symbolic universe of language by the numerical infinity of code.

The reason why the short story form seems a propitious place to begin this radical rethinking of what narrative actually is today, is rooted in its origins in the implicitly 'post-book' conjuncture of the late nineteenth century, and the consequently rich history of formal flexibility it has to draw upon in mapping out a genuinely post-literary cultural space. As the universal plenum of digital connectivity spreads to incorporate more and more of the planet's living subjects, comprehensively reshaping the very notion of 'attention' by the power of annually redoubling zettabytes; and as late capitalism's consumption cycles dissolve the corporeal foundations of circadian human biorhythms in a sleepless, multitasking world of 24/7, such that 'our bodies and identities assimilate an ever-expanding surfeit of services, images, procedures, chemicals, to a toxic and often fatal threshold', what form better recommends itself as a testing ground than one forged on the modern anvil of train timetables, subscription cycles, chronic distraction and an appetite for what Leopold Bloom calls the 'tid-bit'?[20] A further consideration is that, given its inevitable formal association with the anecdote as such, the short story also looks poised to reap whatever rewards are still available to it by blurring the lines we continue, perhaps anachronistically, to draw between fiction and non-fiction, in the face of what David Shields has termed a pervasive cultural 'reality hunger', itself a logical consequence of our wholesale conversion from representation to connectivity. 'Suddenly everyone's tale is tellable, which seems to me a good thing, even if not everyone's story turns out to be fascinating or well told.'[21] The point is, in a connected world, not that these stories tell 'the truth', or conform to aesthetic criteria developed under a different regime, but that they instantiate the very connectivity of which they are crucial existential elements – their *reality* is that they do what Forster once called for the novel to do, 'only connect'.

Rather than the smoothly balanced, symmetrical organization of standard novelistic form, Shields calls for the patching together of 'fragmented materials ... materials yanked out of context', whose underlying logic is curatorial and editorial rather than creative or expressive.[22] And what better aesthetic rationale could there be for a world culture now transcoded into data and rendered 'convergent' within the black boxes of digital consumption? Collage may have been introduced to art through the cut-and-paste provocations of the Cubists, but its truest cultural habitat opened up in an epoch of 'general digitization'.

Perhaps it is possible, then, to extrapolate from these conditions of short-form narrative possibility and anticipate where and in what forms the tale or *récit*, the story as such, is likely to prosper in the years ahead. In the first place, and almost certainly, the abandonment of the printed page as either story's origin or its end will tend to open it up to a genuine multimedia process. One of the more remarkable recent experiments in short-form narrative, *Noah* (Cederberg & Woodman, Canada, 2013) pushes the boundaries between film and text to the point where their distinctions break down. Over eighteen minutes, we see only a 'live' screenshot of the eponymous character's iMac (and once or twice his iPhone), as he operates a number of applications and websites simultaneously – a porn site, Facebook, Skype, iTunes, QWOP, Messages and Chatroulette – in a continuous online multitask that perfectly captures the complex distribution of informational codes today across a range of sonic, visual and textual channels, all of them undergirded by digital technology. Noah no more feels the ontological distinctions between text, image and sound than he questions the difference between truth and lie – the 'real' is the constancy of his live links with friends, girlfriend and strangers.

In this way *Noah* offers a sense of 'narrative' giving way to something else, a regime of connectivity put together piecemeal out of discrete applications, only some of which are text-based. And yet, this 'film' is as textual, as 'written' as it is anything else, and asks us to read it with the attention and exactitude of any inveterate short story reader: the importance of the written word on these screens is, in fact, far weightier than the spoken word or the online facial clue. It is just that we are obliged not only to parse the words that appear and disappear with the characteristic ephemerality of digital messaging, but to hold that information in an interpretive balancing act with what the soundtrack and flashing and fading visuals are simultaneously communicating. *Noah* is an exciting glimpse into the short story's more likely future.

If, in the modern period proper, the principal distinction between language arts and the audio-visual art of film had been the inequality of access to and expertise in the respective means of production, today those boundaries have collapsed. The widespread availability of affordable and intuitive audio-visual production technologies, and the ostensible decline in standards of traditional literacy, mean that the playing field has progressively been levelled. So that today it is as likely that a young storyteller will turn to an application like Mixamo Face Plus to tell her tale, as that she will open Microsoft Word and begin to type it out in words. A demonstration clip like Mixamo's 'Unplugged' makes clear the extraordinary results that can be obtained by 'anybody with Unity, Face Plus and a creative concept', as they put it.[23] Their goal, 'to democratize 3D character art', seeks to wrest the means of short-form story production away from big production studios; if anybody with enough basic competency can put together a rich and emotionally convincing character arc in 3D animation on their home computer, the argument goes, we will see more and more 'Stories of My Life' being told in well-rendered, highly textured, immersive narrative worlds put together as audio-visual files rather than printed texts. The short story, as a form, is facing a momentous transmigration of formal features both into and out of the domain of text, as writers seek to 'upload' the older technology perfected by Raymond Carver and Ernest Hemingway into new media vestments.

Meanwhile, it is not as though text-only forms will cease altogether to find purchase in the new informational economy; rather, those forms will be obliged to undergo mutations specific to a regime of connectivity and ubiquitous file-sharing. In one of the more indicative experiments of recent years, the Australian if:book project entitled 'Lost In Track Changes' challenges the very notion of the single author, or the author function itself, as adequate to a world characterized by what Michael Hardt and Antonio Negri called cooperative immaterial labour.[24] Their website describes the experimental form: 'Five writers have written a short piece of memoir, a vignette. Each work is passed onto another author within the group, tasked with transforming the piece into something else. In the background, if:book tracks the changes. The newly minted remix is passed along again and so on until each of the pieces have passed through all five authors.'[25] The ostensible goal here, to expose the confessional anecdote or memoir form to the exigencies of collage and remix, as well as resurrect the older pleasures of the parlour game, is suggestive of certain directions for future work in the field. Dismantling the aura of the creator, the single literary genius, seems a pertinent move to be making just as the very category of professional writer enters into serious economic jeopardy. Moreover, this promiscuous irradiation of the 'Story of My Life' by the stories and scepticism of others mirrors the established dialogical dynamism between the 'content' and 'comments' sections in any number of text-driven websites, and returns the short narrative form to something like its origins in the comic novellas of the sixteenth century: anonymous anecdotes, replete with irony, of things that most likely never happened, to persons who exist only for the sake of the fictions.

But if these are the more obvious, immanently logical moves we can expect over coming years, what are the outer limits into which the short story may well be absorbed? For a brief period recently, the world of poetry was subjected to an incursion from an unprecedented bastard progeny of Oulipo known as 'flarf' poetry. Here, 'deliberately bad poems' were pieced together out of strings of inane prefabricated content, mostly accessed on the Internet via Google searches. The resultant tongue-in-cheek anti-aesthetic, variously known as 'unoriginal', 'uncreative' and 'flarf' writing, has clear (if not conspicuously enlightening) applications to the production of short narrative texts. To purloin, remix and variously adapt verbatim materials found in the immeasurable reaches of the World Wide Web's archive of the *déja dit*, is to conform to the presiding force-field of cultural activity today. In Kenneth Goldsmith's estimate of the potential, 'confronted with an unprecedented amount of texts and language, writers have the opportunity to move beyond the creation of new texts and manage, parse, appropriate and reconstruct those that already exist'.[26] Such a practice of hypertrophic collage where nothing is actually added other than the ironic conceptual frame, where text, image and sound blend and overlap, and where it is finally impossible to distinguish the real from the fictional, is properly adequate to a regime of computation in a way that none of the experimental fictions analysed above truly is. We await the full development of unoriginal prosaics in the years and decades to come.[27]

Finally, however, there is a last remaining frontier. The most pressing question here concerns the very provenance of narrative itself, which, if it can be analysed and broken down into so many component parts, so many logical elements, and reassembled out of them, it can just as surely be handed over to the fundamental grammarian of our time, namely the algorithm. Rather than sending a human being, with all its existential limitations and inbuilt nostalgias for a lost humanistic framework, into the dense thickets of found text lining the avenues of the information superhighway, why not send an instrument altogether more appropriate to the task at hand: namely, a robot? This is the gamble of some of the more pioneering of textual producers today, who, rather than creating text, or finding and curating it, are writing algorithms capable of doing that work automatically and without the filter of any organic preconceptions. Mark Riedl and his colleagues at the Georgia Institute of Technology have written a program called 'Scheherazade', an automatic story generator that '(a) automatically learns a domain model by crowdsourcing a corpus of narrative examples, and (b) generates stories by sampling from the space defined by the domain model'.[28] There are robots with Twitter accounts (Twitterbots) that post micro-blog entries under usernames like '@chatmundo' (a conversational robot) and '@Horse_ebooks', whose Tweets include gems like 'I m going to outline 14 different ways that I ve found you' (sic) and 'breath, and vice versa. How many of the common things I and others thought we were doing'.[29] These micro-narratives are generated and disseminated without a hint of human participation, and are read by hundreds of thousands of avid followers.

Consider, finally, Darby Larson's 2013 'book' *Irritant*. Comprised of around thirty 'memes' or elemental building blocks of textual thought – 'man', 'balloon', 'irritant' and so forth – and subjected to the logical dictates of formulaic sentence structures like 'So in something of X lived the Y while the Z Z'd in front of the A', *Irritant* inserts the memes into the sentence structures within a dizzying number of permutations and combinations.[30] While a few of these sentences manage to conform to the logic of sense, most veer off into regions of absurdity and meaninglessness that summon up images of a room full of typewriting monkeys. The image is advised, since although there are shades of Gertrude Stein's *Making of Americans* here, 'Darby Larson' doesn't enjoy, at least in the sense that Gertrude Stein did, anything like a direct relationship with this curious post-literary *combinatoire* – which also has an indefinite afterlife on Twitter, where a robot retweets random sentences from *Irritant*.[31] Rather, this textual composition is fully mediated by the kinds of computational code that underwrite all cultural circulation today, for it has been filtered through algorithms and machine syntheses that utterly exceed the imaginative reach of even the most speculative fiction. Larson operates within sets of systemic constraints and limited variables that privilege computational processing. The finite set of possible permutations engendered from within these constraints need not be elaborated by human thought; they can be conjugated by a tailor-made code in PERL (a family of high-level, general-purpose, interpreted, dynamic programming languages), which is what Larson actually writes. If the result looks too mechanical, too predictable on a first output, that too can be adapted through a new code: 'I wanted to mix all these sentences up so it would have a flow that didn't sound like a computer just spit it out. [So] I wrote [a] wrapper for the randomizer function in PERL to spit out all sentences in a random order.' If now the result felt a little too open, too free, all that remained was to expose the text to a new algorithm that effectively imposed higher-order constraints and delimitations on the material – principally a reduction of lexical variables down to variables on only one root.

> Now the work feels good to me, albeit quite long. It is basically moving from sentences like 'The man danced with unicorns.' to sentences like 'The pig pigged with pigs'. For me, what's happening is there is a tightening of constraint as the piece moves forward. Like it's closing in on itself. A pig virus that is slowly eating up all the original sentences. But I wanted to see the reverse, or an opening up. To begin with this pig virus but slowly shed it to eventually reveal the original set.[32]

As a harbinger of textual things to come, Larson's text poses entirely new questions to the inherited hermeneutic apparatuses for the reading of short stories. Drawing its aesthetic impetus from the history of the avant-garde, but predicating its method on codes that belong to an entirely numerical paradigm, 'his' work adapts the art of fiction to a computational horizon where the point is no longer to mediate between human beings, but to encourage human beings to come to terms with their dependency on algorithmic functions to which they only rarely have any direct access. In this brave new world, the short narrative form is being asked to carry unwonted ontological and epistemological burdens, whose proper critical weighing must await the thoroughgoing reinvention of our analytic toolkits. Adapting to its media environment with the precocious rapidity demanded of it by the sheer velocities of technological change, the story form is already well out ahead of its tardy readers, scouting the existential perimeters of a world we are creating with our eyes wide shut.

Notes

1. Henry James, 'Preface', in *The Wings of the Dove*, ed. Peter Brooks (Oxford University Press, 1998), p. xxxvii.
2. Pascale Casanova, *The World Republic of Letters*, trans. M. B. Debevoise (Cambridge, MA: Harvard University Press, 2004), especially pp. 82–124.
3. James, *Wings of the Dove*, p. xxxvii.
4. John B. Thompson, *Merchants of Culture: The Publishing Business in the Twenty-First Century* (Cambridge: Polity, 2010), p. 389.
5. André Schiffrin, *The Business of Books* (London and New York: Verso, 2000), p. 171.
6. Ewan Morrison, *The Last Book You Read* (London: Black and White Publishing, 2005).
7. www.wetellstories.co.uk/stories/week4/about/ (accessed 20 January 2015).
8. Fredric Jameson, *The Antinomies of Realism* (London and New York: Verso, 2013), p. 21.
9. www.wetellstories.co.uk/stories/week2/ (accessed 20 January 2015).
10. Rebecca J. Rosen, 'Authors of Kindle Singles Are Raking in Tens of Thousands of Dollars', *The Atlantic* (March 2012), at www.theatlantic.com/technology/archive/2012/03/authors-of-kindle-singles-are-raking-in-tens-of-thousands-of-dollars/254368/ (accessed 20 January 2015).
11. Schiffrin, *Business of Books*, p. 3.
12. Roddy Doyle, *Two Pints*, Vintage e-book edition (London: Jonathan Cape, 2012).
13. The whole thing is available free of charge at the website http://acalendaroftales.com/, in dynamic multimedia format (accessed 20 January 2015). All quotes taken are from that website.
14. See https://twitter.com/sceptrebooks/timelines/488586138048004096.
15. See http://mashable.com/2014/11/05/sto-margaret-atwood-twitter-contest/ and https://twitter.com/horrorstory_140 (accessed 20 January 2015).
16. See on this Harry Jenkins, *Convergence Culture: Where Old and New Media Collide* (New York University Press, 2006).
17. See N. Katherine Hayles, *My Mother was a Computer: Digital Subjects and Literary Texts* (University of Chicago Press, 2005), pp. 15–38.
18. This is a distinction usefully made in David Trotter's *Literature in the First Media Age* (Cambridge, MA: Harvard, 2014). See, for example, pp. 2–14.

19. Friedrich Kittler, *Gramophone, Film, Typewriter*, trans. Geoffrey Winthrop-Young and Michael Wutz (Stanford University Press, 1999), pp. 1–2.
20. Jonathan Crary, *24/7: Late Capitalism and the Ends of Sleep* (London and New York: Verso, 2013), p. 10.
21. David Shields, *Reality Hunger: A Manifesto*, e-book edition (London: Hamish Hamilton, 2010), sec. 52 and 53, loc. 364.
22. *Ibid.*, sec. 349, loc. 1575.
23. See www.mixamo.com/unplugged (accessed 20 January 2015).
24. Michael Hardt and Antonio Negri, *Empire* (Cambridge, MA: Harvard University Press, 2000), p. 294.
25. See www.futureofthebook.org.au/2014/07/02/introducing-lost-in-track-changes/ (accessed 20 January 2015).
26. Kenneth Goldsmith, *Uncreative Writing: Managing Language in the Digital Age* (New York: Columbia University Press, 2011), back cover blurb.
27. See also Marjorie Perloff, *Unoriginal Genius: Poetry By Other Means in the New Century* (Chicago University Press, 2010).
28. See https://research.cc.gatech.edu/eilab/open-story-generation (accessed 20 January 2015).
29. https://twitter.com/Horse_ebooks (accessed 20 January 2015).
30. Sam Moss, review of Darby Larson's *Irritant*, Small Press Book Review (June 2013), at http://thesmallpressbookreview.blogspot.com.au/2013/05/review-of-darby-larsons-irritant.html (accessed 20 January 2015).
31. https://twitter.com/IrritantTheBook (accessed 20 January 2015).
32. Quoted in an interview with Blake Butler, 'If You Build the Code, Your Computer Will Write the Novel', *Vice* (11 September 2013), at www.vice.com/read/if-you-build-the-code-your-computer-will-write-the-novel.

Select Bibliography

The following suggested items of further reading do not include items already cited in the endnotes.

1. Early-Modern Diversity: The Origins of English Short Fiction

Bush, Douglas, *English Literature in the Earlier Seventeenth Century 1600–1660*, second edition (Oxford: Clarendon Press, 1962).
Clements, Robert J. and Joseph Gibaldi, *Anatomy of the Novella: The European Tale Collection from Boccaccio and Chaucer to Cervantes* (New York University Press, 1977).
Collins, Jane, 'Publishing Private Pleasures: The Gentlewoman Reader of Barnaby Riche and George Pettie', *Explorations in Renaissance Culture*, 29.2 (2003), pp. 185–210.
Munro, Ian, *'A Womans Answer is Never to Seke': Early Modern Jestbooks, 1526–1635* (Aldershot: Ashgate, 2007).
Salzman, Paul, 'Theories of Prose Fiction in England: 1558–1700', in *The Cambridge History of Literary Criticism, Volume III: The Renaissance*, ed. Glyn P. Norton (Cambridge University Press, 1999), pp. 295–304.

2. Short Prose Narratives of the Eighteenth and Nineteenth Centuries

Adburgham, Alison, *Women in Print: Writing Women and the Women's Magazines from the Restoration to the Accession of Victoria* (London: Allen & Unwin, 1972).
Lawrence, John Abbott, *John Hawkesworth: Eighteenth Century Man of Letters* (Madison: University of Wisconsin Press, 1982).
Newman, Donald J., ed., *The Spectator: Emerging Discourses* (Newark, DE: University of Delaware Press, 2005).
Newman, Donald J. and Lynn Marie Wright, eds., *Fair Philosopher: Eliza Haywood and the Female Spectator* (Lewisburg, PA: Bucknell University Press, 2006).
Shevelow, Katherine, *Women in Print Culture: The Construction of Femininity in the Early Periodical* (London: Routledge, 1989).

3. Gothic and Victorian Supernatural Tales

Freeman, Nick, 'Sensational Ghosts, Ghostly Sensations', *Women's Writing*, 20:2 (2013), pp. 186–201.
Harris, Wendell V., *British Short Fiction in the Nineteenth Century: A Literary and Bibliographic Guide* (Detroit: Wayne State University Press, 1979).
Morrison, Robert and Chris Baldick, eds., *Tales of Terror from Blackwood's Magazine* (Oxford University Press, 1995).
Polsgrave, Carol, 'They Made it Pay: British Short-Fiction Writers, 1820–1840', *Studies in Short Fiction*, 11 (1974), pp. 417–21.
Thurston, Luke, *Literary Ghosts from the Victorians to Modernism: The Haunting Interval* (Abingdon: Routledge, 2012).
Wolfreys, Julian, *Victorian Hauntings: Spectrality, Gothic, the Uncanny, and Literature* (Basingstoke: Palgrave Macmillan, 2001).

4. The Victorian Potboiler: Novelists Writing Short Stories

Bauer, Helen, *Rudyard Kipling: A Study of the Short Fiction* (New York: Twayne, 1994).
Chan, Winnie, *The Economy of the Short Story in British Periodicals of the 1890s* (London: Routledge, 2007).
Duncan, Ian, *Scott's Shadow: The Novel in Romantic Edinburgh* (Princeton University Press, 2007).
Gilmartin, Sophie and Rod Mengham, *Thomas Hardy's Shorter Fiction: A Critical Study* (Edinburgh University Press, 2007).
Mossman, Mark, 'Violence, Temptation, and Narrative in George Eliot's "Janet's Repentance"', *Journal of the Short Story in English*, 35 (2000), pp. 9–20.
Niles, Lisa, 'Trollope's Short Fiction', in *The Cambridge Companion to Anthony Trollope*, ed. Carolyn Dever and Lisa Niles (Cambridge University Press, 2010), pp. 71–84.
Orel, Harold, *The Victorian Short Story: Development and Triumph of a Literary Genre* (Cambridge University Press, 1986).

5. Fable, Myth and Folk Tale: The Writing of Oral and Traditional Story Forms

Blackham, H. J., *The Fable as Literature* (London: The Athlone Press, 1985).
Connor, Steven, 'Modernity and Myth', in *The Cambridge History of Twentieth-Century English Literature*, ed. Laura Marcus and Peter Nicholls (Cambridge University Press, 2004), pp. 251–68.
Coupe, Laurence, *Myth* (London: Routledge, 1997).
Tatar, Maria, ed., *The Cambridge Companion to Fairy Tales* (Cambridge University Press, 2015).
Thompson, Stith, *The Folktale* (New York: Holt, Rinehart and Winston, 1946).

6. The Colonial Short Story, Adventure and the Exotic

Fincham, Gail, Jeremy Hawthorne and Jakob Lothe, eds., *Outposts of Progress: Joseph Conrad, Modernism and Post-Colonialism* (University of Cape Town Press, 2013).
Hampson, Robert, *Cross-Cultural Encounters in Joseph Conrad's Malay Fiction* (London: Palgrave, 2000).
McBratney, John, *Imperial Subjects, Imperial Space: Rudyard Kipling's Fiction of the Native-Born* (Columbus: Ohio University Press, 2002).
Ricketts, Harry, *The Unforgiving Minute: A Life of Rudyard Kipling* (London: Chatto & Windus, 1999).

7. The *Yellow Book* Circle and the Culture of the Literary Magazine

Ashley, Mike, *The Age of the Storytellers: British Popular Fiction Magazines, 1880–1950* (London: British Library, 2005).
Beckson, Karl, *Henry Harland: His Life and Work* (London: Eighteen Nineties Society, 1978).
Dowling, Linda, 'Letterpress and Picture in the Literary Periodicals of the 1890s', *Yearbook of English Studies*, 16 (1986), pp. 117–31.
May, J. Lewis, *John Lane and the Nineties* (London: John Lane, 1936).

8. The Modernist Short Story: Fractured Perspectives

Drewery, Claire, *Modernist Short Fiction by Women: The Liminal in Katherine Mansfield, Dorothy Richardson, May Sinclair and Virginia Woolf* (Farnham: Ashgate, 2011).
Hanson, Clare, *Short Stories and Short Fictions 1880–1980* (New York: St Martin's Press, 1985).
Jacobs, Joshua, 'Joyce's Epiphanic Mode: Material Language and the Representation of Sexuality in *Stephen Hero* and *Portrait*', *Twentieth Century Literature*, 46 (2000), 1, pp. 20–33.
Klein, Scott W., *The Fictions of James Joyce and Wyndham Lewis: Monsters of Nature and Design* (Cambridge University Press, 1994).
Sacido, Jorge, ed., *Modernism, Postmodernism and the Short Story in English* (New York: Rodopi, 2012).

9. War Stories: The Short Story in the First and Second World Wars

Liggins, Emma, Andrew Maunder, and Ruth Robbins, 'The Short Story and the Great War', in *The British Short Story* (Basingstoke: Palgrave Macmillan, 2010), pp. 133–54.
McLoughlin, Kate, ed., *The Cambridge Companion to War Writing* (Cambridge University Press, 2009).

Piette, Adam and Mark Rawlinson, eds., *The Edinburgh Companion to Twentieth-Century British and American War Literature* (Edinburgh University Press, 2012).
Tate, Trudi, ed., *Women, Men and the Great War: An Anthology of Stories* (Manchester University Press, 1995).

10. The Short Story in Ireland to 1945: A National Literature

Averill, Deborah, *The Irish Short Story from George Moore to Frank O'Connor* (Lanham, MD: University Press of America, 1982).
Ingman, Heather, *A History of the Irish Short Story* (Cambridge University Press, 2009).
Kilroy, James, ed., *The Irish Short Story: A Critical History* (Boston: Twayne, 1984).
Trevor, William, ed., *The Oxford Book of Irish Short Stories* (Oxford University Press, 1989).
Zimmermann, Georges, *The Irish Storyteller* (Dublin: Four Courts Press, 2001).

11. The Short Story in Ireland since 1945: A Modernizing Tradition

Hogan, Robert, 'Old Boys, Young Bucks, and New Women: The Contemporary Irish Short Story', in *The Irish Short Story: A Critical History*, ed. James Kilroy (Boston: Twayne, 1984), pp. 168–215.
Journal of the Short Story in English. Special Issue: The 21st Century Irish Short Story, 63 (2014), ed. Bertrand Cardin, Presses de l'Université d'Angers.
Rafroidi, Patrick and Terence Brown, eds., *The Irish Short Story* (Gerrards Cross: Colin Smythe, 1979).
Story, Michael, *Representing the Troubles in Irish Short Fiction* (Washington: The Catholic University of America Press, 2004).

12. The Short Story in Scotland: From Oral Tale to Dialectal Style

Carruthers, Gerard and Liam McIlvanney, eds., *The Cambridge Companion to Scottish Literature* (Cambridge University Press, 2012).
Crawford, Robert, *Scotland's Books* (London: Penguin, 2007).
Gifford, Douglas and Dorothy McMillan, eds., *A History of Scottish Women's Writing* (Edinburgh University Press, 1997).
Morrison, Robert and Daniel S. Roberts, eds., *Romanticism and Blackwood's Magazine: 'An Unprecedented Phenomenon'* (Basingstoke: Palgrave Macmillan, 2013).

13. The Short Story in Wales: Cultivated Regionalism

Aaron, Jane, ed., *A View across the Valley: Short Stories by Women from Wales c.1850–1950* (Dinas Powys: Honno, 1999).
Evans, George Ewart, ed., *Welsh Short Stories* (London: Faber, 1959).
Jones, Gwyn, ed., *Welsh Short Stories*, World's Classics series (London: Oxford University Press, 1956).
Richards, Alun, ed., *New Penguin Book of Welsh Short Stories* (Harmondsworth, Middlesex: Penguin, 1993)
Smith, Dai, ed., *Story: The Library of Wales Short Story Anthology*, 2 vols. (Cardigan: Parthian, 2014).
Williams, John, ed., *Wales Half Welsh* (London: Bloomsbury, 2004).

14. The Understated Art, English Style

Baldwin, Dean, *Art and Commerce in the British Short Story, 1880–1950* (London: Pickering and Chatto, 2013).
May, Charles E., *The Short Story: The Reality of Artifice* (New York: Twayne, 1995).
Stinson, John J., *V. S. Pritchett: A Study of the Short Fiction* (New York: Twayne, 1992).
Treglown, Jeremy, *V. S. Pritchett: A Working Life* (New York: Random House, 2004).
Vannatta, Dennis, ed., *The English Short Story, 1945–1980: A Critical History* (Boston: Twayne, 1985).

15. The Rural Tradition in the English Short Story

Baldwin, Dean, *H. E. Bates: A Literary Life* (Selinsgrove, PA: Susquehanna University Press, 1987).
Flora, Joseph M., ed. *The English Short Story, 1880–1945: A Critical History* (Boston: Twayne, 1985).
Shaw, Valerie, *The Short Story: A Critical Introduction* (London: Longman, 1983).
Vannatta, Dennis, *H. E. Bates* (Boston: G. K. Hall, 1983).

16. Metropolitan Modernity: Stories of London

Ackroyd, Peter, *London: The Biography* (London: Chatto & Windus, 2000).
Groes, Sebastian, *The Making of London: London in Contemporary Literature* (Basingstoke: Palgrave Macmillan, 2011).
Manley, Lawrence ed., *The Cambridge Companion to the Literature of London* (Cambridge University Press, 2011).
McLaughlin, Joseph, *Writing the Urban Jungle: Reading Empire in London from Doyle to Eliot* (Charlottesville: University Press of Virginia, 2000).
Phillips, Lawrence, *London Narratives: Post-War Fiction and the City* (London: Continuum, 2006).

Wolfreys, Julian, *Writing London: The Trace of the Urban Text from Blake to Dickens* (Basingstoke: Macmillan, 1998).

17. Gender and Genre: Short Fiction, Feminism and Female Experience

Hanson, Clare, ed., *Re-reading the Short Story* (New York: St Martin's Press, 1989).
Gardiner, Judith Kegan, *Rhys, Stead, Lessing and the Politics of Empathy* (Bloomington and Indianapolis: Indiana University Press, 1989).
Leclerq, Florence, *Elizabeth Taylor* (Boston: Twayne Publishers, 1985).
Malcolm, Cheryl Alexander and David Malcolm, eds., *A Companion to the British and Irish Short Story* (Oxford: Wiley-Blackwell, 2008).
Patea, Viorica, ed., *Short Story Theories: A Twenty-First-Century Perspective* (Amsterdam and New York: Rodopi, 2012).
Sage, Lorna, ed., *Flesh and the Mirror: Essays on the Art of Angela Carter* (London: Virago, 1994).

18. Queer Short Stories: An Inverted History

Burton, Peter, ed., *The Mammoth Book of Gay Short Stories* (London: Robinson, 1997).
Davidson, Toni, *The Gradual Gathering of Lust* (Edinburgh: Canongate, 2007).
Livia, Anna, ed., *Incidents Involving Warmth: A Collection of Lesbian Feminist Love Stories* (London: Onlywomen, 1986).
Osman, Diriye, *Fairytales for Lost Children* (London: Team Angelica, 2013).

19. Stories of Jewish Identity: Survivors, Exiles and Cosmopolitans

Brauner, David and Axel Stähler, eds., *The Edinburgh Companion to Modern Jewish Fiction* (Edinburgh University Press, 2015).
Cheyette, Bryan, *Diasporas of the Mind: Jewish and Postcolonial Writing and the Nightmare of History* (New Haven, CT: Yale University Press, 2014).
Elswit, Sharon Barcan, ed., *The Jewish Story Finder: A Guide to 668 Tales Listing Subjects and Sources*, second edition (Jefferson, NC: McFarland, 2012).
Malcolm, Cheryl Alexander, 'The Anglo-Jewish Short Story since the Holocaust', in *A Companion to the British and Irish Short Story*, ed. Cheryl Alexander Malcolm and David Malcolm (Oxford: Wiley-Blackwell, 2008), pp. 330–41.
Wirth-Nesher, Hana, ed., *What is Jewish Literature?* (Philadelphia, PA: Jewish Publication Society, 1994).

20. New Voices: Multicultural Short Stories

Evans, Lucy, Mark McWatt and Emma Smith, eds., *The Caribbean Short Story: Critical Perspectives* (Leeds: Peepal Tree, 2011).

Gilroy, Paul, *'There Ain't No Black in the Union Jack': The Cultural Politics of Race and Nation* (London: Unwin Hyman, 1987).
Gunning, Dave, *Race and Antiracism in Black British and British Asian Literature* (Liverpool University Press, 2010).
Procter, James, *Dwelling Places: Postwar Black British Writing* (Manchester University Press, 2003).
Ramdin, Ron, *Reimaging Britain: 500 Years of Black and Asian History* (London and Sterling, VA: Pluto, 1999).

21. Settler Stories: Postcolonial Short Fiction

Baldwin, Dean and Patrick J. Quinn, eds., *An Anthology of Colonial and Postcolonial Short Fiction* (Boston: Houghton Mifflin, 2006).
Bennett, Bruce, *Australian Short Fiction: A History* (St Lucia: University of Queensland Press, 2002).
Chapman, Michael, ed., *Omnibus of a Century of South African Short Stories* (Johannesburg and Capetown: Ad Donker Publishers), 2007.
Dvorák, Marta, and W. H. New, eds., *Tropes and Territories: Short Fiction, Postcolonial Readings, Canadian Writings in Context* (Montreal: McGill-Queens University Press, 2007).
Gwynne, Joel, *The Secular Visionaries: Aestheticism and New Zealand Short Fiction in the Twentieth Century* (Amsterdam and New York: Rodopi, 2010).

22. After Empire: Postcolonial Short Fiction and the Oral Tradition

Awadalla, Maggie and Paul March-Russell, eds., *The Postcolonial Short Story: Contemporary Essays* (Basingstoke: Palgrave MacMillan, 2012).
Bardolph, Jacqueline, ed., *Short Fiction in the New Literatures in English* (Nice: Faculté des Lettres et Sciences Humaines de Nice, 1989).
  Telling Stories: Postcolonial Short Fiction in English (Amsterdam and Atlanta, GA: Rodopi, 2001).
Evans, Lucy, Mark McWatt and Emma Smith, eds., *The Caribbean Short Story: Critical Perspectives* (Leeds: Peepal Tree Press, 2011).

23. Ghost Stories and Supernatural Tales

Bown, Nicola, Carolyn Burdett and Pamela Thurschwell, eds., *The Victorian Supernatural* (Cambridge University Press, 2004).
Briggs, Julia, *Night Visitors: The Rise and Fall of the English Ghost Story* (London: Faber & Faber, 1977).
Hay, Simon, *A History of the Modern British Ghost Story* (Basingstoke: Palgrave Macmillan, 2011).

Smith, Andrew, *The Ghost Story, 1840–1920: A Cultural History* (Manchester University Press, 2010).
Sullivan, Jack, *Elegant Nightmares: The English Ghost Story from Le Fanu to Blackwood* (Athens, OH: Ohio University Press, 1978).
Warner, Marina, *Phantasmagoria, Spirit Visions, Metaphors, and Media into the Twenty-first Century* (Oxford University Press, 2008).

24. The Detective Story: Order from Chaos

Knight, Stephen, *Crime Fiction Since 1800* (London: Palgrave, 2004).
Porter, Dennis, *The Pursuit of Crime: Art and Ideology in Detective Fiction* (New Haven: Yale University Press, 1981).
Rzepka, Charles J., *Detective Fiction* (London: Polity, 2005).
Worthington, Heather, *Key Concepts in Crime Fiction* (London: Palgrave, 2011).
  The Rise of the Detective in Early Nineteenth-Century Popular Fiction (London: Palgrave, 2005).

25. Frontiers: Science Fiction and the British Marketplace

Butler, Andrew M., 'The British Science Fiction Story', in *The Cambridge Companion to the English Short Story*, ed. Ann-Marie Einhaus (Cambridge University Press, 2016).
Elkins, Charles, 'E. M. Forster's "The Machine Stops": Liberal-Humanist Hostility to Technology', in *Clockwork Worlds: Mechanized Environments in Science Fiction*, ed., Richard D. Erlich and Thomas P. Dunn (Westport, CT: Greenwood, 1983), pp. 47–61.
Hammond, J. R., *H. G. Wells and the Short Story* (Basingstoke: Macmillan, 1992).
Latham, Rob, 'The New Wave', in *A Companion to Science Fiction*, ed. David Seed (Malden MA: Blackwell Publishing, 2005), pp. 202–16.
Lewis, Mitchell R., 'Science Fiction and Fantasy after 1945: Beyond Pulp Fiction', in *A Companion to the British and Irish Short Story*, ed. Cheryl Alexander Malcolm and David Malcolm (Oxford: Wiley-Blackwell, 2008), pp. 372–83.
Mendlesohn, Farah, 'Science Fiction Stories', in *The Edinburgh Companion to the Short Story in English*, ed., Paul Delaney and Adrian Hunter (Edinburgh University Press, forthcoming).

26. Weird Stories: The Potency of Horror and Fantasy

Harman, Graham, *Weird Realism: Lovecraft and Horror* (Winchester: Zero Books, 2013).
Jones, Darryl, ed., *Horror Stories: Classic Tales from Hoffmann to Hodgson* (Oxford University Press, 2014).
Ligotti, Thomas, *The Conspiracy Against the Human Race: A Contrivance of Horror* (New York: Hippocampus Press, 2010).

Smith, Andrew, *The Ghost Story: 1840–1920* (Manchester University Press, 2010).
Woodard, Ben, *Slime Dynamics: Generation, Mutation and the Creep of Life* (Winchester: Zero Books, 2012).

27. Experimentalism: Self-Reflexive and Postmodernist Stories

Clark, Miriam Marty, 'Contemporary Short Fiction and the Postmodern Condition', *Studies in Short Fiction*, 32 (1995), pp. 147–59.
Iftekharrudin, Farhat, Joseph Boyden, Joseph Longo and Mary Rohrberger, eds., *Postmodern Approaches to the Short Story* (Westport, CT: Praeger, 2003).
Winther, Per, Jakob Lothe and Hans H. Skei eds., *The Art of Brevity: Excursions in Short Fiction Theory and Analysis* (Columbia: University of South Carolina Press, 2004).

28. Satirical Stories: Estrangement and Social Critique

Barreca, Regina, ed., *Fay Weldon's Wicked Fictions* (Hanover, NH, and London: University Press of New Hampshire, 1994).
Faulkner, Peter, *Angus Wilson: Mimic and Moralist* (London: Secker and Warburg, 1980).
Finney, Brian, *Martin Amis* (London: Routledge, 2008).
Hays, Hunter M., *Understanding Will Self* (Columbia, SC: University of South Carolina Press, 2007).
Peach, Linden, *Angela Carter*, second edition (Basingstoke: Macmillan, 2009).

29. Comedic Short Fiction

Gibson, Brian, *Reading Saki: The Fiction of H. H. Munro* (Jefferson, NC: McFarlane and Company, 2014).
Lodge, David, *Malcolm Bradbury* (London: Book Trust, 1988).
McDonnel, Jacqueline, *Evelyn Waugh* (Basingstoke: Macmillan, 1988).

30. Short Story Cycles: Between the Novel and the Story Collection

Lunden, Rolf, *The United Stories of America: Studies in the Short Story Composite* (Amsterdam and Atlanta: Rodopi, 1999).
May, Charles E., ed., *The New Short Story Theories* (Athens: Ohio University Press, 1994).
(The principal studies of the short story cycle are cited in the endnotes for this chapter.)

31. The Novella: Between the Novel and the Story

Clements, Robert J. and Joseph Gibaldi, *Anatomy of the Novella: The European Tale Collection from Boccaccio and Chaucer to Cervantes* (New York: New York University Press, 1977).

Mudford, Peter, *Memory and Desire: Representations of Passion in the Novella* (London: Duckworth, 1996).

Vezhlian, Evgeniia, 'A Portrait of a Genre Against the Backdrop of a Prize: The Contemporary Novella and Tales of the Belkin Prize', *Russian Studies in Literature*, 49:2, (Spring 2013), pp. 59–70.

32. The Short Story Visualized: Adaptations and Screenplays

Bellour, Raymond, *The Analysis of Film* (Bloomington, IN: Indiana University Press, 2000).

Paglia, Camille, *The Birds* (London: British Film Institute, 1998).

Samuels, Robert, *Hitchcock's Bi-Textuality: Lacan, Feminisms, and Queer Theory* (Albany: SUNY Press, 1997).

Žižek, Slavoj, *Looking Awry: An Introduction to Jacques Lacan Through Popular Culture* (Cambridge, MA: MIT Press, 1991).

33. The Short Story Anthology: Shaping the Canon

Enright, Anne, ed., *The Granta Book of the Irish Short Story* (London: Granta, 2010).

Prescott, Lynda, ed., *A World of Difference: An Anthology of Short Stories from Five Continents* (Basingstoke: Palgrave Macmillan, 2008).

Short Stories Volume 1: English and Irish Authors Read Their Own Work (audio CD) (London: The British Library, 2011).

Yentob, Alan, ed., *BBC National Short Story Award 2014* (Manchester: Comma Press, 2014).

34. The Institution of Creative Writing

Galloway, Janice, *Collected Stories* (London: Vintage, 2009).

O'Rourke, Rebecca, *Creative Writing: Education, Culture and Community* (Leicester: National Institute of Adult Continuing Education (NIACE), 2005).

Rogers, Jane, *Hitting Trees with Sticks* (Manchester: Comma, 2012).

Royle, Nicholas, *Mortality* (London: Serpents Tail, 2006).

Tremain, Rose, *The American Lover* (London: Chatto & Windus, 2014).

Woodward, Gerard, *Caravan Thieves* (London: Vintage, 2009).

Index

Authors' short stories are listed before their story collections and longer works.

Aaron, Jane, *A View Across the Valley, Short Stories by Women from Wales, c.1850–1950*, 574
Abbott, Edward, *Flatland*, 431
Abel-Watters, G., *People Your Mother Warned You About*, 306
Academy, 418
Achebe, Chinua, 107, 378, 380, 381, 568
   'Akueke', 379
   'Girls at War', 379
   'The Madman', 379
   'Vengeful Creditor', 379
   Arrow of God, 379
   Girls at War, 379
   Things Fall Apart, 379
Ackroyd, Peter, 318
Addison, Joseph, 37, 44
   The Spectator, 38
Adichie, Chimamanda Ngozi
   'Arranged Marriage', 381
   'The Headstrong Historian', 381
   'Imitation', 381
   'Jumping Monkey Hill', 381
   The Thing Around Your Neck, 381
Adnan, Etel, 288
Aesop, 389
Aesop's Fables, 84
African Literature Today, 378
Aguilar, Grace, 324
   'The Fugitive', 332
   Home Scenes and Heart Studies, 332
   The Vale of Cedars, 332
Ahmed, Sara, *The Promise of Happiness*, 317
   Aickman, Robert, 404, 458–60
   'The Fetch', 460
   'The Hospice', 459
   'Never Visit Venice', 460

   'The Swords', 459
   'The Trains', 405, 459
   'The Unsettled Dust', 459
   'The View', 460
   'The Wine-Dark Sea', 460
   The Attempted Rescue, 459
Aidoo, Ama Ata, 380
   'For Whom Things Did Not Change', 380
   Diplomatic Pounds, 380
   The Girl Who Can, 380
   No Sweetness Here, 380
Ainsworth, Harrison, 564
Albemarle, 124, 129
Alderman, Naomi, 338
   Alice in Storyland, 602
Aldington, Richard, 161
   'The Case of Lieutenant Hall', 158, 159
   'Nobody's Baby', 482
   Roads to Glory, 158
   Soft Answers, 482
Aldiss, Brian, 432, 433, 435, 437, 438
   'Psyclops', 437
   Barefoot in the Head, 437
   The Canopy of Time, 438
   Penguin Science Fiction, 437
   SF Horizons, 437
   Space, Time and Nathaniel, 437
Aldrich, Ann, 311
Aldrich, Thomas Bailey, 'Marjorie Daw', 309
Alexander, William, *Sketches of Life Among My Ain Folk*, 207
All the Year Round, 62
Allan, Nina, 441, 443
Allen, Grant, 80, 414
   Strange Stories, 451
   The Woman Who Did, 127

Index

Allen, Walter, 202
  The Short Story in English, 502
Allingham, Margery, 421, 422
Almond, David, 576
Amazing Stories, 434
Ambit, 439
Ambler, Eric, 423, 561
Amis, Kingsley, 248, 505–8, 509, 511, 572
  'Dear Illusion', 506
  'The Huge Artifice, an interim assessment', 507
  'Mason's Life', 508, 510
  'To See The Sun', 507
  'Who or What Was It?', 506, 507
  New Maps of Hell, 429
  Spectrum, 437
  Stanley and the Women, 506
  The Egyptologists, 506
Amis, Martin, 487, 495, 578
  'Career Move', 484
  'State of England', 494
  'The Time Disease', 486
  'Thinkability', 485
  Einstein's Monsters, 485
  Heavy Water and Other Stories, 494
  Money, 522
  Time's Arrow, 522
Amy, George, *The Letter*, 558
Anand, Mulk Raj, 389
  'Lajwanti', 389
  'Old Bapu', 389
  'The Thief', 389
  Selected Short Stories, 389
And Thus Will I Freely Sing, 317
Andersen, Hans Christian, 85
Anderson, Benedict, 598
Anderson, Jessica, 366, 369
Anderson, Margaret, 131
Anderson, Patrick, *Eros, An Anthology of Male Friendship*, 312
Anderson, Sherwood, *Winesburg, Ohio*, 515, 516, 519
Anthony, Michael, 384
Arabian Nights, 85, 515
Armstrong, Jeanette, 'This Is a Story', 393
Armstrong, Tim, 429
Ascham, Roger, *The Scholemaster*, 24
Asher, Neal, 441
Ashley, Mike, 435, 437
Ashworth, A. J., *Red Room, New Short Stories Inspired by the Brontës*, 577
Astley, Thea, *Hunting the Wild Pineapple*, 516, 517, 520, 521

Astounding, 435
Astounding Science Fiction, 434
Atkinson, Kate, *Not the End of the World*, 513, 519
Atlantic, 503, 603
Atwood, Margaret, 10, 286, 287, 288, 295, 297, 298, 299–301, 369, 589
  'Entities', 301
  'Giving Birth', 300
  'The Grave of the Famous Poet', 301
  'Happy Endings', 300
  'My Last Duchess', 301
  'Simple Murder', 300
  'There Was Once', 300
  'Under Glass', 300
  'Women's Novels', 300
  Bluebeard's Egg, 299
  Curious Pursuits: Occasional Writing 1970–2005, 300
  Dancing Girls, 299, 300
  Good Bones and Simple Murders, 300
  Moral Disorder, 300, 301, 517
  Murder in the Dark, 299
  The Stone Mattress, 369
  Wilderness Tips, 300
Auden, W. H., 'The Guilty Vicarage', 420
Auden, W. H., 411, 492
Auerbach, Nina, 461
Aumonier, Stacy, 161, 236, 238, 561
  'The Friends', 238
  'Overheard', 238
  'Where Was Wych Street', 238
Austen, Jane, 253, 293
Austin, Frederick Britten, 161
Authentic, 435
Awdeley, John
  Fraternity of Vagabonds, 21

Bach, Johann Sebastian, *Goldberg Variations*, 335
Bacon, Francis, *Essays*, 28
Bail, Murray, 365
Bailey, H. C., 420
Bailey, Paul, 318
Bakhtin, Mikhail, 527
Ball, John Clement, 279
Ballantyne, Tony, 441
Ballard, J. G., 280, 432, 435, 437, 438, 439, 441, 470, 486, 509
  'Billennium', 280
  'The Concentration City', 280
  'Dream Cargoes', 580
  'The Terminal Beach', 438

626

Index

'Why I Want to Fuck Ronald Reagan', 508
The Atrocity Exhibition, 439, 508
Balzac, Honoré de, *Lost Illusions*, 599
Bandello, Matteo, 22
Banim, John, 169, 172
Banim, John and Michael, *Tales of the O'Hara Family*, 169
Banks, Iain M., 'A Gift from the Culture', 440
Banville, John, *Long Lankin*, 193
Barbusse, Henri, 161
Bardwell, Leland, *Different Kinds of Love*, 194
Barnes, Djuna
  'Cassation', 312
  'A Little Girl Tells a Story to a Lady', 312
Barnes, Julian, 236, 249–50, 578
  'Appetite', 249
  'Evermore', 249
  'Harmony', 250
  'The Limner', 250
  'The Things You Know', 249
  'Tunnel', 249
  Cross Channel, 249
  Flaubert's Parrot, 249
  The History of the World in 10½ Chapters, 514
  The Lemon Table, 249
  Pulse, 249
Baron, Alexander, 'The Anniversary', 249, 332
Barr, Fiona, 'The Wall-Reader', 196
Barr, Robert, 125
Barrett, Colin, *Young Skins*, 199
Barrie, J. M., 104
  Auld Licht Idylls, 205
  Farewell Miss Julie Logan, 205
  A Window in Thrums, 205
Barry, Kevin
  Dark Lies the Island, 199
  There Are Little Kingdoms, 199
Barth, John, 12, 96, 465
  Chimera, 391
Barthelme, Donald, 12, 465
Bartlett, Neil, 318
Bates, H. E., 9, 152, 160, 236, 237, 239–42, 258, 259, 260–4, 266, 530, 531, 541, 562
  'Alexander', 239, 240, 261
  'The Baker's Wife', 239
  'The Black Boxer', 240
  'Breeze Anstey', 241, 312
  'The Captain', 241
  'The Common Denominator', 242
  'Country Society', 242
  'The Cowslip Field', 261
  'Cut and Come Again', 240
  'The Daffodil Sky', 263
  'The Evolution of Saxby', 242
  'The Fuel-Gatherers', 239
  'The Gleaner', 261
  'The Good Corn', 262
  'The Grass God', 262
  'Harvest', 260
  'The Hessian Prisoner', 240
  'How Sleep the Brave', 241
  'The Idiot', 239
  'The Irishman', 240
  'The Kimono', 241
  'Mr Livingstone', 241
  'The Mill', 240, 262
  'The Mower', 261
  'Now Sleeps the Crimson Petal', 263
  'The Pink Cart', 240
  'Queenie White', 262
  'The Shepherd', 239
  'There's Something in the Air', 160
  'The Triple Echo', 532
  'The Wedding', 262
  'The White Pony', 261
  'The Young Man from Kalgoorie', 241
  An Aspidistra in Babylon, 541
  The Black Boxer, 261
  The Cruise of the Breadwinner, 241, 541
  Cut and Come Again, 240
  The Daffodil Sky, 242
  Day's End and Other Stories, 239, 260
  Death of a Huntsman, 541
  Fair Stood the Wind for France, 241
  The Four Beauties, 541
  The Golden Oriole, 541
  The Greatest People in the World, 241
  How Sleep the Brave, 241
  The Modern Short Story, 91, 157, 237, 465
  My Uncle Silas, 241, 262
  The Nature of Love, 541
  Seven Tales and Alexander, 239, 261
  Something Short and Sweet, 241
  Sugar for the Horse, 262
  The Triple Echo, 541
  The Woman Who Had Imagination, 240
Bauman, Zygmunt, 327
Baxter, Stephen, 440
Bayer, Gerd, 17
Bayley, Barrington J., 435
Bayley, John, *The Short Story*, 456
Baynton, Barbara, 'Squeaker's Mate', 365–6
Beachcroft, T. O., 29
Beacon, 383

Index

Beardsley, Aubrey, 118, 126, 128, 130
   Under the Hill, 129
Beckett, Chris, *The Turing Test*, 441
Beckett, Mary, 185
   A Belfast Woman, 196
Beckett, Samuel, 12, 183, 466–8, 506, 578
   'Dante and the Lobster', 182
   'Ping', 578
   From an Abandoned Work, 466
   More Pricks than Kicks, 182
   Texts for Nothing, 466–8
Beerbohm, Max, 494, 509
   'Enoch Soames', 502
   Christmas Garland, 482
Behn, Aphra, 4, 26–8, 33
   'Adventure of the Black Lady, The', 28
   'The History of the Nun, or, The Fair Vow Breaker', 27
   'The Unfortunate Happy Lady, A True History', 28
   The Fair Jilt, 27
   Love-Letters Between a Noble-Man and his Sister, 27
   Oroonoko, 27, 532
Belgravia, 566
Bell, Julia, *England Calling, 24 Stories for the 21st Century*, 576
Bell, Michael, 96
Bell, Sam Hanna, 185
   Summer Loanen and Other Stories, 189
Bellerby, Frances, 287
Belloc, Hillaire, 482
Bellour, Raymond, 553
Benjamin, Walter, 271, 589
   'The Storyteller', 72
Bennett, Andrew, 278
Bennett, Arnold, 119, 138, 414, 482, 598
   'A Letter Home', 130
Benson, A. C., 482
Benson, E. F., 236, 238
   'A Breath of Scandal', 238
   'The Puce Silk', 238
Benson, Stephen, 96
Bensusan, S. L., 324
   'Death', 326
Bentley, Phyllis, 'Miss Phipps and the Invisible Murderer', 423
Bergonzi, Bernard, *Exploding English*, 583
Berman, Hannah, 325
   'The Horse Thief', 326
Bernières, Louis de, 266–7
   'The Girt Pike', 267

'Obadiah Oak, Mrs Griffiths and the Carol Singers', 266
   Notwithstanding, 266
Berry, Ron, 230
   'Natives', 231
Best American Short Stories, 577
Best British Short Stories, 577
Beta-Life, 442
Bhabha, Homi, 348
Bim, 383
Binchy, Maeve, *Dublin 4*, 194
Bio-Punk, 442
Birdsell, Sandra, 369, 373
   Agassiz Stories, 370
Birmingham Post, 576
Birmingham, George A., *Irish Short Stories*, 574
Bishop, Steve, 575
Black and White, 80, 120
Black Orpheus, 378
Blackwood, Algernon, 406, 407, 449, 450
   'Ancient Sorceries', 406
   'The Kit-Bag', 399
   'Willows', 406
Blackwood's Edinburgh Magazine, 5, 47, 51, 53, 56, 74, 120, 202, 430, 566
BLAST, 131, 488
Bleiler, E. F., 449
Blind, Mathilde, 324
   'Leopold Sontheim's Confession', 326
Bloom, Harold, 423
Bloxam, John Francis, 'The Priest and the Acolyte', 309
Blue Review, 131
Blum, David, 603
Blyth, Harry, 414
Blythe, Ronald, 264–6
   'The Right Day to Kill a Pike', 265
   'The Shadows of the Living', 265
   'The Windfall', 264
   Akenfield, Portrait of an English Village, 264
   The Components of the Scene: An Anthology of the Prose and Poetry of the Second World War, 163
   The Stories of Ronald Blythe, 264
Boccaccio, Giovanni, 4, 13, 22, 360
   The Decameron, 17, 85, 515, 520, 532
Bodley Head, 129, 131
Bond, William, 39
Bonfiglioli, Kyril, 437, 438
Booth, Charles, *Life and Labour of the People in London*, 275
Borden, Mary, *The Forbidden Zone*, 154

Index

Borderline, 317
Borges, Jorge Luis, 449, 527, 600
Boston Herald, 455
Boston, Anne, 164
   Wave Me Goodbye, Stories of the Second World War, 163
Bowen, Elizabeth, 182-3, 272, 278-9, 287, 464, 465, 469, 578, 594
   'The Apple Tree', 312
   'The Back Drawing-Room', 182
   'Careless Talk', 156
   'Charity', 312
   'The Demon Lover', 154, 279, 312, 400
   'The Disinherited', 571
   'The Happy Autumn Fields', 183
   'Her Table Spread', 182, 575
   'In the Square', 278
   'The Jungle', 312
   'A Love Story, 1939', 183
   'Maria', 569
   'Mysterious Kôr', 163, 279
   'The Short Story in England', 278
   'Summer Night', 183, 575
   'Sunday Afternoon', 183
   'Unwelcome Idea', 183
   The Demon Lover and Other Stories, 153, 296
   Faber Book of Modern Stories, 132, 570
   The Heat of the Day, 162
   Joining Charles, 312
   Look At All Those Roses, 183, 296
Bowles, Paul, 207
Boyce, Benjamin, 32
Boyce, Frank Cottrell, 442
Boylan, Clare
   A Nail on the Head, 194
   Concerning Virgins, 194
Boyle, Patrick, *The Port Wine Stain*, 194
Bradbury, Malcolm, 276, 494, 578, 581
   'An Extravagant Fondness for the Love of Women', 494
   'Composition', 494
   'Nobody Here in England', 494
   'Who Do You Think You Are?', 484
   The Penguin Book of Modern British Short Stories, 439, 565, 578, 585
   Who Do You Think You Are?, 494, 509
Braddon, Mary Elizabeth, 59, 61, 68
   'Cold Embrace, The', 58
   'The Dreaded Guest', 77
   'Eveline's Visitant', 60, 567
   'Good Lady Ducayne', 52
   'The Mystery at Fernwood', 60
   Ralph the Bailiff and Other Tales, 58, 60

Bradford, Edwin Emanuel, 'Boris Orloff', 309
Brady, Kristin, 253
Braine, John, 494, 509
Brake, Laurel, 127
Bramah, Ernest, 418
Brand, Dionne, *Sans Souci*, 388
Bray, Alan, 305
Bray, Carys, 591
   'Scaling Never', 595
   A Song for Issy Bradley, 595
   Sweet Home, 595
Brennan, Maeve, 9, 188, 190
Brett, Jeremy, 551
Bridge, Ann, 561
Briggs, Julia, 396
Brissett, Yvonne, *Whispers in the Walls*, 576
Brito, Leonora
   'Digging for Victory', 231
   'Moonbeam Kisses', 231
   dat's love, 231
Brontë, Charlotte, 'Napoleon and the Spectre', 49
Brooke-Rose, Christine, 468, 470
Brookes, Les, 314
Broughton, Rhoda, 59
   'Behold, it was a Dream', 62
   'Poor Pretty Bobby', 62
   'The Truth, the Whole Truth, and Nothing but the Truth', 58, 399
Brown, Eric, 441
Brown, George Mackay, 211, 573
   'Andrina', 211
   'The Eye of the Hurricane', 212
   'Five Green Waves', 211
   A Calendar of Love, 211
   Time in a Red Coat, 214
Brown, Stewart, *Oxford Book of Caribbean Short Stories*, 384
Browning, Elizabeth Barrett, 72
   'The Dead Pan', 452
Browning, Robert, 72
   'My Last Duchess', 298
   The Ring and the Book, 516
Bruce, Nigel, 550
Buchan, John, 119
   'Fountainblue', 207
   'Skule Skerry', 207
   Grey Weather, 207
   The Runagates Club, 207
   The Thirty-Nine Steps, 601
   The Watcher by the Threshold, 207
Bulletin, 364
Bulmer, Kenneth, 435

Bulwer-Lytton, Edward, 430
  The Coming Race, 430
Bunyan, John, *The Pilgrim's Progress*, 84
Burchill, Julie, 575, 576
Burford, Barbara, 317
Burgess, Moira
  Streets of Gold, 575
  Streets of Stone, 575
Burke, Sean, 'The Trials of Mahmood Mattan', 231
Burke, Thomas, 561
  'The Pash', 312
  Limehouse Nights, 275
Burns, Alan, 468
Burns, Robert, 'Tam O'Shanter', 55
Burnside, John, 216
Burr, James
  'Life's What You Make It', 510
  Ugly Stories for Beautiful People, 509
Burton's Gentleman's Magazine, 270
Butler, Judith, *Bodies That Matter*, 145
Butler, Neil, *The Roost*, 214
Butler, Samuel, 430
  Erewhon, 430
Butterworth, Michael, 439
Butts, Mary, 162
  'Speed the Plough', 257
Byatt, A. S., 10, 11, 286, 288, 297, 298–9
  'The Chinese Lobster', 299
  'The Dried Witch', 299
  'The July Ghost', 407, 408
  'Medusa's Ankles', 299
  'Morpho Eugenia', 560
  'Raw Material', 592
  'A Stone Woman', 299
  The Djinn in the Nightingale's Eye, Five Fairy Stories, 299
  Little Black Book of Stories, 299, 592
  The Matisse Stories, 299, 520
  The Oxford Book of English Short Stories, 578
  Sugar and Other Stories, 299
Byron, George Gordon (Lord), 287
  'Augustus Darvell', 50, 51

Cady, Joseph, 306, 307
Calder, Jenni, 573
Calder-Marshall, Arthur, 'After the War', 154
Callender, Timothy, 386
  'The Boyfriends', 386
  'A Deal with the Devil', 386
  'Peace and Love', 386
  It So Happen, 386
Calvino, Italo, 96, 518

Campbell, Angus Peter, 216
  Invisible Islands, 216
Campbell, John W., *Astounding Science Fiction*, 434
Campbell, Joseph, 84
Canetti, Elias
  'The Sacrifice of the Prisoner', 330
  Auto-da-Fé, 330
Cannan, Gilbert, 7, 88
  Windmills: A Book of Fables, 88
Canning, Richard, 315
Cardinal, Agnés, *Women's Writing on the First World War*, 162
Carey, Peter, 359, 369, 373
  'American Dreams', 366
  The Fat Man in History, 366
Carleton, William, 8, 169–70, 175
  Traits and Stories of the Irish Peasantry, 169
Carnell, John, 434, 435, 436, 437, 438
  New Worlds, 435
  New Writings, 439
Carpenter, Edward, *Ioläus, An Anthology of Friendship*, 312
Carr, Emily, *Klee Wyck*, 367
Carr, John Dickson, 423
Carrington, Charles, 102
Carrington, Leonora, 470–2
  'A Mexican Fairy Tale', 471
  'My Flannel Knickers', 579
  'The Seventh Horse', 470
Carroll, Lewis, 431
  Alice's Adventures in Wonderland, 601
Carter, Angela, 13, 287, 296, 297–8, 440, 486, 487, 518, 585, 591
  'The Bloody Chamber', 487
  'The Company of Wolves', 298, 487
  'Elegy for a Freelance', 280
  'The Erl King', 487
  'The Loves of Lady Purple', 567
  'The Tiger's Bride', 487
  'The Werewolf', 298
  Black Venus, 472, 520
  The Bloody Chamber, 96, 298, 472, 487, 520
  Fireworks, 472
  Nothing Sacred, 298
  The Sadeian Woman, 487
  The Virago Book of Fairy Tales, 297
  Wayward Girls and Wicked Women, 567
Carver, Raymond, 585, 609
Cary, Joyce, 572
Cassell's, 119
Castell, Daphne, 438
Casket, The, 270

Index

Castle, Terry, 143, 305
Cavaliero, Glen, 458
Cave, Edward, *Gentleman's Magazine*, 43
Caxton, William, 16
Century Guild Hobby Horse, 119
Cervantes, Miguel de, *Novelas ejemplares*, 22
Chalkdust, The Mighty, 385
Chandler, Blanche Wills, 'Zepp-Proof', 155
Chandler, Raymond, 422, 424
   'The Simple Art of Murder', 420
Chandra, Vikram
   Love and Longing in Bombay, 391
   Red Earth and Pouring Rain, 391
Charles, Gerda, 323
   Modern Jewish Stories, 324, 328, 333
Chase, James Hadley, 422
Chaucer, Geoffrey, 4, 13, 360
   The Canterbury Tales, 16, 17, 85, 392, 515, 532
   'The Miller's Tale', 17
Chekhov, Anton, 9, 172, 174, 175, 179, 185, 191, 235, 239, 247, 360, 456, 598
Chen, Willi, *King of the Carnival*, 385
Cheney, Donald, 20
Chesney, George, 430
   The Battle of Dorking, 430
Chesterton, G. K., 416, 423, 425, 482, 501, 509, 551, 556
   'The Awful Reason For The Vicar's Visit', 501
   'The Blue Cross', 416
   'The Invisible Man', 416
   'The Man in the Passage', 416
   The Club of Queer Trades, 501
Cheyette, Bryan, 330, 338
   Contemporary Jewish Writing in Britain and Ireland, 324, 331
Christie, Agatha, 419–20, 422, 424, 425, 551
   'Tape Measure Murder', 411, 420
   'Three Blind Mice', 420
   'A Witness for the Prosecution', 420
   Autobiography, 420
   The Labours of Hercules, 420
   The Mousetrap, 420
   Murder in the Mews, 419
   The Mysterious Affair at Styles, 419
   Poirot Investigates, 419
   The Thirteen Problems, 419
Christopher, John, 434, 435
   'Christmas Roses', 436
   'Monster', 436
   'The Tree', 436
Cinthio (Giovanni Battista Giraldi), 22
Civil and Military Gazette, 455

Cixous, Hélène, 362
Clarke, Arthur C., 433, 434, 435
   'The Nine Billion Names of God', 436
   'The Sentinel', 556
   'The Star', 436
   2001, A Space Odyssey, 556
   Tales from the White Hart, 435
Clarke, Austin, 384
Clements, Toby, 544
Cliff, Michelle
   Bodies of Water, 388
   The Store of a Million Items, 388
Clifford, Hugh, 105, 106
   'The Amok of Dato Kaya Biji Dera', 106
   'The East Coast', 106
   'The Experience of Raja Haji Hamid', 106
   'The People of the East Coast', 106
   'The Were-Tiger', 106
   East Coast Etchings, 106
   In Court and Kampong, 106
Clute, John, 440
Cocks, H. G., 305
Colburn, Krystyna, 143
Coleridge, Samuel Taylor, 54, 306
Collier, John, 561
Collier's Weekly, 156
Collins, Charles, 70
Collins, Merle, *Rain Darling*, 388
Collins, Wilkie, 57, 59, 69, 77, 273–4, 414
   'The Biter Bit', 274
   'Brother Owen's Story of Anne Rodway', 77–8
   'The Dead Hand', 60
   'The Dead Secret', 77
   'The Diary of Anne Rodway', 273, 413
   'The Dream Woman', 61
   'A Marriage Tragedy', 78
   'The Monktons of Wincot Abbey', 60–1
   'A Terribly Strange Bed', 53
   'Who Killed Zebedee?', 274
   No Name, 60
   The Frozen Deep and Other Stories, 61
   The Moonstone, 77, 273, 425
   The Woman in White, 60
Collymore, Frank, 384
   The Man Who Loved Attending Funerals, 386
Colyer, Mary, 44
Compton-Burnett, Ivy, 312
Congreve, William
   Incognita, 26, 532
Conlon, Evelyn, *My Head is Opening*, 194
Connolly, Cyril, 310

Conquest, Robert, 506
  Spectrum, 437
  The Egyptologists, 506
Conrad, Joseph, 81, 107–8, 110, 482, 530, 533–5
  'The End of the Tether', 108, 533, 534, 536
  'Heart of Darkness', 107, 531, 533–4
  'The Idiots', 130
  'Karain', 105, 107
  'The Lagoon', 105, 107
  'An Outpost of Progress', 107, 109, 533
  'The Tale', 161
  'Typhoon', 108, 533
  'Youth', 108, 533, 535
  Almayer's Folly, 105, 111
  The Nigger of the 'Narcissus', 108, 130
  An Outcast of the Islands, 111
  Victory, 111
  Youth: A Narrative and Two Other Stories, 534
Constantine, Storm, 441
cony-catching pamphlets, 21–2
Coover, Robert, 96
Coppard, A. E., 7, 91–2, 236, 237, 258–60, 562, 571
  'The Bogey Man', 92
  'Dusky Ruth', 258, 579
  'A Field of Mustard', 579
  'The Higgler', 259
  'The King of the World', 91
  'The Princess of Kingdom Gone', 91
  'Some Talk of Alexander', 579
  'Speaking Likenesses', 92
  'The Watercress Girl', 260
  Adam and Eve and Pinch Me, 91, 258
  The Field of Mustard, 92, 260
  Fishmonger's Fiddle, 259
  Ninepenny Flute, 92
Corelli, Marie, 124
Corkery, Daniel, 178–9, 180
  'The Awakening', 179
  'Carrig-an-Afrinn', 178
  'The Emptied Sack', 178
  'Nightfall', 179
  The Stormy Hills, 178
Cornell, Paul, 442
Cornhill Magazine, 119, 270, 498
Cortázar, Julio, 465, 478
Cory, Annie Sophie, 127
  The Woman Who Didn't, 127
Cosmopolis, 124
Costello, Mary, *The China Factory*, 200
Country Matters, 562

Coward, Noel, 313
  'Me and the Girls', 313
  'Star Quality', 313
Cowasjee, Saros, 389
Cox, Andy
  Black Static, 441
  The Third Alternative, 441
Crackanthorpe, Hubert, 124, 129
  'The Haseltons', 128
  Wreckage, 124
Craig, Cairns, 219
Craig, David, 581
Crazy Jig, The, 317
Cripps, Arthur Shearly, 'The Black Death', 372
Crispin, Edmund, 423
  Best SF, 436
Critical Quarterly, 506
Crockett, S. R., *The Stickit Minister*, 205
Croft-Cook, Rupert, 561
Crofts, Freeman Willis, 420
Croker, Thomas Crofton, 172
  Fairy Tales and Legends of the South of Ireland, 168
Crompton, Richmal, *Just William*, 505
Cross, Eric, *The Tailor and Ansty*, 178, 519
Crowe, Catherine, 'A Story of a Weir-Wolf', 52
Crowther, Peter, 441
Csicsery-Ronay, Istvan, 433
Cuddon, J. A., 532
Cunningham, Allan, *Traditional Tales of the English and Scottish Peasantry*, 203
Cunninghame Graham, R. B., 207
Cusk, Rachel
  Arlington Park, 514, 519, 525, 591
  The Bradshaw Variations, 514
  The Lucky Ones, 514, 519, 591
  Outline, 516, 591

D'Arcy, Ella, 80, 130
  'Irremediable', 128
  Monochromes, 129
Dahl, Roald, 561
  'A Piece of Cake', 163
  Tales of the Unexpected, 561
Daily Chronicle, 498
Dalby, Richard, 449
Daly, Ita, *The Lady with the Red Shoes*, 194
Dante, Alighieri, 182
Darwin, Charles, 533
David Constantine, 'Ashton and Elaine', 577
Davidson, Toni, *And Thus Will I Freely Sing*, 305

Index

Davie, Elspeth, 209, 236, 573
  'The Colour', 210
  'The Concerto', 210
  'The Snow Heart', 210
  The High Tide Talker, 210
Davies, David Stuart, *Crime Scenes*, 425
Davies, E. Tegla, 574
Davies, Lewis, *Urban Welsh*, 219
Davies, Peter Ho, 342, 576
Davies, Rhys, 223, 224–5, 236, 237, 574
  'Period Piece', 225
  'The Pits are on the Top', 224
Davin, Dan, 152, 165
  Short Stories from the Second World War, 160, 163
Davis, Bette, 558
Davis, Leith, 55
Dawson, Carrie, 361
Dawson, Paul, 583
Day, Graham, 223
de la Mare, Walter, 92–3, 457
  'Dick and the Beanstalk', 92
  'The Thief', 92
  'The Three Sleeping Boys of Warwickshire', 92
  Broomsticks, 92
  The Lord Fish, 93
De Quincy, Thomas, 202
Deandrea, Pietro, 353
Defoe, Daniel, 28, 269
  'A True Relation of the Apparition of One Mrs Veal', 34
  Robinson Crusoe, 26, 88
Deighton, Len, 556
Deloney, Thomas, 19–20
  The Gentle Craft, 20
  Jack of Newberie, 20
  Thomas of Reading, 20
Denisoff, Dennis, *The Broadview Anthology of Victorian Short Stories*, 566, 567
Desai, Anita
  'The Man Who Saw himself Drown', 391
  'Surface Texture', 391
  Diamond Dust, 391
  Games at Twilight, 391
Devlin, Anne
  'Naming the Names', 196
  The Way-Paver, 196
Dexter, Colin, 423
Dhlomo, R. R. R., 382
Díaz, José María, 136
Dick, Philip K., 433

Dickens, Charles, 6, 56–7, 68, 69, 77, 271–2, 496, 528, 579
  'Arcadian London', 272
  'Barbox Brothers and Co.', 70
  'The Boarding House', 272
  'The Clock-Case', 56
  'The Drunkard's Death', 271
  'The Magic Fishbone', 90
  'Meditations in Monmouth Street', 271
  'Night Walks', 272
  'Our Next-door Neighbour', 271
  'Passage in the Life of Mr Watkins Tottle', 272
  'Shabby-genteel People', 272
  'Shops and Their Tenants', 272
  'The Signal-Man', 6, 57, 69, 406–7, 565
  'Thoughts about People', 272
  'To Be Read at Dusk', 54
  A Christmas Carol, 406
  All the Year Round, 57, 271, 566
  Bentley's Miscellany, 56
  Hard Times, 601
  Household Words, 57, 60, 69, 271, 412, 566
  Mugby Junction, 70–1
  The Old Curiosity Shop, 76
  Our Mutual Friend, 76
  The Pickwick Papers, 515
  Selected Short Fiction, 565
  Sketches by Boz, 271, 515
  Sketches of Young Couples, 483
  Sketches of Young Gentlemen, 483
  The Uncommercial Traveller, 272
Dilworth, Thomas, 140
Disch, Thomas M., 439
Diski, Jenny, *The Vanishing Princess*, 337
Disraeli, Benjamin, 324
  'Ixion in Heaven', 326
Diva Book of Short Stories, 317
Dixon, Ella Hepworth
  'The World's Slow Stain', 482
  One Doubtful Hour, 482
Doctor Who, 561
Dolley, Christopher
  Penguin Book of English Short Stories, 571
  Second Penguin Book of English Short Stories, 571
Dome, The, 135
Donoghue, Emma, 199, 308
  'Night Vision', 198
  'Words for Things', 198, 316
  Kissing the Witch, 197
  The Woman Who Gave Birth to Rabbits, 197

Donovan, Anne, 591
Doolittle, Hilda, 162
Dorcey, Mary, 317
   A Noise from the Woodshed, 194
Dostoevsky, Fyodor, 124, 601
   Poor Folk, 127
Douglas, Lord Alfred, 417
Dowling, Finuala, 486
Dowson, Ernest, 129
Doyle, Arthur Conan, 120, 124, 127, 274–5, 411, 482, 502, 548–51
   'The Adventures of the Norwood Builder', 415
   'A Case of Identity', 274
   'A Scandal in Bohemia', 413
   'The Final Problem', 414
   'His Last Bow', 156
   'The Horror of the Heights', 207
   'The Jew's Breastplate', 417
   'The Man with the Twisted Lip', 275
   'The Prisoner's Defence', 156
   'The Resident Patient', 274, 415
   The Adventures of Gerard, 206
   The Exploits of Brigadier Gerard, 206
   A Study in Scarlet, 413
Doyle, Roddy
   Two More Pints, 603
   Two Pints, 603
Drum, 370, 378
Dryden, John, 506
Drysdale, Russell, 365
du Maurier, Daphne, 461, 552–5
   'The Birds', 552
   'Don't Look Now', 461, 552, 553, 555
   'Ganymede', 313
   My Cousin Rachel, 552
   Rebecca, 461, 552
du Maurier, George, 124
Duberman, Martin, 305
Dublin University Magazine, 62, 169
Dublin University Review, 169
Duffaud, Briege, *Nothing Like Beirut*, 198
Duffy, Carol Ann, 288, 318
Duffy, John-Charles, 309
Duncan, Bill, *The Smiling School for Calvinists*, 214
Duncan, Norman, *The Soul of the Street: Correlated Stories of the New York Syrian Quarter*, 516, 517
Duncker, Patricia, 342, 442
   'James Miranda Barry 1795–1865', 316
Dunsany, Lord, 449
   The Gods of Pegana, 451

Durrell, Lawrence, 310, 494, 509
Dvorak, Martha, 368

Eagle, The, 436
Eckstein, Barbara, 370
Eco, Umberto, 415
Edgeworth, Maria, 69, 168, 169, 173
   'The Limerick Gloves', 566, 575
   Moral Tales, 47
   Popular Tales, 566
   Practical Education, 47
Edinburgh Review, 120
Edwards, Amelia, 70
Edwards, Dorothy, 226
   'The Conquered', 226
Edwards, Malcolm, 440
Egerton, George, 80, 125–6, 173–4
   'A Lost Masterpiece', 126, 173
   Discords, 126, 174
   Keynotes, 174, 481
Egoist, The, 136
Einhaus, Ann-Marie, *Penguin Book of First World War Stories*, 162
Èjxenbaum, Boris, 432
Eliot, George, 6, 70
   'Janet's Repentance', 73, 75
   'Lifted Veil, The', 6, 61–2, 63
   Adam Bede, 75
   Middlemarch, 53
   Scenes of Clerical Life, 73–5
Eliot, T. S., 235, 411, 490, 527
Ellery Queen's Mystery Magazine, 423
Ellis, Edith
   'Dolores', 312
Ellis, Havelock, 304
Empson, William, 254
   Some Versions of Pastoral, 521
Encounter, 439
English jest book, 4, 18
English Review, 159
English Short Stories of Today, 568
Enright, Anne
   'Fatgirl Terrestrial', 197
   'Honey', 197
   'Little Sister', 197
   'What You Want', 590
   The Portable Virgin, 196
   Taking Pictures, 197
   Yesterday's Weather, 590
Epic of Gilgamesh, The, 430
Ernst, Max, 470
Esty, Jed, 235
Eustace, Robert, 'Sorceress of the Strand', 415

Index

Evans, Caradoc, 220–1, 574
  'Be This Her Memorial', 221
  'The Way of the Earth', 221
  My People, 221
Evans, George Ewart, 219, 223
  'Ben Knowledge', 226
Evans, Margiad, 227–8
  'Mrs Pike's Eldorado', 228
  'The Old Woman and the Wind', 228
  Autobiography, 227
Evening Standard, 414
Everyday Matters 2, 317

Faber Book of Gay Short Fiction, 315
Faber, Michel, 216
  'Vanilla-Bright Like Eminem', 216
  The Fahrenheit Twins, 216
Faderman, Lillian, 304, 308, 309
Fainlight, Ruth, 'Another Survivor', 333
Fantasmagoriana, 50
Farwell, Marilyn R., 306
Faulkner, William, 162, 389
Faulks, Sebastian, 161
Fawcett, Frank Dubrez, 422
Feaver, Jane, 591
Female Spectator, 4
Fielding, Henry, 44, 506, 515
Figes, Eve, 468
Fine, Elizabeth, 171
Finlay, Ian Hamilton, 573
  The Sea-Bed, 209
Firbank, Ronald
  'Santal', 311
  'A Study in Opal', 311
  'A Study in Temperament', 311
Fitzgerald, F. Scott, 'The Diamond as Big as the Ritz', 568
Fitzroy, A. T., 310
Five Love Letters from a Nun to a Cavalier, 26
Flaubert, Gustave, 172, 174, 175, 191
Fleming, Ian, 423, 556
Flint, Kate, 309
Ford, Ford Madox, 131
  The Soul of London, 269
Form, 131
Forster, E. M., 7, 93–4, 235, 314, 572, 608
  'Arthur Snatchfold', 311
  'The Machine Stops', 432, 568
  'The Obelisk', 311
  'The Road from Colonus', 93–4
  'The Story of a Panic', 93–4
  'What Does it Matter', 311
  The Celestial Omnibus, 93

  The Life to Come and Other Stories, 311
  Maurice, 311
Forsyth, Frederick, 556
Fort, Charles, *Lo!*, 434
Foster, Jeanette Howard, *Sex Variant Women in Literature*, 305
Foucault, Michel, 587
Fowler, Adrian, 521, 522, 527
Frame, Janet, 359, 362–4, 369, 370, 373
  'The Lagoon', 363
  'Swans', 363
  The Lagoon, 363
  Owls Do Cry, 362
Frame, Ronald, 212
  Watching Mrs Gordon, 319
France, Anatole, 123
Francis, Dick, *Field of Thirteen*, 424
Francis, Stephen, 422
Frankau, Gilbert, 325
  'An Outlier from His Tribe', 326
Fraser's Magazine, 47
Freeman, R. A., 425
Freeman, Richard Austin, *The Singing Bone*, 418
Freewoman, 136
French, Nicci, 601
  Your Place and Mine, 601
Freud, Sigmund, 137, 148, 396, 400, 533
  '"Civilised" Sexual Morality and Modern Nervous Illness', 137
  'Femininity', 402
  'On Narcissism', 137
  The Ego and the Id, 137
  The Uncanny, 141
Friel, Brian, 186
  The Gold in the Sea, 189
  The Saucer of Larks, 189
Friel, George, 212
Fry, Roger, 137
Frye, Northrop, 84, 527
Fryer, Peter, *Staying Power*, 341
Fun, 481

Gaiman, Neil, 510, 604–5
  'The Case of Four and Twenty Blackbirds', 510
  A Calendar of Tales, 604
Gaitens, Edward
  'A Wee Nip', 573
  Dance of the Apprentices, 208
  Growing Up, 208
Gale, Patrick, *Dangerous Pleasures*, 315
Gallant, Mavis, 367–8, 369

Index

Gallant, Mavis (cont.)
  'Baum, Gabriel, 1935–()', 368
  'The Moslem Wife', 368
  Collected Stories, 368
Gallienne, Richard Le, 129, 130
Galloway, Janice, 593
  'Breaking Through', 215
  Blood, 215
  Where You Find It, 215
Galsworthy, John, 138, 482, 568
  'Defeat', 161
Galt, John, 202
  'Buried Alive, The', 53
Gappah, Petina, 382
  'The Annexe Shuffle', 382
  'The Mupandawana Dancing Champion', 382
  An Elegy for Easterly, 382
Gapper, Frances, 'The Secret of Sorrerby Rise', 316
Gardam, Jane
  'Dead Children', 407
  'The First Adam', 520
  'The Last Adam', 520
  Going into a Dark House, 520
  The Pangs of Love, 520
Garnett, Richard, 121
Gaskell, Elizabeth, 6, 57, 68, 69
  'The Grey Woman', 58
  'The Ghost in the Garden Room', 58
  'A Manchester Marriage', 566
  'The Old Nurse's Story', 58–9, 69, 398
  'The Squire's Story', 58
  'The Well of Pen-Morfa', 75–7
  Cranford, 73
Gaudio, Tony, *The Letter*, 558
Gay, Jackie, *England Calling, 24 Stories for the 21st Century*, 576
Gelder, Ken, *The New Diversity: Australian Fiction 1970–88*, 365
Gentle, Mary, 441
Gentleman's Journal, 29
George, W. L., 325
  'Ave, Amor, Morituri Te Salutant', 326
Gerber, Helmut, 481
Germ, 119
Gernsback, Hugo, 435
  Amazing Stories, 434
Gesta Romanorum, 18
Ghose, Zulfikar, 469
Gibbon, Charles, *The Casquet of Literature, being a Selection of Prose and Poetry from the Works of the Most Admired Authors*, 566

Gibbon, Lewis Grassic, 573
  'Smeddum', 208
  Scottish Scene, 208
Gifford, James, 307
Gilbert, William, 'The Sacristan of St Botolph', 579
Gilchrist, Robert Murray, *The Stone Dragon*, 454
Gillette, William, 549
Gillie, R. P., *German Stories*, 51
Gillings, Walter, 434, 435
  Fantasy, 435
  Tales of Wonder, 434
Gilman, Charlotte Perkins, 'The Yellow Wallpaper', 80
Gilman, Sander L., 331
Gilroy, Paul, *The Black Atlantic*, 352
Giraldi, William, 532
Gissing, George, 75, 80, 119, 487
  'Fleet-Footed Hester', 275
  'The Lady of the Dedication', 483
  'The Pessimist of Plato Road', 483
  'The Scrupulous Father', 483
  New Grub Street, 122
Glanville, Brian
  'A Betting Man', 333
  'The Survivor', 333
  A Bad Streak and Other Stories, 333
Golding, Louis, 325
  'The Doomington Wanderer', 326
  Magnolia Street, 326
Goldsmith, Kenneth, 610
Goldsmith, Oliver, 'Adventures of a Strolling Player', 575
Gomes, Albert, 383
Gomez, Jewelle, 317
Goodison, Lorna, 388
  Baby Mother and the King of Swords, 388
  By Love Possessed, 388
  Fool-Fool Rose Is Leaving Labour-in-Vain Savannah, 388
Goodwin, Geraint, 227
  'Janet Ifan's Donkey', 227
  'The Lost Land', 227
  'The White Farm', 227
Gordimer, Nadine, 10, 11, 286, 288, 290–1, 370–2, 373
  'The African Magician', 290
  'The Catch', 371
  'Is There Nowhere Else Where We Can Meet?', 290
  'The Last Kiss', 291
  'Once Upon a Time', 372

'The Soft Voice of the Serpent', 290
'What Were You Dreaming?', 371
Face to Face, 287, 371
Gordon, Samuel, 324
  'The Miraculous Kaddish', 326
Gorky, Maxim, 179
Gosse, Edmund, 100, 119, 121, 129, 482
Gowers, Justin, 318
Grabinksi, Stefan, 449
Grahame, Kenneth, 119
Grahn, Judith, *True to Life Adventure Stories*, 314
Gramich, Katie, 227
Grand, Sarah, 80, 125
  Our Manifold Nature, 125
  The Heavenly Twins, 125
Grant, Damian, 346
Granta, 578
Graphic, 80, 120
Graves, Robert, 420, 572
Gray, Alasdair
  'Five Letters from an Eastern Empire', 213
  Lean Tales, 213
  Something Leather, 214
  Unlikely Stories, Mostly, 213
Green, Henry, 457
Green, Jen, *Reader, I Murdered Him*, 567
Greene, Graham, 9, 112–13, 235, 236, 242–3, 248, 314, 556, 572
  'The Basement Room', 242
  'The Blue Film', 112
  'Chagrin in Three Parts', 313
  'A Chance for Mr Lever', 112, 242
  'The Destructors', 242, 580
  'May We Borrow Your Husband?', 242, 313
  'Men at Work', 163
  'Under the Garden', 243
  Twenty-One Stories, 112
Greene, Robert, 4, 21–2
  A Notable Discovery of Coosnage, 21
  Pandosto, 22
  The Second Part of Conny-Catching, 21
  The Third Part of Conny-Catching, 21
Greenland, Colin, 440
Gregory, Lady, 171
Grier, Barbara, *The Lesbians Home Journal*, 314
Griffin, Gerald, 169, 172
  'The Knight of the Sheep', 169
  Tales of the Munster Festivals, 169
Griffith, Nicola, 305, 440
Grimm, Jacob and Wilhelm, *Grimm's Fairy Tales*, 84
Griswold, Wendy, 219, 232

Grossmith, George and Weedon, 499
Guardian Weekly, 342
Gunesekera, Romesh, 392
  Monkfish Moon, 392
Gunn, Kirsty, *Infidelities*, 591
Gunn, Neil M., *The White Hour*, 209
Gurr, Andrew, 538
Gutter, 304

Haas, Philip, *Angels and Insects*, 560–1
Habila, Helon, 378
  'Love Poems', 381
  Prison Stories, 381
  Waiting for an Angel, 381
Hadfield, Andrew, 17
Hadfield, John
  Modern Short Stories, 569
  Modern Short Stories to 1940, 569
Hadley, Tessa, 594–5
  'A Mouthful of Cut Glass', 594
  Clever Girl, 517, 519, 521
  The Lucky Ones, 520
  Married Love, 594
Haggard, Henry Rider, 100
  King Solomon's Mines, 101, 108
  She, 279
Haldane, J. B. S.
  'The Last Judgment', 433
  Dedalus, or Science and the Future, 433
Hall, Anna, 168, 169
Hall, Radclyffe, 310, 314
  'Fräulein Schwartz', 157
  'Miss Ogilvy Finds Herself', 312
  Miss Ogilvy Finds Herself, 157
  The Well of Loneliness, 305, 316
Halliday, Andrew, 70
Halward, Leslie, *To Tea on Sunday*, 505
Hamilton, Hugo, *Dublin Where the Palm Trees Grow*, 198
Hamilton, Margaret, 573
Hamilton, Peter F., 440
Hammett, Dashiell, 422
Hancock, Joan, *Modern Irish Short Stories*, 574
Hanscombe, Gillian, 312
Hanson, Clare, 88
  Short Stories and Short Fictions, 585
Hanson, Maurice, 434
Hardt, Michael, 610
Hardy, J. E., 317
Hardy, Thomas, 69, 73, 75, 81, 85–6, 239, 253–4, 258, 259, 389, 464, 482, 528, 572, 579
  'The Distracted Preacher', 85, 253
  'A Few Crusted Characters', 86

Hardy, Thomas (cont.)
  'Fellow-Townsmen', 85
  'For Conscience' Sake', 86
  'An Imaginative Woman', 86
  'Interlopers at the Knap', 85
  'The Melancholy Hussar of the German Legion', 80, 85
  'The Son's Veto', 86
  'The Three Strangers', 85, 254
  'A Tradition of Eighteen Hundred and Four', 85
  'A Tragedy of Two Ambitions', 86
  'The Withered Arm', 85, 253
  A Group of Noble Dames, 516, 519
  Jude the Obscure, 78
  Life's Little Ironies, 85
  Tess of the d'Urbervilles, 481, 489
  The Trumpet-Major, 489
  Wessex Tales, 73, 85, 86, 253, 254
Hariharan, Githa
  'Gajar Halwa', 391
  'The Remains of the Feast', 391
  The Art of Dying, 391
  When Dreams Travel, 391
Harland, Henry, 122, 123–4, 129
  'Concerning the Short Story', 124
  The Cardinal's Snuff-Box, 123
  Comedies and Errors, 123
  Grey Roses, 123, 129
Harman, Thomas, *A Caveat or Warning for Common Cursetors*, 21
Harper's Magazine, 566, 577
Harris, Frank, 482
Harris, Robert, *Enigma*, 162
Harris, Wilson, 377
  'Kanaima', 386
Harrison, Harry, *SF Horizons*, 437
Harrison, M. John, 439, 441, 442, 449, 460, 461
  'The Great God Pan', 460
  'Running Down', 460
Harrison, Niall, *Strange Horizons*, 441
Harte, Bret, 'Uncle Jim and Uncle Billy', 309
Harth, Michael, *Eros at Large*, 306
Hartley, L. P., 236
  The Travelling Grave, 311
  The White Wand, 311
Hartnett, P. P.
  The Gay Times Book of Short Stories, 315
  The Next Wave, 318
Hawkesworth, John, 5, 37, 39
  Adventurer, 42–3
Hawthorne, Nathaniel, 598
  Twice-Told Tales, 69, 136, 565

Hay, Simon, 396, 403
Haynes, Dorothy K., 214, 573
  'Dorothy Dean', 210
Haywood, Eliza, 4, 39
  Female Spectator, 39–41, 43
Head, Bessie, *The Collector of Treasures*, 382
Head, Bodley, 119, 121, 123, 126
Head, Dominic, 136, 147, 371, 543
Healy, Dermot, *Banished Misfortune*, 193
Hemingway, Ernest, 162, 207, 609
Hemry, Mark, *Chasing Danny Boy*, 305
Hendry, J. F., *The Penguin Book of Scottish Short Stories*, 573
Henley, W. E., 100
Hennesberger, Clark, *Weird Tales, A Magazine of the Bizarre and Unusual*, 447
Henry, O., 432
  'The Last Leaf', 309
Hensgen, Jörg, *The Vintage Book of War Stories*, 161
Hensher, Philip, 591
  'Dead Languages', 579
Hewison, Robert, *Under Siege: Literary Life in London 1939–1945*, 163
Hewlitt, Maurice, 482
Hickey, Christine Dwyer, *The House on Parkgate Street and Other Dublin Stories*, 199
Higgins, Aidan, *Asylum and Other Stories*, 193
Highsmith, Patricia, 311, 424
Higonnet, Margaret R., *Lines of Fire, Women Writers of World War I*, 162
Hill, Aaron, *The Plain Dealer*, 38
Hill, Susan
  The Mist in the Mirror, 297
  Penguin Book of Modern Women's Short Stories, 566
  The Woman in Black, 297
Hinton, Charles Howard
  'The Persian King', 431
  Scientific Romances, 430
Hird, Laura, *Nail and Other Stories*, 214
Hitchcock, Alfred, 552
  Alfred Hitchcock Presents, 561
  The Birds, 552
  Jamaica Inn, 552
  The Man Who Knew Too Much, 556
  Rebecca, 552
  Secret Agent, 556
Hoevler, Diane Long, 54
Hoffmann, E. T. A., 5, 50, 598
  'The Sandman', 148
Hoffnung, Gerard, 441

Index

Hogan, Desmond, 575
  The Diamonds at the Bottom of the Sea, 193
Hogarth Press, 138
Hogg, James, 51, 69, 73, 76, 202–3, 573
  'The Barber of Duncow – A Real Ghost Story', 203
  'An Old Soldier's Tale', 203
  Noctes Ambrosianae, 203
  Private Memoirs and Confessions of a Justified Sinner, 425
  The Shepherd's Calendar, 203
  Winter Evening Tales, 203
Hoggart, Richard, *The Uses of Literacy*, 448
Holbrook, David, *People and Diamonds: An Anthology of Modern Short Stories for Use in Secondary Schools*, 568
Hollinghurst, Alan, 315, 318
Holme, Constance, 257
  'Second Wind', 257
  The Wisdom of the Simple and Other Stories, 257
Homer, 13
  Odyssey, 514
Hooley, Ruth, *The Female Line: Northern Ireland Women Writers*, 196
Hornung, E. W., 416–17
  'A Costume Piece', 417
  'Gentleman and Players', 417
  'The Gift of the Emperor', 417
  The Amateur Cracksman, 416
  The Black Mask, 416
  The Thief in the Night, 416
Hosain, Attia, *Phoenix Fled*, 391
Howard, Elizabeth Jane, 458, 506
Howard, Robert E., 447
Hudson, Derek, *Modern English Short Stories 1930–1955*, 569
Hughes, Linda, 127
Humble, Nicola, 429
Humphreys, Arthur, 416
Humphreys, Emyr, 'Dinas', 230
Hundred Merry Tales, A, 4, 17–19
Hunt, Leigh, 54
Hunter, Adrian, 47, 85
Hunter, Jim, *Modern Short Stories*, 569
Hussein, Aamer
  Insomnia, 392
  Mirror to the Sun, 392
Huston, John, *The Dead*, 559–60
Hyde, Douglas, 171

Ibsen, Henrik, 172, 174, 176
Idler, 80, 125

Ihimaera, Witi
  Dear Miss Mansfield, 393, 520
  Pounamu, Pounamu, 393
  The New Net Goes Fishing, 393
Illis, Mark, 591
  Tender, 591
Illustrated London News, 120, 270, 310
Impulse, 438
In and Out of Time, 317
Incidents Involving Warmth, 317
Ingram, Forrest, 517, 518, 523
Ings, Simon, 440, 442
  Arc, 442
International Times, 439
Interzone, 440–1
Irigaray, Luce, 362
Irish Homestead, 113, 172, 190
Irish Review, 172
Irish Statesman, 172
Irving, Washington, 5, 50
Isherwood, Christopher, 311, 314
  'A Berlin Diary (Autumn 1930)', 311
  'An Evening at the Bay', 311
  'The Nowaks', 311
  Great English Short Stories, 571
Ishiguro, Kazuo, 578, 585
  Nocturnes, 513, 519, 520, 591

Jackson, Holbrook, 131
Jackson, Shirley, 461
Jacob, Violet
  'The Fiddler', 208
  Tales of My Own Country, 208
Jacobson, Dan, 329, 330
  'The Zulu and the Zeide', 329, 331
James Mirollo, James, 18
James, C. L. R., 383
James, Henry, 46, 64, 69, 80, 103, 119, 122, 130, 296, 432, 464, 482, 530, 535–7, 598
  'The Aspern Papers', 535
  'The Author of Beltraffio', 309
  'The Beast in the Jungle', 531, 535, 536
  'The Coxon Fund', 122
  'Daisy Miller', 531
  'Daisy Miller: A Study', 535, 536
  'The Death of the Lion', 122, 126
  'The Figure in the Carpet', 531, 535, 536
  'The Great Good Place', 309
  'In the Cage', 535
  'The Pupil', 309, 535
  'The Turn of the Screw', 69, 399, 535
  The Bostonians, 122

James, Henry (cont.)
  The Golden Bowl, 122
  Guy Domville, 122
  The Portrait of a Lady, 122
  Terminations, 122, 129
  The Wings of the Dove, 122, 598
James, M. R., 404, 407, 449, 451, 568
  'The Haunted Dolls' House', 602
  'The Mezzotint', 404
  'Whistle and I'll Come to You, My Lad', 404
James, William, 130
  Principles of Psychology, 137
Jameson, Fredric, 3, 601
Jewett, Sara Orne, 528
  The Country of the Pointed Firs, 516
Jhabvala, Ruth Prawer, 248
Johnson, B. S., 12, 468–70, 476
  'Broad Thoughts from a Home', 469
  'Clean Living is the Real Safeguard', 469
  'A Few Selected Sentences', 578
  'Perhaps It's These Hormones', 469
  Albert Angelo, 469
Johnson, Leslie J., *Outlands*, 435
Johnson, Samuel, 37, 39, 41–2
  Rambler, 41
  Rasselas, 87
Jolley, Elizabeth, 366–7, 370, 373
  Five-Acre Virgin and Other Stories, 366
Jones, Glyn, 223
  'The Kiss', 224
  The Dragon Has Two Tongues, 221
Jones, Gwyn, 220, 221, 223, 227
  'The Pit', 223
  Welsh Short Stories, 574
Jones, Gwyneth, 440, 442
Jones, Langdon, 439
Jones, Phyllis M., *Modern English Short Stories*, 569
Jones, Sally Roberts, 221
Jordan, Neil, *Night in Tunisia*, 193
Joseph, Jenny, 288
Joshi, S. T., 449, 458
Josipovici, Gabriel, 13, 335–6, 468
  Goldberg: Variations, 335, 336, 337
Journey into Space, 436
Joyce, Graham, 441
Joyce, James, 5, 113–14, 136, 138, 139–41, 143, 149, 176–7, 182, 191, 192, 310, 494, 508, 530, 600
  'After The Race', 113–14
  'Araby', 176
  'The Boarding House', 569
  'Clay', 177
  'The Dead', 8, 139–41, 177, 525–6, 531, 537, 559–60, 573, 575
  'A Mother', 176
  'Ivy Day in the Committee Room', 114, 573
  'The Sisters', 524, 525
  Dubliners, 113, 139, 173, 174, 176–7, 182, 513, 516, 519, 523, 524, 527, 528, 537, 569, 573
  A Portrait of the Artist as a Young Man, 135, 139, 513, 517
  Stephen Hero, 135, 139
  Ulysses, 113, 131, 138, 235, 514, 537
Joyce, Stanislaus, 176
Judy, 481
Jump, Harriet Devine, *Nineteenth-Century Short Stories by Women*, 566

Kafka, Franz, 449, 457
Karageorgevich, Bojidar, 124
Kaveney, Roz, 440
Kay, Jackie, 317, 318, 342, 350–2
  'Out of Hand', 350, 351
  'Shark! Shark!', 350
  'Shell', 350
  'Trout Friday', 352
  'Why Don't You Stop Talking', 352
  'Wish I Was Here', 590
  Trumpet, 350
  Why Don't You Stop Talking, 350
  Wish I Was Here, 590
Kaye-Smith, Sheila
  'Joanna Godden's Joy Ride', 258
  Faithful Stranger and Other Stories, 258
  Joanna Godden, 258
Keegan, Claire, 199
  'Men and Women', 199
  Antarctica, 199
  Walk the Blue Fields, 199
Keepsake, 53, 54, 56, 564
Kelly, Harold, 422
Kelly, Maeve, *A Life of Her Own*, 194
Kelman, James, 9, 212
  Not Not While the Giro, 212
  Translated Accounts, 214
Kemp, Jeremy, 560
Kennedy, A. L., 476, 584
  'Proof of Life', 590
  'Sympathy', 216
  'The Mouseboks Family Dictionary', 216
  Night Geometry and the Garscadden Trains, 215, 582
  On Writing, 582, 590
  What Becomes, 216

Kennedy, Gerald, 518
Kensit, Patsy, 560
Kenworthy, Chris, 441
Keynotes, 125–7
Kiberd, Declan, 170
Kiely, Benedict, 187, 195
  'A Ball of Malt and Madame Butterfly', 195
  'Bluebell Meadow', 195
  'Proxopera', 195
  A Ball of Malt and Madame Butterfly, 195
  A Cow in the House, 195
Killick, Tim, 32, 38, 51, 55, 252
Kincaid, Jamaica, 388
  'Girl', 389
  'In the Night', 389
  At the Bottom of the River, 389
King, Stephen, 544
King, Thomas
  'The One About Coyote Going West', 393
  All My Relations, 393
Kipling, Rudyard, 7, 69, 81, 100–5, 106, 110, 162, 238, 455–7, 482, 572, 598
  'At the End of the Passage', 455, 456
  'The Courting of Dinah Shadd', 81, 104
  'The Gate of the Hundred Sorrows', 102
  'How the Alphabet was Made', 91
  'How the Leopard Got his Spots', 91
  'How the Whale Got his Throat', 91
  'In the House of Suddhoo', 456
  'The Incarnation of Krishna Mulvaney', 104
  'The Judgment of Dungara', 109
  'Love o' Women', 104
  'The Madness of Private Ortheris', 105
  'The Man Who Would Be King', 101
  'Mary Postgate', 456
  'The Mutiny of the Mavericks', 105
  'On Greenhow Hill', 104, 105
  'The Phantom Rickshaw', 101
  'The Strange Ride of Morrowbie Jukes', 101
  'Swept and Garnished', 156
  'Wireless', 456
  'With the Night Mail', 432
  Barrack-Room Ballads, 104
  In Black and White, 100, 102
  Just So Stories, 7, 91
  Mine Own People, 455
  The Phantom Rickshaw, 102
  Plain Tales from the Hills, 81, 101
  Soldiers Three, 100, 102, 104
  Under the Deodars, 100, 102
  Wee Willie Winkie, 102
Klee, Paul, *Wander-Artist*, 335

Kleinburg, Seymour, *The Other Persuasion*, 314
Kleist, Heinrich von, 600
Kneale, Nigel, 569
Korte, Barbara, *Penguin Book of First World War Stories*, 162
Kranzler, Laura, 58
Kristeva, Julia, 147
Krueger, Kate, 396
Kubrick, Stanley, *2001, A Space Odyssey*, 556
Kunzru, Hari, 347
Kureishi, Hanif, 281–2, 342, 347–50, 584
  'In a Blue Time', 282
  'My Son the Fanatic', 282, 349
  'Nightlight', 282
  'The Rainbow Sign', 347, 348
  'We're Not Jews', 348
  'Weddings and Beheadings', 590
  'With Your Tongue down my Throat', 282, 348
  The Black Album, 349
  The Buddha of Suburbia, 349
  Collected Stories, 590
  Love in a Blue Time, 281, 347
  Midnight All Day, 281
Kyk-over-al, 383

L'Estrange, Sir Roger, *The Fables of Bidpai*, 36
La Fontaine, Jean de, 85
La Guma, Alex, *A Walk in the Night*, 382
Lady's Magazine, 44, 72
Lafayette, Madame de, 26
Lahiri, Jhumpa, 392
  The Interpreter of Maladies, 393
Lambert, Zoe, 591
Lamming, George, 342
Landa, Gertrude, 324
  'My Venetian Singer', 326
Landa, M. J., 324
  'Two Legacies', 326
Lane, Joel, *Birmingham Noir*, 575
Lane, John, 121
Lang, Andrew, 84, 100, 103
Lappin, Elena, 13
  Foreign Brides, 337
Larkin, Philip, 460
Larminie, William, 171
Larriere, Claire, 466
Larson, Darby, 611–13
  Irritant, 611
Latham, Sean, 131
Laurence, Margaret, 369, 373
  A Bird in the House, 370

Index

Lavin, Mary, 9, 185, 186, 188, 190
   'The Becker Wives', 188
   'Chamois Gloves', 188
   'The Convert', 188
   'A Cup of Tea', 188
   'A Gentle Soul', 188
   'Happiness', 188
   'In a Café', 188
   'In the Middle of the Fields', 188
   'Lilacs', 188
   'The Nun's Mother', 188
   'Sarah', 188
   'A Story with a Pattern', 188
   'Sunday Brings Sunday', 188
   'The Widow's Son', 188
   'The Will', 188
Lawrence, D. H., 7, 88, 94–6, 131, 162, 235, 236, 237–8, 239, 242, 310, 314, 530, 539–41
   'The Blind Man', 237
   'The Captain's Doll', 539
   'Daughters of the Vicar', 237
   'England, My England', 159
   'The Fox', 241, 309, 531, 539, 540, 541
   'Fanny and Annie', 573
   'The Horse Dealer's Daughter', 237, 573
   'The Ladybird', 539
   'The Man Who Loved Islands', 95, 237
   'New Eve and Old Adam', 95
   'Odour of Chrysanthemums', 237, 559–60, 568
   'The Old Adam', 95
   'The Princess', 539
   'The Prussian Officer', 237, 309, 312
   'Rawdon's Roof', 237
   'The Rocking-Horse Winner', 94, 401
   'Rupert and Gerald', 312
   'Samson and Delilah', 95
   'St Mawr', 539
   'Tickets, Please', 237
   'The Woman Who Rode Away', 94, 531, 539, 540
   England, My England and Other Stories, 159, 573
   The Escaped Cock, 7, 95–6, 539
   Lady Chatterley's Lover, 542
   The Man Who Died, 95
   The Virgin and the Gypsy, 539
   The Woman Who Rode Away and Other Stories, 94, 520
   Women in Love, 312
Lawrence, T. E., 311
Lawson, Alan, 359, 361
Lawson, Henry, 359, 360, 364, 373
   'The Drover's Wife', 364, 365–6
Le Carré, John, 556
Le Fanu, Joseph Sheridan, 51, 57, 59, 62–4, 407
   'An Account of Some Strange Disturbances in Aungier Street', 398
   'Carmilla', 309
   'Green Tea', 63–4, 406
   Carmilla, 52
   In a Glass Darkly, 63, 170
Leacock, Stephen, *Sunshine Sketches of a Little Town*, 367, 516, 519
Leavitt, David, 305, 307, 309
Ledger, Sally, 127
Lee, Jeanette, 'The Cat and the King', 309
Lee, Richard, 465
Lee, Tanith, 441
Lee, V. G., *As You Step Outside*, 319
Lee, Vernon, 80
   'A Wicked Voice', 402
   'Lady Tal', 482
   'The Phantom Lover', 402
   Hauntings, 460
Leftwich, Joseph, 323, 324–8, 332
   Yisröel: The First Jewish Omnibus, 324
Léger, Tom, *The Collection*, 306
Lehmann, Rosamond, 'A Dream of Winter', 569
Lessing, Doris, 10, 11, 248, 259, 286, 287, 288, 289–90, 436, 509, 578
   'Little Tembi', 290
   'No Witchcraft for Sale', 289
   The Golden Notebook, 289
   The Sun Between Their Feet, 289
   This Was the Old Chief's Country, 289
Levin, Shaun, *A Year of Two Summers*, 315
Levy, Amy, 324, 326–7
   'Cohen of Trinity', 326
   Reuben Sachs, 326
Lewis, Alun, 228
   'The Jungle', 229
   'The Last Inspection', 485
   'The Orange Grove', 229
   The Last Inspection, 159
Lewis, C. Day, 421
Lewis, C. S., 434
Lewis, Damien, *Slave*, 352
Lewis, Percy Wyndham, 136, 138, 162, 209, 487–91
   'A Soldier of Humour', 489
   'Bestre', 147–9
   'Cantleman's Spring-Mate', 138, 488, 490
   'Constantinople our Star', 488
   'Inferior Religions', 147, 489

'Satire and Fiction', 488
'Studies in the Art of Laughter', 488
'The Rot', 490
The Childermass, 434
Men Without Art, 138
Rotting Hill, 488, 490, 491
The Wild Body, 138, 147–50, 486, 488, 489–90, 491
Unlucky for Pringle, Unpublished and Other Stories, 488
Liebowitz, Judith, 533
Life and Letters Today, 226
Liggins, Emma, 75
Linklater, Alex, 588
Linklater, Eric, 236
'The Goose Girl', 211
Sealskin Trousers, 211
Lippincott's Magazine, 455
Litmus, 442
Litt, Toby, 441, 495–6, 509, 586–7, 589, 591
'After Wagamama but Mostly Before', 496
'It Could Have Been Me and it Was', 495
'Please Use a Basket', 586
'The Audioguide', 587
'When I met Michel Foucault', 587
Adventures in Capitalism, 495, 586
Exhibitionism, 586
I Play the Drums in a Band Called Okay, 517, 587
Life-Like, 516, 587, 592
Slice, 602
Littell, Robert, 358
Little Review, 131, 138
Litvinoff, Emanuel
'Fanya', 329
Journey through a Small Planet, 329
The Penguin Book of Jewish Short Stories, 324, 329
Livia, Anna, 317
The Pied Piper, 316, 317
Liyong'o, Taban lo, *Fixions*, 381
Lodge, David, 578
Lokugé, Chandani, 392
Moth, 392
London, 270
London Journal, 270
London Magazine, 270, 575
London Monthly Magazine, 270
London Penny Journal, 270
London Review, 270
London, Jack, 'The White Silence', 309
Lovecraft, H. P., 447, 458
'The Call of Cthulhu', 450

'The Dunwich Horror', 460
Supernatural Horror in Literature, 449
Lovegrove, James, 441
Lovelace, Earl, *A Brief Conversion*, 385
Lover, Samuel, 172
Legends and Stories of Ireland, 168
Low, Sidney, 100
Low, Warren, *The Letter*, 558
Lucian, 'A True History', 430
Lycett, Andrew, 100
Lynch, Eve M., 60

Macaulay, Rose
'Miss Anstruther's Letters', 164
Wave Me Goodbye, 164
MacDiarmid, Hugh, 208
MacDonald, George, 52, 90, 204
'The Carasoyn', 204
'The Golden Key', 90, 204
'The Light Princess', 90, 204
'The Shadows', 90
Adela Cathcart, 90, 204
Dealing with Fairies, 204
Dealings with the Fairies, 90
MacDougall, Sophia, 442
Machen, Arthur, 127, 449, 450, 451–4, 457, 460
'The Bowmen', 155, 402
'A Fragment of Life', 454
'The Inmost Light', 452
'N', 454
'Novel of the White Powder', 452
Far Off Things, 453
The Great God Pan and The Inmost Light, 451, 452
The Hill of Dreams, 453
The London Adventure, 454
The Three Imposters, 452
Mackay, Shena
'The Most Beautiful Dress in the World', 215
Dreams of Dead Women's Handbags, 215
Mackenzie, Henry, 44
Maclaren, Ian, *Beside the Bonnie Brier Bush*, 205
MacLaverty, Bernard, 216, 575
'The Daily Woman', 195
'Some Surrender', 195
The Great Profundo, 195
Matters of Life and Death, 198
A Time to Dance, 195
MacLennan, Hugh, 367
MacLeod, Alison, 584
Thresholds, 585
MacLeod, Ken, 442

MacLeod, Riley, *The Collection*, 306
MacMahon, Bryan, 185
   The Lion-Tamer and Other Stories, 189
Macmillan's, 119
Madox Ford, Ford
   The Brown Owl, 90
   Christina's Fairy Book, 91
   The Feather, 90
   The Queen Who Flew, 90
Maginn, William, 202
Mahabharata, 389
Mahar, Alan, *Birmingham Nouveau*, 576
Maine, Charles Eric, 435
Mais, Roger, 384
   And Most of All Man, 387
   Face and Other Stories, 387
   Listen, the Wind, 387
Maitland, Sara, 442
   'Moss Witch', 442
Man, 362
Mann, Mary E., 255–7
   'Blue Beads', 255
   'Little Brother', 255, 579
   'Wolf-Charlie', 256
   The Complete Tales of Dulditch, 255
   The Fields of Dulditch, 255
Mann, Thomas, *Death in Venice*, 532, 533, 536, 543
Mansfield, Katherine, 131, 136, 137, 147, 148, 149, 162, 277–8, 287, 292, 358, 360–1, 367, 369, 373, 393, 530, 538–9, 594
   'The Aloe', 530, 539
   'At the Bay', 360, 531, 538
   'Bains Turc', 312
   'Bliss', 8, 138, 144–6, 147, 312
   'The Fly', 154
   'The Garden Party', 360
   'Leves Amores', 312
   'Life of Ma Parker', 278
   'The Little Governess', 360
   'Pictures', 277
   'A Suburban Fairy Tale', 95
   Bliss and Other Stories, 287
   The Garden-Party, 287
   In a German Pension, 287
   Prelude, 360, 530, 531, 538
   Something Childish, 95
March-Russell, Paul, 591
Marcus, David, 190
   Tears of the Shamrock, 194
Marechera, Dambudzo, 382
   House of Hunger, 382

Marek, Adam, 442
Markham, E. A., 342, 344–5
   'Mammie's Form at the Post Office', 344
   'A Place for Simon', 351
   The Penguin Book of Caribbean Short Stories, 384
Marquez, Gabriel Garcia, 518
Marryat, Florence, 59
Marsh, Richard, 458
Marshall, Herbert, 558
Mars-Jones, Adam, 578, 585
   'Structural Anthropology', 578
   The Darker Proof, Stories from a Crisis, 315
   Lantern Lecture, 315
   Mae West is Dead, 315, 317
Marson, Una, 384
Martin, Ann, 93
Martin, Carol A., 57
Marx, Karl, 49, 137, 533
   Communist Manifesto, 403
Mason, Simon, *Lives of the Dog-Stranglers*, 519
Masters, Olga, 360
Mathews, Elkin, 121
Mathias, Roland, 'Ffynnon Fawr', 230
Matthews, Brander, 68, 79
Matus, Jill L., 57
Maugham, William Somerset, 101, 108–12, 162, 556–8
   'Before the Party', 110
   'Flotsam and Jetsam', 111, 112
   'The Force of Circumstance', 110
   'Giulia Lazzari', 158
   'The Hairless Mexican', 557
   'The Letter', 110, 557
   'Mackintosh', 109
   'The Outstation', 110
   'Rain', 109
   'The Short Story', 100, 108, 110
   'The Traitor', 161, 557
   'The Yellow Streak', 110
   'Virtue', 112
   Ashenden, Or the British Agent, 557
   The Casuarina Tree, 109
Maughan, Tim, 443
Maunder, Andrew, 75
   British Literature of World War I: The Short Story and the Novella, 162
Maupassant, Guy de, 9, 172, 174, 179, 235, 239, 360, 598
   'Paul's Mistress', 309
May, Charles, 26, 465

Index

Mayhew, Henry, *London Labour and the London Poor*, 275
Mayne, Ethel Colburn, 130
Mayo, Robert D., 32
McAllister, Hayden, *War Stories*, 161
McAuley, Paul, 433, 440, 442
McBratney, John, 101
McCabe, Brian, 212
McCabe, Eugene
   'Cancer', 195
   'Heritage', 195
   'Victims', 195
McCann, Colum, 199
   'A Basket Full of Wallpaper', 198
   Everything in this Country Must, 199
   Fishing the Sloe-Black River, 198
McDermid, Val, 318, 424
   'The Ministry of Whisky', 424
   The Writing on the Wall, 424
McDonald, Ian, 440
McEwan, Ian, 470, 472–4, 476, 486, 530, 543–4, 578, 585, 589
   'In Between the Sheets', 473
   'Solid Geometry', 586
   'To and Fro', 473
   'Two Fragments, March 199–', 280
   Amsterdam, 532, 543
   Black Dogs, 472
   The Cement Garden, 543
   The Comfort of Strangers, 532, 543
   Enduring Love, 472
   First Love, Last Rites, 472, 513, 586
   In Between the Sheets, 472
McGahern, John, 188, 189, 191–2, 195, 199, 575
   'Along the Edges', 191
   'The Beginning of an Idea', 191
   'The Conversion of William Kirkwood', 192
   'The Country Funeral', 192
   'Crossing the Line', 192
   'Doorways', 191
   'Eddie Mac', 192
   'Gold Watch', 192
   'The High Ground', 192
   'Like All Other Men', 192
   'My Love, My Umbrella', 191
   'Oldfashioned', 192
   'Peaches', 191
   'The Recruiting Officer', 191
   'Swallows', 191
   'The Wine Breath', 192
   'Wheels', 191
   The Collected Stories, 192
   Getting Through, 191, 192
   High Ground, 192
   Nightlines, 191
McGregor, Iona, 317
McGregor, Jon, 476–8
   'In Winter the Sky', 476, 477
   'The Last Ditch', 477
   'Which Reminded Her, Later', 591
   This Isn't the Sort of Thing that Happens to Someone Like You, 476, 591
McGurl, Mark, 581, 590
McKay, Claude, *Gingertown*, 386
McKenzie, Alicia, *Satellite City*, 388
McLane, Maureen N., 55
McLaverty, Michael, 185
   The Game Cock, 189
   The White Mare, 189
McLean, Duncan, *Bucket of Tongues*, 214
McLellan, Robert
   'The Falls Brae', 209
   Linmill Stories, 208
McLeod, John, 343
McNeile, H. C. (Sapper), 'The Man Who Would Not Play Cards', 158
McWilliam, Candia, *Wait Till I Tell You*, 215
Meade, L. T., 124, 414
   'Sorceress of the Strand', 415
Méliès, Georges, *A Trip to the Moon*, 555
Melville, Herman, 598
   'Bartleby, the Scrivener: A Story of Wall Street', 70
Melville, Pauline, 342, 377
   'Eat Labba and Drink Creek Water', 347
   'Mrs da Silva's Carnival', 345
   'The Parrot and Descartes', 386
   The Migration of Ghosts, 345, 386
   Shape-Shifter, 345, 347, 386
   The Ventriloquist's Tale, 345
Mendes, Alfred, 383
Mendlesohn, Farah, 429
Mengal, Ewald, 57
Mercanti, Stefano, 390
Mercer, Gina, 363
Meredith, George, 482
Merril, Judith, 437
Metcalfe, Beverley, 491
Mew, Charlotte, 236–7
   'The China Bowl', 236
   'Passed', 236, 309
Meyrink, Gustav, 449
Miéville, China, 433, 450, 461

Mile, Siân, 486
Miller, Henry, 310
Millin, Sarah Gertrude, 325
  'Up from Gilgal', 372
  'Why Adonis Laughed', 327–8
Mills, Joseph, *Borderline*, 305
Milman, Lena, 124
Milne, A. A., 561
Minchin, James H. C.
  Great Short Stories of the War: England, France, Germany, America, 161
Mish, Charles, 29
Mistry, Rohinton, *Tales from Firozsha Baag*, 393
Mitchell, David, 509, 605–6
  'The Right Sort', 605
  'Underground', 525
  Ghostwritten, 515, 525
Mitchell, Gladys, 422
  'A Light on Murder', 423
Mitchell, Juliet, 490
Mitchell, Mark, 305, 307, 309
Mitchison, Naomi, 433, 573
  Beyond This Limit, 209
Mitford, Mary Russell, 252–3
  Our Village, 72, 252
Moers, Ellen, *Literary Women*, 567
Mohin, Lilian
  The Pied Piper, 316, 317
  The Reach, 316
Molloy, Frances, *Women Are the Scourge of the Earth*, 196
Monar, Rooplall, *Backdam People*, 386
Montagu, Ivor, 555
Montague, John
  'The Cry', 194
  The Death of a Chieftain and Other Stories, 194
Montague, C. E., 161
Moon, Lorna, *Doorways in Drumorty*, 207
Moorcock, Michael, 435, 437, 438, 439, 441
  London Bone, 282
  New Worlds, 440
Moore, George, 5, 80, 174–6, 482
  'Alms-Giving', 175
  'Exile', 175
  'Fugitives', 175, 176
  'Home Sickness', 574
  'Homesickness', 175
  'Julia Cahill's Curse', 175
  'Literature at Nurse, or Circulating Morals', 481
  'A Play-House in the Waste', 175
  'So on He Fares', 175

'The Wedding Gown', 175
'The Wild Goose', 175, 176
'The Window', 175
The Untilled Field, 174–6, 527, 574
Moore, John, 569
Moore, Lorrie, 577
Moorhouse, Frank, 365, 373
  'The Drover's Wife', 365
  The Coca-Cola Kid, 366
Moretti, Franco, 275
Morgan, Claire, *The Price of Salt*, 311
Morris, William, *News from Nowhere*, 88
Morrison, Arthur, 276, 414, 415
  'The Case of Laker Absconded', 415
  'The Lenton Mysteries', 415
  'Lizerunt', 276
  'On the Stairs', 276
  Tales of Mean Streets, 276
Morrison, Ewan, 600–1, 602
  The Last Book You Read, 600
Morrison, Toni, 477
Morrow, John, 'Place, Belfast/Time, 1984/Scene, The Only Pub', 485
Mort, Graham, 584
  Terroir, 584
  Touch, 584
Morton, Thomas, *Speed the Plough*, 481
Moskowitz, Sam, *Masterpieces of Science Fiction*, 567
Motteaux, Peter, 33
  Gentleman's Journal, 34
Mphahlele, Es'kia
  In Corner B, 382
  The Living and the Dead, 382
Muddock, Joyce Emerson, 414
Mudford, William, 'The Iron Shroud', 53
Mueenuddin, Daniyal, *In Other Rooms, Other Wonders*, 392
Mukherjee, Bharati, 392
  Darkness, 392
  The Middleman, 393
Mulkerns, Val, *An Idle Woman*, 194
Munro, Alice, 10, 286, 288, 294–5, 360, 368–9, 517, 518, 589, 594
  'Boys and Girls', 369
  'Dear Life', 295
  'Royal Beatings', 524
  'Sowesto', 295
  'Spelling', 526
  'Train', 577
  'Walker Brothers Cowboy', 294
  'Who Do You Think You Are?', 526
  'Wild Swans', 294

Index

'A Wilderness Station', 295
The Beggar Maid, 294
Dance of the Happy Shades, 295, 369
Lives of Girls and Women, 294, 369, 519
Something I've Been Meaning to Tell You, 369
Who Do You Think You Are?, 294, 369, 513, 517, 521, 523, 524, 526
Munro, Neil, *The Vital Spark*, 205
Munt, Sally, 423
Murdoch, Iris, 494
Murphy, Brenda, 'A Social Call', 196
Murray, Ian, *New Penguin Book of Scottish Short Stories*, 573
Murry, John Middleton, 131, 538
Mzamane, Mbulelo, *My Cousin Comes to Jo'burg*, 382

Nagai, Kaori, 104
Naipaul, V. S., 384, 568
   Miguel Street, 381, 383, 385, 516, 519
Nair, Anita, *Ladies Coupé*, 392
Naqvi, Tahira, *Attar of Roses*, 392
Narayan, R. K., 389, 568
   A Horse and Two Goats, 390
   Gods, Demons and Others, 389
   The Mahabharata, 389
   Malgudi Days, 390
   The Ramayana, 389
   Under the Banyan Tree, 390
Nash, Catherine, 367
Nash's, 418
Natzler, Caroline, 317
Navarre, Marguerite de, 22
   Heptameron, 532
Nazer, Mende, *Slave*, 352
Nebula, 435
Needle on Full, The, 317
Negri, Antonio, 610
Neville, Henry, 'Isle of Pines, The', 26
New Review, 130
New Scientist, 442
New Weird, The, 449
New Worlds, 435, 436, 437, 438, 439, 440
New Writings in SF, 437
New Yorker, 186, 188, 290, 368
New, W. H., 518
Newell, Stephanie, 380
Newman, Kim, 440
News Chronicle, 241
Ní Dhuibhne, Éilís, 197, 199
   'The Day Elvis Presley Died', 197
   '*The Inland Ice*' and Other Stories, 197
   'The Mermaid Legend', 197

   'Midwife to the Fairies', 197
   'Oleander', 197
   'The Pale Gold of Alaska', 197
   'The Search for the Lost Husband', 197
   'The Truth about Married Love', 197
   Blood and Water, 197
   Eating Women is not Recommended, 197
   The Pale Gold of Alaska, 197
Nineteenth Century, 129
Nissen, Axel, 310
Nixon, Mark, 466
Noah, 608
Nolan, Maggie, 361
Noon, Jeff, 433, 442
   Cobralingus, 443
   Pixel Juice, 443
Nordau, Max, 64
Novae Terrae, 434, 435
Nwapa, Flora, 380, 381
   This is Lagos, 379
   Wives at War, 379
Nyeko, Monica Arac de, 381

Ó Ceallaigh, Philip, *Notes from a Turkish Whorehouse*, 199
O'Brien, Edna, 187, 190–1, 578, 595
   'Cords', 191
   'Irish Revel', 191
   'My Two Mothers', 191
   'Over', 191
   'The House of My Dreams', 190
   'The Love Object', 190, 191
   'The Mouth of the Cave', 190
   'A Rose in the Heart of New York', 191
   'A Rug', 191
   A Scandalous Woman, 190, 191
   The Love Object, 190, 191
   Mrs Reinhardt, 191
   Saints and Sinners, 191
O'Brien, Flann, 'The Martyr's Crown', 485
O'Connor, Flannery, 585
O'Connor, Frank, 8, 9, 10, 22, 175, 177, 178, 179–80, 182, 185, 186–8, 220, 235, 359, 496, 515, 518, 571, 575, 595
   'The Babes in the Wood', 187
   'The Cheapjack', 186, 187
   'The Cheat', 187
   'The Corkerys', 187
   'Darcy in the Land of Youth', 187
   'The Grand Vizier's Daughters', 186
   'Guests of the Nation', 180, 485
   'In the Train', 180
   'Judas', 187

O'Connor, Frank (cont.)
  'Legal Aid', 187
  'The Late Henry Conran', 180
  'The Long Road to Ummera', 186, 187, 188
  'The Luceys', 186
  'The Mad Lomasneys', 187
  'The Majesty of the Law', 180
  'The Mass Island', 188
  'My First Protestant', 187
  'My Oedipus Complex', 187
  'September Dawn', 180
  'The Sorcerer's Apprentice', 187
  'Uprooted', 187
  'The Weeping Children', 187
  Bones of Contention, 179
  Crab Apple Jelly, 186
  Guests of the Nation, 179
  The Lonely Voice, 187, 188, 590
  Modern Irish Short Stories, 574
O'Faoláin, Seán, 8, 177, 178, 179, 180–1, 182, 185–6, 190, 575
  'Admiring the Scenery', 181
  'A Broken World', 181
  'Fugue', 181
  'Lady Lucifer', 186
  'A Letter', 186
  'Lovers of the Lake', 186
  'The Man Who Invented Sin', 185
  'A Meeting', 181
  'Midsummer Night Madness', 180, 181
  'One Night in Turin', 190
  'The Patriot', 181
  'The Planets of the Years', 190
  'A Shadow, Silent as a Cloud', 190
  'The Small Lady', 181
  'A Touch of Autumn in the Air', 190
  'Unholy Living and Half Dying', 185
  The Bell, 181, 185
  The Finest Stories, 185
  The Heat of the Sun, 190
  I Remember! I Remember!, 190
  Midsummer Night Madness, 180, 181, 571
  A Purse of Coppers, 181
  The Short Story, 185
  Teresa and Other Stories, 185
O'Flaherty, Liam, 177, 179
  'A Wave', 179
  'The Blackbird', 179
  'The Caress', 179
  'The Cow's Death', 179
  'The Rockfish', 179
  The Mountain Tavern and Other Stories, 179
  Spring Sowing, 179

The Tent, 179
Two Lovely Beasts and Other Stories, 188
O'Kelly, Seumas, 'The Weaver's Grave', 178
O'Neill, Jamie, 318
O'Rawe, Geraldine, 559
O'Rourke, Rebecca, 582
O'Sullivan, Vincent, 539
Observer, 209
Ogot, Grace
  Land without Thunder, 381
  The Other Woman, 381
Okike, 378
Okri, Ben, 342
Oliphant, Margaret, 67–8, 69, 78–9, 81, 103, 204, 573
  'The Anti-Marriage League', 78
  'The Library Window', 204
  'Little Pilgrim', 204
  'Mr Sandford', 67
  'A Preface: On the Ebb Tide', 67
  'Queen Eleanor and Fair Rosamond', 79
  'A Story of a Wedding Tour', 79, 80, 566
  'Tales of the Seen and the Unseen', 204
  'The Two Mrs Scudamores', 78
  'The Wonderful History of Mr Robert Dalyell', 67
  Chronicles of Carlingford, 73
  Neighbours on the Green, 73
  The Ways of Life, 67
Orczy, Emma, 418
Orel, Harold, 118
Orwell, George
  'The Decline of the English Murder', 422
  'Raffles and Miss Blandish', 422
Osborne, John, 494, 509
Out There, 304
Overbury, Sir Thomas, *Characters*, 28
Owens, Agnes, 9, 213
  'Arabella', 214
  Gentlemen of the West, 214
Owusu, Kwesi, 354

Pagan Review, 129
Pagel, Stephen, 305
Paglia, Camille, 553
Pain, Barry, 498–500
  'Miss Sakers', 499
Painter, William, *The Palace of Pleasure*, 22, 24
Pall Mall Gazette, 413, 431
Palmer, Paulina, 315
Panchatantra, 389

Panter-Downes, Mollie, 'Meeting at the Pringles', 154
Parker, Michael, *The Hurt World, Short Stories of the Troubles*, 195
Parkes, Adam, 138
Partridge, Mark, *Odour of Chrysanthemums*, 559
Pearson's, 418
Pearson's Magazine, 431
Penguin Book of Lesbian Short Stories, 317
Perrault, Charles, 297
  Tales and Stories of the Past with Morals, 84
Perry, Anne, *Lowest Heaven*, 442
Peters, Catherine, 61
Pettie, George, *A Petite Palace of Pettie his Pleasure*, 23
Phillips, Ambrose, *Free-Thinker*, 38
Phillips, Mike, 344, 351
Phillips, Robert, 311
Phillips, Trevor, 344, 351
Pinter, Harold, 506
Pirkis, Catherine, 416
Pirkis, Catherine Louisa, 413
Plomer, William, 570
Plunkett, James, 185
Plutarch, 'On the Decline of Oracles', 452
Poe, Edgar Allan, 3, 5, 50, 136, 170, 296, 456, 464, 514, 522, 565, 598
  'How to Write a Blackwood Article', 74, 120
  'The Man of the Crowd', 270–1
  'The Murders in the Rue Morgue', 412
  'The Pit and the Pendulum', 53
  'The Philosophy of Composition', 69
Polidori, John
  'The Vampyre', 50, 51, 52–3
  Ernestus Berchtold, 50
Pollard, Velma, 388
  Considering Woman I, 388
  Considering Woman II, 388
  Karl and Other Stories, 388
Pollock, Louis, 561
Pope, Alexander, 506
Porter, Kevin, *Between the Acts*, 310
Potts, Cherry, 317
Pound, Ezra, 136, 482, 490, 533
Powys, T. F., 7, 88–9, 95, 572
  'The Bucket and the Rope', 89
  'The Clout and the Pan', 89
  'Lie Thee Down, Oddity!', 569
  'The Stone and Mr Thomas', 89
  Fables, 88–9
  God's Eyes A-Twinkle, 569

Pratt, Annis, 228
Pratt, Mary Louise, 118
Priest, Christopher, 432, 438, 441
Priestley, J. B., 433
Pringle, David, 440
Pritchard, Hesketh, 'November Joe', 418
Pritchett, V. S., 236, 243–8, 249, 572, 578
  'The Cage Birds', 246
  'A Family Man', 565
  'Greek Theatre Tragedy', 243
  'On the Edge of the Cliff', 247
  'Passing the Ball', 246
  'Pocock Passes', 244
  'The Sailor', 244, 246
  'The Saint', 244, 246
  'The Satisfactory', 245
  'Sense of Humour', 243, 247
  'The Skeleton', 247
  'The Wheelbarrow', 246
  'The White Rabbit', 243
  Blind Love and Other Stories, 246
  A Careless Widow, 247
  It May Never Happen and Other Stories, 244, 245
  The Key to My Heart, 246
  On The Edge of the Cliff, 247, 565
  The Spanish Virgin and Other Stories, 243
  When My Girl Comes Home and Other Stories, 245
Propp, Vladimir, 84
Prospect, 588
Proust, Marcel, 192
Pullinger, Kate, 585
Punch, 126, 481, 482, 498, 499, 500

Quarterly Review, 120
Quatermass Experiment, The, 436
Quiller Couch, Arthur, 73
Quin, Ann, 468
Quinn, Seabury, 448

Radcliffe, Anne, 53
Rahv, Philip, 544
Raine, Allen, 220
  'Home, Sweet Home', 221
Ramayana, 389
Ramchand, Kenneth, *West Indian Narrative*, 384
Ramsay, Allan, 'The Adventure of the Table Foot', 482
Rankin, Ian, 424
  'The Dean Curse', 425
  'The Gentlemen's Club', 425

Rankin, Ian (cont.)
   'A Good Hanging', 425
   'Playback', 425
Rao, Raja, 389
   The Cow of the Barricades, 390
   Kanthapura, 390
   On the Ganga Ghat, 390
   The Policeman and the Rose, 390
Rathbone, Basil, 550
Read, Herbert
   'Killed in Action', 158
   Naked Warriors, 158
Reade, Brian, 307
Reade, Charles, 77
Reid, Coletta, *The Lesbians Home Journal*, 314
Remarque, E. M., 161
Rendell, Ruth, 551
   'The Irony of Hate', 424
   Blood Lines, 424
   The Fallen Curtain, 424
   The Fever Tree, 424
Reynolds, Alistair, 440, 442
Reynolds, G. W. M., *The Mysteries of London*, 270
Rhodes, Neil, 24
Rhys, Jean, 286, 287, 288, 291–2, 388, 578
   'The Day They Burned the Books', 389
   'Good-bye Marcus, Good-bye Rose', 292
   'Heat', 291
   'I Spy a Stranger', 157
   'I Used to Live Here Once', 289
   'Let Them Call It Jazz', 292
   'Mixing Cocktails', 291
   'Pioneers, Oh, Pioneers', 389
   'Rapunzel, Rapunzel', 292
   'Sleep it Off Lady', 292
   'The Whistling Bird', 292
   Left Bank and Other Stories, 291
   Let Them Call It Jazz, 291
   Sleep it Off Lady, 291
   Tigers Are Better-Looking, 287, 291, 389
Rhythm, 131
Rich, Adrienne, 298
Richard Freeman, 419
Richards, Alun, 219, 220
   'The Scandalous Thoughts of Elmyra Mouth', 230
   New Penguin Book of Welsh Short Stories, 574
   Penguin Book of Welsh Short Stories, 574
Richards, Grant, 176
Richardson, Dorothy, 146–7
   'Death', 146
   'Ordeal', 146
   'Tryst', 146
   Pilgrimage, 137
Richardson, Henry Handel
   'The Bathe', 312
   'Two Hanged Women', 312
Richardson, Maurice, *The Exploits of Engelbrecht*, 441
Richardson, Samuel, 44
   Clarissa, 43
   Pamela, 35, 522
Richler, Mordecai, *The Street*, 519
Richmond: Scenes from the Life of a Bow Street Runner, 412
Riddell, Charlotte
   'Hertford O'Donnell's Warning', 62
   'The Old House in Vauxhall Walk', 58, 62
   'The Open Door', 403
   'Sandy the Tinker', 62
   Weird Stories, 451
Riedl, Mark, 611
Robbins, Ruth, 75
Robert Harbinson
   Tattoo Lily, 194
   The Far World, 194
Roberts, Adam, 442
   'Hair', 442
   Adam Robots, 442
   By Light Alone, 442
   Jack Glass, 442
Roberts, Dewi, *Heartland*, 219
Roberts, Kate, 222–3, 574
   'The Condemned', 222
   'Protest March', 223
Roberts, Keith, 438
   Pavane, 438
Robertson, James, 216
Robson, Justina, 442
Rodriguez, Luisa, 466
Roeg, Nicholas, *Don't Look Now*, 553–5
Rogers, Jane, *Mr Wroe's Virgins*, 514
Rohmer, Sax, 415, 425
Rolfe, Frederick
   'In Praise of Billy B.', 309
   'Stories Toto Told Me', 309
Roscoe, Theodore, 448
Ross, Leone, *Whispers in the Walls*, 576
Rossetti, Christina
   'Hero. A Metamorphosis', 90
   'Nick', 90
   Commonplace and Other Stories, 90
Roth, Cecil, 325

'The Martyr', 326
Roth, Philip, *The Ghost Writer*, 334
Rothenstein, William, 502
Royle, Nicholas, 441, 455, 593
  Best British Short Stories, 577, 593
  Book of London Short Stories, 575
Rushdie, Salman, 297, 342, 345–7, 578
  'The Courter', 346
  'Imaginary Homelands', 346
  East, West, 346, 392
  Midnight's Children, 391
Ruskin, John, *The King of the Golden River, or The Black Brothers, A Legend of Stiria*, 90
Russell, George, 113
Rylance, Mark, 560
Ryman, Geoff, 442
  When It Changed, 442
Rymer, James Malcolm, *Varney the Vampire*, 52

Saadi, Suhayl, *The Burning Mirror*, 214
Sagar, Keith, 540
Saki (H. H. Munro), 207, 483, 511, 561, 568
  'The Boar-Pig', 483
  'Cousin Teresa', 484
  'Gabriel-Ernest', 483
  'The Infernal Parliament', 482
  'The Lull', 483
  'The Lumber Room', 483
  'The Open Window', 483
  'Reginald at the Theatre', 484
  'Sredni Vashtar', 483, 502
  'The Toys of Peace', 579
  'Tobermory', 483, 502
  The Chronicles of Clovis, 484
  Reginald, 483
  Reginald in Russia, 484
  The Square Egg and Other Sketches, 482
Sales, Ian, 443
Salinger, J. D., 494
Salkey, Andrew, 384
  Anancy, Traveller, 385
  Anancy's Score, 384
  Stories from the Caribbean, 384
  West Indian Stories, 384
Salzman, Paul, 16, 23
  The New Diversity, Australian Fiction 1970–88, 365
Samuels, Robert, 553
Sandler, Helen, *Diva Book of Short Stories*, 318
Sansom, William, 96–7, 236, 457–8, 460
  'Among the Dahlias', 97

'Fireman Flower', 457
'The Little Fears', 457
'The Vertical Ladder', 97
'The Wall', 97, 163
Fireman Flower and Other Stories, 97, 457
Something Terrible, Something Lovely, 97, 457
Sargeson, Frank, 11, 360, 361–2, 364, 369, 373
  'Conversations with My Uncle', 361
  'A Good Boy', 362
  'I've Lost My Pal', 362
  'In the Midst of Life', 361
  'The Last Adventure', 362
  'A Piece of Yellow Soap', 361
  'White Man's Burden', 362
Savage, H. R., 'Night Attack', 163
Savoy, 128, 135
Saxton, Josephine, 438
Sayers, Dorothy L., 11, 238–9, 419, 421, 551, 561
  'Bloody Sacrifice', 239
  'The Entertaining Episode of the Article in Question', 421
  'The Inspiration of Mr. Budd', 239
  'Nebuchadnezzar', 239
  'The Unsolved Puzzle of the Man with No Face', 419
  Great Short Stories of Detection, Mystery and Horror, 419
  Hangman's Holiday, 421
  In the Teeth of the Evidence, 421
  Lord Peter Views the Body, 421
  Salesman's Handbook, 239
Sayle, Alexei, 576
Scarron, Paul, 26
Schiffrin, André, 599, 603
Schlauch, Margaret, 18
Schlicke, Paul, 56
Scholes, Robert, 131, 530
Schötz, Bettina, 347
Schreiner, Olive
  'Eighteen-Ninety-Nine', 372
  Stories, Dreams and Allegories, 372
  The Story of an African Farm, 125
Schwartz, Bill, 341
Schwarz, Daniel R., 537
Science Fantasy, 435, 436, 437, 438
Scofield, Martin, 429
Scott, Duncan Campbell, 528
  In the Village of Viger, 367, 516
Scott, Walter, 51, 54, 69, 564, 573
  'My Aunt Margaret's Mirror', 54, 55
  'The Tapestried Chamber', 54, 55–6, 58
  'The Two Drovers', 202
  'Wandering Willie's Tale', 203, 206

Scott, Walter (cont.)
  Chronicles of the Canongate, 38, 47, 202, 204
  Ivanhoe, 332
  Redgauntlet, 203
  Tales of My Landlord, 202
Scottish Review of Books, 593
Scott-Moncrieff, Charles Kenneth, 'Evensong and Morwe Song', 309
Scott-Thomas, Kristin, 560
Searle, Ronald, 441
Sedgwick, Eve, 63
Seforim, Mendele Mocher, 330
Self, Will, 272, 487, 495, 509, 510, 544, 584, 586
  'Bull', 181, 185
  'Cock', 509
  'The Nonce Prize', 495
  'The North London Book of the Dead', 495
  'A Rock of Crack as Big as the Ritz', 495
  Cock and Bull, 509
  The Quantity Theory of Insanity, 509
  Tough, Tough Toys for Tough, Tough Boys, 495
Selver, Paul, 325
  'Well, I'm Blowed', 326
Selvon, Sam, 279, 342–4, 354, 384
  'Basement Lullaby', 279
  'Calypso in London', 279, 343
  'Eraser's Dilemma', 279
  'Finding Piccadilly Circus', 342
  'If Winter Comes', 279
  'Obeah in the Grove', 279
  'Waiting for Aunty to Cough', 279
  'Working the Transport', 279
  The Lonely Londoners, 11, 279, 342
  Ways of Sunlight, 279, 385
Senior, Olive, 387–8
  'Ballad', 387
  'Bright Thursdays', 387
  'The Case Against the Queen', 388
  'You Think I Mad, Miss?', 388
  Arrival of the Snake-Woman, 387
  Discerner of Hearts, 387
  Summer Lightning, 386, 387
Sergeant, David, 102
Seth, Vikram, *A Suitable Boy*, 391
Seymour, A. J., *Kyk-over-al*, 384
SF Impulse, 438
Shakespeare, William
  Macbeth, 454
  Much Ado About Nothing, 17
  The Winter's Tale, 22
Sharp, Evelyn, 127
  At the Relton Arms, 127
Sharp, Margery, 'Night Engagement', 164

Sharp, William, 129
Shaw, George Bernard, 129, 136, 482
Shearman, Robert, 443
Shelley, Mary, 54, 432, 564
  'Ferdinando Eboli', 54
  'The Mortal Immortal', 54, 566
  'The Sisters of Albano', 54
  Frankenstein, 50, 51, 54, 61, 430, 447, 566
Shelley, Percy Bysshe, 54
Shiel, M. P., 127, 414
Shields, David, 608
Short Fiction in Theory and Practice, 592
Short Stories, 120
ShortFiction, 584
Showalter, Elaine, *A Literature of their Own*, 567
Shulman, Sheila, *The Reach*, 316
Shurin, Jared, *Lowest Heaven*, 442
Sicher, Efraim, 334
Sillitoe, Alan, 96, 236, 248, 494, 530, 531, 541–3, 578
  'The Loneliness of the Long Distance Runner', 97, 248, 532, 534, 541
  'Out of the Whirlpool', 532, 535, 541, 542
  The Ragman's Daughter and Other Stories, 248
Simmel, Georg, 'The Metropolis and Mental Life', 275
Simpson, Helen, *Hey Yeah Right Get a Life*, 520
Sims, George, 416
Sinclair, Clive, 476, 578, 585
  'The Creature on My Back', 334, 335
  'The Luftmensh', 334, 335
Sinclair, Iain, 269, 272, 281, 453, 454
  'Art of the State (*The Silvertown Memorial*)', 281
  'Horse Spittle (*The Eros of Maps*)', 281
  'The Isle of Doges (*Vat City plc*)', 281
  Downriver, 281
  Slow Chocolate Autopsy, 281
Sinclair, May, 136, 137, 138, 141–3, 149
  'If the Dead Knew', 141, 402
  'The Intercessor', 402
  'The Token', 402
  A Defence of Idealism, 137
  Uncanny Stories, 141, 144, 402, 460
Sindoni, Maria Grazia, 342
Singh, Khushwant
  'Black Jasmine', 391
  'Karma', 391
  The Mark of Vishnu, 390
  The Portrait of a Lady, 391
Sivanadan, A., 342

Sketch, 120, 125
Sladek, John, 439
Slemon, Stephen, 359
Smajić, Srdjan, 399
Smith, Ali, 216, 318, 509, 520, 587–90
  'Present', 588
  'The Second Person', 217, 588
  'The Third Person', 217, 588
  'True Short Story', 588
  'The Universal Story', 216
  Artful, 589
  The First Person and Other Stories, 217, 588
  Free Love and Other Stories, 319
  The Whole Story and Other Stories, 216
Smith, Andrew, 396
Smith, Angela K., *Women's Writing of the First World War*, 162
Smith, Clark Ashton, 447
Smith, Dai, 574
  Story, 220
Smith, George Murray, 119
Smith, Iain Crichton, 211
  'An American Sky', 211
  'The Existence of the Hermit', 211
  The Black and the Red, 211
Smith, Pauline, 'Desolation', 372
Smith, Stevie, 'Not Waving but Drowning', 292
Smith, Zadie, 342, 352–3, 354
  The Embassy of Cambodia, 283, 352
  White Teeth, 352
Smithers, Leonard, 129
Smoke Signals, 575
Smollett, Tobias, 506, 515
Smythe, James, 442
Somerville and Ross, 170–1
  Further Experiences of an Irish R. M., 170
  In Mr Knox's Country, 170
  Some Experiences of an Irish R. M., 170
Soueif, Ahdaf
  Aisha, 383
  Sandpiper, 383
Spark, Muriel, 272, 329, 494, 509, 572, 573, 578
  'The Gentile Jewesses', 329
  'The House of the Famous Poet', 573
  'The Portobello Road', 209
  'The Seraph and the Zambesi', 209
Sparrow, The Mighty, 385
Spence, Alan, 212
  Its Colours They are Fine, 212

Spender, Stephen, 492, 571
  The Burning Cactus, 311
Spinrad, Norman, *Bug Jack Barron*, 439
Sporting Magazine, 46
Sprat, Bishop, *History of the Royal Society*, 28
Springer, Mary Doyle, 536, 537, 540
  Forms of the Modern Novella, 532
St James's Gazette, 100
Stableford, Brian, 431, 438
Staffrider, 378
Stahl, John Daniel, 57
Stapledon, Olaf, 433–4
  Last and First Men, 433
Star, 129
Stavans, Ilan, *The Oxford Book of Jewish Stories*, 324, 330
Stead, Christina, *The Salzburg Tales*, 515, 520
Steele, Alan, *Modern Irish Short Stories*, 574
Steele, Richard, 36, 37, 44
  The Spectator, 38
  The Tatler, 34
Stein, Gertrude, 411
  'Miss Furr and Miss Skeene', 309
  Making of Americans, 611
Steiner, Max, *The Letter*, 558
Stenbock, Stanislaus Eric
  'The True Story of a Vampire', 309
  Studies of Death, Romantic Tales, 309, 454
Stephens, James, 171
Stephenson, James, 558
Stern, G. B., 325
  'Cinderella's Sister', 326
Sterne, Laurence, *The Life and Opinions of Tristram Shandy*, 522
Stevenson, Robert Louis, 47, 69, 76, 81, 86–7, 100, 206–7, 598
  'The Beach of Falesá', 206, 573
  'The Bottle Imp', 206
  'The House of Eld', 87
  'The Persons of the Tale', 87
  'Something In It', 87
  'Thrawn Janet', 73, 86, 206
  'Will o' the Mill', 87
  The Ebb-Tide, 206
  Fables, 87
  Island Nights' Entertainments, 206
  New Arabian Nights, 206
  The Merry Men and Other Tales, 86, 206
  The Strange Case of Dr Jekyll and Mr Hyde, 61, 63, 206, 272–3, 451
  Treasure Island, 87
Stewart, Sophie, 556
Stewart, Victoria, 154

Stoddart, Charles Warren
　'Pearl Hunting in the Pomotous', 309
　South-Sea Idyls, 309
Stoker, Bram, 52
　Dracula, 52, 447, 450
Strachan, Zoë, Out There, 318
Strand Magazine, 80, 120, 125, 127, 156, 206, 270, 413, 415, 420, 423, 431, 500, 551, 566
Street, G. S., 482
Stretton, Hesba, 70
Strindberg, August, 174
Stross, Charles, 440
Sue, Eugène, Les Mystères de Paris, 270
Sullivan, Tricia, 442
Sulter, Maud, 'Blackwomansong', 317
Sunday Pictorial, 310
Sunday-Night Theatre (BBC), 555
Sutherland, Alistair, Eros: An Anthology of Male Friendship, 312
Sutherland, Donald, 554
Sutro, Alfred, 324, 325
　'The Bread on the Waters', 326
Suvin, Darko, 430, 432
Swain, E. B., The Stoneground Ghost Tales, 516, 521
Swanzy, Henry, 384
Swettenham, Frank, 105, 106
　'The Eternal Feminine', 106
　'A Fishing Picnic', 106
　'A Malay Romance', 106
　'The Murder of the Hawker', 106
　'The Noon of Night', 106
　'The Real Malay', 106
　'The Story of Mat Aris', 106
　'The Tiger', 106
　Malay Sketches, 106
Swift, E. J., 442
Swift, Graham, 96, 474–6, 578, 585
　'First on the Scene', 97
　'Learning to Swim', 475
　'Seraglio', 474
　England and Other Stories, 97, 474
　Learning to Swim and Other Stories, 97, 474
Swift, Jonathan, 506
　A Tale of a Tub, 88
　Gulliver's Travels, 88, 515
Sykes, Christopher, 569
Symonds, John Addington, A Problem of Modern Ethics, 306
Symons, Arthur, 128, 129
Symons, Julian, 551
Synge, J. M., 171

Syrett, Netta, 127
　Nobody's Fault, 127

Tagore, Rabindranath, 449
Tales of Wonder, 435
Tate, Trudi, Women, Men and the Great War: An Anthology of Stories, 162
Taylor, D. J., 255, 493
Taylor, Elizabeth, 287, 288, 292–4
　'Better Not', 293
　'The Blush', 293, 294
　'Gravement Endommagé', 165
　'Oasis of Gaiety', 293
　'Perhaps a Family Failing', 293
　A Dedicated Man and Other Stories, 292
　Dangerous Calm, 294
　Hester Lilly and Other Stories, 292
　The Blush and Other Stories, 292
　The Devastating Boys, 292
Taylor, Elizabeth Coles, 286
Temple Bar, 62
Temple, William F., 434, 435
　'The Lonely', 436
Tennant, Emma
　Bananas, 440
　Wild Nights, 297
Tennyson, Alfred, 72
　'The Lady of Shalott', 298
Terrific Register, 56
Thackeray, William Makepeace, The Rose and the Ring, 90
Tharoor, Shashi, The Great Indian Novel, 391
Thieme, John, 359
Thiong'o, Ngugi wa, Secret Lives, 381
Third Alternative, 441
Thomas, Deborah, 68
Thomas, Dylan, 228–9, 457, 506, 574, 578
　'And death shall have no dominion', 229
　'The Burning Baby', 229
　'Red Notebook', 228
　'The School for Witches', 229
　'The Visitor', 228
　18 Poems, 228
　Portrait of the Artist as a Young Dog, 516
Thomas, Gwyn, 223
　'Dust in the Lonely Wind', 225
　Where Did I Put my Pity? Folk Tales from the Modern Welsh, 225
Thorpe, Adam, Ulverton, 519, 521
Thousand and One Nights, The, 391, 392
Time Out, 575
Times, 129
Timmons, Stuart, 304

Tit-Bits, 120
Tlali, Miriam, *Soweto Stories*, 382
To-day and To-morrow, 433
Todd, Richard, *Consuming Fiction: The Booker Prize and Fiction in Britain Today*, 586
Tóibín, Colm, 199
   'The Name of the Game', 198
   'A Priest in the Family', 198
   'Three Friends', 198
   The Empty Family, 198, 319
   Mothers and Sons, 198
Tolstoy, Leo, 124, 172
Tomlinson, H. M., 161
Torgovnick, Marianna, 540
Towers, Frances, 569
Town and Country Magazine, 43, 45
Transition, 378
Trebisz, Malgorzata, 530, 534, 535, 540
Tremain, Rose, 578, 585
Trevor, William, 187, 192–3, 199, 578, 595
   'An Evening with John Joe Dempsey', 192
   'Another Christmas', 193
   'Attracta', 193
   'Autumn Sunshine', 193
   'The Ballroom of Romance', 192
   'Beyond the Pale', 193
   'Death in Jerusalem', 575
   'The Distant Past', 193
   'The Raising of Elvira Tremlett', 192
   'Torridge', 313
   Angels at the Ritz, 193
   Beyond the Pale, 193
   A Bit on the Side, 193
   Cheating at Canasta, 193
   Lovers of Their Time, 192, 193
   The Ballroom of Romance, 192
   The Oxford Book of Irish Short Stories, 575
Trezise, Rachel
   'Jigsaw', 232
   Fresh Apples, 232
Trinidad, 383
Trinidad Guardian, 342
Trollope, Anthony, 67, 68, 69, 70, 81, 487, 528, 579
   'Christmas at Thompson Hall', 482
   'Father Giles of Ballymoy', 170
   'The Gentle Euphemia', 483
   'John Bull on the Guadalquivir', 482
   'The Journey to Panama', 80
   'Never, never – Never, Never', 482
   'Not if I Know it', 482
   'The O'Conors of Castle Conor, County Mayo', 170
   Tales from All Countries, 515
Trumbach, Randolph, 305
Truth, 364
Tubb, E. C., 435
Turgenev, Ivan, 172, 174
   Sketches from a Hunter's Album, 174
   A Sportsman's Sketches, 515, 519
Turner, Reginald, 'A Chef-d'Oeuvre', 123
Tuttle, Lisa, 441
Tytler, Graeme, 57

Unwin, T. Fisher, 124
Urquhart, Fred, 236
   'Namiętność, or The Laundry Girl and the Pole', 210
   The Clouds are Big with Mercy, 210

Vannatta, Dennis, 484
Vassanji, M. G., *Uhuru Street*, 381
Verne, Jules, *From the Earth to the Moon*, 555
Victoria Regia, 81
Voltaire, François-Marie Arouet, *Candide*, 87
Vorticists, 131
Vowler, Tom, 591, 595

Wain, John, 248
Wainaina, Binyavanga, 381
Wales, 226
Wall, William, *No Paradiso*, 199
Wallace, Diana, 60
Wallis, Hal B., *The Letter*, 558
Walpole, Horace, *The Castle of Otranto*, 450
Walter, Elizabeth, 'Come and Get Me', 405
Walter, Melissa, 23
Wandor, Michelene, 337, 582
   'Corridors of Light and Shadow', 337
   'False Relations', 337
   'Song of the Jewish Princess', 337
   'The Story of Esther and Vashti', 337
   'Toccata and Fugue', 337
   'Yom Tov', 337
   False Relations, 337
Ward, Ned, *London Spy*, 34
Warner, Marina, 90, 287, 297, 470, 583
   Fantastic Metamorphoses, Other Worlds Ways of Telling the Self, 298
   Mermaids in the Basement, 298
   Murderers I Have Known and Other Stories, 298
   Wonder Tales, 298
Warner, Sylvia Townsend, 236, 287, 288, 293

Warner, Tom, 304
Warren, Austin, 523
Waters, Sarah, 318
Watson, H. B. Marriott, 'The Dead Wall', 128
Watson, Ian, 439, 441, 442
Watson, Melvin, 39
Waugh, Arthur, 121, 130
Waugh, Evelyn, 491–2, 494
   'The Balance', 484, 494
   'An Englishman's Home', 491
   'Excursion in Reality', 484
   'Love Among the Ruins', 492
   'Mr Loveday's Little Outing', 491, 568
   'Scott-King's Modern Europe', 491
   A Handful of Dust, 496
   Brideshead Revisited, 492
Wedmore, Frederick, 124, 129
Weeks, Jeffrey, 306
   Between the Acts, 310
   Coming Out, 310
Weird: A Compendium of Strange and Dark Stories, The, 449
Welch, Denton
   Brave and Cruel and Other Stories, 311
   The Stories of Denton Welch, 311
Weldon, Fay, 11, 287, 288, 296–7, 486–7, 493, 495
   'Alopecia', 486
   'Down the Clinical Disco', 487
   'Who Goes Where? A Christmas Tale', 296
   Nothing to Wear & Nothing to Hide, 296
   Polaris and Other Stories, 486
   The Spa Decameron, 296
   Watching Me, Watching You, 296, 486
Wellek, René, 523
Wells, Catherine, 'The Beautiful House', 309
Wells, Frank, *H. G. Wells Comedies*, 555
Wells, H. G., 119, 130, 135, 138, 418, 431–3, 443, 482, 485, 509, 511, 555–6, 568, 598
   'Blue Bottle', 555
   'Daydreams', 555
   'The Chronic Argonauts', 431
   'The Crystal Egg', 431
   'The First Men in the Moon', 555
   'The Flowering of the Strange Orchid', 431
   'The Man Who Could Work Miracles', 555
   'The New Accelerator', 432
   'A Slip Under the Microscope', 130
   'The Star', 431, 434
   'The Stolen Bacillus', 431
   'A Story of the Days to Come', 432
   'The Tonic', 555

   'The Truth About Pyecraft', 500
   The Invisible Man, 555
   The Island of Dr. Moreau, 555
   The Time Machine, 431, 555
   The War of the Worlds, 431, 434, 555
   When the Sleeper Wakes, 432
Welsh, Irvine, *Trainspotting*, 214
Welty, Eudora, 585
Wertham, Fredric, *The Seduction of the Innocents*, 448
West, Rebecca, 136
Westminster Gazette, 129
Westminster Review, 413, 417
Wharton, Edith, 162
What Did Miss Darrington See?, 317
Whates, Ian, 442
Whedon, Tony, 533
Whitaker, Malachi, 'Landlord of the Crystal Fountain', 579
White, Edmund, *The Darker Proof, Stories from a Crisis*, 316
White, James, 435
Whitehead, Henry, 447
Whyte, Christopher, 319
Whyte, Hamish
   Streets of Gold, 575
   Streets of Stone, 575
Wickham, John, *Oxford Book of Caribbean Short Stories*, 384
Wicomb, Zoë, 373
   'Another Story', 373
   'Ash on my Sleeve', 373
   You Can't Get Lost in Cape Town, 382, 383
Widrath, Helen, *Reader, I Murdered Him, Too*, 567
Wijenaike, Punyakante, 392
   The Rebel, 392
   The Third Woman, 392
Wilde, Oscar, 69, 80, 119, 128–9, 138, 172–3, 306, 310, 417, 452, 482, 504
   'The Canterville Ghost', 395, 397, 483
   'The Portrait of Mr W. H.', 309
   The Happy Prince and Other Tales, 90, 172, 173, 309
   A House of Pomegranates, 173, 309
   The Picture of Dorian Gray, 128
   Salomé, 128
Williams, D. J., 574
Williams, Liz, 440, 442
Williams, Raymond, 230, 274
Williams, Richard Hughes, 222
   'Siôn William', 222
Williams, Tennessee, *Hard Candy*, 313

Williamson, Kevin, *Children of Albion Rovers*, 214
Wilson, Angus, 236, 492–4, 572, 578, 581
  'Crazy Crowd', 493
  'Et Dona Ferentes', 313
  'A Flat Country Christmas', 493
  'More Friend than Lodger', 578
  'Mother's Sense of Fun', 313
  'Rex Imperator', 493
  'Significant Experience', 493
  'The Wrong Set', 248
  A Bit Off the Map, 493
  Such Darling Dodos, 248, 313, 493
  The Wrong Set, 248, 313, 492
Wilson, Edmund, 411, 448
Wilson, Ethel, *The Innocent Traveller*, 367
Wilson, Janet, 360
Wilson, John, 202
Windsor Magazine, 418
Winning, Joanne, *The Crazy Jig*, 305
Winterson, Jeanette, 296, 318
Wittig, Monique, 308
Wodehouse, P. G., 238, 423, 504–5
  'Comrade Bingo', 504
Wolosky, Shira, 467
Wong, Donna, 171
Wood, Ellen, 59, 413
  'The Unholy Wish', 77
Wood, Lucy, 591, 595
  Diving Belles, 591
Woodhouse, Reed, 314
Woolf, Virginia, 136–7, 138, 142–4, 147, 148, 149, 162, 194, 276–7, 287, 293, 301, 412, 433
  'The Duchess and the Jeweller', 569
  'Kew Gardens', 136, 277
  'The Mark on the Wall', 153, 276
  'Moments of Being, Slater's Pins Have No Points', 143
  'Mr Bennett and Mrs Brown', 137, 571
  'The Mysterious Case of Miss V', 143
  'Professions for Women', 142

  'Slater's Pins Have No Points', 312
  'An Unwritten Novel', 136
  Mrs Dalloway, 235, 537
Wordsworth Book of Horror Stories, 567
Wordsworth, William, 54
Worpole, Ken, 269
Wright, Farnsworth, *Weird Tales*, 450
Wulfman, Clifford, 131
Wyler, William, *The Letter*, 558
Wyndham, John, 434, 435
  'Consider Her Ways', 436
  'Survival', 438
  The Day of the Triffids, 436

Yeats, Jack, 178
Yeats, W. B., 119, 129, 171–3, 451
  Representative Irish Tales, 172
  The Celtic Twilight: Men and Women, Dhouls and Fairies, 171
  The Secret Rose, 173
Yellin, Tamar, 13, 336
  Kafka in Brontëland, 336
  Tales of the Ten Lost Tribes, 335, 336
Yellow Book, The, 5, 80, 118–32, 135, 138, 173, 235, 236
Youd, Sam, 434
Young, Ian, *On the Line*, 314
Young, Roland, 556

Zangwill, Israel, 324, 330
  'The Sabbath Breaker', 326
  'Tug of Love', 331
  Children of the Ghetto, 275
  Ghetto Comedies, 326
  Ghetto Tragedies, 326
Zangwill, Louis, 324
  'Prelude to a Pint of Bitter', 326
Zimmerman, Bonnie, 312, 315
Žižek, Slavoj, 553
Zola, Émile, 179
  Thérèse Raquin, 601
Zoline, Pamela, 439

CPSIA information can be obtained
at www.ICGtesting.com
Printed in the USA
LVHW040942171021
700680LV00001B/3